The Ottoman Army of the Napoleonic Wars 1784–1815

A Struggle for Survival from Egypt to the Balkans

Text and Illustrations by Bruno Mugnai

Helion & Company

Helion & Company Limited
Unit 8 Amherst Business Centre
Budbrooke Road
Warwick
CV34 5WE
England
Tel. 01926 499 619
Email: info@helion.co.uk
Website: www.helion.co.uk
Twitter: @helionbooks
Visit our blog http://blog.helion.co.uk/

Published by Helion & Company 2022
Designed and typeset by Serena Jones
Cover designed by Paul Hewitt, Battlefield Design (www.battlefield-design.co.uk)

Text © Bruno Mugnai 2022
Illustrations © as individually credited. Uncredited images open source.
Colour artwork by Bruno Mugnai © Helion & Company 2022
Maps drawn by George Anderson © Helion & Company 2022

Cover: Provincial *sipahi*, 1800–1802 (Illustration by Bruno Mugnai © Helion & Company 2022)

Every reasonable effort has been made to trace copyright holders and to obtain their permission for the use of copyright material. The author and publisher apologise for any errors or omissions in this work, and would be grateful if notified of any corrections that should be incorporated in future reprints or editions of this book.

ISBN 978-1-915070-48-7

British Library Cataloguing-in-Publication Data.
A catalogue record for this book is available from the British Library.

All rights reserved. No part of this publication may be reproduced, stored in a retrieval system, or transmitted, in any form, or by any means, electronic, mechanical, photocopying, recording or otherwise, without the express written consent of Helion & Company Limited.

For details of other military history titles published by Helion & Company Limited, contact the above address, or visit our website: http://www.helion.co.uk

We always welcome receiving book proposals from prospective authors.

Contents

Chronology	v
Acknowledgements	ix
A Note on Transliteration	x
1. 'The Sick Man of Europe'	11
The Ottoman Empire at the Turn of the Century	20
The Empire: Centre and Periphery	35
The Sultanate	38
Ottoman Geostrategy	42
Between Chaos and Transformation	48
The Sultan's Household	54
2. The Armies of the Sultan	60
The Sources for the Ottoman Military in the Age of Transformation	66
Financing the Army	69
The Standing Army and the Officer Corps	74
Janissaries	88
Cebeci, Armourers	105
Topçu, Artillery	108
Sipahi and *Çavuş* Cavalry	115
Provincial Troops and Private Contingents	117
The Egyptian *Ocaks*	137
The Ottoman 'New Model Army'	148
Supply and Logistics	155
Auxiliary Troops	161
3. Ottoman Warfare: A Struggle for Survival	167
Campaigns Against the Bedouins in Iraq, 1784–1791	195
Expeditions to Egypt, and Factional Struggles in Syria, 1786–1790	202
War Against Austria and Russia, 1787–92	203
Kara Mahmud's Rebellion in Albania, 1792–1796	234
Campaigns Against Pazvandoğlu Osman, 1792–1798	236
The First Ottoman–Saudi War, 1794–1800	241
The War Against France of 1798–1802	243

Rebellions in Syria, 1802–1808	262
Civil War in Egypt, 1803–1804	265
The Second Ottoman–Saudi War, 1802–1807	269
Rebellion in Eastern Anatolia, 1804–1805	273
War Against Russia and Britain, 1806–1812	275
The First Serbian Uprising, 1804–1813	299
The Ottoman–Egyptian Saudi War, 1811–1818	314
The Second Serbian Uprising, 1815	316
4. Dress, Equipment and Ensigns	319
The Sources for Ottoman Military Clothing	320
Generalities	322
The *Kapıkulu* Dress Code	330
Campaign Dress	334
The Uniforms of the *Nizâm-ı Cedîd*	340
Weapons	344
Ensigns	361
Appendix	366
Glossary	369
Colour Plate Commentaries	371
Bibliography	385

Ottoman Chronology

1774–1789	Reign of Abdülhamid I
1774	21 July: Signing of the Treaty of Küçük Kaynarca, Ottomans lose control of the Crimea
1775	March: Iranians besiege Basra. Habsburgs annex Bukovina.
1776	27 April: Loss of Basra to Iran
	2 May: Ottomans declare war on Iran
1779	21 March: Explanatory convention of Ayanalikavak concerning the Treaty of Küçük Kaynarca provides Russia with rights in Wallachia and Moldavia
	April: Recovery of Basra
1781	Plague in Salonika (Greece)
1782	21–22 August: Major fire in Constantinople
	31 December: Halil Hâmid Paşa becomes grand vizier
1783	9 July: Russia annexes the Crimea
1784	Famine in Cairo
1785	Earthquake in Patras
	31 March: dismissal and execution of Halil Hâmid Paşa
1786	Plague in Constantinople; nearly one third of the population dies.
1787	31 August: Ottomans declare war on Russia
	Major fire destroys Constantinople
1788	9 February: Habsburgs declare war on the Ottoman Empire
	8 August: Ottoman victory over the Austrians at Dubica
	17 December: Oçakov surrenders to Russians
	Sweden declares war on Russia. Debasement of coins.
1789–1807	Reign of Selim III
1789	6 April: Death of Abdülhamid I
	11 July: Ottoman–Swedish alliance against Russia
	11 July: Austro-Russian victory at Focşani
	22 September: Austro-Russian victory at Martineşti
	8 October: Belgrade surrenders to the Austrians
	11 October: Russians enter Akkerman
	9 November: Austrians occupy Bucharest
1790	31 January: Ottoman–Prussian alliance
	8 June: Ottomans defeat the Austrians at Giourgiu
	30 October–22 December: Russians seize Kilia and İzmail
	New debasement of coinage
1791	4 April: The Russians defeat the Ottomans at Ibrail

	10 July: loss of Macjn to the Russians
	4 August: Habsburg–Ottoman Peace signed at Sistova; Belgrade and Bucharest return to the Ottomans.
1792	9 January: Peace of Jassy, which provides Russia territorial gains on northern Black Sea shores
	13 September: Major fire in Constantinople
1793	24 February: Formation of the first *nizâm-ı cedîd* military units
1794	16 January–5 August: First modern military hospital
	Series of earthquakes in Constantinople
1795	Opening of the Military Engineering School
	7–8 July: Major fire at Constantinople
1796	26 April: Strong earthquake in Lattakuia
	June: French General Aubert du Bayet with his military mission arrives in Constantinople
1797	Autumn–winter: Military operation against the warlord Pazvandoğlu, who dominates in northern Bulgaria
1798	2 July: Napoleon Bonaparte occupies Alexandria
	21 July: Battle of the Pyramids; French enter Cairo the day after.
	1 August: British destroy the French navy at Aboukir
	10 August: Battle at Salheyeh, French victory
	2 September: Ottomans declare war on France. Ottomans join Russian and British naval forces in the Mediterranean.
	Famine in Aleppo, nearly half of the city's population dies
	7 October: French defeat the Ottomans at Sédiman
1799	3 January: Russian–Ottoman alliance against France
	5 January: Ottoman–British alliance
	11–19 February: The French seize El-Arish
	7 March: Siege of Jaffa, French victory
	18 March: Napoleon besieges Acre
	8 April: Battle at Nazareth, French victory, Junot with 500 men defeats 3,000 Ottomans
	11 April: Napoleon defeats the Ottomans in the battle of Cana
	16 April: Bonaparte relieves the troops under Kléber at Mount Tabor
	21 May: Final defeat of Bonaparte at Acre
	25 July: Ottoman defeat at Aboukir
	22 August: Bonaparte leaves Egypt
1800	February: French troops begin their withdrawal
	21 March: Ionian Islands become Ottoman domain
	14 June: Murder of Kléber in Cairo; General Menou, a convert to Islam, takes over command.
1801	8 March: British landing near Aboukir
	21 March: the French under Menou are defeated at Alexandria; the British–Ottoman troops besiege the city.
	31 March: Ottoman army arrives at El-Arich
	19 April: British and Ottoman forces capture Fort Julien at Rosetta after a four-day bombardment, opening the navigation on the Nile
	27 June: General Belliard surrenders in Cairo

OTTOMAN CHRONOLOGY

	31 August: Siege of Alexandria ends in Menou's surrender
	2 September: French troops evacuate Egypt
1802	25 June: Ottoman–French Peace
	26 October: Earthquake in Constantinople
1803	March–April: Wahhabis occupy Taif and Mecca
	8 July: Muhammad Ali Paşa becomes governor of Egypt
1804	April: Beginning of the Serbian rebellion
	4 June: Earthquake in Patras
1806	Winter: Selim III recognises Napoleon as an emperor
	June: Inability to expand the *nizâm-ı cedîd* conscription to the Balkans due to resistance of the local *ayan* notables
	December: Russians occupy Moldavia and Wallachia
	22 December: Ottomans declare war on Russia
1807–1808	Reign of Mustafa IV
1807	28 January–1 March: British fleet blockades the Dardanelles and threatens Constantinople
	20 March–14 September: British occupation of Alexandria
	12 April: beginning of the military campaign against Russia
	25–29 May: Kabakçı Incident
	29 May: Deposition of Selim III and accession of Mustafa IV
	31 May: End of the *nizâm-ı cedîd* reforms. Agreement between the court and the janissaries
	7–9 July: Treaty of Tilsit
	25 August: Russo-Ottoman armistice. Wahhabis establish their domination over the Hijaz.
	27 September: British forces evacuate Alexandria
1808–1839	Reign of Mahmud II
1808	28 July: Alemdâr Mustafa Paşa occupies Constantinople and becomes grand vizier
	Murder of Selim III; deposition of Mustafa IV and accession of Mahmud II.
	7 October: the Sultan signs the *sened-ı ıttifak*, which acknowledges provincial notables' right to resist unjust policies
	14 October: founding of a new military corps, the *sekban-ı cedîd*
	14–18 November: Janissaries revolt
	15 November: janissaries kill grand vizier Alemdâr Mustafa Paşa; execution of Mustafa IV
	18 November: Agreement between Mahmud II and the janissary corps for the dissolution of the new military units
1809	5 January: British–Ottoman Peace agreement
	23 July: Ottoman army moves against Russia
	24 October: Russian defeat at Silistra
1810	16 February: Catastrophic earthquake at Heraklion
	30 May: Russians seize Silistra
	25 June: Mahmud II declares 'holy war' against Russia
	27 September: Russians occupy Rüsçük (Ruse) and Giurgiu
	Halet Efendi plans the assassination of the Iraqi Mamluk Süleyman Paşa in Baghdad to ensure direct Ottoman administration

	Debasement of coinage
1811	Muhammad Ali Paşa of Egypt destroys the Mamluks
1812	28 May: Russo-Ottoman Peace of Bucharest
	Russia annexes parts of Bessarabia, and Serbs receive limited autonomy
	2 December: Ottoman–Egyptian troops expel the Wahhabis from Medina
1812–13	The governor of Trabzon eliminates the principal notables of the Black Sea region
1813	23 January: Egyptian troops regain Mecca from the Wahhabis
	3–7 October: suppression of the Serbian revolt
	Davud Paşa restores Mamluk rule in Baghdad
1814	Alexander Ypsilantis founds the Greek nationalist society *Philiki Hetairia* in Russia
	27 September–30 December: Suppression of the Hadži-Prodan's rebellion in Serbia
1814–15	The death of the central Anatolian *ayan* Çapanoğlu Süleyman in 1814 provides an opportunity for the Ottoman government to control the Anatolian interior
1815	March: New Serbian revolt led by Miloš Obrenović
	August: Russian pressure forces Mahmud II to acknowledge the Serbian parliament
	Mahmud II leaves Topkapı Palace for Besiktas Palace

Acknowledgements

First conceived as a series of articles written in Italian, this book later evolved in a broader research for a largest audience of readers. Along the way, it has benefited from the support of a large number of people. Therefore, it is a pleasure to thank all those who have been mentors to me over the course of this research. Most of all, I thank my 'agent in Ankara' Demiral Burak, who has helped my work tracing and sending valuable Turkish sources. I am honoured to have him as a friend of mine.

This book would never have been written without the patient solicitation of Andrew Bamford, who provided judicious comments that vastly improved the quality of the work. Many other individuals, among them scholars, friends, and colleagues, have contributed to this study either indirectly with their teaching or directly through criticisms and suggestions. To them, my most sincere thanks.

Many of the facts and places described in this book will probably seem unfamiliar to readers, yet many of them resonate ominously in more recent and even current chronicles. If history is also a means of learning about cultural diversity and aiding mutual understanding, for what it is worth, I hope this book will also serve this purpose.

BM

Florence, 20 March 2022

Notes on Transliteration, Places and Names
Names and titles in Ottoman Turkish are rendered according to modern Turkish usage and not by strict transliteration. Arabic names and titles are transliterated according to a slightly simplified system based on that of the *International Journal of Middle Eastern Studies* (IJMES). For geographical names frequently encountered in material in the English language, common English usage is preferred. Thus, the reader finds Damascus, Smyrna, and Salonika, not Dimashq, Izmir, and Thessaloniki. For all other place names, to avoid confusion, the Ottoman designations or that of the contemporary successor states of the Balkans and Near East have been employed. For personal names, the original diction has been left.

1

'The Sick Man of Europe'

The world is turning upside down, with no hope for better during our reign,
Wicked fate has delivered the state into the hands of despicable men.
Our bureaucrats are villains, who prowl through the streets of Constantinople,
We can do nothing but beg God for mercy.[1]

European diplomacy of the mid nineteenth century portrayed the Ottoman Empire as the paradigm of a state condemned to irreversible decline and with no hope of survival in the scenario dominated by the Western European powers.[2] According to some authoritative scholars, the influx of American silver and an associated price revolution, combined with the demographic pressures, the rise of Western European military states, and their economic hegemony, were instrumental in the corruption of the classical Ottoman administrative system.[3] In other words, the Ottoman Empire simply did not have the means to compete with the European powers, which were undergoing a wide-ranging technological transformation, and consequently

---

1   Shortly before his death in 1774, Sultan Mustafa III composed this quatrain describing the state of the Ottoman Empire. See 'Ataullah Ahmed, *Tarih-i 'At 'nın Eş 'ar Faslına Dair Olan Dördüncü Cildidir* (Istanbul, 1876), p.67.

2   Emperor Nicholas I of Russia (1796–1855) is considered to be the first to use the term 'Sick Man' to describe the Ottoman Empire in the mid nineteenth century. The characterisation existed during the 'Eastern Question' in diplomatic history, which also referred to the decline of the Ottoman Empire in terms of the balance of power in Europe.

3   The decline of the Ottoman Empire was first discussed by Bernard Lewis in 'Some Reflections on the Decline of the Ottoman Empire' in *Studia Islamica*, IX (1958), pp.111–127, and *The Emergence of Modern Turkey* (London and New York, NY: Oxford University Press, 1968), pp.21–39. Among the most recent works, see Rifaat Ali Abou El-Haj, *Formation of the Modern State: The Ottoman Empire Sixteenth to Eighteenth Centuries* (New York: State University of New York Press, 1991); Suraiya N. Faroqhi (ed.) *The Cambridge History of Turkey, vol. 3 – The Later Ottoman Empire, 1603–1839* (Cambridge: Cambridge University Press, 2006); Virginia H. Aksan, *Ottoman Wars, 1700–1870. An Empire Besieged* (London and New York, NY: Routledge, 2007), and Fanani, Ahmad Fuad,'The Otoman Empire. Its Rise, Decline and Collapse', in *Jurnal Salam Pascasarjana Universitas Muhammadiyah Malang*, vol. 14 (2011), pp.93 109.

THE OTTOMAN ARMY OF THE NAPOLEONIC WARS 1789–1815

The Old Sick Man of Europe in a comic by Charles Lewis Bartholomew (1869–1949). From 1787 to 1815 the Ottoman armies were generally defeated, and often in a humiliating way, whenever they saw themselves forced to go toward with one of the great European powers, or whenever an adventurous general such as Napoleon Bonaparte on his Egyptian expedition of 1799–1802 saw an opportunity to attack without risking serious reaction in Europe. Only the English naval expeditions against Istanbul and Egypt in 1807 ended with some kind of Ottoman success. Otherwise, the sultans' armies on their own were never again in a position to efficiently defend the Empire.

its decline was a foregone conclusion.[4]

To these evils, others were added, generated by a system of relations and power now out of control. Corruption and bad governance had already marked the Empire at various stages of its history, but by the second half of the eighteenth century all institutions were in an unprecedented state of abjection. The connivance between the sultan's officials and an underworld system akin to modern organised crime was precipitating a catastrophe in the Empire.

Classic historiography has frequently tended to view the decreasing participation of the sultans in political life as evidence of the 'Ottoman decline', which supposedly began at some time during the second half of the sixteenth century. According to this view, the 'decline' coincides with the period when the reigning sultans became unconcerned with politics, or were minors, or were clumsy men.[5] The statements about the decadence reinvigorated during the eighteenth century, when the Ottoman Empire became a second-tier power, and in the following century many diplomats considered it no power at all, but merely a potential problem. Thus, the Ottoman Empire existed briefly as a full and active member of a concert of European states.[6]

The decline theory as such and its application to the Ottoman context have widely been criticised and investigated. In terms of historiography, this was a rigidly linear perception of history that confined any Ottoman effort at modernisation as an inherently futile attempt. By judging that the eventual collapse of the Empire was evidence of earlier incapability to adopt modern models and reforms, decline theory provided historians with a fundamentally anachronistic framework. Modern scholars have pointed out on the fact that in the eighteenth century, the Ottoman Empire was still a not negligible power, and that noticeable though limited economic recovery followed the 1720s crisis. In the following decades came longer and positive economic growth, and major evidence of the Ottoman decline is not visible before the

---

4 For some classical examples see Hakkı Uzunçarşılı, İsmail, *Osmanı Tarihi*, vol. 3 (Ankara: Türk Tarih Kurumu Basmevi, 1983), pp.270–288; Halil İnalcık, 'The Ottoman State: Economy and Society, 1300–1600' in H. İnalcık and D. Quataert, *An Economic and Social History of the Ottoman Empire, 1300-1914* (Cambridge: Cambridge University Press, 1994), p.22; Ömer Lütfi Barkan and Justin McCarthy, 'The Price Revolution of the Sixteenth Century: A Turning Point in the Economic History of the Near East', in *International Journal of Middle East Studies*, vol. 6, n. 1, January 1975, pp.3–29.

5 Suraya Faroqhi, 'Crisis and Change', in S. Faroqhi, B. McGowan, D. Quataert, S. Pamuk (eds), *An Economic and Social History of the Ottoman Empire* (Cambridge: Cambridge University Press, 1999), vol. II, p.553.

6 Gerald MacLean, *Looking East. English Writing and the Ottoman Empire before 1800* (New York, NY: Pearlgrave, 2007), p.245: 'British attitudes towards the Ottomans and the Ottoman Empire from the mid sixteenth through the eighteenth century were initially and substantively characterised by imperial envy, a structure of feeling that combined admiration with contempt, fear with fascination, desire with revulsion.'

nineteenth century.[7] From the military perspective, declinists have difficulty in explaining the Ottoman victories and military successes, other than pointing out factors such as unusual leadership, geographical difficulties, or simple luck. This difficulty is even more evident when trying to explain the relative ease with which the Ottoman government overcame serious military defeats in the eighteenth and nineteenth centuries. Moreover, someone might argue that the Empire of the descendants of Osman continued to exist until 1922 despite all the problems that plagued it. It is precisely on this apparent contradiction that much of the historiography on the Ottomans has focused in recent years. The judgements hastily expressed since the end of the eighteenth century about the Ottoman ability to resist the expansionism of its closest rivals, such as Austria and Russia, needed to be investigated from a different perspective, especially in the field of the 'New Military History', which often sidestepped or underestimated the remaining strengths of the sultan's empire. On this specific matter the work of authoritative scholars has opened new perspectives, increasing knowledge about the Ottoman Empire and its 'military' in one of the most dramatic phases of its history.[8] According to them, the Ottomans lost the wars of the eighteenth and early nineteenth centuries because the most recent developments in warfare had largely passed them by. However it is remarkable that, despite continuous defeats on all fronts, the Ottoman military did not disintegrate.

Though the idea of a single 'military revolution' in Europe has now largely been abandoned, the cumulative effect of changes in military technology and organisation were particularly significant for the Ottoman Empire. In the second half of the eighteenth century, from the Iberian Peninsula to Russia, standing or state-commissioned armies had achieved a level of discipline and drill and a degree of standardisation of equipment that had been unthinkable a century before. The better discipline and drill improved the tactical co-ordination of the units on the battlefield. The major European powers such as England, France and Prussia led this development; neither the Ottomans, nor any other non-European power succeeded in effectively following their lesson. The Ottomans in particular faced many obstacles to the processes of modernisation, centralisation, and industrialisation that characterised the rise of the European nation states. Historians remark that

---

7   Economic and military historians have shown the remarkable resurgence of the Ottoman Empire in the seventeenth century and argued that the economy and war industry did not substantially decline until about the mid to late eighteenth century. See Gábor Ágoston, 'Military Transformation in the Ottoman Empire and Russia, 1500–1800', in *Kritika* 12, n. 2 (Spring 2011), p.287.

8   Virginia H. Aksan, 'Military Reforms and its Limits in a Shrinking Ottoman World, 1800–1849', in V. H. Aksan and D. Goffman (eds), *The Early Modern Ottomans* (Cambridge: Cambridge University Press 2007), p.118: 'The Ottomans and their successors of the Middle East are generally thought to have failed to impose civilian order over militarised regimes, which is demonstrably the case. Yet studies of nation-state emergence often mute the central role played by violence in constructing all modern state, except in the Middle East, which is relentlessly castigated for its militarism.'

the peoples of the Ottoman Empire never developed an actual national identity comparable to the coeval nation-states.[9] They spoke a plethora of languages; they espoused several religions; their sense of governance was diffused not only by patriarchal and rabbinic authority and power, but also by foreign determination to regulate Ottoman treatment of Catholic and Orthodox subjects; their borders were more and more blurred and malleable because of the insistence of foreign powers on commercial, political, and missionary access. Such manifold barriers to the creation of a national identity proved too many to overcome. All these negative factors represented serious obstacles, and the Ottoman Empire did not, as it probably could not, follow a course parallel to the emerging powers of the modern world.

However, even if it is not correct to consider the last three centuries of Ottoman history as an age of decline, certainly it is possible to speak of poor development, or at least of little progress.[10] As a result, in the eighteenth century the Ottoman 'military' was in disarray. Financial and political crisis after crisis strapped the Empire's ability to maintain an effective armed force throughout its domains. Obviously, this does not mean that every attempt to reform failed, but the matter was not easy to manage. In particular, it is fundamental to consider that the word 'reform' had a changing meaning in Ottoman society.[11] Recently, historians have proposed new interpretations about the period of reforms. Some of them portray the years between the 1720s and the early nineteenth century as 'a long period of transformation of the Ottoman society'.[12] Characteristically the Ottomans attempted to achieve

---

9   Alessio Bombaci, Stanford J. Shaw, *L'Impero Ottomano – Storia Universale dei Popoli e delle Civiltà*, vol. VI (Turin: Utet, 1981), pp.398–402.

10   Bombaci and Shaw, *L'Impero Ottomano*, p.403: 'With regard to its composition and the vastness of the peoples who composed the Empire, it was not possible to find a single explanation capable of encompassing such diverse experiences. The Ottoman state was a multi-ethnic and multi-religious empire, in which varying degrees of autonomy existed between some provinces and the political centre. This aspect alone shows how complex and varied the problem was. Researches showed that, despite the apparent immutability of its institutions, the Empire had sought to reform itself in order to respond to challenges from outside, and how the reforms were implemented since the beginning of the eighteenth century.'

11   Even after the Peace of Carlowitz in 1699, reform meant a search for the old forms which had been the underpinning of earlier Ottoman centuries. See also Bruce McGowan, 'The Age of the *Ayans*', in S. Faroqhi, B. McGowan; D. Quataert, S. Pamuk (eds), *An Economic and Social History of the Ottoman Empire* (Cambridge: Cambridge University Press, 1999), vol. II, pp.639–643.

12   Kadir Ustun, 'The New Order and Its Enemies: Opposition to Military Reform in the Ottoman Empire, 1789–1807' (Submitted in partial fulfillment of the requirements for the degree of Doctor of Philosophy in the Graduate School of Arts and Sciences: Columbia University, 2013), p.14: 'In addition to its anachronism, the decline theory prioritized political and military success by stripping social, economic, and cultural processes of their relevance for history. Economic, social, and cultural histories written on various regions of the Empire over the past several decades have emphasised change as an analytical category as opposed to decline.' See also Jamal Malik, 'Muslim Culture and Reform in 18th Century South Asia,' in *Journal of the Royal Asiatic*

THE OTTOMAN ARMY OF THE NAPOLEONIC WARS 1789–1815

Abdülhamid I (reigning from 1774 to 1789) emerged on the throne with a clear understanding of the need to reform the Empire in order to save it, and he left his mark as one of the strongest reforming sultans of the eighteenth century. While he resorted to the old Ottoman game of playing off parties and changing ministers to keep power in his hands, he promoted traditionalistic reform, seeking to introduce the new military techniques and weapons that were necessary to meet the modern European armies. He was the first sultan to import large numbers of foreign military advisers and to use them without the requirements of conversion and adoption of Ottoman dress and customs, thus inaugurating a transition to the new style of reform that was to dominate throughout the nineteenth century. While maintaining personal direction of reforms, he operated through two grand viziers, Kara Vezir Seyyit Mehmet Paşa (1779–1781) and Halil Hamit Paşa (1782–1785), with the latter especially becoming one of the great Ottoman reformers in the course of his relatively brief term in office.

Sultan Selim III (r. 1789–1807) was a skilled calligrapher and a musician, and cultivated interest in Western technology and art, particularly painting. In this image, Selim's recently modernised naval dockyard at Kasimpağa in Constantinople is shown in the background, and newly cast cannons and mortars are lying in the foreground. Much of Selim III's reign was taken up with the problems resulting from Napoleon's invasion of Egypt in 1798, with considerable revolts on all fronts, in pre-Napoleonic Egypt and the Hijaz, and also in Arabia, Eastern Anatolia, and the Balkans. Selim's attempts to modernise state and army along Napoleonic lines resulted in his deposition and death. His murder in 1808 has resulted in a widespread misperception of Ottoman affairs, causing students and historians to falsely romanticise the reign of Selim III as a struggle between religious reactionaries and the reformers.

this transformation from the top down, via central state power.¹³ Reform and finally modernity often clashed not only with conservative interests but also with those of certain sectors of society favouring other types of transformation.¹⁴ Historians therefore describe two distinct periods of reforms, substantially diverging, and decidedly in conflict with each other. The belief that the failures and the crisis were the consequence of the relaxation of the authority of the sultan and his government, resulted in the 'traditionalist reform', which sought to restore the state to the purity and strength of its origins. After the Peace of Passarowitz (today Požarevac, in Serbia), signed in 1718, the Ottoman policy was therefore oriented to the reaffirmation of internal power, and at least it succeeded in restoring to the sultan a political dignity which seemed to have disappeared after the golden age of Süleyman the Magnificent. As might be expected from a highly conservative and traditionalist approach, the Ottoman reformers identified the main reason behind the deterioration of the Empire (and army too) as corruption and disuse of the classical institutions, which they immediately linked to the lost virtues of a centralised, efficient, and rational classical system.¹⁵ They saw the growth of the *kapıkulu* corps, especially the janissaries, and introduction of foreign elements into the corps, as instrumental in increasing corruption and in causing poor performance.¹⁶ The scenario becomes even more intricate because of the structure of Ottoman power. The Porte constantly exercised control following the traditional policy of balances opposing and equilibrating the different factions, especially the military one represented by janissaries, but the results had often been fraught with unpleasant consequences. Among the most serious and lasting, the transformation of the ancient structure of government and military organisation represented

---

Society 13, no. 2 (2003), p.229, and Bernard Lewis, *What Went Wrong? Western Impact and Middle Eastern Response* (Oxford; New York: Oxford University Press, 2002).

13 Aksan, *Ottoman Wars*, p.2.

14 Suraiya N. Faroqhi (ed.), *The Cambridge History of Turkey volume 3. The Later Ottoman Empire, 1603–1839* (Cambridge: Cambridge University Press, 2006), p, 60: 'Little research has been done on why Ottoman society did not embark on a more holistic approach, and why there have been numerous Ottoman modernities rather than a single version of the modernity project.'

15 Mesut Uyar, Edward Erickson, *A Military History of the Ottomans. From Osman to Atatürk* (Santa Barbara, CA: ABC Clio, 2009), p.82: 'Obviously, a totally new approach is needed to explain the Ottoman military, but the first focus must be on the increased capability of the Ottoman military's logistical and manpower systems in order to explain why this period should be labelled as a 'transformation' rather than a 'decline'.

16 Curiously, the Western commenters' view about the crisis afflicting the Empire identified the presence of a large standing army as the fundamental cause of the corruption. This judgement is decidedly singular, considering that even in the Europe of the *ancien régime*, corruption was widespread at all levels. See Alessandro Barbero, *Il Divano di Istanbul* (Palermo: Sellerio, 2015), p.169.

by the *timar* system disappeared,[17] opening the way to new and particularly aggressive social elites, such as the unscrupulous *ayan* magnates.[18]

The age of traditionalist reforms lasted until the 1790s, but produced few results.[19] Except for the conquest of Belgrade in 1738, the Ottomans were continually defeated and lost strategic territories on the north-eastern frontier and Black Sea. After the bitter defeat suffered in the Russo-Ottoman war of 1768–1774, Sultan Abdülhamid I (reigning 1774–1789) emerged on the throne with a clear understanding of the need to further reform the state. He left his mark as one of the strongest reforming sultans of the eighteenth century. Though he promoted another extensive season of traditional reform, Abdülhamid aimed to introduce new military tactics, discipline and weapons that were absolutely necessary to face the armies of the European enemies. Although he had spent most of his 50 years in the seclusion of the Palace, particularly during the reign of his brother Mustafa III, Abdülhamid I went much further than his predecessors, and although the results were below expectations, his policy represented a transitional phase between old and new viewpoint in matters of reform.[20]

After him, Selim III (sultan in 1789) strongly favoured the rise of original attempts at reform filtered through Western European models. Setting aside any idea of restoring the ancient 'traditional' order, with him the age

---

17 A *timar* was the land granted distributed in the form of temporary concession by the sultans to their bravest soldiers. There were three categories of *timar* estates according to their tax values: *timar* worth between 2,000 and 19, 999 *akçe* (asper), *zeamet* 20,000–99,999 *akçe*, and those with more than 100,000 *akçe*. The revenues produced from land acted as compensation for military service. The *zeamet* estates were generally given to senior military officers according to their ranks, which left the smaller *timars* for common *sipahis* and junior officers.

18 *Ayan* is the plural of the Arabic word *ayn,* meaning 'something or someone that is selected or special'. The term was used differently by different communities within the Ottoman Empire, although in Anatolia the more common term was *derebey*. In the eighteenth century, the term *ayan* was most often applied to an individual who was recognised as a civic leader in a town or village or to a provincial notable, as contrasted with Ottoman officials appointed from Constantinople. Such *ayan* had their own armed forces to support his power and enjoyed varying degrees of autonomy from the central government in provincial administration. Their legitimacy depended on their positions as governors recognised by the Porte.

19 In 1727, a modest Hungarian or Transylvanian renegade named Müteferrika Ibrahim, with the support of Grand Vizier Damad İbrahim Pasha and other prominent court personalities, achieved the most prominent reform effort of this period with the establishment of the first Turkish printing house. Even though this was not a military reform, it affected the military educational system drastically in the coming decades. It also provides a case study to understand the shortcomings and structural problems of both the Ottoman reforms and reformers. See also Faroqhi, p.640.

20 Stanford J. Shaw, *History of the Ottoman Empire and Modern Turkey Volume I: Empire of the Gazis: The Rise and Decline of the Ottoman Empire, 1280-1808* (Cambridge: Cambridge University Press, 1977), p.251. According to the author, Abdülhamid I was the first sultan to import large numbers of foreign military advisers and to use them without the requirements of conversion and adoption of Ottoman dress and ways, thus inaugurating a transition to the new style of reform that was to dominate throughout the nineteenth century.

of modern reforms began, culminating in the reign of Mahmud II and the decisive season of the *tanzimat*.[21]

The period 1789–1815 is perhaps one of the most tumultuous in the long history of the Ottoman house.[22] It has been a crucial moment in world history too, but for the Ottoman Empire it was a do-or-die moment, hardly the period to introduce liberalism, or constitutionalism.[23] In this age, an ever-resourceful government continued to overcome its problems by creative or pragmatic methods, although it must be said that sometimes the solutions themselves were instrumental in the creation of even larger secondary problems. In this perspective, the theory of decline is unable to explain the rapid transformation of the Ottoman military machine against the threat raised by the Habsburgs and Romanovs or its ability to fight on the eastern and western frontiers at the same time. In truth, following contemporary European trends, the Ottoman military transformed itself slowly but decisively by introducing new firearms, and increasingly making use of siege and counter-siege tactics. Still, the picture is very much complicated by the arrival of the seaborne powers of France and Great Britain. For historians of the Eastern Question, the centrepiece of the struggle has been the problem posed by the 'Sick Man of Europe', or, to view the situation from the other side, 'the impediments to modernisation through consensus that were exacerbated by the self-serving policies of meddling foreign powers',[24] but the age of transformation was much more complicated than foreign interference with sovereign rights.

Obviously, a thoroughly new approach is needed to explain the Ottoman military between 1789 and 1815, but the first focus must be on the astonishing capacity of resistance of the 'Old Sick Man'.

The Ottoman Empire at the Turn of the Century

The most salient characteristic of the Ottoman Empire at the end of the eighteenth century was its fragmentation. In several respects, the Ottoman state can only be considered an empire in the loose sense in which the term is used to refer to such medieval states as the coeval Chinese Empire. Its administrative establishment, economic system, and social organisation all

---

21 The word *tanzimat* means 'reforms', 'rearrangement', and 'reorganisation', and in Ottoman history the *tanzimat* period refers to a time of Westernising reforms from 1839 until 1876.

22 Kemal H. Karpat, 'The Transformation of the Ottoman State, 1789–1908' in R. Schulze (ed.). *Studies on Ottoman Social and Political History* (Leiden-Cologne-Boston, MS: Brill, 2002), p.27: 'The study of the Ottoman state in the latter part of the eighteenth century and throughout the nineteenth demands a broader analytical framework than hitherto used if its transformation and the social and political history of the Middle East, the Balkans, and even North Africa, which were parts of the Ottoman state at one time or other, are to be properly evaluated and interpreted.'

23 Aksan, *Ottoman Wars*, p.7.

24 Ann Pottinger Saab, *Origins of the Crimean Alliance* (Charlottesville, VA: University Press of Virginia, 1977), p.161.

call to mind the structure of a pre-modern state. The Ottoman 'Imperial' linguistic usage reflects the social reality, since it divided the population into two basic categories: *askeri*, 'the military class', and *re'aya*, subjects (literally, the sultan's flock). The ruling class often used its power to enrich itself, legally or illegally. Some civilians, mostly merchants, were often in a precarious position and could be exploited and blackmailed by soldiers and emirs. At the end of the eighteenth century, the Empire was still divided into three *beglerbegliks* (Rumelia, Anatolia and Egypt), 22 *paşaliks*, 210 *beylics*, 300 *zeamets* and about 50,000 *timars*.[25] In the major Ottoman provinces, *beglerbegs* and *paşas* were the highest-ranking officials, who as the sultan's representatives administered the province and were responsible for protecting the central government's interests, including collection and delivery of revenues, the maintenance of law and order, and safeguarding the Empire's strategic interests. This venerable structure was replaced in 1795 by a new organisation, when the government launched a major reorganisation of provincial administration. Designed to strengthen central control over the periphery, the new law decreed that there would be 28 *vilayets*, or provinces, in the Empire, each to be governed by a *vizier* or *vali*, who acted like the predecessor, and usually held the title of *paşa*.[26] The *vilayets* were Adana, Aleppo, Anatolia, Baghdad, Basra, Bosnia, Crete, Çıldır, Damascus, Diyarbakir, Egypt, Erzurum, Jeddah, Karaman, Kars, Maraş, the Aegean Islands with Cyprus, the Peloponnese, Mosul, Rakka, Rumelia, Sayda, Şehr-i Zor, Silistra, Sivas, Trabzon, Tripoli in Lebanon, and Van.[27] Each *vilayet* was divided into *sancaks*.[28]

Nominally or directly, the sultan's rule stretched from North Africa to Yemen, Bosnia to the Caucasus, and Ethiopia to Basra, encompassing a vast area inhabited by some 30 million people.[29] As for the singular regions, population estimates wary widely. Though some, like those of the French in Egypt, were based on modern criteria, no census of any part of the Ottoman Empire took place before 1831. Tax records suggest that, while the European population of the Empire outweighed that of Anatolia in the early eighteenth century, 100 years after that they were more nearly equal. The Arab domains generally, with the possible exception of the Arabian Peninsula, were still trending downwards at the time of Napoleon's expedition to Egypt. It is

---

25 Sükrü M. Hanioğlu, *A Brief History of the Late Ottoman Empire* (Princeton, NJ: Princeton University Press, 2008), p.49.

26 Occasionally, the Sultan could award his subject for special merit with the title of *beylerbey* or *mirmiran*. Both titles followed the rank of vizier.

27 Hanioğlu, *A Brief History of the Late Ottoman* Empire, p.50.

28 Madeline C. Zilfi, 'The Ottoman Ulema', in S. Faroqhi (ed.), *The Cambridge History of Turkey, vol. 3 – The Later Ottoman Empire, 1603–1839* (Cambridge: Cambridge University Press, 2006), p.212. Beneath these military-administrative layers, the Ottomans divided their empire into districts (*kazas*), and assigned to them a small army of kadis, jurisconsults (*müftis*) and legal clerks.

29 Hanioğlu, *A Brief History of the Late Ottoman Empire*, p.30. According to McGowan 'The Age of the *Ayans*', p.646, coeval estimates of total population around 1800 vary between 25 and 32 million.

THE OTTOMAN ARMY OF THE NAPOLEONIC WARS 1789–1815

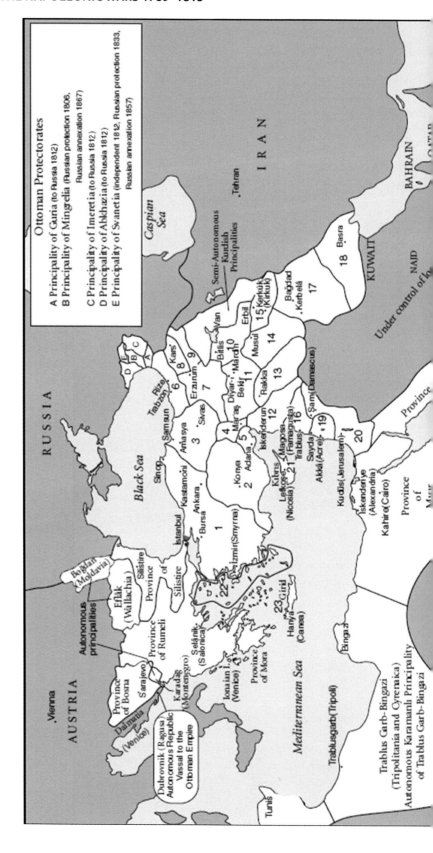

'THE SICK MAN OF EUROPE'

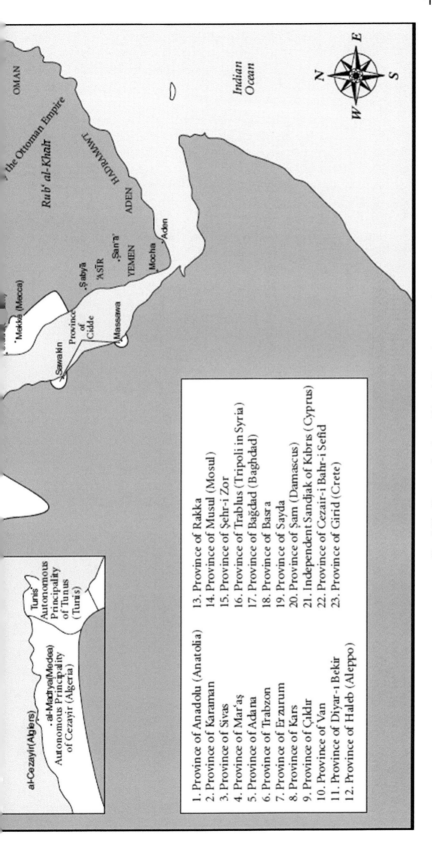

Map 1 The Ottoman Empire and Vassals States (1787–1815)

certain that both Syria and Egypt experienced great losses during the last third of the eighteenth century, owing to the combined scourge of wars, fiscal rapacity, famine and insecurity. Taken as a whole, the Ottoman Empire did not participate in the considerable gains registered in Western Europe and Russia after the middle of the eighteenth century.

Old Constantinople, within the walls, may have held about 300,000–350,000 inhabitants when not devastated by fire or epidemic. The whole population, including suburbs, amounted to about 600,000 in the late eighteenth century. Early in the next century, a French Jesuit estimated among the total about 200,000 Greeks and 80,000 Armenians. Western residents numbered 3,000, not counting 20,000 slave oarsmen and a further 4,000–5,000 domestic slaves of Western origin.[30] Except for Edirne, which had an estimated population of about 100,000, the other European cities of the Empire show an overall downward trend.[31]

Waves of migration already were moving as the eighteenth century progressed. Muslim Bosnian bordermen driven from Hungary returned to settle in Bosnia, or wherever they could, crossing paths with a northbound flow of Orthodox Christian Serbs into southern Hungary, and Bosnian Catholics into Slavonia. Serbia grew swiftly during the eighteenth century, from fewer than 100,000 in 1739 to about 200,000–230,000 by 1800, much of it thanks to the immigration from the south-west.[32] Among the major cities of this area, Belgrade still had a relatively modest population of about 25,000–30,000 in 1816.[33] Sarajevo had an estimated population of 40,000–45,000 around 1800. The demographic mobility of the region generated centres that quickly increased the population to several thousand. For instance, the *Tsintsar* centre of Moscopolje, which may have reached 40,000 before being sacked for the first time in 1769, was almost as large as Sarajevo.[34] The whole population of Bosnia varied at around one to one and a half million in the period 1750–1800.[35] In eastern Bosnia the formerly predominant Muslim population was gradually replaced by northward-bound Serbian Orthodox peasants, some of whom accepted the harsh conditions of Bosnia and some of whom moved on into the reconstituted *paşalik* of Belgrade after 1739. During the 1770s and 1780s there was much spontaneous northbound migration across the Sava and the Danube, in part responding to the attraction of the fortified towns of Zemun and Novi (today Novi Sad in Serbia). The emigration was especially heavy during the war

---

30 Hanioğlu, *A Brief History of the Late Ottoman Empire*, p.652.
31 Yücel Özkaya, 'XVIII Yüzilim Sonlarında Timar ve Zeametlerin Düzeni Konusunda Alinan Tedbirler ve Sonuçlari', in *TD, XXXII* (1979), p.219.
32 Robert Bideleux, Ian Jeffries, *A History of Eastern Europe. Crisis and Change* (London and New York, NY: Routledge, 2007), p.91.
33 Duran Nurbanu, 'Life in the Belgrade Fortress in the First Quarter of the 19th Century', in R. Srdan and S. Aslantaş (eds), *Belgrade 1521–1867* (Belgrade: The Institute of History, 2018), p.288.
34 McGowan, 'The Age of the *Ayans*', p.653.
35 M. Šamic, 'Economski život Bosne i Sarajeva početkom XIX vijeka' in *Godišnjak Istorijskog Društva Bosne i Hercegovine*, IX, pp.111–134.

of 1787–92, when many Serbs were organised into Austrian *Freikorps*, and also during the Serbian wars of independence between 1804 and 1815, when pressure from Ottoman reprisals made life dangerous for the Serbs.[36] Bosnia continued to lose many Serbian 'families' across its northern border as it attracted from still harsher provinces to the south. As a result, many Serbs also crossed the Sava River into Habsburg territory.

Population movements affected one region differently from another. In Bulgaria, however, the population followed a similar trend to that of the neighbouring provinces. During the eighteenth century, Bulgaria had an estimated population of 600,000–800,000.[37] Recovery was slow, since the overall population of the Balkans, according to one estimate, fell from a high of eight million in the late sixteenth century to a mid-eighteenth century low of three million.[38] Each of three Russo-Ottoman Wars between 1786 and 1812 caused waves of Bulgarian refugees, totalling as many as 200,000, to cross over into the Rumanian provinces, and most of them continuing into the newly conquered Russian territories where they replaced the retreating Tatars. The second of these wars also drove many Bulgarians into Thrace and Macedonia. Their fate could not have been happy since this was also a climactic period of two decades in which the newly risen warlords of Ottoman Empire, the *ayans*, where locked in a struggle for dominance. Between 1797 and 1800, in particular, there occurred a large-scale flight of Bulgarian refugees into Constantinople. These movements, like those of the Greeks, brought many Bulgarians into contact with foreign cultures and stimulated their emergence as a modern nation.[39]

In contrast to the previous cases, trade boosted the population of several Albanian towns during the eighteenth century. Shkoder had about 30,000 inhabitants in 1739 but reportedly this doubled to 60,000 by 1793.[40] In Ottoman Albania Muslims were the majority, but there were large areas populated by Orthodox Christians, while Catholic Albanians inhabited the Venetian-controlled regions of present-day Kotor in Montenegro. In 1800, ethnic Albanians numbered about 700,000–800,000 persons, of which 30

36　The Habsburgs wisely permitted Serbian refugees to settle in their southernmost provinces during the disturbed years of the eighteenth and early nineteenth centuries. These émigrés often enlisted in the longstanding *Militärgrenze* under a special regime.

37　Richard J. Crampton, *A Concise History of Bulgaria* (Cambridge: Cambridge University Press, 2005), p.52.

38　McGowan, 'The Age of the *Ayans*', p.653. Bulgarians towns are given impressive, perhaps inflated estimates for the second half of the century: Sofia 70,000, Filibe (Plovdiv) 50,000, Rüsçük (Ruse) 30,000, Şumen 30,000, Vidin 20,000, Nicopolis 20,000, Zistovi (Svistov) 20,000, and Varna 15,000.

39　McGowan, 'The Age of the *Ayans*', p.649.

40　McGowan, 'The Age of the *Ayans*', p.653. Other Albanian towns at the end of the century: Arta held 10,000 persons, and Preveza 10,000–12,000. Elbasan already had 6,000 families, and Berat 5,000 families, implying populations of 30,000 and 25,000 respectively, though these figures could be exaggerated.

percent settled outside Albania's modern borders.[41] Furthermore, Albanian clansmen and mercenaries, migrating from a region that was relatively densely populated at the time, found a place in most of the great retinues of Ottoman Europe during the eighteenth century, especially in Constantinople, and often went much further afield to Syria, North Africa and Egypt.[42] Alongside the Muslims of Bosnia they became the leading mercenaries on the European side. However, they could be difficult to control because of their powerful kinship relations. Largely employed in Greece during the war of 1768–74, the Albanian *arnavut* mercenaries then settled down as predators and usurers, and had to be rooted out long after the war had ended.

The havoc created in the Peloponnese by the Albanian soldiers in the 1770s caused a great portion of the Greeks there to migrate, some into the Pindus Mountains as far as they could go to Italy, to Austria and even to Russia, but above all to the Sporades islands and the Anatolian shore opposite Greece. Many Greeks from the Peloponnese were also sold as slaves during the nine-year Albanian occupation.[43] The population of continental Greece as a whole was an estimated half million on the eve of the revolution of 1821. This represented a comeback from the dark days of the 1770s, when the Peloponnese seems to have lost 30,000–60,000 residents, who had either died or fled to safer places.[44] In the archipelago, Chios was the leading island with almost 80,000 inhabitants at the end of the eighteenth century. The major Greek island in the Mediterranean, Crete, did not experience the same growth and had fewer than 50,000 inhabitants. The port of Salonika was the largest town in Greece, growing spectacularly in the eighteenth century, with a population of 60,000–70,000 by its end.[45]

---

41 Robert Elsie, *Historical Dictionary of Albania. Historical Dictionaries of Europe, No. 75* (Plymouth: The Scarecrow Press, 2010), p.59.

42 Uğur Bayraktar, 'From salary to resistance: mobility, employment, and violence in Dibra, 1792–1826', in *Middle Eastern Studies*, vol. 54, No. 6 (2018), p.880: 'The Porte concerned about the expansion of Albanian migration throughout the Empire during the eighteenth century. Especially following the Patrona Halil Rebellion, which was an urban protest against the new taxes resulting from the dethronement of Ahmed and the execution of the Grand Vizier Ibrahim Pasha, the Ottomans treated the immigrants as a threat to public security in Istanbul. As Halil was ethnically Albanian and as he was able to mobilise 22,000 Albanians in the capital, Ottoman officials chose to replace the word "immigrants" with Albanians.'

43 McGowan, 'The Age of the *Ayans*', p.654. The flight of Greece sometimes was answered by a movement of Turkish peasants to take their place in this account from Larissa dated about 1806: 'The Greece are continually migrating, chiefly to the districts of Ionia governed by the family of Karaosmanoğlu; in return Turkish peasants from Asia Minor have settled on some of the Larissean Farms, and have been able to live better than the Greeks, because they are exempt from the *kharatj* (head tax), and some impositions to which the Greeks alone are liable.'

44 Fariba Zarinebaf, Jack L. Davis, John Bennet, *A Historical and Economic Geography of Ottoman Greece: the Southwestern Morea in the 18th Century* (Princeton, NJ: Hesperia, 2005), p.28.

45 Other major Greek towns around 1800 were Seres with 30,000 inhabitants, Larissa 20,000, Vodina 12,000, Patras 10,000, and Athens 12,000. Yanina, which held a mixed population of Albanians and Greeks, may have numbered 16,000 inhabitants. The demographic situation was

The celebration in the Topkapı Palace after the Eid prayer; detail from a painting of an anonymous artist, early 1800s. With some notable exceptions, most of the sultans until the late eighteenth century reigned rather than ruled. The sultan's authority was limited and often undermined by competing court factions. In the eighteenth century sultanic authority was further limited as an emerging network of *paşa* and vizierial households and their protégés gained power in the Ottoman court. Although Mahmud II (r. 1808–39) reasserted sultanic power for a time, in the following years the powerful grand viziers returned to their prominent role in the administration of the Empire.

Considerable nomadic groups were still widespread throughout the Balkan area, including Macedonia and northern Greece. Among them the Aromanians represented the largest group, which still travelled this area organised in clans of shepherds. They were considered ethnic Rumanians, and possibly numbered 30,000 persons.⁴⁶

Regarding the semi-autonomous Rumanian principalities of Wallachia and Moldavia, the population fell from about a million in 1700 to half that by the mid century. In both the principalities, the harsh Russian occupation during the war of 1736–39 and fear of servitude drove many peasants into Habsburg territory. This trend continued after the war as up to 77,000 Rumanian peasants fled from the renewed Phanariote rule into the Banat and into Transylvania, causing a crisis in government in two nearly Ottoman provinces. These regions, as well as the Ottoman Empire generally, enjoyed relatively greater security during the subsequent

---

much better in the archipelago, where some of the Aegean islands experienced considerable growth, partly as a result of emigration from the mainland. See Antoine, Baron de Jucherau de Saint-Denis, *Histoire de l'Empire Ottoman depuis 1792 jusqu'en 1844* (Paris, 1844), vol. I, p.180.

46 There is still some ambiguity about the actual origin of the Aromanians, Greece considers them Greeks Romanised by language, and Romania takes them as Romanians. The Ottomans had recognised their identity since the fifteenth century. In modern day the Aromanian population is estimated about 200,000. See in Corneliu Zeana, 'The Aromanians, a Distinct Balkan Ethnicity', in I. Boldea (ed.), *The Shades of Globalisation. Identity and Dialogue in an Intercultural World* (Targu Mures: Arhipelag, 2021), pp.39–44.

Pazvantoğlu Osman (1758–1807), portrayed in a contemporary print by unknown artist (author's archive). He was an Ottoman military officer, governor of Vidin after 1794, and one of the major *ayans* who rebelled against Constantinople. After a long and successful struggle against the forces sent against him by the Porte, in 1798 Osman submitted to the Sultan, obtained his pardon, and holding the title of *paşa* ruled large territories in Bulgaria and Serbia, while also extracting tribute from Wallachia. Several factors contributed to the raise of the *ayans*. From the eighteenth century onward the sharp distinction between the military class and the common people, the *reàyà*, gradually blurred. With the crisis of the *timar* system, new provincial figures, the *ayans*, emerged as prominent figures in the provinces. Though never officially acknowledged by the state as a status group, the *ayans* shared at the provincial level, the economic, administrative, and military authority of the *askeri* military class. The ascendancy of local families controlling districts or even whole provinces began in the first half of the eighteenth century but gained momentum later on. Political historians have conventionally regarded this process as part of the central government's collapse. More recent research, however, has demonstrated the interdependence between local power-holders and the Porte.

three decades of peace at mid century. But the Porte allowed many thousands of Moldavians to be carried off in 1758 by the Tatars, as punishment for a rebellion against the intensified state effort to channel grain to Constantinople by forced sales in the two Rumanian princedoms. As a result, the population of Bucharest declined along with it from 60,000 to a mid-century low of 30,000. Much of this loss was down to flight and deportation. Considerable immigration, as well as better administration, increased the population to an estimated one million in Wallachia during the first decade of the nineteenth century, and in Moldavia to one-half million.[47] Bucharest then numbered about 80,000, Jassy about the half of this number.[48] Russian occupation of the Rumanian provinces were more orderly beginning under Catherine's reign. Bucharest began to recover from a mid-century decline and also to attract Bulgarian refugees. After every war, both principalities had been left in devastation by the military campaigns, and the consequent famine and plague had been intensified by the exactions of the Greek Phanariote *hospodar* and *voivoda* (princes) who ruled in the name of the sultan. During the decade following the peace of Jassy in 1792, six princes in Wallachia and five in Moldavia used their short terms to secure vast revenues for themselves, with the intrigues of the Russians and family rivalries in Constantinople further complicating the situation and worsening the plight of the people they ruled.

Further east, the Tatars, who had been allies and useful raiders for the Ottoman armies, became the victims after 1774. In just 10 years from 1774 to 1784, a huge wave of migration of about 200,000 people emigrated out of Russia's orbit. Many Tatars ending up in Dobruja on the western bank of the Black Sea.[49] In connection with the loss of the

---

47 Colin McEvedy and Richard Jones, *Atlas of World Population History* (New York, NY: Facts on File, 1979), pp.93–97. Jucherau de Saint-Denis, in his *Histoire de l'Empire Ottoman*, vol. I, p.25, supplies a slight different estimate of 900,000 in Wallachia and 400,000 in Moldavia.

48 McGowan, 'The Age of the *Ayans*', p.653.

49 Brian Glyn Williams, *Crimean Tatars: the diaspora experience and the forging of nation* (Leiden-Boston, MS: Brill, 2001),

Crimea, a 'deluge' of Slavs and Greeks were driven by the Russians towards Azov, beginning in 1778. Once a grave threat to St Petersburg, and the Russian conquest of Dobruja, the Tatar nation finally survived only as a diaspora.

Alongside the Tatars, also Muslim Circassians and Abkhazians were forced to leave their settlements under Russian pressure. On this side of Black Sea, the sultan maintained an insecure rule on the Caucasus, comprising northern Armenia,[50] the western territories of modern Azerbaijan and the Georgian semi-independent principalities. The Porte also claimed its hegemony over the Circassian and the Abkhazian populations in the area. In this area, Russian and Iranian pressure had confined the Ottoman rule to Batumi and Poti on the coast, Artvin in the interior, the province of Meskheti with Akhaltsikhe, and the enclaves of western Abkhazia. There are few estimates of the population, which possibly numbered 120,000 inhabitants in Ottoman Georgia, but with strong seasonal variations, and possibly a further 200,000 Circassians and Abkhazians under Ottoman rule.[51] In the nineteenth century the Muslim inhabitants of northwestern Caucasia were expelled by the advancing Russians, and forced into Anatolia to serve as low-cost agricultural labourers.[52]

Neither can estimates of Anatolia's population can be offered with confidence, though fiscal records suggest parity with Rumelia in the late eighteenth century. Estimates for Smyrna, the premier port of the Empire, vary between 65,000 and 102,000. Bursa around 1802 is estimated at about 60,000; Ankara was probably equally populous. The cities of Iraq are thought to have lost much or most of their population during the eighteenth century, largely because of epidemic disease. Baghdad at the end of the century numbered perhaps 80,000, Mosul about 65,000. Basra, which survived a long Iranian siege in 1775, was reduced to a fraction of its former population of 40,000, perhaps as few as 4,000 persons. Before the raiding and famine of the 1780s and 1790s, Aleppo's population may have exceeded 100,000, a considerable drop from its previous peak, but still impressive. By the end of the century, Aleppo may have been close to parity with Damascus although both cities' populations had fallen dramatically.[53] Raiding and predation by the Bedouins and other bandits had reduced much of the coastal plain to marsh, thus condemning the coastal towns of Ṭarabulus (Tripoli of Lebanon), Sidon, and Antakya to relative insignificance. The challenge to Ottoman authority by the Bedouin tribes of the desert was a secular factor in Ottoman history. This challenge had increased with the northward movement of the Anazeh tribes into the Syrian periphery in the last decades of the seventeenth century. They were followed by the Shammar tribes in the

---

pp.24–26.

50 The remaining Ottoman Armenia, composed of the six *vilayets* of Erzurum, Van, Bitlis, Diyarbakir, Kharput, and Sivas, and was also referred to as Western Armenia.
51 Amjad Jaimoukha, *The Circassians: A Handbook* (New York, Palgrave, 2001), p.64.
52 R. Toledano Ehud, *Slavery and Abolition in the Ottoman Middle East* (Seattle: University of Washington Press, 1998), p.85.
53 Jucherau de Saint-Denis, *Histoire de l'Empire Ottoman*, vol. I, p.236.

THE OTTOMAN ARMY OF THE NAPOLEONIC WARS 1789–1815

Facing page: Militiamen of the Republic of Ragusa, after Richard Knötel, *Die Grosse Uniformenkunde* (1890). The tributary city-republic and major port of Ragusa (today Dubrovnik in Croatia), a kind of Ottoman Hong Kong on the Adriatic, linking the Balkan heartlands with Europe, was the centre of endless Ottoman, Austrian, and Venetian diplomatic manoeuvres and bargains. Although Vienna became the second protector of Ragusa in 1684, the Ottomans succeeded in re-establishing sole protection in the eighteenth century, and kept this city-republic in the Ottoman fold until the French occupation in 1806. The French integrated Ragusa into their *Provinces illyriennes* in 1808, but ceded it to Austria at the Congress of Vienna, whereby the Ottomans lost this vital trade link forever.

eighteenth century, increasing the pressure on Syrian villagers, especially in the south, and upon the pilgrimage caravans which set out yearly from Damascus. The Anazeh tribes increased their power, especially after the arrival of their Amarat kinsmen from eastern Arabia between 1800 and 1808. The raiding of these decades, the Saudi takeover of the pilgrimage route, and the loss of Ottoman control over the Syrian revenues combined to complete the devastation of the villages around Aleppo. Simultaneously, the Ottoman government was pushing Turkoman and Kurdish nomads to the edge of the Syrian Desert, where it was hoped that they would act as a counterweight to the pressure of Bedouin tribes encroaching upon the towns of Syria and the pilgrimage route. This programme soon failed as the displaced Turkomans drifted back to the better pastures from which they had been driven, though recorded attempts to enforce the programme occurred as late 1745.[54] East of the Tigris, Kurdish tribes, with a predatory reputation far surpassing the Turkomans, drifted southwards from Anatolia.

Following the defeat of the rebellion in 1711, political realignments on Mount Lebanon drove the Druze faction to Hawran, east of Lake Tiberias, while Christian peasants moved southwards across Mount Lebanon under the protection of the now dominant Shihabi princes. The other major port in this area was Beirut, where lived 6,000 persons, of which 4,000 were Christians.[55] Yet at the end of the century, the towns of Palestine were still considerable: Jerusalem had 9,000–10,000 inhabitants; Acre and Gaza 8,000; Nablus 7,500; Safed and Hebron 5,000 each, and Jaffa 4,000. In the early 1800s, in the hills and mountains of this region, out of reach of desert raiders, there lived a population that included fugitives from the plains.[56]

The population of Egypt in 1800 is estimated at four or four and a half million. Cairo was one of the largest cities of the Empire and held 210,000–260,000 people, and Alexandria had another 10,000–15,000. These figures represent the low of a downwards slide owing to increasingly chaotic political conditions and accompanying peasant flights, especially characteristic of the late eighteenth century.[57] The political instability and the continuous struggles between the local factions seriously affected the

---

54 McGowan, 'The Age of the *Ayans*'. p.647.
55 Jucherau de Saint-Denis, *Histoire de l'Empire Ottoman*, vol. I, p.229.
56 McGowan, 'The Age of the *Ayans*', p.654.
57 Michael Winter, *Egyptian Society under Ottoman Rule 1517–1798* (New York and London: Routledge, 1992), p.149.

The vassal principalities of Wallachia and Moldavia, in a map dated to 1786 (author's archive). Both the principalities became a battlefield during the war against Austria and Russia in 1787–92 and 1806–12.

Egyptian economy. The countryside was already battered by repeated plagues, droughts, a pestilence that carried off an enormous proportion of the animals, and a neglect that left its crucial irrigation system in disrepair, to the extent that villages were abandoned and the fields remained unfilled. Rosetta and Damietta lost half or more of their populations. Alexandria was neglected and undefended, its water supply unsecured; Cairo's population lost almost 40,000 people. The population was divided into impermeable classes, with the multi-ethnic Mamluks as the ruling elite. Together with them, Egypt was home for a large variety of ethnic groups, comprising Christian Syrians, Copts, Sudanese Moroccans, Maghrebis, and Arab *fellahins* as well. They were equally closed and homogeneous groups with little assimilation among themselves. In addition, there was a strong division between the urban population and the peasants with the semi-nomadic Bedouins, which were the last major ethnic group. Spread across the Egyptian Delta and in all the provinces of Upper Egypt, Bedouin tribes were a constant irritation both to the authorities in the cities whose caravans and trade had to pass through their territory, and to the farmers who suffered their frequent predations.[58] These tribes migrated over an area that included the pilgrim route along the Arabian coast, the Sinai Peninsula, Palestine, modern-day Jordan and Lower Egypt, and were difficult for the authorities in Cairo to control. Local wars had further devastating effects because they loosened Ottoman control over the Arab provinces. Here, the aforementioned Shammar tribes came into conflict with the expanding Saudi confederation in the 1780s and were pushed into northern Iraq.[59] At this time, Ottoman rule in Arabia was concentrated at a few forts located along the Red Sea coast as stations for the annual pilgrimages to the Holy Cities, the ports of Yanbo and Jidda and the Holy Cities themselves. All of these were under the governorship of the Sherif of Mecca, who, in addition to being the representative of the sultan, was accepted as suzerain by most of the Bedouin tribes who lived in the peninsula.

The sultan's nominal rule extended to the 'Barbary' state of Algiers, Tunis and Tripoli. Algiers was midway on a continuum between the 100,000 estimated as its seventeenth century peak, and the 40,000–50,000 who remained at the time of the French expedition of 1830. By that time Constantine had about 25,000, Tlemcen about 20,000. Algeria's total population in the early nineteenth century was an estimated two and a half to three million. In the same period, Tunisia had a population of one million. Tunisia was on a growth trajectory in the eighteenth century, at least between 1760 and 1784, after which it seems to have declined. In 1800, the city of Tunis had an estimated population of 100,000, and was recovering from the epidemic losses of 1784–85. Tripoli also was hard hit by a combination of famine and epidemic in 1784–85, losing about a quarter of its population of 14,000.[60] The local economy thrived on piracy in the Eastern Mediterranean. But state-sponsored piracy and the regular holding of hostages for ransom inevitably led to trouble with foreign governments.[61] As in other parts of the Empire, the Porte was not always able to control the actions of privateers. Algiers and Tunis were now almost independent states, and only Tripoli remained under the direct rule of Constantinople, albeit with a large degree of autonomy.

---

58 Peter Malcom Holt, 'The pattern of Egyptian Political History from 1517–1798', in P. M. Holt (ed.), *Political and Social Change in Modern Egypt* (London: Routledge, 1968), p.66. It was because of Bedouin control of the area between Alexandria and Cairo, for instance, that travellers (and their goods) proceeded from Alexandria along the coast, either by caravan or by boat, to Rosetta, and thence up the Nile to Cairo, instead of taking the shorter desert route.

59 McGowan, 'The Age of the *Ayans*', p.647.

60 Robert Mantran, 'Le statut de l'Algerie, de la Tunisie e de la Tripolitaine dans l'Empire Ottoman', in *L'Empire Ottoman du XVI au XVIII Siecle* (London: Routledge, 1984), p.6.

61 In 1798, for instance, the governor demanded 100,000 French francs from the Swedish government, in addition to a yearly payment of 8,000 French francs, in return for safe passage for Swedish vessels. The Swedes' refusal prompted an all-out attack on their shipping, and only Napoleon's personal intervention secured the release of hundreds of hostages at a reduced rate of 80,000 French francs on top of the annual fee. See Hanioğlu, *A Brief History of the Late Ottoman Empire*, p.10.

It may seem a paradox that the Ottoman territories were surprisingly urbanised, when compared with Europe. The French traveller Felix Beaujour was amazed to find that only two persons lived in the countryside in Macedonia and Thessaly for every person in town.[62] There is evidence to suggest that flight from the countryside to the towns and cities was one of the main responses to the insecurity and misgovernment of the times. The others were northward migration into the Habsburg or Russian territories, or an escape into banditry when civilised life had become troublesome. To all these concerns, other disasters were added. Practically all the great cities of the Empire experienced natural catastrophes during the eighteenth century. Constantinople was especially vulnerable to fire and suffered tremendous loss of property and life in the great conflagration of 1750, when possibly 80,000 houses were burned. Further fires affected the capital in 1756, 1782 and 1787, when two thirds of the city outside the Byzantine walls burned, with a loss of 40,000 lives.[63] Though Constantinople suffered a great earthquake in 1756, the more usual enemy was epidemic, reflecting the human traffic to which it was exposed. The city often traded epidemics with Cairo, as in 1786, when one third of the inhabitants died of plague. Constantinople experienced many food shortages, but not actual famine because of the government's effort to guarantee its food supply.

The most unlucky cities of the Empire with respect to epidemic disease were those which functioned as ports and as caravan terminals, especially Aleppo and Smyrna. This latter seems to have suffered from one epidemic or another in more than half of the eighteenth century. Aleppo, likewise exposed to both the traffic of ships nearby and caravans, experienced at least a dozen years of epidemic during the century, but underwent its worst catastrophe with the wholesale destruction of the villages by Bedouin raiding in the later years of the eighteenth century, creating a long running famine which by 1798 killed half of the inhabitants. Salonika also experienced a dozen years of epidemic during the century, the most serious being in 1781, when 25,000 persons died.[64]

The cities of North Africa not only dealt with much human traffic, but occasionally were also decimated owing to crop failures which they did not have the resources to recoup. Cairo faced several years of hunger during the eighteenth century, including seven severe years of deprivation owing to Mamluk misrule in the period 1780–1800. In 1784 famine drove Egyptians onto the streets, and every town in the Levant, as far as Tripoli of Lebanon and Tunis, was hit hard by famine in 1784 and 1785 respectively. More isolated cities were often spared for decades, and then smitten lethally. Diyarbakir suffered a serious famine in 1757 in the aftermath of a locust invasion. Famine killed most inhabitants of Baghdad during the siege of 1731; in 1773

---

62 Felix Beaujour, *A view of the Commerce of Greece, Formed after an Annual Average, from 1787 to 1797* (London, 1800), p.134.
63 McGowan, 'The Age of the *Ayans*', p.646.
64 Bruce Brewer, *The Hidden Century. Turkish Rule from the Fall of Constantinople to Greek Independence* (Lindon, New York NY: I. B. Tauris, 2010), p.548.

'THE SICK MAN OF EUROPE'

an epidemic carried off two thirds of Baghdad's people, and the same year also decimated Basra.⁶⁵

With the resumption of war against Russia in 1787 and France in 1798, new waves of migration broke loose, followed by others still later, aggravating the chaos initiated in the period 1792–1815. These new migrations not only affected the Serbs, but also Albanians, Bulgarians, Greeks, Tatars and even the Arab inhabitants of the Syrian periphery.

Sultan Selim III, accompanied by his *silihtar*, comes out of his residence in Constantinople with his escort, including a *sipahi* wearing gilded helm and chainmail. Note the European musket lock. Behind him, a not very reassuring janissary puts his hand to his dagger. (detail from the painting attributed to Konstantin Kapidağli). Often mischaracterised as the result of fanaticism, ignorance, and corruption that swept away all the westernising reforms in bloodshed, the Kabakçı's revolt of 1807 was the result of a political conspiracy carried out by a rival faction in the Palace. This faction, resenting the arrogance and corruption of the reform committee, made use of the discontented janissaries, the *ulemas*, and the Balkan *ayans* whose interests were threatened by the Selim's reforms.

The Empire: Centre and Periphery

To understand the Ottoman policy of this period, historians set it against the background of the European 'absolutist' states of this age focusing the structure of the Empire.⁶⁶ The domains were divided into two major groups.

---

65 McGowan, 'The Age of the *Ayans*', p.645.
66 Faroqhi, 'Crisis and Change', p.553: 'Neither cameralist nor physiocrats, the Ottomans were free traders by default. Like the physiocrats, they placed great importance on agriculture, which directly supplied the great bulk of their revenues. They might almost be called precocious had they been more aware of what they were doing. But in fact they were trading on terms which

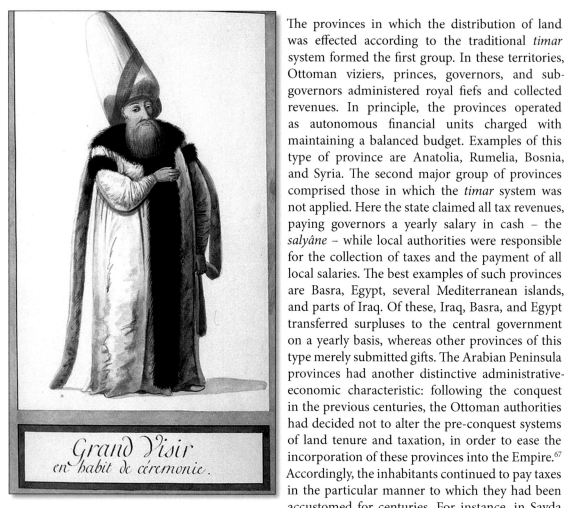

A grand vizier, from the album *Costumes Turcs* of the Diez Collection, 1790s. In the tumultuous years between 1789 and 1815, 17 grand viziers came to power. The succession was not always without conflict and violent depositions. Mouradgea d'Ohsson effectively comments on the tragic events of the janissaries' rebellion: 'In such a disastrous period, in which the authority of the government was powerless, money seemed to be the only method to calm the seditions, but inevitably it ended up provoking new ones. When order was restored, the government demanded an oath of loyalty and obedience from the janissaries. Each soldier swore on the Koran, while a sabre, bread and salt were placed on a silver tray.'

The provinces in which the distribution of land was effected according to the traditional *timar* system formed the first group. In these territories, Ottoman viziers, princes, governors, and sub-governors administered royal fiefs and collected revenues. In principle, the provinces operated as autonomous financial units charged with maintaining a balanced budget. Examples of this type of province are Anatolia, Rumelia, Bosnia, and Syria. The second major group of provinces comprised those in which the *timar* system was not applied. Here the state claimed all tax revenues, paying governors a yearly salary in cash – the *salyâne* – while local authorities were responsible for the collection of taxes and the payment of all local salaries. The best examples of such provinces are Basra, Egypt, several Mediterranean islands, and parts of Iraq. Of these, Iraq, Basra, and Egypt transferred surpluses to the central government on a yearly basis, whereas other provinces of this type merely submitted gifts. The Arabian Peninsula provinces had another distinctive administrative-economic characteristic: following the conquest in the previous centuries, the Ottoman authorities had decided not to alter the pre-conquest systems of land tenure and taxation, in order to ease the incorporation of these provinces into the Empire.[67] Accordingly, the inhabitants continued to pay taxes in the particular manner to which they had been accustomed for centuries. For instance, in Sayda (modern-day Syria and Lebanon with the exclusion of Aleppo province), the inhabitants paid a cash tax on saplings to the Imperial treasury and another in kind of wheat and barley to local state depots. In Mosul, farmers paid half of their harvest as a tithe – the *öşür* – while tribesmen paid taxes based on the number of tents or herds they owned. In Cyrenaica, the determining factor was the number of wells in a given tribe's territory.

The vastness of the domains, however, was based on an economy that showed a strong backwardness in comparison with Western Europe and also with

---

they later would have cause to regret. As fiscalists, rather than economists, the Ottomans were somewhat similar to the 'absolutist' states of Europe but at an earlier stage.'

67 Hanioğlu, *A Brief History of the Late Ottoman Empire*, p.9.

emerging states such as Russia. The Ottoman Empire had a medieval-type agrarian economy, which had limited surplus capacity, was short of ready cash, and possessed scant resources required to support the newly evolving permanent army which had emerged in Western Europe. The Ottomans did not have the means to compete with countries accumulating large amounts of cash from commerce and banking, especially England and France. The conservative governing elite had neither the understanding of economic developments occurring in Western European countries nor was it willing to make drastic changes. Another obstacle was directly linked to the previous limitation. The government was well known for its dislike of making drastic changes or abolishing any traditional military corps or institutions. Understandably, this conservatism resulted from the government's unwillingness to face the socio-political consequences of any radical change. Despite the difficulties in maintaining centralised control, the Ottoman fiscal practices may turn out to have been one of the best cards, enabling them to accumulate significant reserves during the first half of the century. However, the Ottoman Empire did not participate in the new world of credit operations and central banking invented in Western Europe, with the result that prolonged wars found them dangerously short of staying power.

The government tried to solve this problem by introducing classical methods, such as debasing the currency, short-term domestic loans, introducing new taxes, and the sale of excess administrative and military posts. These classical methods did not provide the necessary relief, and instead created new problems including social unrest and insubordination. For this reason the government unwillingly introduced new methods, such as in-cash taxes instead of in-kind taxes, tax-farming, and reassignment of the *timar* and other land estates, which were essentially related to each other. Moreover, the government began to focus renewed attention on effective tax collection, more effective bureaucratic procedures, and better bookkeeping. Except for direct borrowing, tax-farming was an expedient alternative for an agrarian state like the Ottoman Empire to extract surplus resources from its citizens. This evolved in order to produce regular and predictable cash flows to meet the expenses of modern warfare. However, the only lands available for this were the estates of the *sipahi-timars*, and the government was already unhappy with the combat performance of the *sipahis*, who were becoming

A *defterdar* administrative official, after the *Fenerci Albümü* (early 1800s).

militarily useless against the modern European armies.[68] However, the most dangerous problem turned out not to be the increased financial burden but its side effect, the breakdown of law and order, and as a result the fragmentation of the Empire into a cluster of semi-autonomous potentates. In practice, between the middle of the eighteenth century and 1831, the reach of the Ottoman government in Constantinople rarely extended beyond the central provinces of Anatolia and Rumelia, and then only weakly.[69] The remainder of the 'sultanic domains' displayed a rich variety of administrative patterns, the common theme of which was the dominance of quasi-independent local rulers. In the periphery, particularly in Africa and the Arabian Peninsula, fluid boundaries fluctuated in tandem with the vicissitudes of tribal loyalty.

Ottomans defeats at the hands of European powers, and the experience of occupation by foreign armies, also sharpened the awareness of several Ottoman peoples – the Serbs, Rumanians, Georgians, and Greeks first of all – regarding their destinies as conquered nations. There were other sources of disaffection near the centre. The commercial partnership of the Ottoman minorities with European merchants brought knowledge of a world superior to that of the Muslim majority and, often, the possibility of changing status and even loyalty.

The Sultanate

The Ottoman Empire was divided into classes, corporations and religious groups, as established in the early phase of its history. The cement that held these components together was the result of the combination of several unifying factors. Among these there were professional guilds, freedom of confession, and above all the relational ties resulting from economic and professional interests. The guarantor of this system was the sultanate, the only institution in which all the subjects of the Empire recognised themselves under the common name of Ottomans. The sultan or *padishah* was the supreme ruler of the Empire, both in secular and religious matters. All law emanated from him, and he was commander-in-chief of the army. Loyalty to the sultan was the basis on which the Empire was founded and this was demanded of all subjects regardless of their social or court position and religious beliefs. Good or bad, the sultanate had managed to secure the loyalty of the population even when its credibility had been compromised by infighting and revolts caused by recurring economic crises. In fact, the turmoil had never challenged the sultan's authority. On the contrary, he was always invoked as the guarantor of the rights of all subjects. In this context, the sultanate had survived almost unscathed, and even in its less glorious moments, the dynasty had always managed to win the loyalty of the different components of the Empire. To his subjects, the sultan could still claim to be

---

68 Uyar and Erickson, *A Military History of the Ottomans*, p.88.

69 Hanioğlu, *A Brief History of the Late Ottoman Empire*, p.7: 'Everywhere, population data, even vital information on taxpaying households, was hopelessly out of date.'

the legitimate heir of the Roman emperors and the grand lord of Asia and North Africa. To non-Turkish Muslims, particularly Arabs, the sultan could emphasise his primacy as the owner of the holy places and as the successor of the Abbasid caliphs. As for the Christian subjects, the sultan granted them permission to remain in their seats, to guarantee their property, to preserve their customs, religion, language and even a certain degree of autonomy in the administrative field. Moreover, to the non-Muslim Greek, Bulgarian, Serbian and Albanian *millets*,[70] the sultan could easily point out that under his protection they were guaranteed rights that under certain Christian princes they could hardly maintain. It cannot be said, however, that sultans had great power and authority. In the eighteenth century they were very different from the portrait of the 'oriental despot' portrayed in popular literature. Their scope and authority was limited, first by the fact that the government itself had a rather limited scope. Even within the ruling elites, the sultan's power was very limited. The fact that the Ottoman government found it very difficult to control the administration of the Empire was mostly due to its original organisation, which had remained unchanged for centuries, and in the eighteenth century did not appear to be able to provide adequate answers to the challenges ahead. The scenario offered by the Ottoman state was therefore that of a confederation of autonomous and highly decentralised entities. All this was taking place at a time when Western Europe was undergoing a radical change, with the rise of fiscal-military states, which

---

70 *Millet*, 'religious community'. Gábor Ágoston and Bruce Masters, *Encyclopedia of the Ottoman Empire* (New York, NY: Facts on File, 2009), p.467: 'As long as the Sultan was revered, order was respected, taxes were paid, and the army was maintained, individuals were free to practice their religion, speak their language, and live in the private sphere of their *millet* – an institution recognised by the government – all while respecting the basic principles of Ottoman society. The Ottoman Empire was therefore an enormous conglomerate of both large and small communities of greater or less importance that coexisted without any real mixing.' On this topic see also Reina Lewis, *Rethinking Orientalism: Women, Travel and the Ottoman Harem* (London: I. B. Tauris, 2004), p.53: 'These semi-autonomous religious-ethnic units of legislation accommodated (in a somewhat permeable manner) not only the Empire's minority populations but also organised through the Muslim *millet* to manage administrative affairs within the Empire. The concept of the *millet* changed with differing circumstances. The minority millets recognised not only a distinction from the Muslim majority (as in the Jewish *millet*) but came also to accommodate differences within faith communities (as seen in the distinctions between the Gregorian Armenian and the Greek Orthodox *millets*). *Millets* could also traverse ethnic differences: in the Muslim millet between, for example, Arabs, Turks or Kurds, whilst the minority millets also grouped faiths across ethnic divides, such as the Greek Orthodox millet which had itself managed to incorporate previously separate Balkan Orthodox patriarchates. The minority millets were in receipt of differential taxation – in return for being barred/exempt from military service – and had within this system enjoyed for centuries (in theory if not always in practice) greater rights and protections than were available to minorities in Europe. Prior to the *tanzimat* reforms the ruling class had consisted of those involved in the various functions of the Sultan's Imperial household (religious–judicial, military, financial), whose power was derived from "the delegation of the Sultan's authority".'

THE OTTOMAN ARMY OF THE NAPOLEONIC WARS 1789–1815

Muhammad Ali, alias Kavalalı Mehmed Ali Paşa (1769–1849), portrayed by Auguste Couder, collection of the Palace of Versailles. The Albanian Ottoman governor was the de facto ruler of Egypt from 1805 to 1848. Note the Albanian *xhamadan* short jacket with open sleeves and the Mamluk curved sword in foreground.

had already configured an absolutist organisation of power.[71]

Coeval authors focus on the sultan, depicting his life as engulfed in protocol and religious observance. The sultan's isolation meant that his choice of grand vizier was guided not by knowledge of a candidate's merits but by the Palace favourites. The Ottoman government's tradition conferred on the grand vizier the function of 'head of the viziers and commanders. He is greater than all men; he is in all matters the sultan's absolute deputy.'[72]

As long as he held the seal of office from the sultan, the grand vizier wielded great power. He commanded military campaigns, appointing all public functionaries except the *şeyh ul-İslam*, presided over the *divan*s of

---

71 Bombaci and Shaw, *L'Impero Ottomano*, p.421: 'This was also the case among the Ottoman subjects themselves with the application of the traditional law, the *hadd*, which stated that each citizen of the Empire was autonomous within his own sphere of power, and no one could interfere in it, not even the Sultan, as long as he fulfilled the rules required by the law.'

72 Ágoston and Masters, *Encyclopedia of the Ottoman Empire*, p.11.

the Sublime Porte, the assemblies where all the state's affairs were discussed, and conducted inspection tours, usually incognito, to police the marketplace. Upon dismissal, he had to hand over the seal and immediately go into exile. A former grand vizier was never allowed to reside in the capital. The grand vizier had three deputies, usually termed as 'ministers of state'. Of the three, the grand vizier's steward, the *kâhya bey* was his deputy for internal and military affairs. The second steward held the title of *reis ül-küttab*, the chief scribe. reflected his historical role heading the grand vizier's chancery, but the urgency of foreign affairs had begun to turn him into the foreign minister that he eventually became. The grand vizier's third deputy, the *çavuş başı*, chief bailiff, had varied duties, starting with procedural and police functions at the grand vizier's judicial councils and extending into ceremonial when ambassadors paid official visits to the Sublime Porte or the grand vizier participated in Palace ceremonies. The grand vizier presided over the government like a modern prime minister. He also was the chief of the army and held the right to form his own lifeguards, choosing among the soldiers of the *kapıkulu*[73] or enlisting them from his clients and network of relationships. Some grand viziers gathered private corps of 4,000–5,000 men, even in peacetime.[74] In terms of military practice, the nature of these 'private troops' was well established, but there were no rules concerning the strength of the units and for a long time even the establishment of permanent corps was always accomplished by the wealthier *paşas* and *beys*.

The most important decisions concerning war or peace were discussed in the *divan*. The members of the *divan* represented the three major groups of the Ottoman ruling class or *askeri*: the 'men of the sword', namely the military, 'the men of the religious science' known as the *ulema* or the religious establishment, and 'the men of the pen', the bureaucrats. Each member of the *divan* was responsible for a distinct branch of government: politics and the military, the judiciary, and the Empire's finances. In the council, the military was represented by the grand vizier, other viziers whose number had grown over time, and the *beylerbey* of Rumelia, originally the commander of the Empire's provincial cavalry. The *divan* could also include the *kadıaskers*, the judges, who spoke in the council for the religious establishment in military matters and in particular assisted the sultan and the grand vizier as heads of the Ottoman judiciary in the army. The bureaucracy constituted the last group of the ruling class in the *divan*, and it was specially represented by the treasurers, known as *defterdars*. In each province and district, the *defterdar* was responsible for the funds allocated for military purposes, such as pay for garrison soldiers and the maintenance of fortifications. He was assisted by other officials, the *defter kethüdası* or *şehir kethüdasi*, who dealt with the matter for the minor districts. A typical *vilayet* or major province was directed

---

73 The sultan's household troops. For more details, see the following chapter.
74 Özgür Kolçak, 'The Composition, Tactics and Strategy of the Ottoman Field Army', in F. Tóth and B. Zágorhidi Czigány (eds), *A szentgotthardi csata es a vasvari beke: Oszman Terjeszkedes-Europai Osszefogas – La bataille de Saint Gotthard et la paix de Vasvar* (Budapest: MTA Történettudományi Intézet, 2017), pp.82–83.

THE OTTOMAN ARMY OF THE NAPOLEONIC WARS 1789–1815

Alemdâr Mustafa Paşa (1750?–1808), or *bayrakdar*, 'standard-bearer'. He was originally the *vali* of Rüsçük, and one of the most powerful *ayans* of his time. The deposition of the reformer Sultan Selim III in 1807, and his replacement with the reactionary Mustafa IV, provoked Alemdâr Mustafa Pasha to lead his private army to Constantinople in an attempt to reinstate Selim III and restore his reforms. As grand vizier, Alemdâr purged the soldiers who had rebelled against Selim, removed conservatives from government positions and replaced them with men sympathetic to reform. His measures would eventually lay the ground for further reforms in the Ottoman Empire. Meanwhile, the ruling elites were resentful of him. On 15 November 1808 about 1,000 janissaries raided his residence. Realising he could not survive the assault, he ignited the gunpowder reserves in the cellar of his house, killing himself and approximately 400 janissaries in the ensuing explosion.

by the respective *divan*, which consisted of the presiding governor, the *sancakbeys* and their deputies, and occasionally the *kadı*. The council probably functioned in a similar way to the Imperial divan in Constantinople, although assembling less frequently and rarely in full number.[75]

The Empire was an area of boundless proportions. Until the nineteenth-century reforms, the Ottoman government, unlike the governments of modern nation states, was small, employing no more than 1,500 clerks. Its tasks were limited to a few key areas: defence of the Empire, maintenance of law and order, resource mobilisation and management, and supply of the capital and the army. Functions associated with government in modern nation states such as education, healthcare, and welfare were handled by the Empire's religious and ethnic communities and by religious and professional organisations like pious foundations guilds or *vakif*. Therefore, the Ottoman Empire had a less efficient and less centralised government than those of the coeval European powers.[76]

Ottoman Geostrategy

Ottoman frontiers were constantly shifting as the Empire expanded and contracted over its history. They also varied radically in their nature, according to geography, local circumstances, and the nature of the powers contesting the sultan's authority. In Europe, on the front line with the Habsburgs, something akin to a modern frontier had developed by the sixteenth century, with the two powers confronting each other across a delineated border from behind a network of fortresses, even if this frontier line was not always taken particularly seriously in practice. The eastern Danube and Black Sea were closely related with the latter area, since the loss of the Crimea in 1783 had modified the frontier with Russia. The loss of the peninsula, hitherto ruled by the Tatar *khan*s, had wiped out an important buffer zone, and above all had turned the capital of the Empire into a frontline city. In this area, however, the Porte still maintained

---

75 Ágoston and Masters, *Encyclopedia of the Ottoman Empire*, p.16.
76 McGowan, 'The Age of the *Ayans*', p.717.

control over the principalities: an important area protecting the main access routes to Constantinople. In Iraq, the border with Iran was more ambiguous, with numerous tribes of fluctuating loyalties inhabiting the no-man's land between the two empires. In Africa, on the other hand, it remains unclear how far the Empire's reach stretched up the Nile, and it seems more likely that this ambiguity also existed then, rather than there having been a direct frontier with the Ottomans' rivals in the area. In the Arab Peninsula, the Ottomans struggled to control the Hijaz's routes connecting the pilgrimage centres of Mecca and Medina with Syria and ultimately Constantinople. The sultan's prestige could be challenged by local forces such as the Bedouin in Arabia as well as rival states. In the Mediterranean, Ottoman authority was contested by the navies of western powers and by corsairs.

It has often been claimed that the Ottomans were a one-front army with a two-front empire. In the period under discussion, they did indeed have two regular battlefronts, with a third being added by 1798, but that did not mean that mobilisation could not occur on other fronts, although absorption on one front could often lead to the neglect of another, and respite for local populations. Multiple theatres of war also account for the increasing Ottoman systematic reliance on and tolerance of the semi-independent provincial *ayans*, who managed such territories in the name of the sultan.

The first and most often visited theatre of war was the Danubian battlefront, and the chief enemy was the Austrians. Distance to the front was another factor which influenced campaigning in both the Danubian arena and on the eastern frontiers up to the Black Sea, the second of the regions, in which the Ottomans were forced to fight against the Russians. In this area, both sides were constantly plagued by the great difficulties of distance, and losses of 25 or even 50 percent of all soldiers were not uncommon.[77] The Ottomans controlled the border from the Adriatic to the Danube with a relatively stable line of defence, which faced the Austrian *Militärgrenze* to the north and the Venetian Dalmatia to the west. This line ran along the Unna and the Sava rivers, and had in Belgrade its barycentre, with some major fortress at Bihać, Novi, and Šabac. In this area, the most common type of fortress was the *palanka*. Typically, a *palanka* was a wooden structure, but occasionally the term also seems to have been applied to stone fortresses. Apart from the comparatively small *palankas* there were located along the Sava numerous fortress villages. From Belgrade, the eastern defensive axis ran along the two major rivers: the Danube and the Dniester. Chotin, on the latter river, guarded access to the principalities from Ukraine, while the west coast of Black Sea was secured by the enclave of Oçakov, with İzmail, Kinburn, Bender and Akkerman as major strongholds in the Danubian and Dnieper deltas. This line was decisively crushed in 1792, after the Russian occupation of Dobruja and the displacement of the frontier on the Prut. The

---

77 John L. H. Keep, *Soldiers of the Tsar: Army and Society in Russia 1462–1974* (Oxford: Clarendan Press, 1985), pp.225–226. This figure includes plague, famine and desertion. However, there is no equivalent in the Ottoman context, and no reliable statistics have yet been established, but it is possible that Ottoman soldiers resisted better as they were usually used to the hard scenarios.

Russian gains significantly changed the Ottoman defence, since fortresses that had become part of the core Ottoman lands now returned to be frontier places. The new defensive line was now represented by Varna, Vidin, Rüsçük (today Ruse in Bulgaria), Silistra, Şumen and Giugiu in Wallachia. The new frontier forced the Porte to undertake a costly campaign to improve the fortifications, which, however, remained partly incomplete.

The main enemies in the Caucasus were first the Safavids, Shiite Muslims, and then Nadir Shah, the Afghan leader who conquered Iran after the fall of the Safavid dynasty, followed by the Russians in the later period. Here the terrain was far more inhospitable than even the Danubian arena, parts of which after all served as the Ottoman source of supply. Nomadism played a significant role in the eastern context as irregular corps of Tatars, until 1783, and Kurds, all necessitated different techniques of warfare, where horse and cold steel were more effective than the sustained siege. Ottoman commanders had trouble convincing their troops of the need for wintering over at such distances, the janissaries proving unhappy with fighting fellow Muslims and with the prevailing style of slash-and-burn warfare, which inevitably crippled the supply systems. Logistics in this heater of war were paramount, and account for success in the retaking of Basra in 1779.[78]

A third frontier was Egypt and the Hijaz. Here, external and local threats growing out of the French invasion of 1798 forced major reconsideration of the entire military and diplomatic system. Nomadism in the Hijaz potentially interfered with the lucrative caravan and pilgrimage trade, and initially the relationship between the skilled Muhammad Ali of Egypt and the Porte was positively affected by his ability to quell the Wahhabi rebellion and protect both the access of pilgrims to the holy cities and the transit trade.[79]

Egypt had long played the role of client, supplying troops to Ottoman campaigns elsewhere, and was responsible for providing most of the annual subsidies accorded by Istanbul to Mecca. By 1807, with the virtual independence of Muhammad Ali, Greater Syria and Palestine had become a buffer zone, making it a place where internal and external challenges to the Ottomans were played out, with a predictable impact on local populations and resources. Although in the eighteenth century, local households became more powerful and independent, the sultan's suzerainty continued to be recognised everywhere except in Arabia. In fact, in this area coexisted two distinct zones, which were differently affected by the central power of Constantinople. The inner zone consisted of provinces in Syria and Iraq, which were closest to the Ottoman heartland of Anatolia. These were fully incorporated into the Ottoman Empire, and the full measure of Ottoman provincial governance was implemented there. Provinces further afield were usually governed by men sent out from Constantinople. However, they typically relied on local political elites to fill the lower ranks of administration.

---

78 Virginia H. Aksan, 'War and Peace' in S. Faroqhi (ed.), *The Cambridge History of Turkey, Volume 3, The Later Ottoman Empire, 1303–1839* (Cambridge: Cambridge University Press, 2006), p.86.

79 Among the best studies on this topic: Khaled Fahmy, *All the Pasha's Men: Mehmed Ali, his Army and the Making of Modern Egypt* (Cambridge: Cambridge University Press, 1997).

Instead, the Arab cities on the outer zone rarely had Ottoman governors. Here, local warlords ruled, although they also professed loyalty to the sultan and collected taxes in his name. Given the diversity in conditions that existed in the Arab provinces, the local forces making for autonomy differed widely in their origins. Nonetheless, every Arab province witnessed the rise of political movements or personalities who challenged the sultan's monopoly of power in the eighteenth century.[80] Among the most redoubtable opponents, the Saudi Wahhabis[81] contended the primacy in the Hijaz for three decades.

Furthermore, the Ottomans did not possess the will or the military strength to subdue the Bedouin, Kurds, Druze or Berbers completely. Never decisively defeated, the clans waited in their mountain, or desert, strongholds and periodically reconstituted themselves to challenge the Porte. The authority and legitimacy of both the provincial and the centrally recruited military forces rested on the edge of their swords, to paraphrase an eighteenth-century Syrian chronicler.[82]

Ottoman authority also began to wane in Iraq in the last years of the seventeenth century. For over a half century thereafter struggles for power continued without end, with the Bedouins ravaging the countryside and the province falling into political, economic, and social chaos. It was only in the middle of the eighteenth century that the vacuum was at last filled by the Mamluk slaves brought in to serve the Ottoman officials in the same way as they had in Egypt. But unlike the Egyptian example, once the Mamluks gained control in Iraq, they filled all the offices in the Ottoman hierarchy of government, including the governorship, which came to be held by the chief of the dominant party. For this reason, the Porte never was able to maintain competing Mamluk factions for its own benefit, and the sultan's treasury therefore never secured the same sort of financial reward as it had from Egypt. Whilst the Iraqi Mamluks did divide into competing factions, there was always one which was able to achieve unchallenged control for long periods of time. With the fear of oppression removed, their rulers were far freer to develop the security and prosperity of the country and to restore its administration than the Mamluks were in Egypt.

Since the mid eighteenth century, Ottoman rule in Arabia was concentrated at a few forts located along the Red Sea coast as stations for the annual pilgrimages to the Holy Cities, the ports of Yanbo and Jidda and

---

80   Bruce Masters, 'Semi-autonomous forces in the Arab provinces', in S. Faroqhi (ed.) *The Cambridge History of Turkey Volume III* (Cambridge: Cambridge University Press, 2006), p.186.

81   Wahhabi doctrine was strongly based on the traditional belief, in which all the rituals of religion had to be obeyed to the letter as manifestations of full devotion, and all aberrations, including failure to pray even a single time, were considered to be the worst sort of sin, punishable by death. To sins such as the construction of tombs, lighting of candles, and veneration and worship of saints and prophets were added the use of drink and tobacco and the playing of music, which were considered to be heretical innovations since they were not specifically mentioned in the Koran. All Muslims who had not yet accepted the Wahhabi teachings were considered to be pagans or polytheists who had to be converted or killed.

82   Masters, 'Semi-autonomous forces in the Arab provinces', p.187.

the Holy Cities themselves. All of these were under the governorship of the Sherif of Mecca, who, in addition to being the representative of the sultan, was accepted as suzerain by most of the Bedouin tribes who lived in the peninsula. In 1787 this post was assumed by the Sherif Galib ibn Musaid, who bore the brunt of the Wahhabi attacks into the Hijaz during the remainder of the eighteenth century.[83]

As for the last frontier, concerns came once again from Russian expansionism, which coincided with a decrease in Iranian pressure. The authoritative opinion of an official who had familiarity with the Russo-Iranian frontier made him caution the grand vizier about protecting the Ottoman borders. According to him, Egypt, the Black Sea and Northern Anatolia, and Baghdad were vulnerable frontiers, and especially Kars, Van and Erzurum required permanent garrisons and constant vigilance.[84] The Caucasus was a secondary front in the war of 1787–92, but the relative threat turned out to be more serious in the following decades.

In the 1800s the Porte had to deal with additional crises and conflicts on several fronts. The Ottoman–Russian War of 1806–1812 continued amidst the rebellions within the country. Ottoman expeditionary forces, composed of mostly provincial troops of the *ayans*, did show stiff defence and achieved some feats, but they were more like a horde than an army. The two-pronged Russian assault penetrated into Rumelia and Georgia. Luckily for the Ottomans the epidemics, hunger, and the incoming French offensive forced Russians to give up their desire to conquer Moldavia and Wallachia. A minor conflict between Serbs and local janissaries turned into a medium-level rebellion in 1804 and became a full-fledged insurrection with Russian support in 1807. The government managed to suppress the rebellion in 1813 only after the Russians withdrew their support because of the clauses of the Bucharest Peace Treaty of 1812, and Napoleon's ill-fated invasion.

Though the precarious international reputation of the Ottoman government was constantly guarded during the second half of the eighteenth century, this went into a sharp deterioration after 1774. The overall situation of the Empire in the aftermath of the Peace of Küçük Kaynarca was now perceived as critical by all. In order to annex more regions of the Ottoman Empire, and at the same time satisfy the other European powers, Catherine II of Russia devised the 'Greek Plan' in 1780, in agreement with the Habsburg emperor, to sweep the Ottomans out of Europe. The principalities of Wallachia and Moldavia were to be united in a new Romanian state called Dacia, under the influence of the Czars; Thrace and Macedonia, Bulgaria and northern Greece were to form a new Byzantine Empire, with Constantinople as its capital, ruled by Catherine's nephew Constantine. In turn, Austria would receive the western Balkans, Serbia, Bosnia-Herzegovina, and the islands of Dalmatia held by Venice; in return, the Serenissima would be granted the Peloponnese, Crete, and Cyprus. France, which after Louis XVI's marriage to

---

83 Stanford J. Shaw, *Between Old and New. The Ottoman Empire under Sultan Selim III, 1789–1807* (Harvard, MA: Harvard University Press, 1971). p.222.

84 Aksan, *Ottoman Wars*, p.191. The official in question was the seasoned veteran Canikli Ali.

Marie Antoinette of Habsburg had distanced itself from the Ottoman Empire, would receive Syria and Egypt, which it was likely to share with England if London also joined the plan. Despite the large number of players, Britain and Prussia opposed the massive consolidation of the states participating in the plan, realising that the survival of the Empire was now a matter of international policy.[85]

In 1798, with the French invasion of Egypt, a new era of relations with Europe began, which in nineteenth- and twentieth-century historiography reduced the sultan and the Empire to second-class players, waiting to be rescued by their changing protectors: Russia, Britain and France. This period between was a turning point in Ottoman history. From now on there existed an 'Eastern Question' and a relatively weak Ottoman Empire became the object of the political as well as territorial aspirations of the European great powers. With the sultan no longer an important agent at the margins of the diplomatic and military 'balance of power' game played by the European states, his territories were turned into bones of contention for Russian, Habsburg, English and French ambitions. Seeking viable alliances therefore became a matter of survival for the Empire. Already from 1794 the Ottomans maintained permanent embassies in the most important European capitals. Shifting alliances – with Prussia, Sweden, England and France – often served to ward off military attacks. At the same time, however, they served as a means for Western powers to gain economic influence and extraterritorial status for their merchants.[86]

Moreover, Ottoman understanding of the foreign scenario was not always very accurate, and the lack of adequately trained personnel for a modern foreign policy led to unpleasant consequences, or the Ottomans found themselves embroiled in crises and disputes orchestrated from outside.[87] The European powers soon discovered this weakness and acted by encouraging local ambitions for autonomy. In this disturbing action Russia played a leading role, encouraging the Christian populations to revolt, and if in 1775 St Petersburg had to accept failure in Greece, in 1806 the Czar achieved the desired result with the Serbs.

---

85 Bombaci and Shaw, *L'Impero Ottomano*, pp.464–465.

86 Edhem Eldem, *French Trade in Istanbul in the Eighteenth Century* (Leiden, Cologne, Boston MS: Brill, 1999), pp.47–51.

87 Hanioğlu, *A Brief History of the Late Ottoman Empire*, p.18. Among the most outstanding incidents, there is the one concerning Montenegro. In 1797, a man named Vinčić appeared at the Imperial capital with a letter of introduction from the Ottoman ambassador to Prussia, claiming that he was a Montenegrin aristocrat duly elected by a local council. He furnished an election document, dated 1795, and promised to raise a 35,000-man army and collect the poll tax on behalf of the central government. The Ottoman authorities seriously entertained the idea of recognising this person as the new ruler of Montenegro until the French ambassador informed them that he was a charlatan who had already attempted to dupe the French authorities by posing as a Croat prince.

Between Chaos and Transformation

At the end of the eighteenth century the Ottoman Empire was going through the final and most acute phase of the crisis that had begun in the 1730s. High-ranking commanders and officers were constantly changing, and soon administrative authority was becoming paralysed.[88] The administrative chaos observed by some Western observers was taking place on an even larger scale in the provinces. As both edicts from the sultan, grand vizier, and official records attest, an increasing number of people ignored the orders of the government and tried to seize locally even major powers, managing to expand their influence as they saw fit. On the one hand, owners of the *timars* were refusing to meet their military duty yet all the while oppressing peasants; on the other hand, armies of bandits made up of army deserters had emerged. there seemed to be no end to the chaos. The weakness of the central government to act on its authority in such a situation caused local *ayans* to take up administrative control, across Anatolia it passed from cosmopolitan *devşirme* officials to this class of magnates. During the many years of chaos, a new array of individuals came to be appointed by the government: Anatolian soldiers who had gained prominence, local people of influence who had ensured security in their regions, and taxmen who had succeeded in gathering taxes and delivering these to the treasury.[89] The appointment of these officials, called *mütesellim* or even *voyvoda*, instead of governors, represented a drastic change. Young people from Anatolia were now replacing the *devşirme* who had been educated in the Seraglio, which meant that the class of people who had hitherto been referred to in the Ottoman political tradition as uncouth Turks were taking control of the state. Many grand viziers, viziers and commanders of the eighteenth century, such as Nevşehirli Damat Ibrahim Paşa, or Halil Hâmid Paşa, were indeed mostly of Turkish origin.

The turning point in this phase of Ottoman history passes through the reign of Sultan Selim III (r. 1789–1807) and concludes with Mahmud II (r. 1808–1839). In 1792 the Empire emerged from a ruinous war, the cost being the loss of strategic territories on the Black Sea. Peace, however, was illusory indeed, as Selim became embroiled in a series of internal and foreign entanglements.

Further threats emerged in the Balkans and Anatolia, and finally the French invasion of Egypt in 1798 led the Empire to face an increasingly complex political situation. In the midst of this nightmare scenario, Sultan Selim III tried to find a solution by introducing a campaign of reform, which received the designation *nizâm-ı cedîd*. As a prince, Selim III previously gained the confidence of many high officials by showing great interest in scientific and military matters. In 1789, when he succeeded to his uncle Abdülhamid I, Selim was unable to change the course of the war against Austria and Russia started two years before, but used the negative ending of the conflict as a pretext to

---

88   Hanioğlu, *A Brief History of the Late Ottoman Empire*, p.22.
89   Ilber Ortayli, *The Empire's Longest Century* (Istanbul: Kronik, 2021), pp.92–93.

convince the most traditional and conservative officials of the necessity for military and political reforms. In the years following, the season of reforms began, but new internal and external conflicts brought new concerns, while the international scenario involved the Porte in the European arena dominated by the coalition wars against France.

To add to the Sultan's difficulties, a dangerous new threat rose within the Empire during the summer of 1806, making it impossible for him to deal adequately with any of the problems. Opposition to the Sultan had been building for a long time. The janissaries and other *kapıkulu* troops threatened by his reforms had been agitating since early in his reign. Opposition also came from the *ulemas*, most of whom considered every innovation to be a violation of Islamic law and tradition. Many other Ottomans, including some reformers, now began to understand how destructive to the Ottoman system the new secularist ideas could be and therefore demanded that the iron curtain be lowered again before it was too late. Selim's efforts to reform the Empire and the older military corps with it only added to the resentment.

In 1806, Selim III's order to expand the new *nizâm-ı cedîd* military corps in the Empire triggered the revolt which has become known in history as the 'Edirne Rebellion'. Mostly notables feared that they would lose their field of recruitment, and that the Ottoman army might become strong enough to end their independence. Soon, they entered into an alliance with the Constantinople conservatives, led by Grand Vizier Hafiz Ismail Ağa, who plotted to have the *ayans*' troops march to Constantinople and eliminate both the Sultan and his new army. It all started on 18 June, when the Sultan again ordered a *nizâm-ı cedid* force to be assembled in Edirne, which was to be commanded by Kadi Abdurrahman Pasha, one of the few provincial governors and commanders loyal to Selim's reforms. Abdurrahman assembled troops intended for Rüsçük and the Danubian garrisons from all over Anatolia in the new barracks in Üsküdar, on the Asian side of the Bosporus. A few days after, the influent Balkan *ayan* Tirsiniklioğlu İsmail, at the Grand Vizier's secret urging, marched on Edirne with a force estimated at 80,000 men. Deliberately supplied misinformation about the size and strength of the reforms' opponents, and repeated demands for the disbanding of Abdurrahman's troops, led Selim III to capitulate after a series of bloody encounters between *nizâm-ı cedid* soldiers and janissaries in early August.

As was to happen frequently in the last year of his reign, Selim III caved in under pressure, abolished the recruitment in Rumelia, and dismissed the *nizâm-ı cedîd* commanders. The Sultan's capitulation further encouraged the notables. When Grand Vizier Ismail Ağa died in September, Selim replaced him with the janissary commander İbrahim Hilmi Paşa. All the rebels in Edirne were pardoned. Furthermore, the Sultan did not even intervene in the struggles for power among his lieutenants, allowing one of them, the powerful *ayan* Alemdâr (or Bairakdar: standard-bearer) Mustafa, to gain as much power as his master had. Furthermore, in reaction to the threats of the notables, Selim placed command of the *nizâm-ı cedîd* in the hands of his enemies, hoping thereby to satisfy the conservatives, but in the process depriving himself of the means of defending himself. Emboldened by these developments, his opponents proceeded to plan for the Sultan's eventual overthrow. Selim might have stifled the revolt, but he was convinced by the conservatives among his advisers, led by the most reactionary personalities at court, that it would be better to negotiate and conciliate by sending negotiators to the rebels. This gave the conservative party in Constantinople time to use the incident to ignite a general conflagration.

A new revolt broke out on 25 May 1807, when an *ağa* escorted by a company of *nizâm-ı cedid* soldiers went by boat to Rumeli Kavak to pay the *yamaks*[90] their quarterly wage and also to persuade them to accept the new training and uniforms. But as soon as the *ağa* began to distribute the uniforms, the *yamaks* set upon him and tore him apart. The escort managed to escape by boat and land at Büyükdere, hoping to save themselves by going to their quarters, but the *yamaks* caught and immediately executed them.[91] The revolt found its leader in Kabakçı Mustafa, the commander of the Rumelian fortress, and driven by religious scholars, the *ulemas* with the support of the janissaries quartered in Constantinople. Taking advantage of the populace's discontent, who dreaded compulsory military service in the new army, and resented heavy taxation, the *ayans* managed to decisively reject the introduction of the *nizâm-ı cedid* army and reforms in their provinces. The rival faction encouraged the garrisons along the Bosporus to refuse to wear the *nizâm-ı cedid* uniforms and to mutiny. Unaware of the conspiracy, Selim III did not send his new army to suppress the uprising, seeking to avoid a possible civil war while the Empire was facing another war with Russia. When the rebel group headed by Kabakçı Mustafa entered the capital, and joined forces with the janissaries, the mutiny became an open revolt approved by the discontented public. The economic cost of the reforms, together with inter-elite rivalries, contributed to the final demise in the final crisis. The Sultan's legitimacy was also undermined by other events and developments, including the Serbian uprising in the Balkans, the Wahhabi offensive in Arabia, and the war with Russia and Great Britain, which caused the blockade of the Dardanelles and the arrival of a hostile British fleet in the Bosporus. In Constantinople, the discontent of the common people was further exacerbated by the extravagant life led by the court, the debasement of the currency, and periodic food shortages. Realising his failure, a demoralised Selim complied with all the rebels' demands, but was still forced to abdicate on 29 May 1807, and a new sultan, his cousin Mustafa IV, ascended to the throne. Immediately the members of the reform committee, 10 in total, were executed.

---

90 The *yamak* was a janissary who did not perform an active role, and therefore without pay when not engaged. He benefited from full tax exemption like the Janissaries and could exercise a trade waiting for an employment in the corps when a place became available.

91 Shaw, *Between Old and New*, p.378. Jucherau de Saint-Denys, in *Histoire de l'Empire Ottoman*, vol. II, pp.172–173 refers a different version of the episode. A fierce fight occurred between the parts when the official intimated the yamaks to wear the uniforms. However, the fate of the unfortunate ağa and escort did not change. After this brutal murder, the riots spread along the garrisons on the Bosporus, involving the artillery of the Asian side, whose commander was killed by the tumultuous *yamaks* and his body thrown into the sea.

However, the new sultan was only a puppet in the hands of those who had put him on the throne, and the new regime did not last very long. At first, the main rebel groups coordinated their efforts and tried to share the fruits of victory evenly. The janissary elders promised to end their intervention in state affairs in return for assurances that their wages increased.[92] However, about one year later, Constantinople was the stage of a second violent confrontation between the troops of governor of Silistra and Rüsçük Alemdâr Mustafa Paşa on the one side, and janissaries on the other. The plan had been devised in Rüsçük, where the surviving generation of reformers under Abdullah Ramiz Efendi, a judge and veteran of the Egyptian campaign against Bonaparte, persuaded the ambitious Alemdâr of the advantage of reinstalling Selim III by force if necessary. Constantinople needed help against the erstwhile rebels, who, under Kabakçı Mustafa, were terrorising the city. By mid 1808 the original conspirators had fallen out, and administrative disorder ensued as each tried to remove the other from office. The 'Rüsçük Committee' manipulated events to its own ends, persuading Mustafa IV to call on Alemdâr and his troops for support. By early May, Alemdâr had joined the Grand Vizier in Edirne, and many of Selim's supporters had been appointed or reappointed to offices in the government and bureaucracy. On 14 July Alemdâr Mustafa and new grand vizier Çelebi Mustafa marched on Constantinople with 15,000 troops, where *Feyhülislam* Ataullah, still the favourite of the janissary Corps, held sway. The conservative party had the support of Caniklizade Tayyar Mahmud Pasha, former Governor of Trabzon, a Russophile known for his hatred of Selim III. Mustafa IV complicated the situation by courting Tayyar Mahmud and promising to make him grand vizier in order to rid himself of Ataullah and the two remaining princes of the Ottoman dynasty, the deposed Selim III and his cousin, Mahmud. Instead, Ataullah secured the dismissal of Tayyar Mahmud, who then joined the side of Alemdâr Mustafa as *serasker* of Varna. The Rüsçük contingent broke the back of the Bosporus *yamak* rebellion by ordering the rebel chief Kabakçı Mustafa to be secretly attacked and killed.[93] The janissaries and their *yamak* clients, learning the next day of the death of their leader, were encouraged to revolt by Süleyman Ağa, uncle of Kabakçı Mustafa. Chaos and fighting lasted until the end of July. However, by early August the Grand Vizier and Alemdâr Mustafa had restored order to the city and eliminated most of the opposition, largely because the janissaries were disinclined to raise their weapons against their brothers-in-arms of the same *ortas* who had been on campaign on the Danube.

The increasing rivalry between the Grand Vizier and Alemdâr Mustafa, however, determined Selim III's fate. The *ayan* hid his real aim, the assumption of the grand vizierate, until 28 July 1808, when he rose up against Çelebi Mustafa and Sultan Mustafa IV, intending to restore Selim III to the throne. The Grand Vizier surrendered the seal to Alemdâr, who immediately marched

---

92   Shaw, *History of the Ottoman Empire*, vol. I, p.274.
93   Shaw, *Between Old and New*, p.248. A detachment of cavalry was sent to a village on the Bosporus, where Kabakçı Mustafa was living, caught him asleep in his harem, and promptly beheaded him.

on the Palace. In the very final moments of his rule, Mustafa IV sent his own servants to kill Selim III and Prince Mahmud; the latter instead managed to escape over the Palace roofs to Alemdâr Mustafa, who immediately placed him on the throne as soon as he learned of Selim's fate.

Alemdâr Mustafa was also instrumental in collecting important provincial magnates to make a Magna Carta-type agreement with the state, in which the state acknowledged the rights and legitimacy of magnates, and in return the *ayan* magnates were obligated to support his planned reforms. In early August he invited all the important notables to come to Constantinople for a general deliberation on the problems of the Empire. Perhaps no other leader at the time could have persuaded the highly independent and fractious notables to come, but he was able to do so. After being received by the Sultan at his summer residence in Kagithane on 29 September 1808, the notables held a series of meetings to discuss Alemdâr's proposed reforms, resulting finally in a 'Document of Agreement' – the *sened-ı ıttifak* – signed by all present on 7 October.

The notables and provincial governors signing the document confirmed their loyalty to the Sultan and promised to recognise the Grand Vizier as his absolute representative (Articles 1 and 4). The Ottoman tax system was to be applied in full throughout the Empire, in all their provinces, without any diversion of revenues rightfully belonging to the Sultan (Article 3), and in return the Sultan promised to levy taxes justly and fairly (Article 7). Because the Empire's survival depended on the strength of the army, the notables promised to cooperate in the recruitment of men in their provinces. The new army was to be organised 'in accordance with the system presented during the discussion' (Article 2), of which no exact details were indicated. The notables were to rule justly in their own territories (Article 5). They promised to respect each other's territory and autonomy, to act separately and collectively as guarantors for each other's fulfilment of the promises, and to support the central government against any opposition to its reforms, marching to Istanbul whenever they heard of any uprising, without even wasting time to secure the sultan's permission (Article 6). The agreement thus included no specific programme of military reform, but the entire drift of the discussion and the provisions indicated that *nizâm-ı cedid* would be restored with the full support of those present.[94] In accordance with this article, a new corps was raised with the name *sekban-ı cedid*.

The *sened-ı ıttifak* might be important in terms of the history of constitutional law, but in reality it was one of the lowest points in the power of the Ottoman central government. The Rüsçük Committee was successful, but now they had to work to restore the programme of reform through the person of an unscrupulous *ayan* and an unknown and untried prince rather than the sultan whom they had championed. During the short mandate of Alemdâr, the political situation in the capital became unstable again. The

---

94 Shaw and Shaw, *History of the Ottoman Empire and Modern Turkey Volume II: Reform, Revolution, and Republic: The Rise of Modern Turkey, 1808–1975* (Cambridge: Cambridge University Press, 1977), pp.2–3.

new Grand Vizier and his men, unaccustomed to the power of office as well as to life in a great metropolis, soon began to act in such an arrogant and destructive manner as to alienate those who had originally supported them. Behaving as the actual ruler, Alemdâr issued orders without going through the formality of discussion and assent, irritating almost everyone, including the Sultan. When the janissaries rebelled against him on 12 November 1808, he had to fight with only a few supporters; the rebellion lasted nearly a week and caused a new bloodbath throughout the capital. Alemdâr was killed, but again Constantinople fell to the scourge of victorious military rebels, who demanded that the Sultan give them a new commander as well as a Grand Vizier more acceptable to them. Mahmud II was thus in a situation similar to that of Selim III a short time before, but he had learned his lesson well. He knew that concessions would only encourage the rebels to demand more and more until his throne would certainly be lost to the deposed Mustafa, who had many partisans in and out of the Palace. Thus instead of giving in, he temporised while ordering Kadi Abdurrahman and other loyal notables to bring their troops to the Palace on 15 November. He then rejected the rebel demands, and when the janissaries attacked, they were beaten back by the Palace's reinforced garrison. Mahmud further secured his position by ordering the execution of the deposed Sultan Mustafa IV, thus depriving the rebels of the alternative candidate to the throne.

Meanwhile, a full-scale conflict followed in Constantinople. The janissaries obtained the support of the artisans and populace, and on 16 November mounted a general assault on the Topkapı Palace from the direction of the Aya Sofya, cutting off its water supply. The navy in the Golden Horn began bombarding the janissary barracks as well as their barricades around the Palace, but this started huge fires that destroyed large sections of the Sultanahmet, Aya Sofya, and Divan Yolu quarters, with thousands of civilians being killed. The janissary leaders then decided that they could not win and that compromise was best, signing a 'Document of Obedience' to the Sultan in return for an amnesty. The *ulemas* finally persuaded the most radical among the rebellious soldiers to agree the negotiations as the only possible alternative. A truce was agreed, but violence and vengeances resumed. After the massacre of Alemdâr's new military corps, a number of notables who had supported the reforms were killed, including Kadi Abdurrahman. It seemed that reaction had won out again, but Mahmud remained on the throne. He was firmly committed to reform, and now convinced that new military corps could not be effectively

A *solak başi*, after *Les portraits des differens habillemens qui sont en usage à Constantinople et dans tout la Turquie* (before 1809). During the sultan's visit to the capital, the *solaks* marched by the side of his horse. Their assignment was for life and the officers were chosen from among the best of the janissary corps. Officers and common *solaks* wore a colourful dress, comprising *kalafat* headdress and red leather footwear.

built unless the old ones, whose interests were being threatened, were destroyed, that in fact reform could not be limited only to the army but had to span the whole spectrum of Ottoman institutions and society.

The Sultan's Household

All Western travellers who visited the Ottoman Empire described the Sultan's residence as unique in the world. No matter how extravagant or even inhuman the Sultan's court seemed, there was always the feeling of being in the presence of something extraordinary and fascinating. The very structure of the Topkapı Palace, organised like a large encampment, still showed foreigners that the Empire maintained its image of a state ruled by a dynasty of warriors, and despite the crisis it was going through, proudly claimed its origins.

Among the authors who dealt with the Ottoman Empire in the second half of the eighteenth century, Ignatius (or Ignace) Mouradgea d'Ohsson occupies a special place thanks to his *Tableau Général de l'Émpire Othoman*.[95] The work is a very accurate description of Ottoman society in the 1780s and is considered to be the best analysis of the state that has ever been given, since it is written by a native of the country. In the seventh volume of his work, d'Ohsson gives a detailed description of the Empire in the last decades of the eighteenth century. In particular, d'Ohsson describes the Sultan's household, and reports that it retained the structure of the classic age with a few differences.

In the second chapter d'Ohsson deals with the 'officers of the court', meaning those of the 'outside service', the *ağayan-ı birun*, divided into eight classes. Allowed to let their beards grow and to spend the night at home rather than in the Topkapı Palace, the *ağas* of the outside service were very distinct from the *ağas* of the inside service, who had to shave their chins and spend the night in the Palace.

The first class of the outside service consisted of *ulema* attached to the Palace, including not only the sultan's instructor, the *hoca*, and two Palace imams, but also several medical officers and the *müneccim başı*, chief astronomer-astrologer.[96]

The second class in the outside service consisted of the *rikâb ağaları*, namely *ağas* of the Imperial stirrup. This group included officers of the sultan's stables, the Sultan's standard-bearer, the *bostancı başı* or chief

---

95 Born in Constantinople in 1740 into a family of Armenian origin, he was secretary and first interpreter to the Swedish ambassador in Constantinople. He became Sweden's *chargé d'affaires* in 1782, then minister plenipotentiary and envoy extraordinary. He then devoted himself to writing his *Tableau général de l'empire othoman*. He died in Bièvres, France, on 27 August 1807.

96 Mouradgea d'Ohsson, *Tableau Général*, p.286. The medical and astronomical specialties reflected the historical association of nearly all higher learning with the *medreses*. For a serious illness in the Imperial family, the best European specialist in the city might also be brought in for consultation.

gardener, and the *kapıcı başı*, namely the Palace 'gate keeper', a distinguished corps of officers who performed the most secret missions for the sultan.

The third class of the outside service consisted of five *emin*, or intendants, in charge of managing the Imperial buildings, of the mint and the mines, of the Imperial kitchens, of forage for the Imperial stables, and of Imperial expenditures.

The fourth class had titles pertaining to the Imperial hunt. These were the *sahinci başı*, grand falconer, the *çakırcı başı*, the chief keepers of stone falcons, the *doğancı başı*, lanner falcons, and *atmacacı başı*, goshawks. However, these offices had become mere titles since the sultans had ceased hunting.

The fifth class included officers subordinate to the chief 'black eunuch', guardian of the Imperial harem, who belonged to the *enderun* or inside service. Exemplifying his accretion of functions, the *çadır mehter başı*, the master of the Imperial tents, headed 800 men in four companies, whose titular role was to set up tents and pavilions for the sultan's day outings, either inside the palace gardens or in the sultan's many other outing spots. Forty of these men also served as *veznedar*, cashiers, under the *veznedar başı* as first officer of the public treasury, located in the first court of the Palace. Four or five of the lowest-ranking tent-pitchers also served as executioners, always waiting near the *orta kapı* – the gate between the first and second courts of the Topkapı – to carry out the orders of the sultan or grand vizier. In addition to the nominal tent-pitchers, another *ağa* of this class, the *hazinedar başı*, the intendant of the 'outer treasury' and his 20 assistants had charge of storerooms near the divan hall, namely, the depots of the financial records, of robes of honour, and of sacks of satin or cloth of gold used to send out important documents. The *bazırgan başı*, the master purveyor, was responsible for supplying the Imperial household with textiles. Finally the *peşkeşçi başı*, the keeper of gifts, kept custody of all the gifts given to the sultan either by his subjects or on behalf of foreign rulers.

The sixth class of outside *ağas* was subordinate to the *kiler kâhyası*, the Steward of the Imperial Larder, and his assistant the *kilerci başı*. These included the *çaşnigir başı*, the chief taster, with about 50 assistants, whose only job was to serve dinner to the Imperial divan on days when it met. The *mehter Başı*, the master of music and his 62 musicians provided music for the Palace on the two *bayram*s. The sixth class included the personnel of the Palace's kitchen, which included 100 cooks, 100 larders, 150 bakers, and 150 confectioners, each group with a respective chief. The outside service also employed about 300 tailors, furriers, shoe makers, and such, working only for the Palace.

The seventh class comprised two ceremonial lifeguards of foot. When the sultan rode out on horseback to visit the city, or moved to Edirne or elsewhere, they formed a human fence around him. The main corps were the four janissary *ortas* called *solak*, holding the numbers 60 to 63 in the janissary corps series, and each *orta* comprised one *solakbaşi*, two *rekiab-solağis* as lieutenant and 100 footmen. In turn, 60 *solaks* with all four commanders and eight lieutenants formed the sultan's daily escort. The *solaks* were quartered in the capital like the ordinary janissaries, but they received a higher salary, and special prizes during holy festivities.[97] The commanders of the *solak* usually held the rank for life.

Usually the *solaks* were accompanied when they escorted the sultan by other servants in charge of delivering the sovereign's messages. They belonged to the *peik* corps, who formed a single company of 150 men under one *peik başi* as captain. In the procession and in march, 30 *peiks* proceeded at the sultan's side, alternating with the *solaks*. Like these latter, the *peiks* enjoyed special privileges, such as that of announcing good news to the sultan of the arrival of the caravan of pilgrims from Constantinople on its way to Mecca: a task traditionally well rewarded.[98] When the sultan went out on water, members of the two guards accompanied him, adapting the procedure to the long boats.

However, the Palace corps that was most responsible for protecting the person of the sultan and his family belonged to the eighth class. The last of the outside service comprised six units of Palace guards, characteristically performing police duties extending beyond the Topkapı. First were the *bostancis*, who were selected among the most loyal and trusted janissaries, in charge of securing the Palace, the gardens, and the sultan's pleasure palace. The origin of this corps is traceable in the name, since *bostanci* means 'gardener'. It was in fact Mustafa III who, in the mid eighteenth century, transformed the corps of the Topkapı gardeners into a personal guard, the only one that performed armed service in the Imperial residences. According to d'Ohsson, in the 1780s the *bostanci* corps numbered 2,500 men divided into *ortas*, and they enjoyed the same privileges of the janissaries, from whom, however, they differed since they did not join the field army. Their chief was the aforementioned *bostancı başı*, and was chosen personally by the sultan. He was the actual governor of this Palace, and supervised both banks of the Bosporus and Sea of Marmara, with lucrative rights to license building on those shores. Additionally he was the provost marshal in charge of imprisoning, torturing, and executing high-ranking officials who had incurred the sultan's wrath. He held therefore the title of chief of the executioners, and the rank of a *paşa*

A *bostanci başi*, after *Les portraits des differens habillemens qui sont en usage à Constantinople et dans tout la Turquie* (before 1809), wearing ordinary dress. Scarlet kaftan with black piping; turban with white wraps on a green *kavuk*; yellow leather footwear.

---

97 Mouradgea d'Ohsson, pp.25–26.
98 Mouradgea d'Ohsson, p.27.

'THE SICK MAN OF EUROPE'

as governor of Edirne.[99] Further prestigious tasks were entrusted to the *bostanci başi* in 1798, when the new regulations issued by Sultan Selim III gave him the supervision of the four castles guarding the Bosporus.[100]

The *bostancis* continued to fulfil their original functions in caring for the flowers in the seraglio, but at the same time constituted the praetorians designed to protect the sultan in the increasingly frequent overthrows of the throne: a task performed in a not always impeccable manner. The *bostancis* rowed the sultan's barge, and they did the same with the major personalities of the government and the *kapıkulu*'s senior officers. On these occasions, viziers and men of other major ranks were usually escorted by two to four *bostancis*, or by the same number of *çokadars*-valets, dressed and equipped like the *bostancis*. In Edirne were quartered 400 *bostanci* who performed the same tasks as those in Constantinople. The *bostanci başi* directed the work of the *hasseki ağasi*, who served as is lieutenant, and was usually the successor of the commander. The senior officers of the *bostanci* corps included a further six ranks including the 'vice-inspector of the forest', and he who carried communication between the sultan and the grand vizier.[101]

After the *bostanci* there were 300 selected lifeguards who served inside the seraglio, known as *hassekilar*, under the direction of the *hasseki başi*. They served the sultan personally, and whenever he went out 60 of them accompanied him as a bodyguard. If the *hassekis* guarded the Sultan, 400 *baltacis* guarded daily the princes, princesses, and harem, and were subordinated for that task to the chief of the black eunuchs. At the funeral of the sultan or other members of the Imperial family, or harem, the *baltacis* bore the coffin. Their supervisor included a number of officials with duties pertaining more to those of the chief black eunuch. They included a *yazıcı efendi* (secretary), and the aforementioned *hasseki başi*.

The remainder of the eight class of outside service included 120 *zülüflü baltaci* lifeguards, who served the officers of the sultan's private chamber, the *has oda*, and were therefore subordinated to the sultan's own sword-

A *mehter* beating on the *nakkare* or kettledrum, from the album *Costumes Turcs* of the Diez Collection, 1790s.

---

99 Mouradgea d'Ohsson, p.16.
100 Mouradgea d'Ohsson, p.54.
101 They were the *çavuşcibaşi* and the *vezir kara koulak*; the latter also watched for fires in the city. The other officers were the *ocak kyaia* (quarter marshal), *terekeci başi* (adjutant of the commander), the *bostanciler odabaşi* (commander's attaché to the government and seconded to the grand vizier's palace) and the *ağa carakulak* (as the previous but assigned to the janissary commander).

THE OTTOMAN ARMY OF THE NAPOLEONIC WARS 1789–1815

A *hasseki başi*, from *Les portraits des differens habillemens qui sont en usage à Constantinople et dans tout la Turquie* (before 1809). Crimson kaftan with golden edging lace and breastplate; scarlet bonnet, white sash with green and red floral pattern; yellow leather footwear; sabre strap of green-white lanyard.

bearer, the *silâhdar ağa*. He usually accompanied the sultan's pages to carry his weapons when the sovereign personally led the army, an event that never occurred after 1697.

In his work, d'Ohsson also describes the *enderun*, the inside service, divided into six classes, all serving in the third court of the palace, the sultan's private quarters.[102] Most prestigious among these were the gentlemen of the *has odalı*, the privy chamber. Thirty-nine in number, with the sultan rounding out the auspicious 40, these were headed by the aforementioned *silâhdar ağa*, who accompanied him on ceremonial occasions with the sultan's sword over his right shoulder. The *silâhdar ağa* was the master of the household. Most of the other officers had titles implying personal service to the sultan, such as the masters of the turbans, handkerchiefs, keys, and so on, but the list also included a *muezzin*, and a *sır katibi* as private secretary, who received petitions from bystanders as the sultan passed and read them to him afterwards. The *has odalıs* also guarded the room where the sacred relics were preserved, a room adjoining the privy chamber. Next after the privy chamber came the *hazine-i enderun*, the inside treasury, presided over by the *hazine kâhyası*, the steward of the treasury, with a number of specialised assistants.

The next two sections of the inside service were the *kiler odası*, the pantry room, and the *sefer odası*, the campaign room. The former supplied food, beverages, and candles to the sultan and harem. The campaign room had lost its original military function and gained a role as a school training musicians, singers, entertainers, barbers, and bath attendants for the palace. Each chamber of the inside service also had several mutes to serve as messengers for confidential communications, and some of these were also eunuchs to serve in the harem. There were also dwarfs to serve as entertainers. Except for the privy chamber, those who served in the other three chambers were all known as 'inside pages': *iç oğlanları*, *iç ağaları*, and *gilmanan-ı hassa*.

The last components of the inside service were the black and the white eunuchs. The 200 black eunuchs, or *kara ağalar*, were headed by the *kızlar ağa*, the 'aga of the girls', so called because he guarded access to the Imperial harem. The *kızlar ağa* had the rank of military *paşa* of three *tuğ* horsetails, and so did his assistant, the *hazinedar ağa*, treasurer of the harem. The 90 white eunuchs, *ak ağalar*, were headed by the *kapı ağa*, the aga of the gate.

---

102 Mouradgea d'Ohsson, third chapter, pp.1–62.

This was the gate leading from the second court of Topkapı Palace into the third, which was the sultan's private quarters. For the white eunuchs, the Palace was 'their prison and their tomb'. They were not allowed to leave, and they had no other post they could aspire to other than the directorship of the school for pages at Galatasaray. The agas of the Imperial harem were all castrated. The last functionary of the third court was the *dar ül-saade*, meaning 'lord of the abode of felicity'. This latter rank held the control of the three or four *cucu*, or castrated dwarfs, who entertained the harem with buffoonery, and served as messengers between the sultan and his favourites.[103]

The chief white eunuch held the position of chief officer of the Palace, outranked only by the grand vizier and the mufti or *seyh ül-İslâm*. The two chief eunuchs, the *silâhdar*, and the other top positions in the inside service were appointed directly by the sultan and thus were independent of the grand vizier, who otherwise controlled appointments even in the Palace. In addition to these officials, the Palace housed servants and other personnel of various levels. During some periods it was supposed to be 12,000, and this crowd was known collectively as the *kılıç*, 'the sword', in tribute to the military origins of the Imperial household, and to its roots in Turk–Mongol tradition. For all those who served in the Palace, the day began at dawn and ended an hour before sunset. Service had to be provided every day, so licenses were only issued during the *bajram* holidays.[104]

---

103 Mouradgea d'Ohsson, third chapter, pp.45–46.
104 The festivities for the end of Ramadan.

2

The Armies of the Sultan

In 1774, the Peace of Küçük Kaynarca closed the disastrous war against Russia that began six years earlier. The treaty caused the moral collapse of the governing elite and the Empire as a whole. The humiliating agreement had been catastrophic for the Empire, and some contemporaries stated that the consequences were even worse than those of the beleaguered treaty of Carlowitz in 1699.[1] Not only the loss of Crimea irreparably modified the strategic scenario, but also the poor performance of the army surprised even the most pessimistic observers, and showed clearly the futility of the reform efforts introduced in the previous decades. In the two decades prior to 1768, military improvements were certainly no motor of Ottoman transformation. Characteristically the Ottomans attempted to achieve this transformation from the top down, via central state power. The disaster at least served to impose a radical change in the reform programme pursued until then. In this tormented period, reform and finally modernity often clashed not only with conservative interests but also with those of certain sectors of society favouring other types of transformation.[2]

The change occurred in the Ottoman 'military', especially after 1792, has been much described but little investigated. In this period, both Ottoman bureaucratic and military classes adopted western systems and languages, and trained a new elite with aspirations concerning state and constitutionalism,

---

1 The treaty signed on 21 July 1774 had catastrophic strategic consequences: the Ottoman Empire definitively lost its sovereignty over the Crimea, turning the Black Sea into a Russian lake thanks to the acquisition of the ports of Kilburun (Kinburn), Kerch and Yenikale. Moreover, Russia gained freedom of navigation in the Black Sea and Mediterranean, and could now claim the right to protect the interests of the Orthodox Christians of the Ottoman Empire. Much against their will the Crimean Tatars were declared independent, and the Ottomans had to pay a tremendous indemnity of 4,500,000 roubles.

2 Christopher R. Neumann, 'Political and Diplomatic Developments', in S. N. Farouqhi (ed.), *The Cambridge History of Turkey, vol. 3 – The Later Ottoman Empire, 1603–1839* (Cambridge: Cambridge University Press, 2006), p.62: 'Little research has been done on why Ottoman society did not embark on a more holistic approach, and why there have been numerous Ottoman modernities rather than a single version of the modernity project.'

but overall, the imperative of the late Ottoman Empire arose from the need to acquire and mobilise the means of war for survival and defence.[3] Throughout the eighteenth century, the Ottomans had tried to reform their military forces in response to the tactical challenges they faced on their frontier against the Habsburg and Russian field armies. After a few isolated experiments, in the late eighteenth century the trend towards modernisation of the army as a remedy for defeats gained a growing credit among the Ottoman elite. However, among the many obstacles to modernisation the most resistant was the traditional reluctance of the Ottomans to turn the common people, the *raya*, into soldiers even for limited periods. This opposition brought force by the memory of the tragic *celali* uprisings of the seventeenth century, when large numbers of soldiers enlisted for limited periods had severely threatened the stability of the Empire, becoming dangerous armed and trained bandits. Therefore, the Ottoman ruling elite perceived relations between the military and non-military groups in society as an anomaly contributing to the many defeats. Court historians spoke of a golden age when the military and non-military classes in the Ottoman society had supposedly remained within their own classes and avoided intermingling with each other.[4] This viewpoint, however, had brought the Empire to an unsustainable situation. The professional military had become an actual counter-power difficult to control, and the consequences for public order were terrible. Common Ottoman citizens had to deal with various rebels, large groups of bandits, unruly nomads, unemployed religious students, and mercenaries, all of which were the product of the heavy burden of wartime chaos. The government managed to deal with the opposition coming from different groups either by disciplinary measures and using one group against

---

3 Donald Quataert, 'Labor History and the Ottoman Empire, 1700–1922', in *International Labor and Working-Class History* N. 60 (1 October, 2001), p, 96. According to the author, the Ottoman society's belonging to the Islamic world meant that it was supposed to be demarcated from the Western world and would not be influenced by it until it was confronted with the challenge of the West. The problem with this approach, besides its Eurocentric bias, is that it assumes that the West influenced the Ottoman political, economic, social, and intellectual currents in a unidirectional manner; suggesting, 'change in the Ottoman Empire came from without, namely, from the West'. According to this framework, Ottomans were simply imitators who 'could not even appreciate their own backwardness'.

4 Among the historians who have questioned the existence of military and non-military separation, Kafadar Cemal has disputed the idea that the Janissaries were ever in such an ideal state disconnected from society at large. He has shown that the alleged demarcating lines between the subjects (*reaya*) and the military (*askeri*) classes were far from rigid and the engagement of the military classes in the economic sphere need not be interpreted as a sign of corruption and decline of the Ottoman military institutions. Kafadar Cemal, 'On the Purity and Corruption of the Janissaries,' in *Turkish Studies Association Bulletin* XV, N. 1991 (1991): pp.273–279. See also Kafadar Cemal, 'Janissaries and Other Riffraff of Ottoman İstanbul: Rebels Without a Cause?', in *Identity and Identity Formation in the Ottoman World: A Volume of Essays in Honor of Norman Itzkowitz* (Madison, WI: The Center for Turkish Studies at the University of Wisconsin & The University of Wisconsin Press, 2007), pp.113–134.

THE OTTOMAN ARMY OF THE NAPOLEONIC WARS 1789–1815

A janissary, from the album *Costumes Turcs* of the Diez Collection, 1790s. At the turn of the century, the janissaries remained both the Ottoman Empire's most important military corps, and its greatest military weakness. Their reputation was always high in Europe. In his *Travels*, written during the Egyptian campaigns of 1800–1802, William Wittman gave a positive comment of the janissaries, though he admitted that compared to the discipline that in the previous centuries rendered them 'so formidable' their present state was inadequate. Since the state still lacked the funds to pay its swelling troops, the janissaries were allowed to engage in trade and craftsmanship. It is hardly surprising, thus, that in the eighteenth century some 30 percent of the Janissaries were pensioners or second line soldiers, not fit for active military service. By 1750, some 50 to 60 percent exclusively performed garrison duties; thus only a fraction of the force joined the field army on campaigns.

another or simply by introducing new measures and reprisals. Necessarily, there was a military necessity to tolerate the rule of governors who pursued independence from the Porte, or local potentates who became rich illegally.[5]

Historians have focused on the reasons that led the government to leave the crucial matter of military administration unresolved, avoiding the modern criteria introduced in other nations during the eighteenth century.[6] Since the 1750s, the Ottomans had already realised that some army models experienced in Europe were superior to others. This is demonstrated by the admiration aroused by the army of Frederick II of Prussia in the middle of the century.[7] However, the direction of reform was pitted against traditional Ottoman ideas from the classical period, which obstinately continued to oppose the modern tactical innovations of contemporary Europe. Many of the reformers themselves were not exclusively men with military backgrounds, and resistance and thrust to reform efforts varied through the years. Reversals of policy took place as well, which both accelerated and retarded overall progress. Finally, reformers, identifiable by their alignment with contemporary European ideas – mainly those of France – effectively moved the Empire's military in the 1790s towards the attempt to raise a regular army organised and trained according to contemporary European models. Signals of transformation had already appeared in the seventeenth century, but the reformist movement matured into a significant force in Ottoman military affairs in the 1700s. The Ottomans acknowledged the superiority of their enemies and replicated some European institutions. This might suggest that the Empire had adopted a Western culture, but the modernisation was

---

5   Uyar and Erickson, *A Military History of the Ottomans*, p.105.
6   Gábor Ágoston, 'Military Transformation in the Ottoman Empire and Russia, 1500–1800', pp.311–312.
7   Virginia Aksan, 'An Ottoman Portrait of Frederick the Great', in *Ottomans and Europeans: Contacts and Conflicts*, (Istanbul: The Isis Press, 2004), pp.67–80.

carried out primarily as a means to counter the threat posed by their European enemies.[8]

In the eighteenth century, the Porte lost its strategic offensive capability in Europe, and retained only a very limited offensive capability on the eastern border. Therefore, it is no great wonder that the Ottomans were more than satisfied to rely on a defensive strategy first against the Habsburgs and later against the Russians. By this time the army was already overstretched from constant campaigns and rebellions elsewhere, and it was far from the old corps in terms of combat efficiency and discipline. The government reduced the inflated numbers of standing corps by half, but even this harsh measure did not increase the military quality of the remaining soldiers. Consequently, the Constantinople-based standing corps was not the ideal candidate to man distant border fortresses permanently. The Ottoman government's policy basically acknowledged an already ongoing process, which gave the entire responsibility for the defence and interior security of border provinces to their governors and *ayans* – provincial magnates. In this dramatic scenario, the absence of a serious reform policy led the sultans to rely on these notables and regional leaders, who were the only ones able to mobilise soldiers and control them without becoming a problem for public order.

Even the Empire's standing army, the *kapıkulu* with its famous janissaries, ended up being transformed into a self-referential organisation that was increasingly privileged and untrained for modern warfare. Increasingly, the government had to maintain troops in winter quarters near the frontiers to have reserves against possible out-of-season enemy attacks or to start the next campaign early. This new policy created serious tensions within the retained provincial units and created numerous disciplinary problems and occasional disorders. In addition to these problems, winter quartering required strict order and discipline as well as detailed planning beforehand so as to arrange provisions and other logistical needs. As a result, and also to counterbalance enemies' superiority in firepower, the Porte increased the numbers of

Anatolian irregular from the province of Aydin, after the *Fenerci Albümü* (1808). The term *levend* (or its plural form, *levendat*) was the generic name of musket-bearing, mostly infantry but also cavalry, mercenary groups of the seventeenth and eighteenth centuries that were also labelled under different names, including *sekban*, *sarıca*, *deli*, *faris*, *gönüllü*, and the like. Originally, *levend* was the name given to the marines of the Ottoman flotillas during the fifteenth century. Over time, it became the generic name of all mercenaries, but it was most often associated with those recruited as the personal retinue of high provincial officials. Though modern ethic labels all mercenaries as evil, without the presence of large units of irregulars, the Ottomans could not withstand the onslaught of their increasingly powerful enemies, and these became relatively important in reversing numerically inferior odds. Moreover, after the rapid enlargement of the *kapıkulu* corps and the disuse of *devşirme* system the socio-ethnic difference between mercenaries and *kapıkulu* soldiers literally disappeared.

---

8   Ortayli, *The Empire's Longest Century*, p.95.

the existing janissary corps and enlisted other arms-bearing infantrymen joined in irregular bands from among the subject population, indifferently called *miri levend*, *sekban*, *sarica*, *tüfenkendaz*, *panduk* or *arnavut*. Neither method, however, brought the desired result. To the contrary, some measures introduced in the army weakened the government's ability to raise and provide for troops and left it dependent on local 'contractors' and notables in troop mobilisation and war financing. As a result, the Ottoman Empire witnessed a reverse trend, where local notables became virtually autonomous entity with independent armies and support bases. The tremendous demands of war after 1768 had in fact forced the government to rely more and more on these sources for troops, in return granting them official positions that enabled the magnates to strengthen and extend their power. Thus, once the war was over, it was virtually impossible for the government to gain any significant control over them. This situation became a norm, and rarely did the Porte manage to restore its control. In Ottoman Kurdistan, for instance, rival tribal leaders fought each other for dominance without much interference from the centre. Sometimes mere rumours of Ottoman mobilisation were sufficient to trigger a revolt by a major Kurdish tribe. Nevertheless, both in Lebanon and Kurdistan, local chieftains never went as far as the outright rejection of Ottoman suzerainty, and the Ottoman authorities tried to monitor the local political scene.[9]

The rise of the governors and their private armies accelerated the demise of the *kapıkulu* corps, the Sultan's household, and the authority of the Sultan himself. Unfortunately for the Empire, the successful policies and decisions of the past centuries eventually created the nemesis of the system, and successful *ayan* local families, who excelled within the Ottoman military–administrative tradition, used it for their own benefit. Conflicts between the central government and provincial leaders concerned the financial and military obligations of the latter. Despite the fact that most of the *ayans* did not pursue the emergence of an independent rule and were mostly interested in their own welfare and prestige, their increased local autonomy accelerated the decentralisation of the Empire in the last quarter of the eighteenth century until the first decades of the nineteenth century.[10] In this regard, the

---

9   Hanioğlu, *A Brief History of the Late Ottoman Empire* (Princeton, NJ: Princeton University Press, 2008), p.16.

10 Already before the 1720s, the government had successfully balanced provincial units with the *kapıkulu* corps, and even corps within the *kapıkulu* were played against each other. When the military transformation of the eighteenth century effectively destroyed the power base of the provincial *sipahis*, the government lost them as a balancing weight against the *kapıkulu* corps. Historians have debated about the government's acts that tried to use the military potential of the *levends* against the *kapıkulu* corps several times, as in the notorious example of using the *ayans*' armed followers. Nevertheless, none of them brought success and instead made the situation more dangerous. However, the current data does not support the suggestion of wide-scale power struggles between the *kapıkulu* soldiers and irregular mercenaries. See Gábor Ágoston, *Guns for the Sultan. Military Power and the Weapons Industry in the Ottoman Empire* (Cambridge: Cambridge University Press, 2005), pp.178–181.

THE ARMIES OF THE SULTAN

Empire was out of step with Europe, where absolutism was on the rise and strong kings were centralising their power in nation states.[11]

Simultaneously, the traditional military structures were undergoing major transformations as a reply to the new tactical discipline. The first victim of the new warfare was the cavalry. There was no need to gather large contingents of horsemen, either permanent or provincial, and consequently this caused a change in the balance of power in the army and in society, since the cavalry had been recruited through the *timar* system for centuries. However, in the last quarter of the eighteenth century the decrease in cavalry was more of a percentage drop than a numerical one, and in this case, the strength did not fall dramatically. Mounted troops decreased in proportion because the most notable effect was the growth of the janissary corps and the recruitment of large contingents of seasonal irregular infantry. In fact as compared to the coeval European armies, the high number of horsemen that continued to be available to the Porte either in state-financed auxiliary units, or as ethnically raised warrior bands, is striking when warfare turned to armed confrontations of trained regular infantrymen, and cavalry forces increasingly performed only limited functions.[12] It is worth specifying that these changes did not happen unilaterally, but were the result of agreements and accommodations between the centre and the periphery, especially in the provinces where the authority of the government was little more than a formality, for instance in Egypt.

However, neither the increase in the number of janissaries nor the hiring of irregular contingents proved successful in the long run. Ottoman readjustment strategies led to a progressive military decentralisation and weakened the Porte's control over its armed forces and resources, while augmenting its dependence on provincial elites and their military forces in war-making efforts.[13]

Bosnian *panduk* (author's reconstruction after the Diez album, 1790s). Dark red *kavuk* cape and white wraps; black *jacerma* jacket with tin *kov* and *tucle* decorations and red lacing; grey underwear; white shirt; red loose trousers; brown leather footwear. The troops of the *ayans* played leading roles in the wars against the Austrians and Russians, but also contributed to transform the Empire into an aggregation of small sovereigns who watched over each other, whose only political objective was to weaken the power of the sultan, without however ceasing to proclaim him as their sole ruler.

---

11 Uyar and Erickson, *A Military History of the Ottomans*, p.109.

12 Virginia H. Aksan, 'Mobilisation of warrior populations in the Ottoman context, 1750–1850', in *Fighting for a Living* (Cambridge: Cambridge University Press, 2013), p.336.

13 On this specific topic see Halil Inalcik, 'Military and Fiscal Transformation in the Ottoman Empire, 1600–1700', in

Regarding army logistics, instead of institutional change, new combat support tasks were either assigned to traditional military corps or left to perform their old tasks side by side with the new corps, which were essentially founded to deal with the shortcomings of the standing army. The outcome of these two different courses of action was the same: the slow death of the older and obsolescent Ottoman military corps.

After the dramatic and definitive failure of the reform under Selim III in 1807, Sultan Mahmud II's first step had to be to restore the traditional corps so that he would have some force strong enough to defend the Empire against its enemies, particularly Russia, with whom a war was still being waged. Once again, decrees were issued requiring the janissaries and *sipahis* to live up to their traditional regulations, to appoint and promote officers according to ability rather than bribery and politics, and to remove all those failing to train and serve with the corps. Unfortunately, after the disbanding of the forces loyal to him, these decrees could not be enforced effectively. The janissaries remained at best an undisciplined, ill-trained, and poorly armed mob, far better able to act in defence of the old order than to compete with the new armies of Europe.[14]

In the following decades, this situation culminated in the disappearance of the traditional centre of the military power, namely when the elite janissary corps and the associated forces of the *kapıkulu* were destroyed in their entirety in 1826. This ended a military architecture and tradition that had characterised the Ottoman Empire's identity since the 1300s.

The Sources for the Ottoman Military in the Age of Transformation

The analysis and study of the Ottoman army in 'the age of transformation' cannot be separated from an analysis of the sources. Any research on this matter has to face several problems: primarily the accessibility of sources and their reliability. Though the Ottoman army between the eighteenth and nineteenth centuries has been the subject of numerous studies in the last 20 years, the authors have often neglected the organisational aspect and the actual numerical war-force of the units that composed the army. Much documentation concerning this information is probably still waiting to be discovered in the Turkish archives, but some uncertainties and approximations will probably never be resolved. Apart from the dispersion and other incidents suffered by the archives, the Ottoman administration appeared in a chaotic state even to the Sultan's own officials.[15] Examples are

---

Archivum Ottomanicum 6 (1980): pp.283–337.

14 Shaw and Shaw, *History of the Ottoman Empire and Modern Turkey Volume II*, p.6.

15 Virginia H. Aksan, *Ottoman Wars, 1700–1870. An Empire Besieged* (London and New York, NY: Routledge, 2007), p.2: 'The opacity of the Ottoman record in surviving archives, in addition to its daunting volume, also proves a formidable barrier to such a project. For the period in question, archival records are chaotic and disorderly, perhaps reflecting the political confusion

innumerable. According to the authoritative opinion of a historian of the late eighteenth century, the commander of the janissaries himself was unable to determine the correct number of members of the corps.[16]

Among the best sources of knowledge on the subject, the western European authors are still the most informative. They were exponents of the 'orientalist' vogue of that period, who travelled or lived in the Empire between 1790 and 1815. The works of Thomas Thornton, Antoine de Jucherau de Saint-Denys, and Constantin-François de Chasseboeuf de Volnay,[17] contain useful information on the numerical strength of the Ottoman army and its organisation in this age. Further 'classic' sources are represented by Ottoman authors, such as Ignatius Mouradgea d'Ohsson, Rayf Mahmud Efendi, and Colonel Cévad Ahmed Beg, who add several interesting data on the Ottoman 'military' in the period 1789–1815.[18]

As far as the warfare is concerned, the memoirs of William Wittman and John Philip Mercier are certainly two sources of fundamental importance.[19] Their first-hand descriptions of the Ottoman army in the most important and challenging of the conflicts of this period still suffer from Western prejudices, but can nevertheless be regarded as reliable, if only because these are the work of direct witnesses. With them, the Prussian Georg Wilhelm von Valentini offers an accurate study of Ottoman tactics, a matter elaborated when he

---

of the age. Multiple and ill-defined modern cataloguing projects have scattered related materials across confusing collections, and complicated the task of analysis. Nonetheless, we are gradually recovering the Ottomans through their archival history, and rethinking the role that nineteenth- and twentieth-century nationalist rhetoric has played in skewing our observations about the nature of pre-modern societies such as those of the Middle East.'

16 Mouradgea d'Ohsson, p.331. Since its printing, the *Tableau* was considered the more accurate work on the legislation and religion in the Ottoman Empire. Today it is still considered the best description of the Ottoman Empire in the eighteenth century, since it is a work by a native of the country.

17 Thomas Thornton, *The Present State of Turkey; Or, A Description of the Political, Civil, and Religious, Constitution, Government, and Laws of the Ottoman Empire ... Together with the Geographical, Political, and Civil, State of the Principalities of Moldavia and Wallachia*, part I and II (London, 1809); Antoine, Baron de Jucherau de Saint-Denys, *Histoire de l'Empire Ottoman depuis 1792 jusqu'en 1844, Tome I-II* (Paris, 1844); Constantin-François de Chasseboeuf, comte de Volnay, *Voyage en Syrie et en Égypte, pendant les années 1783, 1784 et 1785, tome I-III* (Paris, 1787).

18 Mahmoud Rayf Efendi, *Tableau des Nouveaux Reglemens de l'Empire Ottoman* (Constantinople, 1798); Kabaağaçlızade Ahmed Cévad Beg, *Etat Militaire Ottoman, depuis la fondation de l'Empire Ottoman jusqu'à nos jours* vol. I and *Tarih-i Askeri Osmânî* (Constantinople, 1882), vols II–III.

19 John Philip Morier, *Memoir of a Campaign with the Ottoman Army in Egypt, from February to July 1800: Containing a Description of the Turkish Army, the Journal of Its March from Syria to Egypt, General Observations on the Arabs, and on the Treaty of El-Arish, with an Account of the Event which Followed it.* (London, 1801); and William Wittman, *Travels in Turkey, Asia-Minor, Syria, and Across the Desert Into Egypt During the Years 1799, 1800, and 1801, in Company with the Turkish Army, and the British Military Mission: To which are Annexed, Observations on the Plague and on the Diseases Prevalent in Turkey, and a Meteorological Journal* (London, 1803).

THE OTTOMAN ARMY OF THE NAPOLEONIC WARS 1789–1815

The Ottoman army marching in 1800, after William Wittman's *Travels in Turkey, Asia-Minor, Syria, and Across the Desert* (London, 1803). Coeval authors state that establishing the total strength of the Ottoman field armies is a very difficult task. Estimates about their size are generally out of proportion to reality, largely because the commanders still insisted on travelling with huge baggage trains and many camp followers: 'late eighteenth-century Ottoman camps may be likened to disturbed beehives'.

served In Wallachia and Moldavia as a Russian officer in 1811–1812. His work is virtually forgotten today.[20]

There are very few accounts about the life of the Ottoman common soldiers during this period. Of those that exist, one is the 'diary' of an irregular from Anatolia, who spent the years from 1801 to 1833 in military service. Kabudlı el-Haccî Mustafa Vasfî Efendi served as an irregular horseman from the 1820s becoming a *deli* and a soldier of fortune in

---

20 Georg Wilhelm von Valentini (1775–1834) was a Prussian lieutenant general, inspector general of military education and training, and a military writer. His major work on the Ottoman military is *Précis des dernières guerres des Russes contre les Turcs, avec des considérations militaires et politiques; traduit de l'Allemand par Eugène de la Côste* (Paris, 1825).

Eastern Anatolia;[21] his account is one of the few known pre-First World War Ottoman military memoirs. His narrative provides rare glimpses into the tumultuous everyday life and moral dilemmas faced by countless Ottoman irregular soldiery, most of whom hailed from Muslim peasantry and joined paramilitary bands either because of the opportunities such pursuits provided, or because in this way they could protect their kin and communities from similar bands in the Empire. His service in the irregular cavalry brought him the name Dely Mustafa. His narrative helps scholars understand what common Muslims serving in irregular military forces had to do to make a living during this tumultuous period of Ottoman history, and most importantly, how they explained and legitimated their precarious and contentious way of life.

Financing the Army

In every time and at every latitude, money has always been the fuel of armies. For centuries, the holders of small tax assignments or prebends, *timar*, generally had lived in or near the settlements where the assigned revenues were generated and had consumed a certain proportion on the spot. Since the late seventeenth century the landowners – *sipahi-timars* – were increasingly unwilling to take part in long campaigns, preferring instead to pay exemption fees, and the government chose to finance its new military policy at the expense of the *timars*. By the 1700s tax-farming became the primary Ottoman instrument for raising revenue. The advantages of the new system were obvious, because the tax-farmers, who accounted for a growing share of the taxes, converted almost all the foodstuffs they collected into ready cash. The government began to reassign the estates slowly because of institutional conservatism, the continuing need for light cavalry against non-European enemies, and the potentially disruptive socio-economic problems. Nevertheless, the change from *timar*-based tax collection to the tax-farming system by itself was a very traumatic process, first benefiting the Imperial elites in the capital, but evolving to local families, janissary or otherwise, and their Constantinople clients, as the system expanded across the Empire in lifetime contracts.[22] In the government,

---

21 Esmer U. Tolga, 'The Confessions of an Ottoman Irregular: Self-Representation and Ottoman Interpretive Communities in the Nineteenth Century', in *Osmanlı Araştırmaları – The Journal of Ottoman Studies*, XLIV (2014), pp.313–340. Nothing is known about Deli Mustafa except from what he – or a scribe to whom he most likely dictated his account – writes in the manuscript. In the account, he relates that he and his father were professional, itinerant cavalrymen – *deli* – who travelled together first from their native village of Kabud (near Tokat in the mid-Black Sea region of Anatolia) to the eastern frontier of Anatolia to engage in skirmishes with unruly *paşas*, Georgian or Kurds bandits, and Russians. Deli Mustafa's account is another rare source, and indicates how simple soldiers coped with the fickle patronage of superiors. His account describes the options available to those who suffered the consequences of the intrigues that plagued the Ottoman war machine.

22 This process began in the seventeenth century; see Aksan, *Ottoman Wars*, p.55: 'The tendency was to convert the fiefs into tax collections, and large numbers fell out of the jurisdiction of

THE OTTOMAN ARMY OF THE NAPOLEONIC WARS 1789–1815

Albanian *arnavut* chief (lithography by Achille Devèria, 1825)

this process was not perceived as a drastic change, and most members of the governing elite probably did not understand the potential consequences, as it appeared to be simply a part of an already ongoing process.[23]

Nevertheless, some historians have acknowledged that eighteenth-century fiscal innovation was intensive enough to demonstrate that the Ottoman government was capable of 'moving with the times'.[24] The reforms influencing military recruitment include the placing of tax collection in the hands of the *ayans*, and the concentration of both mobilisation and supply in many of the same officials, collectively known 'committees of notables'. As a result, in the last quarter of the eighteenth century, a considerable part of the military financing was under the control of private individuals.

Whilst the Ottoman government's employment of the *ayan* magnates in wars could be likened to private profiteering coming from the conflicts, the Porte could no longer offer lucrative war contracts in the eighteenth century in the wake of the disastrous wars against the Austrians and particularly the Russians. Soon, the state's regular income from tax collection was not sufficient to remedy the situation.[25] In addition, the introduction of permanent war taxes soured relations between government and subjects even more. However, to meet the increasingly expansive war commitments, extraordinary wartime taxes, the *avarız*, became a part of the regular tax structure in the seventeenth century. Gradually, the *avarız* became an annual tax and was collected according to the subjects'

---

the timariots, as a part of the general trend, by which revenue collection devolved to emerging leaders ... Beneficiaries of the evolving system were the imperial household, administrative officials and Janissaries, the latter coincidentally, who, as noted above, were sent into the provinces to quell the *celali* revolts; by the mid seventeenth century, reassigned *timars* regularly went to members of the janissary corps, sometimes in lieu of pay.'

23 İsmail Hakkı Uzunçarşılı, *Osmanlı Devleti Teşkilatından Kapukulu Ocakları* (Ankara: Türk Tarih Kurumu Basımevi, 1988), vol. II, pp.52–53.

24 Bruce McGowan, 'The Age of the *Ayans*, 1699–1812', in S. Faroqhi, B. McGowan, D. Quataert, S. Pamuk (eds), *An Economic and Social History of the Ottoman Empire, 1300–1914* (Cambridge: Cambridge University Press, 1994), p.710.

25 Kadir Ustun, *The New Order and Its Enemies: Opposition to Military Reform in the Ottoman Empire, 1789 – 1807* (Submitted in partial fulfilment of the requirements for the degree of Doctor of Philosophy in the Graduate School of Arts and Sciences: Columbia University, 2013), p.4.

ability to pay, namely their wealth.[26] Additionally, the government began to insist on turning the in-kind nature of the taxes into in-cash collections. It was an understandable policy change due to the fact that transporting the collected in-kind taxes became a nightmare, frequently resulting in spoilage of the provisions. The in-cash alternative was more elastic and became essential for the payment of the salaries, in addition to monies saved in transport fees. Moreover, the purchase of provisions from the provinces near the war zones helped the economy and created more incentives for agriculture. Most of the villagers and other taxpayers were not happy with the changing nature of tax collection, however, and it created large problems for which the government was unable to find satisfactory solutions.[27]

However, the need for immediate resources forced the government to gradually demand more cash instead of deliveries in kind. One of the most common tax was the *nüzul*, which originally had consisted of foodstuff that the subjects conveyed to fixed stopping points for the army on its march to the front. This tax frequently was demanded from households rather from individual, women, children, disabled and old people generally being exempt. In 1691, when the war against the Holy League was at the zenith, the government introduced a reform in order to increase revenues and reinstituted the principle that every taxable individual was to pay separately. Collection thereafter seems to have proceeded in a reasonably regular fashion, and in the following century the *nüzul* was apparently associated with the *avariz*. A further innovation regarding the military financing was the *imdad-ı seferiye*, or campaign-assistance tax, which became a regular, annual imposition after 1718. These revenues were assigned to local officials, and inadvertently contributed to the ongoing empowerment of provincial grandees, or *ayans*.

With the help of these new fiscal measures, the Ottoman government financed its military policy and was able to pay the garrisons in the key strategic fortresses. Even after internal savings and additional tax revenue, however, it was financially impossible to enlist the necessary numbers of garrisons for all the most important fortresses. In order to utilise the revenues economically, the government could hire more musket-bearing mercenaries for its campaigns and fortresses. As the mercenaries were cheap and could be easily demobilised after the end of campaigns, they were useful for internal security duties as well. Some officials were well aware of the consequences of depending heavily on mercenaries, but it was unable to find any other feasible and satisfactory solution.

Even with this renewed capacity, however, the Ottomans several times fell victim to the massive financial burdens of the wars and the maintenance of the border zones. The government demonstrated its flexibility and pragmatism

---

26   Suraya Faroqhi, 'Crisis and Change', in S. Faroqhi, B. McGowan, D. Quataert, S. Pamuk (eds), *An Economic and Social History of the Ottoman Empire* (Cambridge: Cambridge University Press, 1999), vol. II, p.552.

27   Bruce McGowan, 'The Age of the *Ayans*', in S. Faroqhi, B. McGowan, D. Quataert, S. Pamuk (eds), *An Economic and Social History of the Ottoman Empire* (Cambridge: Cambridge University Press, 1999), vol. II, p.640.

Grand Vizier Kör Yusuf Ziya Paşa in the alleged portrait published in *Moeurs, Usages, Costumes des Othomans*, by Antoine-Laurent Castellan (1812).

during the crises, but very often it paid a steep price for resolution.[28] The comparison with one of its main enemies, Russia, clearly shows that the Porte was in a state of great financial weakness.[29] The economic recovery of the mid 1700s had been nullified by recurrent wars with Austria and Russia, by the 1770s and 1790s, as well as the recurrent riots and uprisings occurred in Europe, Africa and Asia in the same period. These continuous wars brought near-bankruptcy at a time when investment in military technology was imperative.

The ever-increasing requirements of the new combat environment and fiscal limitations were instrumental in forcing the government to make use of two older practices on a wider scale. The first was reducing the real salary payments by debasing the currency. This policy, as before, caused widespread unrest and occasional rebellions, but it achieved several decades of relief for the government. The reduction of the salaries, however, forced the professional soldiers to search for other ways to earn a living. Corruption and abuse were obvious outcomes, but the most important development, which was also very similar to the contemporary European examples, was establishing private small businesses and becoming part of the artisans' guilds and city labour market already at the end of the seventeenth century. Recent research shows that *kapıkulu* soldiers were already part of the Empire's commercial activity, but participation in secondary commercial-artisan related jobs was obviously born out of the government's deliberate policy of reducing the salaries by means of debasement.[30]

Whilst information about budgets and expenditures remains elusive, and may never be available with any degree of certainty, authoritative economic studies have demonstrated that expenditures doubled during military

---

28　Ágoston, 'Military Transformation in the Ottoman Empire and Russia', p.309: 'Whereas in the middle of the century, the revenues of the two empires were comparable: 239 tons of silver in Russia in 1751 versus 214 in the Ottoman Empire in 1748, by 1786 Russian revenues were almost seven times greater than those of the Ottoman treasury, which managed 925 tons of silver versus 136.'

29　Ágoston, 'Military Transformation in the Ottoman Empire and Russia',: 'In Russia, the central government's revenues grew steadily during the eighteenth century, parallel to the increase in the number of male souls, the basis of its direct taxes. Revenues rose from 8.5 million rubles in 1724 to 24.1 million in 1769, to 51.4 million in 1786, and to 74.6 million in 1796. By comparison, in the Ottoman Empire, where the population was stable at about 25–30 million, the revenues of the treasury increased only by 10 percent in the eighteenth century, despite the introduction of lifelong tax farms through which the government hoped to collect more revenues.'

30　Uyar and Erickson, *A Military History of the Ottomans*, p.91.

campaigns.³¹ Annual state expenditure rose by 30 percent between 1761 and 1785, but in the wartime there was a 100 percent increase. Soldiers' salaries comprised 75 percent of expenditure in 1784 and 74 percent in 1785. Meanwhile state revenues remained at much the same level, and efforts to increase revenue failed owing to the general economic stagnation. The lack of financial resources prevented the Ottomans from reacting immediately when the Russians annexed the Crimea in 1783. Three years later, the senior accountant at the treasury stated that 15 million *gurus* were needed to begin the war, an amount equal to the treasury's total annual revenue. Meanwhile the *kapudan paşa* estimated the costs of building a battle fleet at 6–7.5 million *gurus*; he also considered the drafting of 36,000 troops necessary.³² Under such circumstances, it is no surprise that the Porte waited until 1787 before involving itself in a new war. Extractions from the countryside were increased accordingly, but other sources of revenue were tapped as well. Examples might include confiscation of wealthy estates, which continued until abolished by Sultan Mahmud II at the end of his reign.

Despite all the resource-saving solutions and control measures introduced, the financing of military policy was the actual Achilles' heel of the Ottoman Empire. It was not uncommon for the lack of money to pay soldiers' salaries to have disastrous effects on the continuation of a military campaign. In 1801, such were the embarrassments of the Ottoman army, from a scarcity of funds for the payment of the troops in Egypt, that 'the principal Ottoman officers were driven to the necessity of subscribing from three to 5,000 *piasters* each, to furnish a momentary relief'.³³ The scarcity of resources was compounded by corruption and maladministration. Further evidence of this is recognisable in the pay tickets and rations of the janissary muster rolls, the *esame*. In the 1770s, the *esame* had become promissory notes that were sold and traded like securities. It is said that 400,000 pay tickets may have circulated at the end of the century, but this figure never represented the actual number

Topçu başi, the artillery commander, after William Wittman's *Travels* (1803)

---

31 Virginia H. Aksan, 'War and Peace' in S. Faroqhi (ed.), *The Cambridge History of Turkey, Volume 3, The Later Ottoman Empire, 1303–1839* (Cambridge: Cambridge University Press, 2006), p.90.

32 Gábor Ágoston, 'Ottoman Warfare in Europe 1453–1826', in J. Black (ed.), *European Warfare,1453–1815* (London: Macmillan, 1999), pp.142–143. According to the author, the export of raw materials was prohibited, and new restrictions were placed on the export of dressed leather and various fabrics. Price increases between 1760 and 1800 reached 200 percent.

33 Wittman, *Travels in Turkey*, p.269.

of active soldiers, who probably were just a minimal percentage.[34] Moreover, reform of the janissary corps became considerably more difficult, as the circulation of such pay tickets benefited the entire Ottoman administration, which speculated with the illegal selling of fictional posts in the *kapıkulu*.[35] It is all the more remarkable that the agendas for reform that Selim III requested from his entourage in 1789 invariably included reform of the *esame* as an essential measure to recover control over the Ottoman 'military'.

The Standing Army and the Officer Corps

In the last decades of the eighteenth century, the ancient *kapıkulu* still represented the actual Imperial standing army. The core of this venerable corps had been instituted by the first Ottoman sultans and comprised the ancient corps of the golden age as definitively established by Süleyman the Magnificent. In the 1770s, the combined strength of the Ottoman standing and garrison forces fluctuated, on paper, between 70,000 and 140,000 men.[36] Alongside them, there were garrison soldiers who were remunerated not directly from the treasury but from the provincial *ocaks*. In the 1750s there were 55,943 local troops, called *neferat-ı yerliiyan*, remunerated from the respective district.[37] Despite the periodic increases in number, by the 1760s the Ottomans were no match for the Russians as far as army strength was concerned. In 1761–62, Ottoman field troops numbered 55,731 men, with an additional 141,116 men in the garrisons. Of the latter, about 55,000 were janissaries, armourers, artillerymen, and gun-carriage drivers serving in the Empire's garrisons.[38] The remaining 85,395 were infantry and cavalry troops of the provincial levy.[39] With a very Anglo-Saxon capacity for synthesis, John Philip Morier divided the Ottoman troops into two distinct classes; the one receiving pay, and the other serving as 'volunteers', namely receiving salary when engaged on campaigns.[40]

Of the Imperial standing troops, the Sultan's one-time elite infantry – the janissaries – continued to play a central role, despite the decline in their fighting capabilities. Paper figures are misleading, however, since only a fraction of the paid janissaries were in fact mobilised for campaigns. Others

---

34 Aksan, *Ottoman Wars*, p.262. This figure had been questioned in 1882 by Ahmed Cévad Beg, who states that in 1792 the number of the active and non-active Janissaries was 112,000. See in Cévad, *Etat Militaire Ottoman*, vol. I, p.92.

35 Aksan, *Ottoman Wars*, p.262. The ostensible reason for the revolt of 1808 was that those Janissaries who refused to enrol in the New Order Army found themselves off the rolls. Not just Janissaries, but scores of merchants, civil servants, and other beneficiaries of the janissary payroll, themselves in possession of pay tickets – *esame* – had been deprived of a source of income.

36 Cévad, *Tarih-i Askeri Osmânî* (Constantinople, 1882), vol. III, p.181.

37 Ágoston, 'Military Transformation in the Ottoman Empire and Russia', p.307.

38 Cévad, *Etat Militaire Ottoman*, vol. I, p.167.

39 Ágoston, 'Military Transformation in the Ottoman Empire and Russia', p.307.

40 Morier, *Memoir of a Campaign with the Ottoman Army in Egypt*, p.7.

were deployed in frontier garrisons, with strategically important forts having janissary garrisons of 1,000 to 5,000 men.[41] It seems, however, that establishing the total strength of the Ottoman armies with a reasonable approximation is a very difficult task. Estimates in western sources about the size of the Ottoman armies are generally out of proportion to reality, largely because the commanders still insisted on travelling with huge baggage trains and large numbers of camp followers: 'late eighteenth-century Ottoman camps may be likened to disturbed beehives'.[42]

Attempts to establish the strength of the army and its effective employment on campaign have calculated the amount of the expenses, but this method does not allow establishing of the consistency of the troops actually available for a military campaign, considering that many of those who were registered as soldiers were instead just servants or pensioners.[43] Even authors who applied military reasoning, such as Captain Thomas Walsh in 1803, reflected on this matter:

> The strength of a Turkish army can never be ascertained, as all the authority of the grand vizier cannot compel them to be mustered. Several revolts have been the consequence of such attempts. In times of prosperity and success, the army increases in proportion with the hope of plunder; but should it experience a defeat, the general is entirely deserted, and left to seek his safety in flight.[44]

Furthermore, the calculation of the field force became difficult due to the large number of auxiliary personnel and the considerable train that accompanied each Ottoman army. Even though the ratio of soldiers to auxiliary personnel was much smaller in favour of the former than in the past, the armies still appeared as a disorderly mass accompanied by a multitude of non-combatants. In this respect, Count Constantin de Volnay emphasised the issue very effectively when he describes the Ottoman army marching to Syria against the rebel Aly Bey:

> The army arrived at the end of February 1771. The gazettes of the time wrote that they numbered 60,000 men, and led Europe to believe that it was an army similar to those of Russia or Germany, but the Turks, and especially those of Asia, differ from the Europeans even more in their military status than in their morals and customs. It is very difficult for sixty thousand men to be sixty thousand soldiers like ours. On the contrary, the army in question was this, which might amount

---

41 Cévad, *Etat Militaire Ottoman*, vol. I, pp.167–168.
42 Aksan, *Ottoman Warfare*, p.144.
43 Ágoston, 'Military Transformation in the Ottoman Empire and Russia', p.304.
44 Thomas Walsh, *Journal of the Late Campaign in Egypt: Containing Descriptions of that Country, and of Gibraltar, Minorca, Malta, Marmorice, and Macri; With An Appendix; Containing Official Papers And Documents* (London, 1803), p.55. Walsh served as Captain in the 93rd Regiment of Foot, and as Field Adjutant of Major-General Eyre Coote during the Egyptian Campaigns of 1801. He left a detailed account of the field operations especially with regard to the British troops, but with little information about the Ottoman allies.

to forty thousand men in all, which must be classified as follows, namely, five thousand Mamluks, all on horseback, and this was indeed the army; about fifteen hundred barbaries on foot, no other infantry. The Turks know of none among them, the man on horseback being all; besides, each Mamluk having on the fly two foot soldiers armed with sticks, it makes 10,000 foot soldiers; more, a surplus of foot soldiers and 'ferrâdjs' or mounted valets for the *beys* and other chiefs, valued at 2,000, all the rest sutlers and scullions: this was the army.[45]

Thirty years later, the situation had changed little reading the words of Morier, who accompanied the Ottoman army in Egypt in 1800:

Two circumstances render it very difficult to ascertain with accuracy the efficient force of a Turkish army: first, the incredible numbers who follow it for any purpose, but that of fighting, and who are not easily distinguished from the soldiers: secondly, the practice, which is very common with the chief of detachments, of giving in a return of more men then they bring into the field, in order to receive the rations allowed for them and their horses. The one under review was said, when I joined it, to amount to 80,000 men, but a deduction of half that number might fairly be made for idlers of all descriptions. The Grand Vizier camp alone, consisting of his attendants and the ministers of state, amount to 10,000. Every man, according to his rank or his circumstances, has a large or small retinue. The common establishment of a person as low in rank as a clerk to any department of the administration, requires two tents; a servant, a water carrier, a groom, a cook, and a person to pitch and strike his tents, with a proportion of horses and camels.[46]

On the same matter, William Wittman remarks:

So considerable, in a Turkish army, are the numbers of trades people, attendants, domestics, and followers of every denomination, that when it is computed to amount to twenty thousand men, nearly the half of that number must be subtracted, to form an estimate of its real and efficient force, when brought into the field.[47]

For an objective assessment of field force and its actual effectiveness, further considerations would be examined. First of all, the quality of the troops. Since the janissaries and other *kapıkulu* troops became less and less willing to participate in military campaigns, the number of newly recruited soldiers became proportionally higher. To have an idea about this proportion, in the mid eighteenth century, the majority of mobilised janissaries had nothing in common with the once-elite corps, since between 70 and 80 percent of them were fresh recruits, hired before and during

---

45 Constantin-François de Chasseboeuf, comte de Volnay, *Voyage en Syrie et en Égypte, pendant les années 1783, 1784 et 1785* (Paris, 1787), vol. I, p.114.
46 Morier, *Memoir of a Campaign with the Ottoman Army in Egypt*, pp.30–31.
47 Wittman, *Travels in Turkey*, p.157.

each campaign from among the commoners.[48] In addition to the *kapıkulu* salaried troops, the irregulars accounted for an increasingly larger share of new recruits. In the same period, from 13,000 to 16,000 provincial *miri levend* and other irregular troops constituted between 10 and 15 percent of the army quartered in Serbia.[49] However, with all the troops deployed in other fronts, the number of the irregulars reached more than 40,000 men in 1738, and 28,000 men in 1739.[50] The share of combatant janissaries declined further in subsequent decades. Furthermore, those janissaries who actually did participate in campaigns performed poorly. The increased demand for troops required widening the pool of recruitment to include Turks and other Muslim-born subjects, who had previously been barred from the Sultan's elite corps.[51]

The sharp increase in the number of hastily recruited and poorly trained soldiers led to a decisive deterioration in the military qualities of the corps. Therefore, one of the most negative aspects outlined by all observers, including neutral ones, was the lack of training and internal discipline. This problem was a common feature of every corps or unit in the army. Wittman dwells on the violent disputes that occurred during the Egyptian campaign. On the report dated 3 April 1800, he reports that the janissary *ortas* 37 and 65 that came to hostilities for the division of a provision of barley. The dispute involved other soldiers transforming the episode in an incredible and chaotic drama:

> In the quarrel, several janissaries were killed and many others wounded. It happened that an Albanian irregular, who was passing by during the affray, received a slight wound. This Albanian made an immediate representation to his corps, that it was intention of the janissaries to fall on and butcher the Albanians without distinction. The effect of this mis-statement was, that the latter had recourse to their arms, and were proceeding to the most alarming measures, which were, however, fortunately prevented by the strenuous interference of the principal Ottoman officers in the camp.[52]

In his very detailed chronicle of the Egyptian campaigns, Wittman also records the clashes and confrontations between the janissaries and the British infantry.[53] The outcome, the so-called the 'grand army' of Yusuf Ziya Paşa, seems not an actual army but 'a horde without effective command

---

48 Gábor Ágoston, 'Firearms and Military Adaptation: The Ottomans and the European Military Revolution, 1450–1800', in *Journal of World History*, vol. 25, N. 1 (March 2014), p.120.
49 Ágoston, 'Military Transformation in the Ottoman Empire and Russia', p.306.
50 Ágoston, 'Military Transformation in the Ottoman Empire and Russia', p.306.
51 Ágoston, 'Military Transformation in the Ottoman Empire and Russia', p.306.
52 William Wittman, *Travels in Turkey, Asia-Minor, Syria, and Across the Desert Into Egypt During the Years 1799, 1800, and 1801, in Company with the Turkish Army, and the British Military Mission: To which are Annexed, Observations on the Plague and on the Diseases Prevalent in Turkey, and a Meteorological Journal* (London, 1803), p.275.
53 Wittman, *Travels in Turkey*, pp.313–314.

THE OTTOMAN ARMY OF THE NAPOLEONIC WARS 1789–1815

The *turnaci başi*, commander of *Orta* number 63, early 1800s, after the collection of Turkish Costumes of Czar Alexander III (Hermitage Museum, St Petersburg).

and control or a competent officer corps.'[54] In 1800 most of the members of the *kapıkulu* corps remained in and around Constantinople, and only a portion of them participated in the Egyptian expedition, albeit with much protest. Similarly, the janissaries assigned to the border's garrisons also tried their best to evade duty. The government was forced to depend on mercenaries more than ever. Interestingly, for the first time in the history of the Ottoman Empire, Albanian and Caucasian mercenaries were more numerous than the traditional mercenaries of Anatolia and Rumelia. The only positive feature of the field army was the presence of regular artillery and engineer units under the command of trained officers, including the 70-year-old Scottish-born Kampel Mustafa Ağa.[55]

If the poor quality of the troops reached worrying levels in certain cases, the situation was equally deplorable at higher command level. In 1804 the Sultan ordered the *paşas* of Syria and Baghdad to undertake a campaign against the Arab Wahhabis, but such a campaign never took place, since lack of determination of the governors to comply with the Sultan's orders led to no results.[56] Rivalry and mutual suspicion between commanders could lead to disastrous outcomes. In 1801, when much parts of Serbia, Bulgaria, Albania, and Greece were out of Constantinople's control, the Porte decided to issue drastic measures against bandits and rebels. However, the appointment of Hakkı Mehmed Paşa to the governorship of Edirne flamed the rivalry of the former *paşa* Gurgi Osman. In order to issue the prestige and authority necessary to accomplish the mission, the Sultan gave Hakkı Mehmed absolute power to act in any way he wished without question. Hearing this news, Gurgi Osman was terrified, fearing that the new governor had also received secret orders for his execution, a common practice at that time. While Gurgi Osman was soon relieved by the news of his appointment to Salonika, he was still bitterly hostile, and intrigued against Hakkı Mehmed. As soon as Hakkı reached Edirne, Gurgi

---

54 Wittman, *Travels in Turkey*, p.249.

55 Uyar and Erickson, *A Military History of the Ottomans*, p.124. He was a Scottish aristocrat, Count Ramsay Campbell, who enter the Ottoman service in the 1770s as artillery officer. Years later, Campbell converted to Islam and assumed a new Muslim name.

56 John Barret Kelly, *Britain and the Persian Gulf, 1795–1880* (Oxford: Clarendon Press, 1968), p.105.

Osman seized Sofia and began to gather a force of brigands and mountaineers from Bulgaria and Albania. The dispute lasted for a year and the two *paşas* almost came to an armed confrontation, which was averted just in time by the Sultan, who eventually replaced Hakkı with another governor. But he soon proved too weak for the post, and bandits robbed Bulgaria, Thrace, and Macedonia again. Some bold outlaw leaders actually surrounding Edirne and making raids as far as Constantinople, ravaging the villages around Silistra, and occupying Varna in 1802. At the same time, the Albanian troops previously sent to support Hakkı's efforts now refused to obey the new *paşa* and set out on their own to ravage and raid the province.[57]

The original connection between ruler elites and a military commander embodied by the grand vizier, *paşa*, *sancakbeg* and others, remained a constant in Ottoman military history until the 1830s. This means that a first-class military knowledge was not indispensable to gain access to important positions in the Empire's hierarchy. As brave and clever as they were, the grand viziers and their subordinates were often less trained than the opponents they faced. The need to raise a general staff formed by professional commanders was not perceived as a necessary condition to close the gap with their Occidental opponents, or, along with this, the formation of a command made up of professional soldiers would have challenged the whole structure of the state. This awareness would eventually prevail many years later. It is striking to note that the commission set up by Sultan Selim III after 1791 to reform the army included a small number of personalities with experience of military command, and that despite this, each of the 24 members of the commission presented their own observations on how to reform the army properly.[58] Although proverbially pragmatic, the Ottomans considered the army to be an integral part of the state, and consequently any influential person was asked for his opinion.

The Ottomans did not raise an officer corps trained in Western-style warfare until the Tanzimat reforms (1839–76). Moreover, there was no staff comparable to those of the field armies of the major European powers, and the presence of second in command officers and other auxiliary personnel directly subordinate to the commander-in-chief did not follow an established rule. Usually, the grand vizier held the rank of supreme commander of the army and navy. In the official acts of government, its status was widely

---

57 Shaw, *Between Old and New*, pp.308–312.
58 Apart from Grand Vizier Koca Yussuf Paşa, his lieutenant Mustafa Reşid Efendi, and Mehmed Hakkı Bey, who were members of the Imperial class, the committee comprised five religious judges, and a further 13 members came from the bureaucracy and administration. Among these latter there were the chief of the Topkapı's kitchen, and the Imperial chronicler, while the scribe of the 'rapid-fire artillery', the *çavuş* commander and the director of the Constantinople arsenal could be considered personalities with some military background. The advisors included also the interpreter of the Swedish embassy, the Armenian-born Mouradgea d'Ohsson, and the French military instructor Bertrand, who were the two foreigners on the committee. See Stanford J. Shaw, *Between Old and New. The Ottoman Empire under Sultan Selim III, 1789–1807* (Harvard, MA: Harvard University Press, 1971), pp 91–93.

THE OTTOMAN ARMY OF THE NAPOLEONIC WARS 1789–1815

THE ARMIES OF THE SULTAN

Ottoman ambassador Resmi Ahmed Efendi arrives at Berlin in 1763, with his escort. Print after an engraving by Johann David Schleuen (author's archive). Resmi Ahmed was born into a family of Greek descent. In 1757 he was appointed to an embassy to Vienna to announce the accession of Mustafa III to the throne. This was followed by a similar appointment, the first ever Ottoman embassy to the court of Frederick the Great in Berlin in 1763–1764. After both embassies, Resmi Ahmed submitted detailed reports on the geography of his passage and the politics of the courts he encountered. In the case of the Berlin embassy, he left behind not just an account of diplomatic niceties but also a portrayal of Frederick and the description of the Seven Years' War. His observations introduced in the Empire a new interest in the study European politics.

celebrated, since the Sultan qualified him as 'general administrator of the state, splendour of the nation, invincible lion of the battlefields, lightning sabre of victories'.[59] After his appointment, each grand vizier received 40 lifeguards from the Sultan, who joined his households and accompanied him on campaign.

The grand vizier, or the officer in command of the field army, made use of other senior commanders or local officials. It was also the case that government officials accompanied the grand vizier, so the Chief Financial Officer and his staff could join the command headquarters, while stand-ins held their offices in Constantinople.[60] William Wittman provides an accurate description of the Ottoman Major Staff of the army of Egypt in 1800. It included the grand vizier as commander-in-chief, the *serasker,* who had the rank of a *paşa*, the *çarcaci başi*; the *yeniçeri ağasi*, the *cebeci başi*, the *topçu başi*, the *arabaci başi*, the *humbaraci başi*, the *lağimci başi*, the *seymen başi* the *kul-kyaia*, the *kadıasker*s; the *etçi başi*, the *samsoncu başi* and the *zagarci başi*.[61] Of the 14 officers, three – *kul-kyaia, kadıasker*s and *etçi başi* – were administrative officials, and the remaining just two – *serasker* and *çarcaci başi* – were titular of an actual field rank.

According to the classical system, an Ottoman officer could be commissioned in three ways: on-the-job training within the *kapıkulu* corps; attendance at the three palace schools (Enderun, close to the Topkapı Palace, Galatasaray, and İbrahimpaşa); participation in the *timar* system. The officers of provincial units and mercenaries did not have the same rights of the privileged officers of the central government who were part of the military-administrative class. However, with the rise of vizier families, governors, and other grandees, and the vitality of their personal retinue for the conduct of campaigns, their households began to recruit and train prospective officer candidates. The grandees increasingly began to assign personnel from their household to high military posts, and patron–client relations became the most important element in this system.[62] Due to this long-established scenario, the military reformers of the eighteenth and early nineteenth centuries found it difficult to use the formal institutions as a springboard to launch reforms. In fact to the contrary, these institutions became an obstacle blocking the foundation of further modern structures.

The period between 1730s and 1790s was instrumental for the rise of a new generation of reformist personalities who decisively influenced the military organisation. Two important experiences made them distinct from their predecessors: combat experiences and direct contacts with Europe in military capacities. Resmi Ahmed Efendi (1700–1783) was an early example of this new generation. After classical scribal training, Ahmed served as ambassador to Vienna (1757–1758) and Berlin (1763–1764). Additionally, he performed important administrative duties at the front during the disastrous Ottoman–

---

59 Mouradgea d'Ohsson, p.163.
60 Aksan, *Ottoman Warfare*, p.144.
61 Wittman, *Travels in Turkey*, p.227.
62 Uyar and Erickson, *A Military History of the Ottomans*, p.94.

THE ARMIES OF THE SULTAN

Russian war of 1768–1774, and he was the chief Ottoman negotiator of the Küçük Kaynarca peace treaty. Thanks to this unique combination of experiences, he witnessed the direct results of the Empire's structural problems and was familiar with its military deficiencies.

In contrast to previous Ottoman diplomatic reports, Resmi Ahmed gave sound military information about the countries he had visited. His descriptions of the Prussian military are especially revealing in understanding his perceptions and priorities. He noted that living conditions for Prussian soldiers were very hard. Their provisions were meagre and accommodations more than Spartan, but surprisingly they continuously participated in rigorous training and manoeuvres. Similarly, their command control and order were very good. At this point he switched his focus from the soldiers to their officers. Obviously he was impressed by the Prussian *Rittersakademie* gentlemen's school in which boys from aristocratic families underwent a long and application-based military training.[63]

The eighteenth century was also an age of 'men of the pen' or 'Efendi-turned-*paşas*', namely of military governors and grand viziers who came from the *kalemiyye*-civil bureaucracy. Though most commanding officers were ill prepared for campaigning during the 1768–74 Russo-Ottoman war, the able grand viziers Silâhdar Mehmed Paşa (1770–71) and Muhsinzade Mehmed Paşa

Janissary, from the album *Costumes Turcs* of the Diez Collection, 1790s. The janissaries benefited from the possession of numerous privileges. In this regard, Mouradgea d'Ohsson states that 'They hold first place among the military corps; they can only receive punishment from their officers, they pay no taxes, and it is rare for them to have property confiscated. Their leader, the *yeniçeri ağası*, takes precedence over all other military leaders and even over ministers of state. It is only on the occasion of Beyram's festivals that he gives way to the commander of the *sipahis* and *silihitars*, because these two military corps are older than the empire. He has the rank of a two-tailed pasha, but in times of war, he frequently gets a third tail as well.'

---

63 Uyar and Erickson, *A Military History of the Ottomans*, p.116: 'Ahmed Resmi's portrait of Frederick the Great is a combination of his reformist tendency and oriental training. He drew an idealized picture of Frederick for Ottoman consumption in order to voice his ideas about what a savior of the Ottoman Empire might appear as. According to Ahmed Resmi, Frederick was a good leader and governor, who spent most of his time in the act of governance but whose most important identity was his apparent military talent and military leadership. Not surprisingly, Ahmed Resmi's vision of an idealized Prussian military machine would become a format for new generations of reforms, which repeated Ahmed Resmi's themes again and again. Indeed, Prussia/Germany remained a model for Ottoman military behaviours until the very end of the Empire.'

(1771–74) were exceptions, and both came from the civil bureaucracy.[64] However, the *kapıkulu* corps managed to keep these protégés out of the units but not out of the high-ranking positions, and palace school graduates were actually bypassed and most of the time had to satisfy themselves with the intermediate positions within the palace.[65] Though the bureaucrats had to face the strong opposition from the *kapıkulu*, they achieved remarkable success in military as well civil affairs. Moreover, grandees' households provided new opportunities for youngsters with a decent backgrounds, and became a new channel of social mobility, but for obvious reasons these patron–client relations factionalised the Ottoman military-administrative system.[66] The acute shortage of trained officers that characterised the Ottoman army until well into the mid nineteenth century, favoured the appointment of bureaucrats as army officers 'in the heat of the moment to fill the breach.'[67] From a military perspective, however, this practice was instrumental in causing the military training institutions to fall into disuse from neglect.[68]

Many times the excessive and fanatical confidence in the enormous resources of the Empire persuaded many commanders and officers to adopt a presumptuous and superficial attitude. This seems to have emerged in 1787, when the Porte went to war against Austria and Russia, without carefully considering the risk it was about to face. Their traditional outlook led the Ottomans, still almost completely unaware of the extent of European technical progress and seemingly unaffected by the defeats inflicted on the Empire in the war of 1768–74, to assume that a revival of the old Ottoman institutions and ways would be entirely sufficient to restore supremacy over their neighbours.

This does not mean, however, that the Porte remained uninterested in the formation of a properly trained officer corps. In eighteenth and nineteenth centuries, foreign military experts, especially French and English,

---

64 Ágoston, 'Military Transformation in the Ottoman Empire and Russia', pp.314–315.

65 Uyar and Erickson, *A Military History of the Ottomans*, p.95.

66 Christoph Neumann, 'Political and diplomatic developments', in S. Faroqhi (ed.) *The Cambridge History of Turkey, volume 3 – The Later Ottoman Empire, 1603–1839* (Cambridge: Cambridge University Press, 2006), p.90: 'It is now known that the career paths of the military, the palace, the bureaucracy and the specialists in religious learning were not as clearly demarcated as had been assumed during the first half of the twentieth century. Men with a palace background could become military commanders, others switched from the ranks of the *ilmiye* (religious scholars; experts in Islamic law) to the central bureaucracy. Such changeovers had always been part of Ottoman life, but after 1700 we observe an increasingly marked tendency towards aristocratisation. We still lack comparative studies between these new-style Ottoman elites, both within and outside the court, and their European counterparts. In the provinces' local notables' class, the *ayan*, formed a social layer mediating between the interests of the inhabitants and those of the provincial government. Among the *ulema* the development of an 'aristocracy' of great families can be observed from the seventeenth century. By 1730 a limited number of families had come to dominate the upper echelons of the *ilmiye* hierarchy.'

67 Aksan, *Ottoman Wars*, p.144.

68 Neumann, 'Political and diplomatic developments', p.90.

played an important role in the introduction of modern military matters in the Ottoman Empire. Thanks to the French renegade Claude Alexandre de Bonneval,[69] who reformed the ancient *humbaracı*-bombardier corps in 1735, the artillerymen and their officers were, for the first time in the history of the Empire, trained in military engineering, ballistics, and mathematics. Their instructor was another French or English renegade called Mühendis Selim (Selim the engineer, or even *İngiliz Selim:* English Selim), who had been educated in military engineering and fortress building in France. Although the corps faltered after its founder's death in 1747, it was revived under Selim III and Mahmud II.[70] The corps proved to be an ideal environment for acculturation and the synthesis of European and Ottoman culture: an Ottoman engineer, Mehmed Said Efendi, who taught geometry at the corps, invented a new instrument for land surveying by combining the European telescope and the Ottoman quadrant. Another well-known European in Ottoman service was Baron François de Tott, a French cavalry officer of Hungarian origin, and France's consul in the Crimean Khanate in the late 1760s.[71] Although

Hurşid Ahmed Paşa (1770?–1822), portrait published by Adam de Friedel in *The Greeks, Twenty-four Portraits of the principal Leaders and Personages who have made themselves most conspicuous in the Greek Revolution* (1830). Born in Georgia, he entered the janissary corps as a youth, and in 1801, after the French evacuated Egypt, he became governor of Alexandria. In 1804 was appointed governor of Egypt at Muhammad Ali's behest. Allied with Britain's diplomatic representative, Hurşid tried to get Muhammad Ali and his Albanians removed from Egypt, bringing in the *deli* light cavalry from Ottoman Syria to counterbalance them, but failed and was besieged in the Cairo Citadel, which he left only after he saw the Ottoman *firman* investing Muhammad Ali as Egypt's *vali*. In 1808 he became governor of Rumelia, participating in the war against the Serbian rebels. On 5 September 1812 he was appointed grand vizier, a post he held until 1 April 1815. He led the campaign in Serbia as commander-in-chief, and brought the uprising to an end after recapturing Belgrade in 1813. In that year he was named governor of Bosnia and from that position campaigned against the Second Serbian Uprising.

---

69 Claude Alexandre Comte de Bonneval (1675–1747) was an unusual personality. He was a very talented and daring officer, but he was also well known for his incompatible character and a certain tendency for financial malfeasance. Because of this volatile combination he had to take refuge first with the Habsburgs in 1706 and then with the Ottomans in 1729. In order not to be handed back to the Habsburgs he converted to Islam and took a new name, Ahmed. His presence was immediately noticed and Grand Vizier Osman Paşa took him under his protection, invested him with the rank of *beglerbeg* (governor general), and tasked him to reorganise the *Humbaracı* into a modern European-style technical corps.

70 Possibly his actual name was Samuel Bayley, and was a son of a pro-Stuart Englishman who emigrated to France in the 1690s.

71 Baron François de Tott (1733–93), the well-known technical adviser to Mustafa III (1757–74), claims sole responsibility for artillery reform in Constantinople. He was son of a Hungarian émigré, former officer of Prince

Tott remained on France's payroll, between 1770 and 1775 the Ottomans occasionally contracted with him to help them rebuild the forts of the Dardanelles, cast cannons, and train artillerymen.[72]

The systematic translation and publishing of Western military and technical books in the Ottoman Empire began in connection with the military reforms of sultans Selim III and Mahmud II in the late eighteenth and early nineteenth centuries. The first among these, published in Ottoman Turkish in the early 1790s, were French military treatises and textbooks, often older ones such as the treatises on warfare, sieges, and mines by Sebastien le Prestre de Vauban (1633–1707). These texts were originally written between the 1680s and early 1700s, though some were printed only in the 1730s. Many of these works were translated for students in the newly established military technical schools: the Imperial Naval Engineering School (*muhendishane-i bahri-ı humayun*), the Artillery School (*topçu mektebi*), and the Imperial Land Engineering School (*muhendishanei merr-i mumayun*).[73]

Surprisingly, the most important and enduring reform of the *nizâm* period, the establishment of the first modern military school of the Empire, was launched in 1795 without fanfare and was unknown to even some of the reformers. The Imperial Military Engineering School was not only the first modern military school but also the first modern high school of the Empire. Even though it was built on the remnants and legacy of various military technical schools of past reforms, it was the brainchild of two modest reformers, Ebubekir Ratıb Efendi and the official interpreter of the Swedish Embassy, Mouradgea d'Ohsson (Muradcan Tosunyan). Both of them proposed nearly the same ideas, most likely unknown to each other: the establishment of a highly academic military school for all military branches with the help of foreign experts. As a former Ottoman citizen of Armenian origins, d'Ohsson additionally asked for the inclusion of non-Muslim students. Selim III accepted the proposals but limited the broad

---

Ferenc Rákóczi during the Hungarian rebellion of 1703–11. Tott was the author of the *Memoires du Baron de Tott Sur les Turcs et les Tartares* parts I–IV (Amsterdam, 1784), in which he described his experiences in the Ottoman Empire. However, many of the statements are not very reliable, so much so that some scholars compare Tott's *Memoires* with Rudolf Erich Raspe's novel *Baron Münchhausen*. See Aksan, *Ottoman Wars, 1700–1870*, p.13.

72 Gábor Ágoston and Bruce Masters, *Encyclopedia of the Ottoman Empire* (New York, NY: Facts on File, 2009), p.380: 'As a former cavalryman in France's famous hussar regiment, Tott had only limited knowledge of fortress building, siege warfare, and cannon casting, and thus the value of his services the Ottomans is uncertain. However, his Memoirs, in which he unashamedly exaggerated his role in Ottoman service, suited the tastes of his European readers and enjoyed unmatched popularity. His often superficial observations and inflated comments are partly responsible for perpetuating myths regarding the Ottoman Empire and its 'Military', such as the Ottomans' supposed preference for giant cannons and their alleged conservatism.'

73 Ágoston and Masters, *Encyclopedia of the Ottoman Empire*, p.380. In addition to these, lecture notes of French and other foreign teachers at the military and naval schools were also translated and printed in either the French Embassy's Constantinople press or in one of the newly established Ottoman printing houses.

concept to the narrowly defined technical school within the structure of bombardier and miners' corps.[74] This bore fruit, because despite the 1807 and 1808 revolts, the technical schools and the printing house continued to operate, and the technical corps in the army was reinforced through new regulations by the succeeding sultans.

Unfortunately, in this period, teaching based on Western scientific texts concerned only a marginal group of the Ottoman commanders. Though it is difficult to form a general picture of the Ottoman officer corps at the time of the Napoleonic wars, many testimonies tend to confirm a deplorable state. It was not only the insufficient technical preparation of the officers at all levels, but also their ignorance of many of the modern scientific matters, their superstition and reluctance to engage with Western culture as a whole. In this period, solace for the tribulation experienced by the Empire was sought in transforming the Islamic religion into an ideology and this became instrumental to oppose modernisation and influences from the infidels.[75] In this regard, William Wittman recounts an episode that took place in August 1799, during a meeting between the British major staffs and the grand vizier Kör Yusuf Ziya Paşa. Wittman relates that after showing a map of Syria, Brigadier General Koehler gave an explanation on the cartography and added some remark about the Earth's sphericity:

> This information caused no small degree of surprise to the Turkish minister, and it appeared, by his reply, that he was disposed to doubt the truth of the assertion. 'If' he observed, 'the Earth is round, how can the people, and other detached objects on the half beneath, be prevented from falling off?' When he was told that the Earth revolved round the Sun, he displayed an equal degree of scepticism, observing that if the was the case, the ships bound from Jaffa to Constantinople, instead of proceeding to that capital, would be carried to London, or elsewhere. So much for the astronomical and geographical knowledge of a Turkish statesman![76]

However, in the course of the campaigns, Wittman's judgement becomes less negative. He recognises the Grand Vizier's quality as a military commander, and acknowledges his human qualities, as well as his distinctly solemn figure. Together with the Grand Vizier, Wittman expresses positive opinions about other Ottoman senior officers, among them the vanguard's commander Tahir Paşa, and especially his fellow countryman Kavalalı Mehmet Ali, the future Muhammad Ali ruler of Egypt.[77]

---

74 Uyar and Erickson, *A Military History of the Ottomans*, p.123.
75 Ilber Ortayli, *The Empire's Longest Century* (Istanbul: Kronik, 2021), pp.92–93.
76 Wittman, *Travels in Turkey*, p.133.
77 Wittman, *Travels in Turkey*, p.133.

Janissaries

The most prestigious and renowned speciality of the *kapıkulu* were the feared janissaries, which represented four fifths of the whole corps. According to d'Ohsson, in the 1780s the janissaries formed four divisions, *cemaat*, *bölük*, *sekban* and *acemi-oğlani*. Each division comprised *ortas* of different strength; a variable number of *odas* in turn composed the *orta*. In overall, there were 229 *ortas*, of which 77 permanently quartered in Constantinople, while the others were assigned to the garrisons in the Empire. The *cemaat* division numbered 101 *ortas*, and were the most prestigious units of the corps because their functions or origins.[78] The first five of this division were normally reserved for the most important garrisons of the Empire,[79] but *ortas* 39, 59, 64, 71, 73, 94 and 101 never left their quarters in Constantinople except in case of war, unlike the *ortas* of the *solaks* of the Sultan's household. The other *ortas* were assigned to the peripheral garrisons, and usually changed the location every three years.[80] The privileges accumulated by the janissary corps did not only concern those quartered in Constantinople. There were *ocaks* that detained special concessions. The janissaries of Cairo, who already held permission to march on horseback for military campaigns, had become a semi-sedentary corps, as well as the 500 of Damascus, who now formed a permanent garrison exempt from mobilisation in wartime.[81]

The *bölük* division comprised 61 *ortas*, of which 30 were quartered in Constantinople and the rest in the Empire. The *segmen*, which originally represented the janissary reserve corps, numbered 36 and only *Orta* 33 had its permanent barracks in the capital. Each *orta* had its own symbol and a number, which did not follow the natural series, because in the hierarchical sequence the first *orta* had '19' and belonged to the *cemaat* division.[82] There was a vacant number 65, the former *zagarçi* (greyhound keepers), suppressed in 1623 because the involvement in the murder of Osman II, and therefore 'constantly cursed' for this infamous act.[83] Some *ortas* had special honour assignments, such as numbers 16 and 18, which were responsible for forming an artillery escort when the army marched on campaign.[84] *Ortas* 1 and 5,

---

78 Mouradgea d'Ohsson, *Tableau Général de l'Émpire Othoman*, vol. VII, p.309.

79 Jucherau de Saint-Denys, *Histoire de l'Empire Ottoman*, vol. I, p.349.

80 Cévad, *Etat Militaire Ottoman, depuis la fondation de l'Empire Ottoman jusqu'à nos jours* (Constantinople, 1882), vol. I, p.156. According to d'Ohsson, the *ortas* were replaced when animosity began to spread among them. Mouradgea d'Ohsson, *Tableau Général*, vol. VII, p.320.

81 Stanford J. Shaw, 'Origins of Ottoman Military Reform' in *The Journal of Modern History*, vol. XXXVII (1965), p.301.

82 The number 1 was an *orta* of the *segmen* division, alongside numbers 5, 6, 9, 10, 11, 13, 15, 19, 23, 24 28, 32, 33, 36, 38, 39, 41, 42, 43, 44, 45, 47, 49, 51, 52, 53, 54, 56, 59 and 61.

83 Mouradgea d'Ohsson, *Tableau Général*, vol. VII, p.312. Originally, the *ortas* involved in the murder of the Sultan were numbers 64 and 65. Their quarters were converted into stables for horses, and 'the curses against these cohorts are repeated every fortnight, when the candles are distributed to the janissaries'. *Orta* 64 was newly formed after 1648.

84 Jucherau de Saint-Denys, *Histoire de l'Empire Ottoman*, vol. I, p.362.

the *deveci*, originally comprised the drivers and the guardians of the army's camels, and number 19 provided the sentinels in the encampment. Further *ortas* maintained particular but only traditional tasks, such as *orta* number 35, known as the *avcilar*, which escorted and helped the sultan on hunting trips, or number 54, the *talimhanecilar*, originally entrusted for training recruits in the use of the bow, while number 102, the *zemberekci*, performed the same with the crossbow.

Finally, the *acemi-oğlani* division comprised 34 *ortas*. They were the pupils of the *kapıkulu* troops, and used to top up janissary numbers as necessary. Originally assembled through the *devşirme* practice, namely the levy of young Christians by the conscription and forced conversion, the *acemi-oğlani* received training and military training like the *kapıkulu* troops. At the end of the apprenticeship period, they became a *civelek*, juvenile soldier, and could be added to the *orta* to serve alongside the veteran janissaries. Unlike other authors, d'Ohsson includes the *acemi oğlani* as a part of the janissary corps. This could be not a simple mistake, but the actual transformation of this institution into a reserve of recruits with any connection to the original model, since in the 1780s the *acemi-oglani* were mostly sons of enlisted janissaries, known as the *kuloglu*. According to some authors, after the mid seventeenth century, the greater part of the recruits came from western and northern Anatolia, especially from Smyrna, Denizli, Aydin, and even from Lazistan or from the Aegean Archipelago and Albania.[85] However, the term *devşirme* continued to identify all the young recruits, including ethnic Turks, destined for the *kapıkulu*. Much evidence indirectly confirms the decline of this practice. Earlier prohibitions against marriage and living outside the barracks fell away and gradually the sons of city-dwelling janissaries replaced the peasant boys of the *devşirme* recruitment. By the early eighteenth century, this firearmed infantry had become hereditary and urban in origin, a position passed from fathers to sons who were Muslim not Christian by birth. One of the last registered *devşirme* occurred in Greece in 1705, and in that occasion the recruitment party sent from Constantinople was massacred by the population of the township of Náoussa.[86] However, according to d'Ohsson, in the last years of

The *serdengeçdi agaşi*, after the *Fenerci Albümü* (early 1800s).

---

85 Robert Mantran, *L'Empire Ottoman du XVI au XVIII siecle* (London: Variorum Reprint, 1984), p.326.

86 According to D. Quataert, in *The Ottoman Empire, 1700–1922* (Cambridge: Cambridge University Press, 2000), p.45, the last *devşirme* levy was in 1703.

the eighteenth century Christian and Muslim families from Albania, Bosnia and Bulgaria still offered their children for a profitable employment in the *kapıkulu*.[87] Alongside them, also the Caucasus continued to supply young recruits to the Egyptian Mamluk households and Ottoman sultans as well, some of whom performed successful careers, such as the Georgian Süleyman Paşa 'the Great', governor of Iraq between 1780 and 1802, or Hürsid Ahmed Paşa, grand vizier from 1812 to 1815, who also came as 'slave-recruits' from Georgia. The *acemi-oglanis* permanently resided in Constantinople divided in two groups, one of Rumelia and the other of Anatolia, and every seven years they were selected for entry into the janissary corps. In wartime, they replaced the janissaries who joined the field army in the capital's garrisons.

In Constantinople, the janissaries resided in three large barracks. The first two were the Eski Odalar, the old barracks and the Yeni Odalar, new barracks, in which the *bölük* division and *orta* 34 of the *segmen* were quartered. The third was called Ağa Capusi and housed the *cemaat* division. The *acemi oğlani* resided in the barracks of Kişlassi.[88]

The janissary corps served under the direction of the senior commander, the *yeniçeri ağasi*. This position was one of the most prestigious and politically relevant in the Empire, especially for the considerable financial needs required by the corps. He managed the administration through a secretariat directed by the *yeniçeri kiatibi*, and was assisted by his own ordinance, the *ağa yamaği*. Further two 'ranks of ordinance' were under the control of the *yeniçeri ağa*: the *neubeci* and the *moumci*, which could number several posts, since the latter were usually appointed junior officers *odabaşi* in the janissary units.[89]

As for the janissary 'major staff', there were one *kethüda bey* as second in command, and one *kethüda yeri* as senior adjutant. Traditionally, another primary officer was the *segmen başi*, but the ancient custom of accessing the rank of commander after holding this title was no longer respected. According to d'Ohsson, in the eighteenth century the rank of *yeniçeri ağa* was usually assigned to the *silâhdar ağa*, or the senior commander of the *sipahis*, or a high official of the court. The *yeniçeri ağa* was in charge of an organisation that was a law unto itself, but he was appointed by, and subject to, the authority of the office of the grand vizier, who was considered the Sultan's absolute deputy in the army. Within the organisation itself, promotion was based almost entirely on seniority and favouritism, as such influences were pervasive throughout the Ottoman system. This first group of senior officers was assisted by the *kapu çukadar* chief orderly, and the *bas çavuş* senior provost.[90] In 1792 Sultan Selim III introduce a new rank with the task of supervisor of the corps, the *yeniçeri nazir*, who, however, lost much of his importance after 1807.

---

87 Mouradgea d'Ohsson, *Tableau Général*, vol. VII, pp.326–327.
88 Mouradgea d'Ohsson, *Tableau Général*, vol. VII, p.340.
89 Cévad, *Etat Militaire Ottoman*, vol. I, p.186.
90 Cévad, *Etat Militaire Ottoman*, vol. I, p.184. The author also mentions the rank of *tekkeli*, senior fourier, which, however, does not seem to have been awarded for some time.

THE ARMIES OF THE SULTAN

After the *segmen başi*, the fourth in command was the *kul kâhya* who served as an intendant-warrant officer of the commander, and usually appointed after the indication of the grand vizier.[91] The other ranks followed in order of importance: the *zagarçi başi*, commander of *Orta* 64; the *samsoncu başi*, commander of *Orta* 71; the *turnaci başi*, commander of *orta* 63, both of which had the task of watching the Sultan's hunting animals like the *zagarçi*; all these belonged to the *cemaat* division.[92] All these senior officers, collectively known as *ocak ağalar*, composed the military council of the janissary, housed in the residence of the *yeniçeri ağa*. *Segmen başi* and *kul kâhya* could be appointed at the ranks only after served as commander in *ortas* 63, 71 or 64. Dismissed or disgraced council officers were either exiled from the capital and assigned to a secondary post, or were appointed commanders in a border garrison, with the rank of *serrhad ağa*. However, if the government called him to Constantinople, a *serrhad ağa* recovered his rank in the council. They usually held the command of the most important

Above, left: *kapu kâhya*, designed as *falakaci*. They formed the guard of the grand vizier's palace, and served as military police in the capital.

Above, right: a *harbaci*, who attended the executioner in Constantinople.

Fenerci Albümü (early 1800s)

---

91 Mouradgea d'Ohsson, *Tableau Général*, vol. VII, p.315.

92 Among the *ortas* that derived their denomination by traditional tasks, *Orta* 63 was in charge of watching cranes, peacocks and ducks in the Topkapı gardens.

border garrisons and in the 1780s there were 32 *serrhad ağas*; among them, that of Vidin, in Bulgaria, held the first rank.

Further senior officers belonged to a second class, since they did not join the council. Some ranks had been created after 1730; however, this class comprised the commander of the *acemi-oglani*, designated as *Istambol ağa*. He occupied the eighth position in the hierarchy of the corps, and had two lieutenants under him: the *Roumili ağa*, and the *Anadoli ağa*, each at the command of 17 *ortas* of *acemi-oglani*. The second class also included the four commanders of the *solak*, who occupied the same hierarchical position of the *zagarçi başi*. After the *orta* under prominent senior commanders, there were the *ocak imam*, chaplain, who held the command of Orta 94; the *beit ul malci*, the treasurer, in charge of commander of Orta 101, both belonging to the *cemaat* division; the *bas çavuş*, and chief of Orta 5 of the *bölük* division. He also supervised the work of the *çavuş* assigned to the janissary corps.

Some officers held the command of an *orta* assigned to particular tasks, like the *muzir ağa*, commander of Orta 28, which formed the guard at the residence of the grand vizier; or the *kâhya yèri*, who had the same rank in Orta 32, in charge of escorting the *yeniçeri ağasi*. This rank occupied the same place of the *muzir ağa* in the hierarchy of the corps, but the latter could replace the *yeniçeri ağasi* in the council if the titular was sick.[93]

While most of these functions originated in centuries-old traditions, others became established in more recent times, such as Orta 32, which in 1803 was granted the privilege of forming the guard corps at the French embassy in Constantinople.[94] Orta 56, under the *Çardak çorbaci*, performed the same task in the principal guardhouse of Constantinople, in the quarter of Çardak. This *orta* also formed the escort for the government's commissioner during the inspection of the prices in the markets of the city. The last of these officers who occupied a special place were also assigned to specific duties: the responsibility for the military training, the *talim kaneci*, was that of the commander of Orta 54; the *assas başi* attended during the public executions in Constantinople. The *avci başi*, chief of Orta 36 of the *segmen* division, alternated his residence, being in the capital in winter and in Istranca (today Binkılıç), on the Black Sea in summer. The *assas başi* was usually appointed as commander of a simple *orta* belonging to the *segmen* division. Hierarchical relationships were not an end in themselves, but were of substantial importance, as they guaranteed additional allowances, and various rights to the inheritance of officers and soldiers who died without heirs.

These rights also affected to varying degrees the simple commanders of the *ortas*. They held the title of *çorbaci*, meaning 'the ones who supply the soup', since the janissaries, as descendants of the corps formed in the fourteenth century by slaves, held a special privilege of receiving food from someone representing the monarch, in continuity with the symbolic meanings of the nomadic societies from which the Ottomans came. The same terminology

---

93   Cévad, *Etat Militaire Ottoman*, vol. I, p.42. The *muzir ağa* had the task of representing the Janissaries to the grand vizier.

94   Jucherau de Saint-Denys, *Histoire de l'Empire Ottoman*, vol. II, p.173.

also occurs in other ranks. Each *çorbaci* occupied a place according to his seniority, and usually moved from one *orta* to another, but if the *çorbaci* had started with the command of an *orta* belonging to the *cemaat* division, he could not be transferred to another category.[95] The *çorbaci* had under him a variable number of *oda başi* who held the command of an *oda*, or chamber, which formed the *orta*. According to Cévad Ahmed Beg, there was another senior officer in the *orta* designated *usta başi*, the 'grand master', whose tasks are not clearly indicated.[96]

The *oda* also included one *vekilharc* as fourier,[97] one *bayrakdar* as ensign, one *başesky* as veteran NCO, one *imam*, one *asçi* as cook, one *baş karakoulluk* as first potholder, one *sakka* as water carrier, and one *karakoulluk* as simple potholder. These officers and NCOs were permanent ranks and their numbers did not change in case of war; only the first and fifth *orta* of the *bölük* division added another NCO, the *zembilci*, in charge of distributing the water in his *oda*, and followed the *sakka* in the internal hierarchy. As for the *sakkas*, the British artillery officer William Wittman remarks that they supplied a very useful service and were generally well equipped.[98] The water carriers had their own commander, the *sakka başi*, in charge of controlling the service. In the janissary corps, there were further ranks comparable to NCO, corporal, or only temporary titles for special assignments and tasks. They were the *koulloukci çavuş*, comparable to a NCO adjutant serving in the major garrisons; the *kuloğlu baş-çavuş*, a junior officer representative of the *kuloğlu*, namely the janissaries' sons; the *muteveli*, administrator of the assets of the mortmain; the *kalloukçi zabiti* soldier assigned to the *orta*'s corps of guard.[99] Another corps formed for combat purposes is often mentioned in the sources. This is the *serdengeçdi*, the voluntary janissaries who composed the assault party. They received a supplementary income and the soldiers who survived this risky task formed a permanent unit under their *serdengeçdi ağasi*.[100]

Regardless of the three main divisions of the corps, further 10 *odas* were added to the corps, each in charge of special duties. Some of these companies

---

95 Cévad, *Etat Militaire Ottoman*, vol. I, p.48. The author adds some special titles associated to the senior officer of the *ortas*, such as the *oturakçi kalfa*, the *kulkutçi kalfa*, the *théllai kalfa*, *çeurekçi kalfa*, and the *ğeuzlemeci kalfa*, which qualified the veteran *çorbacis*.

96 Cévad, *Etat Militaire Ottoman*, vol. I, p.47.

97 The Ottoman term *vekilharc* means 'keeper of funds' or 'cashier'. Thornton, in *The Present State of Turkey*, vol. I, p.228, qualifies this rank as a 'commissioner'.

98 Wittman, *Travels in Turkey*, p.303: 'In the field, the Ottoman army has, among other beneficial regulations, that the establishment of sackers (*sic*), a corps selected among the Janissaries, to attend and supply the troops of water. On this service, they were also constantly employed on a march. They are mounted on horses provided with bells, to the end that their approach may be known to the troops, and each horse carries two leathern sacks containing about forty gallons of water.'

99 Cévad, *Etat Militaire Ottoman*, vol. I, pp.45–54. The author lists other titles and ranks that are not always easily attributable to the Janissaries or the whole *kapıkulu*. Among these, the *sou başi*, the post of chief of gendarmerie, and the *bocek başi*, a gendarme specialising in catching thieves.

100 Midhat Sertoğlu, *Osmanli Kiyafetlerı. Fenerci Mehmed Albümü* (Constantinople: Vehbi Kaç Vakfi, 1986). Plate *serdengeçdi ağasi*.

Janissary *yamak* in ordinary dress, 'as he goes out of the quarter in Constantinople', after *Les portraits des differens habillemens qui sont en usage à Constantinople et dans tout la Turquie* (before 1809). The Turkish word *yamak* means 'assistant' or even 'friend'. In the Balkans, the Bosniak surname Jamaković is derived from the Ottoman term. Initially, *yamaks* were civilians who were mobilised for different tasks during wars or as volunteers who wanted to be recruited as janissaries, especially in borderland fortresses. Local craftsmen, who associated with the janissaries, were referred to as *yamaks* because they assisted the *kapıkulu* soldiers. Eventually they became poorly paid and trained Muslim infantry, particularly in the garrisons of Bosporus, Black Sea and Danube, and for this in some sources, they are referred to 'janissary border guards'. However, the *yamaks* also performed on campaign, at least in not far region. In this regard, in the 1760s and 1770s, during the mobilisation of troops against Russia, it is noticed the enlistment of 1,000 *yamaks* from Sarajevo, who were dispatched against Montenegro. At the end of the eighteenth and beginning of the nineteenth centuries, they became a source of unrest and resistance to reforms. The number of *yamaks* who assisted the few active janissaries was growing because of the business opportunities this position provided. There was a pattern that become characteristic in the provincial garrisons, especially in the Balkans.

had been established in the eighteenth century to grant special privileges in return for the loyalty of their members, or for closer control of the corps. The *yazicis*, role masters, were administrative personnel in charge of recording the strength of the *ortas* and their variations registered in the musters. They numbered 100 men under the *yeniçeri kocakhan*, who served as senior secretary of the corps, even he was a civilian official. After them, there was 60 *oda yazicis*, who managed the archives of the corps and served under the *baş yazici*. This official had the rank of *çorbaci*. The *kiarkanés* was a special *oda* formed by 34 guilds of workers, each formed by 25 artisans who had the special permission to exclusively supply the janissaries. Each group had its NCO who held the title of *usta*. Another special body of janissaries was the *tulumbaci*, in charge of the task of firefighting. It had a strength of 300 men and its commander was the *tulumbaci başi*, who ranked as a *çorbaci*. This *oda* was raised in 1720 by Sultan Ahmed III to exploit a very useful service in a city where the fires were frequent, and they were trained for the first time by a Frenchman who had served as *pompier*.[101] The *oda* of the *mumcis* comprised 24 NCOs assigned six each to the residence of the *yeniçeri aga*, and to the *orta* of the *muzir ağa*, *kâhya yèri*, and *assas başi*. They attended to the public executions ordered by these senior officers. They had their own commander with the title of *mumci başi*. Another company of attendants was that of the *kapu kâhyas*, composed by 60 men under a commander holding the title of *baş kapu kâhya*, and joined to the *orta* of *mizir ağa*. They formed the guards of the grand vizier's palace and served as military police in the capital. They were employed to search for janissaries and other military personnel who were outside the quarters without permission. The ordinary punishment was the beating of the soles of the feet, known as *falaka*. Five *kapu kâhyas*, designed as

---

101 Mouradgea d'Ohsson, *Tableau Général*, vol. VII, pp.323–324.

falakacis performed this task holding the convicted by the ankles under the supervision of the officer.[102]

Employed in a similar function, the *oda* of 60 *harbacis* attended the executioner in Constantinople. On campaign, 40 of them laid the tents close to the grand vizier's pavilion, and the other 20 did the same with the *yeniçeri ağa*. Their role appeared similar to the late Renaissance *Hartschieren* of the German armies, and indeed the designation derives from *harba*, namely the halberd they carried in active service. The *oda* of the *şadis* also numbered 60 men and their employment consisted in the supply of wood for the fireplaces of the Imperial residences. The *oda* of the *hu keşans* supplied the religious service in the janissary corps. After 1591 a whole *orta* hosted the members of the Bektaşi dervish order, which became number 99 of the *cemaat* division. Then, in the eighteenth century, the supernumeraries formed a further unit to ensure religious service for all the garrisons. Finally, the *oda* of the *çavuş* formed a large unit of 330 men ranking as NCOs, selected among the veteran janissaries. In wartime they served as messengers and junior adjutants of the commanders. In peacetime the assured the communications between the government and the garrisons of the Empire. In Constantinople, the *çavuş* attended the corporal punishment for the janissary officers. Their commander held the title of *kul çavuş*, to distinguish himself from the *çavuş* of the seraglio and the navy.

An attempt to restore the corps occurred after 1774, and within a short time the *ortas* were as they had been before the war with Russia: no better but at least no worse. However, all the coeval authors recount that the janissary had become a caste jealous of their privileges and always ready to claim more. Throughout the years, belonging to the janissaries became an entitlement and an honorific status. Like the other *askery*-military members, they did not pay taxes,[103] and extra privileges were accorded, included annual allotments for clothing. Incentive bonuses before and after battles; 'healing money' for meritorious battle wounds; and money for retirees and widows constantly increased through the years. Such entitlements were regularly distributed to members of the corps in its heyday, and continued to be part of the demands in the eighteenth century.[104] Privileges extended also to other matters. In the 1780s the janissary escort to the foreign ambassadors and consuls became

---

102 Mouradgea d'Ohsson, *Tableau Général*, vol. VII, .325. The author does not specify whether these soldiers had replaced the *acemi-oglanis* who traditionally performed this task as early as the sixteenth century.

103 Membership of a *kapıkulu* corps was sufficient to obtain exemption from all duties, and it was not always possible to determine with certainty whether or not they were real Janissaries, given the large number of fictitious positions. In 1782, a certain Osman, responsible for the collection of the tax in the district of Iştib (today Štip, in Northern Macedonia), informed his superiors that 'some Muslims in the aforementioned district, claiming to be Janissaries, oppose the paying of the duty for the sheep in their possession'. See Michael Ursinus, *Grievance Administration (şikayet) in an Ottoman Province. The Kaymakam of Rumelia's 'Record Book of Complaints' of 1781–1783* (London-New York, NY: Routledge, 2005), p.93.

104 Aksan, *Ottoman Wars, 1700–1870*, p.50.

also protégés. Technically they were the only Muslim protégés, who, in theory, enjoyed the same privileges as the dragomans.[105]

The *ortas* developed an *esprit de corps* that resembled an extended family. To encourage participation in campaigns, provincial governors promised registration in the corps. Artisans of all kinds found it convenient to become attached to the corps for physical and economic protection. Furthermore, throughout the eighteenth century budgetary constraints and currency devaluation encouraged the spread of trade and other occupations within the corps.[106] The one-time professional soldiers had become a group who first of all were artisans and guildsmen and were only incidentally on the military payroll.

The engagement of the janissaries in crafts and trades became highly visible as suggested by a coeval account: 'most of the *yeniçeris* pursued non-military trades and most artisans were affiliated with the corps.'[107] Some *ortas* specialised in certain trades and became actual guilds. For instance, confectioners served in *Orta* 14 belonging to the *bölük* division, butchers were in *Orta* 24 of the *cemaat*, while other units comprised tilers, glaziers and blacksmiths.[108] Very often, these trades represented an additional opportunity for fraud and extortion against the population, since the chronicles recount that 'a lot of harassment is tolerated by the officers, who do not disdain to share the earnings with their soldiers'.[109]

The janissaries retained the status of a privileged caste, a praetorian guard, long after their usefulness on the battlefield had declined. Even more buoyant due to their growing political strength, the janissaries even refused to participate in military campaigns, or reduced the field contingent to a minimum, as occurred during the war against the French in 1798–1802.[110]

Regarding the total number of the janissary corps, sources are often discordant and always approximate. In his authoritative work, d'Ohsson estimates an overall strength of 120,000 janissaries in the 1780s, of which 20,000 resided in the capital, but only 3,000 were actually quartered in the barracks.[111]

---

105 Maurits H. van den Boogert, *The capitulations and the Ottoman legal system: Qadis, Consuls and Beratlıs in the 18th Century* (Leiden: Brill, 2005), p.64.

106 Mehmet Mert Sunar, 'When grocers, porters and other riff-raff become soldiers: janissary Artisans and Laborers in the Nineteenth Century Istanbul and Edirne', in *Kocaeli Üniversitesi Sosyal Bilimler Enstitüsü Dergisi* (17) 2009, 1; p.179. According to the author, the janissary corps became an instrument through which impoverished artisans, petty tradesmen, and men of odd jobs could live parasitically off the government treasury, and that many of the rebellions in the eighteenth and nineteenth centuries were carried out by impoverished artisans through their janissary connections.

107 Cemal Kafadar, *Yeniceri Relations*, cited in Baki Tezcan, *The Second Ottoman Empire. Political and Social Transformation in the Early Modern World* (Cambridge: Cambridge University Press, 2010), p.202.

108 Mouradgea d'Ohsson, *Tableau Général*, vol. VII, p.342–343.

109 Mouradgea d'Ohsson, *Tableau Général*, vol. VII, p.350.

110 Morier, *Memoir of a Campaign with the Ottoman Army in Egypt*, pp.8–9.

111 Mouradgea d'Ohsson, *Tableau Général*, vol. VII, p.331.

He outlines that there existed three categories of janissaries, depending on their status. The first category comprised the janissaries in active service, called *eskinci*. In the second category were registered the janissaries who did not perform and active role, and therefore were without pay, but exercised a trade while waiting for an employment in the corps when a place became available. They were the infamous *yamaks*, whose main goal was to enjoy the social prestige and tax privileges that derived from membership in the janissary corps. According to coeval estimates, their total number increased to at least 150,000 men in the 1790s,[112] and they were widespread in almost all major garrisons in Europe as well as in Asia. These local janissaries often waited in vain for their pay, and this contributed greatly to the unrest that shook the Empire in the eighteenth and early nineteenth centuries.[113]

The last category comprised people who adopted the headgear of the janissary and assumed the title of *tasslaşci*, namely aspirants. None of these categories concerned the *acemi-oglanis*, only the actual janissaries. The same author adds further information about the janissaries, referring to the category of *oturak*, which comprised the retired veterans who received a pension from the Imperial treasury. In the janissary corps there were also many honorary appointments granted to personalities of the court and to the Sultan himself.[114] Baron François de Tott, in the Crimea as French consul, was made an honorary member of the janissary corps in Perekop in 1770, a common practice of the period.[115] Moreover, it proved easy to buy one's son into the corps, and hence, promotion likely followed much the same pattern.

Even reconstructions based on the economic expenditure incurred by the treasury to maintain the janissaries are not always reliable. Though there are hundreds of archival records of the janissaries concerning the pay register in the late eighteenth century, these documents seem to have been arranged by region, with one record book listing the janissary troops for the garrison in an entire province, or several neighbouring districts. Thus, the records for Serbia can often be found in the same *defter* (register) as those for Sarajevo. Some troops temporarily assigned from Constantinople to the frontier garrisons may also still be listed in the capital's payroll. Difficulties arise when scholars try to reconcile data from the documents that list only the janissaries with those that list all the other garrison troops. All this contributes to making any reconstruction carried out on military expenditure calculations very complicated.

The surviving janissary rolls are a reminder of a well-documented problem of controlling registration: for example in 1771, 30,000 names were stripped from inaccurate, often corrupted registers.[116] Functionaries as well as grand

---

112 Mouradgea d'Ohsson, *Tableau Général*, vol. VII, p.341.

113 Ágoston and Masters, *Encyclopedia of the Ottoman Empire* (New York, NY: Facts on File, 2009), p.92.

114 Usually the sultans were enlisted in the first *orta* of the *bölük* division. See Cévad Beg, *Etat Militaire Ottoman*, vol. I, p.171.

115 Tott, *Memoires*, part II, p.176.

116 Aksan, *Ottoman Wars, 1700–1870*, p.52.

viziers had always to contend with inflated muster rolls, often benefiting themselves from pocketing salaries of non-existent soldiers. The government alike faced the increasing debt burden not just of army wages, but also of the 'accession gift', which had become the obligatory contractual agreement between the janissaries and any new Sultan who took the throne. These data too do not allow the total strength of the corps to be reconstructed, given the large number of fictitious soldiers.

Even coeval authors, when attempting to provide the total number of Ottoman military forces, propose very different results. This problem affected every component of the army, and the fact that there is so much uncertainty even regarding the number of the janissaries alone, who should have been the most carefully administered corps, gives an idea of how difficult the matter is to solve. Some reconstructions are blatantly exaggerated. The Franco-Hungarian Baron François de Tott claimed that by the mid 1770s almost 400,000 janissaries were registered in the whole of the Empire.[117] An English author, the diplomat Sir James Porter, states that in the 1760s, the total number of janissaries was 200,000–300,000, including honorary and retired members.[118] Reconstructions from archival registers propose a field force of 61,239 janissaries in 1775–76.[119] After Porter, William Eton in 1798 established in 113,400 the overall number of janissaries, included 20,000 in the garrisons of Constantinople. However, Eton's deductions seems to be the result of some wrong identifications of troops.[120] Thomas Thornton doubles the garrisons proposed by Eton for Constantinople, but suggests an overall 'active force' of 40,000 men in all.[121]

Even one of the first authors to investigate the Ottoman archives, namely Kabaağaçlızade Ahmed Cévad, encountered some difficult to estimate the exact number of janissaries at the end of the eighteenth century. The Ottoman colonel contests the figure proposed by Thornton and proposes 80,000 men under Selim III.[122] As for the field force, he provides a very concise list of garrisons but dating from 1750.[123] This valuable document is taken from the payroll records of janissaries actually in service. Each *ocak* is registered with the strength, and the final sum shows a force of 53,966 men. This figure does not include the janissaries resident in Constantinople.

---

117 Tott, *Mémoires*, vol. I, part II, p.70.

118 James Porter, *Turkey: Its History and Progress. Journals and Correspondence of Sir James Porter* (London: 1854), p.323.

119 Ágoston, 'Military Transformation in the Ottoman Empire and Russia', p.305.

120 William Eton, *A Survey of the Turkish Empire* (London, 1798); vol. I, pp.60–61. The author suggests further data on the *kapıkulu* forces: 12,000 *bostanci*, 5,000 artillerymen, 2,000 bombardiers, 10,000 *sipahis* and 13,000 *cebecis*. Concerning Eton's reconstructions, already in 1809 Thomas Thornton questioned the figures expressed by Eton, claiming that these came largely from an apocryphal text by a 'pseudo-Greek' named Elias Habeschi, published in 1784. See Thornton, *The Present State of Turkey*, vol. I, p.232.

121 Thornton, *The Present State of Turkey*, vol. I, p.233.

122 Cévad, *Etat Militaire Ottoman*, vol. I, p.92.

123 Cévad, *Etat Militaire Ottoman*, vol. I, pp.167–168.

With regard to peripheral garrisons, Vidin and Belgrade quartered the largest forces, with 5,440 and 5,039 janissaries respectively. As for details of the garrisons' strength, d'Ohsson reports that in the 1780s there were 12 *ortas* in Belgrade, 14 at Chocin, 16 at Vidin, and 20 at Baghdad.[124] Both documents demonstrate that the northwestern theatre was the sector from which the most concern came. In fact, almost two-fifths of the total was on the Danube and the Dnestr area, with Bender that housed 4,134 janissaries. Like d'Ohsson, the Ottoman colonel estimates the number of janissaries in Constantinople by calculating the *zemistani*, namely the payment of wages in the winter season, and proposing the number of 45,241 men.[125]

The difference between this estimate and the figures proposed by other authors is only apparent, as both totals include aliquots of semi-active personnel, described by Thornton as janissaries, but actually *yamaks*, 'who, though enrolled, are not embodied into *odas*, are dispersed throughout the Empire, living as burghers, mixed with the people, and following different trades and professions, or idle vagabonds, or at best but labouring peasants.'[126] The janissary corps did not only include males. According to the sources, in 1790, it was estimated that of the 12,000 names registered in the janissary rolls, only 2,000 could or would perform service when needed in campaigns. Most of the corps members actually were not only artisans, and merchants untrained in the military arts, but included even women and children, holding their memberships only for their revenues, and completely unable and unwilling to perform the military services supposedly required of them in return for their salaries.[127]

In the 1790s, with the reforms introduced by Sultan Selim III, there is more light on the strength of the janissaries.[128] Selim officially began his military reforms with the publication of new regulations for the *kapıkulu* corps in 1792. The officially announced aim was the reorganisation of the corps according to classical regulations and ideals. Nor were the military reforms any more successful. The janissary corps absolutely refused to accept the Sultan's decrees. While its members were no longer capable of fighting the armies of Europe on an equal basis, they still had enough power to impose their will at home by force if need be. Selim's agents were simply murdered whenever they tried to find out which members of the corps were serving and which were not, which of the officers and men were capable of further service and which should be removed. Whenever the Treasury cut off the salaries of janissary members who were not performing their duties, the entire corps revolted, whether at home or on the battlefield, and the grand vizier was usually forced to yield to their demands as the result of the

---

124 Mouradgea d'Ohsson, *Tableau Général*, vol. VII, p.321.
125 Cévad Beg, *Etat Militaire Ottoman*, vol. I, p.169.
126 Thornton, *The Present State of Turkey*, vol. I, p.231.
127 Shaw, *Between Old and New*, p.82, and p.84: 'Sultan's agents were simply murdered whenever they tried to find out which members of the corps were serving and which were not, which of the officers and men were capable of further service and which should be removed.'
128 Cévad, *Etat Militaire Ottoman*, vol. I, p.318.

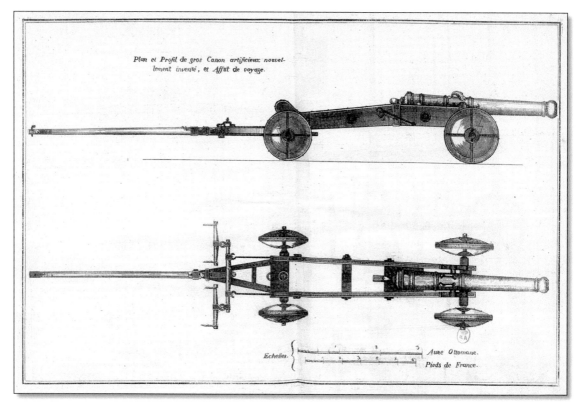

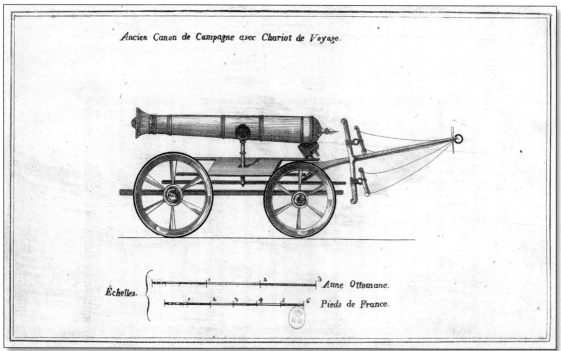

THE ARMIES OF THE SULTAN

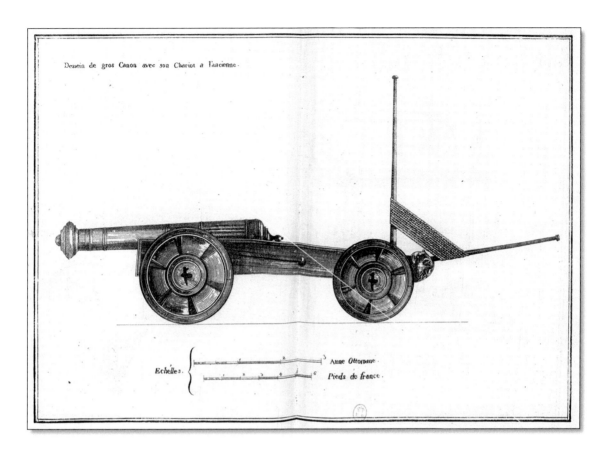

Above: Ottoman *gros canon* or *sahi* gun with the old type of carriage, after the work of Rayf Mahmoud Efendi, *Tableau des Nouveaux Reglemens de l'Empire Ottoman* (Constantinople, 1798).

Facing page, top: Ottoman *balyemez* heavy field gun trained by the 'new invention carriage', after Rayf Mahmoud Efendi, *Tableau des Nouveaux Reglemens de l'Empire Ottoman* (Constantinople, 1798). Note the solid wooden wheels with metal fittings.

Facing page, bottom: Field gun on 'travel carriage', after Rayf Mahmoud Efendi, *Tableau des Nouveaux Reglemens de l'Empire Ottoman* (Constantinople, 1798).

Below: Ottoman *abus* and tripod on wheels, after Kabaağaçlızade Ahmed Cévad Beg, *Etat Militaire Ottoman, depuis la fondation de l'Empire Ottoman jusqu'à nos jours*, vol. I (Constantinople, 1882).

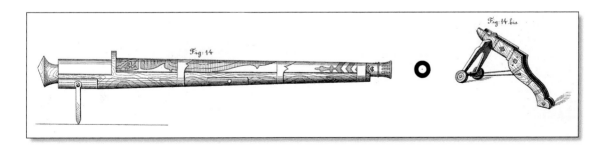

THE OTTOMAN ARMY OF THE NAPOLEONIC WARS 1789–1815

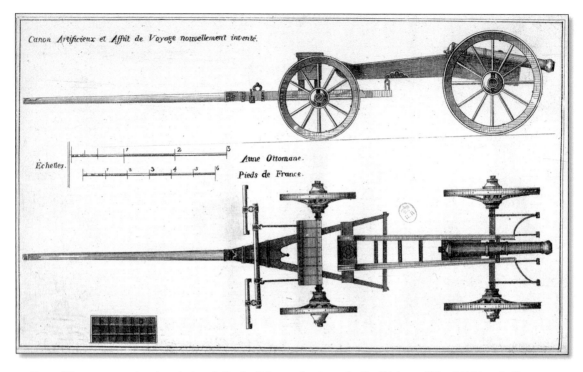

Above: Ottoman gun and carriage designed after the Gribeauval system, after Rayf Mahmoud Efendi, *Tableau des Nouveaux Reglemens de l'Empire Ottoman* (Constantinople, 1798).

Below: Ammunition wagon of new model, after Rayf Mahmoud Efendi, *Tableau des Nouveaux Reglemens de l'Empire Ottoman* (Constantinople, 1798).

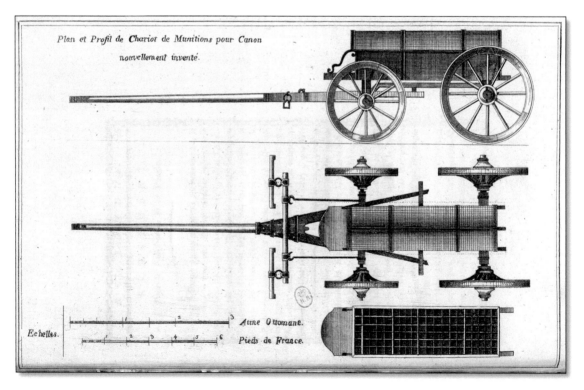

exigencies of war. The problematic reforms ended with very modest success, and only a few targets were achieved. The numbers of janissaries rose against all attempts of reduction from 54,458 in 1794 to 55,256 in 1800, 98,539 in 1806, and 109,791 in 1809.[129]

In addition to the rise in the numbers of janissaries serving in the provinces and frontier regions, their temporary rotational service system was also changed in the meantime. At the end of the eighteenth century, most of them were serving in the same province permanently and had already established family and socio-economic relations with the local society. In doing so they became part of local politics and power struggles, much like their predecessors had in Constantinople and Egypt. Whatever the merits of this policy in the short and middle term, the janissaries who were assigned to provinces permanently lost their military value and became more or less a police force. Therefore, any statistics that count them as combatants give a false picture of their actual strength. The dramatic increase in strength transformed the corps drastically, contributing to decrease its military efficiency.

Some recent studies propose a figure of 30,000–40,000 mustered janissaries as the most probable active field force for the period 1790–1815.[130] This number is consistent with Thornton's evidence, but strongly disagrees with the figure proposed by the Baron Antoine Jucherau de Saint-Denys, who was a French military advisor in Constantinople in 1806–07 and 1829–35.[131] He states that the janissary corps comprised tens of thousands of honorary members, but the active force available for a military campaign consisted in only 25,000 men, as occurred in all the wars after 1798.[132]

According to some authors, in wartime each *orta* gathered at least 500–700 men; while those assigned to the peripheral garrisons had to deploy between 200 and 300 men.[133] There were, however, some particularities, generated by very different situations, to which the government had tried to give a rule, according to the all-Ottoman characteristic of regulating even the most total chaos. In peacetime the *ortas* garrisoned in Constantinople usually consisted of 100 janissaries. However, the *orta* of the *kul kâhya* constantly deployed 500 men, that of the *zagarci başi* had 300, the *samsoncu* 200, and the *turnaci* 150.[134] Some indications suggested that other *ortas* deployed 150 men even in peacetime, but very often, the actual field strength was half. Some authors state different figures. This is the case of *Orta* 31 of the *cemaat* division,

---

129 Uya and Erickson, *A Military History of the Ottomans*, p.121 and Shaw, *Between Old and New*, p.120.
130 Aksan, *Ottoman Wars, 1700–1870*, p.53.
131 Antoine Jucherau de Saint-Denys (1778–1850). He was the author of the *Histoire de l'Empire Ottoman depuis 1792 jusq'en 1844,* published in two volumes in 1844. Despite being a source from an undoubtedly authoritative author, the information from this work has been little studied by contemporary researchers.
132 Jucherau de Saint-Denys, *Histoire de l'Empire Ottoman*, vol. I, p.351.
133 Mouradgea d'Ohsson, *Tableau Général*, vol. VII, p.320, and Cévad Beg, *Etat Militaire Ottoman*, vol. I, p.92.
134 Mouradgea d'Ohsson, *Tableau Général*, vol. VII, p.336.

French General Jean-Baptiste Annibal Aubert du Bayet (1757–1797), portrayed by Jean-Baptiste Paulin Guérin. In 1796, Aubert du Bayet was appointed as Ambassador-Minister of the Republic to the Ottoman Empire. He was sent to Constantinople with artillery equipment and French artillerymen and engineers to help with the development of the Ottoman arsenals and foundries. Infantry and cavalry officers were also to train the *kapıkulu* foot and horse, but they were frustrated by the opposition of the janissaries. Ironically some of these troops, trained to Western methods, were successfully employed against Bonaparte in Egypt.

which was credited with 10,000 enlisted men, many of whom held ranks and titles other than that of soldier.[135]

As usually denounced by the Western commenters, there was a general tendency to enlist as many men as possible, in open violation of the law, but with the complicity of the officials and the higher commanders themselves, who profited from the salaries. janissary officers also competed by favouring the inclusion of their servants in the ranks of the corps, 'and as a consequence the pensions of extinct veteran *oturaks* also accumulated in the name of a courtier or servant, while the pay destined for the janissaries was subjected to an agiotage favourable to embezzlement, so much so that it ended up ruining the soldiers' wages.'[136] As a consequence, the government issued more payment tickets – *memhour* – than there were soldiers in the roles. The payment of the salary, the *esame*, became a veritable source of illicit speculation and scandalous clientele. Realising the government's need for infantry troops, the janissaries themselves seized the moment and used it to strengthen their privileges and enlist their sons in the corps. Selling janissary certificates that enabled their holders to draw pay and receive daily food rations also became a lucrative business for officers and bureaucrats.[137] About this deplorable traffic, d'Ohsson provides an eloquent comment:

> These tickets have a different value, and are sold at the price of twelve or twenty piasters per akçe. The Grandees extort from the officers a percentage of the favours granted by them to the servants and customers, who in turn receive income from the trades authorised by the officers. Consequently, a multitude of people of all classes receive the salary of a janissary or artilleryman. … Each war increases the number of tickets dispensed to the army, and deaths do not diminish this proliferation, but on the contrary, even the killed soldiers and officers continue to receive wages.[138]

Obviously, this was a ruinous policy, which fell by the wayside as the economic crisis deepened at the end of the eighteenth century, but the payment for valour, special duties, captives, wounds, and numbers killed in

---

135 Jucherau de Saint-Denys, *Histoire de l'Empire Ottoman*, vol. I, p.351.
136 Jucherau de Saint-Denys, *Histoire de l'Empire Ottoman*, vol. I, p.350.
137 Ágoston, 'Military Transformation in the Ottoman Empire and Russia', p.315.
138 Mouradgea d'Ohsson, *Tableau Général*, vol. VII, p.337.

battle continued until the next century. The venality had deplorable effects during the military campaigns. In 1787, the janissaries sent with the field army to Sophia began to desert to return to Constantinople. The chronicles report that due to the excessively long campaign, the soldiers did not want to continue serving. To try to remedy this, contests and other exercises were held and, as the grand vizier promised, the most skilled would be rewarded with money. Some janissaries, on the pretext that the prizes were too low, attacked the tent of the grand vizier and in an instant other janissaries joined the assailants. Order was only restored after the intervention of their commanders and it almost degenerated into a general mutiny.[139]

As rightly pointed out by an authoritative historian, 'the janissaries embodied a pre-modern social welfare system, which extended throughout Ottoman society.'[140] Small wonder, then, that there was a clamour to join the ranks as volunteers, and a vigorous resistance to change. Some sources indicate that in 1808, Grand Vizier Alemdâr Mustafa proposed reforms for the older military corps, including an end to irregularities in appointments, requirements for unmarried members to live in the barracks and for all members to accept obedience and training in order to receive their salaries, and even the use of European-style weapons, but such plans did not appear in the famous deed of agreement signed in Constantinople.[141]

Despite all the efforts towards a modernisation, the janissaries and their allies managed to derail all military, bureaucratic, and financial reforms tried by the sultans, even killing the 'infidel Sultan' Selim III himself. It was not until the 1830s that fundamental reforms could be started under Mahmud II, who finally destroyed the janissaries in 1826.

Cebeci, Armourers

As far as the other *kapıkulu*'s corps are concerned, the uncertainties regarding their number diminish considerably, but only because these are much smaller contingents. This is the case of the *cebeci* – armourers – in charge of preserving and maintaining the portable firearms. The custody of the muskets was a consequence of the regulation imposed within the *kapıkulu*'s corps to avert, as far as possible, any acts of violence, especially when the use of firearms significantly increased. For this purpose, it was forbidden for the janissaries to keep firearms in their residences, or to circulate with them in the city. This measure to prevent violence had the undesirable effect that, on the occasion

---

139 Cévad, *Etat Militaire Ottoman*, vol. I, p.317. Days after, the army finally marched on, and when it arrived near Vidin the janissaries mutinied again. Under the pretext that they had not yet received their salaries, they surrounded the tent of the grand vizier and asked their commander to join them. When the *ağa* objected, the most excited of them hurled themselves at him, wounding him with their daggers, and it was only by the intervention of his guards that he managed to save himself.
140 Aksan, *Ottoman Wars, 1700–1870*, p.52.
141 Shaw, *History of the Ottoman Empire and Modern Turkey*, vol. II, p.2.

THE OTTOMAN ARMY OF THE NAPOLEONIC WARS 1789–1815

Ottoman *topçu* artillerymen, and bronze guns, after the *Augsburger Bilder* or *Charakteristische Darstellung der Vorzüglichsten Europäischen Militairs* (1802–1810).

of internal uprisings, such as the memorable one in 1730, soldiers loyal to the government had to face the rioters armed only with sticks and knives, while the seditionists had stormed the arsenal and forcibly taken their firearms. In Constantinople all the firearms were kept in the city arsenal located near Aghia Sophia, and the personnel assigned to their custody also belonged to this corps. Among the main tasks, the *cebecis* maintained the firearms and therefore they were assigned to all the garrisons that comprised janissaries. Moreover, the *cebecis* performed also as marksmen and employed special weapons when joined the army on campaign.

According to some authors, they also escorted the supply, ammunition and baggage train, and guarded these in battle.[142] The corps had two divisions according to the location with the designation of *bölük* and *cemaat*, which formed an undefined number of *odas*. The *cebeci* contingents were usually small, compared to the overall size of the garrison. Most often there were one or two *odas* of around 10 men, plus NCOs known as *oda başi*. The senior commander held the rank of *cebeci-başi* with the *cebeciler kethüda başi* as second in command, They had his residence in Constantinople in

---

142 Jucherau de Saint-Denys, *Histoire de l'Empire Ottoman*, vol. I, p.376.

THE ARMIES OF THE SULTAN

the quarter of the *cebeciler kapu*, close to the city arsenal, where resided the *cebecis* assigned to the capital.

Once again, the actual number of the *cebeci* is hard to determine. Thornton specifies that they deployed 60 *odas* in overall, and 'their number is not correctly ascertained,'[143] but according to the annual cost, the *cebecis* could have been about 2,000.[144] Other authors do not add much to this matter, except Jucherau. He reports that Sultan Selim III tried to re-establish the original function of the corps, and had allocated substantial funds to maintain 4,000 specialists, but this number resulted in only 500 soldiers, because the money was diverted by corruption.[145] According to another author, in the 1790s, the corps of the *cebeci* received recruits from the disbanded corps of the provincial infantry.[146] As for the personnel employed in the other provinces of the Empire, the Egyptian armourers were called *azab*, but their commander held the rank of *cebeci başi*.[147] As in Constantinople, also in Cairo there was an important production centre of muskets, which still followed the traditional Ottoman pattern in matter of firearms.

Well into the eighteenth century, the Ottoman infantry of all classes used flintlock musket equipped with the same technology introduced in the late seventeenth century. The Ottoman battery still resembled the ancient Spanish *patilla*-lock, which, however, was still used in Spain by the mountain marksmen known as *miqueletes*. The only variant introduced in the Ottoman arsenal was the *Vauban*-lock, produced after 1688.[148] Whatever type of mechanism was fitted, the Ottomans referred to the muskets as *tüfenk*.

A janissary in ordinary dress by William Page, 1823 (author's archive). White turban with gold spiral; dark blue jacket with red-yellow edge; dark blue breeches; dark blue *yelek* with yellow embroideries; red shoes and gaiters with yellow piping and embroidery; red cloak piped of yellow. Note the *kandjal* dagger carried under the waist sash.

---

143 Thornton, *The Present State of Turkey*, vol. I, p.252.
144 Uzunçarşılı, *Osmanlı Devleti Teşkilatından Kapukulu Ocakları*, p.77.
145 Jucherau de Saint-Denys, *Histoire de l'Empire Ottoman*, vol. I, p.377. Corruption was compounded by resistance to innovations that threatened privilege and speculation: 'In 1796, the Sultan (Selim III) was trying to reorganise the corps by re-establishing discipline and bringing musket production under one direction in order to standardise the calibre. The attempt was unsuccessful. In Constantinople, firearms manufacturers, mostly belonging to the *cebeci* corps, violently opposed this attempt, on the pretext that the reform would change the production of weapons that had enabled the conquest of many kingdoms. The guilds of the capital joined them and the Sultan, advised by his ministers, was forced to stop his project.'
146 Mouradgea d'Ohsson, *Tableau Général*, vol. VII, p.303.
147 Mouradgea d'Ohsson, *Tableau Général*, vol. VII, p.363.
148 Ágoston, *Guns for the Sultan*, p.89.

Topçu, Artillery

The artillery personnel known as *topçu* (gunners), alongside the *humbaraci* (bombardiers), and the *mimar* (carpenters and engineers for the artillery) formed the standing artillery corps of the *kapıkulu*. Like the *cebeci*, they were specialised personnel who joined the janissaries in the peripheral garrisons, but had its main quarter in Constantinople. The internal structure of the artillery corps was similar to that of the janissaries, since the artilleryman were divided into *ortas* formed by one or more *odas*. The senior commander was the *topçu başi*. He directed the corps from his residence in Constantinople and managed the activity of the city's foundry of Tophane. The *topçus* were entrusted not only with the use of cannons, but also with the preparation of gunpowder, maintenance, and the production of guns in the main foundries of the Empire. As privileged officers, the *topçu basi* could inherit properties and riches of his subordinates who died without heirs. His command was directly subordinated to the authority of the grand vizier, to whom he had to notify the days in which the cannons were cast. In each main arsenal served a *dokuku basi* as technical director and instructors of personnel. The major staff was completed by the *katib*, who served as adjutant and a first secretary of the *topçu basi*. These officers had their residence in the capital, where an *oda* under an *odabasi* formed the standing artillery in the capital. Like any other *kapıkulu* corps, the *topçu* comprised active personnel, pensioners, reservists and honorary members. According to Thornton, before 1796 the corps numbered about 30,000 men dispersed throughout the Empire and joined to the garrisons where the janissaries were quartered.[149]

In the eighteenth century fundamental changes in casting technology influenced battlefield tactics, and marked the end of the artillery tactics based on static defence and siege warfare. The Ottoman Army became acquainted with these tactics in the wars against Austria and Russia. However, testimonies regarding the efficiency of the Ottoman artillery are unflattering. Primarily, the problem was technological, since the Ottoman artillery had a slower rate of fire compared to the European weapons. Furthermore, the artillery relied on outdated tactics and was essentially a static element in the siege as well as in the battlefield. In addition, personnel training and military knowledge appeared to be in a poor state. In 1796, reports stated that the *kapıkulu* artillery was filled 'with ignorant persons entirely incapable of using the weapons which they had'.[150] The results were disappointing, despite the government always investing significant resources for training the artillerymen and paying them with high salaries. Since the beginning of the century, foreign technical advisors had been appointed to improve the artillery, and modern training had been introduced under Sultan Abdülhamid I after 1774. A new corps of 2,000 artilleryman had to be raised by selecting the best gunners of the *kapıkulu*, and transferring them to the direct command of the grand vizier. The new corps received quarters outside Constantinople at Kagithane, near the old Sa'dabat palace, in order to

---

149 Thornton, *The Present State of Turkey*, vol. I, p.250.
150 Shaw, *Between Old and New*, p.104.

separate them from the janissaries. French officers joined the *sürat topçulari okağı*, the name assumed by the unit meaning 'fast' because the corps had to be trained as light field artillery.[151] The first 250 gunners began training with guns designed according to the Gribeauval system supplied by the French embassy. The indefatigable François de Tott drilled his men in modern tactics, assisted principally by a Scottish officer named Campbell (who, unlike most of his colleagues, converted to Islam and took the name Mustafa, becoming known, inappropriately enough, as Ingiliz Mustafa, 'Mustafa the Englishman') and a Frenchman named Aubert.[152] De Tott also built a modern cannon foundry at Hasköy, on the Golden Horn, and finally contributed to the raising of the *Hendesehane*, the new mathematics school next to the artillery corps barracks, more or less a reincarnation of the Engineering School of the Tulip Period and the forerunner of the Army Engineering School later established by Selim III. Following de Tott's departure, the *sürat* corps and school continued operating under Aubert and Campbell respectively, and while they were disbanded for a time under janissary pressure, they were rescued and continued their work during the grand vizierate of Halil Hamit Paşa, largely under the protection and encouragement of *kapidan paşa* Gazi Hasan, who emerged as the leading naval reformer of the time.

The humiliating defeats suffered in the early stage of the war of 1768–74 overhauled the Ottoman artillery, and favoured the establishment of the rapid-fire field guns. Although training proved successful, the first action against the Russians in 1774 was a complete failure owing to erroneous tactics, and even the desertion of the gunners from the battlefield in their very first campaign. However, the Ottoman government did not abandon the idea of creating a modern field artillery to support the cavalry and infantry. To compete with the Russian and Habsburg armies, the Ottomans continued to drill the rapid-fire artillery corps and manufacture ammunition for the new type of cannons. However, in the war of 1787–1792 the performance of rapid-fire artillery corps was, once more, critically inadequate. Needless to say, the problems in manufacturing, transportation, provision and funding were important in this result but these were not indigenous for the Ottoman Army. The reorganisation of the artillery corps in general and the integration of field artillery gunners in this new organisation was the result of the lessons learned on the battlefield. During the reign of Selim III, not only was the organisation of the artillery changed, but also the casting technology and standards of the cannons were rearranged in line with French standards.

In 1791 Selim III added a company of *tüfenkci*s as infantry fusiliers, and appointed as commander a war veteran, Ömer Ağa, who had spent some months as a prisoner in Russia. One year later, most of the soldiers serving in

---

151 Baron Françoise de Tott was also involved in the training of the corps, and he refers that the *süratçi*s were paid regularly, while the Janissaries claimed 27 months in arrears. See *Memoires du Baron de Tott*, Part III, p.174.

152 Stanford J. Shaw, *History of the Ottoman Empire and Modern Turkey Volume I: Empire of the Gazis: The Rise and Decline of the Ottoman Empire, 1280–1808* (Cambridge: Cambridge University Press, 1977), p.252.

the corps were dismissed, but new ones were enrolled, mainly from Bosnia. The artillery was reorganised in 25 regiments, each with 10 cannons, of which four normally were the new rapid-fire *sürat* cannons, two were the smaller *abus* and four consisted of the older *balyemez* and *şâhî*, making a total of 250 cannons in all. Ten men were assigned to each cannon, forming a squad.[153] Expansion of the corps went ahead rapidly, and by the end of 1796 there were 2,875 well-trained artillerymen stationed at the Tophane, organised in companies of 115 officers and men each along with an additional company of specialist with 115 technicians. Within a few years the corps grew to 4,000 men and became the artillery of the *nizâm-ı cedîd*, the New Order Army raised by Selim III.[154] The expansion of the corps went ahead rapidly and by the end of 1796 there were 2,875 well-trained gunners stationed at the Tophane along with an additional company of 115 men stationed at Levénd Ciftlik to assist the new *nizâm-ı cedîd* army. In 1806 the force still numbered 4,910 men.[155]

Further innovations concerned the production of guns. In the early 1800s the foundries started to regularly cast calibres more suited for the field artillery, especially 4, 8 and 12 lb guns designed after the Gribeauval system.[156] This followed the introduction of 6-pounder field guns after the Austrian model. Regarding internal organisation, Selim III did not alter the titles and privileges of the artillerymen, but reformed the *topçu* corps into 110 *odas* of 120 men each. The Sultan confirmed for officers and NCOs the same privileges granted to the janissaries, and considerably increased the pay for the common gunners to make the service more attractive. The *topçu başi* was elevated to the rank of *paşa* with two horsetails, and the staff increased with the appointment of one *nazir* as senior intendant for the administration of the corps. Because of the special skills and training required, 125 members of this corps ordinarily were not allowed to marry, regardless of rank, and had to live in the barracks at all times. Salaries and wages were higher than those paid for service in the other corps, and the pensions were considerably better.

The artillery train's personnel, which maintained the ancient denomination of *arabaçi*, and hitherto recruited for the duration of a single military campaign, was also organised militarily under Selim III. The cannon-wagon corps was originally given a complement of 600 men and officers organised into five regiments, but it expanded almost continuously to keep pace with the increasing needs of the cannon corps: 759 men and officers in 1793, 902 in 1803, and 2,129 in 1806.[157] Strenuous efforts also were made to attract the ablest artisans to serve the corps. Special bonuses were provided in addition to their regular salaries, and in peacetime artisans were allowed to work privately in their own shops when the corps had no immediate need for them. The Sultan appointed an officer trained according to the modern criteria

---

153 Shaw, *Between Old and New*, p.122.
154 Mouradgea d'Ohsson, *Tableau Général*, vol. VII, p.371. According to the author, one cavalry corps was joined to the *süratçis*, but probably this is the independent horse artillery raised in 1796.
155 Mouradgea d'Ohsson, *Tableau Général*, vol. VII, p.373.
156 Jucherau de Saint-Denys, *Histoire de l'Empire Ottoman*, vol. I, p.364.
157 Shaw, *Between Old and New*, p.123.

A print from Mouradgea d'Ohsson's *Tableau Général de l'Empire Othoman*, depicting the exercise of the *kapıkulu sipahis* in the 1780s.

with the original title of *arabaçi başi*, but the expectations were not met. The conductors remained a small corps and far from being a true military unit.

In 1796 the French military advisors showed the Sultan the effectiveness of the horse artillery. The 'ready and accurate' manoeuvres and the rapid movements of the cannons, which could follow the cavalry over all terrain, enchanted the Ottoman court. Immediately it was decided to create a similar corps and, forced by a desire to emulate, several *topçu* gunners asked to join the new unit.[158] The good will and excellent quality of the Turkish horses produced excellent results and in the opinion of foreign observers, the Ottoman horse artillery was able to compete in firing efficiency and mobility with the contemporary European units.[159] In the early 1800s the horse artillery companies assembled 800 men. The whole artillery was subjected to strict discipline in order to preserve its members 'from the vices that had corrupted the janissaries'.[160] New artillerymen were not allowed to marry and had to stay overnight in barracks. Training in the manoeuvring of pieces was intensified and took place three times a week. Regrettably, after the deposition of Selim III, the efficiency of the artillery soon declined, but the officers, formed under the rule of the clever but unlucky Sultan, remained

---

158 Jucherau de Saint-Denys, *Histoire de l'Empire Ottoman*, vol. I, p.366.
159 Jucherau de Saint-Denys, *Histoire de l'Empire Ottoman*, vol. I, p.367.
160 Jucherau de Saint-Denys, *Histoire de l'Empire Ottoman*, vol. I, p.367.

loyal to the government. This made it easier for his successor, Mahmud II, to resume the reform where it left off.

The most relevant reform before the 1790s was that of the *humbaracı ocağı*, the bombardier corps. This specialty was not an independent corps and played a minor military role throughout the classical period. During the seventeenth century it even lost its minor role and became more or less extinct, namely an organisation on paper only. According to the reformers, however, under the leadership of grand vizier Topal Osman Paşa the corps became an ideal laboratory for transformation. The corps had no effective socio-economic power base and its personnel strength was minimal. Moreover, it was a totally technical corps, and changing it would not provoke the resistance of conservatives. Osman Paşa had an additional asset in the person of a French aristocrat, Claude Alexandre de Bonneval, who had taken refuge in the Ottoman Empire and willing employment in the Sultan's army. Bonneval, or with his new name and title, Humbaracı Ahmed Paşa, immediately started the reorganisation with the help of three other renegades and two French officers, who were assigned by Louis XV's government. First, a new salaried corps with a strength of 300 personnel was established in the 1730s, followed by the construction of custom-built barracks. Due to the legacy of the corps, nearly all the personnel were recruited from Bosnia. The mortar corps continued to survive through difficulties until September 1792, when strenuous attempts were made to revive the *humbaracı* with the assistance and advice of the French military advisor Aubert and Cuny. New barracks, stables, and storehouses were built for them at Hasköy and Sütlüje, on the northern shore of the Golden Horn in Constantinople. As was the case with the other corps, a supervisor was appointed to handle financial and administrative matters, while the former chief, the *humbaraci başi*, was limited to military affairs. The new organisation laid out for the mortar corps during the spring of 1793 was somewhat special by virtue of the special nature of its military task. The corps had 50 mortars in all and to each of them there were assigned teams of nine mortar men commanded by one *halife* assistant helped by nine apprentices. The teams were organised into five companies, each composed of 191 officers, men and assistants, under the command of a *ser halife*. This organisation provided a total of 450 men, 450 apprentices, 50 *halifes* and five *ser halifes*, with the superintendent, the commander, and three subordinate corps officers bringing the total of men and officers to 960 in all. Whenever new cannons or mortars were added to the corps along with their men, new companies were created for them, so that the size and organisation of the existing companies remained as they were established in the regulation.[161]

But the most important part of the reform in matter of artillery was the establishment of a technical school, the *hendesehane* (Geometry School). Though the *hendesehane* was a modest school with limited enrolment, it was the first European-style military high school in the Empire and turned out to be the ancestor of all Ottoman military technical schools. Historical

---

161 Shaw, *Between Old and New*, p.123.

information about the new corps and the school is very limited, but it is known that because of the secretive and timid approach of the governing elite it did not become a springboard for progress as planned. It affected only several hundred soldiers and suffered huge problems due to constant interventions, financial problems, and simple ignorance. The ambitious political manoeuvres of the complex Bonneval did not help, and he was exiled in 1738 due to his political activities, which were unrelated to his role in military reforms. Like the ones before this, the *humbaracı* reforms faded away in the meantime. Previously, another grand vizier, Koca (also known as Mektupçu) Ragıb Paşa (1755–1773), tried to re-energise the corps and its school by collecting the old *humbaracıs* while continuing its modern training and education system. He even managed to conduct field exercises. However, these efforts also failed and did not produce any meaningful or permanent results.[162] The Geometry School was renamed the Engineering School in 1781. The number of graduates of these schools, however, was negligible compared to those trained in comparable technical and military schools in Western Europe.[163]

The reforms introduced in the field of artillery show that on the Ottoman side interest in technological progress outweighed traditionalist resistance. However, many Western commentators point to the persistence of old and obsolete technology in matter of artillery. By the end of the eighteenth century, the existence of large cannons in coastal batteries or Asian fortresses may have reinforced the Western view of the persistent and obsolete Ottoman tendency to insist on these huge weapons. In this regard, Count Jucherau de Saint-Denys reports 700 or 800 lb cannons still in service in the early nineteenth century.[164] According to the same author, the bulwark defences of some important strongholds consisted of cannons positioned on long and massive carriages that fired 120-pound shells, and required 20 artillerymen to reposition the battery after firing. This and other similar observations suffer from the Eurocentric conditioning that relegated Ottoman

The commander of the miners' corps, *lağımcıs başi*, from the album *Costumes Turcs* of the Diez Collection, 1790s. Headdress of black sheepskin with golden brim; red kaftan with brass buttons, green *entari* waistcoat laced of yellow, yellow-red sash.

---

162 Gábor Ágoston, 'Firearms and Military Adaptation: The Ottomans and the European Military Revolution, 1450–1800', in *Journal of World History*, vol. 25, N. 1 (March 2014), p.115.

163 Ágoston, 'Military Transformation in the Ottoman Empire and Russia', pp.281–319.

164 Jucherau de Saint-Denys, *Histoire de l'Empire Ottoman*, vol. I, p.361.

technology to a lower rank, but these great cannons were essentially 'weapons of prestige', preserved by virtue of their historical value, as was the case in some old fortresses in Western Europe.[165]

However, among the traditional artilleries still employed by the Ottomans in the period 1790–1815, there were some models designed in the seventeenth century and cast until 1730–40. The classic, large, Ottoman cannon was named *şaika*. This designation derived from the Slavic *chaika*, or 'seagull' boats, which usually were equipped with three guns. Later, the term designated the large cannons in the riverside forts, which enabled the Ottoman commanders to install *şaika* guns of ever larger bore size. These huge weapons became the trademark of the Ottoman artillery until the end of the eighteenth century, but the sources show that the Ottoman foundries considerably reduced the various type of *şaika*. In the late 1770s, newly cast guns, designated as large *şaikas*, were mainly 44 and 22-*okka* calibre,[166] and fired shots of 56 and 28 kg in weight.[167] Among the old Ottoman models of guns, the late eighteenth century sources still registered the *kolumburna* and the aforementioned *şâhî*. The classical Ottoman field guns usually measured 220, 264 and 330 cm in length. Ottoman *kolumburna* are indifferently indicated as *şâhî*, which differed little with the previous one.[168] The classic *şâhî* was a reduced version of the *kolumburna*, and indeed this was a relatively long cannon, especially considering their very small calibres. Weapons inventories list *şâhî* measuring up to 330 cm long, but the great majority were smaller-calibre pieces firing shots ranging from 150 g to 1.8 kg in weight. The weight of the guns varied according to the length of the barrel. The minimum and maximum weight of these guns cast in Constantinople in the first half of the eighteenth century varied from 159 to 182 kg.[169]

The cannon called a *balyemez* was originally a large siege gun similar to the *saika*. In the 1790s, Rayf Mahmud Efendi refers to this weapon as *cannon de batterie*, implicitly demonstrating its transformation into a multi-purpose heavy cannon. This kind of *balyemez* measured 350 cm long, and fired shots of some 27–35 kg.[170] Alongside the *şâhî*, this was the most widespread gun of the Ottoman field artillery at the turn of the century. In the late eighteenth century, another widely widespread field gun was the aforementioned *abus*. This derived from an early form of howitzer created by the Ottomans in

---

165 Ágoston, *Guns for the Sultan*, p.68.
166 One *okka* is equal to 1.28 kg.
167 Ágoston, *Guns for the Sultan*, p.76. It is easy to identify the culverin used in Europe behind the Turkish term. Like the European weapons, the Ottoman culverin varied in size from 2-*okka* through 10-*okka* calibre, and occasionally 11, 14 and 16-*okka* guns that fired balls from 2 to 20 kg in weight.
168 See Mahmoud Rayf Efendi, *Tableaux des nouveaux reglemens de l'Empire Ottoman*, figure 12, where is depicted a gun about 260 cm long that could have fired projectiles of 13–15 kg in weight. These characteristics qualify this weapon as a *kolumburna*, but the author talks about it as a *şâhî*.
169 Ágoston, *Guns for the Sultan*, p.86.
170 Mahmoud Rayf Efendi, *Tableau des Nouveaux Reglemens de l'Empire Ottoman* (Constantinople, 1798), p.20, plate II.

the seventeenth century. The *abus* were small, but often too heavy to carry, and many were equipped with a tripod. The most widespread models had a calibre between 7.6 cm to 23 cm and fired a shot of 1.92 kg. This gun, despite deriving from the howitzer, was primarily used as an anti-infantry weapon. Given its small size, the *abus* was also easy to transport, and two of them could be carried by one horse or mule.[171] Possibly, this kind of weapon is the same referred to in a French account of the engagement that occurred before the Battle of the Pyramids in 1798. The report states that Bedouins on camels fired shots with small cannons mounted on the saddle.[172]

In siege warfare, the Ottoman artillerymen used an even greater variety of mortars. The largest mortars were the 85-*okka* through 200-*okka* calibre pieces charged with stone balls of 104–246 kg in weight. Yet, mostly of the mortars were smaller weapons, like the 14 *okka* and 45 *okka* calibres, that fired balls weighing 17–55 kg, and were dominant across the whole eighteenth century. In 1771–72, only 14, 18 and 32-*okka* calibre mortars were cast in the Tophane, and these pieces fired shots weighing 18, 23 and 41 kg.[173]

In addition to the Constantinople gunpowder works, the Ottomans produced gunpowder in their provincial centres, including Cairo, Baghdad, Aleppo, and Yemen in the Arab provinces and Belgrade, Salonica, and Gallipoli in the European provinces; as well as Izmir, Bor, Erzurum, Diyarbekir, Oltu, and Van in Anatolia. These works met the demand of the army, navy, and garrisons well into the eighteenth century. However, in the 1770s diminishing production forced Constantinople to import substantial quantities of powder from Europe. At the end of the eighteenth century the new Azadlı gunpowder works in Constantinople, modernised with French assistance, were again able to manufacture sufficient quantities of gunpowder of a much better quality.[174]

Sipahi and *Çavuş* Cavalry

The cavalry constituted the oldest corps in the whole *kapıkulu*. However, apart from maintaining a few symbolic privileges, such as the pre-eminence of its commander over other senior officers, the cavalry had lost its importance for over a century. The janissaries, as well as all musket-bearing light infantrymen, were the ideal corps for the new battle environment. For this reason the government understandably increased the personnel strength of the foot and tasked them with additional duties. More and more janissaries and other footmen were trained and sent to provinces for policing due to the increased unreliability and ineffectiveness of the *sipahis*, as well as to frontier regions because of the changing nature of war from the pitched

---

171 Ágoston, *Guns for the Sultan*, p.84.
172 General Jean-Pierre Doguereau, *Journal de l'expédition d'Égypte, publié d'après le manuscrit original, avec une introduction et des notes, par C. de La Jonquière, chef d'escadron d'artillerie breveté* (Paris: 1904), p.198.
173 Ágoston, *Guns for the Sultan*, p.71.
174 Ágoston, *Guns for the Sultan*, p.87.

battles to the siege and counter-siege operations. Being a very expensive light cavalry corps, the *sipahis* became unable to withstand the financial compromises of the transformation and could not protect their privileges effectively. However, the decreasing of the cavalry was not only due to the transformation of warfare, but above all to the political rivalry between the *sipahi* and the janissaries, which ended with the defeat of the former and their relegation to a secondary role.

In the 1780s, the *kapıkulu* cavalry still comprised the traditional two divisions: the *sipahi ulufely*, and the *çavuş*. The first division formed six large squadrons called *bölük*, each with different strength and ensign, under the command of the respective officer, designated *bölük başi*. The general commander held the title of *sipahilar ağasi*, and directed a 'major staff' composed by one *baş kâhya*, one *kâhya yéri*, one *baş çavuş*, and one *bas-bölük başi*. These officers were in active service also in peacetime, and in case of war they could not join the field army if there was not at least one *paşa*.[175] The commander of the corps also held the command of the first squadron, which was the largest one. The second squadron was under the *silâhdar ağa*, the Sultan's household esquire, but fielded a very lesser number of cavalrymen. However, they had the rank of officer and were usually rewarded with the assignment of a *timar*.[176] The third and fourth *bölüks* had the same strength, while the last two *bölüks* numbered half of the strength of the previous ones.[177] Among the *sipahi*'s cavalry, the grand vizier usually chose his personal lifeguard, formed by one or more squadron of elite horsemen, designated as *mutefferika*.

In the mid eighteenth century the *kapıkulu* cavalry amounted to about 12,000 horses, as established by Sultan Ahmed III in 1721. This number oscillated through the years. According to d'Ohsson, they still numbered about 12,000 in the 1780s.[178] Thornton raised their number to 15,000 in the 1790s,[179] but all these estimates seem inaccurate because should include active and honorary members as well. In 1796 the statements concerning the strength of the *kapıkulu* cavalry reported that of the 30,000 men registered on the rolls, only 2,000–3,000 horsemen were 'ready to march' when summoned for battle, although all of them managed to show up whenever wages were paid.[180] Regarding the field strength, Jucherau reports that the *sipahi* had fallen from 12,000 to less than half, and in the early 1800s the government severely reduced the replacement of horses to save money, and at the same time got rid of these 'useless soldiers'.[181] Moreover, according to a coeval author, the *sipahis* did not have quarters in Constantinople, and therefore

---

175 Mouradgea d'Ohsson, *Tableau Général*, vol. VII, p.368.

176 Jucherau de Saint-Denys, *Histoire de l'Empire Ottoman*, vol. I, p.379.

177 Jucherau de Saint-Denys, *Histoire de l'Empire Ottoman*, vol. I, p.379. According to Jucherau, the original strength of the *bölüks* was 8,000 horsemen the first, 500 the second, 1,000 the third and the fourth, and 750 each the fifth and sixth.

178 Mouradgea d'Ohsson, *Tableau Général*, vol. VII, p.367.

179 Thornton, *The Present State of Turkey*, vol. I, p.253.

180 Shaw, *Between Old and New*, p.104.

181 Jucherau de Saint-Denys, *Histoire de l'Empire Ottoman*, vol. I, p.379.

they were scattered in the provinces.[182] Indirect confirmation of the numerical irrelevance of the *sipahis* comes from Selim III's reform of the *kapıkulu* in the 1790s. The *kapıkulu* cavalry had to form a corps of 10,000 newly hired salaried *sipahis* maintained by the Imperial Treasury and by contributions of provincial notables in times of emergency.[183] Each corps would have received modern weapons and come to Constantinople for training from Western advisers for six months every two years. However, the attempt to reform the *sipahis* failed, not because of their reaction, as happened with the janissaries, but because by this point they had no organisational structure at all.[184]

The *çavuş* formed the second division of the *kapıkulu* cavalry. They were horsemen employed as junior officers or adjutants as well as messengers for the Sultan, grand vizier or other senior commanders. Their rank in the army was considered like that of a junior officer. In the cavalry, they immediately followed the *bölük başi*. When important orders were sent, the *çavuş* formed an escort for the messenger. The *çavuş başi* had the command of the corps. The overall number of the *çavuş* was about 300–400 men in the 1790s. As occurred for the whole *kapıkulu* cavalry, their importance strongly declined in the early 1800s, and probably the *çavuş* diminished to a few dozen under Selim III and Mahmud II.[185]

Provincial Troops and Private Contingents

> The Empire is governed by independent Aghas, or chief of districts; revolted from oppression, every man asserting and maintaining his own … and defending his estates with resolution and effect. In the exigencies of war, they have made common cause with the state they have contributed a quote of soldiers to the war, but upon no account have they suffered Paşas or officers of authority to come amongst them to govern.[186]

By the end of the sixteenth century the Porte began to reinforce its permanent *kapıkulu* troops with contingents enlisted for the duration of a campaign. With their various categories and constantly changing names, even identifying the roles of each of these units and their development is often very difficult. These were mainly infantry, originally intended to replace in the garrisons the janissaries and other *kapıkulu* foot troops when these marched on campaign. These replacements were *azab* and *segmen* infantrymen equipped as musketeers, *hisar erler* artillerymen and other

---

182 Mouradgea d'Ohsson, *Tableau Général*, vol. VII, p.368.
183 Shaw, *Between Old and New*, p.120.
184 Uyar and Erickson, *A Military History of the Ottomans*, p.121: 'Their system and organisation existed only on paper for many years, and, while the government, on one hand, tried to revive the organisation, on the other hand, by allocating the land estates to new reform projects it destroyed any chance of resurrecting this class.'
185 Jucherau de Saint-Denys, *Histoire de l'Empire Ottoman*, vol. I, p.380.
186 Volnay, *Voyage en Syrie et en Égypte*, p.326.

Above, and facing page: Ottoman *sipahi* and *deli* cavalrymen in two Austrian prints published in 1818.

corps to support the army on campaign, such as pioneers and diggers, designated as *musellimi*. These specialties formed the *serhaddkulu*, who also included special units of light cavalry, which comprised several categories depending to their use and size. Thus, there were *deli*, *beslü*, and *gönüllü* cavalry corps assigned to the border garrison in Europe. The *serhaddkulu* had much in common with the Prussian *Landwehr* of the Napoleonic age, however the *deli* border cavalry served permanently, as was the case in the opposite camp with the Austrian *Grenzer*.

Originally the *serhaddkulu* also included the *lağımcı* miners corps. In the past, this speciality had brought great reputation to the Ottoman army, who employed them in large numbers from the late sixteenth century onwards. However, like many other traditional corps, the miners were undergoing a deep crisis. In the war against the Russians of 1768–74, despite the sacrifice of many miners, the Porte had lost important strongholds without being able to regain them. These failures persuaded the government to completely reform the corps by establishing a new speciality trained according to the criteria of Western European military engineers. The efforts to reform the technical corps were somewhat more successful, but the difficulty of obtaining experts from abroad combined with the opposition of the janissaries to every move limited the progress. In 1787–88, fewer than 1,000 miners were recruited to serve alongside the janissaries, but their refusal to serve with them forced the grand vizier to leave them at home whenever campaigns were undertaken.[187] After 1800, the miners of the *serhaddkulu* practically dropped out of the military history of the Ottoman Empire, with the exception of limited cases where they were employed as a basic labour force during the few sieges sustained in this period.

The other major reserve corps of the Ottoman army was the provincial cavalry, named *sipahi toprakli*, or even *timarli*, *askeri elayet* or simply *sipahi*. The calculation of the recruit quota was based on the income of each province and district.[188] This system, in which the *sipahis* were allocated *timar* or land estates, continued without significant variation for centuries, but in the eighteenth century the change in the balance of power with enemies like the

---

187 Shaw, *Between Old and New*, p.85.

188 The requirements for military service and supply were determined in proportion to the annual value of the *timar* holdings, which ranged from 5,000 to 20,000 *akce*. These resources permitted to recruit fully equipped horsemen from each village and township. On paper, with this system, the Porte gathered one horseman for every 5,000 *akce* of income.

Austrian Habsburgs and the Russians caused the downsizing of this kind of cavalry.

The more serious problem for Ottoman stability was that the *timar* land could no longer support the cavalryman's obligations to report to campaign. Gradually, the revenues of entitlement from the *timars*' revenues were not sufficient, and many *timars* simply could not afford the cost of campaigning. The horsemen who did turn up for a campaign were ill-equipped to face the firepower of the Western armies, and were increasingly reluctant to fight. Furthermore, during the eighteenth century, the strategic scenario became increasingly unfavourable for the large masses of cavalry. The Ottoman Empire, now on the defensive, needed foot soldiers rather than mounted warriors. This transformation caused a rapid decline of the provincial cavalry, accelerated by the reluctance of *timar* holders to serve on foot. Thus, if in the second half of the eighteenth century the provincial cavalry could, on paper, gather 120,000 horsemen, the overall strength was not more than 30,000.[189] Provincial cavalrymen were initially drawn from the earliest and central Ottoman territories of Anatolia and parts of Rumelia. Tributary and frontier territories added at a later date were governed more loosely, or submitted annual tax revenues, called *salyaneli*.[190]

However, this process did not affect all the provinces. Some scholars have recently theorised that the persistence of nomad populations facilitated some cavalry roles, such as protecting the *hajj* route caravans to the Holy Cities, and defending the eastern border against the Iranians. The failure to impose a sedentarisation on such tribal structures ultimately caused the Porte endless problems in the nineteenth century, especially in forging a modern, conscripted, and well-trained military force from such populations.[191]

As for their efficiency in the battlefield, records are unanimously unflattering. The always precarious cohesion, the uneven level of training, the desertion and the poor combativeness were more of a hindrance than an advantage on the battlefield.[192] Ahmed Resmi noted a few stragglers in 1769, old men calling themselves *timarlıs*, encumbered with too much baggage and too many retainers. The provincial horseman are rarely mentioned in

---

189 Jucherau de Saint-Denys, *Histoire de l'Empire Ottoman*, vol. I, p.382.
190 Aksan, *Ottoman Wars*, p.55.
191 Aksan, 'Mobilisation of warrior populations in the Ottoman context', p.336.
192 Aksan, *Ottoman Wars*, p.55, and Thornton, *The Present State of Turkey*, vol. I, p.91.

THE OTTOMAN ARMY OF THE NAPOLEONIC WARS 1789–1815

Ottoman *deli* light cavalrymen, from *The Military Costume of Turkey*, by Thomas McLean (1818). In 1802 John Philip Morier describes the *delis* as the most numerous and famed of Ottoman cavalry: 'This name, which signifies "madmen", is well applied to them: they form a light cavalry, and boast of never refusing to undertake the most hazardous enterprizes: they are the enfans perdus of the Turkish army.'

the sources, and no official Ottoman counts of soldiers for the 1768–74 war include *timariots*.[193] *Sipahis* from Anatolia are noticed by Wittman in Egypt in the army led by Grand Vizier Ziya Yusuf Paşa in 1799–1801.[194] In the 1790s estates were no longer issued to the *kapıkulu* horsemen, instead, janissaries were continuously demanding that they be given *timars* as supplementary income. Most of the remaining *timars* had long been converted into taxes to replace military service, or otherwise absorbed into tax revenue farms, and no longer represented soldiers required to report to the military campaign.[195]

Even the once celebrated mounted frontiersmen had lost much of their renown, and were no longer a threat to the Empire's enemies. Only *deli* light

---

193 Aksan, *Ottoman Wars*, p.56.

194 Wittman. *Travels in Turkey*, p.255.

195 Uyar and Erickson, *A Military History of the Ottomans*, p.88. Already in the previous century, the Ottoman government granted *timars* to other military groups and non-military individuals. Fortress guards, gunners, bombardiers, and regional militia officers were the main non-cavalry groups that were granted *timars*. Differing from the Mamluks, who did not receive *timars*, the Ottomans included native higher aristocrats in the Balkans, who received parts of their former lands as *timars* in exchange for loyalty and military service.

horsemen are still registered in the order of battle, like those registered in the Ottoman cavalry in Egypt during the campaigns of 1800, organised in squadrons under the respective *başdeli*.[196] In March 1800 Wittman related that the *deli* corps numbered about 450 horsemen, and formed the vanguard of the 5,000 soldiers promised by Cezzar Paşa: 'who now manifested his intention to cooperate strenuously with the combined British and Turkish forces against the common enemy'.[197] Their employment on campaigns suggests that they were essentially light cavalry used as screen or scouts, and no longer carried out wide-ranging raids as in the previous century, but possibly the *delis* formed the bulk of the mounted force that successfully operated in 1788 into the Banat of Temesvár and Croatia.[198] Morier saw the *delis* in action during the Egyptian campaigns of 1800–1801, leaving an ambivalent description about their quality:

> [The *delys* are] the most numerous and famed of Ottoman cavalry ... they form a light cavalry, and boast of never refusing to undertake the most hazardous enterprises: they are the enfans perdus of the Turkish army ... In case of defeat they are the plunderers of their own camp, and frequently when the body of the army is engaged. During the march, they infest the country through which they pass, for the purpose of pillaging the unfortunate peasants.[199]

Though the *deli* comprised a large variety of mounted soldiers according to their provenance, in the 1810s Mahmud II strengthened this light cavalry and created new standing corps of border horsemen with this title.[200]

Except for the *delis*, the *serhaddkulu* and *toprakli* had in common that they were mobilised only in case of war. About the *toprakli*, the largest contingents came from the major governors, namely from the *beglerbegs* and *paşas*, who gathered the troops in their provinces. Each governor dealt with the war equipment, the appointment of the *ağas* and other officers, and with the control of the recruits assigned to the governors of the minor divisions, namely the *sancakbeg*, *zeamet* and *timar*. *Sancakbeg* and *zeamet* were both taxed with a contingent of soldiers to be led on campaign, while each *timar* had to present himself to the call-to-arms along with another equipped and mounted horseman. Alternatively, he could pay the *bedel*, a tax for recruiting a substitute. However, the ability to gather large armies seemed a distant memory. After all, each *timar* holder could choose whether to present himself for the call-to-arms. Surprising as it may seem, each landowner was allowed to refuse to join the army on campaign up to a maximum of six

---

196 Wittman, *Travels in Turkey*, p.257.
197 Wittman, *Travels in Turkey*, p.257.
198 K.u.K. Kriegsarchiv, 'Eine Episode aus dem Feldzuge 1788', in *Österreichische Militärische Zeitschrift* (1893), vol. I, pp.301–302.
199 Morier, *Memoir of a Campaign with the Ottoman Army*, p.17. 'The Volunteers, as well as all other descriptions of troops which compose a Turkish army, receive a daily ration of bread: the cavalry receive a ration of barley for their horses.'
200 Uyar and Erickson, *A Military History of the Ottomans*, p.126.

Tepeleni Ali Paşa (1740?–1822), portrayed by Spyridon Ventouras in 1820. The famous 'Lion of Janina' was an ethnic Albanian who ruled as *ayan* in central and southern Albania, most of Epirus and the western parts of Thessaly and Greek Macedonia. He first appears in historical accounts as a bandit leader who became involved in many encounters with the Ottomans, but later he joined the administrative-military system of the Empire, holding various posts until 1788 when he was appointed *paşa*. His diplomatic and administrative skills, his interest in modern technology and concepts, his popular Muslim piety, and his respect towards other religions were unconditionally praised by contemporaries. As military leader, it was said that he could assemble an army of 50,000 men in a matter of two to three days, and could double that number in two to three weeks. He was able to increase his power while continuing to remain loyal to the Porte until 1820, when his involvement in Ottoman politics increased culminating in his active opposition to the ongoing reforms introduced by Sultan Mahmud II. After being declared a rebel in 1820, he was captured and killed in 1822. In Greece, he is considered one of the fathers of independence.

times, and only in this case did he lose his status. Once the military campaign was over, those who returned hastened to resume their original occupations, and if a campaign ended unfavourably, just as quickly these troops tended to return to their homes. One of the principal causes of Ottoman failure in the wars with Austria and Russia in 1735–39 and 1768–74 was the insistence on the part of the provincial cavalry that they be allowed to return home to administer their lands during the winter months. Under the traditional *timar* system it was, indeed, necessary for them at some point to collect the revenues they needed to maintain themselves and their suites in the field army. As a consequence, much territory taken by successful military action against the enemy during the summer was lost without a fight during the winter months. Only the major governors, such as the *beglerbeg*, *paşa* and some wealthy *sancakbeg*, could maintain a standing force, occasionally established in corps known as *alay* under the respective *alay beğ* or *alay bey*.

Like the other major governors, the grand viziers also raised their own military contingents. Morier states that the grand vizier's household depended upon his wealth, 'or upon his ideas of grandeur'.[201] According to the court's rule, the sultan provided 40 *solaks* as lifeguard for his prime minister, and further soldiers were raised as his personal retinue. At the battle of Heliopolis in March 1800, Wittman reports that the grand vizier's lifeguard included

---

201 Morier, *Memoir of a Campaign with the Ottoman Army in Egypt*, p.15.

both cavalry and infantry,[202] while in 1811 Laz Aziz Ahmed Paşa had a lifeguard of 600 horsemen from Rumelia.[203] The *paşa* of Damascus' personal retinue in 1799 was seen on parade by the English traveller William George Browne, who relates that it was a mounted and well-armed corps of 400 men. This included two separate units of 'dellis' cavalry, 'mounted on Arabian horses, variously armed and clothed, but on the whole forming no mean display'. One unit had 300, and the other 400 men. The *paşa* of Damascus is also recorded as having 150 Albanian infantrymen.[204] The *paşa*'s retinue also included two group of 15, and 30 men mounted on dromedaries, with 'musquetoon' large carbines fitted to the saddles on a swivel mounts: These troops, it was said, were a 'destructive instrument of war that has passed from the Persians to the Syrians'.

In the 1790s the Porte tried to issue a new regulation for restoring its provincial mounted troops, since the cavalry was less needed in modern warfare, but the army could not be deprived of a mounted force for basic tasks such as reconnaissance, escort and pursuit. The *alay bey* and other officers of each *sancak* district drew up new registers of all the fiefs under their supervision together with the names and descriptions of the individuals to whom they were assigned. They then travelled around their districts to make sure that the nominal fief holders were permanently residing on them and performing the required duties, and that they were persons who were able and willing to supply military service to the army when required. In addition inspectors were sent from the Porte every three years to make sure that *timars* and officers alike were performing their duties and that the commanders were really eliminating all those who violated the regulations. If the *timars* were not present on their fiefs when the inspectors came, or if they did not respond to calls for their military service, they were supposed to be dismissed at once, but the frequency with which this regulation was repeated during the reign of Selim III seems to indicate the difficulty which the government had in enforcing it.[205] Efforts were made to revive and reorganise the apprentice system. The number of apprentices in each district was limited to 10 percent of its active fief holders, and it was stipulated that only these apprentices could replace the feudatories when the fiefs became vacant. Inheritance was allowed here much more than in the salaried infantry corps. The government tried to satisfy the needs of the *timar* system without disrupting the army by decreeing that the feudatories no longer had the absolute right to return to their fiefs during the winter months; it was now to be only a privilege granted them by the Sultan at his pleasure. Every 10 *timars* in the army holding lands in the same or neighbouring districts were allowed to get together, and choose one of their number to go

---

202 Wittman, *Travels to Turkey*, p.266.

203 Carl von Martens, *Allgemeine Geschichte der Türken-Kriege in Europa von 1356 bis 1812* (Stuttgart, 1829), vol. II, p.287.

204 William George Browne, *Travels in Africa, Egypt, and Syria, from the Year 1792 to 1798* (London, 1799), p.396.

205 Shaw, *Between Old and New*, pp.118–119.

home for a time to administer their own lands and the lands of the others, who continued to serve on campaign.[206] In the 1770s and 1780s, attempts to restore this source of recruitment failed, since the horsemen enlisted by the districts did not join the field army regularly, a fact that accelerated the decline and the effectiveness of the provincial cavalry as a whole.

Decline was also a common feature of the *azabs* as well as the other *serhaddkulu* foot troops, which gradually became forces under the direction of semi-autonomous local governors. As the Porte faced internal unrest and financial collapse, the need for short-term troops was left to local governors. Already at the end of the seventeenth century, the government authorised *beglerbegs* and *paşas* to arm themselves with contingents of troops to join the Sultan's army. Not only had the governors organised private contingents, but also some wealthy families who did not belong to the ruling elite had managed to consolidate their own territorial rule exploiting the tax-farming system: namely the aforementioned *ayans*. In this scenario, the *ayans* began to emerge as one of the most politically relevant figures. The family-clan Çapanoğlu in northeastern Anatolia, the Janikli in eastern Anatolia, and the Karaosman near Smyrna could act like semi-independent lords, and through their collateral branches were able to collect large private contingents. Europe also witnessed the rise of prosperous and powerful figures who deeply influenced the history of the Empire in this age. Among the most prominent, Pasvanoğlu Osman, Tepeleni Ali and Alemdâr Mustafa became the Sultan's allies or enemies depending on the case.

The notables were responsible for every kind of revolt, and often they acted like gangster bosses extorting tributes in the area under their control. In the second half of the eighteenth century the affirmation of these local notables and magnates became definitive, and their positions often became hereditary. Individuals and families who were locally prominent because of wealth, or religious and social prestige, had come to occupy influential places in their communities. They were looked to as arbiters and leaders by those around them. Because of their influence with the people, they were increasingly consulted and used by Ottoman officials to secure local compliance with their orders and desires. They assumed the function of mediating between the people and the government officials and, as the latter became more corrupt and tyrannical, of intervening to protect the people from the officials. Exploiting the absence of the army, which was weighed down on the war fronts, the *ayans*, whose power relied in part on their public

---

206 Shaw, *Between Old and New*, p.118: Efforts were also made to curb the practice of giving military fiefs to persons serving the government in Istanbul to provide them with revenues in addition to their salaries without requiring them to perform the military services for which the fiefs in question were originally set aside. This practice had deprived the state of a great deal of needed military service and at the same time had made the officials in question much more independent of the Sultan and the grand vizier than they would have been if they were dependent for their maintenance on Treasury salaries alone. About 500 fiefs held in this way were abolished, and only a small number was set aside to support certain palace and scribal officials who were not given regular salaries in return for their work.

function and in part on landownership, or *ciftlik*, acted independently of the central government.[207] Soon, the local elites took advantage of the power vacuum to increase their autonomy, becoming actual warlords, able to gather private armies of many thousands of soldiers from their own fiefdoms. Their rise was also facilitated by the fact that the central power, threatened on several occasions by the janissaries, had to rely on these private contingents to counterbalance the supremacy of its praetorians.[208]

From 1768 onwards the Ottomans begun to increase their recourse to the *miri levendat* system, since volunteerism was still very much in evidence, and participation was limited to a single campaign, renewable thereafter dependent upon the situation. In the following decades, state-financed irregular infantry and cavalry contingents in great numbers became a standard of the Ottoman army. Mouradgea d'Ohsson stated that in 1769 there were 97 'regiments' each of 1,000 soldiers, thus totalling 97,000 irregulars.[209] The troops supplied by the *ayans* played a major role during the wars against Austria and Russia in 1787–91, and in some cases numbered up to 30,000 men, including cavalry, artillery, logistic facilities and train.[210] In these dramatic years, turning to these troops allowed the Porte to make considerable economic savings. The irregular mercenaries provided by the *ayans* were in every way cheaper than *kapıkulu* soldiers. Their salary was relatively low, and they received it haphazardly. Most often, their equipment and weapons were second rate, and surprisingly, they proved to be as willing and warlike as the *kapıkulu* soldiers. However, they were not equipped and guaranteed as the standing corps. They had no job security, and at the end of the campaign season they had to find other jobs in order to survive during the winter. It was very difficult – but not impossible – to find temporary jobs in the inelastic Ottoman economy. These winter period jobs mainly involved guarding frontier fortresses, serving in military construction work, or policing the provinces against bandits. In contrast, the *kapıkulu* soldiers increasingly spent these winter periods working in their well-established

---

207 Jucherau de Saint-Denys, *Histoire de l'Empire Ottoman*, vol. I, p.385. Concerning the *ayans*, the French baron reports that 'Some of these wealthy lords, such as those from Macedonia and Thrace, had managed to amass impressive fortunes and thanks to these and their personal qualities had subjugated the governors of the neighbouring provinces and made themselves useful and formidable for the Porte.'

208 Jucherau de Saint-Denys, *Histoire de l'Empire Ottoman*, vol. I, p.385. In this regard, Ágoston states in *Explorations in Russian and Eurasian History*, p.303: 'Apart from the Janissaries, provincial governors and local notables profited from the devolution of power. In return for their military assistance, they continued to have access to state revenues through the various tax farms. They obtained more and more such revenue sources for life; and many appointments as *muhassils*, *mütesellims*, and *voyvodas* managed to turn them into inheritable revenue farms.'

209 Mouradgea d'Ohsson, *Tableau Général*, vol. VII, pp.381–82.

210 Virginia H. Aksan, 'The Ottomans, Military Manpower and Political Bargains 1750–1850' in M. Sariyannis (ed.) *Political Thought and Practice in the Ottoman Empire*' (Rethymno: Crete University Press, 2019), p.436.

civilian secondary jobs.[211] As a consequence, after discharge from the military, mercenaries returned back to their provinces with their personally owned firearms. Thus, the accumulated knowledge of manufacturing and using firearms was instrumental in the creation of rebel armies headed by chiefs able to collect a force of more than 30,000 musket-bearing men. While the government still had enough power to control this diffusion by enforcing import bans – in fact, only a very few provinces had foreign supply channels – this scenario could be controlled, especially collecting all firearms from non-military classes. In reality, it was the Ottoman policies that created 'the volatile atmosphere of rebellion and banditry in which government-trained disaffected officials led the unemployed villagers, students, *timariot*s, and mercenaries, who manned the rebel armies and bandit gangs'.[212] At this point, the government also exploited the situation for its own benefit, in terms of financing the military and war effort more effectively by increasing the tax-burden of villagers and by employing armed groups as cheaply as possible and then getting rid of them as soon as possible. Interestingly, the rebels and bandits actually acted as additional tax collectors by squeezing villagers more, but of course, they did not share their collections with the state. Nevertheless, by using these financial tricks as a kind of salary, or to provide equipment and weapons as well, the bandit armies became another cheap and ready source of labour for the government. It is not surprising to note that the willingness of rebels and bandits to join the troops hired by the government came with the promise of a good salary or a position as governor.[213]

The wars and the business of mercenaries served to increase the strength and bargaining power of the notables as opposed to the governors and the *sehir kethüdasi* sent from Constantinople.[214] Since the regular Ottoman standing army was unable to supply sufficient numbers of trained men to fight the Russians and Austrians, the Porte became increasingly dependent for such troops on the *ayans*. In return for military contributions at critical times, they gained further privileges. However, just as easily as one may obtain an important position during the wars, one may also lose everything. During the war of 1787–92 against Austria and Russia, the Caniklizade family – who were extremely wealthy and powerful, despite a conflict that emerged between one of them and the Porte in 1779 – did not provide the Sultan with the requested aid and personnel. Their failure to carry out the will of the Sultan resulted in executions and the stripping away of all posts and offices. Caniklizade family would not hold another office until 1799, and in the meantime some members of the family offered their services to

---

211 Uyar and Erickson, *A Military History of the Ottomans*, p.95: 'Last, but not least, the irregulars following the tradition of their predecessors sought employment in foreign countries, including the erstwhile enemy of the Ottoman Empire, Iran. Unfortunately, there exists very limited information about the real dimensions of Ottoman mercenaries serving abroad.'

212 Uyar and Erickson, *A Military History of the Ottomans*, p.96.

213 Robert Zens, 'Provincial Powers: The Rise of Ottoman Local Notables (Ayan)' in *History Studies*, vol. 3, March 2011, p.446.

214 Administrative officials. See Chapter 1.

the Russians.[215] Nine years later Kahraman Paşa, a wealthy commander of Albanian irregular troops on the Danube, met a similar fate. Just released from prison to lead the troops on campaign, he was accused of disruption and desertion of the battlefield, and summarily executed.[216]

In 1789 Sultan Selim III declined to continue his predecessors' efforts to control the *ayan* magnates. One year later the position of governor was abolished, and orders were issued for the Ottoman officials to accept as 'notables' anyone who was able to get the approval of the local population, namely local leaders who had the force to establish their domination. In many cases the Sultan had to go even further than this and appoint the notables as governors to secure their military support. Under existing conditions, this was the only thing he could do. The notables were in fact far more able to perform the duties of local administration and provide military contingents than the regular Ottoman officials.

In general, the recruitment of irregular troops was in the hands of provincial officials and magnates in Anatolia and Europe, both those who were state-appointed such as *valis* and *kadıs*, and the *ayans*. The Sultan gave them the freedom to recruit in their provinces anyone able to fight. Thus, to encourage the recruitment effort, the government issued formal orders which offered recruits a sign-on bonus – *bahşiş* – which was significant enough to pay off much of an individual's debt, a monthly salary – *ulufe* – in six-month lump sums, daily rations, and the ability to re-enlist for additional two-month service periods. Officers were also allotted a 10 percent commission or *ondalık*. All salaries were paid by the central government and guaranteed by the notables who recruited them. *Ayans*, or other recruiters, were fined double the amount which they were advanced by the government for any desertions in order to ensure morally sound soldiers as well as to prevent provincial authorities from merely pocketing the large sums of money passing through their hands. However, these fines were rarely imposed.[217] In addition to supplying men, the *ayans* sold foodstuff to the army. During the war of 1787–92, the request addressed to the Karaosmanoğlu family asked them to supply recruits and foodstuff. Ömer Ağa, the *voyvoda* of Bergama, and Hacı Ahmed Ağa, the *mütesellim* of Saruhan, took 2,500 men plus supplies to join the army on campaign, for which the latter was presented with a sable-lined *kaftan* by Sultan Selim III.[218]

---

215 Zens, 'Provincial Powers', p.444. The Caniklizade family is an excellent example of the benefits that could be gleaned from the state during wartime. Their rise to power through a combination of tax farming privileges and landholdings and, ultimately, a demonstration of their physical and financial might during wartime was rather typical of the *ayan* dynasties that existed in Anatolia.

216 Virginia H. Aksan, 'Mutiny and the Eighteenth Century Ottoman Army', in *Turkish Studies Association Bulletin* 22, 1 (1998), pp.116–125.

217 Cezar Mustafa, in *Osmanlı Tarihinde Levendler* (Istanbul: Çelikcilt Matbası, 1965), pp.353–354, states that the bonus was intended to enable the recruits to purchase a gun and horse, if they did not already possess one.

218 Zens, 'Provincial Powers', p.444.

The contingents were organised on a local basis and reflected patterns and structures typical of the places from which they came. In the Balkans, the Albanian clan and the Bosnian *zadruga*[219] formed the basis for the structure of these corps, and hence the strong bond of cohesion between them and the leaders. The variety of designations assumed by these troops denote their origin: from the *miri levend* to the *arnavut*, they comprised mercenaries with different salary treatment, and indifferently coming from Europe or Anatolia, as well as the Caucasus or even Egypt and Syria.[220] The private armies of the *ayans* were mainly composed of Albanians, who were everywhere, and increasingly by *Lazs* from Trabzon, Bosnians as well as the Circassian communities from the Caucasus, Tatars, Arabs and, finally, Kurds from eastern Anatolia. Such mobile soldiers and their leaders would become the officer corps and 'cannon fodder' of the reformed armies of Muhammad Ali of Egypt.[221] One interesting characteristic of the Ottoman mercenaries was their preference to seek employment distant from their original province. For example, the most famous mercenary group, the Western Anatolians, sought employment in European and North African provinces while the Albanians took opportunities in Anatolia and Egypt.

Provincial levies were raised by local magnates, but paid for from the central treasury, and distinguished both from the *kapıkulu* soldiers and the magnates' own household troops, usually designed as *kapı halkı*. The fact that these were fierce and even feared contingents is amply proved by numerous episodes, such that in July 1808, when thousands of irregulars gathered by Alemdâr Mustafa marched on Constantinople and took control of the city from the janissaries.[222]

Some detailed studies deal with the composition of these formations.[223] In the European provinces, the governors already had powerful personal contingents, financed by seizing estates and assigning them to their household members. The weakness of the central government gave them rights to create or reorganise provincial units according to the geography of the border. All of the soldiers, including artillerymen, were to be locally recruited from volunteers or villagers and organised into *oda* companies. One or several companies would be grouped under a field officer, who was responsible

---

219 The *zadruga* was an institution of an aristocratic nature found among the South Slavs since before their settlement in the Balkans. It can be defined as a rural community of life, goods and work between families and individuals linked by a kinship, who recognise the authority of a single leader.

220 Concerning the *levends*, the standard work remains Cezar, Mustafa, *Osmanlı Tarihinde Levendler* (Istanbul: Çelikcilt Matbaasi, 1965); see also Virginia Aksan, 'Ottoman Military Recruitment Strategies in the late Eighteenth Century', in V. Aksan (ed.), *Ottomans and Europeans. Contacts and Conflicts* (Constantinople: Isis Press, 2004), pp.191–207.

221 Aksan, *Ottoman Wars*, p.250.

222 Alessio Bombaci, Stanford J. Shaw, *L'Impero Ottomano – Storia Universale dei Popoli e delle Civiltà*, vol. VI (Turin: Utet, 1981), p.469.

223 See Michael Robert Hickok, *Ottoman Military Administration in Eighteenth-Century Bosnia* (Leiden-Boston, MS: Brill, 1997), pp.63–54.

for a border region that included small fortresses, towers, and *palanka* guardhouses. In Bosnia, for example, a *kapudan* (captain) was responsible for an area called a *kapudanlık* or *kaptanija*. Bosnia provided the best and most important example of these new border defence units. Thanks to the efforts of a series of competent governors, in the eighteenth century Bosnian irregular border units achieved a high standard of effectiveness and kept it for a century. Highly motivated and well trained, Bosnian frontiersmen not only defended their respective regions properly but also conducted offensive operations against the Habsburg *Militärgrenze* on the border region, and even against the Austrian regular forces. They played an important role in all the wars between 1736 and 1798. In 1768, a strong irregular mobile force numbering 5,000 *panduks* was called to reinforce the Russian front, which crippled the defence of Bosnia.[224] In the 1790s indigenous soldiers almost always outnumbered Ottoman standing troops in the province, and formed the garrisons of the major fortresses.[225] In each garrison a *kapudan* held the command of the troops who were more regularly drilled and equipped compared to the irregulars from Anatolia and elsewhere. Though these troops were controlled by the local notables, they maintained a much higher loyalty to the Porte, which maintained a durable control over them.[226]

Not all the provinces followed the Bosnian pattern, and in most of the southern and eastern provinces, and in northern Black Sea region, the Ottoman government had to depend more on tribal leaders, including Kurdish chiefs, Arab sheikhs, and other local lords, and acknowledge their already well-established semi-autonomous rule. However, their loyalty was always problematic and their frequent underhand deals with enemies were notorious. Of course, constant negotiations and bargaining was the norm. As a result, the massive Ottoman northern and eastern fortresses like Kili, Özü, Akkirman, Kars, and Erzurum were tasked not only to stop enemy advances until the arrival of the main army and act as forward staging bases, but were also necessary to keep the locals loyal. The government had to solve difficult problems such as allocating financial resources for the maintenance of the increasingly expensive fortresses, providing up-to-date weapons and equipment, and procuring massive amounts of gunpowder. In terms of recruiting fortress garrisons in the east, the government had to depend more on mercenaries and tribal warriors because of the proven uselessness and unwillingness of the janissaries. Even though both of these groups were very problematic and rebellious, in order to carry out the tedious and dangerous

---

224 Uyar and Erickson, *A Military History of the Ottomans*, p.106.

225 Hickok, *Ottoman Military Administration*, p.41: 'Some scholars have labeled the eighteenth century as a period when the provincial elite (*ayans*) were in ascendancy. Bosnia with its traditional history of a strong provincial nobility was surely no exceptions, or so we might believe.'

226 Hickok, *Ottoman Military Administration*, p.140. The author states that Ottoman officials in Bosnia were as effective as their western neighbours in dealing with foreign and local challenges, that they were by and large honest and dedicated public servants, and that their skill ensured that Bosnia would remain part of the Ottoman Empire for several more generations.

job of guarding the fortresses, the government had no alternative but to keep them in line using all sorts of methods and tools.[227]

In Asia, the province of Damascus provides another unique example of provincial military organisation. In the early eighteenth century, the Porte surprisingly lifted the obligation of Damascus to provide units for military campaigns while, at the same time, tried desperately to mobilise unexploited manpower sources. Instead, it tasked Damascene units with the responsibility for the organisation and execution of the pilgrimage to Mecca and Medina and also for interior security duties, especially against unruly nomadic tribes. Actually, by rendering this difficult and strange decision, the government was openly recognising its limitations and difficulties in mobilising and transporting soldiers from Damascus to the faraway theatres of war and, at the same time, stabilise the province during the absence of its military. In the eighteenth century, Damascus never provided enough recruits and always experienced difficulty in fulfilling its military obligations. Moreover, the meagre Damascene garrison with only 500 janissaries was available for campaigns and after 1721, they became an *ocak* permanently quartered into the capital. As occurred in Constantinople and in the European provinces, local janissaries increased their number with *yamaks* and fictional soldiers. Therefore, from a military perspective the absence of the Damascus troops had little effect on the overall combat efficiency of the Ottoman army. In turn, they would be more useful by stabilising the province, and providing protection for the pilgrimage. The successful execution of the yearly pilgrimage was very important for the prestige and legitimacy of the Porte in the eyes of the entire Muslim world. However, increasing Bedouin attacks on pilgrimage convoys and other difficulties in execution, including billeting and providing transport, caused the Ottomans to come under serious criticism. Thus, from a political perspective the allocation of Damascene units for the pilgrimage was a wise decision. Additionally, the Damascus governor was obligated to pay an exemption fee for not participating in campaigns, which generated revenues for the state.[228] Surprisingly, the policy

---

227 Virginia H. Aksan, 'Manning a Black Sea Garrison in the Eighteenth Century: Ochakov and Concepts of Mutiny and Rebellion in the Ottoman Context', in *Ottomans and Europeans: Contacts and Conflicts* (Constantinople: The Isis Press, 2004), pp.253–255.

228 The complex composition of the Damascene military is important in understanding the difficulties of the Ottoman government in terms of making use of the Empire's potential. There were four main military groups in Damascus. The first group was composed of local janissaries, designated as *yerli*, who were the successors of the janissary unit left to guard the city after its conquest in 1516. The second group was the so-called Imperial janissaries (commonly called *kapıkulu* by the locals), who were positioned in Damascus after a large military rebellion in 1659. Both of these groups had already become part of local society and politics and had practically no military value. The third group was composed of mercenaries, in general service to the governors as a part of their retinue. This group was actually a strange mixture of Anatolian *levends*, Kurdish musketeers, and North African mercenaries. The fourth group was the provincial-timariot cavalry. They were the biggest group, but their numerical and military strength reduced rapidly after the last quarter of the seventeenth century. Most of the estates were allocated or captured

worked and produced results until the 1750s. The government effectively curbed the numbers of janissaries, sometimes violently as in the example of the local janissary rebellion and suppression of February 1746, and used different groups to balance different interests. By limiting the Damascus governors' opportunity for promotion within the system, the government forced them to focus more on local matters and achieved effective control over the province.

Both the Bosnian and Damascus models are instructive in understanding the difficulties facing the Ottoman Empire and its pragmatic solutions in meeting them. While the government managed to defend its borders by using locals more and giving them freedom of action in Bosnia, it managed to fight effectively against internal troublemakers and rebels by following a different formula in Damascus. Moreover these two divergent, but complementary, policies limited the ambitions of governors and *ayan* provincial magnates for the whole century and helped make them dependent on the central government.

In the case of the Albanians, an officer appointed by the *ayan* as his lieutenant held the command of the irregular corps in his absence, and usually took care of training and internal discipline. In some case, he was designated the rank of *bölük başi*. The troops were divided into 'battalions' of 200–300 men, under a *serçesme* (sergeant major) proposed by the soldiers and approved by the *ayan* or by his lieutenant. Within the corps, veterans were selected at the rank of NCO, each commanding a squadron of 40–60 men.[229] Soldiers provided arms by themselves and were usually engaged for a period of two months, four months, or maximum six months, or seasonal engagement. If they served in summer, they left the army at November and went back to home no matter what the current military situation was.[230] Obviously, this was true if the service took place in Europe, but in the case of the Albanian mercenaries who went to Egypt, their engagement was unlimited. Although many of the details of these capitulations are still unknown, there was no fixed scheme for payment. Usually, the Porte paid the hire of mercenaries to the commander, while in other cases it was the *defterdar* who issued the salaries as he did for the soldiers of the regular army. In this case, the government wanted to secure a guarantee to better control these often-turbulent mercenaries. Even though the government more or less gave free hand to the governors, it still held sanction authority and paid special attention to the commissioning and assignment of officers.

---

by the governors, *ayans*, or janissaries. As a group, they ceased to exist at the beginning of the eighteenth century. All of these groups had difficulty cooperating with each other and preferred to spend their time in local politics and trade rather than on military matters. However, instead of abolishing them the Ottoman government mobilised them for pilgrimage and stabilisation duties. See Uyar and Erickson, *A Military History of the Ottomans*, pp.106–107.

229 Ali Fuat Örenç, 'Albanian Soldiers in the Ottoman Army during the Greek Revolt at 1821' in B. Çinar (ed.) *The Balkans as a Crossroad: Evaluating Past, Reading Present, Imagining Future* (Tirana: IBAC, 2012), p.511.

230 Örenç, 'Albanian Soldiers in the Ottoman Army', p.506.

Additionally, by keeping the assignment and allocation of cash funds – *ocaklık* – for the wages of these units, the government had a strong lever to control them.[231] At the end of their contract, company commanders tried to find another employer in order to keep their private units intact since otherwise they had little means to keep them together. In the worst-case scenario, company commanders sometimes chose banditry.[232]

In the European provinces, irregulars were mostly infantry, but Bosnia in particular supplied horsemen alongside the infantry. The mounted corps were organised in tactical troops called *faris*, ranging between 20 and 50 men divided in *odas*. The total number of *faris* took the name *cemaat*. Within the major corps, further officers were in charge of administrative services, with one or more *çavuş* as adjutants. Each detachment usually included a standard-bearer, the *bayrakdar*, plus a certain number of *odabasis* according to the number of *odas* forming the *faris*. Horsemen barely formed half of the forces gathered by the *ayans* in Anatolia. For instance, Canikli Ali Bey, an *ayan* from Trabzon, in 1774 actively recruited 1,500 cavalrymen and 1,500 infantrymen and sent them against the Russians, in addition to many supplies.[233]

By focusing on the fluid military employment practices of the highlander *arnavuts*, in the late eighteenth and early nineteenth centuries, some factors reinserted these irregular bands into the political turmoil of the period. Rather than rogue bandits, these mercenaries constituted a significant group of military labourers offering their services to several patrons. Bosnian and Albanian mercenaries' motivation for joining the army was, at best, questionable. Yet, there were no promising means for replacing them. The veteran Yusuf Paşa of Serres, who became commander in Patras and Lepanto in 1822, criticised most of the Albanian mercenary troops he could mobilise for his upcoming role. He complained that the soldiers, who would be of great importance if dispatched according to the right conditions – which stipulated basically the mobilisation of adult and able males in arms in return for tax exemptions – did not meet expectations, as the bulk of the soldiers were merely peasants and shepherds.[234] Several Ottoman commanders and officials complained about these mercenaries. Süleyman Penah Efendi, a seasoned bureaucrat in the military accounting offices, refers to the Albanians' disorder and ferocity, which caused untold suffering and flight after their arrival in the Peloponnese to suppress the rebellion in 1770.[235] The irregulars were nothing but scum who would obey no one. Furthermore, they spoke Albanian among themselves and did not understand Turkish, so they were untrustworthy and difficult to train.[236]

---

231 Uyar and Erickson, *A Military History of the Ottomans*, p.106.

232 Uyar and Erickson, *A Military History of the Ottomans*, p.94.

233 Zens, 'Provincial Powers', p.444.

234 Uğur Bayraktar, 'From salary to resistance: mobility, employment, and violence in Dibra, 1792–1826', in *Middle Eastern Studies*, vol. 54, N. 6 (2018), p.888.

235 He was the author of *Mora Ohtilâli Tarihi*, a description of the massive Greek rebellion of 1770. See Aksan, *Ottoman Wars*, p.189.

236 Aksan, *Ottoman Wars*, p.189.

Another acute observer, the English artillery officer William Wittman, reports that in February 1800 a corps of 600 Albanian infantrymen, who had joined the army before Jaffa a few days before, suddenly left the camp and headed to Acre, 'and the defection was supposed to have been occasioned by the want of money and provisions at the encampment'.[237] Two years before, a similar incident occurred when *Kircaali* (Turkish speaking inhabitants of the Kircaali valley in Thracia) and Albanian irregulars marching into Greece to embark for Egypt became the object of the government's complaints. Since they were waiting for their salaries, the soldiers refused to leave the army whether their service duration was complete or not, and their chiefs demanded extra payment for this delay. The Ottoman authorities laconically informed the Porte that 'the mercenaries did not fight for the Sultan or religion, but money', and because of the lack of money the soldiers, led by their own chiefs, plundered villages and towns.[238]

Though these troops represented a source of serious problems, the Ottomans continued to employ irregular forces, no matter how self-ordained they were. The Albanians formed a considerable part of the forces sent to Egypt against the French. No less than 20,000 mercenaries left the 'country of eagles' in three successive expeditions, and in 1802 formed the largest contingent in Egypt, under the orders of Tahir Paşa and his most famous lieutenant Kavalalı Mehmet Ali, later Muhammad Ali. They became much appreciated as warriors, and their service expanded throughout the Empire. Concerning their attitude to war, the Prussian General Valentini remarks:

> They are a kind of voluntary militia of the Turkey of Europe, who leave it unclear whether they recognise Jesus Christ or Mohammed. They put themselves in the pay of the pashas or whoever can pay them, and at the same time engage into brigandage.[239]

However, the transformation of these soldiers from irregular to regular was not straightforward. Though the initial aim of the government had been to form private contingents in imitation of the Habsburg *Freikorps*, the outcome had negative consequences for the Empire as well as for the army. Since the government had only authorised the formation of these contingents for the duration of a campaign or the war, the *ayans* opposed the disbanding of the personal armies, arguing that the troops needed to be kept in service to survey the public order. When the government insisted on disbanding the contingents, the *ayans* did not hesitate to provoke rebellions and riots. This was the trajectory of personalities such as Cezzar Ahmed, governor of Sidon, became famous for his defence of Acre in 1799 against Bonaparte. Previously, in 1776–77, he recruited troops to suppress the Druze rebellion supported by the *paşas* of Aleppo and Damascus, and after this commitment he became so powerful that he could ignore the central

---

237 Wittman, *Travels in Turkey*, p.252.
238 Örenç, 'Albanian Soldiers in the Ottoman Army', p.506.
239 Valentini, *Précis des dernières guerres des Russes contre les Turcs*, p.40.

government's orders when these did not suit his particular interests. By the end of the eighteenth century, and throughout the next century, notables and *ayans* ruled all of eastern Anatolia and much of the west, with only Cilicia and the districts of Kütahya, Manisa, Aydin, and Menteşe in the south-west remaining under some sort of direct administration by officials sent from Constantinople.[240] By the end of the eighteenth century further *ayans*, such as Tepeleni Ali Paşa of Janina, Pazvantoğlu Osman of Vidin, Canikli Ali Paşa of Trabzon, Çapanoğlu Mustafa Paşa of Yozgatand, Alemdâr Mustafa of Rüsçük, the Karaosmanoğlu family in western Anatolia, and the Janikly in the east, begun to pursue their own foreign policy. Pazvantoğlu Osman In the following century, Muhammad Ali in Egypt and Alemdâr Mustafa Paşa in Anatolia continued this trend, but with the opposite outcome.

When the irregular troops turned into bandits, they imposed tributes or 'protection' on the civilians under the threat of reprisals. By specifically dealing with the military recruitment dynamics present in some provinces, the chronicles demonstrate that incidents of violence occurred in tandem with the Empire's increasing practice of irregular recruitment.[241] The government received a seemingly unending stream of reports in the 1780s, 1790s, and 1800s, which detailed the depredations of marauders in all corners of the Balkans. In the late eighteenth century, Albanians functioned as mountain bandits at times and armed irregulars at other times, particularly following the war of 1768–74.[242] As the legal system in the provinces became less effective in this period of turmoil, those who lost positions and possessions to powerful local notables also recruited Albanian *arnavuts* and other irregulars to strike back at those above the law. Late in 1788 the powerful *ayan* of Siroz (today Serres in northern Greece), İsmail Beg, returned home after the first campaign season of the 1787–92 war against Austria and Russia, only to find that a number of his properties had been sacked by bandits. The destruction affected not just the district of Siroz, but that of nearby Siderokastro as well. The main force of the bandits consisted of 2,000 Albanian followers of a certain Orhan Beg of Beraştann, near Permet, southern Albania. One of the leading outlaws, who had recruited Orhan and his men, however, also sent a complaint to Constantinople, charging that İsmail Beg had illegally seized

---

240 Among the most important and long-lived ruling families of this kind in Selim's time were the Küchük Alioğlu around Payas and Adana, the Ilyasoğlu in the area of Milas and Menteşe,the Tekeli Ibrahimoğlu at Antalya, the Tuzjuoğlu at Rize, the Jemshitoğlu around Trebizond, the Nazuhoğlu at Gediz, the Kalyonjuoğlu in Bilecik, the Ajemoğlu at Ushak, the Yilanlioğlu at Sparta, and the Katiboğlu family of Izmir. See Shaw, *Between Old and New*, p.215.

241 Uğur Bayraktar, 'From salary to resistance', pp.878–879: 'The mountain bandits' reign stemmed mostly from the state of the Ottoman army, which 'evolved from a combination of voluntary feudatory militias and janissary-style conscripted infantry into a system of state-funded militias, with periods of short-term conscription.'

242 Frederick Anscombe, 'Albanians and Mountain Bandits' in F. Anscombe, *The Ottoman Balkans, 1750-1830* (Princeton, NJ: Markus Wiener Publishers, 2006), pp.89–90.

THE ARMIES OF THE SULTAN

Mamluk horsemen training in Cairo in a late-eighteenth century print (author's archive). Because Mamluk troops were generally mounted, they moved at considerable speed, capable of sustaining a rate of 30 or 40 miles a day when necessary, and customarily averaging at least half that. In order to facilitate this performance, populated districts were obliged to provide the army with food and fodder, while in the desert region supplies marched on dromedaries.

his *çiftliks* estates. İsmail naturally managed the problem by recruiting his own retinues from Albania.[243]

It would almost seem that an actual 'Bandit Kingdom' existed, stretching from Albania to Macedonia, even tolerated by the Ottoman government, because it ultimately guaranteed control of the territory through people who often had important contacts with the central power. Incidents happen without the local authorities doing anything to prevent them, as occurred in 1792 in Prilep (today in the Republic of Northern Macedonia), when Osman of Mat, an Albanian bandit leader, assaulted the town with 300 men to claim the local military commandership. Following their surrender, the inhabitants of Prilep were forced to deliver a ransom to the bandits while Osman roamed the town's surroundings:

> The desperate deputy governor of Prilep asked Yusuf Bey of Dibra for help. He in turn dispatched mullah Yunus of Peshkopi with 800 men to Prilep. The moment the mullah arrived at Prilep, however, Osman of Mat left for Stip, a nearby town, to help another patron, Torkullu Mehmed Sipahi. Osman's departure, however, did not relieve the inhabitants of Prilep. They asked Mulla Yunus to return later

---

243 Anscombe, p.91: 'In 1799, the brother of the *nazir* (supervisor of revenues) of Drama (Greece) joined forces with one of the most notorious leaders of Albanian Mountain Bandits, Manav İbrahim, to pillage the district of Nevrekop (Gotse Delchev, Bulgaria) as part of a long struggle against İsmail's domination.'

Mamluk *bey*, watercolour from the *Fenerci Albümü*, 1800–1809. Each *bey* could gather their own contingents, which alongside the troops recruited for a single campaign increased the Egyptian *ocaks* to several thousands of men. However it is difficult to establish the actual strength with accuracy, not least because each Mamluk household had its own *saraçes* or assistants.

as his services were no longer needed. To this, the mullah responded indifferently, saying, 'I want the payment [*ulüufe*]'. Once the deputy governor found out that he would not be able to handle the problem on his own, he fled the town. In the meantime, the judge of the town alerted the government in his petition that more than 2000 bandits led by Mulla Yunus, Yaşar Bey, Yusuf Bey, Hasan Dora, Receb Dora, and Osman of Mat had ravaged the town and harassed the people. The inhabitants had to pay roughly another 266 kuruş to the mullah to ensure his departure for another town.[244]

No matter how striking this episode of violence may have been, the case was not peculiar to this region, but was, rather, an Empire-wide phenomenon. This was both the immediate result of the collapse of Ottoman central authority in the Balkans, as well as a typical episode in the era of the irregular military corps raised in the Empire. The long-lasting period of internal struggle in eastern Anatolia presents similar episode, and sometime there was the legitimate authority who acted like outlaws. It was in Erzurum, in 1816, that some mounted irregulars came into the employment of a certain Baba Paşa, who sent them to the Georgian borderland to lay siege to the fortress of Ahıska occupied by a *paşa* whom the Porte had declared an outlaw. Weeks later, the irregulars accused the *paşa* of deceiving them and their comrades into believing that they would be paid salaries for their services, when indeed, the *paşa* had no intention of paying them and simply abandoned them along with 15,000 other irregular soldiers.[245]

In other provinces, the situation was not less critical, since at the beginning of the nineteenth century the Porte lost control of many of the Empire's outer zones. A serious crisis began in 1803 when the Wahhabis, led by the Saudi emirs, took control of the Hejaz, Mecca and Medina, and maintained control of some centres until 1814.[246] Even in the Ottoman core provinces, the Balkans and Anatolia, the Sultan's rule was under threat. The Serb uprising of 1804 marked the beginning of a series of wars of national liberation.

---

244 Uğur Bayraktar, 'From salary to resistance', p.879: 'At about the same time, Torkullu Mehmed Sipahi was intimidating the inhabitants of Stip in order to become the notable of the town.'

245 Esmer U. Tolga, 'The Confessions of an Ottoman Irregular: Self-Representation and Ottoman Interpretive Communities in the Nineteenth Century' in *Osmanlı Araştırmaları – The Journal of Ottoman Studies*, XLIV (2014), p.320.

246 Ágoston and Bruce, *Encyclopedia of the Ottoman Empire*, p.594.

Meanwhile Ottoman power in Egypt was challenged by the Mamluk emirs and by the French invasion of 1789–1802. Finally, in 1805, Kavalalı Mehmet Ali, an Albanian mercenary of the Sublime Porte, seized power in Egypt. Relying upon his European-style army, he held power for 40 years, becoming Muhammad Ali. In several respects, the military history of Egypt exemplifies the trajectory of this complex phenomenon of transformation of Ottoman army and society between the end of the eighteenth and the beginning of the nineteenth century. This trajectory was decisively shaped by another clash with Western Europe, this time represented by revolutionary France.

Less known, but no less disruptive and historically significant, was the autonomy experienced by the *eyalet* of Diyarbakir in 1808, under Şeyhzâde İbrahim (1747 or 1748–1814). İbrahim's visionary project was aimed not so much at overthrowing Imperial power, but at transforming the Ottoman state into a great federation of peoples. The experience ended in 1819 with the siege of Diyarbakir, which surrendered to the Ottoman army under Behram Paşa after three months of hard fighting.[247]

The Egyptian *Ocaks*

Egypt had not been an easy province to govern. The Mamluk class was still strongly entrenched in the key posts of the state and enjoyed privileges granted to no other ethnic group in the Empire.[248] In addition, Bedouin nomads and aggressive Arab clans were a constant source of unrest and instability.[249] Thus,

---

247 The only surviving source giving a detailed account of the events is the manuscript of Haci Regeb Bey, who survived the siege and spent the rest of his life in exile. The Diyarbakir 'Commune' was an unfinished revolution at the end of the old regime. Among the Ottoman stoics, Cevdet Paşa devotes a few pages of his *Tarihi* to the federation and its eventual defeat in 1819. Later historians show little sympathy for the cause of İbrahim's followers. In their descriptions of events, they suggest that the armed intervention ordered by the Porte was a consequence of feuds between the local elites and the local Kurdish tribes. See Ariel Salzmann, *Tocqueville in the Ottoman Empire. Rival Paths to the Modern State* (Leiden-Boston MS: Brill, 2004).

248 Bruno Mugnai, *Wars and Soldiers in the Early Reign of Louis XIV, Volume Three: The Armies of the Ottoman Empire* (Warwick: Helion and Company, 2020), p.23: 'After the occupation of Egypt in 1517, the Ottomans replaced the Mamluk Sultan with a *beglerbeg* sent from Constantinople, but the social structure of the province remained unchanged. The Ottomans were pragmatic and realised that the special nature of the Egyptian economy favoured minimal intervention in its administration. Then, Egypt did not become a regular Ottoman province; the *timar* system, which marked the full integration of a province into the Empire, was never applied there, and the province was registered in the *salyane* category alongside Baghdad, Basra, Yemen and Habesh. The governor received an annual salary, the *khazina* (or *khazna*), which he drew from the Egyptian treasury in accordance with the aforementioned *salyane* category. This office was considered one of the most important of the Empire, and often the Egyptian *beglerbeg* was promoted to the grand vizierate after completing his term in the province.'

249 Around 1740 the Hawwara, under the leadership of Shaykh Humam, extended its control in Western Egypt. The Shaykh Humam's rise to power was impeded by the strong rule of the

Egypt was an ideal political laboratory for a leader who could exploit the circumstances and transform the province into an independent state.[250]

The deterioration of Ottoman authority in eighteenth-century Egypt becomes evident, focusing the waning of the governors' influence within the Egyptian political scenario. Though the Ottoman *vali* (governor) was still a central figure in the violent dramas being enacted in Cairo, he could act into a very limited space. These limitations turned him into a hostage of the country's influential potentates. The governor took sides in the factional strife, and continuous riots occurred after the civil war of 1711, trying to manipulate different forces for his own political and financial gain. As leading authority in the province, he benefited substantially from the extensive purges in the ranks of the warring military grandees, because all newly appointed office-holders – the *kashif*s, *multazim*s and the like – had to pay him the *hulwan* tax. Some strong governors did not hesitate to resort to the most drastic measures. In the upheavals during which many emirs were executed, assassinated, or fled the country, the Porte was keen to get hold of their possessions.[251] Numerous decrees were dispatched to Egypt, warning against neglecting this matter, and special agents of the central Treasury were sent to make certain that Constantinople got its share. The governor was formally the head of all military forces in the province, but even in this matter, his authority was limited by many factors.

In the eighteenth century the army of Egypt was still organised in the traditional seven *ocaks*, corps: two of infantry and five of cavalry. The infantry *ocaks* were the *mustahfizan-i qal'a-i misir* (guardians of the citadel), later known as Cairo's janissaries, and the *azabs*, organised like their European and Anatolian counterparts. The mounted corps were the *sipahis*, and included two elite units, the *muteferrika* and *cavuş* corps, who naturally were the best paid. The fifth corps was the *cherakise*, the Circassians; then the other two corps were the *gonullu* and the *tüfenk*, light horseman equipped with firearms. These latter corps were formed by local recruits. In the early eighteenth century the Egyptian *ocaks* were typical Ottoman garrisons, although a particularly large, strong force of approximately 10,000 men, of which about 8,800 were 'native Egyptians' and formed the permanent

---

Ottoman governor Ketkhüda Ibrahim, but after his death in 1754, Hawwara's control of the Sa'id was undisturbed. See Michael Winter, *Egyptian Society under Ottoman Rule 1517–1798* (New York, London: Routledge, 1992), p.102.

250 Daniel Crecelius, 'Egypt in the Eighteenth Century' in M. W. Daly (ed.), *The Cambridge History of Egypt, Volume 2, Modern Egypt, from 1517 to the end of the twentieth century* (Cambridge: Cambridge University Press, 2008): 'The Ottoman central government had already lost its ability to direct the affairs of Egypt in the seventeenth century as most of the leading positions within the administration and the garrison corps (*ojaqat*, sing. *ojaq*) had been taken by Emirs.'

251 This emerges clearly in the words of Bakir Pasha (1728–9), concerning the accounts of Mehmet Pasha, his predecessor. The latter claimed that his balance was merely 275 purses (*kises*), but Bakir refused to give him a receipt in full, saying: 'This man was the governor of Egypt for seven years, and has killed 40 *sanjaq beyis* and 12 *ketkhudas*, *aghas*, and other officers'. See Winter, *Egyptian Society Under Ottoman Rule*, p.8.

military force.²⁵² Some 1,000 troops, a tenth of the army, were stationed in Upper Egypt alone. Usually, the Ottoman governor disposed of a lifeguard of about 400 Turkish horsemen, known as *müteferriqa*, from which key officials of the Egypt's administration had been selected. During the century, the *ocaks*' strength increased with the entry of fictitious recruits, as happened in Constantinople, reaching a paper strength of 18,309 men in 1797.²⁵³

The agreed conditions between Mamluk elites and the Porte included the sending of the annual remittance to Constantinople and some points concerning the Ottoman army stationed in Egypt. The most important concerned the demand that a contingent of soldiers – usually up to 3,000 men – join the army for the campaigns in Asia, Europe or the Mediterranean. Moreover, the Mamluk *beys* could gather their own contingents, which in the late eighteenth century numbered on paper about 40,000 horse and foot,²⁵⁴ but possibly the actual military strength was 20,000 in all.²⁵⁵ However, these figures are recurrent when reports refer to military contingents in Egypt. In the 1770s the famous Mamluk chief Ali Bey el-Kabir, from Abkhazia, reputedly had 25,000 to 40,000 troops at his disposal.²⁵⁶ However, the actual strength is difficult to establish with accuracy, not least because each Mamluk household had his own *saraçes* or assistants, who could number a third of the whole force.²⁵⁷ Some estimates suggest that the average Mamluk cavalry corps numbered from a minimum of 500 to 1,000 or more horsemen under the command of a *bey*, whose 'power and influence were proportionate to the number of Mamalukes [sic] that composed their household.'²⁵⁸ Morier and Walsh report that each corps had its own officer staff, which comprised one *cashefs* as a *bey*'s lieutenant, who was a vassal-lord governing five or six villages within the district of his master. There were also junior officers with the rank of *gindees*.²⁵⁹

---

252 Winter, *Egyptian Society Under Ottoman Rule*, p.38.

253 Aksan, *Ottoman Wars*, p.232.

254 Temel Öztürk, 'Egyptian Soldiers in Ottoman Campaigns from the Sixteenth to the Eighteenth Centuries' in *War in History* (vol. 23, 2016), p.17.

255 Volnay, *Voyage en Syrie et en Égypte*, vol. I, p.114. The same author reports that in October 1783, Ibrahim Bey only had under his command 3,000 Mamluk horsemen. According to Daniel Crecelius, in the 1770s the Mamluk chief Aly Bey reputedly had 25,000 to 40,000 soldiers (*The Roots of Modern Egypt: A Study of the Regimes of 'Ali Bey al-Kabir and Muhammad Bey Abu al-Dhahab, 1760–1775* (Studies in Middle Eastern History, number 6 – Chicago, Bibliotheca Islamica, 1981), p.55).

256 Daniel Crecelius, *The Roots of Modern Egypt*, p.55. In 1769, Ali Bey deposed the Ottoman governor, and challenged the sultan by refusing to submit the annual tribute to Istanbul, even though he did send the 3,000-troop contingent to the campaigns unfolding in the Balkans in the same year.

257 Volnay, *Voyage en Syrie et en Égypte*, vol. I, p.117.

258 Walsh, *Journal of the Late Campaign in Egypt*, p.172.

259 Walsh, *Journal of the Late Campaign in Egypt*, p.172, and Morier, *Memoir of a Campaign with the Ottoman Army in Egypt*, p.16.

THE OTTOMAN ARMY OF THE NAPOLEONIC WARS 1789–1815

Upper Egypt chief, from *The Military Costume of Turkey*, by Thomas McLean (1818). Mercenaries from the Upper Nile and Sudan joined the Mamluks from the beginning of the French invasion in 1798. In the following decades, Muhammad Ali turned to this source during his infamous campaign of recruitment in Sudan for his personal army.

Other cavalry contingents grew from similar backgrounds and contexts, such as the clan-based warriors who characterised some areas in Syria and Druze Lebanon.[260] Nomadic groups of Turkmens or Bedouins might serve as temporary local mounted contingents, or protectors of the caravan routes. Inter-tribal warfare made that kind of force problematic for the Ottomans, and the centrally appointed governors often found themselves pawns of local events. A third kind of local force commonly seen elsewhere were the *levends*: cavalry of mostly Anatolian and Balkan origin, who essentially became soldiers-for-hire when they were demobilised by the Ottoman army itself. They could be Albanians, Kurds, Libyans, or even Maghrebins, the latter also known as *delis*, or the later *başı bozuk* cavalry. Local *ayans*, such as the famous Cezzar Ahmed Paşa, made extensive use of the *levend* horsemen against the French during the campaigns of 1799–1800, as well as independent groups of Bosnians and Albanians. The war of 1798–1802 added the mix of foreign soldiers even with Wahhabi Arabs, who served as seasonal mercenaries.[261] The British artillery officer William Wittman reports that in 1800, the Ottoman–Egyptian army under Ziya Yusuf Paşa comprised janissaries, Albanian *arnavuts*, Mamluks, *delis*, 'Asiatics' (Anatolians), Tatars, Maghrebins, Avarees (Hawwaras), and Bedouin Arabs.[262] In April 1800 Wittman records that a whole contingent of 2,500 Arabs and Hawwara Bedouins joined the Ottoman army under Ziya Yusuf Paşa in Egypt.[263] In the following decades, the ethnic variety further increased with the arrival of Greek pioneers and artillerymen, French deserters from *l'Armée d'Orient*, and, after 1806, Italian renegades and even Scottish and English prisoners of war who converted to Islam and joined Muhammad Ali's army.[264]

The main task of the standing *ocaks* was the control of the internal order of the newly acquired province and the securing of the countryside from the marauding Bedouins. The Porte constantly maintained any effort

---

260 Aksan, *Ottoman Wars*, p.231.
261 Aksan, *Ottoman Wars*, p.231.
262 Wittman, *Travels in Turkey*, p.249.
263 Wittman, *Travels in Turkey*, p.274.
264 Carlo Giglio, 'La Questione Egiziana dal 1798 al 1841', in *Oriente Moderno*, Anno 23, Nr. 11/12 (November–December 1943), pp.45–46.

not to lose control of the Egyptian *ocaks*, because of the local revolts. No appointments, even of the lowest-ranking soldiers, were allowed without confirmation from Constantinople. Initially discipline was extremely severe and insubordination was punishable by dismissal from service or by death. The Porte's thriftiness is also evident when it specified the maximum number of soldier in each *ocak*, and a stern warning is given against enlisting men before a vacancy occurred. However, discipline was very relaxed.[265] The seven *ocaks*, especially the local janissaries, became even more demanding and conditioned the governors' actions. In the eighteenth century the *ocaks* were the most powerful bodies within the Egyptian ruling class. The soldiers of the garrisons used their functions as police officers and guardians of the capital to exploit the most lucrative sources of revenue.[266]

As in Constantinople, where a violent rivalry between janissaries and *sipahis* had arisen, the military history of Egypt was also marked by bitter local factional struggles. In the eighteenth century the military class of Egypt was still divided into two 'households', the *faqariyya* and the *qasimiyya*.[267] The Egyptian household had its own *sancak bey* – chief – and their bond resembled the one existing in the janissary corps.[268] The Ottoman governors attempted to control the two factions by dividing the control of territories and key administrative positions evenly between them. However even a weak governor could make his will prevail if he acted with determination, but the reprisals brought peace for a short time. As happened in other parts of the Empire, economic and financial crisis worsened the scenario. Hurt by inflation, the soldiers tried to compensate themselves by forcing artisans and

---

265 Michael Winter, *Egyptian Society under Ottoman Rule 1517–1798* (New York and London: Routledge, 1992), p.57.

266 Winter, *Egyptian Society*, p.57. To sum up the relations between Constantinople and Egypt: the Porte had three objectives in Egypt, namely recognition of the Sultan, payment of the *khazina* tribute, and dispatch of Egyptian troops to the Ottoman wars, were attained in the eighteenth century. But the fulfilment of each of these objectives underwent considerable erosion.

267 Winter, *Egyptian Society*, p.39: 'A myth mentioned in the introduction of 'Abd al-Rahman al-Jabarti's history of Ottoman Egypt, explains that the eponyms of these factions were two young Mamluks, whose competition as horsemen before Sultan Selim I developed into bitter strife. In fact, the Qasimiyya and the Faqariyya are not mentioned before the beginning of the seventeenth century, and the appearance of the two factions and their rivalry is related to the advent of the beylicate. Each faction had its Bedouin allies: the Faqariyya, the Sa'd; the Qasimiyya, the Haram. Among the *ocak*s, the Azabs were traditionally Qasimis, whereas the majority of the janissaries were Faqaris.'

268 Though in Egypt the title *sancakbeg*, or *bey*, never acquired a territorial connotation, local elites controlled territories and the people linked to them like clients and protégées. It was the intention of the Ottoman government that the number of *beys* in Egypt should not exceed 12, yet it is obvious from numerous decrees that, contrary to the Porte's wish, the number reached at least 40 in some periods.

tradesmen into partnerships, extorting protection money in the cities and imposing an illegal tax, the *tulba*, on the peasants.[269]

The central government's inability to block takeover of its administration by local households resulted from its loss of a loyal garrison. Prominent power had passed from the *muteferriqa* corps, the small cadre of Ottoman troops attached to the governor's suite, to the janissaries, and to a lesser degree to the *azab* corps, both of which had their barracks in the Citadel of Cairo. Locally based household leaders had penetrated the highest ranks of these and other Ottoman corps and already by the early eighteenth century had filled virtually half the ranks with Mamluks from their own households.[270] As this process continued, the corps were completely debilitated. In 1786 the Ottoman governor Ghazi Hasan Paşa tried unsuccessfully to reconstitute the *azabs*, but there is no evidence that the corps were part of the army that faced the French invasion in 1798. Although each corps might still be headed by an *ağa*, effective command was in the hands of a locally appointed *katkhuda*, an officer appointed for one year, during which he was known as *katkhuda alwaqt*. These officers and their sub-commanders had previously derived profits from control of urban tax-farms in Cairo and surroundings.[271] This financial strength made the janissary corps the dominant power in Egypt too, and its senior officers played a leading role in the politics of the capital.

A third, more relevant, element made the Egyptian scenario even more complex and insidious. The Mamluks had long been a stable and dominant group in Egypt, yet they continued to fill their ranks with recruits coming from a wide variety of countries. A lesser immigration of Circassians and Georgians continued to provide leadership for the Mamluk households in the second half of the eighteenth century. Another ethnic group, Russians captured during the Ottoman wars and sent into military slavery in Egypt, represented a distinct social body in the Mamluk ranks, particularly in the household of Ibrahim Bey, during the last decade of the century.[272] A fourth group comprising Anatolian Turks came to Egypt in the 1700s.[273] Indifferent to their origins, the Mamluks considered themselves as *khushdāsh*, namely 'brothers in arms'.

---

269 Jane Hathaway, *A Tale of Two Factions. Myth, Memory, and Identity in Ottoman Egypt and Yemen* (Albany NY: State University of New York Press, 2003), p.6.

270 Stanford J. Shaw, *The Financial and Administrative Organisation and Development of Ottoman Egypt, 1517–1798* (Princeton NJ: Princeton Legacy Library, 1958), p.8.

271 Through supervision of the Suez customs the janissaries had become involved in the immensely lucrative coffee and spice trade of the Red Sea. As their power increased, they competed with the beys for control of agricultural tax-farms. See Crecelius, 'Egypt in the Eighteenth Century', pp.62–63.

272 Winter, *Egyptian Society*, p.51.

273 Peter Malcolm Holt, 'The pattern of Egyptian Political History from 1517–1798', in P. M. Holt (ed.), *Political and Social Change in Modern Egypt* (London: Routledge, 1968), p.84. The author suggests that the various households at the beginning of the eighteenth century were to some extent based on ethnic solidarity. The *Fiqariyya* were of Circassian origin; the *Qasimiyya* had a noticeable Bosnian connection; and the *Qazdagliyya* enrolled Anatolian Turks.

Some changes occurred as a consequence of the rivalry between the households. The two great households, the *faqariyya* and the *qasimiyya*, were superseded by the mid eighteenth century by a new combination of households, both of which had their origins in the late seventeenth to early eighteenth centuries as allies of the *faqariyya* household. The lesser household, the *jalfiyya*, was led by officers of the rank of *katkhuda* in the *azab* corps, while the dominant household, the *qazdagliyya*, traced its origins to Mustafa al-Qazdagli, who had been a janissary *katkhuda*. *Qazdagliyya* leaders, while continuing to base their power in the janissary corps, advanced increasing numbers of personal Mamluks to the rank of *sancak bey*, a policy that had enormous consequences for the subsequent history of Egypt. In the confusion and factional strife of the 1770s and 1780s the Ottomans were able to re-establish a relationship with the *qazdaglis* which lasted until the French invasion in 1798, but which did not include secure administrative control of such an important province.

By the mid eighteenth century most of the Cairo *ocaks* had come under the control of Mamluk households, and were packed with local residents seeking to benefit from the salaries and protection of the corps. In the following years the Mamluks enfeebled the Ottoman garrisons, took control of the financial administration of Egypt, and seized revenues assigned to the corps. Meanwhile, when other provincial leaders – such as Cezzar Ahmed (known locally as Ahmad al-Jazzar) in Palestine – were creating autonomous regimes and instituting new economic policies, the Mamluk *beys* plotted an autonomous foreign policy by means of which they once more tried to make Egypt independent from Constantinople. Egyptian households founded by freeborn adventurers successfully combined Mamluk *beys* and freeborn Muslims holding key offices in the garrison corps, but the second half of the eighteenth century saw this system evolve into a powerful Mamluk regime in which freeborn members were excluded from leadership.[274] By the mid eighteenth century the Egyptian household system also resembled the Ottoman-style client system. The distinct style of the Mamluks, however, was that membership of the households was said to be restricted to formally manumitted slaves, largely from the Caucasus.[275]

So long as the governors were able to maintain such a balance, the Ottoman treasury secured sufficient revenues to fulfil its financial needs in Egypt, and was content to leave the actual functioning of the government in the hands of the Mamluks. But after 1779, Egypt fell under the control of a Mamluk coalition led by Murad and Ibrahim *Beys*, who ruled almost continuously for the rest of the century. For a time they continued to pay their taxes and tribute. But once they had eliminated their rivals and established virtually unopposed rule after 1783, they reduced and largely ended their payments. Only then did the Porte send a military expedition to curb them, under the leadership of the *kapudan paşa*, Gazi Hasan Paşa, in the spring of 1787. His object was not to restore direct Ottoman administration since he was well

---

[274] Crecelius, 'Egypt in the Eighteenth Century', p.64.
[275] Aksan, *Ottoman Wars*, p.232.

Caricature illustrating the introduction of the 'French method of training' in the Ottoman army, in a British print dated 1797 (author's archive).

aware that the Porte would lack the power to enforce such a position once his expeditionary force returned to Constantinople. Rather he sought only to restore the various Mamluk factions so they would be able to administer the country while paying for the governor's encouragement and support. Since the outbreak of a new war with Russia forced Gazi Hasan to leave before he could bring about a satisfactory solution, it was not long before Murad and Ibrahim returned to power. Since the defence of the northern borders obsessed the inner circle in Constantinople, the Egyptian theatre remained a crisis front, but secondary.[276]

The most powerful confederation of Bedouins was the Hawwara, which was sedentary and dominated the entire area of Upper Egypt from its capital at Farshut. Hawwara *shaykhs* maintained close relations with the authorities in Cairo, purchased positions in the military garrisons and accepted clientele, hence protection, from garrisons' officers. Relations between the Hawwara *shaykhs* and the janissary corps were particularly close.[277]

---

276 Aksan, *Ottoman Wars*, p.235.
277 Crecelius, 'Egypt in the Eighteenth Century', p.66.

The French invasion of 1798 was the detonator that exploded the contradictions existing in the old skeletons of Egyptian-Ottoman *ocaks* and Mamluk households. The Mamluk army that faced the French on 21 July 1789 in the famous Battle of the Pyramids appears as a result of adaptations and compromises, since it comprised household cavalry as well as *fellahin* militia acting as infantry.[278] The struggle that unfolds after 1800 concerns the last of the great Mamluk households, local Bedouin groups, and the imported Albanian soldiers who constituted a good proportion of the Ottoman armies sent to Egypt. However, during the short time they ruled in Egypt, the French removed the old ruling class. It was replaced by native Muslims, in particular by the village chiefs and members of the *ulema* and by the Coptic intendants. The Mamluks who had dominated the country for two centuries lost not only their positions in the army, but also their revenues so that even when they returned after the French left the country, they found the entire basis of their power undermined.[279]

The Ottoman governor of Egypt was caught in the middle unless he was able to construct an alliance with the local brokers, because at the moment he had no other solution than to resort to the mercenaries provided by the *ayans*. As chance would have it, among the chiefs of the relief army there was a commander with not only military talent but also considerable political skills. Though he is considered the father of modern Egypt, Muhammad Ali was a leader whose objective was to aggrandise his personal position, and his main objective was not the creation of a new Egyptian nation, but the creation of a domain for him and his sons. Though in the period from 1801 through 1818, the composition of the military force in Egypt was a mixture of ethnic Albanian mercenaries and native Egyptian recruits,[280] Muhammad Ali resorted to other sources of manpower, including those who were unrelated to him. Initially he was largely dependent on the Albanian *arnavuts* who had been supplied to him from the Porte. They were mercenaries supplied and paid for by Constantinople, and at least until 1803 were loyal to the Sultan, not Muhammad Ali. The largest contingent of Albanian mercenaries was under the command of Çarhaci Tahir Paşa, and numbered about 2,000 men.[281] These and the other mercenary *bölüks* constituted the core of the expeditionary force that include Muhammad Ali, which totalled 8,000 men with five guns in April 1800.[282]

After the French army left Egypt in 1801, the Muhammad Ali's task was to protect Egypt from another foreign invasion. Ali sought to transform his

---

278 Fahmy, *All the Pasha's Men*, p.96.
279 Shaw, *Between Old and New*, p.262: 'Their revenues and positions were in the hands of native Egyptians who had been shown for the first time that it was to their benefit and interest to manage the affairs of their own country, a lesson which was not lost on them in the years which followed.'
280 'Egyptian' simply means coming from Egypt and not necessarily ethnically Egyptian.
281 Örenç, 'Albanian Soldiers in the Ottoman Army', p.504. Tahir Paşa, or Thir Paşa, was an ethnic Albanian born in Kavala, son of the older sister to the future Muhammad Ali of Egypt.
282 Wittman, *Travels in Turkey*, p.276.

Ebubekir Ratıb Efendi (1720?–1799), the principal supporter of the *nizâm-ı cedîd* reform. The path of reform was long and difficult, and faced many obstacles, not only from the traditional military corps, but also from large sectors of the bureaucracy and the religious. However, there were some among the senior officials who supported the policy of Selim III. Ebubekir Ratıb Efendi served as temporary ambassador to Vienna in 1791–1792, and at the end of his mission he wrote a very detailed memorandum on the military, economic and social organisation of the European states in that time. There are also recommendations to the Sultan on basic issues such as reducing the budget deficit, introducing postage stamps, developing domestic trade and domestic arts, and promoting the use of domestic goods. With him, Tatarcikzade Abdullah Efendi, the oldest of Selim's major advisor, was another important supporter. Born in 1730, he was son of a member of the *ulema*, and himself a judge in Jerusalem, Cairo, and Medina before Selim III came to the throne. He served as *kadiasker* (judge) of the army during the campaigns of 1789. A firm advocate of reform in his own profession, he also became an expert on military matters and helped to direct the reorganisation and modernisation of the Imperial cannon foundry as well as instruct the soldiers of the artillery corps in the new ways until his death in 1797.

army into a personal army corps by mandating training and other performances outside of their orders by The Porte. After a brief period of success, Muhammad Ali encountered determined resistance once the Albanian troops recognised he sought to transform them into a regular army. The loss of trust in them seems to emerge in 1811, when he assembled 14,000 'Turks' and Maghribis for the campaign in the Hijaz against the Wahhabis.[283] However, one year later, he relied on the Albanians for the campaigns of 1812 and 1818. For the campaign of 1818, Muhammad Ali gathered a composite corps of 2,500 men, which included Maghribis, Sudanese, Greeks and even Armenians, mixed with the last Albanians still in service.[284] The campaign encountered serious logistical problems and the expeditionary force resulted in a badly trained soldiery.[285]

The introduction of regular training sessions was another difficult problem to solve. The Albanian troops were initially gathered by Muhammad Ali in Cairo for training, which essentially consisted of firing volley shots at static targets within the confines of the Citadel. This method approximated the French system. However, it was after a number of training sessions that the Albanians began to oppose resistance to regular training, but Muhammad Ali relied on them to capture and enslave Sudanese men, whom he wanted to use in an army structure once the Albanians proved unwilling to become a force under his command. Muhammad Ali hastily decided on the transition from the Albanian corps to utilising Sudanese recruits once he encountered Albanian opposition and recognised that they were verging on insurrection.

---

283 Pascal Ghazaleh, 'Governance in transition: Competing immigrant networks in early nineteenth-century Egypt', in I. Freitag, M. Fuhnnann, N. Lafi, F. Riedler (eds), *The City in the Ottoman Empire. Migration and the Making of Urban Modernity* (London – New York, NY: Routledge, 2011), p.140.

284 Fahmy, *All the Pasha's Men*, p.46.

285 Henry Dodwell, *Founder of Modern Egypt – a Study of Muhammed 'Ali* (Cambridge: Cambridge University Press, 1967), p.48.

During the war against the French the Mamluks resorted to Sudanese recruits, but most of them entered the service as volunteers. Collecting recruits in Sudan was also becoming a difficult and costly task. It was not long before Muhammad Ali realised that the army sent to Sudan was much larger than the number of slaves captured, which defeated the purpose for which it was sent in the first place, and so it was decided that for every 1,000 soldiers employed 3,000 slaves must be collected. However, even this principle now did not make sense, since those who had been collected were in very poor health and were dying 'like sheep with the rot'.[286] Furthermore, the Sudanese recruits were understandably unwilling to serve as soldiers. It soon became obvious to the *Paşa* that something was going drastically wrong with his plans to raise an army this way. When, for example, he knew that out of 2,400 slaves arriving in Aswan only 1,245 managed to reach Cairo, he said 'We spend so much energy to fetch these slaves, healthy and capable of work, from remote areas only to perish in our midst and in front of our eyes.'[287] In desperation, Muhammad Ali wrote to Boghus Bey, his Armenian adviser on foreign affairs, ordering him to hire a number of American physicians to treat the slaves. These were preferred to Europeans since they had experience of dealing with 'this race'.[288]

This change in policy occurred after 1815 and initiated a process that would culminate between 1820 and 1822 with the creation of a regular 'Egyptian army'. During this period the army was no longer Mamluk–Albanian but rather Albanian–Sudanese. There are indications that already in 1810 Muhammad Ali attempted to conceal his project to raise a modern army.[289] Initially he imitated the Ottoman *nizâm-ı cedîd* reforms and even called his new army by the same name, but later, with the arrival of foreign experts who were mainly French officers, the Egyptian reforms changed course.[290] During this period Muhammad Ali communicated to various subordinates that he wished to purge the Albanians from the army. Therefore, when the Porte ordered him to support the war effort in the Hijaz against the Wahabbis he immediately sent his mixed contingent in 1812 to

Gunner of the *nizâm-ı cedîd* army, by Antoine-Laurent Castellan, *Moeurs, Usages, Costumes des Othomans* (1812). The opening of new military technical schools and restructuring of the artillery corps were followed by the foundation of the infantry of the *nizâm-ı cedîd* army in 1794, on the European model with Western-style uniforms, equipment, and – most significantly – modern military training.

---

286 Fahmy, *All the Pasha's Men*, pp.88–89.
287 Fahmy, *All the Pasha's Men*, p.89.
288 Fahmy, *All the Pasha's Men*, p.89.
289 James Bowden, 'The Army of Egypt in the Years 1801–1832', in *History & Uniforms N. 7* (2016), p.70.
290 Uyar and Erickson, *A Military History of the Ottomans*, p.127.

deal with this. The remaining Albanian corps were used in Sudan for the enslavement process.[291]

At the same time as the Albanians were beginning to leave Egypt, Muhammad Ali moved away from the former method of training and instituted different types of training for the Sudanese recruits. It appears that at this stage two training camps were established, one at Farshut and one at Aswan, along the Nile.[292] From 1815–1822 Sudanese conscription was still the active policy of Muhammad Ali and the army would continue to enlist Mamluk, Albanian, and Sudanese recruits, however, the traditional problems of rampant disease and high mortality still, and quite literally, plagued the men. It was in 1822 that Muhammad Ali began to look for an alternative and found it in the native *fellahin*.[293]

The Ottoman 'New Model Army'

The eighteenth century witnessed experimentation with various forms of recruitments and military systems in the Ottoman Empire, ranging from standing troops to state-contracted mercenaries, and private contractors, leading to the *nizâm-ı cedîd ordusu* – New Order Army – of Sultan Selim III.[294] When Selim III succeeded his father in April 1789 he found the Empire embroiled in a disastrous war with Russia and Austria, already in progress for over a year, and his long-awaited plans for reform had to be subordinated to more pressing military needs. On 17 May 1789, a little over a month after Selim came to the throne, he inaugurated his reforms by calling a general consultative council of notables, which met in the Revan Pavilion of the Topkapı Palace. Over 200 leaders of the ruling class, comprising judges

---

291 Bowden, 'The Army of Egypt in the Years 1801–1832', p.71.

292 Fahmy, *All the Pasha's Men*, p.85 and p.97. The first attempt of conscripting the Egyptian *fellahin* stemmed from the desire to relieve the Ottoman soldiers in Muhammad Ali's pay from serving in the remote and hot lands of the Sudan. The 4,000 peasants who were gathered from villages in Upper Egypt to replace the Albanians were to be conscripted for only three years at the end of which they would each be given a stamped certificate and allowed to return to their villages and resume their normal, civilian lives.

293 Bowden, 'The Army of Egypt in the Years 1801–1832', p.87: 'What is presented here is the emergence of a pattern that would engender much confusion. The Albanians had presented resistance of an unexpected nature to Muhammed's methods and his intentions. The execution of the process, however, would involve an indistinct transition that was overlapped by various sub-plots and motivations. The contemporary documents also tend to portray several different currents of thought in Ali's mind at this time. Mostly, it is a distinct break between the written instructions and the benevolence conveyed in those instructions and the hard reality of their execution. Ali never worked to redress the failure of carrying out his instructions.'

294 Ágoston and Masters, *Encyclopedia of the Ottoman Empire*, p.434: 'By the reign of Selim III (r. 1789–1807), the general term *nizâm-ı cedid*, which the Ottomans had hitherto used to describe minor administrative and financial reforms, took on a new meaning: the opposite of *nizâm-ı kadim*, an ambiguous term signifying the traditional Ottoman system.'

THE ARMIES OF THE SULTAN

A private soldier of the first regiment of the *nizâm-ı cedîd* army, portrayed in the *The Military Costume of Turkey*, by Thomas McLean (1818). This is the best known images of these troops, but contemporary Ottoman iconography shows a slightly different version of the same uniform.

and administrators, scribes and teachers, active and retired military officers and veteran soldiers, were invited to discuss what could be done to save the Empire.[295] However, it was only after peace was concluded in 1792 that the Sultan and his associates could move ahead to examine the ills of the Empire and attempt to solve them. The war ended in another military frustration, but diplomatic success was the background to Selim's achievements and failures in the following years.

Launched in the aftermath of the war, the reforms had to involve military, financial and administrative branches of the Empire.[296] While the entire reform is said to have included 72 clauses on a variety of topics ranging

---

295 Shaw, *Between Old and New. The Ottoman Empire under Sultan Selim III, 1789–1807* (Harvard, MA: Harvard University Press, 1971), p.73.

296 After the reorganisation of the Empire in 28 provinces, promotion and appointment in the civil service were governed by new rules; attempts were made at economic development; in particular, encouragement was given to the consumption of locally produced goods, in an effort to reduce the effect of the capitulations. The first permanent embassies were also established in Paris, London. Berlin and Vienna. See also Somel, Selcuk Aksin, *Historical Dictionary of the Ottoman Empire* (Lanham, MD: Scarecrow Press, 2003), p.216.

from the military and judicial institutions to the central and provincial administration, the most tangible results of the *nizâm-ı cedîd* were seen in the spheres of the military and diplomacy. The formal *nizâm-ı cedîd* reform programme was carried out by a dedicated reform committee that secretly worked in 1796 to implement more than 20 reform proposals in all, the most influential of which was the report on the Habsburg Empire written by Ebubekir Ratıb Efendi, who had been the Ottoman ambassador to Vienna.[297]

The reforms provided for the raising of a new, well-trained, European-style army equipped with up-to-date weaponry, dressed in modern uniforms, and financed by funds from an independent treasury.[298] Recruitment had to involve only Anatolian Turks, preferably peasants and tribesmen.[299] Early on the Balkans were excluded as an area for recruitment, since the strong *ayans* were opposed to the reform programme that threatened their mercenary business. The new army was organised as a 'National Guard' force rather than a professional standing army in the Western sense, but the project had been carefully examined in order to raise an efficient standing force. From a historical point of view, this was an event of the utmost importance, because for the first time in Ottoman history, the Turkish peasants of Anatolia would be conscripted into the military service on a large scale. The original plan provided that once trained, the peasants would be stationed near their own homes, but under the command of these central government officers rather than the governors, and supported both by the Central Treasury of Constantinople and provincial sources. The plan forecast that within eight years a force of about 42,000 men could be prepared in this way.[300] Other advisors expressed a different opinion. In order to provide the new soldiers with European officers and instructors, food, clothing, supplies, and modern weapons, and to make them into the new military elite, the corps had to be a standing force. In return, the recruits of this new corps would agree to serve the Empire all their lives, to remain unmarried so they could live in their barracks at all times, and to pledge loyalty to the Sultan. To avoid trouble with the older corps, this new unit would be attached to the *bostanci* at the start until it had 20,000 to 30,000 well-trained infantry and artillery,

---

297 The committee included all the major advisors of the Sultan, comprised two foreigners, the well-known Armenian chief dragoman of the Swedish Embassy in Istanbul, Mouradgea d'Ohsson, and a French artillery officer named Bertrand, one of the French officers who trained the Ottoman *humbaragi* corps.

298 Bombaci and Shaw, *L'Impero Ottomano*, p.467: 'To finance this project, a special budget item, called irad-ı cedid (new revenue fund), was created with resources collected from confiscated *timars*, tax collection contracts and previously untaxed land, so as to disturb existing institutions as little as possible. Selim III hoped that the new army would be strong enough to defend the Empire, while avoiding the need to change traditional institutions too drastically. However, he did not consider any extension of the authority of the government, and the extension of reforms to other aspects of state organisation, a feature that would be introduced by his successor Mahmud II after 1826.'

299 Shaw, *Between Old and New*, pp.76–77.

300 Shaw, *Between Old and New*, p.107.

after which it could become fully independent since it would beat off any attacks that might be made. Some of the Sultan's advisors recommended that the members of this corps be given salaries almost twice those paid to the members of the older corps at that time, so the very best men would be attracted to and retained in the new corps, but that this high salary be paid them only so long as they were able to train and participate in battles. If they became old and infirm, they would be retired at once on special pensions provided by the government so their salaries in the corps could be used to pay newly enlisted younger men.[301]

Selim and his intimate circle of consultants launched this radical plan secretly behind the cover of *kapıkulu* reform attempts. The main idea was to establish a modern European-style infantry corps and later use this corps as a core around which a totally modern military could be created. Indeed, the name of the new infantry corps, the *nizâm-ı cedîd* became the name of the entire reform package and era. Fortunately, a quick start was possible because Grand Vizier Koca Yusuf Paşa had already selected 120 deserters and prisoners of war of the Russian and Austrian armies, enlisted with the promise of a non-commissioned officer's post. He collected them into a company-size infantry unit as a personal lifeguard, armed with captured weapons, and conducted several training exercises and manoeuvres. This improvised unit took the first steps towards the creation of a new infantry corps. In April 1792 the company was secretly stationed away from public eyes in barracks near Constantinople, the Levénd Çiftlik, and reinforced with recruits from the unemployed citizens of Constantinople. The British Embassy provided some infantry weapons and equipment, and French soldiers of fortune were hired as trainers and advisors. The new unit secretly continued its training for two more years, wearing dress and distinctions like the *bostanci* gardeners, in order not to create suspicion among the janissaries. For this reason, the corps assumed the denomination *bostanci tüfenktçisi ocaği*. The regiments continued to grow under this camouflage, with the introduction of additional recruits coming from contingents of the Anatolian *ayans*. The first regiment was established in Levénd in 1795, and the second one in Üsküdar in 1799, completed with prisoners of war from the Russian army, especially Poles and other minorities who did not return under the Czar.

With growing confidence, Selim III ordered the establishment of further units, albeit under the control of the *ayans* in Anatolia. At least nine provinces carried out the order, and for the first time recruitment of villagers began. After this strategic decision, the size of the corps rose rapidly from 9,300 in 1801 to 24,000 in 1806.[302] Not all the governors recruited and trained men for the new corps, but nine did, of whom the most active were Abdurrahman Paşa, governor of Karaman and Alaiye, who was appointed *colonel* in 1801. With him, Jebbar Zade and Süleyman Paşa met the *nizâm-ı cedîd* project. Starting

---

301 Shaw, *Between Old and New*, p.108.

302 Stanford J. Shaw, 'Origins of Ottoman Military Reform', in *The Journal of Modern History*, vol. XXXVII (1965), p.297.

in 1802, Abdurrahman Paşa developed a system of military conscription throughout Anatolia to provide men for raising in Karaman nine regiments in all.[303] Each provincial and district official and notable was required to send a certain number of recruits to Üsküdar for training in the new army, for periods of between six months and one year. Generally, half the contingent was trained as infantry for service in the regular Levénd Çiftlik and Üsküdar corps. The other half was trained as cavalry so that they could return to form the local militias of the provincial governors and district notables.[304]

The internal organisation of the regiments followed the traditional European pattern, and some bilingual terms, with one *colonel-binbaşi*, one *lieutenant colonel*, and one *adjutant major* forming the regiment's major staff. These latter rank had the tactical denomination of *ağa-ı yemin* (commander of the right wing) and *ağa-ı yemin* (commander of the left wing), each in charge of a *tabor*, or battalion. *Capitaine-bölükbaşi, lieutenant, sous lieutenant* and *porte drapeau-bayrakdar* were assigned to the companies, which also comprised *çavuş* and *onbaşi* as not-commissioned-officers in Western style.[305] Each *orta*, or regiment, comprised 12 *bölüks* or *compagnie* with 1,602 men in all. To each *bölük* was added one cannon served by eight *topçu* artillerymen, one *top ustasi* cannon master, five *arabaçi* wagoners and six *kullukçu* assistants. The lieutenant of the first company hold the title of *kolağasi*. A music band, an *imam* and a company of artillery were also attached to each regiment.[306] To coordinate the activities of the two regiments, a new rank was created, the *ocak kethüdabaşi* (lieutenant of the corps), and it was given to one of the *binbaşi*s of the two regiments. Two renegades were appointed to command the two regiments, one Greek named Ahmed Ağa, and the other Prussian, Süleyman Ağa.[307] The initial plan was implemented with the transformation of the second regiment into a dragoon unit, but the attempt was abandoned.

While the *nizâm-ı cedîd* reform programme was successful and far-reaching, it was not, of course, without critics. In the battle between supporters and opponents of reform, the pro-reform group presented the modern *nizâm-ı cedîd* troops as an effective instrument against the Russian threat, for during this period the modernisation of Russia had become both a threat to the Ottomans and a model to emulate. Some Ottoman notables regarded Russian reforms as a danger to their own state, but others admired Russia's modern military or saw in the industrialisation and progress of Russia an example for domestic change.[308]

For the government, the outstanding performance of the newly formed infantry in the war against France of 1798–1802 represented the confirmation of the project's success. Soldiers from the two *nizâm* regiments quartered in

---

303 Théophile Lavallée, *Histoire de l'Empire Ottoman* (Paris, 1855), p.432.
304 Shaw, *Between Old and New*, p.132.
305 Rayf Efendi, *Tableau des nouveaux règlements*, note to plate XXVI.
306 Jucherau de Saint-Denys, *Histoire de l'Empire Ottoman*, vol. II, p.113.
307 Jucherau de Saint-Denys, *Histoire de l'Empire Ottoman*, vol. II, p.115.
308 Ágoston, 'Military Transformation in the Ottoman Empire and Russia', p.299.

Constantinople joined the Ottoman expeditionary force in Egypt in 1799. A battalion-size *nizâm* reinforcement turned the tide in the defence of Acre, and the 3,000 well-trained *nefer*-soldiers fought proficiently in the next campaigns, while the remaining Ottoman units performed poorly.[309] In 1800, when the British fleet blockaded the French in Alexandria, 2,000 *nizâm-ı cedîd* soldiers were landed along with 6,000 regular Ottoman troops, and they managed to maintain a successful blockade against the French at Rosetta, eventually forcing them to surrender in April 1801. During the next six years the new army soldiers performed significant, although somewhat limited, service against the mountain bandits in the Balkan and Rhodope Mountains.[310] In 1807 about 2,000 *nizâm-ı cedîd* troops took part on the campaign against the Serbs, and a further 4,000 from the disbanding regiments filled the ranks of the army that faced the Russians in the Principalities until 1808.[311]

After 1804, an effort was made to transform the entire *timar* system into the base for the new order army. The fiction of feudal organisation was preserved by the application of the name *sancakbeğ* to their officers, but these were in fact salaried personnel sent to the provinces by the existing regiments.[312] Because of the war and domestic struggles, the corps, while expanding in size, rapidly became weaker instead of stronger. The government was unable to increase the numbers of trained officers, and except for the original two regiments, all other *nizâm* units became liabilities rather than assets. The newly raised regiments were poorly trained, lacked effective command and control, and, like the retinues of *ayans*, showed limited loyalty to the central government. The commanders encountered difficulty in mobilising them during the campaigns. Furthermore, following in the footsteps of the janissaries they created the same type of problems against civilian populations, such as looting, robbery, and abuse of all sorts. Contemporary European witnesses testify to the unfinished result of the project, when in February 1804 Selim III decided to enforce his New Order in the Balkans, unknowingly triggering a tumultuous chain of events for him and his empire. The failure of *nizâm* units to stabilise the provinces and widen the control of the central government further weakened the reformist camp. It also gave encouragement to increasing opposition against reform, as happened after the failure of the important pro-*nizâm* commander Kadı Abdurrahman Paşa in Konya between 1803 and 1804. Early in 1805, Selim III issued an order for the establishment of a new *nizâm-ı cedîd* military corps in Rumelia to be quartered at Edirne, with men secured by general conscription in the Balkans, but the disastrous attempt to spread the *nizâm* turned into the revolt of 1806. In early June the Balkan notables who refused to cooperate with the sultan's orders formed a strong coalition that fielded a force misleadingly

---

309 Uyar and Erickson, *A Military History of the Ottomans*, p.124.
310 Kabaağaçlızade Ahmed Cévad, *Tarih-i Askeri Osmânî*, vol. II, p.43. The *nizâm-ı cedid* troops formed a 'brigade', comprising the three regiments of Karaman, one of Constantinople, one artillery company and one cavalry company.
311 Jucherau de Saint-Denys, *Histoire de l'Empire Ottoman*, vol. II, p 155.
312 Shaw, *Between Old and New*, p.133.

estimated at 80,000. Selim III delayed sending Abdurrahman and his loyal troops, numbering 15,000–20,000, against them. When they did march in mid July, they were confronted outside Edirne by a force of 10,000 janissaries and *yamaks*. Sustaining considerable losses, the *nizâm-ı cedîd* troops retraced their route to Silivri, a suburb of Constantinople, where they were halted by Selim III himself.[313] In the open conflict between the janissaries and soldiers of the New Order army, the British Ambassador to the Porte, Charles Arbuthnot, described the fight that occurred between them in the streets of Constantinople as follows:

> The janissaries, it is true, were not sufficiently to be depended upon, either in point of obedience or training. Individually, however, they are expert in the use of the weapon to which they have been accustomed, and altho' they are very inferior to the disciplined troops of European powers, it is to be doubted whether they do not preserve some advantage over the soldiers of the New Turkish Institution who have not yet been taught to act with confidence in a collective body, and whose mode of training must debar them from the separate feats of personal prowess by which the janissaries have ever been distinguished.[314]

Despite these failures, the government did not stop its plan to extend the *nizâm-ı cedîd* in the Empire. In Rumelia the last unlucky attempts occurred on 25 May 1807. The rebellion marked the definitive end of the *nizâm-ı cedîd* reforms. Though the government had established a second army parallel to that of the janissaries and provincial troops, the fine-tuning of it was still a long way off. Furthermore, the *nizâm-ı cedîd* army required a restructuring of state finances and administration to favour growth and expansion. The rebels attacked and massacred the *nizâm* soldiers who had been left to their fate by the government. From 1798 to just before this dramatic episode, some 22,700 troops and 1,600 officers had been recruited and quartered in Constantinople.[315]

After his appointment as grand vizier in 1808, Alemdâr Mustafa tried to revitalise the military reforms and enlisted his own mercenaries as 'state soldiers' to form the nucleus of another new army. In the role of kingmaker, the Grand Vizier confidently tried to continue the reforms under a new name, while simultaneously hunting down the rebels. To avoid resistance from the janissaries, the new troops took a different designation: *sekban-ı cedîd*. The nucleus for the new force was the 3,000 foot brought to Constantinople by Kadi Abdurrahman Paşa, to which he added other *nizâm-ı cedîd* survivors and soldiers brought by the other *ayan* leaders convened in the capital in September 1808. The old *nizâm-ı cedîd* barracks were repaired and turned

---

313 Aksan, *Ottoman Wars*, p.244.

314 Fatih Yeşil, 'Drill and Discipline as a Civilizing Process: The Genesis of the Modern Soldier in the Ottoman Empire, 1789–1826', in S. Faroqhi and B. Ergene (eds), *Ottoman War and Peace. Studies in Honor of Virginia H. Aksan* – The Ottoman Empire and Its Heritage Politics, Society and Economy, vol. 68 (Leiden and Boston MS: Brill, 2020), p.101.

315 Aksan, 'War and Peace', p.104.

over to the new corps in October. About 5,000 volunteers were enrolled, and orders were issued for recruitment around the Empire as soon as possible. As commander, the Grand Vizier appointed a former *nizâm-ı cedîd* officer, Süleyman Ağa, but Kadi Abdurrahman Paşa served as actual military leader. While it was not given a separate treasury, a fund was established to secure the necessary revenues managed by the newly established Ministry for Affairs of the Holy War – *umur-u cihadiye nezareti* – a name with particular appeal to the *ulema*. A force of some 160,000 men divided into 100 *bölüks* and three divisions was envisaged, but for the moment, the corps numbered about 10,000 men and officers in all.[316] They had their first engagement on 16 November 1808, during the rebellion against Grand Vizier Alemdâr Mustafa. In the encounter, the *sekban* troops responded with sorties outside the walls of the Topkapı to repulse the janissary assault, but they were not yet fully organised and trained, and against the numerical superiority of the attackers they could not break out of the circle.

Sultan Mahmud II was forced to consent to all the demands of the rebels. The fate of the new corps was the most difficult issue to solve. Finally, after long discussions, on 17 November an agreement was reached by which the *sekban-ı cedîd* would be disbanded, but their members would be allowed to leave the capital without harm, and the sultan would not be required to surrender any of his supporters who had taken refuge in the palace. With the abolition of the corps, all the privileges of *kapıkulu* corps were renewed. As the *sekban* left the palace in accordance with the compromise, disarmed and without their uniforms, they were set upon by those waiting outside, while other mobs attacked and destroyed their barracks, killing those inside. After the destructive janissary rebellions of 1807 and 1808, Sultan Mahmud did not make any overt reform attempts, but waited patiently for the 'Auspicious Event' of 1826.

Supply and Logistics

The Ottomans were justly proud of their supply system. In the seventeenth century the Ottoman army disposed in Europe as well in Asia of a well-established network of warehouses for food and other stuff much earlier than the magazines created by Louvois in the 1670s. While the miseries of war were universal, the sultans' armies were on the whole somewhat better supplied than their European counterparts. Peasants provisioned the stopping points along army routes, and craftsmen were drafted to accompany the soldiers, so as to obviate recourse to urban markets, where military discipline would have been difficult to maintain.

The co-ordination of supplies and the preparation of ammunition and food for the troops fell within the sphere of activity of the supreme financial authority of the Empire, the *defterdar paşa*, who made use of a corps of commissioner-employers, the simple *defterdar*-superintendent, in turn

---

316 Shaw, *History of the Ottoman Empire*, p.3.

THE OTTOMAN ARMY OF THE NAPOLEONIC WARS 1789–1815

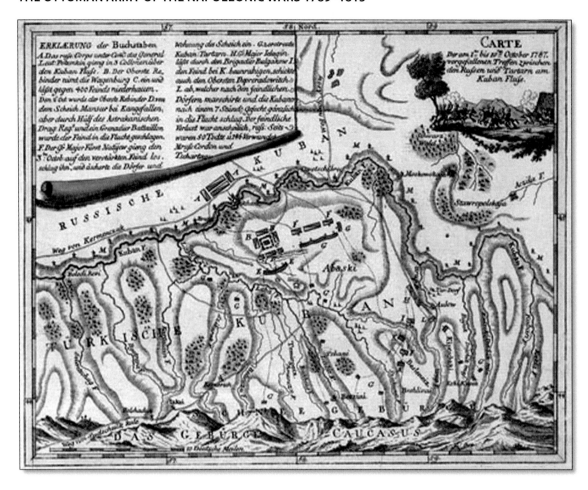

A map showing the actions and positions of the Russians and Tatars in the Kuban region from 1 to 10 October 1787. The map is oriented with north-north-east to top. This is one of 15 numbered maps and views published by Trattnern relating to the Russo-Turkish War of 1787–92 (Royal Collection Trust).

assisted by the administrative officials of the provinces, the *defter katibi*. The army *defterdars* were the administrators responsible for the field army, and occupied an important place in the Empire, since he administered the supply and funds for the local garrisons and other permanent forces. Before each military campaign, in anticipation of the number of men mobilised, a network of supply facilities was set up. Each warehouse had its superintendent, who was also responsible for seeing to the purchase of foodstuff, namely barley, wheat and flour, as well as *peksimed* biscuit. This was shipped from all over the Balkans.[317] Around the warehouse operated the personnel in charge of preparing the necessaries for the army, joined in the *matbah* corps. This term identified the personnel in charge of the provisioning, along with the drivers and other service personnel, usually recruited for a single campaign in the provinces close to the war theatre.

The janissary rations were highly regulated, including clothing allotments and special funds for equipment. Individual corps often had a provisions

---

317 Aksan, 'War and Peace', p.94. In 1769, multiple orders to individual *mubayaacı*-state provisioners indicate the concern of Constantinople about provisioning the fortresses from the recently harvested crops. The orders contain specific cautions about sifting the grain for impurities.

fund, contributed by the members themselves, which served the common good. The *timars* were expected to feed and outfit themselves, but were often given a food ration, or its cash equivalent, at the beginning of a campaign. The irregulars received a similar treatment, and were usually supplied through the network of the *defterdar*s. Both irregulars and *timars* received paid sign-on bonuses, six-month campaign wages and rations. A gratuity often preceded a major battle or siege, and certainly rewarded the especially valorous afterwards. Complaints about the lateness or non-arrival of these 'fringe benefits' were used as excuses for failure to show up on the battlefield, universal problems in all early modern military contexts.[318] All these funds were supplied by the central treasury, although theoretically supported by the local *imdad-ı seferiye* tax.[319] However, given the Empire's limited productivity in agriculture and crafts, this was an expensive way of going to war. Collaboration and negotiation around different needs for the army had the unintended result of aggrandising the many families of magnates, who could speculate on supplies.

Tatar courier, from an Ottoman print published by Eugenio and Raffaele Fulgenzi di Loreto in *Litographie et Taille Douce* (Smyrna, 1838). He wears a dark brown jacket trimmed with white sheepskin on a green doublet, white shirt, multicoloured sash, blue trousers, white embroidered flaps and black boots. The headdress is of black felt with yellow top.

Sustaining the war effort meant considerable investment in other aspects of warfare, such as artillery and its train, as well as transportation of supplies and enlistment of new recruits. This was a common matter of all the coeval armies, but for the Porte resulted in a more expansive need of funds. For this reason, on the European front river transport was a convenient solution and consequently, control of the Danube was vital to supply the breaks in that region. On this river the Porte continued to maintain a war fleet with armed vessels and barges. Every time the Empire was engaged in war, the supply system had to be reactivated after the period of peace and during the wars in Europe, Bosnia and Bulgaria always bore the heaviest load. However, biscuit and foodstuff was requisitioned from as far away as Crete and Egypt by *mübayaacı* state-appointed commissioners and local officials.[320]

After the defeats suffered in the seventeenth and early eighteenth centuries, a large part of the supply network in the Balkan had been destroyed. Then in 1768–74 the war against Russia had meant a neglect of the roads and warehouse systems which guaranteed their ability to function in the eastern border. The collapse of the army supply system in the second half of the eighteenth century seems to have been at the root of the military debacle

---

318 Aksan, 'War and Peace', p.94.

319 Aksan, 'War and Peace', p.104.

320 Aksan, 'War and Peace', p.104.

THE OTTOMAN ARMY OF THE NAPOLEONIC WARS 1789–1815

Left: A Tatar horseman, after Dalvimart's *The Costume of Turkey* (London, 1804). According to the artist, 'no nation throughout the eastern part of the world has preserved the various customs of their ancestors'. Certainly, the essential simplicity of Tatar clothing represented an element of primitiveness in the eyes of Europeans. The predominant use of natural colours also helped to reinforce this impression.

Right: Kurdish Chief, after Carl Max Tilke's *Orientalische Kostüme in Schnitt und Farbe* (Berlin 1923). Kurdish dress had more in common with the Anatolian tribesmen with some influence also from Iraq and Persia. Note the multicoloured turban and embroidered kaftan with loose sleeves.

of those years.³²¹ The war of 1787–92 required the restoration of fortresses, supply depots, and means of transportation which disabled much of the field action of those years. In this regard, the Rayf Efendi's *Tableau des Nouveaux Reglemens de l'Empire Ottoman* complains about the absence of sufficiently stocked warehouses and that the little that did exist was plundered by starving troops. According to the author, in 1790 the Danube route and all border fortresses lacked storages capable of supporting the army in the countryside.³²² Supply warehouses on the south shores of the Danube were absolutely pivotal to the well-being of the Ottoman army as it marched north into the territories between the Prut and the Dniester. In this area, the principal frontline supply depot was at Hantepesi, halfway between Jassy and Chotin. The passage between was punctuated with bivouacs, which were also generally supplied with pack animals and food levied from the countryside.

In each war against Russia, enemy pressure in the Black Sea had the effect of strangulating the Ottoman supply system terminal at Constantinople. For this reason, each time the Porte imposed on the Romanian vassal principalities the provision of supplies for the army. But the limited availability of resource in these territories, as well as the unreliability of their princes, did not allow for adequate supplies for the troops on campaign. Combined with disorderly retreats, and the invidious habit of fleeing troops to plunder their own camps, the renowned Ottoman supply system fell apart. When food, clothing and tents were no longer supplied, soldiers attacked townsmen and villagers in order to provision themselves 'at source'.³²³ Even worse, Orthodox villagers taxed beyond the limits of endurance now tended to side with the Tsar, while in previous centuries, projected incursions into Ottoman territory on the part of Christian rulers had in most cases attracted but minimal support from the sultans' non-Muslim subjects. By the second half of the eighteenth century military demand had reached a level that was simply too high for taxpayers to support any longer. From the Ottoman perspective, it was a major military catastrophe.

During the war of 1768–74 Ahmed Resmi, an acute critic of the state of the Ottoman army and logistics, wrote an interesting essay and submitted it to Grand Vizier Halil Paşa while on the battlefront. It contains a list of 13 issues concerning mobilisation and provisioning that he thought needed attention, following the disasters of the early years of the war. The most significant issues included the problem of Anatolian troops, described as 'a filthy horde

---

321 Virginia H. Aksan, 'War and Peace', p.103.
322 Rayf Efendi, *Tableau des Nouveaux Reglemens*, p.14.
323 Suraya Faroqhi, 'Introduction. Massive Size and Central Control' in in S. Faroqhi (ed.), *The Cambridge History of Turkey, vol. 3 – The Later Ottoman Empire, 1603–1839* (Cambridge: Cambridge University Press, 2006), p.8: 'In all probability the supply system collapsed when it did due to overload. It had long been customary in the Ottoman realm to demand deliveries for the military at prices that in many cases did not even cover production costs. Artisans responded by lowering the quality of their goods, and presumably the grain supplied at stopping points by hapless peasants must often have been inedible.'

Wallachian *boyar*, from *Les portraits des differens habillemens qui sont en usage à Constantinople et dans tout la Turquie* (before 1809). The Romanian elite are described as wearing Ottoman dress, except for the headdress, which for the Wallachian was the *kalpak* of black lambskin, while in Moldavia the cloth bonnet with fur trim was the most common.

of thieves and vagabonds', who plundered their way to the battlefront.[324] His particular targets were the governors, who raised sufficient troops but could not control them, meanwhile demanding cash and foodstuff for this useless soldiery. Among the most serious flaws, Ahmed outlined the huge size of the supply train, estimated at 20,000–30,000 camp followers, who burdened the army. He was incensed, for example, that those who pitched the tents for the troops were Druzes from Syria, who essentially went on strike if not properly compensated. Lack of control over prices for goods delivered to the camp meant extortion. Similarly, lack of control over those responsible for the delivery and maintenance of the pack animals, as well as mounts, meant considerable abuse and unnecessary waste.[325] Regarding the supplies, he added that the complete breakdown in shipments of flour and bread meant men were dying by eating loaves adulterated with dirt. At his angriest here, Ahmed was indignant that the staff of life should thus be abused. Remedies he suggested included foresight in warehousing, a central commissary system and incorruptible officials.[326]

Another seasoned veteran of the Russo-Turkish wars, Canikli Ali Paşa, later awarded with a *sancak* in the Trabzon province, wrote between 1780 and 1782 his *Nasayih al-Muluk*, an indictment, among other things, of the provincial supply system, based on fixed prices and state purchase. The individuals involved, he claimed, had no stake in seeing their duties carried out properly. The state made requests for provisions based on historical lists, without checking on a region's current ability to provide the foodstuff, animals and/or other types of supplies required for the army. When a *mubayaacı* state purchaser was appointed, local *ayan* were happy because they could collude on the enumeration of individual holdings. For example, a peasant had one ox; it was recorded and taxed as a pair. Furthermore, the *ayan* confiscated and hoarded the food supplies, in the hopes of a higher price and were not above selling rotted grain to the state. Even the captains of the foodstuff transport ships in the Black Sea and on the Danube were involved. They shipped barley mixed with chaff, and wheat cut with sand. One of Canikli Ali's suggestions was to bypass the corruption, and institute a system of direct buying, half at fixed and half at market price. As with others on the same matter, Canikli Ali was calling on the Sultan and his grand viziers to exert some leadership, and address the undue oppression of the peasantry.[327]

---

324 Aksan, *Ottoman Wars*, p.188.
325 Aksan, *Ottoman Wars*, p.188.
326 Aksan, *Ottoman Wars*, p.188.
327 Aksan, *Ottoman Wars*, pp.191–192.

Auxiliary Troops

Probably the most problematic, least understood, and largely ignored parts of the classical Ottoman 'military' were its auxiliary corps. Even though their numbers increased the field army with several thousands of soldiers, they often remained in the shadows. These troops comprised Tatars from the Dobruja, Turkmen and Kurds from eastern Anatolia, Georgians, Abkhazians and Circassians as well as a myriad of tribesmen from the Caucasus. Their participation in the military campaigns on the Ottoman side was usually negotiated by the local governors, or directly by the Porte.

Although they were local troops, some of these contingents could also serve far away from their bases. Wittman and Morier note the Caucasian horsemen who joined the Ottoman army in Egypt in 1800. Both authors refer to them as *Leghis*, adding that they were Georgian and Circassian light cavalrymen. These troops were warlike 'and inured to war, from the constant hostile state in which they live among themselves in the inaccessible heights of the Caucasus, and from the frequent skirmishes that they have with the Russians'.[328]

As the Caucasian auxiliaries, the Tatars also served in different war theatres. The Crimean Tatars had been separated from the Ottoman empire in 1783, and after this date the only significant presence still under Ottoman control was the Buçak Tatars of Dobruja. They were organised in clans each with a *mirza* as chief, who usually held the rank of *beg*, coinciding with the military command. The number of Buçak Tatars had grown with the arrival of many refugees from the Crimea, but the population possibly totalled 150,000 inhabitants in all.

The one-time reputed strong contingent of light cavalry, in the 1780s was just a minor force of about 10,000 horse and foot.[329] However, already by the early eighteenth century, the Tatars had lost much of their ability to support the Ottomans in the campaigns against the modern armies of their enemies. Furthermore, the period of peace and further neglect of regular training taken its toll, and the absence of skilled and experienced military leadership had spawned an ill-trained, spiritless, and

Portrait of Dimitrios Makris (1772–1841), a powerful chief of the *armatolís* in Central Greece, by unknown artist. By the 1820s the Greek warriors became a favourite subject of the Romantic painting. In early 1806, the expulsion of the bands of *klepht* brigands from the Peloponnese marked the relation between the Greek *armatolís* and the Porte. At the end of the previous year, a *firman* from the Sultan reached the Ottoman authorities in the Peloponnese ordering that all *klepht* bandits should be apprehended and brought to justice. The *firman* was accompanied by a formal epistle written by the patriarch Kallínikos IV, which reinforced the Sultan's order. The patriarch condemned any who failed to support the Ottomans against the *klephts*, while those who did give support were offered remission of sins. The operations began in early January 1806, and for the next three months the Ottoman troops harried the *klephts* all over the central and southern Peloponnese. The bands of *klephts* were constantly on the move, unable to retreat for safety to the mountains because these were covered with winter snow. The Ottomans employed 2,000 soldiers in the operation.

---

328 Morier, *Memoir of a Campaign with the Ottoman Army in Egypt*, pp.14–15.
329 Bryan Glyn Williams, *The Crimean Tatars: the diaspora experience and the forging of a nation* (Leiden, Boston, MS: Brill, 2001), p.140.

THE OTTOMAN ARMY OF THE NAPOLEONIC WARS 1789–1815

A Circassian warrior portrayed by Charles Parsons for *The Oriental Album of the people and Scenery of Turkey* 1862 (Collection of the New York Public Library). Caucasian tribesmen's clothing and equipment differed little between one region and another. John Philip Morier described the Circassian and Georgian warriors: 'The lesghis are the troops that come from Georgia and Circassia; they form a light cavalry, and are a fine manly race, extremely handsome, fair, and well-shaped. They are inured to war, from the constant hostile state in which they live among themselves in the inaccessible heights of Mount Caucasus, and from the frequent skirmishes which they have with the Russian troops on their frontiers. Their dress resembles, in some respects, that of the Tartars; but their heads are not shaved, and, instead of a turban, they wear a cap made of sheep's skin.' This figure wears the typical Circassian headdress of black Astrakhan sheepskin, and the long undyed coat. Note the ammunition pouch carried on the breast, typical also among the Ottoman irregulars.

totally unreliable force. The war of 1787–92 saw the Tatars engaged against the Russians on the eastern border. Skirmishes occurred in October 1787 on the Kuban River; then a contingent of approximately 7,000 horse under their *begs* joined the Ottoman-Rumanian army camped between Jassy and Sirlai in late summer 1788; their contribution to the campaign was minimal.[330] In the following campaigns, the Tatars were employed conducting foraging raids deep into enemy territory, in order to keep them occupied, and to provide additional sources of supply.

Then, after the Russian annexation of Dobruja in 1792, the Tatar contribution to the Ottoman military campaign virtually disappeared. The Russian government took preventive measures against the Muslim population and expelled them from many villages on the southern shore and confiscated their vessels.[331] In 1806 about 3,200 Tatars immigrated to Anatolia,[332] and some of them joined the Ottoman army in Egypt in 1800–1802. In this regard, Wittman specifies that the Tatar horsemen were entrusted as messengers to deliver 'public dispatches'. According to him: 'a certain number of Tatars, under a *khan*, or chief of their nation, were constantly stationed with the army of the grand vizier, to receive his Highness' commands, and to proceed on the different missions.'[333] Wittman remarks that the Tatars are 'strong and hardy race', capable of enduring the greatest fatigue, and perform their journey with celerity, seldom or never sleeping on the route.[334] Other sources confirm that the Ottoman commanders used the Tatars as postal couriers. They enjoyed a reputation as honest, reliable, strong, fit and quick people and they could complete the route in a short time. Messenger Tatars were also responsible for bringing

---

330 Carl von Martens, *Allgemeine Geschichte der Türken-Kriege in Europa von 1356 bis 1812*, vol. II (Stuttgart, 1829), p.225.
331 Williams, *The Crimean Tatars*, p.142.
332 Williams, *The Crimean Tatars*, p.242.
333 Williams, *The Crimean Tatars*, p.243.
334 Williams, *The Crimean Tatars*, p.243.

summoned individuals to court or to a government office, and they guided travellers.[335]

Tatar horsemen and scouts participated also in the war against Russia, but their numerical strength did not exceed 5,000–600 men in all. They and other Turkish and Cossack irregulars formed the cavalry 'regiment' quartered at Silistra, raised under Mahmud II in 1822.[336]

Before 1774 Tatar contingents were also associated with the troops from the Romanian principalities. After the annexation of Crimea, the Tatar horsemen who had joined the Ottoman border garrison in 1787 formed a corps in the army that faced the Russian on the Prut. This army was under the command of princes Alexander Ypsilantis of Moldavia and Nicolai Mavrogenes of Wallachia. Despite the nominal rule of the princes, with the definitive installation of the Phanariots from Constantinople in the early eighteenth century, the principalities were completely integrated into the Ottoman military and political systems, and their independent foreign policy and diplomacy ceased to exist.[337] In 1739 the Porte dismantled the old military organisation entirely, as it had no purpose under the new circumstances. Romanian historians stated that this measure was intended to weaken Moldavia and Wallachia, and to leave them unprotected at the mercy of the Ottomans.[338] The native boyars repeatedly asked for the re-establishment of the army, and troops from the principalities fought in all the Russo-Austrian wars against the Turks, but a regular army did not reappear even partially until 1831.

In wartime, the Porte asked each of the principalities to gather a contingent of 12,000 men, half of them cavalry.[339] These troops could be supported by local peasants assigned to many of the less demanding tasks of warfare, such as building defences or digging ditches. The Rumanian contingent comprised local recruits and mercenaries from the Balkans and Greece. Valentini reports that both the princes had their own lifeguard to foot formed by Albanian *arnavuts*, and 'the boyars themselves have them at their service and in their retinue, both for their safety as well as for luxury.'[340] The irregular mercenaries of foot were also designated *segban*, while the cavalry usually comprised local recruits known as *calarasi*, under

---

335 Akşin Somel, *Historical Dictionary of the Ottoman Empire* (Lanham, MD: Scarecrow Press, 2003), p.233.

336 Stanford J. Shaw, Ezel Kural Shaw, *History of the Ottoman Empire and Modern Turkey Volume II: Reform, Revolution, and Republic: The Rise of Modern Turkey, 1808–1975* (Cambridge: Cambridge University Press, 1977), p.24.

337 Their foreign policy was limited to representing the interests of the Empire, to plotting occasionally with the Russians and Austrians, and to being the Porte's informant about events in Europe. See Vlad Georgescu, *The Romanians. A History* (Columbus, OH: Ohio State University Press, 1984), p.75.

338 Robert W. Seaton-Watson, *Histoire des Roumains de l'époque romaine a l'achèvement de l'unité* (Brussels, 1941), p.110.

339 Georgescu, *The Romanians*, p.76.

340 Valentini, *Précis des dernières guerres des Russes contre les Turcs*, p.40.

the command of the local boyars. Generally, these troops were even less reliable than the more undisciplined Ottoman irregulars, and the immediate solution was to assign them to the less exposed garrisons. Each time, the Ottoman commanders relied on these contingents and invariably there were desertions and resounding changes of front. In the war against Russia and Austria, Ypsilantis and most of his troops went to the Russian camp in 1788, while Mavrogenes did not due to the close presence of Ottoman troops. Although the Romanians looked to Russia as a guarantor of their autonomy, the Czars' policy disappointed their expectations.[341]

However, the Principalities' troops did not always receive the blame of the Porte. In 1769 a small Russian corps was harboured near a village not far from Craiova. The *ban* of the village was a Greek called Manolaki, who had been appointed by the *hospodar* of Wallachia, himself a traitor who had fled to the Russians. This Manolaki, incensed by the treason of his Prince, requested aid from the *paşa* of Vidin. Gathering around him the Albanians scattered throughout Wallachia, and with some help from the Vidin *paşa*, he successfully defended Craiova. His fame reached the ears of the Grand Vizier, who was persuaded that any individual, no matter his religion, merited compensation for his loyalty, and commanded his appearance to him in order to be recognised.[342]

If from the military point of view the principalities were almost useless, they represented for the Porte a buffer territory, which could be exploited for the sustenance of the troops in the wars against its Austrian or Russian enemies. The exploitation of resources could also take place without the direct involvement of the principalities. In early April 1798, during the operations against the rebel *ayan* Pazvandoğlu Osman, the Ottoman army marched through Thrace with approximately 50,000 men. This force was considerably enlarged by men and supplies contributed by the notables through whose territory he passed, so that it had almost 100,000 men by the time it reached Vidin early in May. At the same time, an Ottoman fleet sailed through the Black Sea and up the Danube, bearing supplies, artillery, and heavy siege equipment. Wallachia, now under the rule of Constantine Hangerli (prince from 1797 to 1799), was forced to provide most of the wheat and animals needed by the besieging army, and these were secured by large-scale confiscations which ravaged the province just as it had begun to recover from the events of the 1787–1792 war.[343]

---

341 Valentini, *Précis des dernières guerres des Russes contre les Turcs*, p.40: 'In 1792, the boyars protested the seizure of Bessarabia; in Bucharest the people demonstrated their joy at the withdrawal of the imperial Russian armies by setting fire to Russian uniforms in the town square. Dionisie Eclesiarhul, a contemporary chronicler, best expressed the sentiments of the inhabitants for the army (which came to liberate them but stayed to treat them almost more harshly than the Ottomans): There were not houses or places enough to hold them … nor food and drink enough for them, and still they stole everything they found.'

342 Aksan, *Ottoman Wars*, p.152.

343 Shaw, *Between Old and New*, p.246, and Georgescu, *The Romanians*, p.77, 'The Ottoman demands for supplies, which were frequent and heavy despite the official edicts that regulated

Wallachians and Moldavians were not the only Christians who provided aid to the Ottoman army. Although not a military corps in the true sense of the word, the *armatolís* of Greece were another of the significant exceptions of non-Muslims allowed to bear arms. *Armatolí* or *armatolikia* corps were created in areas of Greece with high levels of brigandage, especially the *klepht* brigands of Epirus, or in regions that were difficult for Ottoman authorities to govern due to the inaccessible terrain, such as the Agrafa mountains of Thessaly. In this region, the first *armatolí* were established in the fifteenth century and employed as territorial police force. Over time, the roles of the *armatolís* and *klephts* became blurred, with both reversing their roles and allegiances as the situation demanded, all the while maintaining the delicate status quo with the Ottoman authorities. According to some testimonies, most *armatolís* were former *klephts* who had received amnesty, and sometimes there were men serving in one district as *armatolí* and as bandit in another.[344] The *armatolís* were organised in feudal levy in exchange for titles of land. The Ottomans employed units of *armatolí* or *kapetanioi* (after καπετάνιοι, captains, meaning the troops under a captain) to control mountain passes or areas where resistance to Ottoman rule entailed acts of theft by the *klephts*. The commanders were appointed with an agreement between the local *paşa* and Muslim and Christian community representatives. The *armatolís* were mostly concentrated in Macedonia, Thessaly, Epirus, Acarnania, and Aetolia. In the late eighteenth century, there were 17 *armatolikia*; 10 of them were located in Thessaly and in the eastern regions of Central Greece; four in Epirus, Acarnania, and Aetolia, and three in Macedonia; the overall strength varied from 10,000 to 15,000. A single corps numbered about 800–1,000 *palikaria* (παλικάρια, from ancient Greek *pallix*) under the respective *kapetanio* with two or more *protopalikara* as junior officers. A *kapetanio* was not only a military leader. He was in effect the governor of his area, *capitanlik* in the Ottoman sources, and the *capitanliks* broadly coincided with the *armatoliks* that were controlled by *armatolí* leaders appointed by the Porte. In his *capitanlik* he alone was called captain rather than plain *kírios* (sir), and he alone made appointments. The *armatolís* were paid by the district's authorities but some time they made use of force to exert additional incomes. Discipline was a recurring problem. The most serious breaches were theft and rape, and though rare, anyone found guilty of it was expelled from the corps; in some cases he could be also executed.[345]

The Serbs were the last Christian minority authorised to raise a military militia to support the Ottoman army. Serbs and non-Muslim Bosnians had been employed in the past as pioneers and labourers to accompany the Ottomans on campaign, but only in 1800 did the Porte ask for a direct support against its rebellious janissaries. During the war against Austria and Russia of

---

them, also had a ruinous effect on the economies of Moldavia and Wallachia. Great quantities of grain, cattle, lumber, and saltpeter made their way to Constantinople without payment, or were bought at a price well below market value.'

344 Bruce Brewer, *Greece: the Hidden Centuries. Turkish Rule from the fall of Constantinople to Greek Independence* (Lindon: I. B: Tauris, 2010), p.187.

345 Brewer, *Greece: the Hidden Centuries*, p.187.

1787–92 thousands of Serbs had joined the Habsburg army or at least provided it with sympathy and supplies as it passed through their lands. Moreover, many Serbs had joined the Austrian army as volunteers in the *Freikorps*. Once peace was reached and the Porte regained the lands south of the Danube and the Save, many more Serbs fled across the Danube in 1792 in fear of Ottoman vengeance for their wartime treason, and those who remained behind were certain that they would not easily escape the wrath of the Porte. However, Sultan Selim III had no thought of exacting vengeance from his reluctant Serbian subjects. His main desire was to remedy the sources of their discontent, in particular the power of the local Ottoman garrisons that exerted illegal incomes and acted like actual outlaws. The repression of the rebel garrisons took place with difficulties, and also involved some of the turbulent *ayan* magnates, who sided against the Sultan. In the summer of 1800 the Ottoman governor accepted the offer of the Serbian leaders to support the government in the fight against the rebels. Instead of relying entirely on Ottoman troops maintained by Serbia, the Sultan would allow the Serbs to raise native troops as auxiliaries, and these would be supported directly by the local population without the necessity of new Ottoman taxes.[346] The plan provided for the raising of 10,000 *haiduks* equipped like the Ottoman infantry. The corps was divided into small units numbering each about 100 men, with a *buliakbasha* as commander.

While the new Serbian units were being assembled and trained, the Ottomans withdrew more and more of their regular men to meet the needs of the Egyptian campaign. In November, the Serbian *haiduks* received a baptism of fire when they repulsed the rebels in the attempt to storm the citadel of Belgrade. In this episode the Christian *rayas* rose in defence of their Ottoman overlords, a unique action in the long history of the Ottoman Empire.[347]

The Serbian militia was to be disarmed once control of the province was re-established, but the events that followed persuaded the parties not to demobilise the *haiduk* corps. In 1804, these troops formed the backbone of the forces that rebelled against the Sultan's authority.

---

346 Shaw, *Between Old and New*, p.306.

347 Shaw, *Between Old and New*, p.306: 'This successful defence only stimulated new complaints on the part of the janissaries and Ulema and their supporters, not only in Belgrade, but also in Istanbul and Sarajevo. How could infidels be armed and used against believers in the true faith, whatever their crimes might be? What would the consequences be? To calm their hostility, Selim pardoned the rebels crowded into Vidin and allowed them to return to Belgrade on condition that they agree to obey the orders of his governor there. They promised but of course had no intention of obeying.'

3

Ottoman Warfare: A Struggle for Survival

Ottoman self-confidence in its own military abilities disappeared completely in 1718 after the Peace of Passarowitz. By this date, the Ottoman ruling elite began to acknowledge Western European technological superiority. With the terrible defeats suffered in the Danubian campaigns of 1716–17, the Porte had effectively ended its expansionist phase. The new situation deeply modified the geostrategic scenario in the remaining decades of the eighteenth century. This was a tormented period with many shadows and few lights. With the exception of the recovery of Belgrade in 1737, and some modest successes in the war against Persia of 1742–46,[1] the Ottomans were defeated every time they opposed their western enemies, and each time they were forced to cede important strategic provinces, or to grant increasing concessions to their rivals. When the Porte did manage to prevail, as in Egypt, it was only thanks to the help of a powerful ally.

Other concerns emerged throughout this period from autonomous rebellions in the Balkans, Anatolia and Egypt. To further darken the scenario, a bewildering sequence of plots, betrayals, feuds and mutinies followed one another uninterruptedly between conflicts, often directly linked to these, or resulting from unwise attempts to restore order with further violence and intrigues. The struggle took place on different terrains and fought by

---

1 The conflict erupted after Iranian Prince Nadir Şah made an unsuccessful effort to get the support of the Sunnis of Dagestan in May 1741, and then in April 1742 he demanded an equal share in the right to rule and maintaining the Holy Cities, something the Sunni *ulema* would not approve and the Porte could not grant. Sultan Mahmud I replied by declaring war, supporting the Safavid prince Şah Safi as ruler of Iran in place of Nadir Şah. The war was fitful and bloody. At first, the Iranians attacked Kirkuk, Mosul, and Baghdad but was beaten back with heavy losses in the summer campaign of 1743. They were more successful in the Caucasus, particularly after the Anatolian notables disrupted the Sultan's effort to mobilise the army. The desultory nature of the war finally convinced both sides that they could not win a decisive victory, and an agreement was reached on 4 September 1746. The long and debilitating war brought no major border alterations, whereby the pre-1742 boundaries were again restored.

Bilingual plaque commemorating the Battle of Kozluca in modern Bulgaria (author's picture). Here, on 20 June 1774, inferior numbers of Russians routed the Ottoman field army, and the last available forces melted against the advancing Russian units without any effective resistance at Şumnu on 30 June. After this bitter defeat, the Ottoman government had no alternative than to ask for peace and throw itself on the mercy of Russia.

local forces composed mainly of irregulars, since the standing troops were engaged in the defence of their privileges. During this age, the Ottomans experimented with some changes in war tactics, and new technologies were also introduced, especially in the field of artillery and engineering, but were hardly ever conclusive.

Even in the isolation of the Topkapı palace, anyone understood that a series of changes had taken place in Western Europe in terms of military technology, discipline, tactical organisation, and regularised drill. Here, strengthening of the relationship between financial profit and military adventures was the crucial characteristic that made innovations possible and sustainable in the long run. Furthermore, regular tax income allowed the maintenance of permanent armies in all the modern fiscal-military states.[2] The Ottoman Empire, with all its backwardness, was no longer able to fuel an expansion sufficient to keep under control the destabilising forces of the ruling military class. In other words, the Ottoman state's financial ability to make wars profitable and desirable enterprises was compromised at all.[3]

---

2   According to the most recent historiography, a fiscal-military state was one capable of sustaining large-scale warfare through taxation and fiscal innovation, such as the creation of a national debt or credit-providing institutions. See also C. Storr (ed.), *The Fiscal-Military State in Eighteenth-Century Europe: Essays in honour of P. G.M. Dickson* (London: Routledge, 2009).

3   'The military reform measures were part of the bargaining process and both the state elites and different political actors often shifted their positions depending on the political circumstances.

The emergency favoured the full establishment of the *ayan* notables, the only ones able to recruit large contingents at low cost. Consequently, the presence of these troops caused the decentralisation of the Ottoman 'military'.[4] Some scholars suggest that the ad hoc measures that eventually led to fiscal and military devolution in the Ottoman Empire were originally introduced because, in the eighteenth century, the Porte had to fight rivals, especially Russia, who had access to much richer human and military resources and hence possessed larger military capacities.[5]

The military superiority of the Europeans had been the subject of careful observation by one of the most acute Ottoman intellectuals of the eighteenth century. In his reform treatise written in 1732, Müteferrika Ibrahim praised the structure and good order of the 'Christian' (by which he meant European and Russian) armies, focusing on the balanced proportions of infantry strengthened with grenadiers, cavalry, and dragoons, and the excellent cooperation among these components. He also noted that Western military writers considered army organisation so important that they developed a new branch of study that examined the structure and order of armies.[6] The conventional view argues that the Ottomans tried to follow the West in military matters, but failed because they did not go far enough and their conservative society did not allow them to introduce modernity. However, the whole eighteenth century witnessed increasing Ottoman acceptance of foreign discipline and technology, especially from France.[7] In the 1780s a French military mission introduced unprecedented change in Ottoman military history. After the

---

It is crucial for us to have an in-depth understanding of the reasons for resistance from various groups such as the janissaries, local notables, and common people, as their resistance shaped the possibilities of the Ottoman military reform.'

4   Ágoston, 'Military Transformation', pp 287.

5   Ágoston, 'Military Transformation', pp.287: 'Scholars suggest that the decentralisation could be examined in the wider context of military devolution and the emergence of the military contractors and entrepreneurs. Notwithstanding the political risks involved in the system, it is generally accepted that the contract system was an effective way to overcome limited fiscal, organisational, and administrative capabilities, especially in smaller states that thereby managed 'to maintain a military capacity that far exceeded their direct access to resources.'

6   Ágoston, 'Military Transformation', p.318: 'According to Ibrahim, other laudable qualities of the 'Christian' armies, included superior methods of training and drilling soldiers that strengthened discipline; military regulations and laws that were read to the troops monthly; the high proportion of officers, which ensured order and discipline; the possibility for advancement based on merit; the multiple competence of the high command; the order and defence of military camps; military intelligence and counterintelligence; geometric troop formations; uniforms that helped prevent confusion and desertion on campaigns; and volley technique to maintain continuous fire. The Ottoman troops lacked most of these qualities, and hence were repeatedly defeated by their European adversaries. Therefore, Ibrahim argued, the Ottomans had to emulate the European armies and their new order armies.'

7   Among the first foreigners to introduce western techniques into the Ottoman army was the Italian gun founder Pietro Sardi, who in the seventeenth century introduced new technique of production in Constantinople.

THE OTTOMAN ARMY OF THE NAPOLEONIC WARS 1789–1815

OTTOMAN WARFARE: A STRUGGLE FOR SURVIVAL

THE OTTOMAN ARMY OF THE NAPOLEONIC WARS 1789–1815

Previous page: The Ottoman artillery and cavalry engaging the Austrians in open field; detail from a print illustrating the campaign of 1788 in Moldavia. At the end of the eighteenth century the wars against Austria and Russia had demonstrated that the Ottomans' military superiority was a thing of the past; but this did not mean that they were no longer a considerable military power. However, eighteenth-century warfare proved to be both costly and unpopular. In the war and society debate, the Revolutionary and Napoleonic wars act as the end of a particular kind of warfare which led to an impasse in all military systems of Europe, just prior to the French innovations by which the state-under-arms became a reality. The ability to sustain long campaigns, and feed and care for upwards of 100,000 men, their equipment and transportation, had reached a breaking point. The impact of that kind of warfare on the populace at large was reflected in rebellions and desertions of villages, and often also in resistance to taxation and billeting. This unrest, as well as the responses of the elite groups – central and provincial – to the opportunities represented by the upheavals of constant warfare, are two points of comparison that also work well in the Ottoman context.

Russian annexation of the Crimea in 1783, the French government revised its Eastern policy according to which the Ottoman Empire had to be strengthened militarily against Russia through technical assistance. A group of French officers in the Antoine Chaboit mission undertook to reinforce many major fortresses including Chotin, Oçakov and the castles along the Dardanelles, and renovate the gun foundry and the naval arsenal.[8] Acceptance of the French mission encouraged the Duc de Luxembourg, a relative of Louis XVI, to visit Constantinople with an interesting military project in 1784. He connected the Ottoman defeats with the incompatibility of the Ottoman troops in contemporary European warfare. Accordingly, he was proposed raising an Ottoman force of 1,200 men in Rhodes or Crete, and the troops were to be disciplined and trained by French officers. However, the reforming grand vizier Halil Hâmid Paşa turned down the proposal, for he was aware of French ambitions in the Levant.[9]

Another group of French officers arrived in İstanbul the same year under the leadership of De Lafitte-Clavé, alongside a French geographer. These officers were specialists in siege techniques and fortification. They supervised a number of fortresses in the Black Sea region. Meanwhile, Monnier, Aubert and Granper were commissioned to revitalise the neglected field artillery corps together with some other experts in ship construction and gun casting. De Lafitte, Monnier, and Mehmed Ağa – a Prussian convert – established the School of Fortification with the intention of training engineer officers expert in siege techniques and fortification.[10]

The instructors who came from France therefore initiated a major transformation of the Ottoman fighting systems and tactics. The development of modern drill was the single and most visible part of this transformation. This drill was first applied in the infantry, and the new practice eventually revolutionised both the structure of the traditional army, and its tactics, identifying the contrasts between the janissaries' practices of war and the drills of the *nizam-ı cedid* – the New Order Army. All this provides clues about the transformation of military culture during this period. The differences

---

8   Virginia H. Aksan, 'Choiseul-Gouffier at the Sublime Porte 1784–1792', in S. Kuneralp (ed.), *Studies On Ottoman Diplomatic History* (Constantinople: The Isis Press, 1992), pp.30–31.
9   Aksan, 'Choiseul-Gouffier at the Sublime Porte 1784–1792', p.31.
10 Aksan, 'Choiseul-Gouffier at the Sublime Porte 1784–1792', p.32.

between the two types of military training are evident in the establishment of modern barracks, which were first constructed during the reign of Selim III, and the lifestyle that came with these barracks.[11] However, the limits of this transformation were the limited expansion of the new, modern trained infantry corps. To try to overcome this, the supporters of transformation proposed to extend the new drill to the *kapıkulu* corps. Ingeniously, in 1794, orders were issued for the provision of new European-type muskets and ammunition to the janissary corps as soon as possible, and it was hoped that they would be entirely armed with the new equipment by the end of the year. Each *orta* had to include eight trained riflemen and eight assistants to teach the men to use the new weapons and to lead them in campaigns.[12] However, the janissaries absolutely refused to accept the Sultan's order concerning modern drill.

Neutral observers reported that by the second half of the eighteenth century the level of training had significantly declined across the *kapıkulu*.[13] However, some of them pointed out that generally the Ottoman soldier had in average good military quality, stating that they were reputed solid in defence, and showed greater individual initiative than the Western infantry, but in the field performed poorly when opposed to regular troops. Though the Ottoman was sturdier, consumed fewer luxury goods and contended more easily with the difficult conditions of the campaigns than his fellow European counterpart, the tactical gap between him and his Austrian or Russian counterparts seemed unbridgeable. Some coeval writers stated that the Ottoman soldiers generally withstood the hard conditions on campaign, and when the government was unable to pay salaries or unable to feed the army, they continued to fight rather than desert.[14] Nevertheless, they were prone to rebellion, and if the delay in payment persisted, they did not hesitate to plunder villages and even towns, friend as well as foe. If led to exasperation, soldiers and even junior officers were very difficult to placate afterwards.[15] To avoid these excesses and to maintain order, the camps were free of alcohol, which not only reduced the need to allocate transportation for carrying barrels of beverages, but also reduced alcohol-related troubles

---

11 Yeşil, 'Drill and Discipline as a Civilizing Process', p.102.

12 Shaw, *Between Old and New*. pp.119–120: 'It is not known whether Selim and those around him actually believed they could reform the *sipahis* and Janissaries by these methods, but it is known that all efforts made to enforce these regulations were vigorously and violently opposed. The inspectors sent to examine the provincial fiefs had to rely on information supplied by the local feudal officers and men, who managed to conceal anything which it was not to their advantage to reveal.'

13 Uyar and Erickson, *A Military History of the Ottomans*, p.91, and Johann Schels, 'Die Treffen zu Lande und auf der See, bei Kinburn und Oczakow 1787–1788 nebst Eroberung der letzteren Festung durch Fürst Potemkin', in *Österreichische Militärische Zeitschrift*, (1829) vol. I, pp.341–342.

14 Uyar and Erickson, *A Military History of the Ottomans*, p.86.

15 Wittman, *Travels in Turkey*, p.202.

as well.[16] These judgements concerned mainly the *nizâm-ı cedid* troops, and some elite forces, while the janissaries became increasingly useless on campaign. Already in the 1770s, the seasoned bureaucrat Süleyman Penah, had warned the Sultan that:

> with such soldiers [the janissaries], all order had been overturned. There was no way either to make them fight, or to keep them from flight. Such an army was worse than a rag-tag general call-to-arms ... Their inexperience had brought defeat, rout and a loss of zeal.[17]

Irregular troops were valued even less. This was, very probably, due to their part-time employment as soldiers and, while working mainly as independent villagers, their inability to participate in regular military training. Obviously, the level of efficiency was uneven between the different irregular corps. Bosnian and Albanian footmen, for instance, excelled in skirmish, ambush, and as marksmen, especially in wooded terrain and mountain, without taking into account their significant numerical contribution in all the military campaigns fought by the Porte.

Technical weapons suffered the most for the opposition of the traditionalist party comprising *ulemas* and janissaries, and all commenters pointed to the backwardness of the Ottoman artillery. Jucherau de Saint-Denys wonders about the Ottoman obstinacy to maintain the ancient bronze guns without handles and breech pin with calibre of 700 and even 800 lb. The main defence of the fortresses relied on outdated guns with massive carriages, served by up to 20 men and shooting projectiles of 120 lb or more. Despite reforms introduced in the 1770s, most Ottoman commanders did not distinguish between siege and field artillery, and gathered guns of all calibres between 40 and 12 lb, 'which they continued to use out of hatred for all innovations.'[18] Finally, the French author deplored the general use of oxen, strong but slow animals that worsened the performance of artillery on campaign.

Almost all commenters agree that one of the reasons for the poor performance of the Ottoman armies was their officers, because they generally possessed very limited tactical and technical skills. According the experienced veteran Canikli Ali, the Ottoman officer corps could not produce good officers because of the high turnover to which it was subjected. The frequency of changes of personnel, requiring constant mobility of governors and other officers, had a deleterious effect not just on loyalty, but overall on the stability of the Empire, when the state was relying on unknown and unreliable men. Furthermore, the 'men-of-state' (bureaucrats) and the *ulema* were making military decisions, 'rather than those with the experience of

---

16   Uyar and Erickson, *A Military History of the Ottomans*, p.86.

17   Aksan, *Ottoman Wars*, p.189: 'Secondly, for those with official entitlements, there was no indication where they were posted, so that a janissary could claim his right to a posting anywhere. This, Süleyman Penah continued, would be easy to fix, if a proper registration were undertaken, and the number who should be in the fortresses was well established and maintained.'

18   Jucherau de Saint-Denis, Antoine, Baron de, *Histoire de l'Empire Ottoman*, vol. I, p.360.

OTTOMAN WARFARE: A STRUGGLE FOR SURVIVAL

An image well fixed in the public mind: the impetuous Mamluks in their exotic dress, being used as if for target practice by the French infantrymen who shot them at point-blank range at the battle of the Pyramids. Painted by Wojciech Kossak (1857–1942), in 1900.

warfare who should be the ones consulted to advise and restore order in the garrisons'.[19] Canikli Ali was equally critical of the lack of order in the artillery corps. He devoted several pages to the need for order in the camp, and the organisation of the artillery as well as its emplacement on the battlefront. Present-day warfare, he asserted, was a matter of sabre and cannon rather than raiding and words.[20]

Since many officers owed their position to corruption or factional interests, almost none applied themselves to the study of matters related to warfare.[21] There was not only the refusal to accept modern 'infidel' theories to fuel this position, even stronger was their unwillingness to engage in matters that would have questioned their abilities. Not surprisingly, many Ottoman officers were celebrated more for their courage than for their technical authority. This was typical for the officers of the *kapıkulu*, while the *ayans* and the commanders of the irregular troops were differently motivated on this issue, and indeed, it was mainly from them that the best Ottoman commanders emerged. This problem existed at all levels. In this regard, British Brigadier General George Frederick Koehler told his superiors in London that the Ottoman senior commanders

---

19 Aksan, *Ottoman Wars*, p.191.
20 Aksan, *Ottoman Wars*, p.191.
21 İsmail Hakkı Uzunçarşılı, *Osmanlı Devleti Teşkilatından Kapukulu Ocakları* (Ankara: Türk Tarih Kurumu Basımevi, 1988), vol. II, p.72.

showed no foresight in operation against the French during the Egyptian campaign of 1800. Koehler wrote:

> What is expected from such troops, or rather mobs, thus commanded? Nothing but shame or disgrace, and yet they have fine men, excellent horses, good guns, plenty of ammunition, and provision, and forage, and in short great abundance of all materials required to constitute a fine army, but they want order and system, which would not be difficult to establish if their principal officers were not so astonishingly adverse to anything tending towards it.[22]

In the same year, Wittman confirmed that the Ottoman soldiers had good basic qualities, such as bravery, resistance and will to fight, and motivated and aggressive soldiers formed some irregular corps. However, due to the lack of efficient officers, basic military training and discipline, they were more or less useless against European modern armies.[23]

Another British observer, John Philip Morier, comments:

> It is, perhaps, a fortunate circumstance for Europe, that the efforts which have been made at different times, and which are still making, by European officers, to introduce a discipline among the Turks, have proved ineffectual; for, if they are considered in regard to their personal courage, their bodily strength, or their military habits, they will be found to equal, if not surpass, any other body of men.[24]

In another passage of his work, Morier summarises effectively the characteristic of the Ottoman army and its commanders marching on campaign in Egypt in 1800:

> A Turkish army well be compared to an armed rabble; with this difference, that instead of being a lawless mob, led away by the impetuosity of passion, or by the impulse of the moment, the power of a chief may keep up a certain degree of subordination, which however, goes only as far as he possessed of more or less energy and character, and often will not prevent disorders, such as the plundering of villages, and quarrels between whole corps of the same army.[25]

The same author provides an insightful observation on Ottoman commanders and subordinates:

> The yeniçeri-agasi, or 'generalissimo' of the janissaries, ranks with a Pasha of three tails. But the rank of the officers below him carries none of that respectability

---

22 Cited by Edward Ingram, 'The Geopolitics of the First British Expedition to Egypt – II. The Mediterranean Campaign, 1800–1', in *Middle Eastern Studies* vol. 30, N. 4 (October 1994), p.711.
23 Wittman, *Travels in Turkey*, p.250.
24 Morier, *Memoir of a Campaign with the Ottoman Army in Egypt,* p.17; Wittman, *Travels in Turkey,* p.303.
25 Morier, *Memoir of a Campaign with the Ottoman Army,* p.19.

which is attached to the same rank in our armies: the Turkish ensign and captain attend upon the colonel as menial servants.[26]

Morier and Wittman were astonished to find that even in proximity to the enemy, the disorder and quarrels did not end, and reported that notwithstanding 'the great and recent successes' achieved at Damietta and Rahmaniye in May 1801, the officers and soldiers resumed their usual trend:

> The Turks sill continued to display the total disregard to discipline and good order, without which a happy and successful issue cannot be expected from any military operations. This neglect had been frequently urged to them, and pointed out in the strong terms of reprobation. It cannot, indeed, be expected, while they continue to entertain the prejudices by which they are now governed, and while they pay so little attention to discipline in the field and in the camp, but that they will be constantly inferior to their enemies, although there are very many among them who are by no means deficient in personal bravery.[27]

Prior to them, Count Constantin-François de Chasseboeuf de Volnay was even more negative when dealing with the matter:

> [The Ottoman] armies are mobs and their marches are pillaging, their campaigns are incursions, their battles are skirmishes; the strongest or boldest goes after the other, who often flees from combat without a fight; if he waits with a firm foot, he is boarded, mixed up, rifles are drawn, spears are broken, sabres are cut, there is almost never a cannon; and when there is one, it is of little use. Terror often spreads it without reason: one party flees; the other presses it, and cries victory. The vanquished suffers the law of the victor, and often the campaign ends with the battle.[28]

The Prussian general Georg Wilhelm von Valentini expresses a similar judgement:

> The campaigns against the Turks are more like the wars of antiquity than modern ones, both in terms of the theatre in which they take place and the way in which the armies fight and camp. The battles are reminiscent of those narrated by Polybius, because the Turks, like the Romans, fight exclusively on the front of their camp.[29]

The Russian diplomat Lazarev gives an even more negative picture. When the Ottomans complained the violation of the Treaty of Tilsit in 1807, the Russian agent Lazarev replied that:

---

26 Morier, *Memoir of a Campaign with the Ottoman Army*, p.11.
27 Wittman, *Travels in Turkey*, p.303.
28 Volnay, Constantin-François de Chasseboeuf, comte de, *Voyage en Syrie et en Égypte, pendant les années 1783, 1784 et 1785*, (Paris, 1787), vol. I, p.116.
29 Valentini, *Précis des dernières guerres des Russes contre les Turcs*, p.10.

the Ottomans had failed to provide sufficient order and protection in the Principalities, and their troops had served mainly to pillage.[30]

Considerations such as these are probably exaggerated, as is the judgement on their old-fashioned tactics, and both statements cannot be generally applied. Although most commanders opposed modern tactical discipline, the best among them were able to achieve good results by applying traditional tactics. In 1788 against the Austrians, and in 1809–10 against the Russians, the Ottoman commanders successfully opposed the enemies by exploiting the elusive tactics of the irregular infantrymen, consisting in ambush, small-scale counter-attack and skirmish, as well as avoiding open battle. Ultimately, the Ottoman foot soldiers were essentially light infantrymen, and in this respect their tactics were effective, because while the Sultans sought to turn their foot soldiers into line infantry, the armies of the Western European powers increased the presence of light troops. A Prussian tactical school oriented officer like Valentini also confirms the Ottoman advantage in this kind of warfare.[31]

For this kind of warfare, musketry fire was predominant. At the beginning of the nineteenth century foreign commenters such as Thornton and Jucherau de Saint-Denys stated that Ottoman infantry drill was preoccupied only with shooting at targets, but neither provided detailed information about the drill practiced in the *nizam-ı cedid* regiments.[32] Other contemporary documents indeed suggest that the Ottoman military elite had enough knowledge of modern drill. As persistently underlined by some of the Sultan's advisors and officials, soldiers who became objects of modern drill moved in lines as a unified whole, and learned to load their weapons and shoot synchronously. A description of the first stages of this training process appears in a passage of the *Buyuk Lāyiha* – 'Great Treatises' – written by Ratib Efendi, who was the Ottoman envoy to Vienna in 1791. According to him, the Ottoman officers trained the troops following the current drill regulation-*Exerzierreglement* of the Austrian army:

> The drill officer first hands the rifle to the recruit and teaches him how to hold it and when he gets used to it, he will have him carry it holding up for a few days and then teach him how to stick his breast out and pull his belly in. Next, he will show the recruit how to hold the rifle in this position and teach him how to turn right and left while the rifle is in his hand. When the recruit gets used to this, then, he will train him to hold the rifle in accordance with the drill [regulation]. And he will teach him how to load it rapidly. However, the experienced [soldiers] should not demonstrate them hastily but slowly, first explaining a few issues nicely. Next, he will train the recruits to load it slowly and then rapidly, and teach him how to hold the bandolier and pull out and hold the cartridges to load it…[33]

---

30 Shaw, *Between Old and New*, p.392.
31 Valentini, *Précis des dernières guerres des Russes contre les Turcs*, p.10.
32 Yeşil, 'Drill and Discipline as a Civilizing Process', pp.105–106.
33 Yeşil, 'Drill and Discipline as a Civilizing Process', pp.105–106.

When Ratib Efendi wrote his treatises Grand Vizier Yusuf Paşa, together with 18 selected Russian prisoners of war, demonstrated for Selim III the particulars of the tactical formation practised in European armies. This new organisational form called 'battalion battle-drill' in contemporary Ottoman military literature was categorically different from the traditional training, which aimed to make the recruit to be 'the master of his person' and the firing drills that taught synchronous musket use and basic manoeuvre movements. The battalion drill was also a form of training in which officers received information about how to conduct whole corps of trained soldiers on the battlefield following the Western tactics, as the ones introduced in the *nizam-ı cedid* units years later.[34]

Nevertheless, these remained isolated successes, as the vast majority of the Ottoman officers and were firmly opposed to the tactics of the infidel *gavurs*. Coeval Ottoman commentators did not fail to extol the exploits of their soldiers when they prevailed against European adversaries. In the early 1800s the Ottoman chronicler Wassif emphasised the success achieved in Egypt against the French, writing that the Ottoman soldiers fought with great determination if they were protected by the walls of a fortress or an entrenchment. He proudly outlined Bonaparte's judgement, who stated that 10,000 well-trained soldiers could defeat an army of 100,000 Muslims in the open field, but an army of 100,000 men would have been unable to prevail against 10,000 Muslims inside a fortress.[35] Certainly, the Ottoman chronicler had in mind the fierce defence of Acre led by Cezzar Ahmed Paşa between March and May 1799. However, several accounts and reports seem to confirm that under skilled officers the Ottoman troops performed positively in defensive tasks. In these sorts of actions the common soldiers demonstrated a fatalistic attitude, which strengthened their bravery and determination to resist. In some cases their resistance took on fanatical overtones. The hardened veteran irregulars, as well as the elite soldiers, led an existence dominated by violence, which was reflected in their approach to combat and especially in their cruelty towards the civilian population. In his simplistic and semi-literate description of battles, sieges, looting, and pillaging, *Deli* Mustafa Vasfî Efendi reveals the features typical of this world, and some passages are evocative of the common soldier's life, including descriptions of ruthless attitudes towards civilians. Mustafa narrates an episode that took place in Greece in the 1820s:

> The janissaries, because they were on foot, soon fell behind. We, who had good horses, went on ahead. We were altogether eighteen horsemen. Anyway, we went off and arrived in an infidel village. They sat down under two mulberry trees, whereupon some local inhabitants approached them, and said: 'We are afraid of you. We have wives and daughters on that mountain over there. If you give us protection, we will come down.' The Ottoman soldiers answered: 'the pasha has

---

34 Yeşil, 'Drill and Discipline as a Civilizing Process', pp.105–106.
35 Johann von Hammer-Purgstall, *Geschichte des Osmanischen Reiches* (Budapest, 1827–1835), vol. XVI, p.361.

sent us and we have orders to protect you.' The infidels were extremely glad, went away and brought lamb and bread to us. About twenty to thirty women and girls came with us. The cavalrymen grew afraid of being outnumbered, and isolated for the night, when we assumed the infidels would slay us, so we took the infidels, cut off their heads, captured these thirty women and girls, and took off. We came upon a church, captured the infidels who were inside the church, cut off their heads and hid in the church for the night. They found 5,000 sheep beside the church the next day, and with sheep and captives, returned towards their camp. On the way back, an encounter with a troop of janissaries resulted in the losing captives and booty at gunpoint. I had a girl and woman with me, and two mules. They [the janissaries] arrived, plundered all my possessions. I remained behind as a simple foot soldier. Then, running into other janissaries, I pretended to be of their number and complained of the treatment by my comrades. A Kurdish servant of the janissaries addressed those who had abused me: 'you have taken this man's possessions, slave girls, and severed infidels' heads. Things like this do not befit our corps. Now give this man his belongings.'[36]

Mustafa thus retrieved his booty, and returned to camp. His commander rewarded him with two coins for the heads, but chastised him that the *deli* horsemen (possibly his units) had no business advancing ahead of the main army corps. His escapade here appears to have been a private enterprise, and evoked no discipline other than a scolding from his commander.[37] In other passages, he suggests that his world was bound by an intricate set of beliefs and values, forming an ethos or unwritten code that revolved around notions of religious duty, honour, as well as vengeance. The harshness of military life and the continuous coexistence with violence and death caused horrific consequences on the battlefield, especially when the fight took on the character of religious hatred. In the eighteenth century, Ottoman Muslims had experienced an alarming phenomenon, namely the massacre of many of them in lost territories, which ushered in the dismal season of 'ethnic cleansing'. This remained a feature of the wars in the Balkans, and contributed to making the war an all-out struggle. In the course of the wars against the

---

36 Jan Schmidt, 'The Adventure of an Ottoman Horseman: the Autobiography of Kabudlı Vasfî Efendi, 1800–1825', in J. Schmidt (ed.), *The Joys of Philology: Studies in Ottoman Literature, History and Orientalism (1500–1923)* (Constantinople: The Isis Press, 2002), vol. I, pp.284–285. 'Deli Mustafa's narrative presents an interesting snapshot of a broader Muslim, military laborer community around the turn of the nineteenth century. The religiosity and honour codes apparent in Mustafa's narrative had a special flavour to it reminiscent of other borderlands of the Ottoman world in previous centuries. This preoccupation with honour was not unique to Ottoman soldiery but was typical of communities inhabiting contested borderlands and frontiers. In the eighteenth and nineteenth centuries, this borderland ethos became a fact of life *within* Ottoman hinterlands as Rumelia was gradually transformed from a "core" Ottoman province into a borderland contested not only by imperial rivals, but now, also by Ottoman subjects.'

37 Esmer U. Tolga, 'The Confessions of an Ottoman Irregular: Self-Representation and Ottoman Interpretive Communities in the Nineteenth Century' in *Osmanlı Araştırmaları – The Journal of Ottoman Studies*, XLIV (2014), p.320.

OTTOMAN WARFARE: A STRUGGLE FOR SURVIVAL

Austrian print illustrating the surrender of Novi in October 1788 (author's archive). The Ottoman garrison resisted the siege for almost seven months. The Ottomans remained committed to siege warfare, and had consolidated the border fortress line early in the century. It was in entrenched positions at major fortresses where the janissaries excelled, and one of the reasons they so hated eastern campaigns, where the horse and sabre still ruled supreme.

Austrians and Russians, as well as in the campaigns against the Serbs or even the Arab Wahhabis, it was rare for prisoners to be treated differently from slaves. In other, non-infrequent, cases, neither side took prisoners, and the captives had their fate sealed. Friedrich von Schubert, a German officer in the service of the Czar, witnessed the ruthless treatment reserved for the wounded Russian soldiers during the siege of Rüsçük in 1810:

> Finally at around 9 o'clock, the officers managed to force a withdrawal and our troops returned to the cover of the trenches. Now the most terrible, repulsive drama began to unfold as the Turks came out of the fortress and entered the ditch. They began to decapitate the dead and wounded alike whilst we, only 60 yards away, had to watch this barbaric spectacle and listen to the frantic screams of our unfortunate wounded as they awaited their turn. We dared not even fire in case the defenders turned on us for we seemed to have been reduced to a few hundred men and the artillery.[38]

In the defence of fortresses or entrenchments, the Ottoman infantry was considered a particularly formidable enemy by the West, especially in close combat. Generally, neither the janissaries nor other foot troops used bayonets, except for the *nizâm-ı cedid* soldiers, but all had a sabre and one or more knives: very useful weaponry in hand-to-hand combat.

---

38 Erik Amburger, *Friedrich von Schubert. Unter dem Doppeladler: Erinnerungen eines Deutschen in russischem Offiziersdienst, 1789–1814* (Stuttgart, Koehler, 1962), p.203.

THE OTTOMAN ARMY OF THE NAPOLEONIC WARS 1789–1815

OTTOMAN WARFARE: A STRUGGLE FOR SURVIVAL

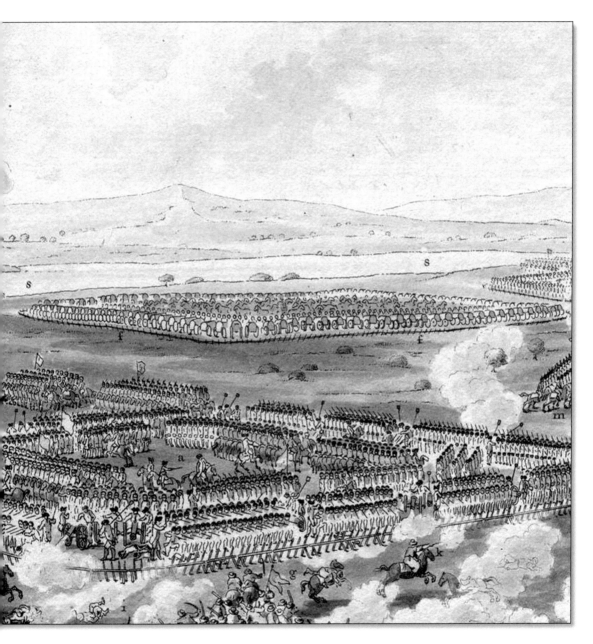

Ottoman cavalry charging the Austrian infantry squares, particular form an episode of the 1788 campaign in Moldavia. In matter of update tactics, the Ottomans reacted slowly, since on several occasions, the cavalry continued to fight in the traditional manner, often paying a high toll in casualties. Similarly, the Mamluks paid a heavy price for their repeated charges on French infantry squares in 1798.

This way of fighting, or rather, this 'savage attitude'[39] of engaging opponents in close combat was also practised by the cavalry.[40] Though the *sipahis* and the Ottoman cavalry as whole had been the powerful element of the Ottoman army, in the last quarter of the eighteenth century their relevance on the field had much decreased. Their role on campaign was similar to the coeval hussars or even Cossacks, as for the irregulars from Anatolia. Equipment and weaponry also qualified the Ottoman horsemen as light cavalry, which employed firearms and usually the lance, especially the irregular *delis*. Usually the Ottoman commanders used the cavalry to form a protective screen around the infantry, carrying out the basic tasks of reconnaissance, scouting and escort, and rarely engaged the heavier Western cavalrymen. However, their skill when operating on broken ground, where the enemy cavalry dared not follow, astonished many observers. In this context the ordinary *sipahi* marched on horseback but fought on foot as the European dragoon.

In 1788 the Ottoman cavalry played a central role against the Austrians under Liechtenstein in northern Bosnia.[41] The Ottomans were not only able to prevail over the opposing cavalry, taking advantage of their numerical superiority, but also bested in the encounters with the infantry in the rough terrain around the Sava and Drava rivers. Their tactic is described by Velentini:

> The Ottoman cavalry hides from the sight of the enemy, in the shelter of hills or scrubs. Then the horsemen suddenly appear from the narrowest paths, not caring about the disorder they find themselves in, as they are not used to any orderly formation as we know it. They are therefore very dangerous on broken ground. They come from places that seem impassable and suddenly appear on the flanks or behind, Two or three horsemen advance looking around, then in a moment 500 or 600 arrive and then misfortune for that battalion that is marching recklessly without proper reconnaissance.[42]

The Ottoman cavalry achieved further, modest, successes in the war against Russia of 1806–1812, especially when they faced the Cossacks and Kalmyks, who acted similar tactics. However, every time the Ottoman commanders tried to engage in open field the Western regular infantry with their cavalry, the outcome was always disappointing.

The massive assault with fast retreat, trying to draw the enemy in and then surprising them with a new charge, had been the trademark of the Ottoman cavalry in the past. This kind of tactic had been interrupted after

---

39 Tolga, 'The Confessions of an Ottoman Irregular', p.331.

40 In this regard, the Prussian General Valentini states: 'If the Turks still retain some superiority in combat, it is only in the use of bladed weapons. Their cavalry always engages ours and the charge is always preferred to the square or ordered fire.' Valentini, *Précis des dernières guerres des Russes contre les Turcs*, p.23.

41 Konrad Thielen, 'Geschichte des Feldzuges', vol. II, pp.166–168.

42 Valentini, *Précis des dernières guerres des Russes contre les Turcs*, p.11.

1718, but was still practiced in eastern Anatolia and in Egypt. In Egypt, the French faced the Mamluks as Prince Eugene of Savoy did with the Ottoman *sipahis* one century previous. In fact, the Mamluks' tactics were still those of centuries before, except for a few differences. Unlike the Ottomans, the Mamluks fought in larger corps and, above all adopted firearms in large numbers. They were reputed as brave warriors and according to an eyewitness who participated at the battle of the Pyramids in July 1798, the French were frightened by the prospect of the expected encounter with the Mamluks, 'those famous warlords who had been in effective control of Egypt for centuries'.[43] As one French officer reported:

> Every horseman has two big muskets that are carried by two of his servants, and which he uses only once. Then he uses two pistols that he carries in a belt around his waist. Then eight arrows that he carries in a quiver and which he aims with extreme precision. Then he uses a mace to smash his enemy. Finally, he carries two swords, one in each hand, and catches the reins of his horse between his teeth, and woe to him who cannot evade his blows, the strength of which can easily cut a man in two. We will fight such a sort of men.[44]

However, the Mamluks' fire seems to have been less effective, at least considering the low rate of casualties suffered by the French. When compiling his report of the battle of Mount Tabor, which occurred on 17 April 1799, the French General Jean-Baptiste Kléber declared that in 10 hours of fighting he had lost only two men and another 60 were wounded. The figure seems surprising, but in all probability it is true. According to an authoritative opinion, it was the most convincing demonstration of the superiority of disciplined infantry deployed in solid squares over the haphazard charges of cavalry, still fighting with such outdated tactics.[45]

It was not just two opposite worlds that faced each other in those fateful campaigns, but two different eras of history. Commenting on the battle of the Pyramids, the Egyptian chronicler al-Jabarti says of the Mamluks that:

> they were irresolute and at odds with one another, being divided in opinion, envious of each other, frightened for their lives, their well-being and their comforts, immersed in their ignorance and self-delusion, arrogant and haughty in their attire and presumptuousness, afraid of decreasing in number, and pompous in their finery, heedless of the results of their action; contemptuous of their enemy, unbalanced in their reasoning and judgement.

Immediately after such a harsh rebuke of the Mamluks and their ineffective style of warfare, al-Jabarti describes the performance of the French during the same battle, much contrasting with that of the Mamluks:

---

43 Chandler, *The Campaigns of Napoleon*, vol. I (Italian Edition; Milan: Rizzoli, 1992), p.295.
44 L'Adjudant-General Boyer, on 10 Thermidor, Year 6, in Boustany (ed.), *Bonaparte,* vol. X, p.59.
45 Chandler, *The Campaigns of Napoleon*, p.319.

> The French were a complete contrast in everything mentioned above … They never considered the number of their enemy too high, nor did they care who among them was killed … They follow the order of their commander and faithfully obey their leader … They have signs and symbols which they all obey to the letter.

From their perspective, the French realised that the Mamluks' reputation was completely unwarranted. The entrance to Cairo would certainly cause an uproar in France, as General Boyer wrote home: 'when the people know what kind of enemy we were fighting, this campaign will cease to be seen as a miracle … These Mamluks, famous among the Egyptians for their bravery, have no idea about military tactics, except how to draw blood with their weapons.' Describing the battle itself, he writes:

> I have never seen soldiers who charge with such valour, depending on nothing but the speed of their horses. They were descending like a torrent on our soldiers … [who] stood still waiting for them until they were only ten feet away and started firing at them and, in a twinkle of the eye, 150 Mamluks fell to the ground and the others fled.

The Mamluk attitude to war and fighting shown in the first battles against the French was an example of a method of warfare made obsolete by the new evolving drills and technology. Al-Jabarti's and Boyer's accounts of the battle of the Pyramids, show clearly how the Mamluks relied on their own strength; how decisions to charge or retreat were left to the personal initiative of the warriors; how their dress in its embroidered kaftans and colourful turbans was an expression of their social status, not of their military ranks; and finally how out of date their weapons were, comprising as they did swords, lances, maces and muskets.[46]. Cavalry was such an important element of the Mamluk army, that nearly no infantry is mentioned in the accounts of the battle.

In Egypt as well as in Syria and Iraq, cavalry maintained a prominent role even in the late phase of the war against the French, as stated by such a well-informed eyewitness as William Wittman, who outlined how in the Ottoman army 'the number of the cavalry is much greater than that of the infantry.'[47]

As for their tactics, Wittman writes that in battle:

> The [Ottoman] cavalry do not engage en masse so much as the janissaries, but are more dispersed.' He also remarks the good cohesion and order, and that 'on these occasions each troop or squadron whatever may be its strength, keep together without mixing with the other troops.[48]

---

46 Fahmy, *All the Pasha's Men*, pp.112–113.
47 Wittman, *Travels to Turkey*, p.240.
48 Wittman, *Travels to Turkey*, p.240: 'In rushing forward, at a given signal, to encounter the enemy, each of the horsemen exclaims with vehemence, *Allah! Allah!* Invoking the aid of the deity to the enterprize.'

Plate A

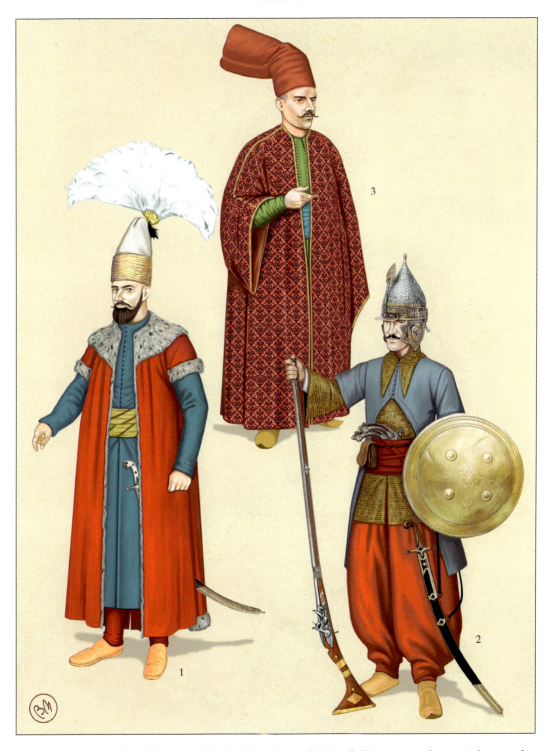

1. Janissary *çorbaci* (1790–98); 2. *Sipahi ulufely* in full armour, late eighteenth century; 3. *Hasseki agasy*, 1790–1810

(Illustration by Bruno Mugnai © Helion & Company 2022)

See Colour Plate Commentaries for further information

Plate B

1. Janissary *kara koullaçi*, 1807; 2. Janissary on campaign, 1790–1800; 3. Janissary junior officer, *cavuş*, 1800–1802

(Illustration by Bruno Mugnai © Helion & Company 2022)

See Colour Plate Commentaries for further information

Plate C

Ottoman Kaftan and *Ciubbeh*, 1790–1826
1. *Erkan-i kürkü* kaftan; 2. *Ust kürkü* kaftan; 3. and 4. Janissary *dolama* kaftans
(Illustration by Bruno Mugnai © Helion & Company 2022)
See Colour Plate Commentaries for further information

Plate D

**1. Irregular infantryman, 1786–1800; 2. Anatolian *levend*, 1800–1809;
3. Anatolian irregular infantrymen**

(Illustration by Bruno Mugnai © Helion & Company 2022)

See Colour Plate Commentaries for further information

Plate E

1. Provincial *sipahi*, 1800–1802; 2. *Delibaşi*, 1800–1809;
3. Georgian horseman, 1780–1815

(Illustration by Bruno Mugnai © Helion & Company 2022)

See Colour Plate Commentaries for further information

Plate F

Mamluk and Egyptian Clothing
1. Mamluk striped kaftan; 2. and 3. Egyptian *gibbeh*; 4. *Faragieb*;
5. Egyptian *eri* cotton shirt; 6. Cotton *eri* shirt
(Illustration by Bruno Mugnai © Helion & Company 2022)
See Colour Plate Commentaries for further information

Plate G

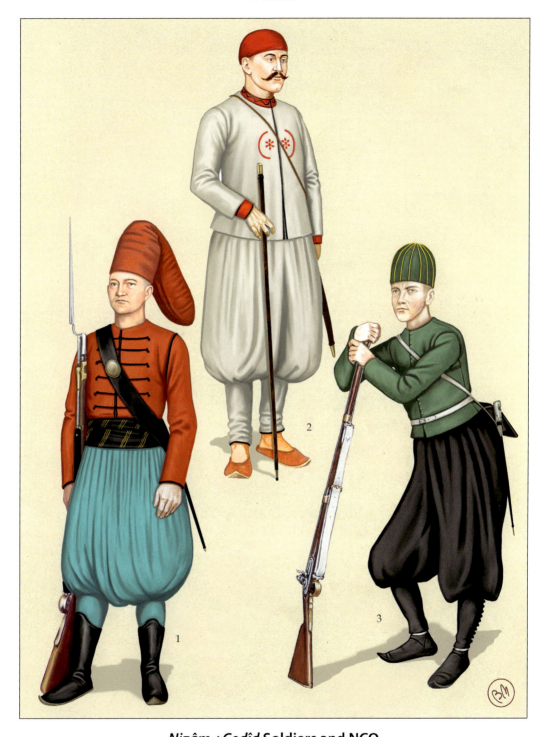

Nizâm-ı Cedîd Soldiers and NCO
1. Private soldier, *Levend* (1st) Infantry Regiment, 1800–1808; 2. NCO in quarter dress, 1800–1808; 3. Anatolian *nefer* private soldier, 1802–1808

(Illustration by Bruno Mugnai © Helion & Company 2022)

See Colour Plate Commentaries for further information

Plate H

1. *Humbaraçi* bombardier officer, 1808–15; 2. Artillery officer, 1800–07; 3. Horse artillery trumpeter, 1800–1807

(Illustration by Bruno Mugnai © Helion & Company 2022)

See Colour Plate Commentaries for further information

Plate I

Ottoman, Balkan and Mamluk Clothing

1. Ottoman-Turkish *salta* jacket; 2. Ottoman-Turkish *mintan* jacket; 3. Bosnian *jacerma* doublet; 4. Greek-Albanian doublet; 5. Ottoman-Turkish *yelek* doublet; 6. Greek-Albanian *fustanela* skirt; 7. Balkan loose trousers of coloured cotton; 8. Ottoman-Turkish *salvar* loose trousers; 9. Mamluk *sernali* trousers for cavalrymen; 10. Ottoman-Turkish trousers; 11. Albanian trousers

(Illustration by Bruno Mugnai © Helion & Company 2022)

See Colour Plate Commentaries for further information

Plate J

Mamluk Elite *Amir* Horseman
(Illustration by Bruno Mugnai © Helion & Company 2022)
See Colour Plate Commentaries for further information

Plate K

1. Egyptian Mamluk, 1790s; 2. Syrian mounted marksman and dromedary, 1797
(Illustration by Bruno Mugnai © Helion & Company 2022)
See Colour Plate Commentaries for further information

Plate L

1. Bosnian cavalryman, *c.* 1800; 2. Kurdish horseman, late eighteenth century

(Illustration by Bruno Mugnai © Helion & Company 2022)

See Colour Plate Commentaries for further information

Plate M

Albanian Foot Soldier of Muhammed Ali
(Illustration by Bruno Mugnai © Helion & Company 2022)
See Colour Plate Commentaries for further information

Plate N

Albanian *Arnavut* Infantrymen

(Top, left and right: From *Wittman's Travels in Turkey*; bottom left: from *Fenerci Mehmed Albümü* (1800–1825); bottom right: from *Costumes Turcs* of the Diez Collection)

See Colour Plate Commentaries for further information

Plate O

1. Cavalry standard; 2. Infantry ensign, Egyptian campaigns 1800–1802; 3. Infantry ensign depicted in the *Fenerci Mehmed Albümü* (1800–1825); 4. *Humbaraci* artillery standard; 5. Ensign of janissary *orta* 25; 6. Ensign of an unknown infantry regiment; 7. and 8. Ensigns of Muhammad Ali

(Illustration by Bruno Mugnai © Helion & Company 2022)

See Colour Plate Commentaries for further information

Plate P

1. *Sancak*, late eighteenth century; 2. Ensign of janissary *orta* 56; 3. Inscriptional *sancak*, early nineteenth century; 4. Late eighteenth-century *sancak*; 5. Large *sancak* with *zulfiqar* and inscriptions dating to 1819. (1, 2, 4: Hermitage Museum, St Petersburg; 3: Private Collection, Malaysia; 5: Askery Museum, Constantinople)

See Colour Plate Commentaries for further information

However, from a tactical point of view, the Ottoman cavalry offers a contrasting picture. According to Constantin de Volnay, who travelled Egypt and Syria in the 1780s, the Mamluks still appeared as remarkable horsemen. In particular, he praises their training, especially the use of the javelin, or *cerid*, which he considers a very lethal weapon against cavalry and infantry as well.[49] Conversely, Valentini states that both the Mamluk and the Ottoman horsemen were unable to break a well-formed square, because they did not exploit the impact of the charge adequately.[50] Wittman remarks that the Mamluk horseman carried six firearms and his European counterpart only one or three at maximum, but whilst the Europeans adapted their tactics according to the capabilities of their firearm, the Mamluks adapted the weapon to their tactics.[51]

Ultimately the Ottoman cavalry tactics were no longer able to withstand confrontation with the West, and not even numerical superiority alone could ensure victory, especially as both the Austrians and the Russians – the main European enemies of the Porte – could deploy equally large armies. In general the Ottomans were less able to effectively coordinate infantry, cavalry and artillery as their European adversaries did, and each corps was managed as a separate element, which was certainly their greatest tactical limitation. For instance, the Ottomans proved repeatedly unable to defeat the weak and isolated French forces in Egypt for lack of co-ordination between infantry and cavalry; similarly, the amphibious operation of Aboukir in 1799 ended in total failure. In the meantime, the government spent enormous amounts of money recruiting all available manpower and bribing standing units to mobilise for war.

Recognising all these weaknesses, the 'progressive' members of the government were summoned together by Sultan Selim III to examine in depth the question of how to reform the army. Selim actually started discussions for reform during the war of 1787–1792, collecting more than 200 high officials and other dignitaries as a kind of advisory council in May 1789. After several heated gatherings a select few of the participants, totalling 24 in all, were summoned. These restricted meetings occurred between 1791 and 1792. Each advisor and minister presented a report and submitted it to the Sultan. These documents are very instructive about the detail of the problems and dysfunctions of the Ottoman army in the aftermath of the war against Austria and Russia. The desire to set aside any attempt at traditionalist reform emerges clearly in the reports, but resistance to introducing Western European methods and forms of modern military organisation *tout court* were still strong.

Ebubekir Ratib Efendi, one of the most authoritative members of the commission, wrote in detail about what he had learned of the military and civil organisations of the European states, their methods of taxation, their military and financial organisations and practices, their postal systems,

---

49 Volnay, *Voyage en Syrie et en Égypte*, pp.160–161
50 Valentini, *Précis des dernières guerres des Russes contre les Turcs*, p.18.
51 Wittman, *Travels to Turkey*, p.236.

roads, mines, agriculture, industry, trade, banks, and army. He praised the freedom left to individuals to do what they wanted without restriction by the state. He stressed the European idea that government was instituted to look out for the welfare and security of individuals, a concept in stark contrast to the traditional Ottoman idea that the sole purpose of government was to extend, defend, and exploit the wealth of the Empire for the benefit of the ruling class.[52]

According to almost all the Sultan's advisors, a major cause of the decay of military effectiveness was the practice of selling the leading positions of the corps to the highest bidders regardless of their military qualifications or experience, although the question of whether this was the cause or result of decay was not considered. The result of this practice was said to be that even the few soldiers who did remain in the army and did report for training and service were poorly led. In addition their officers withheld all or most of the wage money and supplies sent by the Treasury, even going so far as to conceal vacancies resulting from illness or death and continuing to collect for their own profit the salaries and wages for vacant positions. The result was that only a small portion of the names on the rolls of the corps actually assembled when they were called up on campaign, and those who did join the army were riotous, undisciplined, liable to run in the face of danger, and dependent for their subsistence on booty secured from friends and foes alike along the road of march.[53] An initial solution proposed for these conditions by almost every member was to appoint only 'able and honest officers' and abolish the fees required in return, although how this was to be accomplished in the face of an Ottoman society that was almost entirely built around such a system was not discussed.[54]

For the most part, the advisors gave primary emphasis to military reform. This emergency was considered an actual danger even by advisors who were not members of the military corps or had no direct connection with them. Since few of the committee members had any military experience or knew anything of the European techniques they wished to imitate, many of their recommendations were of limited value. However, there was a matter on which all the advisors agreed: military decay was due mainly to a failure of the discipline in the individual corps, and some of the members stated that it could be remedied by the restoration of the traditional laws. Though some

---

52 Shaw, *Between Old and New*, p, 96. According to the Selim III's advisor, 'the Sultan had to face was the immense size of the Empire and the consequent difficulty which the central government had in controlling the various officials and provinces. To him, the essential bases of European greatness were: (1) the organisation and obedience of the soldiers; (2) the efficiency and fullness of the Treasury; (3) the honesty, ability, and loyalty of the ministers and bureaucrats; (4) the arrangements for the tranquillity, comfort, and protection of the people; and (5) the ability of the European states to cooperate for their mutual benefit and to make agreements for mutual assistance. These were the objects which the Sultan would have to keep in mind in reforming his state if he wished to achieve the grandeur and power of those he sought to imitate.'

53 Mouradgea d'Ohsson, *Tableau Général*, vol. VI, pp.273–274.

54 Shaw, *Between Old and New*, p.97.

OTTOMAN WARFARE: A STRUGGLE FOR SURVIVAL

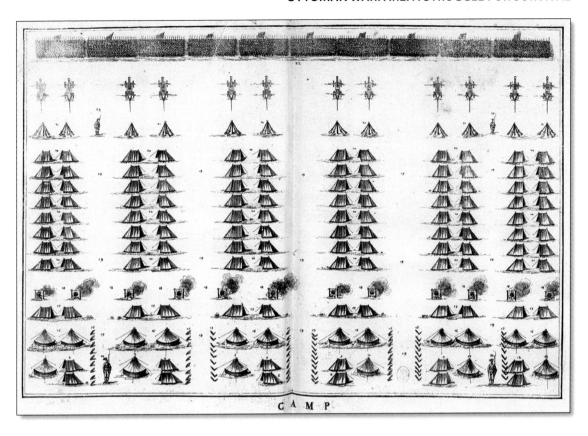

Ottoman encampment according to the modern technique, after Rayf Mahmoud Efendi, *Tableau des Nouveaux Reglemens de l'Empire Ottoman* (Constantinople, 1798).

difference of evaluation emerged among the committee, all the members agreed that officers should be chosen for ability alone, and the corps should be inspected to determine which members were able and willing to serve, and which held the positions only for the revenues which they made possible. The latter should be dropped from the rolls as soon as possible to make room for youths who could be moulded into expert and brave officers from an early age. The soldiers had to be kept together in the barracks in order to be subjected to discipline, and they should be prevented from accepting outside employment and income. Preferably, they would be unmarried in order to be available at all times for regular military training and service.

Once these almost universally accepted diagnoses were set down, the advisors became much more varied in their proposals on how new and able men and officers should be recruited, organised, and trained. Some reports stated that the decline of the janissaries in particular was due to their resentment of the government's increasing neglect of them in favour of the experimental new weapons and their consequent loss of prestige in Ottoman society. These advisors remarked that, if they were given the proper support, and if they were given able officers exempted from all fees – in other words, if they were given their old prestige and esteem – they would automatically return to their own discipline and ways, and they might even be willing to accept new weapons and methods. European military advisors could be summoned to train the janissaries and the other old corps, but they would have to accept Islam since true believers could not be expected to accept the statements and teachings from infidels. Such were the words of two of the most enlightened members of the Ottoman ruling class.

Other members attributed many of the army's difficulties to its annual winter dispersal. Many of the enemy gains had occurred after the Ottoman army had evacuated its advanced positions for winter quarters leaving behind only token guards. As a solution they suggested the division of the entire army into summer and winter contingents, each serving six months and spending the rest of the time training and working at other gainful occupations which would give them sufficient revenue to maintain and supply themselves at minimum cost to the state. On this matter, Ahmed Kamil Paşazade Hakkı Paşa, who had acquired an excellent reputation for honesty and efficiency, suggested that the winter soldiers be drawn from the janissary corps and provincial contingent of Rumelia, and the summer soldiers from the other standing corps and the Anatolian contingents. In addition, each minister and official in the service of the sultan, especially each provincial governor, would assume the burden of recruiting, training, and maintaining a certain number of disciplined soldiers in his own entourage, supplying them as recruits to the regular corps whenever vacancies occurred, and also for special service with the field army in summer or winter, as they were needed. The cost of maintaining this force would be met partly by the Imperial Treasury, partly by the officials involved and partly by wealthy judges in the provinces. Thus for the first time in Ottoman history a kind of Reserve Army similar to the European militia was proposed. Some advisors felt that the army's disorderliness in peace and war was due mainly to the enlistment of far more men than the corps' old regulations permitted and to the government's insistence that they remain in service during peacetime. To remedy this difficulty, they recommended that vacancies be ignored until the corps were reduced to their original numerical limits, and after that time they be filled only by youths willing to serve all their lives. He felt that only a few janissaries and members of the other corps should be kept in Constantinople, and that these should be kept busy training in the use of weapons and tactics. The remainder would be sent to serve with the provincial governors and along the borders for terms of five years, afterwards returning to the capital for further training. On the other hand, one advisor proposed a partial demobilisation of the corps in peacetime, with their members forming a kind of ready reserve force available for service at a moment's notice. They would return to their homes and keep up their skills by participating in weekly training periods directed by the local governors and officers. At the same time, they would serve periodically in the governors' retinues to assist in the task of maintaining peace and security.

Some authoritative advisors proposed a plan which would revive the ancient *devşirme* recruiting system, which had manned the janissary corps during the past centuries. However, the willingness of the subject Christians to cooperate in such a plan was not discussed. A variant of the *devşirme* was also discussed. An advisors felt that the best way of securing a steady flow of qualified recruits for the army was for the corps themselves to maintain auxiliary groups of trainees, numbering 100 or 200 youths each, who would serve as apprentices and assistants to the regular soldiers while in training, and who would have first call at filling vacancies in the corps. In addition, all ministers and officers assigned to duty in the provinces would have to take along with them between 100 and 1,000 young recruits each. These levies would be drilled and maintained at the expense of the state and officers concerned, and would form an additional pool of 10,000 to 15,000 trained recruits ready to fill vacancies in the corps.

Concerning the lack of loyal officers, some advisors felt that a major difficulty with the corps was that their officers came from their own ranks and essentially represented them against the central government. The solution was for the chief officers of the corps to be appointed from among the sultan's men in the inner palace service. Such men would be far more loyal to him, they would prevent any independent action on the part of the corps, and they would keep the soldiers disciplined and obedient. No mention was made of how such palace men without military experience would be able to improve the military abilities of the corps in question. The authoritative Şerif Efendi concentrated his attention on the salaried border guards stationed along the Danube, contending that their officers kept most of the salaries and supplies sent from the Porte, and actually maintained only a very small number of men for border duty. His solution was the abolition of this corps, with half their salaries being eliminated and the other half given as bonuses to the officers and men serving on the frontier with Russia. Another advisor perceived the same weakness in the border organisation; but instead of eliminating it, he suggested that it be reorganised and reformed, with the local judges supervising wage distribution so that only persons actually performing the service would be paid and vacancies would be uncovered and filled.

Many of the reports devoted particular attention to the established artillery corps, including the guns, train, wagons, rapid-fire weapons, mortar and miners corps, since it was they who showed the clearest inferiority to the Austrians and the Russians, and also since the tradition of reform in this field had already been established in previous reigns. Yusuf Paşa and others stated that the older artillery corps had been demoralised by the attention paid to the new light artillery, and that the latter were of little use and should be abolished and replaced with a system in which each high official in Constantinople and the provinces would be given two modern cannons and one mortar and required to train and maintain seven men for each of them. In this way a large number of trained artillerymen would be available for service with the infantry and cavalry corps whenever needed. Another advisor said that the rapid-fire artillery corps should be retained, but only as a training and recruiting vehicle, with its men being assigned to the regular artillery corps for service in battle.

Two prominent advisors felt exactly the opposite. Instead of abolishing the light artillery corps or limiting its importance, they wanted it to be expanded and sent on campaign as an independent unit rather than as a part of the older corps. While they felt that efforts should certainly be made to reorganise and restore the older artillery corps, to them only the rapid-fire artillery offered a possibility for immediate reform, hence they had to be expanded and put under the direction of foreign officers as soon as possible.

Koca Yusuf Paşa (1730–1800), a Georgian convert to Islam, was twice grand vizier in 1786–89 and in 1791–92. Despite his advanced age, he was one of the best Ottoman commanders during the war against Russia and Austria. In 1788, he managed to repel the Austrian offensive in Bosnia and kept his enemies under constant threat until the end of the campaign. For his merits as a military leader, he was called back into service in 1791 in a desperate attempt to stop the Russians on the Danube.

To restore the artillery and its train, another authoritative counsellor proposed that since both the corps were complementary they should be united into a single service, given 200 of the most modern guns available, with 100 men assigned to each of the large army divisions and 50 to the small, forming a corps of about 15,000 men. With the distinction between those who fired the weapons and those who moved them eliminated, in his opinion improved efficiency and discipline would be possible. Moreover, each group of men would be assigned to a specific gun which they would be in charge of maintaining, moving, and firing in battle. If it was disabled, they would have to repair it, or at least make sure that it did not fall into enemy hands. If a cannon was left behind in battle, the men attached to it would be dismissed from service and held up to scorn and mockery by the people. An advisor proposed that an elite of 100 master gunners could be trained to act as supervisors for the older corps and that special funds be provided to assist them in their efforts, and to provide them with the new cannons and equipment they needed. In turn, some advisors felt that the best solution was to cut the number of men in each artillery corps in half and double their salaries to assure that they got the best possible men. Fifty men would be attached to each cannon and given special prizes in return for their standing in turns by their weapons 'day and night, year after year', so that they would be prepared to take them into action at a moment's notice.[55] When they were fully trained, they would be sent in rotation to the various border garrisons, provincial governors, and others needing their services, and would serve for periods from six months to a year before returning to Constantinople for further training.

Grand Vizier Koca Yusuf Paşa also proposed that the previous system by which the officers and more experienced men in these artillery and miners corps were rewarded with fiefs instead of salaries be abolished, since it enabled them to become independent of their officers and to leave their positions to sons or relatives regardless of ability. Salaries would have to be provided for all members of the two corps as the best means of keeping their members disciplined and orderly.

The statements concerning the standing cavalry were of a similar nature. The solutions proposed by almost every advisor involved the usual combination of weeding out incompetents, raising salaries, and training the men in the use

---

55 Mouradgea d'Ohsson, *Tableau Général*, p.267.

of modern weapons. The advisors despaired entirely of making the *sipahis* into an efficient and useful military force in a reasonable time because of the tremendous stake of the vested interests in the status quo. One of them suggested that an entirely new, regular, salaried cavalry corps be formed from the *deli* light horsemen, who in the past had been recruited from the 'bandits' of Rumelia for service during campaigns as mounted irregulars and had been supported entirely by the booty they were able to amass for themselves (*sic*!). He felt that this reorganisation would require so much energy and effort, however, that it would have to be postponed until after the reorganisation of the janissaries was completed, and that the new corps would therefore have to be developed quickly to perform cavalry service in the meantime. Another advisor also realised the vast difficulties involved in attempting to restore the cavalry, but suggested that the reforms be introduced very gradually, with experts spending a number of years investigating conditions before any final programmes were put forward. Some advisors attributed much of the cavalry's difficulty to the addition of over 20,000 men above the numerical limits established in 1720 and recommended a return to the original number as the best way to restore the corps.

Bertrand and d'Ohsson, the two foreign experts who submitted reports, were much more hesitant to include details, apparently because of a realisation that they could easily disturb their own position by angering one or another of the many factions within the Imperial court. They did, however, at least risk such difficulties by referring to the problem with which they were most familiar – that of the foreign advisers in the Ottoman service – and blamed much of their lack of success on betrayal by the Ottoman officials with whom they came into contact, on their neglect in carrying out the recommendations of their advisers, and on their acceptance of many reform ideas without making any further effort to carry them out, coordinate them, or consider their effect on the state and army as a whole. Bertrand stated that most of the Ottoman reformers seemed content just to issue orders, without bothering to see that they were properly executed. He suggested that they be required to inspect their commands regularly to eliminate difficulties as they arose, instead of letting them drag on interminably until the entire reform programme was undermined. D'Ohsson disapproved of the Sultan's excessive focusing on the artillery corps and emphasised that new weapon and techniques should be given to all soldiers and in particular to the old infantry and cavalry corps, since they remained the bulk of the standing army. It is not clear how and to what extent the work of the reform commission was actually processed by the Sultan for the creation of the new army he planned. However, the initiative did not bear the desired fruit, and his attempt to modernise the army failed with his dismissal in 1807 and elimination one year later, leaving the Empire's armies to fight the campaigns for survival in an uncertain position.[56]

In terms of accurate studies covering warfare and campaigns, the period 1792–1815 belongs to the most neglected of all Ottoman history. The long series of conflicts between the Empire and his European enemies resulted

---

56 Shaw, *Between Old and New*, p.99.

THE OTTOMAN ARMY OF THE NAPOLEONIC WARS 1789–1815

Ottoman infantry and cavalry in a last stand at the second battle of Aboukir, 25 July 1799, by Louis-François Lejeune (Chateau de Versailles). Note the short sleeveless jackets, *yelek*, worn by the soldiers in the foreground centre and right.

in a spiral of defeat for the Sultan and a relentless southward march of the border. Yet the campaigns were punctuated with a few successes, just enough to have blinded Ottoman commanders to the necessity for overhauling outmoded fighting styles and cumbersome supply systems. Economically, the Ottoman warfare was again a mixture of success and failure. With raw recruits, fractious elites, incompetent leadership and obsolete equipment, the Ottomans faced Russians and Austrians on the Danube frontier in 1787–92, and only Russians in 1806–12. Scholars invariably ascribe any Ottoman successes to luck, or to Austrian lack of central command and incompetence in leadership, Russian overextension and distances from sources of supply, or difficulties that invariably emerge in coalition warfare. Western European military historiography is dismissive of pre-Napoleonic warfare in general, and makes even shorter shrift of the Ottomans, who by that assessment never faced any significant enemies until the modern Austrian and Russian armies.[57] Even less investigated are the campaigns that the Porte sustained against internal threats that were disintegrating the state, those against the Bedouin tribes, or against enemies who contended for the Sultan's supremacy over the Muslim world, such as the fearsome Wahhabis.

---

57 Aksan, 'War and Peace', p.99.

Campaigns Against the Bedouins in Iraq, 1784–1791

The obsession with the northern frontier led the Porte to neglect the southern tier of the Empire, allowing the expansion of nomadic and mobile populations, such as the Arab Bedouins and Kurdish tribes, which maintained autonomy by their original submission to Ottoman hegemony and payment of annual tributes to the Porte. As a result, in the eighteenth century the local households became more powerful and independent, but the Sultan's suzerainty continued to be recognised everywhere except in the Arabian Peninsula. In fact two distinct zones coexisted in the area, which were differently affected by the central power at Constantinople. The inner zone consisted of provinces located in Syria and Iraq, which were closest to the Ottoman heartland of Anatolia. These were fully incorporated into the Ottoman Empire, and the full measure of Ottoman provincial governance was implemented there. Provinces further afield were usually governed by men sent out from Constantinople. However, they typically relied on local political elites to fill the lower ranks of administration. Instead, the Arab cities on the outer zone rarely had Ottoman governors. Here, local warlords ruled, although they also professed loyalty to the sultan and collected taxes in his name. Given the diversity of conditions that existed in the Arab provinces, the local forces making for autonomy differed widely in their origins. Nonetheless, every Arab province witnessed the rise of political movements or personalities who challenged the sultan's monopoly of power in the eighteenth century.[58]

In Iraq the political scenario was dominated by the greatest of the Mamluk rulers, the Georgian-born Süleyman Paşa 'the Great'. His enlightened 22-year rule largely coincided with the age of Selim III. When Süleyman came to power as Ottoman governor in 1780, he found that the six months of interregnum following his predecessor's death had been used by the Bedouins of the Middle Euphrates, Arabia and Syria to ravage the countryside and defy the central government's authority. At the same time local rulers had declared their independence in the north at Mosul and Mardin and in the south at Basra, withholding their local tax revenues for their own treasuries. To meet these challenges Süleyman first had to establish his position in Baghdad itself. By restoring order and security in the capital he gained the support of the local merchants, whose businesses had been threatened by the previous disorder. At the same time he found the long-established janissary corps in Baghdad, which on paper numbered almost 5,000 men, to be as disorganised and ill-fitted for fighting as their comrades in Constantinople, while the Mamluks were dispirited and reduced in numbers as a result of the long years of factional disputes. Süleyman decided to rebuild the Mamluk forces to provide the base for his power. Thus he imported large numbers of slave-recruits from Georgia and quickly trained them into an effective fighting force. He then appointed the best of them as officers in the janissary *ocak*, and used the Mamluk army to force the janissaries to accept discipline, training, and new weapons. Within a short time he created an effective

---

58 Masters, 'Semi-autonomous forces in the Arab provinces', p.186.

THE OTTOMAN ARMY OF THE NAPOLEONIC WARS 1789–1815

Mamluks and Bedouin from Thomas Walsh's *Journal of the Late Campaign in Egypt* (London, 1803) and the same subjects reproduced in a later album of Ottoman military costumes. Much of the knowledge about the dress of the Ottoman army is still controversial. Many albums and collections of costumes published in Western Europe show in detail clothing and accessories, but these sources are often unfaithful copies from original sources, and the latter are not always accurate in identifying the figures. Furthermore, many mid to late nineteenth century illustrations are highly romanticised, and these have often been used for modern reconstruction, repeating such errors.

OTTOMAN WARFARE: A STRUGGLE FOR SURVIVAL

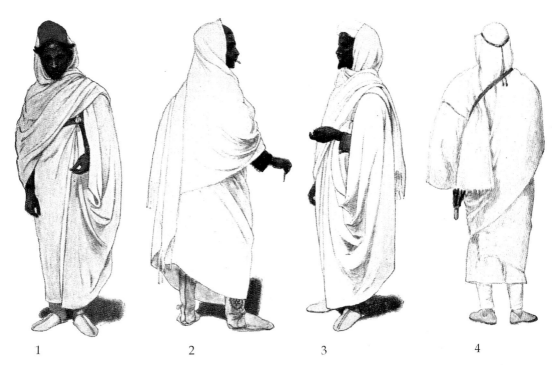

Above: Bedouin clothing. The traditional shawl draped over one or both shoulders developed in the *haik* of North Africa and the Arabian Peninsula. In the Maghreb it is commonly called the *hauly* or *usera*, while in Egypt it is known by the name *hiram*, which is the same term used by the Bedouins. In its most common form, the *haik-hiram* is a woollen shawl of natural colour, up to 4.5 m long and 1.20 m wide, and in some cases, it can be used with the end flap as a turban, wrapped around the body or left loose at the hips or on one arm. Even in the early twentieth century, this was the basic garment of many desert peoples, and in many cases the only one used by the more isolated Bedouin tribes.

Figures 1 and 2 show the simple *hiram* style widespread in Egypt, while figure 3 shows the one typical of the Arabian Peninsula. Figure 4 depicts a Bedouin from Upper Egypt. Under the *haik*, he wears a simple shirt with sleeves and loose riding trousers.

Carl Max Tilke, *Orientalische Kostüme in Schnitt und Farbe* (Berlin: Verlag E. Wasmuth, 1923).

Overleaf, top:

1) With the *haik-hiram*, the *aba*, *kofia*, and *ogal* were worn in Mesopotamia, Syria, Palestine, Arabia, and Egypt by both the settled and semi-nomadic population. The *aba* is the typical mantle usually manufactured of black hard woollen material and consists of two pieces sewn together. The shoulder-seam, neck-slit, and front seam are more or less ornamented with silk cords or embroidery. In this shape, it was used as a mantle by the upper class of Arabs and Bedouin chiefs.

The *kofia* or *kefijah* is a square piece of cotton cloth interwoven with vertical silk stripes. Thin cords with small tassels are fixed on both sides. The *kofia* is generally worn diagonally, so that the cords hang over the shoulders and back. The *ogal* is used to fasten the *kofia* on to the head. It is usually made of natural colour camel's wool around which silk, gold, or silver threads are wound at intervals. In Palestine and Syria, the ogal consists of a ring-like roll wrapped with black wool and folded twice round the head.

2) The *kapanica* is the weather cloak of the Balkans. It is semi-circular, and made to fit the shoulders by the insertion of a gore. It is made of a fulled wool, a sort of rough hunter's cloth, on the outside of which the hair is sometimes left. The favourite colours are black, or black-brown; more seldom white. The opening for the neck and the seams over the chest are trimmed with the customary coloured braid. The inside of the *kapanica*, and the shoulder parts are often lined with silk or calico on the most precious items. The *kapanica* is tied at the neck with strings. The hood is a complement to the *kapanica*, the base of which is secured around the back of the neck.

Carl Max Tilke, Wolfgang Bruhn, *Das Kostümwerk. Eine Geschichte des Kostüms aller Zeiten und Völke* (Berlin: E. Wasmuth, 1941).

THE OTTOMAN ARMY OF THE NAPOLEONIC WARS 1789–1815

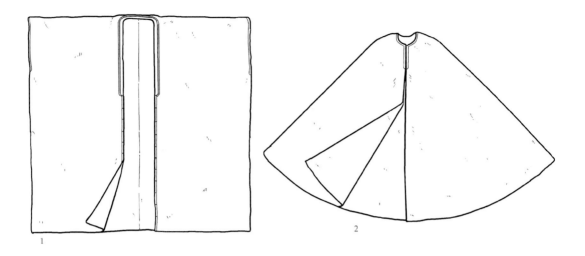

1

2

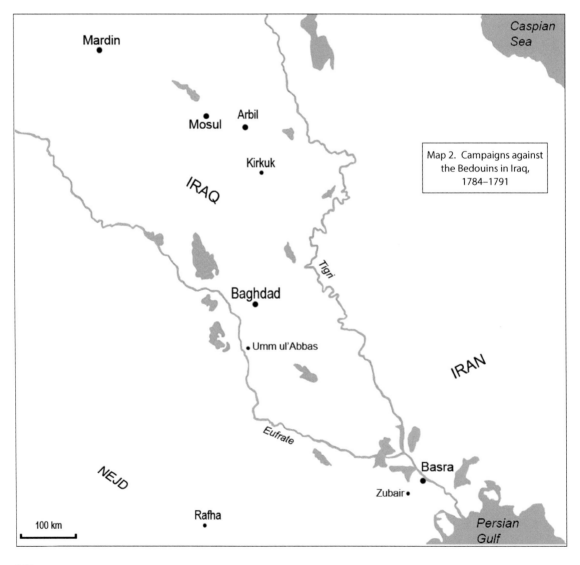

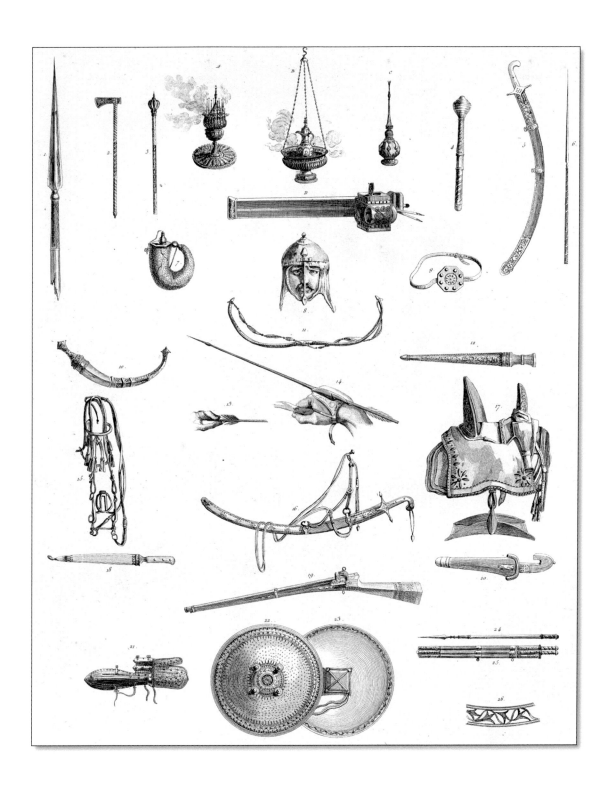

THE OTTOMAN ARMY OF THE NAPOLEONIC WARS 1789–1815

Previous page: Mamluk weapons and equipment, in a print by Auguste Claude Simon Legrand, dating 1802 (author's archive). Note the hand accessories for the arrow. Despite the extensive use of firearms by the Mamluks, archery was still practised as a sporting activity. This was also the case in the eastern provinces of the Ottoman Empire. The Mamluks also had a dangerous training method, which was to let the 'defender' run on the trajectory of the javelin while trying to receive the javelin empty-handed. The javelin (*djerid* or *cerid*) did not have an iron spear head and was theoretically not lethal, but occasionally during training someone was seriously injured. As for the javelin used in wartime, according to General Bardin, the editor of the *Dictionnaire de l'armée de Terre* (1800), the javelin was really a 'horribly lethal projectile weapon'. The Frenchman Miot, who experienced the expedition to Egypt, also confirmed the widespread use of the javelin in wartime. He pointed out that '[The] Mamluk's saddle has a sabre on one side, and a carbine on the other side, and there is usually a javelin'. Denon, the founder of Egyptology, even mentioned the case of throwing three javelins before swinging a sabre.

Below: A Mamluk with horse, engraving by Carle Vernet (1758–1836). Note the pattern of saddle cover and harness, which were common in Egypt as well as all the Ottoman Empire in the elite class.

fighting force for himself. Once this was accomplished, Süleyman moved to restore order in the province.[59]

In the early 1780s Süleyman organised and personally led expeditions against the Bedouins and forced them to perform in his service, both to guard caravans and boats, and to serve in his armies against those of their fellows who had not yet accepted his rule. The river and road bandits were almost entirely eliminated, and once again the Tigris and Euphrates were open for communications. Bedouin raids resumed with a certain intensity in 1784, when Sheyh Thuwaini, leader of the Muntafik tribe of Suk ul-Shuyuh, became the leader of the opposition to Süleyman's power in Iraq. Between September and December 1784 Thuwaini captured Zubair and Basra, arrested the Ottoman officials, and forced the local notables to petition the Sultan to appoint him to Süleyman's place in Baghdad. Süleyman managed to thwart the threat and with support from the Middle Euphrates Bedouins and some northern Kurdish tribes, led a series of campaigns against Thuwaini and in October 1787 finally defeated him at Umm ul-Abbas. Süleyman re-established his direct authority in Basra, but Thuwaini managed to escape and took refuge in Arabia, where the rising Wahhabi movement based its power. With Thuwaini encouragement the Wahhabis turned their attention to Iraq, and their raids in subsequent years came to occupy most of Süleyman's attention. In Arabia, revolt against Ottoman rule during the late eighteenth and early nineteenth centuries was focused in the Wahhabi religious movement and the armed forces of the Saudi family, who first rose to power in the middle of the eighteenth century as the main opponent of Ottoman rule in the region.[60]

Abd ul-Aziz I Ibn Saud had assumed actual political and military leadership of the Wahhabi-Saudi state in the 1760s, and the Bedouin tribes which had declared allegiance to his father did not hesitate to transfer their support. It was under Abd ul-Aziz that the state expanded out of the Nejd to rule most of Arabia and in fact to threaten the foundations of the Ottoman Empire. With no effective internal opposition, his leadership maintained a strong vitality and continued to expand.

For the moment the Saudis preferred to avoid open conflict with the Ottoman forces, so continued to concentrate their activities in the north and east of the peninsula, with their occasional raids into southern Iraq hardly noticed by the centre of power as anything more than the usual Bedouin attacks on settled areas. Raids and counter-raids continued until triggering the first confrontation between Ottomans and Saudi Wahhabis in 1792.

---

59 Shaw, *Between Old and New*, p.221.
60 Shaw, *Between Old and New*, p.221.

Expeditions to Egypt, and Factional Struggles in Syria, 1786–1790

After 1779 Egypt fell under the control of a Mamluk coalition led by Murad and Ibrahim *Beys*, who ruled almost continuously for the rest of the century. For a time they continued to pay their taxes and tribute to the Sultan, but once they had eliminated their rivals and established virtually unopposed rule after 1783, they reduced and largely ended their payments. Only then did the Porte send a military expedition to curb them, under the command of the *kapudan paşa* Gazi Hasan Paşa in 1786. His object was not to restore direct Ottoman administration since he was well aware that the Porte would lack the power to enforce such a position once his expeditionary force returned to Constantinople. Rather he sought only to restore the various Mamluk factions so they would be able to administer the country while paying for the governor's encouragement and support. Since the outbreak of a new war with Russia and Austria in 1787 forced Gazi Hasan to leave before he could bring about a satisfactory solution, it was not long before Murad and Ibrahim returned to power.

As a result of Gazi Hasan's work in building up the other Mamluk factions, however, Murad and Ibrahim were never able to eliminate their rivals entirely thereafter, and they remained sufficiently dependent on the Porte to be forced to pay taxes and tribute although at an ever-decreasing rate. However, during the last quarter of the eighteenth century, there were constant struggles among the rival Mamluk factions, with Murad and Ibrahim never being able to achieve sufficient strength to overcome them and establish relative calm. Each faction extorted tributes in town and country alike to finance its efforts, and none of *beys* had the ability or strength to perform the duties of police and administration needed to keep order and security in the province. Egyptian chaos became chronic, as reported by European travellers of this age.[61]

In Syria, the scenario was decisively less turbulent. Here, the outstanding leader was Ahmed Cezzar Paşa. Born a Christian Bosnian, he entered Ottoman service in 1756 and after an outstanding career as Mamluk in Egypt, he managed to build his personal domains in Palestine and Syria. As governor of Sidon and Damascus, Ahmed attracted into his service large numbers of Bosnians and Albanians into Syria to reinforce the Ottoman garrisons, and he soon built them into the strongest army in the area. With his base continuing at Acre, he expanded his authority and influence throughout much of Syria, Lebanon, and Palestine. Local ruling families had to accept his authority both as Ottoman governor and local notable, and they paid tribute in return for his 'protection'. With these revenues, he not only paid all the taxes he owed to the Sultan, but also enlarged his army, built a small navy, and so extended his power that he was by far the strongest ruler in Syria during the last quarter of the century. The only successful opposition he met came from Mount Lebanon and in particular from the Shihabi Emir

---

61 Gerald MacLean, *Looking East. English Writing and the Ottoman Empire before 1800* (New York, NY: Pearlgrave, 2007), p.188.

Bashir II, who was first chosen as governor of the Lebanon by the local leading families in 1789. Bashir was actually given power by the Janbulat chiefs with the assistance of Cezzar's soldiers, but successfully countered Cezzar's efforts to extend his power into the mountains.

Despite his ostensible submission, Bashir gradually increased his own power in the Lebanon by playing off the various families against one another and gradually confiscating their properties for his own benefit. As a result, by the end of the century he was a powerful rival to Cezzar.[62] Small-scale engagements soon occurred between Cezzar and Bashir in the early 1790s, but no one was able to say who legitimately represented the Sultan's power in the region.

War Against Austria and Russia, 1787–92

The treaty of Küçük Kaynarca, concluded between the Porte and Russia in 1774, was looked on by both as no more than a truce. The treaty marked only one more step along the road towards driving the Ottomans from Europe and the Straits and replacing them with Russian dominion, a dream that Russia nurtured since the time of Peter the Great. Russian championship of Byzantine revival was given its modern expression in Catherine's 'Greek Scheme', embodied in a secret agreement of monarchs concluded with the Emperor of Habsburg Austria in 1783. The essential basis of the agreement was the division of the spoils among the signatories in a mutually satisfying way.

At the same time, France inaugurated a political of friendship with Russia and as a consequence gradually withdrew her support and assistance from the Porte. In 1786 the French officers and technicians who for over a decade had been training units of the Ottoman army were recalled. In January of the next year, France signed a new treaty of trade with Russia, and allowed a similar one with Britain to lapse, thus exposing her new orientation unmistakably.

Confident of its own strength, in August 1783 Russia annexed the Crimea to its empire, and six months later the Porte was forced to recognise this annexation in the Treaty of Aynalikavak. Soon after, Russian soldiers entered the Caucasian principality of Georgia under the pretext of protecting the local prince from his Ottoman suzerain. The Crimean example left the Porte with little doubt as to ultimate Russian intentions east of the Black Sea as well.[63] In May 1787 Russian ambitions were publicly demonstrated by Catherine's

---

62 Shaw, *Between Old and New*, pp.218–219.

63 In addition, Admiral Potemkin was beginning to undertake positive military measures north and west of the Black Sea. At the southern tip of the Crimea, to which the Greek name Thauridia was now given, the great new port of Sevastopol was built to serve as the base of the Russian fleet created to challenge the Ottoman naval monopoly in the area. To the west, at the mouth of the Dnieper, a small but no less important base was built at the ancient Greek colony of Kherson to receive and store the ships and supplies being sent down the Dnieper and the Bug in ever-increasing amounts for service in the Black Sea area. See Shaw, *Between Old and New*, pp.23–24.

THE OTTOMAN ARMY OF THE NAPOLEONIC WARS 1789–1815

THE OTTOMAN ARMY OF THE NAPOLEONIC WARS 1789–1815

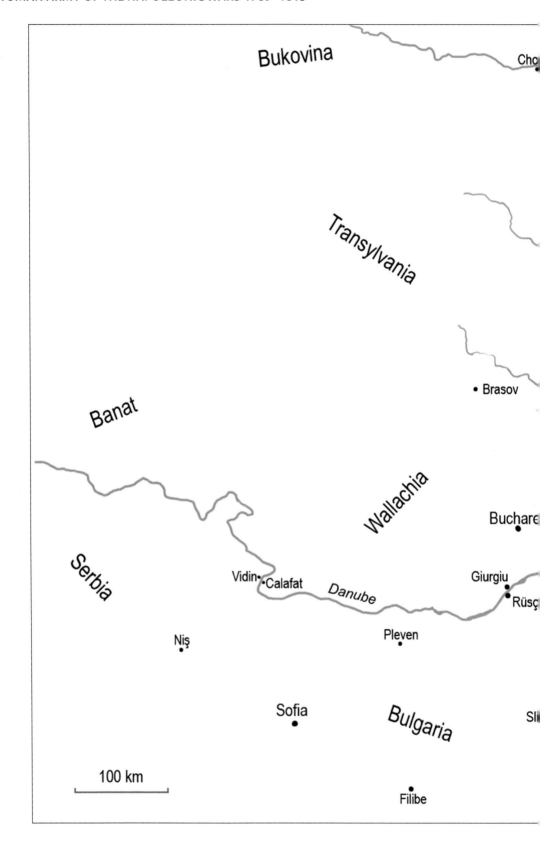

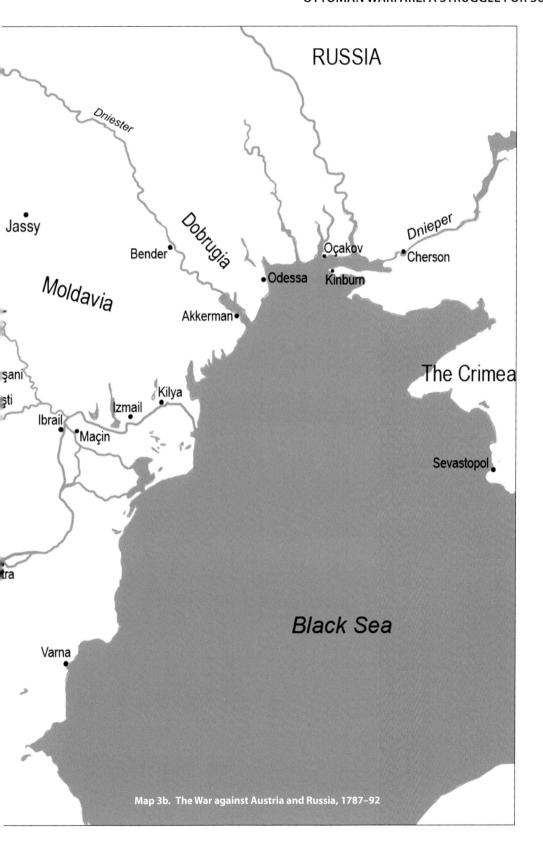

Map 3b. The War against Austria and Russia, 1787–92

triumphal tour through her new province, accompanied by the chief personages of her court and the ambassadors of Austria, Britain, and France.

While Britain and Prussia were encouraging the Porte to stand up against further Russian encroachments, no firm commitments had been made for financial and military support in case of war. The influential *kapudan paşa* Cezayrli Gazi Hasan Paşa warned the government that without such assistance a new war could only be useless, if not ruinous.[64] However, the desire for revenge was very strong. In the court itself the general, almost universal, reaction to the events of May 1787 was an increasing hatred of the infidel and, in particular, the determination to regain the Crimea by force if necessary. But there was great disagreement among the Ottoman leaders as to how and when this could be accomplished. Notwithstanding the attempts of reform perorated by Abdülhamid, the bulk of the army and navy was in the same disorganised and backward state which had led to defeat in the previous war. However, as Catherine's ambitions became more apparent and her insults more frequent after 1783, the partisans of war, led by the grand vizier Koca Yusuf Paşa, rose towards ascendancy in the Sultan's court. This group felt confident that the 'traditional' reforms introduced during the past decade had restored the Ottoman army to a state in which they could defeat anything the European powers could mount against them, and restore Ottoman prestige and authority to the position which they had held in the previous centuries.[65]

An overconfident Yusuf Paşa argued that the informal encouragements which he had received from the British and Prussian ambassadors would inevitably be followed by open assistance if the Ottomans would only have the courage to open the challenge against their bitter enemy. In the spring and summer of 1787, conditions in the domains of the enemies seemed to confirm the arguments of the 'war party' and make the time right for a new Ottoman move. Even while Emperor Joseph II accompanied Catherine through the Crimea, news came of a revolt in the Austrian Low Countries, where he was forced to rush with most of the army which he had been preparing to move south across the Danube into Ottoman territory. In Russia, drought and famine were causing increasingly serious internal discontent that any foreign adventure could only intensify. At the same time, in Constantinople Gazi Hasan's departure for Egypt at the head of an expeditionary force intended to reduce the rebellious Mamluk rulers there left Ottoman policy entirely in the hands of the advocates of immediate war. The Porte's demands that Russia evacuate Georgia and its refusal to accept Russian intervention in the Principalities strained relations even further and made conflict inevitable. Relations further deteriorated in August 1787, when Grand Vizier Yusuf Paşa demanded removal of the Russian consuls in Egypt, and the Principalities, on the grounds of their encouraging and assisting local revolts, and ordered an inspection of all Russian merchant ships passing through the Straits. In the absence of any firm Russian reply, on 14 August the Grand Vizier

---

64 Shaw, *Between Old and New*, p.25.
65 Carl von Martens, *Allgemeine Geschichte der Türken-Kriege in Europa von 1356 bis 1812* (Stuttgart, 1829), vol. II, p.203.

OTTOMAN WARFARE: A STRUGGLE FOR SURVIVAL

Austrian print depicting the Ottoman field army marching to Sofia in the spring 1788 (author's archive). The confusion that reigned in the Ottoman armies both on the march and in the camps is a recurring theme in the reports of their Western adversaries.

pushed the *divan* to an open declaration of war together with a demand for immediate Russian evacuation of the Crimea and the Caucasus as the only way to avoid the conflict. Mediations attempted by more or less interested powers did not produce results. Sultan Abdülhamid rejected all efforts of mediation and replied that peace could be made only on the basis of the conditions set out in his ultimatum, in particular he reiterated the Russian evacuation of the Crimea and Caucasus. Catherine rejected the ultimatum and finally issued a formal declaration of war on 15 September, a full month after that of the Sultan.

Although the declaration of war was not directed against Austria, Joseph was even more alarmed, because he was fully occupied with internal discontent. Austria wanted to keep the Russian alliance in order to secure support against Prussia.[66] Joseph's entry was delayed, both to enable him to move his armies back to the Danube from the Low Countries and to try to get the Ottomans to make the quick peace which he and his ally wanted at

---

66 The Austrian ambassador at the Porte, Baron Herbert de Rathkeal, was ordered to offer 'disinterested' Austrian mediation, with the implied threat of intervention on behalf of Russia if some kind of peace was not made. The French ambassador at the Porte, Choiseul-Gouffier, made similar representations for Catherine. But the Porte rejected all efforts at mediation and replied that peace could be made only on the basis of the conditions set out in his ultimatum, in particular by immediate Russian evacuation of the Crimea and Caucasus. See Hochedlinger, Michael, *Krise und Wiederherstellung. Österreichische Großmachtpolitik zwischen Türkenkrieg und Zweiter Diplomatischer Revolution 1787-1791* (Duncker & Humblot, Berlin 2000), pp.200–201.

this time. The Austrian mobilisation began in September 1787,[67] Joseph and his major staff inspected the border between the Sava River and Danube. The preparative were impressive. The Austrians marched up the long southern front with about 245,000 men,[68] who operated in five large corps, supported by 898 field guns and 252 siege guns, but it was only because of the failure to persuade Abdülhamid to an agreement that Austria finally declared war on 19 February 1788.

However, none of the belligerents were ready to move the troops on the field; therefore, the 1787 season campaign was devoted mainly to preparations on both sides. The Porte had high expectations on a motivated army, purged of negative elements, and above all supported by a completely renewed field artillery, and served by personnel trained to modern standards. The mobilisation of the contingents, directed as always by the grand vizier in charge, involved the formation of a main army to be gathered in Vidin, and another six smaller corps under the orders of their respective *paşas*, deployed along the frontier from west to east, each with its own operational base, and logistical centre in Travnik, Sarajevo, Gradiška, Smederevo, Orşova, Giurgiu, Pleven, Varna, and Sofia. Strong garrisons were quartered at Belgrade, Smederevo, Novi, Vidin, Orşova, Niş, Chotin, Bender, Izmail and Oçakov. This latter stronghold was the last remaining Ottoman major outpost on the Black Sea, which closed the strategic line along the Danube that stretched from here to Belgrade: the main Russian objective in the war.[69]

It was hoped rather naively that tens of thousands of recruits could be gathered within a couple of months, in order to assemble a field army that would have been strong enough to reject the enemies' offensive, and then strike taking advantage of the stall.[70] The strategic contest required the formation of an additional field army to guard the principalities of Wallachia and Moldavia, but since the possibility of a Russian attack was underestimated, it was not until the spring of 1788 that preparations began to raise a mobile corps of 30,000 men comprising half troops from the principalities and Tatar auxiliaries. These contingents quartered between Bucharest and Braşov under the Moldavian *hospodar* Alexander Ypsilantis and Wallachian *voievoda* Nicolai Mavrogenes, waiting for further troops from Constantinople.[71]

Russian preparations were delayed by the sloth and indecision of Catherine's commander-in-chief, Prince Grigorij Aleksandrovič Potemkin. The Russian general, and the court at no lesser extent, were worried by the formation of a

---

67 Michael Hochedlinger, *Austria's War of Emergence 1683–1797* (London and New York NY: Routledge, 2013), p.383.

68 Hochedlinger, *Austria's War of Emergence 1683–1797*, p.383. The size of the Austrian army was to rise further to 294,000 men, but a sizeable proportion of the army had to stay behind in Bohemia to guard the frontier with Prussia.

69 Aksan, *Ottoman Wars 1700–1870*, p.161. For the Ottomans, recovery of the Crimea was the main reason for the war.

70 Martens, *Allgemeine Geschichte der Türken-Kriege*, vol. II, p.204.

71 Martens, *Allgemeine Geschichte der Türken-Kriege*, vol. II, p.233.

new Triple Alliance of Great Britain, Prussia, and the United Provinces, signed on 13 June 1788, directed mainly against Catherine, and by Sweden's effort to take advantage of Russia's Ottoman diversion, and regain Finland by surprise attack. Adding insecurity to the military action was the fact that the Ottomans now seemed better prepared to sustain a war against a modern army than they had been in 1768. Moreover, the strategic situation had not been established, because of differences among the major staff of the navy.[72] The Russian plan was roughly based on two offensives: one army was to advance towards Oçakov in the Dnieper estuary, while a second had the task of covering the flank in Poland and – joining the extreme Austrian left wing in Galicia and Bukovina – could invade Moldavia.[73] Although goaded on by Vienna, Russia was very slow to mobilise fully, and in early 1788 St Petersburg fielded two armies: the first, 60,000 strong with 120 guns, commanded by Golitsyn in Poland and aimed at Wallachia and Moldavia, and the second, 40,000 troops with 48 pieces of artillery, under Rumiantsev across the Crimea. More than half of the army in the Crimea was made up of irregulars, especially Cossack and Kalmyk cavalry.[74] While command gave the Russians considerable advantage over the Ottomans, supply remained the greatest imponderable, affected by dreadful terrain and uncertain weather, and consequently levelling the presumed advantages of either side.[75]

The initial cautious strategy adopted by Russia appeared in stark contrast to the ambitious Austrian war aims. According to the plan devised by the Emperor's first military advisor, Franz Moritz Lacy, no fewer than six 'armies' of varying strength were to cover the whole stretch of the Habsburg–Ottoman frontier, from the Adriatic to the Dniester. The main task was to be performed by the largest army of the Banat, which, supported by another large contingent, was to seize Belgrade first, while by means of a pincer movement the smaller Croatian and Slavonian armies were to invade Bosnia via Una and Sava. Alongside the troops of Transylvania, the corps of Galicia–Bukovina was to undertake a diversion towards the Danube further east and capture Chotim on the Dniester. Meanwhile, the Austrians would take contact with the Russians coming from the east. It was optimistically hoped that after the first campaign the left bank of the Danube would be under Austrian control as far as its confluence with the river Aluta; that done, the road to Edirne and Constantinople would be open. However, the usual problem of coalition warfare surfaced once again.[76]

---

72 Shaw, *Between Old and New*, p.29. The two naval commanders in the Black Sea, the German Prince Charles of Nassau-Siegen and the American revolutionary hero, John Paul Jones, continually fought with each other and with Potemkin over who should take the lead (and the credit), and as a result there was a complete absence of co-ordination of the various Russian military groups in the area.
73 Martens, *Allgemeine Geschichte der Türken-Kriege*, p.212.
74 Aksan, *Ottoman Wars 1700–1870*, p.146.
75 Aksan, *Ottoman Wars 1700–1870*, p.146.
76 Hochedlinger, *Austria's War of Emergence*, p.383.

THE OTTOMAN ARMY OF THE NAPOLEONIC WARS 1789–1815

The storm of Oçakov, in December 1788, painting by January Suchodolski (Military Historical Museum of Artillery, Engineers and Signal Corps, St Petersburg). The artist depicts the Russian troops with great detail, but as for the Ottomans, he gives the figures in the centre of the painting a curious grenadier-style headdress with a yellow metal plate. After the surrender, the city was the scene of a ruthless reprisal that affected the civilian population.

The Ottoman side also faced similar problems. Cooperation between the corps scattered along the frontier and the main army was made difficult by different strategic emphases, and the subsequent problems of co-ordination fuelled mutual distrust. Before the end of the year the Ottoman commanders realised that the triumphal announcement of gathering a large contingent was illusory. The troops, including those of the *kapıkulu*, consisted largely of newly enlisted and untrained recruits; the cavalry was without mounts; the artillery train had oxen and mules instead of horses, and even the irregulars recruited in Anatolia mustered half the expected strength.[77] The start of the operations had been disastrous. During the march from Sophia to Vidin the janissaries had mutinied twice, and many had deserted due to the procrastination of the campaign.[78] To make matters worse, desertion increased as money and supplies began to run low. The contingents gathered in late 1787, on the eve of the impeding campaign, had been reduced into a miserable condition.

Grand Vizier Koca Yusuf Paşa, based in Niş, could field 86,000 troops, including 6,000 artillerymen and 300 cannons. A further 27,000 troops were in Bosnia, 7,000 at Chotin, 40,000 at Izmail, and 12,000 at Oçakov,[79] but

---

77 Thielen, 'Geschichte des Feldzuges', vol. II, p.178. According to the author, the estimate came from the Austrian intelligence in Serbia.
78 Kabaağaçlızade Ahmed Cévad Beg, *Etat Militaire Ottoman, depuis la fondation de l'Empire Ottoman jusqu'à nos jours* vol. I (Constantinople, 1882), p.317
79 Aksan, 'War and Peace', p.103.

the garrison of Belgrade could muster two-thirds of the expected strength, established at 12,000 men. The main army, which according to the government's plan was to have at least 160,000 men resulted in barely the half of this figure and mainly formed with unpaid *kapıkulu* soldiers ready to mutiny.[80]

There was another front where the Ottomans had to provide a defence: the Caucasus. Here the Porte turned to the local *ayans*. This compulsory choice did not protect the Empire from inconveniences, since the Porte's unscrupulous policy of divide and rule was bound to have devastating effects. The rivalry between the region's leading families of notables led to disastrous results when the Janikli Battal Paşa and his son Tayyar Mehmed were assigned to defend Anapa against the Russians. Unfortunately, they betrayed and surrendered the fort and its environs to the Russians, whose service they soon entered.[81]

At the Porte, the vastness of the fronts and the overestimation of its own strength emerged in all its gravity in the first weeks of war. Delay and shortage of troops had also destroyed any chance of gaining the initiative. In September 1787 the decision to wait for the enemies' first move originated from the lack of intelligence on the Austrian and Russian unpreparedness. If the Ottoman main army had been poised on the Danube–Dniester border waiting for the signal to attack, it might well have achieved significant gains and at least captured some important strongpoints before the Russians or Austrians could organise themselves to meet the threat. In absence of any significant synergy, the Ottoman military action turned in a mere diversion for slowing down the enemies' progress. In fact, one of the main reasons for the Austrian and Russian lack of preparation was the certain knowledge of Vienna and St Petersburg that there had been no Ottoman build-up for such a campaign.[82] On the basis of their efficient spy networks in the south, the Austrians and Russians could prepare their forces with a relative tranquillity.

The few engagements which did take place were indecisive but indicative of what was to follow over the following months. In October 1787 an Ottoman effort to storm the great Russian fort at Kinburn, located at the point where the Dnieper and Bug join and flow into the Black Sea, was repulsed by the vastly outnumbered Russian garrisons, as a result of a series of brilliant tactical manoeuvres on the part of their commander, General Alexander Suvorov, who took advantage of confusion and inefficiency of the Ottoman troops. However, the attempts to supply Kinburn through a series of convoys from the Russian ports in the Black Sea were frustrated more by storms than by the Ottoman fleet. The allied initiative came on 2 December, when the Austrians tried to seize Belgrade by a surprise attack in advance of their war declaration, but were repulsed because of their own blunders and lack of co-ordination at the crucial time. However, in February

---

80   Edward S. Creasy, *History of the Ottoman Turks* (London, 1878), p.429.
81   Shaw, *Beyond Old and New*, p.216. In Constantinople, father and son were accused of treason, their families and relatives were executed, and their lands and properties were confiscated and turned over, at least in part, to the rival Çapanoğlu family.
82   Hochedlinger, *Austria's War of Emergence*, p.384.

THE OTTOMAN ARMY OF THE NAPOLEONIC WARS 1789–1815

The Austrian siege at Dubica in a coeval print by unknown artist (Royal Collection Trust). The fortress surrendered on 26 August 1788, but 18 days beforehand the same location was the battlefield of the unexpected Ottoman success in the opening phase of the war.

1788 the Austrians entered Drežnic after a short siege, and in April resumed the offensive with better preparation. The main army seized the Ottoman fortress of Šabac under the command of Joseph II, assisted by *Feldmarschall* Franz Moritz von Lacy. The right flank was secured by the corps under *Feldmarschall-Lieutenant* De Vins, who advanced into Bosnia, while the Slavonian corps under Mittrowsky besieged Novi. Both corps belonged to the army led by Prince Liechtenstein operated in Croatia, while a large contingent under Wartensleben was in the Banat, and another corps under Fabris was quartered in Transylvania. The corps of Bukovina, commanded by Prince of Saxe-Coburg-Saalfeld, joined the Russian army in Moldavia. In late April the Austrians headed to Belgrade. Joseph's headquarters was placed at Peterwardein, thus opposite Belgrade, whose siege, however, proved to be unexpectedly time-consuming. The Austrians dug themselves in around Belgrade, but without seriously starting the siege, suffering 200–300 men falling ill per day.[83] Meanwhile, in July, the vanguard of the Ottoman field army reached the Danube, joining the garrison of Vidin.

Liechtenstein advanced to Dubica and laid siege to the fortress, but unexpectedly, on 8 August, he was defeated by the Ottoman relief force. The success had great resonance, but actually the battle was a series of uncoordinated clashes in which the Ottomans achieved the victory since Liechtenstein did not realise that he was facing only a relief force and not the main enemy field

---

83   Hochedlinger, *Austria's War of Emergence*, p.384.

army.[84] The day after, Baron De Vins re-established the situation, forcing the Ottomans to withdraw and resuming the blockade of Dubica.

The other Austrian corps were also unsuccessful, except in Moldavia, where Saxe-Coburg-Saafeld occupied the northern region with the help of its Greek *hospodar*, Alexander Ypsilantis, who deserted the Porte at a critical moment. In April the Austrians headed south and captured Jassy without resistance.[85] Koca Yusuf partially re-established the strategic situation, exploiting the mobility of his forces which were facing the Austrians in the Banat. He managed to delay Austrian progress before Belgrade, forcing Joseph to dispatch 20,000 men from the main army to relieve the retreating Lichtenstein. The Austrians took up a defensive position in the upper valley of the Temeş to stop the Ottoman advance. Increasing their numbers, the Ottoman horsemen continued to harass the enemy for the next three months, assaulting their front, flanks and rear 'with great impetuosity' and obliging the Austrians to transfer more troops from the other fronts.[86] By mid September most of the Austrian bridgeheads on the Danube's northern bank had been lost, and the whole river as far as Belgrade was now under Ottoman control. As a result, this area became the base for the future Ottoman incursions in Croatia and in the Banat of Temesvár. Unfortunately, Koca Yusuf's cavalry was exhausted after the operation against Liechtenstein, and was reorganising before resuming the action. Moreover, the Grand Vizier had an insufficient mounted force for a large-scale offensive. The war turned into a bitter reprisal, since the Ottomans did not advance further, but in mid October 1788 they began to clear the Banat, wreaking enormous havoc. As they moved, in the immediate border zone alone 36,000 civilians were killed, abducted or forced to flee.[87] Before the end of October the Ottomans took winter quarters at Orşova, north of the Danube, firmly based to repeat their work of destruction whenever they wished.

Months before, a demoralised Emperor Joseph II dismissed Liechtenstein in mid August, summoned Field Marshal Gideon Ernst von Laudon out of retirement, and on 24 August 1788 appointed him as commander of the Croatian corps. On the same day the Austrians overran the entrenched camp near Dubica on the Una River. Two days later the *paşa* of Travnik led a column to succour Dubica but was defeated by Laudon, who inflicted 700 casualties.[88] The garrison of Dubica surrendered on 26 August. In September Laudon headed south, and with the help of the flanking corps under Mittrowsky outmanoeuvred the *paşa* of Travnik who stood in the entrenched camp at Donji Jelovac. This allowed Laudon to move against the fortress of Novi (today

---

84 Johann Schels, 'Feldzug des k. k. kroatischen Armeekorps gegen die Türken 1788', in *Österreichische Militärische Zeitschrift*, vol. 2 (1823), p.271.

85 Aksan, *Ottoman Wars*, p.164. The Ottoman garrison were given ten days to evacuate the fort at Jassy, with full honours, which infuriated Field Marshal Rumiantsev, commander of the Russian army of the Pruth,

86 Schels, 'Feldzug des k. k. kroatischen Armeekorps gegen die Türken 1788', p.273.

87 Hochedlinger, *Austria's War of Emergence*, p.384.

88 Schels, 'Feldzug des k. k. kroatischen Armeekorps gegen die Türken 1788', p.274.

Cezayirli Gazi Hasan Paşa (1713–1790) in an Italian print of the 1790s (author's archive). He is known to have been brought up as a Georgian slave in the Ottoman Empire by a merchant of Tekirdağ, who raised him in that city, considering him on a par with his own sons. He served through the ranks of the Ottoman military hierarchy and was for a time with the Barbary pirates based in Algiers. He became *kapudan paşa* and grand vizier, and alongside Koca Yusuf, he was another skilled commander, both by sea and land.

Novi Sad in Serbia), which had been blockaded since April. The siege resumed on 10 September. After repulsing an Ottoman relief column on 20 September, Laudon ordered an assault the next day. This failed, with 80 killed and 210 wounded, but a second assault on 3 October entered the fortress. The Austrians suffered losses of 220 killed and 353 wounded while total Ottoman casualties during the siege were 400.[89] The conquest of Novi closed the campaign of 1788 in the Sava and Unna theatre. In Moldavia the loss of Jassy broke the Ottoman land connections of the great Dniester fort of Chotin which supported the Ottoman field army, and enabled the Austrians to take it on 19 September after a long siege. Ottoman rule in northern Moldavia thus came to an end, and an Austrian push against Bender during the next year's campaign was made possible.[90]

In the north-eastern theatre, no major events occurred in the opening months of 1788, with the exception of the frequent skirmishes between Ottoman and Russian cavalry parties. Moreover, the Austrian offensive in Bosnia led the Ottomans to maintain a defensive strategy against the Russians in Moldavia and Black Sea. As a result, neither side took the initiative until the summer was almost over. On 28 June, Gazi Hasan Paşa's fleet was routed by the Russian navy under Nassau-Siegen and Jones at the mouth of the Bug, but the lack of cooperation between the two Russian admirals made possible an Ottoman withdrawal with relatively minor losses. On 9 July Gazi Hasan forced the return to Sevastapol of a Russian fleet attempting to supply Kinburn, but his own effort to reinforce Oçakov was in turn beaten off by the Russians. Meanwhile, Sweden's defeat in Finland caused its withdrawal from the war in late July, and this enabled Catherine to transfer troops to Moldavia. Potemkin, meanwhile, gradually encircled Oçakov by land and finally opened the siege on 1 September. In times of peace the Ottoman garrison numbered perhaps 6,000 to 8,000 soldiers, but during the campaign, the strength increased to 20,000 men.[91] A total of 50,000 Russian troops crossed the Bug, and by mid July Potemkin had spread his forces in an arc around the town. He chose in the end to delay the final assault to mid December. However, General Mikhail Illarionovič Kutuzov, later commander in the

---

89 George Bruce Malleson, *Loudon: A Sketch of the Military Life of Gideon Ernest, Freiherr von Loudon* (London, 1884), p.227.

90 Oskar Criste, *Kriege unter Kaiser Josef II* (Vienna, 1904), pp.153–154.

91 Aksan, *Ottoman Wars 1700–1870*, p.161.

1806–12 Russo-Ottoman war, was more impatient, and in late July engaged with a sortie of 50 Ottoman cavalrymen, which proved disastrous when a superior force of Ottomans forced the Russians back to their lines. About 200 Russian soldiers were killed, their heads displayed on stakes around the fortress. In mid August the Ottoman garrison made another sortie, during which Kutuzov himself was wounded and blinded in one eye. Russian ships fired on the Ottomans, forcing the end of the engagement. Part of the reason for Potemkin's delay until winter was the presence of the Ottoman fleet, which as late as October had managed to break the Russian blockade and disembark 1,500 soldiers at the fortress of Oçakov. Potemkin also hoped to negotiate a surrender rather than force a bloodbath. Waiting took its toll on the besiegers: fresh water was scarce; winter arrived early, with temperatures of −15° Celsius; 'the camp became snow and shit',[92] making life unbearable for the soldiers in the trenches, who created burrows for themselves. The final assault on 16 December 1788 occurred after a month of Russian shelling from the harbour, and delays due to the severity of the winter. The violence of the fight was unparalleled. 4,000 Russians fell, 'but the survivors bore down all resistance, and forced their way in to the city, where for three days they revelled in murder and pillage.'[93] No mercy was shown to age or sex, and out of a population of 40,000 human beings, only a few hundred escaped.

The siege and capture of Oçakov was the only important action in the east. On the whole, both the Russians and Ottomans remained quiescent. Although the season was too far advanced for the Russians to take advantage of the victory, it prepared the way for an advance to the Danube and beyond as soon as spring arrived. During the winter both sides were diverted by bitter internal disputes and consequent delays in war planning and preparations. Gazi Hasan Paşa, now returned from Egypt, quarrelled bitterly with the grand vizier over the management of the military campaigns.[94]

To further stress enemy resistance, Austrians and Russians tried to open a new front in the Balkans. Russia called on all Balkan Christians to revolt against the Porte and help the Russian army and fleet which would soon arrive on the Danube and in the Mediterranean. Vienna sent Colonel Vukacevich to Montenegro and Albania with a similar proclamation, promising independence under Austrian protection once the war was over. Arriving with 2,000 Austrian soldiers and 400 Serbian *Freikorps*, Vukacevich set to work to organise and train the Montenegrins wishing to fight the Sultan. Then he made contact with one of the ambitious *ayans* in Albania in order to exploit the weak cohesion between some regions and the central government. The instrument for this action was the *ayan* Bushati Mahmud Paşa, governor of Scutari, best known as Kara Mahmud, who by 1778 had achieved such

---

92   Creasy, *History of the Ottoman Turks*, p.431
93   Creasy, *History of the Ottoman Turks*, p.432. Creasy's description is likely hyperbolic, operating by his time on the then common assumption that Eurasian warfare was somehow more barbaric than other kinds. Potemkin is said to have ordered a stop to the slaughter after four hours. He reported 9,500 Ottomans killed, and 2,500 Russians. See in Aksan, *Ottoman Wars 1700–1870*, p.179.
94   Shaw, *Between Old and New*, p.29.

THE OTTOMAN ARMY OF THE NAPOLEONIC WARS 1789–1815

The Austrian seizure of Chotin on 19 September 1788, in an engraving by Carl Schültz (Royal Collection Trust). The loss of this strategic fortress enabled the Austro-Russians to isolate the Ottomans in Moldavia.

complete control in northern Albania that the Porte was forced to appoint him governor in 1779. His continued expansion and attacks on Ottoman governors and vassals alike, combined with a failure to pay his tribute to the Sultan, finally led to an attack against him by a combined land and sea expedition under the command of Gazi Hasan Paşa in 1784–1785. Mahmud was forced to surrender, but thanks to the support of his clients and proxy at the Imperial court, he was pardoned and restored as governor in return for large payments of tribute and promises to restrain his territorial ambitions in the future. But as soon as the Ottoman army departed, Mahmud turned his attention to Montenegro, which he invaded for the first time in October 1785. Fearful of a new Ottoman attack as a result, he contacted Austrian agents in Montenegro in the hope of securing an alliance against the Sultan. Since the Emperor and Czar were then meeting to prepare the war against the Porte, Mahmud's offer was greeted favourably, and he was promised Austrian recognition as ruler of an independent Albania in return for his assistance against the Porte and his conversion to Christianity. On his return to Albania he assembled all the Christian chiefs with the Muslim chiefs especially loyal to him and swore them on the Bible and the Koran to fight the Ottomans until the death. This led to a second Ottoman expedition against him late in 1786, which comprised troops provided by the neighbouring *ayans*. Mahmud took possession of the fortress of Rusafa, on the hill overlooking Scutari, and successfully held off the besiegers for several months. Finally, by feigning surrender, with the assistance of some allies within the besieging army, he surprised and routed it. His position had become very insecure, but the war with Russia and Austria in 1787 forced the Porte to abandon the efforts to suppress Mahmud and instead to offer him a full pardon on condition that he provide military assistance to the Ottoman army. Mahmud cleverly continued his double game, and in May 1788 Vukacevich sent to Scutari an agent named Brugnard with several soldiers and splendid gifts for Kara Mahmud. But when Vienna was carrying out its plan in Albania, the Ottoman army was overrunning the Austrian positions and advanced in Croatia and into the Banat of Temesvár. Fearing that his new friends would be unable to help him, in August 1788 Mahmud massacred the Austrians and sent their heads to the Sultan along with a declaration of submission and a promise to join the Ottoman army. As a result, Kara Mahmud Paşa became military commander of Novi. Mahmud's defection left the Montenegrins without the expected assistance from Albania, but this did not stop several thousand of them from joining the Herzegovinians and Serbs in the Austrian *Freikorps*.

The events in Montenegro and Albania had few consequences for military operations on the other fronts. In early April 1789, the Austrian corps in Transylvania had anticipated the enemy and gone on the offensive, invading Wallachia. But soon, effective Ottoman counter-attack directed against the mountain passes forced the Austrians onto the defensive. Koca Yusuf's successful actions through the Carpathians into Transylvania in the spring of 1789 were disrupted by death of Sultan Abdülhamid, and the predictable change of power under his successor Selim III, who aimed to remove the Grand Vizier himself and other senior commanders.[95] This left the Ottoman armies disorganised and enabled the enemy to retake the initiative.

In the Banat theatre, after the armies went into winter quarters, Emperor Joseph fell ill and transferred command of the main army to the aged Field Marshal András Hadik. On 14 May 1789 Laudon returned to command the corps in

Bushati Mahmud, also known as Kara Mahmud (1749–1796), was the son of Bushati Mehmed Paşa, the governor and *ayan* of Scutari. In the 1780s, his rebellious temperament brought him into open conflict with the Porte. This conflict is regarded in Albanian historiography as a bid to create an independent principality, but the immediate cause of the conflict was his clash with the powerful governor of Southern Albania, Tepeleni Ali Paşa. Kara Mahmud Pasha continued to quarrel with the Ottoman Empire, however, by annexing the Sanjak of Prizren and parts of Montenegro and by instituting military and political reforms in his state without permission from the Porte. He was able to conduct a dangerous double game with Austria and the Porte until 1788, when he definitively sided with the Sultan. After the war, Kara Mahmud continued to plot against the Porte and in 1796 he launched an offensive against Montenegro, following its proclaimed unification with Ottoman-ruled Brda district. However, his troops suffered an initial defeat in July at Martinići, but Kara Mahmud continued military operations until September, when the Montenegrins from Piperi and Bjelopavlići defeated him in the Battle of Krusi. Kara Mahmud was captured and decapitated by the Montenegrins. His brother Ibrahim Paşa continued to rule Scutari under the Ottoman sultan until his death in 1810. Ibrahim served as governor of Rumelia and played an important role in crushing the First Serbian Uprising.

---

95 The eccentric but clever Selim III had wanted to dismiss Koca Yusuf as soon as he became Sultan, for the Grand Vizier had played an active role in suppressing the abortive attempt to bring Selim to the throne in place of Abdülhamid in 1775.

THE OTTOMAN ARMY OF THE NAPOLEONIC WARS 1789–1815

The battle of Focşani, in a print by Johann Hieronymus Löschenkohl (author's archive). The Austrians deployed 18,000 German and Hungarian troops, the Russian contingent numbered up of 7,000 soldiers, and the Ottomans were about 30,000 troops under Osman Paşa. The battle began in the morning of 1 August 1789, as the Russian and Austrian artillery opened fire on the Ottoman lines. Osman had fortified the camp with a line of entrenchments; Ottoman troops in the Balkans were experienced at erecting field fortifications, which could include ditches, earthen ramparts, and wooden palisades and towers. The Ottomans sortied to attack the allies all along their battle line, but Austro-Russian artillery and musket fire drove them back. Suvorov then attacked the Ottoman right flank, the Russian cavalry was repulsed, but the infantry was successful. The Ottomans were pushed back into their entrenchments under close range Russian fire. On the Ottoman left, the Austrian infantry also threw back the enemy, and defeated on both wings of their line, the Ottomans fled. The Ottoman casualties numbered 1,500 dead and 2,500 wounded; allied casualties amounted to 800. The allies had captured 12 guns.

Croatia which numbered 34,500 infantry and 3,000 cavalry. On 23 June Laudon began operations against the fortress of Gradiška on the Sava. The Austrian troops crossed the Sava above and below Gradiška and began building trenches that approached the fortress. Before the place was completely invested, the Ottoman garrison slipped away on the night of 8 July. They left behind a single man who was supposed to blow up the powder magazine, but this individual did not carry out the plan.

The Austrian Field Marshal Charles-Joseph Prince of Ligne arrived in May to assume command at Semlin (today part of Belgrade but a separate town in 1789), for siege preparations against Belgrade. Ligne was informed that there was a truce in force at the time and that of his corps of 30,000 soldiers, only 15,000 were fit for duty because of sickness. The Austrian general complained in a letter that the truce allowed the Ottomans to bring food supplies into Belgrade.[96] In June Hadik became seriously ill

---

96 K. u. K. Kriegsarchiv, 'Belagerung und Einnahme von Belgrad im Jahre 1789' in *Österreichische Militärische Zeitschrift* (1812), p.235.

and had to be relieved of command. In his place the Emperor appointed Laudon on 28 July, and this change of command caused a further delay.

However, for the Ottoman side the situation was getting worse every day. It was at this point that politics emerged to further undermine the Ottoman military effort, as the Sultan moved to secure a grand vizier more to his liking. Selim also was unhappy with the Grand Vizier's rival Gazi Hasan and his associates, and he further wanted to secure in his place a man who would be more sympathetic to his own reform plans. But Yusuf and Hasan had a good military reputation and a strong following among the conservatives in the court and government, and among the *ulemas*, so for the moment Selim dared not dismiss him. The climate of insecurity and conspiracy further undermined Ottoman morale. The enemy victories in Bosnia and Moldavia gave Selim the pretext he needed, and it did not take very long to tear down the reputation Yusuf had built up. Selim stated that his grand vizier had failed to make proper preparations for the campaign during the previous winter and that 'he spent most of his time with his concubines and cronies instead of caring for the affairs of state and of the army'.[97] On 7 June 1789 Yusuf Paşa was replaced as grand vizier and commander-in-chief by Cenaze Hasan Paşa, who had distinguished himself as commander of Vidin during the previous year's campaign against the Austrians. Yusuf Paşa was given the choice of becoming second in command in Wallachia or at Vidin, and he chose Vidin. Unfortunately, the new grand vizier set in motion a new series of military moves which led to the major Ottoman disaster of the war and began the process by which the Ottoman army dissolved in the months which followed. On 28 August 1789, in the east, the Russians and Austrians went on the offensive, moving through Wallachia into Moldavia. In response to reports that Suvorov's main Russian force in Moldavia was about to unite with the Austrians under Saxe-Coburg to seize Bucharest and occupy the whole Wallachia, the Grand Vizier sent the vanguard of his army and Mavrogeny's auxiliaries and Tatar forces to Focşani to keep the two enemy forces apart. In July, the Grand Vizier gathered new troops, increasing his army and spreading the false report that he had under him 100,000 men.[98] Furthermore, Hasan Paşa had learned of the events at Karánsebes the year before,[99] and by exaggerating the negative reports from his spies about the

---

97 Shaw, *Between Old and New*, p.36.

98 Konrad Thielen, 'Feldzug des k. k. galizischen Armeekorps im Jahre 1789 gegen die Türken', in *Österreichische Militärische Zeitschrift* (1825) vol. I, p.112.

99 The Battle of Karánsebes was a friendly fire incident in the Austrian army, supposedly occurring during the night of 21–22 September 1788. While the Austrian army was marching, Hungarian hussars and German infantry entered in contact and without recognising each other engaged them in combat. During the encounter, some infantry began shouting, Turks! Turks! The hussars fled the scene, thinking that the Ottoman attack was imminent. Most of the infantry also ran away; the army comprised Austrians, Croats, and Italians from Lombardy, as well as other minorities, many of whom could not understand one another. While it is not clear which one of these groups did so, they gave the false warning without telling the others, who promptly fled. The situation was made worse when officers, in an attempt to restore order, shouted, 'Halt! Halt!' which was misheard by

Austrian commanders, he was confident that he could inflict a decisive defeat on the Allies. Reconnaissance by the Tatar cavalry and Romanian auxiliaries did not spot the approaching Russians and by means of a brilliant forced march, Suvorov managed to reach the Austrians on the River Rimnik, shortly before the Ottomans arrived. Then on the morning of 1 August, the two allied armies surprised and completely routed the Ottomans at Focşani. The Austro-Russian victory was itself of little strategic significance since the routed Ottomans were still only auxiliaries and irregulars of the main army, which remained at Ibrail (today Braila in Romania) waiting for the order to move into Wallachia. Coburg and Suvorov had too few cavalry to follow up the advantage by pursuing the routed enemies, completing their destruction, and occupying new ground. But the rout was important in that it manifested and stimulated a growing disorder and lack of discipline in the Ottoman ranks which began with Yusuf Paşa's replacement and which had first shown itself in the failures of 1788. Following Focşani, the disorder spread rapidly. The Ottoman army began to fall apart, with massive desertion and confusion spreading like a disease. This news in turn caused the Ottoman troops in Serbia and Bosnia to break up as well.

On 30 August 1789 Laudon gave orders for his army to concentrate at Novi Banovci, north-west of Belgrade and Semlin. His plan was to cross the Sava on 13 September, but the timetable was accelerated when intelligence indicated that 30,000 Ottomans under Abdy Paşa were approaching from Smederevo. On 9 September the Austrian vanguard reached Novi Banovci and the following day crossed the Sava at Boljevci. Here, Laudon established his headquarters on high ground near Ostružnica, not far from where Prince Eugene of Savoy had led his army in triumph 72 years before. By 15 September the bulk of the Austrian army was south of the Sava. Laudon had 120,900 soldiers, but although 33,000 men were not fit for duty because of sickness,[100] he had enough to face the Ottoman relief corps and the garrison inside Belgrade, which numbered about 9,000 with 456 guns of various calibre.[101] The Ottoman garrison under Osman Paşa fought valiantly, but the Austrian siege progressed well since no external help came to the besieged city. After a late, but inconclusive attempt to push the Austrians back from Belgrade failed near Mehadia, on 30 September, the Austrians advanced on the suburbs, and forced their way through the palisades. The Ottoman resistance

---

soldiers with no knowledge of German as Allah! Allah! In determining losses, accounts of this incident do not distinguish between losses that were caused by friendly fire, those that were caused by the Ottomans, and those that resulted from pillaging by the Austrians or by the local Wallachian auxiliaries. One report states that the Austrian rearguard suffered 150 casualties. Another account states that in the days following the incident, 1,200 wounded men were taken at Arad. Another source claims that 538 men, 24 *Jäger*, and one officer went missing after the incident, but most returned to duty. Also lost were three cannons and the chest containing the army's payroll. See in Durschmied, *How Chance and Stupidity Have Changed History: The Hinge Factor* (Ney York NY: Simon and Schuster, 2016), pp.76–77.

100 Hochedlinger, *Austria's War of Emergence*, p.385.
101 K. u. K. Kriegsarchiv, 'Belagerung und Einnahme von Belgrad', p.38.

Field Marshall Laudon besieges Belgrade in September–October 1789, in an Austrian print of unknown artist (author's archive). The Austrians stormed the city on 30 September, and advanced on the suburbs forcing their way through the palisades. For four hours the Ottomans fought stubbornly in a house-to-house struggle. Finally they retreated within Belgrade's citadel after suffering 800 casualties and losing 12 guns. The Austrians lost 110 killed and 357 wounded. On the morning of 6 October 1789 the Austrian artillery began a very intense bombardment, under which the Ottoman defences rapidly crumbled, forcing the commander to surrender. The Austrian commander claimed that his artillery fired 5,662 round shot and 6,083 bomb shells during the siege.

continued until 6 October, when negotiations were finally opened. Two days later Osman Paşa signed the surrender of Belgrade. In exchange the Ottoman garrison was given a free passage to Orşova with their personal and private possessions. A prisoner exchange was also arranged. While the fighting raged in Belgrade, in Wallachia the Austro-Russians scored another decisive victory on 22 September 1789 at Martineşti on the River Rimnik. After these defeats the Ottomans were now unable to arrest the Austrians, who moved rapidly through Serbia to Niş, while the Russians under Potemkin reached the Dniester on 1 October. The Russians were soon able to take the fortresses of Akkerman, on 11 October, and Bender, on 14 November, both without resistance due to shortages of men and supplies, but failed at Izmail, tenaciously defended by Gazi Hasan.

In Wallachia, Saxe-Coburg came out of winter quarters in mid October on the direct order of Joseph II. The Austrians crossed back through the Carpathians and occupied on 9 November, Bucharest, again without resistance, while the Ottoman garrison fled towards the south.[102] A few days later, rumours warned that the Austrians were already heading for Niş, and towards mid month 5,000 janissaries were sent from Constantinople to Sofia, despite the critical need for their services to keep order in the capital.[103]

Ottoman operations on the internal front with Montenegro were not successful either. In October 1789 Kara Mahmud Paşa led his army from Scutari against a Montenegrin force near Podgoritza. The encounter resulted in an Ottoman defeat; the victors then ravaged and burned the Muslim villages in

---

102 Martens, *Allgemeine Geschichte der Türken-Kriege*, p.242.
103 Shaw, *Between Old and New*, p.43

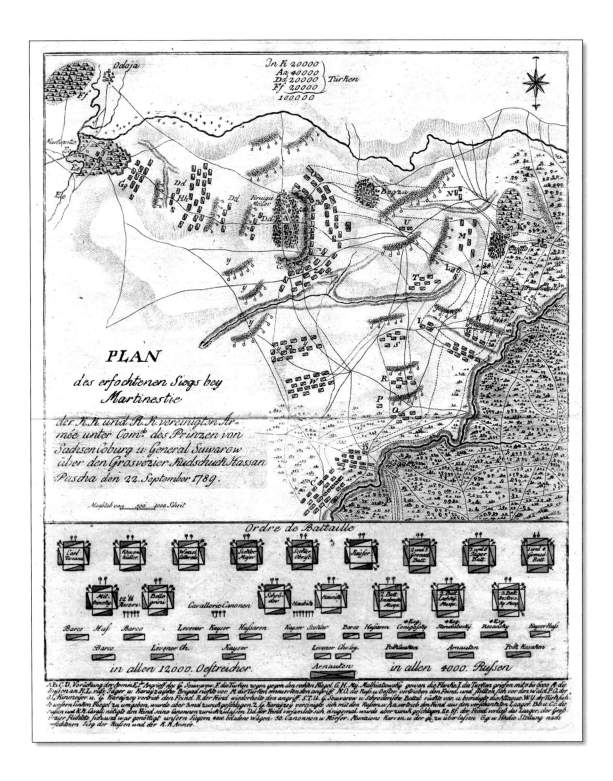

Facing page: The initial deployment of the Allied and Ottoman armies at Martinești on 22 September 1789; engraving by Anton Balzer (author's archive). The Ottomans designate it as the battle of the Boza (or Buzau) River, for the Austrians is the Battle of Martinești, and for the Russians the Battle of Rymnik. According to Suvorov's report, on 21 September he divided his 16,000 men combined army into two columns to advance towards the Ottomans, who were entrenched in two large camps and estimated as 100,000 men, but were probably half of this force. The next morning, after crossing the River Râmna (Rymnik), Suvorov ordered the assault, trusting to take his enemies by surprise. As the Russians approached the entrenchments, they managed to silence the enemy artillery, and immediately formed square formations to face the Ottoman cavalry counterattacks, which tried to separate the enemies. After two hours of fierce fighting the Russians successfully stormed the Ottoman camp. At 5:00 p.m., after seizing the Ottoman fortifications near the village of Vrancea and reuniting with the Austrians, the Allies advanced against the main Ottoman camp in the forest nearby. While the Austrian advance was arrested, Suvorov outflanked the enemy and routed the Ottomans with his cavalry. With almost nowhere to retreat, the Ottomans tried to cross the river, but most drowned. The Russians claimed 1,000 casualties, inflicting about 20,000 and taking all the artillery and the baggage train.

the vicinity. These negative events ended the disastrous Ottoman campaigns of 1789 and opened the way for a joint push towards Constantinople the following spring.

For the moment, Selim III's response was a desperate need to find more soldiers, while for the first time he began to consider the possibility of accepting the peace offers coming to him through neutral channels.[104] He was still determined to regain the Crimea before peace was made, however, and he hoped he could get better terms by continuing the war until his enemies were desperate enough to give him anything he wanted. Therefore, he raised new troops in Anatolia and Bosnia and ordered the army reformed and moved to the attack once again. Months before, on 11 July 1789, Selim gained what seemed to be a major diplomatic triumph when he signed a treaty of alliance with Sweden agreeing to provide annual cash subsidies over a period of 10 years, in return for a renewal of the Swedish land and naval attacks against the Russians in the north. The allies bound themselves to continue the war until both secured satisfactory settlements, with neither making a separate peace without the agreement of the other. The treaty was a victory for Prussia, which had urged Selim to continue the fight, while it was a defeat for France, which had taken the lead in trying to arrange a negotiated peace, just a few days before the Revolution of 14 July. Selim tried to follow up this alliance by securing similar agreements with Prussia and Great Britain, but here he was less successful. While they were willing to encourage and, to a certain extent, assist continued Ottoman campaigns against the Austrians and Russians, they were not willing to join the war openly or to commit themselves to assisting the Ottomans in any formal way.

As the winter began, the Ottoman Empire was on the brink of disaster. The new grand vizier was unable to administer the government and the army at the same time, and both were falling apart as a result. The Danube defence line had been broken in Serbia, Bosnia, and in the Principalities. The new army hastily gathered during the winter was not able to perform a regular campaign. The inefficiency and disobedience shown by Ottoman commanders and men alike showed clearly that the untrained peasants and tribesmen who now formed the bulk of the army were incapable of

---

104 Shaw, *Between Old and New*, p.40.

performing the simplest manoeuvres and were no match for the well-trained and brilliantly led allied forces. Once again there were no immediate results of the battle. The surviving Ottoman forces now saw it would be impossible for them to retain their positions on the left bank of the Danube, so they retired to Kilya, Izmail, and Vidin, which they hoped to hold to defend the Danube line in the east.

Unprecedented measures were introduced to fuel the war. All male Muslim subjects between the ages of 15 and 60 were ordered to prepare themselves to serve in the army if they were needed.[105] The bitter failures suffered in 1789 persuaded Selim III to remove the Grand Vizier and replaced him with the former *kapudan paşa* Gazi Hasan, the skilled and loyal commander who had been able to resume the fight after the debacle at Focşani.[106] Gazi Hasan now went to work with a ferocity and energy which astonished his colleagues and European observers alike. Most of the officers whom he considered responsible for the disasters of the previous year were executed, including all the garrison commanders who had surrendered their posts without resistance. He appointed his predecessor as governor of Rüsçük, with the responsibility of preparing to resist any Austrian effort to push south across the Danube from Bucharest. Selim III issued a decree giving his new grand vizier absolute authority in all matters and stating that no one else should interfere in state affairs or dispute what he ordered. In the middle of January Hasan Paşa was so satisfied with his work that he left his camp, led a force of 10,000 men into northern Bulgaria, and successfully wiped out the bandits who had been interrupting his communications with the capital.[107]

During the winter of 1789–1790 all sides in Europe called for a peace. St Petersburg was diverted by the Sweden's resumed offensive in Finland, Vienna by nationalist uprisings in the Low Countries and Hungary. In addition, the French Revolution and an increasing desire to stifle its growth before its 'seditious' doctrines could spread over the entire continent, led the Triple Alliance formed by Britain, Prussia and the Dutch Republic to try even harder to secure a peace with the Porte as rapidly as possible. Prussia hoped to act as a mediator who could dictate terms to the belligerents in such a way as to secure advantages for Berlin. The Prussians felt that the Ottomans had suffered such staggering defeats in 1789 that they would have to agree to make some concessions to Austria in the Principalities in order to save themselves. Austria, weakened by internal troubles, would have to

---

[105] Hanioğlu, *A Brief History of the Late Ottoman Empire* (Princeton, NJ: Princeton University Press, 2008), p.71.

[106] Gazi Hasan Paşa had opposed the war right from the start. While he still was commander at Izmail, he had sent the Sultan a long and detailed report describing in agonizing detail the plight of the army and strongly recommending that peace be made at once. Now that he was grand vizier, he continued to recommend strongly that the European offers be accepted as soon as possible.

[107] Shaw, *Between Old and New*, p.44

accept the dictates of the balance of power while enlarging its territory at Ottoman expense.[108]

The Prussian ambassador at the Porte, Heinrich Friedrich von Diez, led a group which advocated a far more aggressive policy, involving the cooperation of the Triple Alliance with the Porte, Sweden and Poland in order to dictate their will to Austria and Russia, by force if necessary. Selim III strongly favoured the Prussian plan; in fact, he had been pushing for an open alliance with Prussia and Britain since 1787. But after the defeats suffered in 1789 he reluctantly decided that if he could not get such assistance from his European friends, he would have to make peace without achieving the territorial ambitions for which Abdülhamid had entered the war. The Sultan was fully informed about events in France and elsewhere in Europe. The British ambassador in particular pointed out to him how much the French Revolution was changing the diplomatic alignments of Europe and causing all its monarchies to end their foreign wars so they could join their forces against the contagion of revolution. On 26 November Diez had offered a formal alliance to the Porte in order to keep it in the war. He told Selim that a Prussian war with Austria would divert the Habsburgs from the Ottoman front, and supported this argument by pointing out how the Prussian alliance with Britain had prevented the Russian Baltic fleet from passing to the Mediterranean, and how recent Prussian purchases of large quantities of supplies from Poland had already caused considerable difficulties to the Russian armies in getting their own supplies for the new campaign. Diez promised Selim that Prussia would declare war on Russia and Austria in April if the Porte agreed to the alliance, and that it would fight on until both the Crimea and the Caucasus were evacuated by the Russians, as well as all their territorial gains in the current campaign.[109] In return he asked only for Ottoman support of Prussian claims to Danzig and Thorn and for the return of Galicia to Poland.[110]

At the same time as the peace talks had opened in Şumen, on 15 January 1790, Selim III summoned a formal Imperial Council to discuss the matter, but he had already resolved to accept the Prussian proposal and sign the alliance despite the anguished protests of his grand vizier. He allowed debate only on the question of whether such an alliance with the infidels would be legal. The formal alliance was signed on 31 January 1790. Prussia agreed to demand the return to the Ottomans of Bender, Oçakov, the Crimea, and other areas lost in the current war before it would make peace. The Porte promised to make no peace in which Prussia, Sweden, and Poland were not

---

108 Shaw, *Between Old and New*, p.41. In return for her acquisitions along the Danube, she would have to give all or part of Galicia back to Poland. The Poles would reward Prussia by ceding it Danzig and Thorn, which would give the Prussians complete control of the Vistula.

109 Shaw, *Between Old and New*, p.45. Although Britain and Prussia were closely allied, the British ambassador in Constantinople, Sir Robert Ainslie, was not informed about these negotiations, since Britain now preferred to end the war with the Porte as soon as possible by peaceful means rather than by an enlargement of the conflict.

110 Aksan, *Ottoman Wars, 1700–1870*, p.138.

THE OTTOMAN ARMY OF THE NAPOLEONIC WARS 1789–1815

The siege of Izmail, by Mikhail Ivanov (1748–1823)

included, and once peace was concluded, to regard as an attack on itself any attack made by Austria and Russia on any of those powers.[111]

As a result, by February Selim III wanted to continue the war through another summer so that both his enemies would become anxious enough that they would at least return their conquests of the current war in exchange for peace. Orders were issued for the levy of 200,000 additional men in Anatolia and the Balkans. According to Austrian intelligence the Ottomans gathered 120,000 men on the Danube and a further 60,000 at Silistra to face the Russians.[112] Work was resumed on several new warships. Rumours were spread that Selim himself would go to Edirne to lead the new campaign.[113]

---

111 Shaw, *Between Old and New*, p.46. The latter engagement was to be reciprocal among the four courts, who thus were to be joined in a mutual assistance pact once peace was concluded. It also was agreed that the Porte would not make peace with Russia except through the mediation of Britain and the Dutch Republic. A relatively long term of five months was set for ratification of the treaty in order to give Prussia a chance to use all possible means to get Russia and Austria to accept a peaceful solution before it accepted the obligation to attack them.

112 Martens, *Allgemeine Geschichte der Türken-Kriege*, p.249

113 Shaw, *Between Old and New*, p.47.

The peace talks, which had been carried out in Constantinople through the mediation of the French embassy as well as in the camp of the Grand Vizier, were now suspended, but keeping the treaty secret and continuing the talks with the enemy representatives in order to deceive them into foregoing their spring preparations. Orders were sent to the governors to redouble the preparations for war. Decrees were issued to provide regular provisions and pay for the army, which was to be newly created to go on the campaign. Selim also participated in restoring order and discipline in his government and army. Said Ahmed Paşa, the able commander of the fortress at Sofia, was appointed governor of Rumelia in place of Abdi Paşa who, it was widely rumoured, had accepted Austrian bribes to prevent the reinforcement of Belgrade at the critical time.[114] The Sultan's brother-in-law, Mustafa Paşa, was sent to replace him as governor of Sofia, with orders to prepare it for a last-ditch stand if necessary against the expected enemy offensive.

As for other fronts, Kara Mahmud was compelled to make peace with the *vladika* (Prince Bishop) of Montenegro, who agreed to pay tribute to the Sultan

---

114 K. u. K. Kriegsarchiv, 'Feldzug des k. k. kroatischen Armeekorps im Jahre 1790 gegen die Türken', in *Österreichische Militärische Zeitschrift*, (1827), vol. I, p.153.

in return for the annexation of the entire valley of the Moraka River, together with the fortresses of Podgoritza and Zabliak. However, not all the Montenegrin chiefs had the intention of keeping this peace, and in April 1790, after new arms and ammunition arrived from Trieste, they attacked again and pursued Kara Mahmud's forces into Albania. In a three-day battle, which included a direct clash between Ottoman and Montenegrin boats on the lake of Scutari, the invaders emerged victorious once again, taking and destroying the fort of Zabliak before retiring to the north with the spoils of victory. They then moved into Bosnia and Herzegovina and ravaged large areas, thus undermining the entire Ottoman effort against the Austrians along the Sava. For the moment, however, Kara Mahmud ignored the Montenegrins as he turned back to the job of building his power within Albania.[115]

Although Selim III ratified the treaty at once, Prussian ratification experienced various delays and difficulties. The Prussian government recalled Diez soon after the treaty was signed on the grounds that he had exceeded his authority, and he was replaced as ambassador at the Porte by Knobelsdorf. Final ratification was postponed despite urgent Ottoman inquiries and requests for some definite statement on the subject. But in spite of the delay, the treaty had a tremendous effect in Constantinople. Gazi Hasan himself was bitter and disappointed, but he resumed military preparations with his accustomed vigour and made such strenuous efforts to discipline and reorganise the army, that the janissaries revolted against the Porte on 15 February, forcing him to flee until the dispute was settled. The Grand Vizier sent large numbers of men to strengthen his advanced posts, especially at Giurgiu in Wallachia, where the Prince of Wallachia was building up a force to defend his position against an expected Austrian offensive in the spring. Then Gazi Hasan tried organise a new supply system, and seemed to be achieving some positive results when he died suddenly of fever on 29 March 1790, leaving the army to fall apart once again.[116]

After three weeks of manoeuvre and factious rivalry a new grand vizier, the obscure Rüsçüklu Şerif Hasan Paşa, was appointed. However, to govern such situation was a complex task for anyone. The defeats suffered and the war expenses had produced a domestic crisis. The loss of Wallachia also deprived the capital of a major source of grain, and shortages of food added to popular dissatisfaction as the winter approached. Crowds were coming into the streets of Constantinople, looting shops and homes and setting fires to show their discontent and alarm. Demands for the deposition of the Grand Vizier and his associates were increasing in frequency and intensity. In reaction to this popular protest, a large number of Selim's ministers wanted to make peace. Because of the Sultan's opposition, however, nothing was decided, and instead

---

115 Shaw, *Between Old and New*, pp.232–233.
116 Shaw, *Between Old and New*, p.48. The British and French ambassadors in Constantinople circulated reports that Gazi Hasan had been poisoned by his political enemies. or by the Sultan in an effort to offer up a scapegoat to the public for the defeats of the previous year. But most Ottoman and Western observers who were witnesses to his fatal illness reported that it came from natural causes, and the rumours of foul play seem to have been without foundation in fact.

orders were sent out to prepare for the new campaign.[117] Unfortunately the Grand Vizier revealed himself incapable of carrying out the difficult military and political tasks which fell to him. For the moment, at least the political crisis was solved and the increasingly powerful and vocal factions were satisfied, if not contented. Selim III at once sent his new grand vizier to end bribery and misrule and prepare the army for the spring campaign.

Meanwhile, the international situation pushed the major powers to open talks for a peace agreement, but King Friedrich Wilhelm II of Prussia did not ratify the treaty of alliance with the Porte, thus defusing a dangerous dispute with Austria and Prussia. In Austria, the death of Joseph II marked a further change of direction, as his successor Leopold II imposed a pacifist policy to avoid internal conflagration of the Habsburg state. While the peace negotiations waxed and waned, the armies of the belligerents moved back into the field. Şerif Hasan led the army out of Constantinople towards Vidin and Nicopolis, with the intention of fortifying the last remaining portion of the Danube defence line against enemy attack. But he soon found that it took more than good intentions to revive the army, which had received such a severe beating in the previous month. Weapons, ammunition, equipment and tents had been lost to the enemy in large quantities, and after Gazi Hasan died his successor's efforts to replace them had been swallowed up in the struggles for positions and revenues on the part of the political parties in Constantinople. Therefore, little had been done to fill the storehouses and send out the food and supplies which the army would need. The frontier fortresses still in Ottoman hands were badly in need of reinforcements and supplies if they were to meet new enemy attacks; wagons and horses were needed to transport them; men had to be mobilised and sent where they were needed. Various Balkan notables and *sancaks* had been ordered to send contingents of mounted men to the Grand Vizier as soon as possible, but almost no preparations had been made and the army remained immobilised. The British ambassador in Constantinople made a new effort to mediate a peace, but Selim said he would do nothing without the agreement of his Prussian and Swedish allies. For the moment, however, neither the Austrians nor the Russians moved to take advantage of the Ottoman difficulties. Emperor Leopold still was hoping that peace might be concluded, while the Russians suffered from Potemkin's annual spring lethargy. However, in March the Russian offensive anticipated the Ottomans, when the brilliant general Kutuzov besieged Izmail with 30,000 men. The city had a strong garrison and the expectation of a long siege soon became a reality. Selim was pouring hordes of Anatolian troops across the Bosporus with their own ammunition and supplies in the hope of reinforcing the Grand Vizier before it was too late. In mid May, the Austrian command became aware of

---

117 Shaw, *Between Old and New*. p.43. To provide the money, Selim publicly sent his own gold and silver plate to the Imperial Mint to be melted down and made into coins, and he ordered all the notables of the Empire to do likewise. Orders were again sent out prohibiting the use of gold or silver plate on houses, persons, and horses, and requiring all persons to deliver their valuable utensils to the Mint as soon as possible.

these activities and decided that a show of strength was needed to press the Ottomans towards an early settlement. Saxe-Coburg headed towards Rüsçük, with the implied threat of crossing the Danube unless the Ottomans began to negotiate in good faith. When he reached Giurgiu on the Danube, however, the Ottoman garrison resisted so fiercely that the arrival of reinforcements from Rüsçük panicked the Austrians, who fled back towards Bucharest, leaving all their equipment and supplies behind.[118]

On the western side, in the spring of 1790, the Austrians under *Feldzeugmeister* Joseph Nikolaus de Vins set out for the territories of Ottoman Croatia. With this campaign the Austrians wanted to stop the Ottoman incursions into the border area, seizing the forts of Furjan, Bužim, Ostrožac, Tržac and some other frontier *palankas*. By July the Austrian corps had succeeded in capturing several *palankas* and fortresses, including Cetin, on 20 July, which had a garrison of about 4,000 men.[119]

However, the news from Giurgiu strengthened Sultan Selim III's determination to resist, exactly contrary to Leopold's intention. It also encouraged the Ottoman commanders to make a new push across the Danube in pursuit of the fleeing Austrians, but after a series of indecisive skirmishes the strong resistance by the Austrian rearguard at Kalafat caused the Ottomans to retire in early June 1790. For all practical purposes, military contact between Austria and the Porte was ended and awaited only a political settlement to confirm the fact. Despite the Sultan's intransigence, the Triple Alliance had Austria sign a separate agreement at Reichenbach on 5 August 1790 by which it agreed to abandon all its Ottoman conquests in return for peace. The Sultan at first was extremely unhappy at what he considered to be betrayal by Prussia in negotiating for him without the presence of his representatives, but he finally accepted the arrangement and signed a peace with Austria at Sistova on 4 August 1791, which confirmed the arrangement of Reichenbach. Austria surrendered its conquests in Bosnia, Serbia, and the Principalities in return for the Sultan's promises to treat his Christian subjects well and to allow them to be protected by the Austrians.

As occurred in 1739, Austria had deserted Russia in the heat of a joint campaign against Constantinople. Selim III now restored Koca Yusuf to the grand vizierate in the hope that he could repeat his earlier successes, but the Ottoman army by now was in a miserable state and weakened by desertion and shortage of supply, such as it could do anything. Although he brought a large number of men together, they lacked discipline, morale, and training. During the summer the Russians besieged Kilia on the left bank of the Danube, which surrendered on 30 October, and finally stormed Izmail in December 1790. The fortress was under siege from March, but the Russians hesitated to attack the strong Ottoman garrison. After a heavy bombardment in the night between 21 and 22 December, the Russians entered the city with an assault on the breaches and engaged in fierce fighting with the Ottoman

---

118 Martens, *Allgemeine Geschichte der Türken-Kriege*, p.233.
119 K. u. K., 'Feldzug des k. k. kroatischen Armeekorps im Jahre 1790 gegen die Türken', p.167.

OTTOMAN WARFARE: A STRUGGLE FOR SURVIVAL

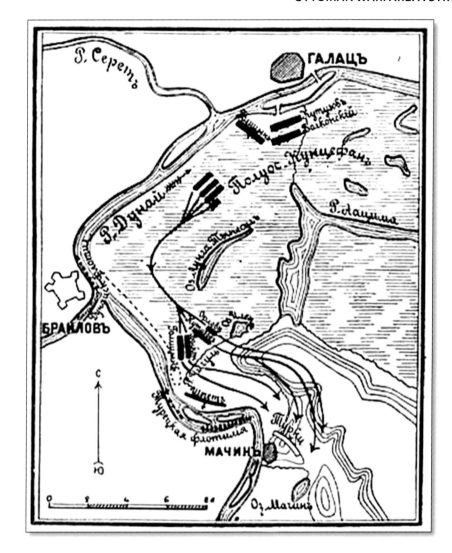

Map of the Battle of Măcin, fought on 9 July 1791; illustration from *Sytin's Military Encyclopedia* (St Petersburg, 1911–1915). The Russian army of 30,000 was commanded by Prince Nicholas Repnin, whereas the Ottomans, numbering twice as many, were led by Koca Yusuf Paşa, appointed grand vizier for the second time. At first the victory was in doubt, but then the Ottomans were routed by a charge of the Russian left, under Kutuzov, and started retreating in disorder.

garrison.[120] The Russian forces suffered 4,330 casualties, while the Ottomans claimed more than 26,000 dead and wounded, military as well as civilians, and just a few survivors were taken prisoners.[121] The loss of Izmail was another serious defeat for the Porte, which feared the collapse of the entire north-eastern front.

Hence, in 1791, it was not difficult for the Russians to besiege Ibrail and rout the Ottoman relief army led by Koca Yusuf Paşa at Măcin, on 9 July, leaving again the Empire defenceless. The defeat proved once again that well-conducted manoeuvre and co-ordination between infantry, cavalry and artillery could prevail over the sheer number and static mass of the undisciplined and untrained Ottoman troops. Russia now controlled the mouths of most

---

120 In the fighting, General Kutuzov received the wound that caused him to lose the right eye.
121 Christopher Duffy, *Russia's Military Way to the West: Origins and Nature of Russian Military Power 1700–1800*. London: Routledge & Kegan Paul Books, 1985), p.189.

of the major rivers emptying into the Black Sea, and transforming the basin in a Russian lake. Sultan Selim therefore was forced to accept Triple Alliance mediation, resulting in a peace agreement with Russia signed at Jassy on 8 January 1792. The Ottoman Empire had entered the war to regain the Crimea but instead had seen its boundaries driven back to the Dniester and the Koban. Russia returned Chotin and the Danubian fortresses to the Porte, but was finally and definitively entrenched on the shores of the Black Sea, with Kherson and Sevastopol established as great naval bases, and the territory provided for the emergence of Odessa as the new instrument of Russian naval supremacy. The Porte had been saved from even greater danger more by the grace of the French Revolution and the dictates of European concert diplomacy than by its own efforts. The war had revealed the extent of Ottoman weakness not only to all of Europe but also to Selim and to his associates, and they emerged from it with a determination to reform the Empire at once before it was too late.[122]

Kara Mahmud's Rebellion in Albania, 1792–1796

Once the peace with Austria and Russia was signed in 1792, governor of Scutari Bushati Kara Mahmud continued to quarrel with the Porte, until he rebelled again in September. Before the end of the year he annexed the *sangakbeylik* of Prizren, raided Montenegro, and instituted military and political reforms in his governorship without permission from the Porte. Through these efforts he aimed to create an independent state free from Ottoman control. Kara Mahmud's domains extended from Scutari to northern Macedonia, and included modern-day Kosovo and southern Serbia. In 1793 he assisted a number of French royalists who escaped through Germany across the Alps. Since this violated Selim III's effort to remain neutral, a new Ottoman expedition was sent against him in May 1793, this time under the command of the governor of Bosnia, Ebu Bekir Paşa. Scutari was besieged, but the siege was lifted and the Ottoman expedition retreated, then returned but failed to complete the siege, since Mahmud routed the Ottomans and captured its supplies.

In the meantime, in the south, Tepeleni Ali of Janina responded to the increasing Bushati threat by emphasising his loyalty to the Sultan and serving him wherever desired. In 1792 and 1793, his sons Muhtar and Veliuddin led a highly successful series of campaigns against brigands in Macedonia. In return, and also to balance the power of the clan Bushati, in 1794 the Sultan gave Ali the rank of *mirmiran*,[123] and gave the governorship of Ohrid to his son Muhtar Paşa, and ordered both to prepare a campaign against Kara Mahmud as soon as possible. Happy to comply with this order, Tepeleni Ali moved into the mountains separating middle Albania from Macedonia, taking Ohrid and Goritza from Kara Mahmud. These conquests cut Kara Mahmud off from possible assistance from the east and at the same

---

122 Shaw, *Between Old and New*, p.68.
123 *Mirmiran* is the military title of the *paşa*. The term itself means 'commandant over commandants'.

OTTOMAN WARFARE: A STRUGGLE FOR SURVIVAL

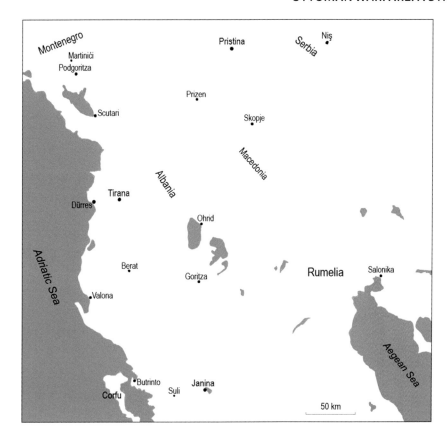

Map 4. Kara Mahmud's Rebellion in Albania, 1792–1796

time opened the way for Ali to make new conquests into Thessaly. He now reached new heights of power, extending his influence among the Albanian clans by marriage alliances as well as by force. His main opposition came from Ibrahim Paşa, who had succeeded his old enemy Kurt Paşa at Berat, allied with the highlanders of Suli and Shimari. Venice, from its coastal naval bases at Parga, Preveza, Vonitza, and Butrinto, provided them with material assistance in order to prevent Ali from overwhelming them as well.[124]

In response to this pressure, Kara Mahmud once again asked for and received a pardon from the Sultan, agreeing to pay all his back taxes and to participate in a new expedition being prepared against Montenegro in 1794. There, the *vladika* and his people had been bitterly disappointed by the peace treaties. While Russia and Austria had persuaded the Porte to give amnesty to those people of the Balkans who had helped their war efforts, nothing had been done to diminish Ottoman sovereignty, establish their autonomy or independence, or, in the case of Montenegro, confirm the conquests they had made in northern Albania, Herzegovina, and elsewhere. However, the *vladika* refused to recognise the peace and continued to harass the Ottomans. At the same time, representatives were sent to St Petersburg demanding that Russia fulfil its promises, but the Czarine replied that for the moment the new peace

---

124 Olsi Jazexhiu, *The Albanian Pashalik of Shkodra under Bushatlis 1757–1831* (Kuala Lumpur: IIUM, 2002), p.169.

made it impossible for her to do anything to help them against the Sultan. During 1796 Kara Mahmud led two expeditions against the Montenegrins. He suffered an initial defeat in July at Martinići, but continued military operations until September when the Montenegrins defeated him again in the battle of Krusi. Kara Mahmud was captured and beheaded along with almost 3,000 of his men.[125] For Tepeleni Ali and the Porte, this event marked the end of the Bushati danger, at least for the moment, since Mahmud's brother and eldest son began a struggle for power which effectively diverted their interests from their neighbours for two decades, until it finally was settled in favour of Mahmud's brother Bushati Ibrahim Paşa. He continued to rule Scutari as an Ottoman governor until his death in 1810. Ibrahim also served as *vali* of Rumelia and played an important role in crushing the First Serbian Uprising.

Campaigns Against Pazvandoğlu Osman, 1792–1798

The rise of the *ayans* in the European provinces of the Empire was marked by strong conflicts with the Porte. By the middle of the eighteenth century the Balkan *beys* and *ayans* were so powerful around the Bosnian capital of Sarajevo that the Ottoman governors virtually abandoned it to them and took up their headquarters at Travnik.[126] Other areas along the Danube and Bulgaria were under the control of local notables and the most extended domain stretched from Vidin to Sofia and was administrated by Pazvandoğlu Osman Paşa.

Osman's father, Ömer Ağa Pazvandoğlu, was a member of the janissary corps who in 1739 received two villages near Vidin in return for services in the war against Austria. Because of his rebellious tendencies, however, he was executed by the local Ottoman governor and Osman himself saved from the same fate only by fleeing to Albania. At the age of 25 he had lost his patrimony, 'and was no more than one among thousands of landless men then roaming the Balkans as robbers and thieves in search of their fortunes.'[127]

Osman participated in the war of 1787–1792 as an irregular in the Ottoman army and on his return to Vidin with a number of his army friends formed a bandit force and began raids into Serbia and Wallachia. When the Ottoman governor of Vidin tried to suppress his band, Osman went into the mountains, built up a large robber army, openly declared a revolt against the Sultan and began to devastate the area. Within a year he had captured Vidin and built it into a major fortress. He now attracted into his service thousands of bandits from all over Bulgaria, Serbia, and Wallachia, and also large numbers of janissaries, driven from Belgrade after 1792. At the same time, he joined the opponents to Selim's reforms, and Osman himself became a leading adversary of the entire *nizâm-ı cedid* programme. He attracted the allegiance and support of other opponents, not only in the Balkans but also

---

125 Shaw, *Between Old and New*, p.234.
126 Michael Robert Hickok, *Ottoman Military Administration in Eighteenth-Century Bosnia* (Leiden and Boston, MS: Brill, 1997), p.38.
127 Shaw, *Between Old and New*, p.237.

in the conservative faction in Constantinople. With their assistance he was able to conceal the extent of his power from the Sultan and his ministers until he was ready to meet them in open conflict. In 1795 he openly declared his independence from the Sultan, beat off an attack by the governor of Belgrade, and rapidly extended his power in western Bulgaria, from the Danube south almost to Sofia and east to the environs of Pleven. Unlike his contemporary Balkan *ayans*, Pazvandoğlu was in a state of open revolt from the start. He refused to recognise the Sultan's authority and drove out Ottoman officials wherever he went. All Ottoman efforts to conciliate him with pardons, flatteries, appointments and honours were brusquely rejected. Once his power around Vidin was consolidated he began to extend his protection, extracting tributes north into Wallachia and west into Serbia.[128] No Ottomans could enter it without his permission, and he usually provided far more orderly and efficient government than was the case elsewhere in Serbia. However, with Pazvandoğlu's invasion all this changed. The local *beys* was quickly driven out and replaced by men loyal to Pazvandoğlu. Taxes were increased to pay for the unscrupulous *ayan*'s military activities, and many of the outlaw *yamak* janissaries fleeing from Belgrade were settled there to administer the new order in their own ferocious way. At the same time, intrigues by Pazvandoğlu's friends in Constantinople led in the spring of 1795 to the appointment of Şaşit Paşa as governor of Belgrade in place of Ebu Bekir Paşa, who was transferred back to Bosnia, where he supported the programme of reforms introduced by Sultan Selim III, curbing the power of the *yamaks* and the *timars* in favour of the local population. In Serbia the new governor vigorously restored the 'old order', and entered into close relations with the *yamaks* serving Pazvandoğlu as well as those in Bosnia, who now fled from Bekir Paşa and returned to Belgrade in large numbers. These acts forced the Serbs to protest and signed a collective petition to the Sultan warning him of the possibility of a revolt if the governor was allowed to continue his policies.

In July 1795, the Porte used this as a pretext to replace Şaşit with Hajji Mustafa Paşa, chief architect of Belgrade, who was much more sympathetic to the Sultan's reforms. Hajji Mustafa immediately moved to restore Ebu Bekir's policies, and once again the local Serbian *obor-knez* (chief) could collect taxes for his village and district. The *yamaks* left in large numbers and asked for support from Pazvandoğlu, who took up their cause and ravaged large areas of Serbia while retaining his control over the Kraina. Mustafa Paşa was able to continue and extend his reforms in 1796 and 1797, increasing the privileges to the Serbs, because Pazvandoğlu now was diverted by a new danger from the east by the Ottomans and their supporters.

---

128 Shaw, *Between Old and New*, p.240. Pazvandoğlu extended his power in Serbia, and in particular in the Kraina. This district was located at the north-eastern tip of Serbia between the Timok and the Danube. It was ruled by an autonomous Christian *bey* who paid a regular annual feudal tribute to the private treasury of the daughters of the Sultan, and it was therefore subject not to the regular Ottoman taxes but only to those which the *bey* chose to levy to fulfil his obligations to the fief holders. The area was under his direct administration.

Frustrated by incompetence and political interference, Selim III finally decided that stronger, more determined, measures were needed to remedy the situation in the Balkans while there was still a chance to do so. In January 1796, the Sultan appointed as governor of Rumelia, with the specific duty of crushing rebel bandits and disloyal notables, Ahmed Kamil Paşazade Hakkı Paşa, who had demonstrated great determination in his previous efforts to repress corruption in the Empire.[129] To carry out his mission Hakkı was given direct command of a force comprising 2,000 artillery, cannon-wagons, and *humbaraci* mortar troops. In addition, the *mutasarrif* of Kojaeli in Anatolia contributed with 1,000 riflemen under his direct order, while the Karaosmanoğlu family contributed with 500 foot, and the Çapanoğlu family with 1,000 horsemen, 'all well trained and disciplined.'[130] Hakkı Paşa's reputation preceded him, and as he left Constantinople on 21 February 1796 and marched towards Edirne, most of the bandits operating in that area fled north to safer places. Many of the local notables were overawed and sent protestations of loyalty and contributions of assistance. Ali Paşa of Janina even sent his son Veliuddin Bey to Hakkı's camp, ostensibly to assist him, but actually as a hostage for his father's good behaviour. In addition, *ayans* were officially charged with the duty of clearing out the bandits in their districts, an obvious move which previous governors had not dared to attempt for political reasons. Hakkı attempted to divert Pazvandoğlu and prevent him from helping his bandit friends by appointing Ahmed Paşa *sancakbey* of the Bosnian district of Srebrenitza, to replace him as governor of Vidin, and charging Hajji Mustafa with the task of installing him in this new position, with the support of the Serbian troops. Informed about the incoming danger, Pazvandoğlu quickly reacted and in April 1796 decisively defeated the Ottoman-Serbian forces in the Kraina, killing Ahmed Paşa and forcing the enemy to return to Belgrade. Meanwhile Hakkı Paşa had his most successful campaign against the Bulgarian bandits during the spring and summer that followed, defeating their forces and executing many of the notables who had assisted them. But many of them managed to escape into the Rhodope Mountains, establish themselves in fortified villages, and emerge from time to time to ravage the area between Filibe (today Plovdiv in Bulgaria) and Pazarjik. As the weeks passed they began to establish a regular system of heavily fortified posts in the valleys as well. Whenever Hakkı approached, they were able to hold out until assistance came from the hills, and the Ottoman force was usually routed in the end. The fight continued until the end of the summer, when finally Hakkı prevailed on the rebels after

---

129 Bruce McGowan, 'The Age of the *Ayans*', in Suraya Faroqhi; B. McGowan; D. Quataert; S. Pamuk, *An Economic and Social History of the Ottoman Empire, vol. II, 1600-1914* (Cambridge: Cambridge University Press, 1999), p.658.

130 Robert Zens, 'Provincial Powers: The Rise of Ottoman Local Notables (Ayan)', in *History Studies* Volume 3, March 2011, p.441. Hakkı also was authorised to requisition all the additional men and supplies he needed from the Ottoman governors and local notables in the areas of his operations, and the Sultan assured him that the Imperial Treasury would provide necessary funds so that sufficient numbers of soldiers would be available at all times.

a surprise move through the mountains. This defeat demoralised the bandit opposition and enabled Hakkı to clear out the entire area between Filibe and Sofia. In the winter of 1796–97 Pazvandoğlu maintained control only in the areas around Vidin, Nicopolis, Rüsçük, and Silistria because of the strong support and material assistance given him to his allies in the area. When the Ottoman army retired to Edirne for the winter, Pazvandoğlu's lieutenant Kara Feyzi captured Tirnovo in southern Bulgaria and raided the environs of Filibe.

In April 1797 Hakkı Paşa moved back from Edirne, and within a short time was able to drive out the rebels and establish a state of security which had not been seen in Rumelia since the early years of the century. However, his successes caused the local notables to abandon their differences and come together for a supreme effort against him. Publicly they promised to obey his orders and help his campaigns, but secretly they sent large sums to Constantinople to finance the activities of his enemies, now led by Grand Vizier Kör Yusuf Ziyaüddin Paşa, commonly known as Yusuf Ziya Paşa, who feared that Hakkı would use his victories to take his place in the government. Orders were sent to Hakkı's subordinates to sabotage his efforts and ignore his orders. They created confusion, allowed trapped bandits to escape, and at times openly supplied them with arms and ammunition. When Pazvandoğlu ordered large-scale attacks in the areas of Tirnovo and Pleven, the Grand Vizier was able to use them and the complaints to ask for Hakkı's dismissal and transferral to Aleppo in May 1797, since his efforts had been unsuccessful.[131]

With Hakkı Paşa out of the way, it was not long before the notables and bandits of Rumelia resumed their former activities. In the early summer of 1797 Kara Feyzi and others ravaged the area of Philippopolis. When Hajji Mustafa Paşa moved against them, they routed the Ottoman force, after which he pardoned them and returned to his base, allowing them to plunder at will.

Since neither the Porte nor Pazvandoğlu were able to prevail, the stalemate turned into a truce in July 1796. Surprisingly, Pazvandoğlu now declared his loyalty to the Sultan, but at the same time moved to take advantage of the political and military vacuum by occupying the entire area between the Danube and the Balkan range. He extended his authority to the east, taking Nicopolis, Tirnovo, and Sistova, and then drove the *ayan* Tirsiniklioğlu Ismail Ağa out of Şumen as the year came to an end.

Selim III removed the unable Hajji Mustafa Paşa in June 1797, and replaced him with Ali Paşa of Janina as governor of Rumelia. For the moment, the Porte was forced to rely on Tirsiniklioğlu Ismail to stop Pazvandoğlu. With the assistance of the governors of Silistria and Belgrade, Ismail routed Pazvandoğlu near Şumen in October, and re-established his own position in eastern Bulgaria. Of course, Tirsiniklioğlu Ismail had his own ambitions

---

131 Shaw, *Between Old and New*, p.244. Bitterly disappointed, Hakkı Paşa obeyed the order, and with a small personal army crossed into Gallipoli on his way to Syria. Even here, he managed to eliminate several bandits whom he encountered along the way, but the grand vizier used these skirmishes to secure his banishment to Istanköy Island, where he remained for two years while Rumelia lapsed again into chaos.

in Bulgaria, but for the moment he was happy to cooperate with the Sultan since this alliance served to weaken the only real rival he had in the area. Blocked in the east, Pazvandoğlu moved west and south, besieging Belgrade and Niş, but in both cases he was driven off by the local governors assisted by Tirsiniklioğlu Ismail. In January 1798 Ali Paşa regrouped the Ottoman forces and moved against the bandits in western Bulgaria, defeating Pazvandoğlu's lieutenants in a series of encounters between Sofia and Nicopolis and pacifying the area between Rüsçük and Belgrade. Under his leadership, Gurgi Osman Paşa entered Rüsçük and Tirnovo and Kurd Osman Paşa captured Sofia, thus limiting Pazvandoğlu to Vidin itself, to which he withdrew in early February, fortifying himself for an expected attack. No actions occurred, and Ali Paşa and his lieutenants retired to Gallipoli and drilled and provisioned their troops. At this time Russia proposed joint intervention to protect Wallachia from bandits, but the Grand Vizier rejected the idea. Then, he ordered *kapudan paşa* Küçük Hüseyin to gather the army with the intention of definitively ending the Pazvandoğlu threat before the foreigners could intervene unilaterally. In early spring of 1798, by mobilising all available resources, the Porte was able to forge an impressive coalition of *ayans* of about 60,000 soldiers. The troops were mustered in preparation for a siege of Vidin and in early April began to move through Thrace. This force was considerably enlarged by men and supplies contributed by the notables through whose territory it passed, so that it had almost 100,000 men by the time it reached Vidin in early May.[132] At the same time, an Ottoman fleet sailed through the Black Sea and up the Danube, bearing supplies, artillery, and heavy siege equipment. On 20 June 1798, after careful preparation, the siege began. At long last it seemed that the Porte had managed to organise an attack which would eliminate Pazvandoğlu once and for all; whilst he managed to hold out against repeated attacks during the summer, his defeat still seemed inevitable. However, in September it was becoming clear that the siege would have to be lifted without result, since Bonaparte's invasion of Egypt left the Porte hardly any other choice but to leave Vidin. In view of the probable dissolution of his army during the winter months, this turn of events may have permitted the Sultan to save face. In early 1799 Osman Pazvandoğlu was not only pardoned, but also appointed commander of Vidin and also granted the titles of vizier and *paşa*.

With the French established on the Ionian Islands since October 1797, it was only a matter of time before the virtual civil war in Rumelia attracted the attention of Western Europe. For the French, Pazvandoğlu was a prospective ally, and he was sensitive to these overtures, because he feared Russian or Austrian interference as a result of the involvement of his lieutenants in Serbia and Wallachia, and also because he expected the two Continental empires to eventually intervene in order to defend the Sultan against Revolutionary France. In contrast, Ali Paşa of Janina, the other great figure in the Ottoman Balkans, needed to be more wary of his French neighbours, who were obviously planning to use his territory as a springboard for further conquests in the east.

---

132 Shaw, *Between Old and New*, p.246.

The First Ottoman–Saudi War, 1794–1800

In 1787, the governorship of the Sherif of Mecca was assumed by the Sherif Galib ibn Musaid, who bore the brunt of the Wahhabi attacks into the Hijaz during the remainder of Abdülhamid I's rule. For the moment the Saudis preferred to avoid open conflict with the Porte, so continued to concentrate their activities in the north and east of the peninsula. The Porte did not perceive their occasional raids into southern Iraq as anything beyond ordinary Bedouin attacks. Sherif Galib was much more aware of the religious and political threat of the Wahhabi Saudi movement, and he considered it his duty to do all he could to stamp it out before it became an important danger. His reports to the Porte had little impact among the increasingly decadent and worldly members of the *ulema*, however, and without their support he was unable to persuade the Sultan that major reinforcements were required to quell the movement. At the same time he also was diverted by internal difficulties, with a revolt led by his brother Abdullah preventing him from doing much about the Wahhabis for some time after his accession.

In the meantime Saud ibn Abd ul-Aziz increased his power, becoming the first Saudi leader capable of holding political and spiritual leadership among the various tribes. He also prevented disputes over the right of succession and assured a continuity of the vassals' loyalty. In early 1790 the elimination of the last important rivals to Abd ul-Aziz's power within the Nejd, the Beni Halid princes of al-Ahsa, set the stage for expansion to the north and south on a scale not attempted previously.

Despite the absence of Ottoman reinforcements, as soon as Abdullah's revolt was put down, Sherif Galib organised a force of about 10,000 men, including irregulars form Anatolia and Bedouin vassals summoned from all over the Hijaz, and even a few places in the Nejd. Then in September 1790 he marched towards Dariye, intending to eliminate the Saudi threat once and for all. However when he failed to seize the fortified town of Kasr Bassam, the lure of booty was effectively dissipated and the army broke up before reaching its objective.

During the next two years the Saudi Abd al-Aziz scattered the Nejd Bedouin tribes which had responded to Galib's call, thus making very sure that they would not respond again. At the same time the death of Muhammad ibn Abd al-Wahhab, at the age of 89, left Abd al-Aziz as the undisputed spiritual as well as political leader of the community. Between 1792 and 1794 he conquered al-Hasa and made it an integral part of his state, and with its wealth he was able to build a standing army for the first time. The desert kingdom now was becoming a state, and the danger which Galib had feared a reality. Wahhabi forces began to move out of the Nejd on a large scale. Various groups pillaged the frontiers of the Hijaz and Iraq and moved into Qatar and al-Kuwait along the Persian Gulf, with their preachers going along, arousing scorn for everything the Sultan stood for. The continued Wahhabi successes and the huge amounts of booty secured in these raids attracted the fealty of more and more tribes, including many of the Iraq and Syrian frontier Bedouins who were severely harried by the raids and discouraged by the failure of Baghdad and Damascus to defend them. As a result the Saudi army

THE OTTOMAN ARMY OF THE NAPOLEONIC WARS 1789–1815

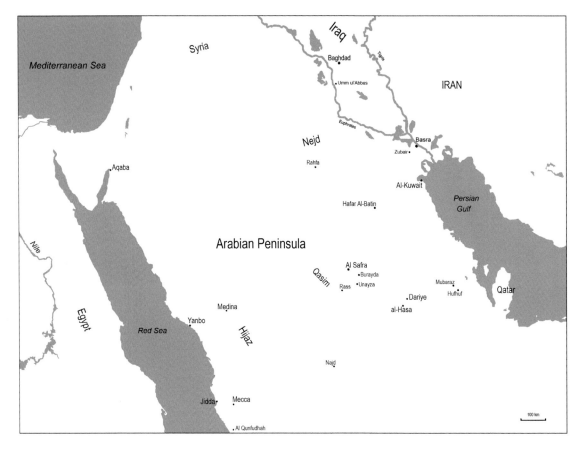

Map 5. First Ottoman–Saudi War, 1794–1800

now became by far the strongest military force in the Arab world. Up to this time, the extent of the Saudi threat was not understood in Constantinople, and the complaints arriving from Mecca, Damascus, and Baghdad continued to be received with scorn. The Saudis were still considered to be no more than another of the innumerable Bedouin forces which had troubled the Empire over the centuries, and the regular defences were felt to be quite adequate to deal with them, especially in view of the Sultan's desire to concentrate on internal reforms at this time. But starting in 1796, this situation changed rather quickly as a result of Saudi attacks on the centres of Ottoman power in the Arab world, attacks which were at least partially provoked by Galib's efforts to crush the movement before it became a threat. Galib's first attack, in the spring of 1796, was repulsed by the Saudis at Nil, on the caravan trail between the Nejd and the Hijaz. Süleyman Paşa of Baghdad persuaded Sheyh Thuwaini to return from exile and organise a coordinated campaign of all the Bedouin princes and chiefs driven out of northern Arabia and southern Syria by the Wahhabi advance. In July 1797, just as they were about to meet the Wahhabi army at al-Hasa, Thuwaini was assassinated by a slave and his forces broke up, thus ending disastrously the first important Iraqi counter-attack against the Saudis. The threat of continued attacks both from Mecca and Iraq caused Saud to attack and ravage al-Kuwait in the spring of 1798 in order to obtain needed supplies and camels to defend himself. This victory caused most of the Hijaz tribes to transfer their allegiance from Mecca to

Saud, thus becoming a major factor in advancing the Wahhabi cause. In the summer and autumn of 1798 and winter of 1799, a regular Ottoman force sent from Baghdad under the command of Süleyman's chief lieutenant, Kethüda Ali Paşa, moved into the Nejd and captured a number of villages. But despite the use of regular janissary and Mamluk soldiers and artillery, he was unable to take the important forts of Hufhuf and Mubaraz. When Saud moved north with a relief army in April 1799, Kethüda Ali, fearing he would be cut off, abandoned the siege, destroyed all his heavy equipment, buried his ammunition, and fled towards the coast with Saud in hot pursuit. The Ottomans thus retired and left the Saudis in control of al-Hasa without having to pay any tribute or indemnities for their previous attacks. As a result, Galib despaired of being able to defeat the Saudis by force so agreed to make peace with them, and in 1799 and 1800 Wahhabi pilgrims were allowed to come to the Holy Cities for the first time. As the century came to a close, all Ottoman efforts to check the Saudis had failed. This dangerous political and religious movement ruled without check in most of Arabia. The Sultan's failure to defeat the Saudis caused him tremendous loss of prestige in the Muslim world, and left his enemy in a position to gain new adherents and new power at the expense of the Ottomans in the following years.[133]

The War Against France of 1798–1802

> *Europe is a rat hole. We must go to the East; the real glory has always been won there!* (Napoleon, *Memoires*)

After 1798 Franco-British commercial rivalry, played out all over the world, was intensified in the Mediterranean with warships as European conflicts spread to the Near East. In 1797 the Habsburgs had abandoned their allies Russia and Great Britain, and at Campoformido the Emperor had signed a treaty with France: one of the first pieces of news reported home from Vienna by Ambassador Ibrahim Afif Efendi.[134] That treaty dismembered the Republic of Venice, and gave France the Ionian Islands, making France a neighbour of the Ottoman Empire for the first time and exacerbating Selim III's complicated Balkan relationships with Pazvandoğlu Osman of Vidin and Tepeleni Ali Paşa of Janina.

In early 1798 Bonaparte proposed a military expedition to seize Egypt. In a letter to the Directory, he suggested this would protect French trade interests, attack British commerce, and undermine Britain's access to India and the East Indies, since Egypt was well placed on the trade routes to these places. Bonaparte wished to establish a French presence in the Middle East,

---

133 Shaw, *Between Old and New*, p.227.
134 Aksan, *Ottoman Wars 1700–1870*, p.229.

THE OTTOMAN ARMY OF THE NAPOLEONIC WARS 1789–1815

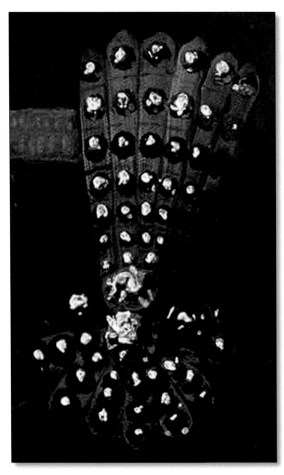

Nelson's distinctive *celeng* depicted in his 1799 portrait. This shows the special design ordered by Sultan Selim III for commemorating the battle of Aboukir, in 1798. The 13 crest rays represent the number of French ships captured and destroyed.

with the ultimate dream of linking with France's ally Tipoo Sahib Sultan, ruler of Mysore in India.[135]

On 1 July 1798, after successfully eluding detection by the Royal Navy for 13 days, the French landed at Marabut, 23 kilometres west to Alexandria, preferring that place instead of the better landing place offered by Aboukir because of General Bonaparte's great desire to see his men safe and sound ashore. Two days later the landing operations were successfully completed. They were 35,000 troops and a 500-strong team of scientists, archaeologists, linguists and scholars.[136] The first action took place on the morning of 2 July, when General Menou stormed the triangular fort defending the western side of Alexandria, while Kléber and Bon seized the gates of Pompeii and Rosetta respectively. The French troops, heated and thirsty, broke the resistance of the terrified Egyptian garrisons, about 500 infantrymen under Koraim Paşa. Although the fighting continued for some time in the narrow streets of the city, the defenders gave up and fled, and by midday Alexandria was under French control. The French had lost 300 men in this action, and the wounded included Generals Kléber and Menou.[137] On the same day Bonaparte issued a proclamation to the population, stating that the arrival of the French had been at the behest of Allah and assuring them that his intention was to free Egypt from the enslavement of the Mamluks. The Corsican general also promised that the Muslim religion would be respected and protected by the French soldiers. Bonaparte left a garrison of 2,000 men under Kléber to secure Alexandria, and on 6 July left the city with the whole army. The French started a long, tedious march to Cairo under the blazing summer sun. The soldiers were suffering from fatigue, thirst and hunger. They were also considerably frightened, and even the presence of the charismatic Corsican general in their midst could not dispel the feeling of estrangement caused by a landscape and a people that were unfamiliar, exotic and often hostile.

---

135 The project of annexing Egypt as a French colony had been under discussion since François de Tott undertook a secret mission to the Levant in 1777 to determine its feasibility. Tott's report was favourable, but no immediate action was taken. Nevertheless, Egypt became a topic of debate between Talleyrand and Napoleon, which continued in their correspondence during Napoleon's Italian campaign. See Watson, William E., *Tricolor and Crescent: France and the Islamic World* (London: Greenwood, 2003), pp.13–14.

136 Chandler, *The Campaigns of Napoleon*, vol. I, p.295.

137 Chandler, *The Campaigns of Napoleon*, vol. I, p.295.

OTTOMAN WARFARE: A STRUGGLE FOR SURVIVAL

Napoleon Bonaparte and his Major Staff in Egypt, painting by Jean-Léon Gérôme (1824–1904) (Hermitage Museum, St Petersburg). Continuing Russian military successes in Eastern Europe seemed to foreshadow imminent collapse of the Ottoman Empire, and seizure by the Russians of Constantinople itself and strategic ports along the Mediterranean's northern rim. Partly to secure its position along the Levant and Egyptian coasts, recoup losses, and guarantee its trade, the Directory sent Bonaparte to occupy Egypt and Palestine and destroy the local regimes responsible for the losses suffered by French trade in the Levant before 1789.

The Mamluks, for their part, were thrown into great panic and confusion upon hearing of the French landing in Alexandria. The war caught the government unaware and completely unprepared. It did not have combat-ready forces, other than the personal retinues of governors and other local magnates, in position to resist the invaders.[138] The Ottoman governor, Ebu Bakri Paşa, summoned the war council in Cairo, in which the two ineffable masters of Egypt, Murad Bey and Ibrahim Bey took part. Their advice prevailed and the available forces were divided in two corps. Murad Bey, with 4,000 Mamluk cavalry and 12,000 Egyptian *fellahin* infantry was approaching the French along the Nile. Ibrahim, in turn, had to gather the rest of the forces and enlist more soldiers by forming a force able to protect Cairo and gathering it at Bulaq. With much optimism, the two powerful emirs declared that they could raise at least 100,000 men.[139]

On 10 July the Mamluks made contact with the division of General Desaix at Rahmaniye, and engaged in a skirmish that ended in the Mamluks' defeat. The day after, Bonaparte inspected the French troops and examined the position of the enemies who were camped 13 km south on the west bank of the Nile. On 13 July the French advanced and engaged in a series of indecisive

---

138 Uyar and Erickson, *A Military History of the Ottomans*, p.123.

139 To exhort his men, Ibrahim gave a vehement but somewhat bizarre description of the French soldiers: 'The infidels who come to fight us have finger nails a foot long, huge mouths and fierce eyes. They are savages possessed by the devil and fight bound together with chains.' Captain Vertray, *Journal d'un officier de l'armée d'Egypte*, cited in Chandler, *The Campaigns of Napoleon*, p.298.

THE OTTOMAN ARMY OF THE NAPOLEONIC WARS 1789–1815

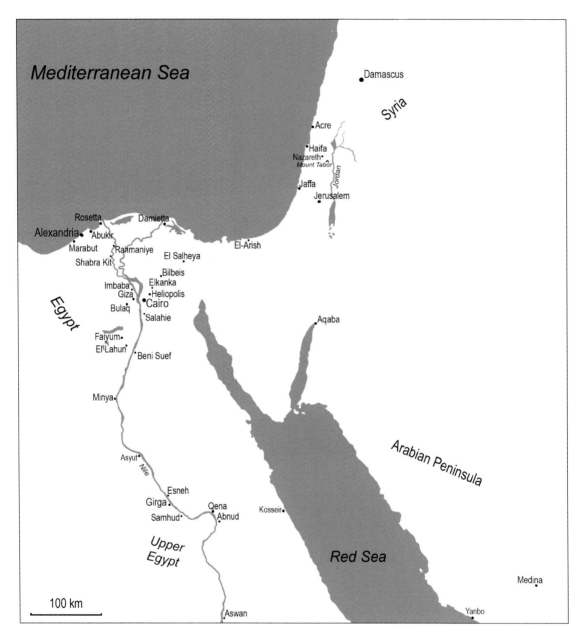

Map 6. Campaigns in Egypt and Syria, 1798–1802

encounters at Shabra Khit. The main action was in fact fought by the river fleets on the Nile. The naval battle lasted almost four hours and the Mamluks almost prevailed over the smaller French fleet. Artillery fire from the shore restored the situation and the Egyptian flagship was hit and blown up, killing the Ottoman commander and his crew. Two days afterwards Murad Bey, the most powerful of the Mamluk emirs, crossed the Nile at Giza and in haste started setting up entrenchments in the area bounded by the village of Giza to the south, Imbaba to the north, the Pyramids to the west and the Nile to the east. The following day he issued a general call-to-arms and the people were summoned to the entrenchments.[140] The French advance resumed the day after, while the Mamluk cavalry did not stop to engage the enemy with sudden skirmishes. At two o'clock on the morning of 21 July the French army raised the camp and marched on the village of Imbaba, and 12 hours later they sighted Cairo. They were given an hour's rest and then the divisions took up the battle position designed by Bonaparte, consisting of large and deep squares with the cavalry and army train in the centre and the corners protected by artillery batteries positioned outside the perimeter of the squares.

The French divisions advanced south in echelon, with the right flank leading and the left flank protected by the Nile, approximately 15 km from the Pyramids of Giza. From right to left, Bonaparte posted the divisions of Louis Charles Antoine Desaix, Jean-Louis-Ébénézer Reynier, Charles-François-Joseph Dugua, Honoré Vial and Louis André Bon.[141] In addition, Desaix sent a small detachment to occupy the nearby village of Biktil, just to the west. Murad Bey anchored his right flank on the Nile at the village of Imbaba, which was fortified and held with infantry and some guns. The Mamluk cavalry deployed on the desert flank. Ibrahim Bey, with a second army, watched helplessly from the east bank of the Nile, unable to intervene. The two forces were estimated at 21,000 to 40,000–50,000 men, including possibly 5,000–6,000 Mamluk horsemen. However, the two *beys* relied mostly on untrained and poorly equipped troops, and only the Mamluk cavalry squadrons could hold their own against the French, at least in terms of equipment and individual courage. It has never been clarified why the Mamluks decided to engage the battle. It is likely that Murad Bey had received incomplete and not entirely true information about the French being without water and food, and therefore weakened and unable to withstand an assault.[142] Mid afternoon the Mamluk cavalry approached, deployed in five large corps, assaulting the French without warning. The divisional squares of Desaix, Reynier and Dugua held firm and repelled the horsemen with point-blank musket and artillery fire. An Egyptian chronicle reports the clash between the Mamluk cavalry and the French infantry and artillery, when, on 21 July, the French columns were seen to the

---

140 The Egyptian chronicler al-Jabarti, who witnessed these momentous events, describes the scene: 'People closed their shops and markets, and everyone was in an uproar. The noise and confusion were very great. The shaykhs, the dignitaries and the common people set out with clubs and arms'; cited in Fahmy, *All the Pasha's Men*, p.111.

141 Chandler, *The Campaigns of Napoleon*, p.301.

142 Fahmy, *All the Pasha's Men*, p.114.

THE OTTOMAN ARMY OF THE NAPOLEONIC WARS 1789–1815

The Battle of the Pyramids, by Louis-François Baron Lejeune (Château de Versailles). On 21 July 1798, Napoleon defeated a Mamluk army double in size at the Battle of the Pyramids. In the annals of military history, the battle stands as the great east–west encounter, with Bonaparte's hollow squares of infantry cutting down Mamluk cavalry mainly armed only with swords and lances.

north of Imbaba: 'an innumerable throng surpassing all description gathered at Bulaq (on the other side of the river)' when the actual fighting began. In the meantime and on the other side of the Nile a band of Mamluks charged upon the French who fired at them 'in successive volleys.'[143] On retreating to their entrenchments and seeing that shells were still pouring down on them 'some of the Mamluk emirs started to cross (the Nile) to the other side on horseback.'[144]

Unable to disrupt the French formations, some of the frustrated Mamluks charged Desaix's division. This was also a failure. Meanwhile, nearer the Nile, Bon's division deployed into attack columns and charged Imbaba. Breaking into the village, the French routed the garrison. Trapped against the river, many of the Mamluks and infantry tried to swim to safety and hundreds drowned.[145] The French reported a loss of 29 killed and 260 wounded. Murad Bey's losses were far heavier, perhaps as many as 6,000 dead and wounded, including

---

143 Fahmy, *All the Pasha's Men*, p.112.

144 Fahmy, *All the Pasha's Men*, p.112: 'They jostled with each other on the ferryboats [and] sand rose in clouds which the wind blew in their faces. [The battle continued] and the muskets of the French were like a boiling pot on a fierce fire.'

145 Chandler, *The Campaigns of Napoleon*, vol. I, p, 303. About 1,000 Mamluks drowned and a further 600 were killed by the French who targeted them from the banks of the Nile.

2,000 of his elite Mamluk cavalry, and all the artillery, consisting of 50 guns.[146] Murad Bey escaped to Upper Egypt with his 3,000 surviving cavalry.[147] During the night that followed Ibrahim Bey abandoned Cairo and retreated eastwards, burning the boats in the harbour. Dupuy's brigade pursued the routed enemy and at night entered Cairo. In the morning an observation corps was put in place at Elkanka to keep an eye on the movements of Ibrahim Bey, who was heading towards Syria. Bonaparte personally led the pursuit and routed again the Mamluks at Salahie on 24 March.

On 25 July Bonaparte entered Cairo, but remained precariously perched on the mouth of the Nile. In fact, the French troops had already been in Africa for a month when on 1 August their connection with France was abruptly cut off. That day, British Admiral Horace Nelson discovered the French warships anchored in a strong defensive position in the Bay of Aboukir and destroyed them in a few hours. After the bitter naval defeat, Bonaparte's campaign remained land-bound, but his army still succeeded in consolidating power in Egypt. After his defeat at the Pyramids, Murad Bey retreated to Upper Egypt. On 25 August 1798 General Desaix embarked at the head of his division on a flotilla and sailed up the Nile. On 31 August the French arrived at Beni Suef where it began to encounter supply problems; then Desaix went up the Nile to Behneseh and progressed towards Minya. The Mamluks did not oppose the enemy and the flotilla returned on 12 September at the entrance of Bahr Yussef. Desaix learned that the Mamluks were in the plain of Faiyum by 24 September. The first contact between the two sides occurred on 3 October and a second minor fight took place, which began to deplete the food and ammunition of the French forces. Meanwhile Murad Bey reconstituted a fighting force with troops from the Arabian Peninsula ,and by then had at least 10,000 men at his command,[148] half of them on horseback or dromedaries. Desaix, on the other hand, had only 3,000 men and two cannons. On 7 October the Mamluks came out of their entrenchments near Al Lahun and attacked the French, who formed themselves into three squares, one large and two small at its angles. As on 21 July the Mamluks charged furiously but were repulsed again. They attempted to use their four cannons, but a vigorous attack led by the French managed to capture them. After several hours of fighting the French went on the offensive and the Mamluks fled southwards. Desaix continued to face Murad until March 1799, and defeated him again on 22 January 1799 at Samhud, and on 8 March at Abnud. Because of the continuous defeats the Mamluk cohesion broke, and Murad disappeared from the scene for a few months.

Between July and December 1798, while Bonaparte's army was in Egypt, other European states sided with Britain, which had never laid down its arms, in a second coalition against France. In Constantinople the government received news of the French fleet's destruction at Aboukir in August, and believed this spelled the end for Bonaparte and his expedition trapped in Egypt. Thus, in September, the Porte entered the war with France, and two

---

146 Jucherau de Saint-Denis, *Histoire de l'Empire Ottoman,* vol. II, p.72.
147 Jacques-Olivier Boudon, *La campagne d'Egypte* (Paris: Belin, 2018), p.102.
148 Chandler, *The Campaigns of Napoleon*, vol. I, p.307.

Murad Bey (1750–1801) portrayed by Dutertre in *Description de l'Égypte* (1809). While the Georgians and some historians claim Murad as born in Tiflis, several others believe he was a Circassian, because in 1768 he was sold in Egypt to the Circassian Mamluk Muhammad Bey Abu al-Dhahab. After the death of his master, he was in command of the household, and shared the power in Egypt with the other *bey*, Ibrahim. During the war against the French he maintained the military leadership, raising troops as far as Upper Egypt and in the Arabian Peninsula. Murad had reportedly offered money to the French forces to leave Egypt, while offering to ally with the British in exchange for his recognition as a ruler and allowing the British to occupy Alexandria, Damietta and Rosetta. In 1800, Murad agreed a peace with Jean Baptiste Kléber, but died of bubonic plague on his journey to Cairo.

months later concluded an unprecedented treaty of alliance with Russia, Great Britain and the Kingdom of Naples, which was joined shortly afterwards by the Ottoman Empire's other arch-enemy, Austria. The German states and Sweden also followed before 1799.

Sultan Selim III ordered the gathering of two armies for the Egyptian campaign. The first, the Army of Damascus, comprised 12,000 *kapıkulu* soldiers, but when the actual strength of the available soldiers decreased to just 4,000, this was reinforced with troops from Damascus, Aleppo, Iraq and Jerusalem, which joined the army with a further 22,000 men.[149] For this reason it was necessary to reach an agreement with the local leaders. In Syria the outstanding personality was Ahmed Cezzar Paşa, and almost as an obligatory choice, Selim III appointed him as commander.

The second army began to assemble in Rhodes with about 8,000 men from southern Anatolia, waiting for the British fleet to take it to Egypt. The government also knew it would get about 42,000 soldiers from Albania, Constantinople, Asia Minor, and Greece.[150] The command was entrusted to the aged Seid Mustafa Paşa.

The Ottomans planned two offensives against the French in Egypt: one from Syria, across the desert of El Salheya-Bilbeis-Al Khankah, and the other from Rhodes by sea landing in the Aboukir area or the port city of Damietta. Unfortunately the army of Rhodes was still behind schedule, and for the time being the campaign was carried out only by the Army of Damascus.

The French *Armée d'Orient* was now in a critical situation. On 7 October 1798 discontent against the French led to an uprising by the people of Cairo, which was brutally repressed the day after.[151] The British had severed the

---

149 Temel Öztürk, 'Egyptian Soldiers in Ottoman Campaigns from the Sixteenth to the Eighteenth Centuries', in *War in History* (2016), vol. 23, p.19.

150 Shaw, *Between Old and New*, p.259.

151 The French General Dominique Dupuy was killed by the rioters, as well as Bonaparte's aide-de-camp, Joseph Sulkowski. The rebellion occurred while Bonaparte was in Old Cairo, and when he and his soldiers moved to the city centre, the crowds rallied at the gates to keep out Bonaparte, who was repulsed and forced to take a detour to get in via the Boulaq gate. The French reacted, however,

French links from the homeland; Ibrahim Bey was still in the field; generals Menou and Dugua were only just able to maintain control of Lower Egypt, since the Mamluks had common cause with the Bedouins against the French, transforming the whole Upper Egypt in a powder keg.

On 29 December 1798, the French division under Desaix arrived at Girga, capital of Upper Egypt, and waited there for a flotilla to bring them ammunition. However, 20 days passed without hearing of the flotilla. In the meantime Murad Bey had contacted Bedouin chieftains from Gidda and Yanbo to cross the Red Sea to join him. He also sent emissaries to Nubia to recruit mercenaries and Hassan Bey Jeddaoui, another Mamluk household chief, to enter the 'Holy Alliance' against the French. Upon hearing this news General Davout mobilised his forces on 2 January 1799, where he met a few thousands of armed men near the village of Sawaqui. The insurgents were easily routed, and 800 of them remained on the battlefield. However, the locals kept gathering around Asyut to resume the fight against the French. On 8 January Davout defeated and put to flight another local forces at Tahta.

Ahmed Cezzar, alias Ahmad Paşa al-Jazzar (1730?–1804) was a Christian native of Bosnia who converted to Islam and served as a Mamluk under Ali Bey al-Kabir, whom he eliminated in 1774. His stoic defence of Acre against Bonaparte in 1799 earned him a reputation as a brave commander.

By early January 1799 Murad Bey's retinue had been reinforced by 1,000 of Bedouins from beyond the Red Sea, 250 Mamluks with Hassan Bey Jeddaoui and Osman Bey Hassan.[152] In addition to Nubians and North Africans led by *sheikh* Al-Kilani, inhabitants of Upper Egypt supported Murad Bey. This composite force marched on 21 January 1799 in the desert to Samhud near Qena. On 22 January, Desaix moved to encounter the approaching enemies. The French formed three squares, two infantry and one cavalry; the latter was placed in the centre. The Mamluk–Arab cavalrymen surrounded them, while another column of Bedouins targeted their left. French suffered some casualties, but the continuous fire of the infantry and a well-directed cavalry charge disrupted the disorganised Egyptian and Bedouin bands. Afterwards the Murad Bey's cavalrymen rallied and came back to attack, trying to capture the village of Samhud, which gave the name to this encounter, but the French infantrymen directed against them a deadly fire, which

---

and responded by setting up cannons in the Citadel and firing to the crowd. During the night, French soldiers advanced around Cairo and destroyed any barricades and fortifications they came across. The rioters soon began to be pushed back by the strength of the French forces, gradually losing control of their areas of the city. The French broke down the gates and stormed into the building, massacring the inhabitants. At the end of the revolt, 2,000 people were dead or wounded, and many prisoners, included 6 sheiks and 80 members of the newly formed *Conseil pour la Defence*, were executed in the Citadel. See Chandler, *The Campaigns of Napoleon*, p.308.

152 General Jean-Pierre Doguereau, *Journal de l'expédition d'Égypte, publié d'après le manuscrit original, avec une introduction et des notes, par C. de La Jonquière, chef d'escadron d'artillerie breveté* (Paris: 1904), p.221.

Ibrahim Bey (1735–1817?), portrayed by Dominique Denon. A Georgian from the southeastern province of Kakheti, or a Circassian, he was sold out in Egypt where he was converted to Islam and trained as a Mamluk. Through loyal service to Muhammad Bey Abu al-Dhahab, the Mamluk ruler of Egypt, he rose in rank and attained to the title of bey. With time, he emerged as one of the most influential Mamluk commanders, sharing a de facto control of Egypt with his fellow Murad Bey. The two men became a duumvirate, Murad Bey managing military matters while Ibrahim Bey managed civil administration. Ibrahim fought against the French but was always defeated. These failures effectively ended his power. He died in obscurity in 1816 or 1817, having survived Muhammad Ali Paşa's massacre of the Mamluks in 1811.

forced them to withdraw after suffering heavy casualties. The battle turned into a confused struggle and involved the French squares under Friant and Bellard. Preceded by their frightful cries of encouragement, the Mamluks and Bedouins charged one more time but clashed against the French artillery fire and musketry.[153] The final charge of the French cavalry routed the Mamluk–Bedouin bands. The French pursued their enemies until the next day and did not stop until they were pushed beyond the Cataracts of the Nile, but Murad and his allied chiefs avoided capture. Desaix continued to march south, and reached Esneh on 9 February. Meanwhile Osman Bey Hassan held the command of a large force stationed at the foot of a mountain near Aswan. On 12 February the French cavalry under Davout discovered the enemy positions and immediately formed two lines, and in this order of battle charged the Mamluk–Bedouin camp, overwhelming the enemy and forcing them to leave the battlefield in a disorderly flight. In the action, Osman Bey was seriously wounded, and died days later.[154]

Meanwhile, in late January 1799, the French headquarters in Cairo learned that Cezzar Ahmed with his Army of Damascus was marching to the border between Syria and Palestine, and that the Mamluks under Ibrahim Bey had joined the Ottoman army days later. Rather than becoming mired in Cairo, Bonaparte headed to Palestine in February 1799. He prepared about 13,000 men in four infantry and one cavalry division, with further corps including one infantry and one cavalry brigade, one camel company, artillery and engineers. In Egypt remained 10,000 men, supported by the local militia organised by the French. Bonaparte intended to prevent the Ottoman offensive and then to seize Acre, defeating the Ottomans in a field battle at the first opportunity. As would later become known, speed was an essential element of Bonaparte's plan, since after the first part of the campaign,

---

153 Various authors, *Dictionnaire historique des batailles, sièges, et combats de terre et de mer, qui ont eu lieu pendant la Révolution Française. Avec une table chronologique des évènements, et une table alphabétique des noms des Militaires et des Marins français et étrangers qui sont cités dans cet ouvrage.* (Paris: 1818), vol. III, p.443.

154 Doguereau, *Journal de l'expédition d'Égypte*, p.255.

View of El-Arish in a 1916 photo. The fortress wall is visible in the background (Matson Collection, The Library of Congress, Washington, USA). The French under generals Kléber and Reynier laid siege to El Arish on 8 February 1799. The fortress finally fell on 20 February 1799 after bitter resistance from the Mamluk and Albanian garrison. The siege of El-Arish was a minor operation compared to the other military episodes of the Egyptian campaign, but the Ottoman resistance put Bonaparte 11 days behind schedule and compromised the success of the plan for 1799.

the French had to return to Egypt just in time to repel the incoming assault by the army of Rhodes.[155]

The French command had calculated crossing 190 km of desert. The calculation was correct, but due to a hasty reconnaissance Bonaparte had an incorrect idea of the size of the garrison at El-Arish, which was halfway between Cairo and Acre. Cezzar Ahmed did not yet have all his troops available, which were still gathering in Damascus, and estimated they would not arrive until late April. Informed by the network of spies in Cairo that Bonaparte was marching eastwards, he had no choice but to reinforce the fortified points on the coastal route to Palestine. The Ottoman commander reinforced the 800 Mamluk garrison of El-Arish with 1,700 Albanian infantrymen.[156] Furthermore, the Mamluk forces under Ibrahim Bey were converging on El-Arish, and laid the camp not far from the fortress. On 6 February the French vanguard quickly arrived before El-Arish, and found a solid and well-manned stone fortress. The sudden need to besiege El-Arish meant that precious time was lost. On 8 February the French attacked the Mamluk encampment and entered the village, but against the fort, any attempt to conquer was in vain. In the following days the garrison of El-Arish defended itself valiantly and the siege did not produce any appreciable results until 19 February, when French mortars opened fire and forced the 800 surviving defenders to surrender the day after.[157]

After marching 50 km across the desert the French arrived before Gaza, where they rested for two days, and then moved on to Jaffa on 3 March. This city had a medieval curtain with high walls flanked by towers. Cezzar Ahmed

---

155 Chandler, *The Campaigns of Napoleon*, vol. I, p.310.
156 Chandler, *The Campaigns of Napoleon*, vol. I, p.314.
157 Doguereau, *Journal de l'expédition d'Égypte*, p.233.

Facing page: French map depicting the main towns and village on the two banks of the Nile, after the Hauet's manuscript *Théatre des operations Militaires* of 1799–1800 (American University in Cairo).

had entrusted its defence to a strong garrison with 5,000 men, including elite troops and the artillery manned by 1,200 men. He left one of his most loyal followers at the command, the resolute Abdallah Bey. Jaffa was a strategic objective of great importance, since its port could be used by the Ottoman fleet and a large part of the expedition's success depended on its resistance.

On 5 March Bonaparte sent a couple of messengers to Abdallah Bey to demand the surrender, but the Ottoman commander executed them despite the envoys' neutrality and ordered a sortie as an answer. The Ottomans were repulsed and on the evening of the same day the French artillery caused one of the towers to crumble. Despite the desperate Ottoman resistance, Jaffa fell. Two days and two nights of carnage were enough to assuage the French soldiers' rage. About 4,400 prisoners were shot or beheaded. Napoleon also had Abdallah Bey executed, reportedly in retaliation for the brutal killing of the messengers, who were tortured, castrated and decapitated, with their heads impaled on the city walls.[158]

Before leaving Jaffa Bonaparte set up a council for the city along with a large hospital on the site of the monastery at Mount Carmel. A report from his generals on the plague's spread seriously worried Bonaparte and his major staff. On 14 March, the army left Jaffa and headed to the coastal town of Acre, but leaving in the hospital another 300 sick soldiers. En route the French seized Haifa and the munitions and provisions stored there by the Ottomans. The French advanced further and enter Nazareth and even the town of Tyre much further up the coast. Bonaparte rested his troops and then advanced towards Acre. The city has a significant strategic importance due to its commanding position on the route between Egypt and Syria. Cezzar Ahmed himself had confided to the Royal Navy Commodore Sidney Smith that Acre was the 'key to Palestine'.[159] A siege by land could prove difficult, since Acre was right on the coast, enabling it to be reinforced and resupplied by the British and Ottoman fleets. Inside Acre, Cezzar Ahmed personally held the command with 4,000 Albanians[160] and some companies of *nızam-ı cedid* infantry, alongside local militia and 40 guns, for 5,500 men in all. On 18 March the French attempted to lay siege using only their infantry. Napoleon believed the city would capitulate quickly to him, but he faced a stiff resistance. After 60 days of siege and two inconclusive assaults, the city firmly remained in Ottoman hands, but even so, it was still awaiting reinforcements by sea as well as the large army from Asia on the Sultan's orders to march against the French. To find out the latter's movements Cezzar Ahmed ordered a general sortie against the French camp,

---

158 *Memoirs of Napoleon, completed by Louis Antoine Fauvelet de Bourrienne* (London, 1832), p.172. This vengeful execution of prisoners found different explanations. According to Chandler, *The Campaigns of Napoleon*, vol. I, p.313, Napoleon could neither afford to hold such a large number of prisoners nor let them escape to rejoin the Ottoman side, or because he did not have sufficient resources to feed such a large number of prisoners. But this act was probably due to Bonaparte's desire to impress Cezzar Ahmed, who was said to be known in the Empire by the nickname 'the executioner'

159 Chandler, *The Campaigns of Napoleon*, vol. I, p.316.

160 Uyar and Erickson, *A Military History of the Ottomans*, p.123.

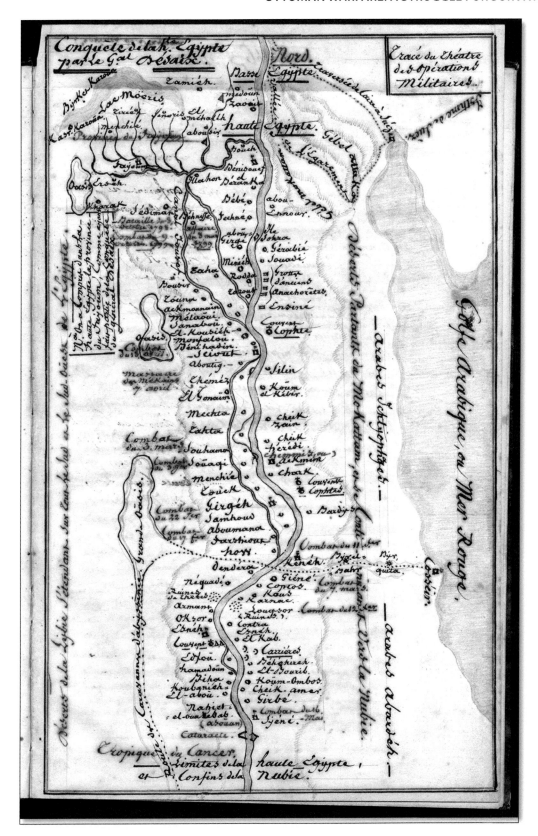

supported by its own artillery and the guns of the British fleet. Furthermore, Commodore Smith helped to reinforce the Ottoman garrisons and supplied the city with additional cannon manned by sailors and marines. Smith used his marines to capture the French siege artillery being sent by a flotilla of gunboats from Cairo, and then bombarded the coastal road from Jaffa. In Acre, the Ottoman resistance continued. Cezzar Ahmed personally visited his troops and encouraged them with prizes. Sitting pompously in an armchair, he watched the fighting without ever losing control of the defence.[161] On 2 April the French sappers triggered a mine, but the wall was barely cracked by the explosion and the subsequent assault was no better. Days after, Bonaparte received information that 7,000 Ottomans were coming from the Jordan River converging to Galilea. and the French cavalry made contact with the approaching enemy at Nazareth on 8 April. The Ottomans did not exploit their numbers and failed to relieve Acre, and withdrew after the few enemy squadrons routed the Ottoman *deli* and *sipahi* cavalrymen. Another Ottoman attempt to succour Acre from land was rejected at Cana on 11 April. This time about 6,000 horse and foot were routed by Junot and Bonaparte with half of this force.[162] On 15 April Murat, with a couple of battalions, routed the Ottomans near the lake of Tiberias capturing valuable resources and pack animals.

On 16 April a large Ottoman relief force was sighted while crossing the pass at Mount Tabor.[163] The *paşa* of Damascus with approximately 25,000 horse and 10,000 foot was faced by just 2,000 French under Kléber deployed at the defence of the road to Acre. The day after, before dawn, notwithstanding the ratio of 1 to 17, the French assaulted the enemy encampment, but the surprise failed and Kléber and his men were involved in a desperate fight that continued until the afternoon. Bonaparte re-established the situation at four o'clock in the afternoon, when Bon's division arrived just in time to assault the Ottomans from behind and force them to a disorderly retreat.[164]

Despite this success, Bonaparte had to deal with the stubborn resistance of Acre and the terrible toll of losses caused by the plague, which by mid April numbered 270 new cases. By early May a new French siege artillery train had arrived by sea and soon opened fire against the wall. The siege artillery managed to make a breach, and between 1 and 8 May the garrison was able to reject four assaults inflicting heavy casualties to the besiegers. The last assault managed to enter Acre, but the French found that the defenders had built another defence, several metres deeper, within the city.[165] Discovery of this new construction convinced Napoleon and his generals that the probability of

---

161 Chandler, *The Campaigns of Napoleon*, vol. I, p.317.

162 Doguereau, *Journal de l'expédition d'Égypte*, p.240.

163 Chandler, *The Campaigns of Napoleon*, vol. I, p.318.

164 Chandler, *The Campaigns of Napoleon*, vol. I.

165 The new defence was designed by a French émigré engineer serving with the British Navy, Louis-Edmond Antoine le Picard de Phélippeaux, who died during the siege. Alongside him, Haim Farhi, the Cezzar's Jewish adviser and right-hand man, played a key role during the siege of Acre, directly supervising the operation of defence. See in Kobler, Franz, *Napoleon and the Jews* (Jerusalem: Masada Press, 1975). p.51.

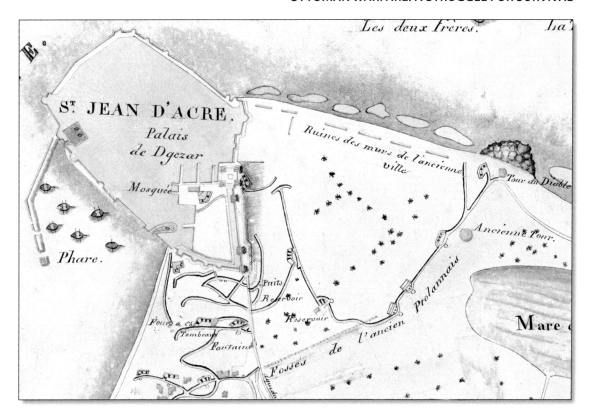

Map of Acre indicating the position of the French army and the works which served in the siege of this place, begun on 29 Ventose An 7 and surveyed on 30 Floréal same year (1799).

them taking the city was minimal. Moreover, after another French assault was repulsed on 10 May, further Ottoman reinforcements from Rhodes were able to land. The French withdrew on 20 May, after a violent fusillade from the siege artillery, which bombarded Acre with all the projectiles still available. Due to the impossibility of transporting the artillery by sea, guns and mortars were nailed down and abandoned. Of 13,000 troops under Bonaparte at beginning of the siege, 2,000 died, included two generals, and another 3,000 men were wounded: heavy casualties even for the period.[166] Ottoman losses are uncertain. But the fight continued on 21 May, when Cezzar Ahmed launched his cavalry to pursue the retreating French columns, and engaged the Reynier Division in a violent rearguard encounter. Skirmishes continued until 24 May. The march of the French columns was painful, as it was slowed down by the large number of invalids and the sick who were forced to continue on foot due to the lack of wagons and draught animals. The French retreat headed to Gaza and finally ended at Katia on 3 June.

In the meantime the fighting in Upper Egypt had never stopped. By the end of February 1799 an occasional skirmish had engaged Desaix and Murad Bey. The encounters, although short-lived, were conducted with ferocity by both sides and prisoners were rarely spared. On 27 February Şerif Hassan with 2,000 footmen from Arabia surprised a French river flotilla with wounded and sick soldiers near the village of Qena. About 500 French, the whole force,

---

166 The generals were Louis-André Bon and Louis-Marie-Joseph-Maximilien Caffarelli.

Mustafa Paşa (drawings after *Denon's Voyage dans la Basse et la Haute Egypte*, Paris 1802). The aged commander of the Army of Cyprus became a French prisoner at Aboukir on 25 July 1799, alongside 2,500 Ottoman soldiers.

were mutilated and killed.[167] On 8 March 1799 General Belliard led his forces against about 3,000 Arab Infantry and 350 Mamluk cavalry in the plain of Abnud, located on the right bank of the Nile to the south of Qena. The French with their square formation managed to approach the Muslim forces who later garrisoned themselves inside the village of Abnud. The fighting lasted for hours; afterwards the French managed to reach the courtyard of the village and set the houses on fire. The Muslims were forced to escape and the remaining injured were all killed. Murad Bey maintained his strategy of inciting the locals against the French. Further episodes of brutality marked the campaign. On 1 May 1799 General Davout's division isolated and routed at least 2,000 armed *fellahin* at Beni Adi near Asyut and killed everyone. The French attempt to expel the last Mamluk forces in Upper Egypt scored another victory on 29 May 1799, with the conquest of Kosseir, which removed Murad Bey from any connection with his followers in Arabia.

The French success in Upper Egypt did little in the way of restoring the strategic balance. However, Bonaparte's design had now changed radically, and after one year of hard campaigning in the desert, Egypt as well as Palestine and Syria were no longer significant targets. During his absence from Cairo two new revolts had threatened the French garrison. Moreover, Murad Bey had reappeared in the vicinity of Cairo with his own army, and this news was followed on 11 July by the arrival of the Ottoman army of Rhodes in the bay of Aboukir, escorted by British ships. The 15,000 Ottoman soldiers landed under the aged Mustafa Paşa easily prevailed on the little French force, which, however, resisted in the castle of Aboukir until 18 July. The Ottomans did not suspect that Bonaparte had decided to intervene immediately to throw them back into the sea. On 25 July about 10,000 French, who had marched 240 km, surprised the enemy by exploiting the Ottoman lack of cavalry, which was still travelling on the ships. Though the Ottomans had dug three lines of entrenchments, their poor discipline and the brilliant manoeuvres of Joachim Murat's cavalry decided the battle.[168] The army of Rhodes was defeated in a few hours; the French captured Mustafa Paşa with other senior commanders, and a further 2,500 soldiers surrendered days later after a vain defence inside the castle of Aboukir. The Ottoman casualties were about 2,000 dead; the French claimed 220 dead and 750 wounded.[169]

On 17 August 1799 Bonaparte left Egypt for France, from where he would embark on his irresistible ascent, but leaving the languishing *Armée d'Orient* in a critical situation. A very contrite Jean-Baptiste Kléber assumed

---

167 J. Christopher Herold, *Bonaparte in Egypt* (New York, NY: Harper & Row, 1926), p.255.
168 Chandler, *The Campaigns of Napoleon*, vol. I, p.324. It was said that Mustafa had promised rewards for every French head, and that the Janissaries had abandoned their position to take the trophies.
169 Chandler, *The Campaigns of Napoleon*, vol. I, p.324.

the command of the 30,000 French and local militiamen deployed between Alexandria and Cairo. No major actions occurred until November 1799. The Ottomans and their British allies spent this time for planning a new operation against the French. Troops from Albania, Thrace and Anatolia gathered near Constantinople waiting for the British fleet. The plan intended to expel the French from Alexandria and Cairo with a direct assault from land and sea.

Problems in the Allied camp affected the preparation of plans for the new offensive against the French in Egypt. Concerns came when the Adriatic naval campaign culminated with the allied occupation of the Ionian Islands. After an initial agreement between the parties, in the final months of 1799 the tension between Constantinople and St Petersburg heightened when over 8,000 Russian soldiers were brought through the Straits and landed at Corfu, ostensibly to help the King of Naples against the French but in fact to strengthen the Russian position in the islands if a showdown came. Ottoman admiral Kadri Bey, who held the governorship of Corfu, opposed the Russian claims in the negotiations, while still striving to retain a good working relationship with the ally. Complains and protests came from many of his officers and crews, who bitterly resented the Russian demands and wanted forceful action to remove them from the Ionian Islands.[170] Controversy spread among the Ottoman admiralship when *kapudan paşa*, Küçük Hüseyin Paşa ordered Kadri to sail at once to Alexandria with a large squadron to support the operations against the French in Egypt, now that the Adriatic campaign was over. Kadri refused to go because of the justifiable fear that he would be dismissed as soon as he joined the *kapudan paşa*. A number of his captains then openly revolted against his authority and sailed out of Corfu harbour towards the south. When Kadri tried to pursue them his own crew mutinied, and together with the crews of a number of other ships landed on the Albanian coast and joined the rebelled Ali Paşa of Janina.[171] Kadri Bey, left with only six ships manned by reduced crews, was forced to take them back to Constantinople and the Russians remained alone in occupation of the islands. In the end, an Ottoman–Russian convention was signed on 21 March 1800. By the terms of the agreement, the Ionian Islands together with a number of smaller islands along the Albanian coast were organised into the 'Republic of the United Seven Islands' or 'Septinsular Republic'. This union was given virtual independence, but was placed under the suzerainty of the Sultan, to whom an annual tribute had to be paid, and under the joint guarantee and protection of Russia and the Porte.[172]

---

170 Shaw, *Between old and new*, p.268. In addition to the question of garrisoning and protecting the Ionian islands, the allies also disputed the question of whether their vacant orthodox clerical positions should be filled by priests trained in Russia or Constantinople, namely, those under the influence of the Czar or the Sultan.

171 Shaw, *Between old and new*, p.268. Ali Paşa, also bitterly hostile to Kadri, accepted these men into his own army despite the Admiral's orders that they be captured and returned to the fleet.

172 Shaw, *Between old and new*, p.269. The Russians thus were left with the naval base at Corfu they had long sought, while the independence given to the republic, together with the right of Ottoman troops to garrison the island, seemed to provide the Porte with sufficient assurance that the Russians would not be able to extend their influence in the islands, and use them as bases for later

On 1 November the British fleet commanded by Admiral Sidney Smith unloaded 26,000 Ottoman soldiers near Damietta. This time, Grand Vizier Yusuf Ziya Paşa led the field army. Immediately, he besieged Damietta, which had a little garrison with 800 infantry and 150 cavalry under General Jean-Antoine Verdier. The siege resulted in a costly action, which caused 2,000–3,000 casualties for the Ottomans, including the janissary commander Ismaël Bey. The Ottomans also lost five guns.[173]

However, the French surrender was just a question of time. In January 1800 Kléber opened a negotiation with Smith and Yusuf Ziya in order to obtain the free evacuation for the remains of the French troops from Egypt. An accord was agreed on 23 January 1800. The Convention of El-Arish allowed such a return to France for Kléber and his troops, but it proved impossible to apply due to internal dissensions among the British and the dithering of the Porte, and so the conflict in Egypt restarted. The British and the Ottomans believed the French were now too weak to resist, and in early March Yusuf Ziya marched on Cairo, where the local population obeyed his call to revolt against the French. Without the support from Yusuf's army, which was still far from Cairo, the uprising failed. On 20 March a large battle was fought between about 25,000 Mamluks and Egyptian *fellayn*s under Ibrahim Bey, opposing 10,000 French. Having defeated the Mamluks who formed the vanguard, the French engaged the main army under Yusuf Ziya near Heliopolis. The Ottoman commander disposed about 12,000 cavalry, 7,000 infantry and 1,000 artillerymen with 40 guns.[174] Once again the French squares were able to break the enemy's disordered waves and soon panic spread, transforming the Ottoman retreat into a rout. Eventually the French also reached the Ottoman camp. Their losses were very small, about 600 casualties, whilst Kléber stated that the Ottomans suffered at least 8,000.[175] Yusuf Ziya's army suffered high casualties but possibly not that many since, despite the defeat, he reorganised his troops and soon resumed the campaign, approaching Cairo. The Grand Vizier gathered the remaining forces of the armies of Damascus and Rhodes, increasing the strength of his army. However, the march was not an easy task. The French opposed resistance and even worse for the British–Ottomans was the epidemic of 'malignant fever' that plagued the troops.[176]

---

expansion into the Balkans and the eastern Mediterranean. While this assumption subsequently proved to be without foundation, and led to a good deal of friction between the allies, for the moment both parties were satisfied.

173 Doguereau, *Journal de l'expédition d'Égypte*, p.317.

174 Wittman, *Travels in Turkey*, p.314: 'At this time the Ottoman army, under the command of his Highness the grand vizier, amounted to about 12,000 cavalry, 7,000 infantry and about 1,000 artillery , with a large battering train, and forty pieces of light artillery.'

175 Wittman, *Travels in Turkey*, p.320

176 Wittman, *Travels in Turkey*, p.316: 'I was informed that there were several cases of malignant fever among the troops, who were also attacked very generally by dysentery, diarrhoea, and ophthalmy [*sic*]. In the latter of these complaints, the eyes became red and painful, and the lids so swollen almost immediately after the attack, that in the course of a few hours the eyes were

OTTOMAN WARFARE: A STRUGGLE FOR SURVIVAL

The Battle of Heliopolis, 20 March 1800, by Leon Cogniet (Chateau de Versailles).

Kléber was managing to save the seemingly desperate situation, at least for the time being. The French were further strengthened with his recruitment of local auxiliaries and his alliance with his former enemy Murad Bey. However, on 16 June 1800 Kléber was assassinated and replaced by Jacques-François de Menou, who revealed to be a less capable commander. The British–Ottoman offensive resumed in April, and after a pause in the summer it continued until November. The allies aimed to isolate the main garrisons of Alexandria and Cairo. During the first weeks of 1801 the allied position extended across the area encompassing the isthmus, the right wing resting upon the ruins of Nicopolis and the sea, the left on the lake of Aboukir and the Alexandria canal. On 21 March 1801, the British–Ottomans launched their land offensive, defeating the French in the Battle of Alexandria, which followed the surrender of Fort Julien in April. The next month the British–Ottomans managed to seize Damietta and Rahmaniye, after that a talk for a truce had failed. By 12 May strong Ottoman cavalry parties approached Cairo and Alexandria for reconnaissance, but French resistance continued until June, when Cairo finally surrendered. Then the allies besieged Alexandria from 17 August to 2 September 1801, and Menou eventually capitulated to the British. Under the terms of this capitulation, British General John Hely-Hutchinson allowed the French army to be repatriated by the British ships. After initial talks in

---

entirely closed. In addition to these diseases, the prickly heat and inflammatory eruptions of the skin were very prevalent, and appeared to have been brought on by irritation on the surface of the body, which, in consequence of the excessive heat of the weather, was covered by copious transudation from the pores.

Al Arish on 30 January 1802 the Treaty of Paris ended the hostilities between France and the Ottoman Empire, returning Egypt to the Sultan. A general peace was signed with the Treaty of Amiens on 25 March 1802. The treaty had given Selim III a providential respite from involvement in the wars of Europe, but this did not mean he or his domains were removed from the conflicts of European diplomacy. Though the Sultan preferred neutrality, Britain insisted on involving the Ottoman Empire against Bonaparte in the Third Coalition with Austria and Russia in 1803. According to the British plan, the Porte would raise a land army of at least 100,000 men and would use its entire fleet in cooperation with those of Britain and Russia.[177] The Sultan did not join the coalition, but expressed gratitude to Britain for its aid in Egypt and established a medal, called the Order of the Crescent, which he bestowed on the British officers 'to perpetuate the signal services rendered.'[178]

Rebellions in Syria, 1802–1808

In 1800, taking advantage of the French presence in Egypt, the Jebel Druzes returned to power in Lebanon. In 1802, with the assistance of the British and the additional help of the powerful Janbulat family, the Druzes built up an army capable of both beating off the attacks from the neighbouring Ottoman-held provinces and eliminating their rivals within the Lebanon. Aleppo and northern Syria were under the control of Ibrahim Ağa Katar *Ağası*, who since 1792 had managed to maintain and extend his own power by playing off the local Ottoman *ocak* and notables against each other, and against the Ottoman governors of Aleppo, reducing them to little more than ambassadors to his court. Finally the Ottomans controlled Damascus, where the strong and able governor al'-Azm Abdullah Paşa continued to keep the province loyal to the Porte through the garrisons left there by Grand Vizier Yusuf Ziya Paşa, as he passed on the way back to Anatolia from Egypt. The city of Damascus, situated on the pilgrimage route to Mecca, had enjoyed a long-lasting stability under the al-'Azm family, members of whom were also Ottoman governors of the province at least nine times between 1725 and 1808.[179]

However, the Porte had lost the local support of the powerful Cezzar Ahmed Paşa, who controlled Palestine, much of the Lebanese coast north to Tripoli, Sidon and the Bikaa. Since Cezzar had cooperated with Ottoman in the war against France, he had expected to receive the governorship of Egypt

---

177 Shaw, *Between Old and New*, p.328. Bonaparte's invasion of Egypt thus had transformed Ottoman enmity for Russia and Britain into an alliance with them against France, and a new phase of the Eastern Question was about to begin.

178 Thomas Walsh, *Journal of the Late Campaign in Egypt*, p.35.

179 Aksan, *Ottoman Wars*, p.232. Abdullah Paşa, one of the last of the family, governed intermittently from 1795–1807, and assisted the Ottomans against Bonaparte. He was dismissed when he could no longer control the local military factions, who could attack the annual *hajj* caravan at will.

in return. When in 1802 Koca Mehmed Hüsrev Paşa was appointed instead,[180] Cezzar returned to his former intransigence, attacking the Ottoman supply lines and preparing to move once again against the Druzes. Yusuf Ziya Paşa was determined to suppress the rebellious Cezzar Ahmed, but he was recalled to Constantinople immediately after the French evacuation, before he could undertake the task. As he passed through Palestine, he left one of his lieutenants, Abu Merak Mehmed Paşa, as governor of Jaffa with a force of approximately 2,000 men, mainly to watch Cezzar Ahmed. In September 1802, Cezzar drove out this Ottoman force and also began to fight with the Ottomans quartered in Gaza. Sultan Selim therefore declared him a rebel, dismissed him from all his positions, and ordered his properties confiscated.[181] Cezzar Ahmed, not at all intimidated, remained at his post, and the Sultan's order remained a dead letter since the Porte had no armies to enforce it. Finally, in October 1803, because of the Egyptian turmoil and the increasing Wahhabi menace, Selim pardoned Cezzar and appointed him governor of Damascus on condition that he serve as commander of the expeditionary force being against the Saudis in Arabia. But by this time Cezzar was old and ill, so he sent his lieutenant Süleyman Paşa in his place to take over Damascus. As soon as the news of his illness reached the Porte, Selim III secretly appointed Ibrahim Paşa of Aleppo as governor of Damascus, Tripoli, and Sidon and commander of the Arabian expedition, and ordered him to confiscate Cezzar's possessions and property as soon as he died, which was on 23 April 1804. On 12 May Ibrahim left Aleppo with 3,000 janissaries and local irregulars, and left his son Mehmed Paşa to administer northern Syria.[182]

On 1 July, taking advantage of Ibrahim's absence in Aleppo, the local notables and janissaries rebelled and expelled Mehmed Paşa and his troops from the city. The Porte immediately sent an agent to try to settle the revolt, while the Druzes of Lebanon managed to interfere in the talks in the hope of using the affair to extend their influence in the region. In the meantime Mehmed Paşa rallied his forces, gained the assistance of some Kurdish tribes from the north, and in early September began to besiege Aleppo. The Ottoman agent was unable to mediate a compromise, and the siege dragged on. In

---

180 Koca Mehmed Hüsrev Paşa (1769–1855), was a typical figure of this age, constantly at the top of Ottoman politics despite failures. After the negative experience as governor in Egypt, he was appointed to other posts including that of governor of Bosnia during the Serbian revolt of 1806 and later as governor of Erzurum during the Kurdish rebellion of 1818. In December 1822, Hüsrev was finally appointed as Grand Admiral of the Ottoman navy during the Greek insurrection. In 1826, Hüsrev played important roles both in the 'Auspicious Incident' (the annihilation of the janissary Corps in 1826) and in the formation of the new 'Mansure Army', modeled after those of the European Powers. Appointed as *serasker* in May 1827, Hüsrev reformed and disciplined the corps. Though ignorant of modern military matters, he assembled a staff of foreign experts and other personnel to assist him. Due to his early championing of military reform and virtual control over the new Ottoman army, Hüsrev was able to install many of his protégés in senior military positions. In total, Hüsrev's household produced more than 30 generals for the Ottoman army.

181 Shaw, *Between Old and New*, p.292.

182 Shaw, *Between Old and New*, p.292.

THE OTTOMAN ARMY OF THE NAPOLEONIC WARS 1789–1815

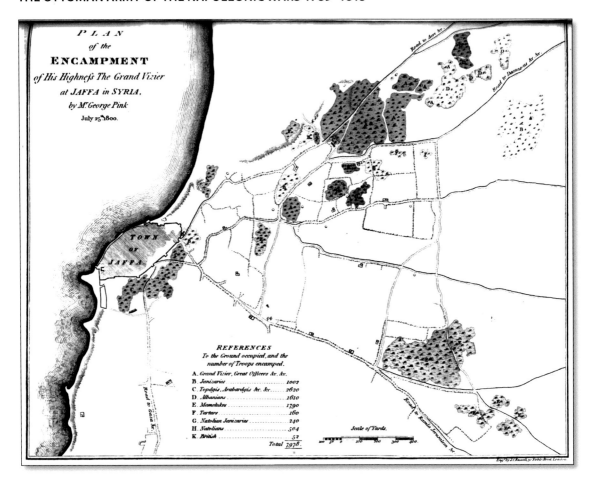

Map depicting the Ottoman Army camped at Jaffa on 25 July 1800. Note the 'References' with the strength of the different corps. In general, in the vicinity of the enemy, the Ottomans defended their camps with entrenchments and artificial defences. On several occasions they faced their enemies in open field relying on these defences, which, however, turned into a trap. (Wittman, *Travels to Turkey, Asia-Minor, Syria, and Across the Desert Into Egypt During the Years 1799, 1800, and 1801*, London, 1803)

late October a compromise was reached by which Mehmed was appointed as governor, but sharing the power with local janissaries and notables, who were given all the other important positions of government. During 1805 Mehmed Paşa gradually regained his former power by stirring up friction between the allies, who finally began to fight each other openly in the streets of the city. While the people suffered at the hands of both parties, Mehmed held his troops back, hoping that the allies and the janissaries would exhaust each other. But the janissaries defeated the notables, forcing the governor to defend himself in the Citadel, now supported by the surviving notables. Both sides used artillery inside the city, which suffered increasingly from famine and plague as well.[183] With the dismissal of Yusuf Ziya Paşa on 24 April 1805, the political scenario changed, involving all his protégés. On 9 June Mehmed Paşa was ordered to move to Tripoli of Lebanon as its governor, replaced by the Sultan's brother-in-law Alauddin Paşa. Ibrahim Paşa tried to join his son to prevent the transfer as it threatened the power they had built up in Syria over the years, but Ibrahim also was dismissed at Damascus and ordered to go to a lesser post at Diyarbakir. Riots and troubles in Kars forced Alauddin to

---

183 Stanford J. Shaw, *History of the Ottoman Empire and Modern Turkey*, vol. I, p.271.

delay his arrival in Syria in early 1805. At the same time, Ibrahim and Mehmed refused to go to their new posts, instead bringing their armies together and lingering between Aleppo and Damascus. In Syria, the local notables were able to use the threat of these armies, combined with the absence of the new governors, to re-form their alliances and restore their power. This situation remained without change during the next three years. Disorders and change of power in Constantinople contributed to leave the question unresolved. Aleppo and Damascus were officially governed by a series of Ottoman governors who were actually under the control of local factions. But so long as the possibility persisted of an Ottoman expedition, or an attack by Ibrahim and Mehmed, the janissaries and notables were compelled to continue to acknowledge the Sultan's suzerainty and remit their regular tribute and taxes. Although Ibrahim and Mehmed tried to get the Porte's help to reconquer the cities, they were unsuccessful because the new Sultan Mustafa IV was satisfied by the continued payment of financial obligations by the local factions who were in control. Between 1805 and 1808 Mehmed and Ibrahim were able to stir up disputes between the notables and janissaries, but whenever they moved to take advantage of the disputes, the alliances were always restored and the attacks repelled. In Palestine in the meantime, Cezzar's lieutenant, Süleyman Paşa, made an agreement with Ibrahim and Mehmed to take over most of Cezzar's possessions himself while father and son went north to deal with the trouble in Aleppo. He now took advantage of the new uncertainty to regain most of Cezzar's territories, while the Druzes consolidated their power in Mount Lebanon. The struggle resumed in the following decade, but the situation remained essentially deadlocked until Sultan Mahmud II gained enough political power to intervene in the 1820s.

The Ottoman ambassador to Paris, Halet Efendi, portrayed (centre) by Jacques Louis David in the painting representing the Napoleon's Coronation as Emperor in 1804. Before 1798, isolationism had been the trademark of Ottoman foreign policy, but now it was no longer practicable, since the war against France, alongside the powers of the Second Coalition, had the effect of bringing the Ottoman Empire back into the European political arena. The traditional policy of isolation from the 'infidels' had proven unworkable in the face of new threats from rising European powers. Averting wars originating in Europe necessitated active Ottoman participation in the European diplomacy. The habit of isolationism thus gave way to the principle of engagement, which governed the conduct of Ottoman foreign policy until the collapse of the Empire.

Civil War in Egypt, 1803–1804

After the Peace of Amiens, the British continued to maintain themselves in Alexandria, while the Mamluk households struggled among themselves and with the Ottomans, Albanians, and popular elements led by their religious leaders. The British supported Elfi Bey, but when late in 1802 he went to London to get their help for an open revolt against the Sultan, he was met with no more than good wishes, for the cabinet now understood the effect such an action would have on its own position in Constantinople. The French supported the Mamluk chiefs Ibrahim Bey and Osman Bey ul-Bardisi. The Ottomans were divided into two hostile camps. Governor Koca Mehmed Hüsrev Paşa had the support of the garrison of 5,000 Ottoman soldiers left by the grand vizier plus a small force of *nizâm-ı cedid* soldiers brought from Constantinople and recruits whom he hurriedly trained locally. On the other side, Çarhaci Tahir Paşa was supported by the Albanian mercenaries and he had thrown off all pretence of obedience, while with his clients was working openly to secure power and revenues for his cause, in the process cooperating with the Mamluks in extorting tributes from the local population. So long as the British remained in Egypt they managed to limit the excesses of the conflicting parties and balance them off; but with their evacuation on 14 March 1803 the situation was altered considerably as each group moved without restraint to further its interests. During the following spring, Hüsrev Paşa tried to curb the Albanians by reducing their salaries in order to pay for the *nizâm-ı cedid* troops he was training. The result was a number of armed encounters between the two groups, with the Albanians invariably emerging as victors. On 1 May 1803 Tahir led his troops in an uprising to secure back pay. Within a few days they took over all of Cairo, seized many of the boats on the Nile to secure food and supplies, and forced Hüsrev Paşa to flee for his life to Damietta. Tahir Paşa declared Hüsrev deposed because of misrule, assumed the position of *kaymakan* for himself, and asked the Sultan to send a new governor, who would be more amenable to his wishes. Mamluks all over the country now openly revolted against the Porte, and a number of them returned to Cairo from Upper Egypt to join Tahir's army. Manipulated by his maternal Uncle Muhammad Ali, on 25 May Tahir was killed by two janissaries in circumstances that have never been fully clarified.[184] Muhammad Ali became *kaymakan*, replacing Tahir, and assumed leadership of the Albanian–Mamluk coalition. The dispute became more bitter, since the Ottomans fought back on two fronts. Ahmed Paşa, governor of Medina, arrived in Cairo and tried to assume command of the Ottoman garrison fighting against the Albanians, but Muhammad Ali defeated and killed him in July. In Alexandria, Hüsrev Paşa tried to gather the Ottoman forces scattered in the Delta for an attack on the usurpers, but Muhammad Ali anticipated him by marching on Alexandria before he was ready, defeating Hüsrev's garrison, and bringing him back to Cairo as a prisoner.

The situation returned to normal for a while, when the new Ottoman governor, Trabluslu Ali Paşa, arrived in Egypt in September to replace Hüsrev, and he was formally installed at the Citadel by Muhammad Ali and his Mamluk friends. Trabluslu was no more willing than his predecessors to accept this sort of local control, and tried to separate the Albanians and Mamluks by pardoning only the latter, and then negotiating with Muhammad Ali against the Mamluks. But Muhammad Ali was not an appropriate leader for that kind of intrigue and the Ottoman governor died, assassinated, on 31 January 1804. In the following weeks Muhammad Ali consolidated his power joining an alliance with Osman Bey ul-Bardisi and with him defeated

---

184 Fahmy, *All the Pasha's Men*, p.286.

the pro-British Elfi Bey on 14 February, forcing the latter to flee to Upper Egypt. With his proverbial unscrupulousness, Muhammad Ali did not follow Bardisi when Elfi Bey was preparing to assault Cairo to overthrow him, and taking advantage of the discontent of the capital's population he stirred up a revolt against the Mamluk chief.[185] Taking advantage of popular support, he attacked and defeated Bardisi and his Mamluks in mid March, forcing them to flee to Upper Egypt and thus leaving himself in sole control in Cairo.

Muhammad Ali knew that the time for ruling Egypt alone had not yet come, and therefore sought to reinstitute Hüsrev Paşa as governor on behalf of the Porte. But his Albanian troops refused to allow the candidate because they held Hüsrev responsible for Tahir's death. The Porte tried to appoint Cezzar Paşa to the post, hoping he would be able to bring Muhammad Ali into line. But Cezzar, now old and ailing, wisely declined. Muhammad Ali then proposed the governor of Alexandria, Hürsid Ahmed Paşa, who was much more acceptable to the Albanians, and when his confirmation came from Constantinople he was installed at the Citadel with the traditional ceremonies. Now having the support of the Ottoman governor, Muhammad Ali raised a large army and marched into Upper Egypt to crush the Mamluks once and for all.

The governor tried to take advantage of Muhammad Ali's absence to build a new army in Cairo, and summoned a large number of Ottoman troops from Syria for this purpose in the spring of 1805. When Muhammad Ali heard the news, he immediately returned to Cairo on the pretext that the Porte had not paid the salaries due to his men and officers. This was enough for Hürsid to dismiss Muhammad Ali as *kaymakan*. The Ottoman forces marched out of Cairo in early April hoping to meet the Albanians before they could reach the environs of the capital. When the two forces approached each other at Kasr ul-Ayni, however, Muhammad Ali managed to get the support of the Ottomans by spreading rumours that they also would not be paid once they had accomplished their mission, and the latter joined the Albanians in entering and ravaging Cairo to get their money. With flattery and threats, Muhammad Ali obtained the consent of the notables and religious of Cairo to remove Hürsid and the Ottoman troops from Egypt on 14 May, and Muhammad Ali was proclaimed as governor in his place. While many of his soldiers remained with Muhammad Ali, Hürsid still was able

Trabluslu Ali Paşa (1740?–1804), portrayed by an unknown artist (Swedish National Museum). He was born in Georgia and kidnapped together with his brother. He was a slave owned by the *dey* of Algiers, but was eventually appointed to a post in the provincial government. After hearing about the overthrow of the governor Koca Hüsrev Mehmed in 1803, Trabluslu Ali asked to be made the governor of Egypt, a position attained months later.

---

185 Shaw, *Between Old and New*, pp.287–288. Muhammad Ali refused assistance unless his troops were given all the back pay due them from the Treasury. This forced Bardisi, in the absence of the governor, to levy a heavy new tax on the merchants of Cairo to get the money. In response to this, the people of Cairo revolted against him and asked for the help of Muhammad Ali.

to gather sufficient Ottoman regulars to hold out in the Citadel, while the Albanians and the populace besieged it. The siege began on 18 May and went on for one month, with the governor heavily bombarding Cairo in order to maintain his position. In reply, Muhammad Ali brought his artillery to Mount Muqattam and began to bombard the Citadel from the rear.[186]

By this time Selim was very anxious to settle the Egyptian problem because of the increasing Wahhabi danger in Arabia. Therefore in mid June, he sent Salah Ağa as agent to Cairo with the duty of investigating the situation and giving official support to whichever party was in control so peace and order could be restored as soon as possible. The Ottoman agent understood the situation at once, thus confirmed Muhammad Ali as governor, and ordered Hürsid to leave the country with him. So long as the Mamluk danger remained, Muhammad Ali was satisfied to perform the duties of *vali*, recognising Ottoman suzerainty and paying the regular tribute to the Sultan. At the same time, he began to prepare the Ottoman garrison and his old Albanian army for a new expedition against the Mamluks. The Mamluk opposition was always led by Elfi Bey, who managed to eliminate most of the old factional rivalries in order to meet the danger posed by Muhammad Ali's rise to power. Elfi Bey had the support of Britain and a considerable number of Ottoman ministers in Constantinople, who intrigued to have Muhammad Ali transferred from Egypt and appointed governor of Salonika. The Mamluk leaders promised faithfully to pay their full annual taxes to the Sultan if only he would help them. Sultan Selim III needed to secure peace in Egypt at any price, in order to get local military assistance against the Wahhabis. Commenters stated that he always had wanted to rid Egypt of Mamluk rule, but he did not want it to be replaced by another dominating party.[187]

Selim accepted the Mamluk demands, and appointed the governor of Salonika, Musa Paşa, as governor of Egypt, and named Muhammad Ali to replace him at Salonika. In May the Ottoman fleet was sent with 1,000 *nizâm-ı cedid* soldiers to enforce the order since it was feared that if janissaries were sent they would only go over to the Albanians or the Mamluks on their arrival. Elfi Bey also was given permission to build up his force with slaves purchased in Constantinople, in return for his paying the back taxes which he owed. On 28 June 1804 the Ottoman fleet arrived off Alexandria, and it received large amounts of food and supplies from Elfi Bey, whose army was then operating in the Delta. At the same time, Elfi turned over one third of his tax debt to convince the Porte of his sincerity and good intentions. Orders were immediately dispatched to Muhammad Ali in Cairo to prepare himself and his men for relocation to Greece.[188]

When the orders arrived, Muhammad Ali refused to depart on the pretext that he was needed in Egypt to prevent revolts and violence. On 28 July, Musa Paşa landed at Alexandria and prepared to march to Cairo with Ottoman and Mamluk support. In the meantime, however, Muhammad Ali had left Cairo

---

186 Shaw, *Between Old and New*, p.289.
187 Fahmy, *All the Pasha's Men*, p.304.
188 Shaw, *Between Old and New*, p.290.

secretly with his best troops, and on 30 July he routed Elfi Bey's Mamluks at Rahmaniye. The Mamluks' defeat deprived the Ottomans of their main local support. This also convinced the Ottomans that a major expedition would be needed to dislodge Muhammad Ali from Egypt. Furthermore, Muhammad Ali had been paying his tax obligations on time and in full, while the Mamluks had paid only a part of what they owed. As a result, the Porte finally decided to support him and in mid October officially confirmed Muhammad Ali as governor of Egypt. The Ottoman fleet then sailed away carrying Musa Paşa back to Salonika, and also bearing Muhammad Ali's son Ibrahim, who went as a hostage to Constantinople. Elfi Bey took refuge in Upper Egypt, however, began to organise a new Mamluk army, and again appealed for British assistance. As a result of this threat, Muhammad Ali continued to accept the Sultan's suzerainty. It would not be many years before Muhammad Ali finally settled accounts with the Porte.

The Second Ottoman–Saudi War, 1802–1807

The major threats to Ottoman interests in this area continued to come from Arabia and southern Iraq. Here, the Saudi-Wahhabi danger flared anew during the last five years of Selim's reign. Since 1800 a truce had been arranged and maintained between the Saudis and their principal opponents, Süleyman Paşa of Iraq and Sherif Galib of the Holy Cities, with the Wahhabis refraining from anything more serious than normal Bedouin skirmishes and raids in return for permission to participate regularly in the annual pilgrimages.[189] By the end of 1801 Süleyman Paşa was a helpless invalid and the strong administration which he had established in Iraq was rapidly falling apart. His sons were disputing among themselves over the succession, and his army had to spend most of its time fighting the Bedouin tribes in the Middle Euphrates and the Kurds in the north. In March 1802 the Saudi Abd ul-Aziz and his son, Saud, took advantage of the situation to undertake a number of destructive raids into southern Iraq. Abd ul-Aziz then moved back into the Hijaz and captured and sacked Taif, which Sherif Galib left without defence when he saw the size of the attacking enemy army. For the moment, however, the attacks were limited to raids, and Abd ul-Aziz retired back into the Nejd with his spoils, but before the end of the year 12,000 Wahhabis sacked Karbala in Iraq, killing up to 5,000 people and plundering the Imam Husayn Shrine.[190]

This act meant that war had in fact been declared, and the Wahhabis were on the prowl once again. Saud immediately inaugurated a series of raids in Iraq and the Hijaz which shook the Empire. In the spring of 1803, he seized Mecca without resistance after the heavily guarded pilgrims' caravan returned to the north, and Galib retired to the fort of Jidda without daring to resist the Wahhabi hordes openly. Saudi rule was proclaimed in the Holy Cities. All the

---

189 See section, 'The First Ottoman–Saudi War, 1794–1800'.
190 Wayne H. Bowen, *The History of Saudi Arabia* (Westport, CT: Greenwood Press, 2008), p.153.

The fortified town of Jidda in an eighteenth-century print (author's archive).

notables assembled at the great mosque, where the Wahhabi precepts were read publicly and all present forced to declare their adherence.[191]

However, Saud's warriors were unable to penetrate the strong fortifications of Jidda and Yanbo, so they finally retired to the Nejd with their booty at the end of May. Although garrisons were left at Taif and Mecca, Galib was able to drive them out and retake the cities within a short time. The Saudi gains of 1803 proved only temporary, but the attacks for the first time made Constantinople aware of the extent of the threat. Up to now no one at the Porte really had known what the Wahhabi movement represented as a political or religious challenge to the established order. The Ottoman *ulemas* were so uneducated and ignorant that few of them knew or cared about the theological debates inspired by the Wahhabis in much of the Arab world under the Sultan's dominion. Militarily the brunt of the Wahhabi attacks had been borne by nomadic tribes and relatively minor governors in Mecca and Baghdad. But now they had ravaged holy places which the Sultan was supposed to defend as part of the basic duties of his office. They had challenged the official state religion of the Empire in the streets of the holiest place of Islam. And when Selim III finally turned his attention to them, he found that they controlled all of the Nejd, Bahrein, Lahsa, Oman, and Muscat, and were threatening to take over southern Iraq, Hijaz, and even the Yemen. Their successes were attracting the allegiance of most of the nomadic tribes of the Arabian Peninsula as well as of southern Syria and Iraq. These victories were inevitably strengthening the Sultan's opponents in Constantinople. In the summer of 1803 the Porte realised that the Saudi threat had become serious and tried to deal with it. Orders were sent to Hüsrev Paşa in Egypt and Ali Kethüda in Baghdad, ordering them to prepare military expeditions against the Wahhabis as soon as possible. Meanwhile, the governors in Anatolia and the Balkans were ordered to raise and send

---

191 Shaw, *Between Old and New*, p.295: 'The Saudi forces then spread out through the city, killing those who refused to accept the new doctrines and destroying tombs and other objects of veneration. All hookahs and intoxicating beverages were confiscated and destroyed. Theological discussions were held between the Wahhabi preachers and the local orthodox religious leaders, and those leaders who refused to accept the new doctrines were eliminated.'

Wahhabbi raiders engaged in close combat in a print dated 1830 (author's archive).

contributions of soldiers and supplies to help in the effort. Letters were sent to the Bedouin tribes throughout Arabia, reminding them of their loyalty to the Sultan and forbidding them any relations with the Saudi-Wahhabis.

Nonetheless the reassertion of power, there was little response to the Sultan's appeals. The only immediate help came from Ali Kethüda of Baghdad, who in the autumn of 1803 attacked and scattered the Iraqi tribes who had accepted Wahhabi suzerainty. In November the assassination of Saudi Emir 'Abd al-'Aziz by an Iraqi was suspected of being orchestrated by the Ottoman governor of Baghdad. However, the government in Constantinople still did not realise the extent of the Wahhabi military power, so Kethüda Ali's appeals for reinforcements were denied and he therefore had to avoid any sustained contact with the Wahhabi armies.

Internal political disputes in Egypt and Syria at the time prevented the local authorities from organising any expeditionary forces. The Sultan himself had too many other problems in the Balkans to allow him to divert troops and resources from his garrisons there and in Anatolia. The way was therefore wide open for further Wahhabi advances. They were not long in coming. In 1804, the Saudis took and ravaged Medina and then moved into Iraq, routing the pro-Ottoman Shamiye and Muntafik tribes and advancing all the way to Baghdad. The following year Saud defeated Galib's forces and took Medina once again, and only his inability to break into the fort at Jidda prevented him from making his conquest permanent. While the annual pilgrims' caravan was able to get as far as Mecca, Saud refused to allow it to complete the rest of the ceremonies in Medina and at Jebel Arafat without

Pilgrims performing the *Hajj*, in a print of the early 1800s (author's archive). The *Hajj* is the annual Islamic pilgrimage to Mecca, the holiest city for Muslims. The control of the routes to Mecca gave great prestige to the Ottoman Sultans across the Islamic world.

acknowledgement of the Wahhabi doctrines, so it turned back. The next year it was able to get through only by acceding to Saud's demands, thus further damaging Ottoman prestige in the Muslim world. The Porte was unable to do anything. Abu Merak Mehmed Paşa arrived in Jidda from Egypt to replace the deceased governor, but the 500 men he brought with him were unable to do anything more than defend Jidda. Sherif Galib finally despaired of getting any effective assistance against the Wahhabis, so at long last he tried to accommodate them, allowing a Wahhabi preacher to come to Jidda and read the Wahhabi treatises publicly.[192] These measures did not satisfy Saud, however, who was determined to show that he and not Selim was the real master of the Holy Cities. To do this, in February 1807, he assembled a large army outside Medina and ordered it not to allow the entry of the Syrian pilgrimage, which was then on its way from Damascus.

Word of this action came to the Emir ul-Hajj (the leader of the pilgrimage) while he was marching through the desert, so he turned around at once and returned without performing any of the rituals. Saud then entered Mecca and Medina once again, carried out the pilgrimage, and completed his earlier efforts to destroy the tombs and carry off the jewels and valuables. He substituted his

---

192 Shaw, *Between Old and New*, p.297.

own name for that of the Sultan in the Friday prayers, the most important symbol of sovereignty in the Muslim world. Saud added insult to injury by inviting Selim himself to come to Mecca and accept the Wahhabi teachings. Not only was the Sultan's prestige in the Islamic world further damaged by these events; even more important at the moment, the Bedouin tribes of the Hijaz, who previously had accepted Ottoman suzerainty, now came forward to declare their loyalty to Saud, who thus for all practical purposes replaced the Sultan as ruler of Arabia.

Rebellion in Eastern Anatolia, 1804–1805

In Anatolia the situation remained relatively quiet after 1792. Çapanoğlu Süleyman Bey and Karaosmanoğlu Ahmed, who governed in the eastern provinces strongly supported the Sultan and collaborated to suppress the brigands and introduce the *nizâm-ı cedid* reforms in their areas. A third powerful family, the Janikli, had been exiled in 1787 because of its intelligence links with the Russians. After the peace of Jassy, the Russian ambassador in Constantinople compelled the Sultan to restore Janikli Battal Paşa to his posts at Sinop and Janik. His son Tayyar remained in Russia in the service of General Suvorov, but in 1793 he was dismissed and imprisoned on the grounds that he had been in secret correspondence with the Porte and was attempting to organise a revolt of the Crimean Tatars against the Czar. Within a year Tayyar was able to escape from Russia; but since he still was accused of conspiracy in Constantinople he begged for pardon, asking for help for his friends and clients at the Porte. In the meantime Russia's loss of influence in Constantinople, combined with the intrigues of the rival. led to Battal Paşa's dismissal from his posts. Janikly's friends soon managed to secure pardons for father and son, however, and Battal Paşa was restored to the governorship of Trebizond and Erzurum in 1798. In return he agreed to raise and lead an army of 20,000 men to assist the Ottoman army, thus indicating that all the most powerful *ayans* were now accepting Selim's reforms.[193]

With the death of his father in 1801, Janikli Tayyar Paşa returned to Eastern Anatolia to take over the family possessions, becoming governor of Janik and Samsun and *muhassil* (district administrator) of Amasya, Merzifon, and Sinop. He also was appointed governor of Erzurum and Diyarbakir. Despite his service being positive, in 1803 Selim III took away some of his positions and limited his power to the Black Sea coast. The Porte suspected him for his links in Russia, but this action was the result of intrigues of the Çapanoğlu family, which convinced Selim and his ministers that the Janikli family was becoming too powerful and would revolt unless curbed. The lands taken from Tayyar Paşa were given to Çapanoğlu Süleyman Bey, who became the principal *ayan* of Anatolia. However, Tayyar refused to accept the Sultan's order, and made himself entirely independent in his own provinces, ravaging the neighbouring

---

193 McGowan, 'The Age of the *Ayans*', p.700.

THE OTTOMAN ARMY OF THE NAPOLEONIC WARS 1789–1815

Map 7. Eastern Anatolia

districts.¹⁹⁴ Furthermore, he expanded his territory to Samsun and Amasya and declared his complete opposition to the *nizâm-ı cedid* reforms, refusing to allow the levy of men or provision of funds or supplies for the new army.¹⁹⁵ In 1804 Selim dismissed Tayyar from all responsibilities and Çapanoğlu Süleyman was ordered to lead an expedition against him. Çapanoğlu's army was organised and trained according to the new methods and armed with modern weapons, while the troops of Tayyar Paşa were a traditional Turkoman bandit force. However, some European observers felt that Tayyar had the advantage because his own men were hardy mountaineers while Çapanoğlu's men were mainly peasants conscripted for service and unaccustomed to the difficult terrain of northeastern Anatolia. While Çapanoğlu prepared his expedition, Tayyar moved to take the initiative. In January 1805 he established his main base at Sinop, leaving a garrison of about 50,000 men, including a trained artillery corps with modern guns, under the direction of two Russian deserters from Georgia. He then took an army of equal size into Çapanoğlu's territories, seized

---

194 Shaw, *Between Old and New*, p.284. The plunders reached such an extent that he came to be known as the 'chief of thieves' among Europeans resident in Constantinople.

195 Shaw, *Between Old and New*, p.284. By these acts, Tayyar he gained the encouragement and support of Selim's cousin Prince Mustafa, eldest son of Abdülhamid I, who long had sought to secure the throne for himself through opposition to the reforms, as well as of Yusuf Agha and Ibrahim Nesim Efendi, two powerful leaders of the secret opposition among the viziers.

Amasya, Çorum, and Sivas, and marched on Süleyman's capital, Yozgat, which he conquered after routing the defending troops and capturing Süleyman himself. Tayyar Paşa was now the ruler of eastern Anatolia as no Ottoman force of any size remained there to oppose him. Bandits from all over Anatolia now saw in him a man who could successfully lead them to booty, and they came to join him in increasing numbers.

Selim III offered talks to Tayyar, offering a full pardon if only he would end the revolt, and sent the former grand vizier Yusuf Ziya Paşa to negotiate with him. Intrigue and sabotage from court circles caused the negotiations to fail in 1806. When an increasingly irritated Selim posed an ultimatum, Tayyar reacted by attacking and pillaging the camps of negotiators and sending them fleeing back to Constantinople. He openly declared his disdain for the Sultan and established himself in full independence, extending his influence until it stretched from Trebizond west to Bursa by the end of Selim's reign.

War Against Russia and Britain, 1806–1812

The turbulence in European politics and the consequences of the coalition wars against France also produced friction on the borders of the Ottoman Empire. In 1803 the rapprochement of the Porte with France did not go unnoticed by the European chancelleries. Russia and Britain could not allow France to exploit a geostrategic space as large as that offered by the Ottoman Empire. The Porte showed a growing interest in France, and Paris was prodigal in offering military advisers and technicians to modernise the army, giving new impetus to the reform projects undertaken by the Sultan in the 1790s, which had long been thwarted. Selim III's Francophilia was tested once again when he wavered over recognising Napoleon Bonaparte as Emperor of France in 1804. Pressured by British and Russian diplomacy, he did not pronounce. Napoleon broke off relations with Constantinople, and the Ottomans were forced to rely on Russia, allowing warships through the straits, and further intervention of Russia on behalf of Ottoman Orthodox subjects. Russophile princes were appointed in the Principalities as a result of the Russo-Ottoman Treaty of Alliance, signed by Czar and Sultan in October 1805. Two secret articles proposed by the Russians and rejected by the Ottomans continued the decades-long and unresolved problem of the Russian presence in the Principalities and the Caucasus. Two months later, emboldened by news of a massive French victory at Austerlitz, Selim III recognised Bonaparte as emperor, formalising his decision in February 1806, and counting on help from the French against the Serb uprising. In fact, with the Treaty of Pressburg on 2 December 1805, Austria ceded Dalmatia to France, connecting the borders between Paris and Constantinople in the Balkans, and raising the concerns of St Petersburg.

In August 1806 Selim III, now under the influence of the French colonel and ambassador Horace François Bastien Sébastiani, and encouraged by the Russian involvement against Bonaparte, deposed Constantine Ypsilantis as *hospodar* of Moldavia and Alexander Mourousis as *voivode* of Wallachia, and replaced them with princes not appreciated by the Czar. The dispute mobilised diplomacy, but after months of fruitless negotiations, the settlement of the

THE OTTOMAN ARMY OF THE NAPOLEONIC WARS 1789–1815

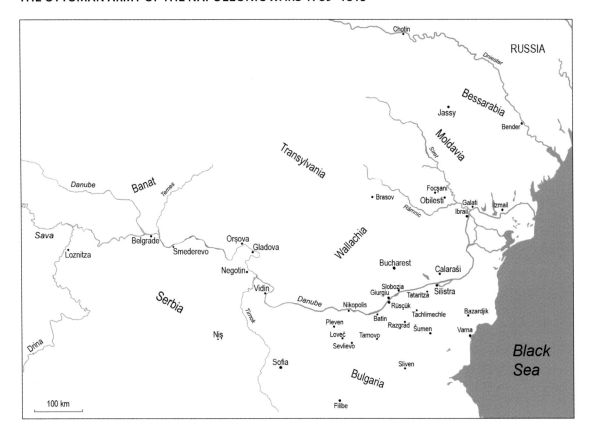

Above, and facing page: Maps 8 and 8a. War against Russia and Britain, 1806–1812

dispute was still far from being resolved. To make relations even worse, the Porte accused the Russians of supporting the Serbian rebellion, which had started in 1804.

Knowing the Ottomans' habitual slowness in preparing their campaigns, and the poor state of the border forts on the Dniester and Danube, the Russians decided to start hostilities without waiting for the outcome of negotiations. In November 1806 the Russian 40,000-man Observation Corps on the Dniester under General Mikelson was ordered to cross the river and invade the principalities of Wallachia and Moldavia.[196] The Russian plan was to quickly conquer the principalities and seize or at least blockade the main Ottoman fortresses on the Danube. As occurred in 1787, supply remained the greatest problem, but the winter offensive could turn into an advantage because snow would have made it easier to transport supplies on sled wagons. Like a stream, the Russians conquered without resistance the Ottoman posts on the border; in just a couple of weeks they entered Jassy, seized Bender and Chotin, and besieged Izmail. The Sultan reacted by blocking the Dardanelles to Russian ships and finally declared war on Russia on 22 December 1806.

Once again caught unprepared, the Porte resorted to the local *ayans* to raise a force to oppose the Russians. The former rebels Alemdâr Mustafa

---

196 Mikhaïlovskiï-Danilevskiï, Aleksandr Ivanovich, and Mikaberidze Alexander (editor), *Russo-Turkish War of 1806–1812*, (West Chester OH: Nafziger Collection, 2002), vol. I, p.24.

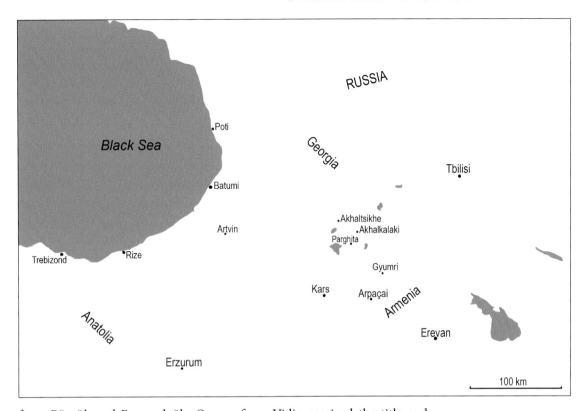

from Rüsçük and Pazvandoğlu Osman from Vidin received the title and honour of a *paşa* and the Sultan appointed them as military commanders in the Principalities.[197] They gathered considerably forces at Focşani,[198] but failed to arrest the Russian offensive with the forces at their disposal. In January the Russians besieged Bucharest, and entered the city shortly after. In revenge, Alemdâr Mustafa kidnapped and took as prisoners the Russian General Consul in Wallachia.[199] Russia's attempt to expand its conquest in Wallachia was successfully faced by Alemdâr, who checked a Russian Division at Giurgiu in late January.[200] After a series of unsuccessful skirmish between February and March the *ayans* withdrew to the south and reinforced the garrison of Giurgiu. Alemdâr Mustafa returned to his possession, leaving the unscrupulous Pazvandoğlu alone in command. Despite the unsuccessful outcome of the campaign, the *ayans'* troops had performed positively and even their commanders 'had enthusiastically

---

197 Jucherau de Saint-Denys, *Histoire de l'Empire Ottoman*, vol. II, p.132.
198 Jucherau de Saint-Denys, *Histoire de l'Empire Ottoman*, vol. II, p.173. Alemdâr had 12,000–15,000 irregulars from Rumelia.
199 Mikhaĭlovskiĭ-Danilevskiĭ, and Mikaberidze, *Russo-Turkish War of 1806–1812*, vol. I, p.49.
200 Aksan, *Ottoman Wars*, p.244: 'In the encounters against the Russians, Alemdâr triumphed, causing many losses among the enemies. The news of the victory of Muslim over Russian soldiers, with few casualties, arrived in Istanbul Alemdâr and caused great joy. Selim III appointed him *serasker* of the Danube with the rank of Vizier, and Governor of Silistra in February 1807.'

joined the defence of the Empire in the name of Islam'.[201] In January 1807 the Ottoman preparations were proceeding, when news came in from Constantinople warning about the arrival of the Royal Navy in the Aegean Sea. Days later, the British ambassador left Constantinople and with him, all the British residents evacuated the city. A formal declaration of war had not yet been sent by London and the two powers were still technically allied. Friction between the Porte and London had begun in November 1806, when Admiral Thomas Louis, with four sailing ships, anchored in the Bosporus to ask for the removal of Sébastiani, his engineers and artillery advisors engaged in improving the Dardanelles defences. The demand was ignored by the Sultan; thus, as diplomacy had failed, so action was required.

In response to the Ottoman blockade of the Dardanelles, and fearing that the Russians would be distracted from the war against France by keeping a large army in the Principalities, the British decided to intimidate the Porte with a naval action direct against Constantinople. The expectation was that a show of force and a few well-aimed rounds into the city would be all that was necessary to scare the Porte into submission. Thus in January Admiral Sir John Duckworth had received order to assemble a squadron of 11 men-of-war at Tenedos.[202] On 19 February, the British fleet was sighted off the Dardanelles, and the day after the ships entered the channel. Taking advantage of the favourable wind, the British ships proceeded rapidly and before noon they were sailing into the Bosporus. No fleet had attempted to cross the straits since the Venetians were repulsed at the end of the Fourth Battle of the Dardanelles in 1657. By that time, the channel had already been protected with fortifications, castle and artillery batteries to discourage anyone from attempting such a daring action. In the months preceding the arrival of the British fleet, the French advisors had warned the Porte about the poor state of the defences. The report containing the required works had been delivered for the maintenance of the fortifications and to provide ammunition and tools, but the works had been neglected, and the funds allocated for the works had taken another destination, namely the bags of some corrupt officials.[203] The artillery still comprised ancient guns cast in the sixteenth century, and numbered 306 cannons and 16 among mortars

---

201 Jucherau de Saint-Denys, *Histoire de l'Empire Ottoman*, vol. II, p.173.

202 Duckwort's squadron comprised the flagship *Royal George* (100-gun first-rate), *Windsor Castle* (98-gun second-rate), *Canopus* (80-gun third-rate), *Repulse* (74-gun third-rate), *Thunderer* (74-gun third-rate), *Pompée* (74-gun third-rate), *Standard* (64-gun third-rate), and the frigates *Endymion* (40-gun fifth-rate) and *Active* (38-gun fifth-rate). Two brigs, four sloops, and two gunboats – *Lucifer* and *Meteor* – accompanied the rated ships. The gunboats were specialised craft with very strong hulls, as each mounted a 10-inch and a 13-inch mortar, the latter capable of firing a 200lb explosive shell to a distance of 2,600 mt. *Ajax* caught fire on 14 February, ran aground on Tenedos, and blew up on 15 February. See in Brenton, Edward Pelham, *The Naval History of Great Britain, from the Year MDCCLXXXIII. to MDCCCXXXVI.* (London, 1837), vol. II, pp.186–187.

203 Jucherau de Saint-Denys, *Histoire de l'Empire Ottoman*, vol. II, p.149. According to the author, the fortifications had been refreshed with white paint, in order to deceive the government.

and bombards, but many batteries were inadequately manned.[204] Even the order to fire on the ships came late, and when the gunners rushed to the guns, 'everyone acted with great indolence'.[205] The *kapudan paşa* went personally to the castles and exhorted the artillerymen to their task, but the resulting fire was ineffective and just a few shots hit the ships. The British fleet replied, including the gunboats, but one of these burst, rendering the ship less than capable of carrying out its role to bombard Constantinople.

Meanwhile in the city, the Grand Vizier and all the Sultan's ministers were bewildered and everything seemed to herald an ignominious surrender. But the thunder of the guns had raised the alarm among the population, who had flocked to the shores. The janissary *ocaks*, the two *nizâm-ı cedid* regiments and all the available soldiers rushed to the castles and batteries. Each post was armed with all available guns and others came from nearby towns. Volunteers from the city's population helped the troops to carry ammunition. In a short time, popular reaction showed the government that the will of the inhabitants and soldiers of Constantinople was to resist at all costs.[206]

Although the British ships successfully reached Constantinople, they had sustained some damage and casualties when the shore batteries had fired to protect an Ottoman ship from capture. The British fleet anchored about eight miles from Constantinople, close to an island named Prota (today Kinaliada), one of the Princes' Islands in the Bosporus, where fresh water was available. Admiral Duckworth did not shell Constantinople, preferring to try to negotiate the surrender of the city from a position of strength or to draw out from Galata the Ottoman fleet to fight, but neither of these eventualities happened, only an encounter that involved janissaries and Royal Marines. This occurred when the Ottomans briefly occupied a shore in Prota and positioned some guns to threaten the anchored British ships, but the Royal Marines chased them off, taking some casualties but capturing two bronze guns.[207]

The Basilica, or Great Turkish Bombard, is a fifteenth-century siege cannon, specifically a supersized bombard which saw action in 1807 during the British action in the Dardanelles. In 1866, on the occasion of a state visit, Sultan Abdülâziz gave the gun to Queen Victoria as a present. The bombard is preserved at Fort Nelson, Hampshire.

---

204 Théophile Lavallée, *Histoire de l'Empire Ottoman* (Paris, 1855), p.443.
205 Lavallée, *Histoire de l'Empire Ottoman*, p.146.
206 Lavallée, *Histoire de l'Empire Ottoman*, p.159.
207 One of these guns is now preserved in the Royal Hospital School, Holbrook.

The spontaneous reaction of the population had enabled the Porte to respond to the threat posed by the Royal Navy, making it risky for ships to approach the shore to bombard Constantinople. After weeks of frustration Admiral Duckworth decided to withdraw to the Aegean, knowing that this time the Dardanelles fortresses were better prepared than before. On 3 March 1807 the British ships ran the gauntlet of heavy guns and ancient bronze bombards once again, with those placed at Abydos and Sestos, on either side of the channel, being particularly destructive. Most of the vessels were damaged, but finally all escaped into the Aegean.[208]

As the war continued on the Danube, involving the interests of the European powers, diplomacy worked according to its own interests. France and Austria wanted to preserve the integrity of the Ottoman Empire, and both agreed that the immediate threat was Russia. Paris had an obvious interest in keeping the Porte in the war by diverting large Russian forces from Poland, and according to Berthier, in January 1807 Bonaparte was ready to support the Ottomans sending 25,000 French soldiers to Vidin.[209]

On 5 February 1807 Pazvandoğlu died after a long illness. His chief lieutenant, Molla Idris Aga, was chosen by the other chiefs to take over his master's position and property in Vidin. Selim III immediately tried to restore Ottoman power in the province by appointing Hürsid Paşa, already governor of Niş, instead of Molla Ağa as military governor of Vidin. The latter, with the support of Sébastiani's lieutenant Mériage, refused, offering instead to pay tribute and make an immediate contribution of soldiers to the Ottoman army: the Sultan was forced to agree. At the same time, Alemdâr Mustafa Paşa now commanded the area from Nicopolis to the mouths of the Danube with an army of 60,000 of the best Ottoman troops. During the winter a Russian corps had moved through Wallachia to the Danube opposite Rüsçük, but Alemdâr Mustafa had repulsed it with a series of successful actions. It was obvious that he was the only *ayan* capable of stopping the Russians; accordingly, late in February, the Sultan appointed him governor of Silistria and commander of the Danube front, putting him in charge of preparations for the spring campaign in this area. The French agents immediately moved to get the support of both notables.[210] Mériage then had Molla Ağa move his troops into Little Wallachia and occupy Craiova in order to prevent a Serbian–Russian conjunction there. The main offensive aimed to retake Bucharest by forcing the Russians to withdraw and avoid the isolation from their bases across the Dniester. In addition, a second army had the task of

---

208 The mainmast of *Windsor Castle* was destroyed by a 300 kg stone ball from a bombard located at Abydos; *Royal George* was also hit by a ball from a coastal bombard; and *Canopus* had its wheel shot away. According to Jucherau de Saint-Denys, *Histoire de l'Empire Ottoman*, vol. II, p.165, British casualties in the action of 20 February were 38 killed and 100 wounded, while the loss of 3 March were 175 killed and 512 wounded. The Royal Hospital House states an overall loss of 42 killed, 235 wounded and 4 missing.

209 Lavallée, *Histoire de l'Empire Ottoman*, p.444.

210 Mériage persuaded Sebastiani to support Molla Ağa's confirmation by the Porte, with the understanding that otherwise Molla Agha would be forced to support the Russians.

engaging the Russians in the Caucasus, merging the forces of the Anatolian *ayans* into the Army of Georgia.

The main Ottoman army was delayed in Constantinople by the British naval attack by the usual physiological delays, and the need to find sufficient fodder for the cavalry and train. Finally, the first columns moved to Edirne in late April 1807. At the same time the news that large Russian forces were moving through the Caucasus towards Ahiska and Kars caused Sultan Selim to appoint the former grand vizier Yusuf Ziya Paşa as governor of Erzurum and commander of the army of Georgia. Here, he had to gather further troops in order to organise a force capable of facing the Russians if they came.

In the meantime Bonaparte disappointed the Sultan by replying evasively to his offers in January, and was open to a settlement with the Russians, and no longer anxious to take important offensive actions against them. Selim III heard rumours to this effect but discounted them, believing that Bonaparte would never desert him. Without the expected military assistance, however, Selim was compelled to limit his plans for the current campaign against the Serbian rebels and the Principalities. Soon after the departure of the Grand Vizier, the Porte sent its remaining reserves through Thrace to Niş and appointed its governor, Hürsid Ahmed Paşa, as governor of Rumelia and commander of the Army of Macedonia, with orders to gather the loyal Balkan *ayans* and then move up the Morava Valley to cooperate with the Grand Vizier. The Ottoman plan was for the governors of Bosnia, Vidin, and Niş to attack the Serbs on both sides to prevent them from joining or helping the Russians. At the same time, the Grand Vizier would march from Edirne through the Dobruja to Ismail, where he would join the irregulars under Pehlivan Ağa, cross the Danube, and move against the Russians in Moldavia. A part of his force would remain at Silistria to march on Bucharest from the east in conjunction with Alemdâr Mustafa, who would cross the Danube at Rüsçük and attack it from the west. The Russians in Moldavia and Wallachia would thus be cut off from each other, and from the Serbs too, and could be defeated, or at least forced to withdraw from most of their conquests. On the other hand Mikelson planned to establish a defence line all the way from the Black Sea to the Adriatic, along the north bank of the Danube to Orşova and from there through Belgrade, Herzegovina, and Montenegro. This would prevent any French effort to move inland from Dalmatia to support the Ottomans in the Principalities.

Vladika Peter I of Montenegro was willing from the start, while the Serbs had toyed with the idea of a separate peace with the Porte, but the execution of the Ottoman envoys in March 1807 had convinced their leaders that it would be prudent to cooperate with the Russian officers sent to Belgrade. In the east, the strategic scenario was quite different. The French gained Molla Idris Ağa's unqualified support by supplying him with arms and money, and by getting Sébastiani to use his influence at the Porte to gain Selim's recognition of him as Pazvandoğlu's legitimate successor. Molla Ağa completely blocked any direct Russian-Serbian union by means of his well-manned forts at Vidin and elsewhere. Mériage also tried to get Molla Ağa to provide military assistance for Alemdâr Mustafa Paşa's advance into Wallachia, but in this he was less successful because of the conflicting territorial ambitions of the two notables and because of Alemdâr's dislike of the idea of bringing a French army to the Danube, so Mériage's plan was quietly abandoned. For the moment at least, Molla Ağa successfully prevented Mikelson and the Serbs from joining forces.[211]

In Albania, Ali of Janina's bitterness at Russian occupation of the Ionian Islands and Parga made the mission of Britain's agent Morier entirely useless, so he departed in March, leaving the way entirely open for France. The French agent Pouqueville's offer of arms and officers to help Ali conquer the islands and coastal ports was warmly received. Since the British and Russian fleets were now operating in the Aegean and eastern Mediterranean, the way was open for Ali and the French to move. Marmont began to send him by sea large quantities of cannons, rifles, and ammunition together with officers to organise and lead his army, which now was assembled at Preveza. At the same time, under French direction, fortifications were prepared along the coast, and a small fleet was built to carry this army to its objectives. At the same time, the Septinsular Republic assembled its own army and built fortifications to resist the attack, wherever it might come. While the main Russian fleet was now with Admiral Senyavin, a number of ships arrived from Venice with some arms and ammunition. In early April Ali made a preliminary attack on Santa Maura to size up its defensive positions and found them so formidable that he decided to postpone any attacks until he could get further assistance from the French. As a result, although preparations continued at Preveza, the attack was never launched, and it was not long before the Treaty of Tilsit gave the islands to France, thus frustrating Ali once again.

In Bosnia, the French agent Pierre David had no difficulty convincing the governor and the Muslim *beys* of the necessity of defending their province against a Russian or Serbian attack from the east. However, they equally feared any infidel army, and the governor informed him that neither he nor the *beys* would ever permit the French to march across their territory to the Danube. In early February, Selim instructed Hüsrev Paşa to allow the passage of a few French officers and artillerymen who were being sent to Constantinople to the Dardanelles, but there was no mention of anything more than this.[212] In April, following the defeat of the British attack on Constantinople, Selim ordered Hüsrev not only to raise troops against the Serbs and Russians but also to call for French aid and allow the passage of French troops from Dalmatia whenever it was deemed necessary.[213] A large number of Bosnian *beys* vigorously opposed the execution of these orders, however, and Hüsrev therefore delayed the negotiations interminably with such questions as whether the French should dress in Ottoman or French uniforms.

In the spring, the Russians and Montenegrins after wintering at Cattaro received invitations from the Christians of Herzegovina asking for their assistance against the Ottomans. An allied force moved to help the district

---

211 Edouard Driault, *La politique orientale de Napoleon: Sébastiani et Gardane 1806–1808* (Paris, 1904), p.229.
212 Shaw, *Between Old and New*, p.354.
213 Shaw, *Between Old and New*, p.354.

in April, but was beaten back. Now, the Bosnian *beys* had been sufficiently frightened that they allowed the entry of a small French contingent, which helped the governor to repulse another enemy offensive in late May and to suppress the Christian notables and *beys* who had provoked the attacks in the first place. However, the Bosnians continued successfully in their opposition to any French movement to the Danube.

As spring arrived, the Ottoman position in the Principalities seemed far more favourable than it had only a short time before. Vidin was heavily manned, and Molla Ağa had strung out a large number of irregulars between there and Gladova to block any attempt by the Serbs and Russians to join forces. Strong Ottoman garrisons were quartered at Rüsçük, Silistria, Ibrail, and Ismail. Newly appointed grand vizier Çelebi Mustafa Paşa brought an army of 30,000 men to Edirne where he remained during April, gathering the *sipahi-timars* and notables of Macedonia and Thrace, and planning his campaign. He finally arrived at Silistria on 24 May, and shortly thereafter crossed the Danube and captured Calaraši, which then became his beachhead for the attack on Bucharest. At the same time, Alemdâr Mustafa crossed the Danube at Rüsçük and moved on Bucharest from the south. Months before, the Ottoman garrisons successfully prevented the Russian–Serbian conjunction, when, in mid April, the Serbs tried to reach the Danube at Negotin, but they were pushed back with heavy losses. When Mikelson tried to establish a bridgehead close to Orşova at Giurgiu soon after, he was repulsed by Alemdâr Mustafa's garrison from Rüsçük. A Russian effort to take the Danubian island of Ostrova on 29 May was equally unsuccessful, but on 2 June a badly coordinated Ottoman assault at Obilesti met an outnumbered Russian corps under Miloradovich, which repulsed the threat inflicting heavy casualties on the Ottomans.

Finally, an Ottoman corps from Bosnia crossed the Drina and with the assistance of the artillery sent by General Marmont routed the Serbs at Loznitza on 3 June, causing the rebels to retire from the Danube in the fear that the Ottomans were beginning a major offensive from Bosnia. Meanwhile Mikelson ordered the commander of Bucharest to evacuate it as soon as the enemy approached, but the Ottoman forces arrived from Rüsçük and Silistria before he escaped, and a siege began on 2 June. The population immediately fled from the city, and the *boyars*, fearing what would happen if the city were taken by storm, entered negotiations with Alemdâr Mustafa and the Russians to secure its surrender. Thus, Ottoman victory in the Principalities seemed near: the Russian effort extend their control on the area had failed; Bucharest and southern Wallachia were about to come under Ottoman control once again; the combined campaign of the Grand Vizier and the *ayans* had checked the potential Russo-Serbian conjunction on the Danube. By mid 1807, the line between the Russian and Ottoman armies was drawn.

Meanwhile the war continued in the Caucasus with the short siege of Anapa conquered by Admiral Pustoshkin. On 18 June the Russians under Gudovich defeated the *ayans* when they were crossing the Akhurian River in Northern Armenia. Gudovich led his main force towards Akhaltsikhe but lost 900 men while trying to assault Akhalkalaki and then retreated to

Georgia. Secondary Russian campaigns against Kars and Poti also failed in August. From the Russian strategic point of view the Caucasus was a less important front, and in addition, the Russians were involved into a double war in the region, one against Persia and the other against the Porte. Although Ottomans and Persians did not ally against the common enemy until 1811, the Russians had little interest in an offensive war. Unlike the Caucasus, the Black Sea and Aegean Sea could be exploited to disrupt enemy sources for supplies. The Ottomans managed to limit the damage, when in response to the Russian attempt to block the Dardanelles they engaged the enemy fleet in a series of battles between May and June. Despite heavy casualties the Ottoman navy forced the enemy fleet to repair on the Russian-held island of Tenedos.

Ottoman involvement in the war extended on further fronts. After the failure in the Bosporus, Britain turned to Egypt. The British signed a treaty with Muhammad Bey Al-Alfy, a local Mamluk leader, to ensure his support in return for a guarantee that the Mamluks would share control over Egypt. An expeditionary corps with 6,000 soldiers was gathered for a landing at Alexandria to establish a connection with the Mamluk households. On 20 March 1807 General Alexander Mackenzie Fraser entered Alexandria and was welcomed as a liberator from the inhabitants, who had little tolerance for the despotism of Muhammad Ali's Albanian troops but even less for the Mamluks. Everything seemed to presage a positive outcome until on 23 March the British encountered the first problems: Muhammad Ali had not been inactive and sent his troops towards the coastal towns, thwarting the enemy plans. At Rosetta Major General Patrick Wauchope with 1,200 men[214] entered the city, lured with deception by the garrison commander, Ali Bey Al-Selaniki, and with his 700 Albanians defeated the enemy after a fierce street fight. The British suffered heavy casualties and Wauchope was also killed in the early stages of the battle.[215] Meanwhile Muhammad Ali arrived in Cairo, returning from Upper Egypt, where he had defeated the Mamluk *beys* at Assiut on 12 April. He was briefed on the news about the British defeat of 23 March, and days later knew that Fraser was resuming the offensive. He ordered the reinforcement of Rosetta and improved the defence with embankments, works that began under his direction. He also added ditches, connecting Cairo to the Nile and filling them with water, then scuttled several boats between the island of Bulaq and the beach to prevent the passage of British ships in the Nile if they came from Rosetta. Artillery was also placed in Shubra and Imbaba and on the island of Bulaq. The works

---

214 Robert T. Harrison, 'Alexandria, British occupation of 1807', in J. S. Olson and R. Shadle (eds), *Historical Dictionary of the British Empire* (London: Greenwood, 1996), p.324. Wauchope's force comprised troops from the 31st Foot and the *Chasseurs Britanniques*, accompanied by a section of the Royal Artillery.

215 Harrison, p.324. The British casualties were 185 dead, 282 wounded and 120 prisoners.

proceeded with extraordinary rapidity, since the locals participated in the operations in exchange for generous prizes.[216]

On 3 April the British moved from Alexandria with 4,000 men heading to Rosetta, and secured their back with a battalion at Al-Hammad. This village is located south of Rosetta between the Nile and Lake Idku, and the purpose of its occupation was to cordon Rosetta, preventing the arrival of supplies from the south, and protecting the water source for the soldiers. The British also captured Akam Abi Mandour, and installed artillery near the village for targeting Rosetta. General Fraser assumed that a continued bombardment would cause a loss of morale among the city garrison and compel them to surrender, but instead the besieged garrison resisted and the governor repulsed the offer for an honourable surrender. The garrison occasionally left the city during the bombardment to skirmish with the British forces encamped around. The bombardment lasted for 12 days but was unable to achieve any results, and Rosetta remained in Egyptian hands. Whilst not personally commanding the garrison, Mehmed Ali's reputation grew with the victory.[217]

On 20 April news about the arrival of a relief force persuaded the British commander to interrupt the siege and prepare for facing the incoming threat. The Ottoman–Egyptian force under Tabuzoğlu Hasan Paşa outnumbered the British four to one. Tabuzoğlu divided his force in two corps, the cavalry in the vanguard under Hasan Paşa, and the infantry at his own command. During the night of 20 to 21 April the cavalry clashed with the British observation pickets and dispersed them. A concerned British headquarters deployed part of the forces in the village of Al-Hammad to seal off the access to the isthmus that joined Rosetta with the mainland, but in doing so weakened the blockade around the town. Colonel MacLeod held the command at Al-Hammad, with the task of holding out as long as possible against the enemy advance and retreating to Rosetta before being overwhelmed. This difficult task was entrusted to only 1,600 men. On 21 April, early in the morning, the Ottoman–Egyptian cavalry executed an accurate reconnaissance and informed Tabuzoğlu about the situation on the field. He could either outflank McLeod in a wide circle and assault the besiegers at Rosetta, or engage the British at Al-Hammad and then reach Rosetta across the isthmus by penetrating through the weak enemy defence. Encouraged by the success achieved by the cavalry of Hassan Paşa the day before, he decided to follow the second plan. Tabuzoğlu crossed the Nile with the infantry, and the boats transported his troops east to Al-Hammad, then he joined Hassan Paşa's cavalry in preparation to engage the enemy defending the village. MacLeod watched the Ottoman–Egyptian forces approaching, and soon the terrain became full of enemy cavalry and infantry. He immediately sent Fraser the news and asked him to withdraw to the British

---

216 Fahmy, *All the Pasha's Men*, p.167. Muhammad Ali managed to get the money needed for the army's expenses, and peasants and scholars helped him to collect the money, which was allocated for the expenses of advance.

217 Aksan, *Ottoman Wars*, p.243.

positions around Rosetta. Fraser approved the request, and sent the answer with a platoon of soldiers, but the messenger did not reach Al-Hammad, because the Ottoman–Egyptian cavalry cut off the communication between Al-Hammad and Rashid. MacLeod began to withdraw from Al-Hammad, but at this point the British forces were dispersed, so the Ottoman–Egyptian cavalry managed to engage them one by one, while the infantry occupied the village. MacLeod and his right wing fought desperately, but were eventually defeated and only 50 prisoners survived. As for the British left flank, it lasted longer but was surrounded from all sides. Its commander, Major Wigsland, agreed to surrender and at this point the battle ended. In less than four hours the British lost 816 men dead or taken prisoner.[218] The British troops that were besieging Rosetta retreated to Alexandria as soon as they learned of the disastrous outcome of the Al-Hammad encounter, having abandoned their baggage and nailed the siege guns.

The defeat at Rosetta forced General Fraser to reconsider his plan, and British troops were ordered to reorganise inside Alexandria, which was soon besieged by the Ottoman–Egyptian troops from Cairo. Muhammad Ali offered Fraser the chance to surrender and receive supplies from the Royal Navy's transports as well as an agreement for supplying Alexandria, with an added assurance of security for any trade routes to India in return for the British recognition of his independence from the Ottoman Empire. The agreement was accepted, and supplies continued to be delivered to the British troops in Alexandria, but London did not accord the formal recognition of independence, since the British Government did not intend to see the Ottoman Empire dismantled in the face of an expansionist Russia.[219] Muhammad Ali in Cairo released the British prisoners of war as a goodwill gesture, sparing them the usual fate of becoming slaves to their captors. In September, when no further use could be gained from the occupation of Alexandria, General Fraser was permitted to surrender the city and withdraw to Sicily on 25 September with the rest of the expeditionary force.

While the events in Egypt focused the attention of the European chancelleries, further diplomatic efforts involved the Porte in the international arena, and the operations of both sides were paralysed by startling news from outside. On 24 June 1807 the French Emperor and the Russian Czar came to Tilsit and began to negotiate a settlement which would recognise Bonaparte's conquests in Europe in return for peace for all concerned. During the course of the negotiations the news of Selim's deposition increased Bonaparte's determination to abandon the Porte. After all, although Selim had been under French influence, the new Sultan and government seemed not be sympathetic. Moreover, Selim's removal provided Bonaparte with the excuse that any personal obligation to consult the Sultan on peace negotiations was now nullified. Czar Alexander I also wished to discuss Ottoman dissolution and partition of the spoils, but Bonaparte was able to use the continued

---

218 Alsager Pollock, and Arthur William (eds), *The United Service Magazine, Notes of an Expedition to Alexandria of the year 1807* (London, 1837), pp.65–66.

219 Shaw, *Between Old and New*, p.378.

uncertainty about events in Constantinople to avoid any agreement on these points. While the treaty signed on 7 July was concerned primarily with European matters, there were a number of important points of direct concern to the Porte. Russia agreed to conclude an armistice with the Ottomans, to turn over the Ionian Islands and Cattaro to the French immediately, and to evacuate the Principalities, although the Ottomans were not supposed to move into them until a final peace was reached. France would mediate a peace settlement between the adversaries in return for a similar effort by the Czar for a Franco-British agreement.[220] Alexander now sent orders to the commanders of all his ships in the Mediterranean and Adriatic to return to the Black Sea via the Straits if the Porte permitted, otherwise to the Baltic. The Russian troops at Cattaro and the Ionian Islands were to go to Trieste or Venice as soon as possible. At the same time, General Marmont was ordered to send a garrison to Cattaro and Corfu and to re-establish friendly relations with the Montenegrins who previously, under Russian influence, had raided Dalmatia almost continuously. From Tilsit, Bonaparte and the Czar sent agents to General Mikelson, the Grand Vizier, and Selim's successor Sultan Mustafa IV, to obtain their agreement on an immediate armistice, Russian withdrawal, and peace negotiations. Sébastiani was instructed to work towards these ends and to maintain Ottoman–French friendship by pointing out that the Tilsit agreement had been made to help the Porte against its enemies. He was to get the new sultan to negotiate for peace with the Russians, to refrain from occupying the Principalities until peace was signed, and to accept French occupation of the Ionian Islands and Cattaro.

During the spring and early summer of 1807, before the Porte heard about the agreement at Tilsit, Sébastiani had made considerable progress in getting the support of the new government. Despite their rejection of Selim's internal policies, Mustafa IV and the men around him had early decided to maintain the alliance with France so long as Russia remained in the Principalities and Britain in Egypt. In this sense, orders were issued prohibiting British commerce in the Empire and organising an inventory of British properties and goods in preparation for their eventual confiscation. When the details of the Franco-Russian agreement finally became known in Constantinople on 18 July, the initial Ottoman reaction was one of intense fury. Sébastiani was hurriedly summoned to the Porte. The Sultan's ministers told him that Bonaparte should not have ratified the peace without prior consultation with his ally, the Sultan; the Ottoman Empire had been sacrificed, left in the hands of Russia to do with as it wished; all the promises made on the subject of its integrity had been violated. The next day, all the French officers and soldiers in Ottoman service were sent back to Dalmatia.[221]

In Constantinople and along the Danube, wild rumours accompanied the news: the Empire would be divided: Bosnia and Herzegovina would

---

220 Shaw, *Between Old and New*, p.389. Bonaparte also agreed that if the negotiations between Russia and the Porte failed, he would join the war against the Ottoman Empire and make further arrangements to divide the European provinces of the Sultan's domains.
221 Shaw, *Between Old and New*, p.390. With the sole exception of Juchereau de Saint-Denys.

be joined to Dalmatia; the Peloponnese to the Kingdom of Italy; Serbia to Austria; Moldavia and Wallachia to Russia.[222] Mobs began to roam the streets, attacking Ottoman officials and foreigners alike in protest against this new betrayal by a Christian ally. The Grand Vizier was so angry that he arrested the French courier bringing the news, and refused to allow him to proceed on to Constantinople. Intestine chaos and rivalry in the struggle for power involved the army, since the influent *ayan* Alemdâr Mustafa became so furious with the government that he and his troops abruptly departed for Rüsçük, taking with them all who wished to go. Alemdâr suspended all relations with the army, refused to supply it with food and provisions, and invited all those wishing to desert to join him.[223]

However, it was not long before there were second thoughts at the Porte. When Sébastiani communicated the full text of the agreement, it was seen that there was a great deal to be said for accepting it. Russia had agreed to abandon its conquests in Wallachia and Moldavia; this meant an end to its assistance to the Serbian rebels, who could therefore be suppressed easily once peace was secured. The negotiations were set for the Slobozia fortress near Giurgiu, but it was not until three weeks later, on 12 August, that work actually began because of a delay in sending the diplomat documents from Constantinople. The discussions then dragged on for two weeks, with the parties disputing bitterly the question of whether the Porte would occupy the Principalities immediately after the Russian evacuation and whether guarantees for a Serbian settlement would be included. On 24 August 1807 the armistice was signed at Slobozia for a term ending on 21 March 1808. Within 35 days Russian troops would leave Moldavia and Wallachia, while the Ottoman army would move south of the Danube, with the right to leave garrisons only at Izmail, Ibrail, and Galati to provide for policing and security. The last Russian ships in the Mediterranean, now at Tenedos and in the Archipelago, would leave and presumably be allowed passage through the Straits into the Black Sea.[224]

On 21 September 1807 the Porte ratified the armistice, and the Ottoman troops immediately withdrew to Silistria. However, mutual distrust influenced the course of the events. General Mikelson died soon after the agreement was signed, and although it was ratified by his successor, General Meyendorff, the Russians never fulfilled it. As soon as the Czar returned from Tilsit, he refused to ratify the armistice, stating that Meyendorff had no authority to sign it. The Russians left Bucharest and Orşova, thus temporarily severing their connections with the Serbs, but they remained in Craiova and Moldavia and refused to budge any further without orders from the Czar confirming the agreement. When the Porte complained, the Russians replied that the Ottomans had failed to provide sufficient police protection in Bucharest and the area between it and the Danube,[225] and

---

222 Shaw, *Between Old and New*, p.390.
223 Shaw, *Between Old and New*, p.386.
224 Jucherau de Saint-Denys, *Histoire de l'Empire Ottoman*, vol. II, p.202.
225 Driault, *La politique orientale de Napoleon*, pp.233–234.

that the Czar had ordered the evacuation to cease until further instructions arrived from St Petersburg. At the same time, the Russian fleet remained at Tenedos with the same pretext.[226] The Russian reversal aimed to continue Russian occupation of the Principalities and Tenedos, as well as to maintain the pressure on the Porte to accept his conditions on Serbia, trade, and other matters. Since the Czar added new conditions, no further evacuation could take place without further negotiations. The talk closed days later, and in October both sides did their best to prepare for resuming their campaigns for the next spring. The Czar took the opportunity to transfer troops from Poland to Bessarabia, while the Porte exploited the pause for a retaliation against the Serbs. The Russians became the object of fierce hatred. Their agents engaged in inciting the Serbs and Principalities against the Porte, as they had already done with the Greeks in 1770, were relentlessly pursued and with them, all foreigners were viewed with suspicion as potential spies of the Czar.[227]

In early 1808 the war went on, albeit somewhat sporadically. After a cold winter, frosts were experienced with shortages of food and wood. The situation of the Ottoman army was dramatic. Recruits were requested from the provincial governors, but some soldiers came from a few places near Constantinople. In the capital the internal struggle was at its highest point, causing delay in the preparation of the spring campaign.

Although on the Danube front the fighting had stopped, in the Caucasus Russians and Ottomans resumed the fighting. In May 1808 the Ottomans took the offensive in Armenia. 30,000 men under the former grand vizier, Yusuf Ziya Paşa, now governor of Erzurum, advanced without resistance, but failed three times to take Gyumri. The Russians relief force led by Gudovich surprised the Ottomans while marching and defeated them at Arpaçai.

At the same time, in the west, 10,000 Russian soldiers moved across the Dniester, and took up positions in Moldavia and Wallachia in preparation for a new advance. Preparations were also made in Constantinople to move along the Black Sea coast in the late spring. Orders were sent out to Anatolia, Bosnia, and Macedonia for troops to be raised and sent for the incoming campaign. Hundreds of men were soon crossing the Bosporus and moving through the capital on their way to Edirne. In Bosnia the governor assembled a field force of 10,000 men ready at Travnik to move towards the Drina. Efforts were made to replace Yusuf Ziya at Erzurum and send him as governor to Baghdad, but when he refused to leave he was retained in his post and ordered to reorganise his army as soon as possible. On 23 March a full Imperial Council, meeting at the Porte in the presence of all the military, administrative, and religious leaders of the ruling class, decided to gather the

---

226 Jucherau de Saint-Denys, *Histoire de l'Empire Ottoman*, vol. II, p.203.
227 Shaw, *Between Old and New*, p.392: 'The immediate Ottoman reaction in Constantinople was renewal of the earlier anti-French feeling; once again, it was felt that Bonaparte had betrayed the Sultan at Tilsit, that Bonaparte never intended that the Russians evacuate their positions, and that Sébastiani had intentionally been trying to deceive the Sultan.'

Imperial army at Edirne and send it north as soon as it was ready[228] The events at Constantinople in the spring–autumn of 1808 paralysed government action, and caused a stalemate in the military operations. The Russians did not take advantage of the Ottoman chaos, leaving the strategic scenario, already in their favour, unchanged, but uncertainties about Bonaparte's potential attack on Russia contributed to delay a resolution. Therefore in 1808, both sides limited their warfare to reconnaissance and occasional raids behind the lines, although the Russians managed to supply their Serbian allies with weapons and military advisors. Military actions ended with winter, leaving both sides awaiting for another negotiate or the next campaign.[229]

Peace talks over a possible treaty broke down as Franco-Russian relations grew frosty. New Sultan Mahmud II would not entertain the surrender of all of Wallachia and Moldavia. In turn Alexander I, similarly, required something to show for years of campaigns and occupation that had yielded little. In March of 1809, the Czar sent an ultimatum to Mahmud II, affirming that he was determined to annex the Principalities to the Russian Empire applying the clauses of the Treaty of Tilsit. The Sultan responded that the frontier should be remain the River Dniester, thus military operations started again. After the Russian army in the Principalities was augmented to 80,000, the hostilities were resumed. Nor did the Ottomans neglect their preparations. Though the Empire was recovering from another dramatic change of power, the government managed to assemble a field army of 50,000 men, but to complete this force turned again to the local *ayans*. The Russians, under the 76-year-old commander-in-chief Alexander Alexandrovich Prozorovsky, failed to capture Ibrail although he had superior forces, despite the Ottomans were still involved in the preparative for the campaign. After this failure, in August 1809, Prince Pyotr Ivanovich Bagration succeeded Prozorovsky. The Russians resumed their offensive and advanced in Dobruja, while Bagration proceeded to lay siege to Silistra with 30,000 men. He met the Ottoman governor, Laz Aziz Ahmed Paşa, who resisted for 20 days and repelled the Russians causing them heavy casualties, when a relief force defeat the Russians at Tataritza on 21 October. Meanwhile, on hearing that the main Ottoman field army marched to Danube, he deemed it wise to evacuate the Dobruja and retreat to Bessarabia. The successful defence of Silistra was highly celebrated in Constantinople, and the brave governor acquired great fame as a military commander. No major events occurred in the following weeks and in early October both the armies moved into winter quarters.

In early 1810 Count Nikolai Kamenskoi assumed command of the Army of the Danube. He gathered 100,000 men around Bucharest and declared himself ready not only to defeat the Ottomans but also to advance onto Constantinople and achieve the final Russian victory, putting an end at the series of stalemates and indecisive campaigns that had characterised the conflict.[230] In May 1810 Kamenskoi crossed the Danube and invaded Ottoman

---

228 Shaw, *Between Old and New*, p.394.
229 Martens, *Allgemeine Geschichte der Türken-Kriege*, vol. II, p.262.
230 Valentini, *Précis des dernières guerres des Russes contre les Turcs*, p.74.

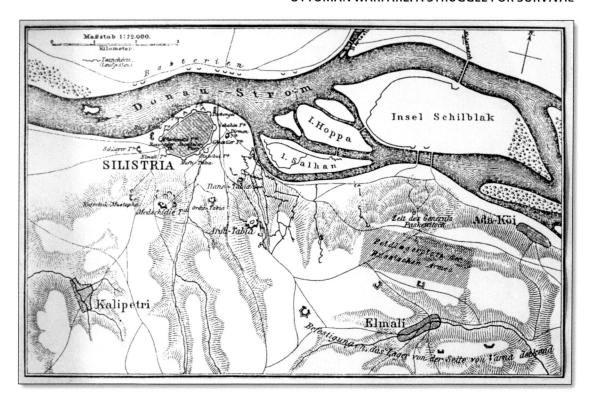

The Russian siege operation at Silistra, 1809, in a German print relating to the Russo-Ottoman War of 1806–1812 (author's archive). The defence of this strategic fortress on the Danube was the only success achieved by the Ottoman in the second phase of the war.

Bulgaria accompanied by a mass of wagons, horses, oxen, mules, and camels. The Russians advanced aimed to engage the main Ottoman field force commanded by the powerful *ayan* Bairakdar Mustafa. However, the Porte had managed to gather just 25,000 men for the field army, since the need to defend the fortresses along the extensive theatre of war was a main concern for Constantinople. After a series of skirmishes and minor encounters in May, on 3 June Bairakdar Mustafa was surprised and routed by the Russian assault on the fortified camp near Bazardjik. The 23,000-strong Russian corps overwhelmed the 5,000-man Ottoman garrison, killing or wounding 3,000 and taking the rest captive. Then Kamenskoi left two divisions under the French émigré Louis Alexandre Andrault de Langéron to secure Silistra, and prepared to strike the Ottoman bases along the Danube, seizing the strategic key positions on the road to Constantinople. On 5 June Langéron blockaded Silistra, supported by a small Russian flotilla on the Danube. On the night of 6 June the Russian batteries began to bombard the town. A mortar shell fell into the Citadel, burst and ignited a powder magazine, triggering a massive explosion. On the next day the Ottoman commander sought capitulation and on 8 June the 4,000 Ottomans were allowed to evacuate the fortress.[231] The loss of Silistra was a serious defeat, since this stronghold secured the Ottoman navigation on the Danube and the vital flow of supplies for the field army and the garrisons in all the Danubian area.

---

231 Louis Alexandre Andrault de Langéron, *Memoires* (Paris, 1902), p.102.

Kamenskoi's advance was proving more problematic. The Russians secured their flanks seizing Razgrad, but were forced to proceed under the threat of the Ottoman cavalry, who ambushed them taking advantage of the wooded terrain. Under this constant threat, the Russians had to form wagon circles when they camped at night. For days, the Ottoman cavalry pressed so heavily on the Russian vanguard that the artillery had to be brought into action. Emboldened by the success, the Ottoman commanders continued to harass the advancing Russians, attacking their front, flanks and baggage train on the rear and obliging the Cossacks and their supporting artillery to repeatedly halt in order to repulse them with cannon fire.[232]

The painful march came to a halt before Şumen on 12 June. On the same day, the Russians immediately faced a large force of Ottoman cavalry with infantry in support. The Russian infantry formed squares with regimental artillery positioned at each corner and wagons and cavalry in the centre. A Russian officer reported that the Ottoman horsemen were so enraged by the failure of their charges that they dismounted before the squares and engaged in close combat with the Russian infantry.[233] Though the Russians resisted the assaults, the outcome remained indecisive for a long time. The next day, the Ottomans kept Kamenskoi under pressure, who eagerly awaited the troops who had seized Razgrad and were now supposed to be approaching Şumen with 7,000 men. Unfortunately their commander took the wrong road and just two *Jäger* battalions arrived at the destination, while the rest joined Kamenskoi days later. The Russians experienced their first setback of the campaign. On 15 June, leaving a force of some 30,000 men to block Şumen under the command of his brother Sergei, Nikolai Kamenskoi turned northwards towards the Danubian port of Rüsçük with further 30,000 men. Seizing this vital fortress would guarantee an excellent base for any further campaigning and would also shorten the communications with Bucharest and bring closer the much-needed reserves and supplies from Moldavia. Furthermore, the conquest of Rüsçük would isolate the Ottoman fortress of Giurgiu on the opposite bank of the Danube.[234]

Further attempts to relieve Şumen failed, and in late June a sortie did not achieve significant results, except for the loss of 600 Russian soldiers. Since the frustrated Ottoman army was unable to arrest the enemy's progress on the field, the only possible option was to reinforce the garrisons of the strongholds in the war theatre. Before the arrival of the Russians the garrison of Rüsçük had grown to 20,000 men, well supplied with ammunition and food in order to sustain a long siege. The Ottoman commander was confident of relief, which was organising in western Bulgaria under the *paşa* of Sofia, Kuçanz Ali. Rüsçük had an ancient curtain with high walls, but strong bastions reinforced the defence system and the entire perimeter was protected by a deep and wide ditch. The Russian vanguards arrived before Rüsçük on 20 July, and the siege started the next day. The Russians continued digging

---

232 Amburger, *Friedrich von Schubert. Unter dem Doppeladler*, p.190.
233 Amburger, *Friedrich von Schubert. Unter dem Doppeladler*, p.194.
234 Martens, *Allgemeine Geschichte der Türken-Kriege*, vol. II, p.264.

throughout July, and repulsed a strong sortie on 26 July, but Kamenskoi came under pressure from his subordinates, who were concerned at the slow progress, to launch a massive assault on the town and take the place by storm. Kuçanz Ali managed to assemble a relief force and on 2 August sent it north, but the Russians intercepted the Ottomans at Tachlimechle and routed them, inflicting 3,000 casualties.[235]

Dismayed by the slow progress, and concerned by reports of Ottoman troops gathering in Sofia, Kamenskoi felt unable to withstand pressure to mount the assault on Rüsçük, and the night of 4 August 1810 was decided upon for the assault. The Russian commanders favoured an escalade, not waiting for a practicable breach but relying on the impetus of their soldiers to scale the walls and take the city by storm.[236] The attempt failed, since the ladders were too short. Furthermore, the Ottoman garrison offered a strong resistance and the besiegers were repulsed suffering heavy casualties. The siege turned into an exchange of artillery fire, and again the Ottomans countered the enemy bombardment, targeting the more exposed Russian batteries. On 7 August the Russian artillery intensified the fire against the city's walls. The bombardment lasted throughout the day but had little effect.

An ever more frustrated Kamenskoi managed to seize Rüsçük with another night assault. Early on 8 September the Russians approached the walls on a dark moonless night, but at the decisive moment the defenders sounded the alarm and engaged in a fierce fight against the enemies who were already penetrating the city. The fighting raged on until the morning with furious assaults and counter-assaults. The Russian commander, finally realising that no progress could be achieved, ordered a general retreat. The aftermath of the fighting was perhaps even more horrible than the storming itself, since the defenders came out to slaughter the wounded Russian soldiers who lay in the ditch. A Russian officer described the final stage of the assault, focusing on the state of exaltation of the Ottoman soldiers, who, however, did not exploit the favourable occasion to defeat the weakened besiegers:

> Had they wanted to, the Turks could have taken our entire artillery, looted our camp and destroyed our entire army. But they were too happy with their victory that they did not think for a moment of exploiting it. The days following this attack were the saddest of my entire military career. The defeat, the dreadful scenes that followed, the loss of so many friends and acquaintances, and the fear that should the Turks attack we were doomed, all had a devastating effect on the entire army. Over the coming days, things began to improve as order was restored, men returned to the ranks and we consolidated our position. But the effect of our defeat was enormous – it had given the Turks fresh hope and courage to resist. We had started the assault with some 25,000 men and had lost 8,000 killed and wounded including 300 officers.[237]

---

235 Amburger, *Friedrich von Schubert. Unter dem Doppeladler*, p.196.
236 Amburger, *Friedrich von Schubert. Unter dem Doppeladler*, p.202.
237 Amburger, *Friedrich von Schubert. Unter dem Doppeladler*, p.203.

Kamenskoi, although stunned, still had troops over from Moldavia and brought up Langéron's division from Sergei Kamenskoi's covering force near Şumen in order to fill the losses suffered during the last assault on Rüsçük. Meanwhile Kuçanz Ali had gathered sufficient troops in central Bulgaria, joining janissaries, with irregulars from Albania, Bosnia, Macedonian and Anatolian *sekban*s. To raise the strength also contributed Muktar Paşa, son of Tepeleni Ali Paşa of Janina with 4,000 Albanian cavalrymen.[238] The army numbered 35,000 men with 34 guns, and on 10 August the first columns headed to relieve Rüsçük.[239] The *paşa*'s first task was to march towards Rüsçük and await for the arrival of the force under the Grand Vizier encamped south of Şumen. The plan was to interrupt the communications between the Kamenskoi brothers at Şumen and Rüsçük and defeat both separately, seizing the most favourable opportunity. Kuçanz Ali marched directly on Rüsçük, and on 15 August his vanguard met the Russian outpost at Batin that barred the way to the besieged fortress. The Russians withdrew, but with their great surprise they saw the enemy who, instead of advancing, was halting and digging in. General Kamenskoi, before Rüsçük, heard about the Ottoman movements and sent an urgent appeal to his brother calling upon him to send further reinforcements from the troops blockading Şumen. Here the Grand Vizier was still inactive, and had yet to set out. At the beginning of September Kamenskoi estimated that he had sufficient forces to storm the enemy camp and defeat it before the grand vizier's troops arrived. After leaving a cordon of troops around Rüsçük, Kamenskoi planned an assault on 9 September. The Ottomans were deployed in five large camps with the village of Batin in the centre. Russian reconnaissance revealed that the northern sector were less fortified. Kamenskoi ordered a demonstration against the exposed Ottoman flank with the assistance of the Russian gunboats, while the cavalry took position undiscovered on the edge of the enemy deployment. The gunboats caught a small Ottoman flotilla, anchored close to the enemy position on the Danube; they sank two boats and captured a further five. The naval encounter opened the battle.

On the centre and on the left, the Russian infantry advanced towards the enemy covering further two columns behind them. Within a short time the Ottoman cavalry emerged from the camp to engage the enemy, forcing the approaching Russian troops to move in square. Emerging from the shallow ravine before ascending the slope towards the enemy camps, the Russian squares became the targets of Ottoman artillery, which halted their advance and inflicted heavy losses. It was at this time that the Russians launched the cavalry assault, which successfully charged the enemy flank. A corps of Albanian horsemen fled in the direction of the camps, and taking advantage of the chaos, the Russian infantry resumed the advance. In this phase of the battle the Russian artillery advanced with the support of the cavalry and opened a deadly fire on the enemy defences from very close range. After a

---

238 Jonathan North, 'Attack along the Danube: The Russo-Turkish War of 1810' in *The Napoleon Series* (July 2000), p.5.

239 Valentini,, *Précis des dernières guerres des Russes contre les Turcs*, p.78.

series of bloody assaults the Russian infantry charged with bayonets, entered the Ottoman encampment and routed the disordered enemy. Only Muktar Paşa escaped with his Albanian cavalrymen and took shelter inside Turnovo. The battle of Batin resulted in 1,542 Russian dead and wounded; the Ottoman casualties were 5,000 dead and wounded and 5,086 prisoners. The Russians also took 14 guns and 178 flags.[240]

The Ottoman defeat effectively sealed the fate of Rüsçük. The siege progressed methodically as the Russians severed all links between the fortress and the surrounding area. On 26 September the Ottoman garrison surrendered and the remaining 15,000 men evacuated Rüsçük without their weapons. While the fighting was going on in Rüsçük, the Russians entered Şumen on 12 September.

Kamenskoi did not stop operations and pushed the offensive southwards. The Ottomans had no other option but to try to thwart the enemy by assaulting them with cavalry or by engaging the Cossacks who carried out deep-seated raids. Skirmishes and ambushes occurred in October, but before the end of the month the Russians seized Loveč, Pleven, with 3,000 prisoners,[241] and Sevlievo, welcomed everywhere by the inhabitants, who were mostly Christians.[242] With most bases on the Danube secured and new strategic possibilities opened by the fall of Rüsçük, Nikolay Kamenskoi resumed the march south and aimed at seizing Sliven, an important fortress on the road to Constantinople. The Russians took Sliven by storm on 11 February. However, Kamenskoi succumbed to a fever and was forced to resign his command and return to Russia in the spring of 1811.[243] The Czar appointed General Mikhail Kutuzov in command of the Russian forces along the Danube and urged him to end the war as soon as possible, due to the worsening of Russo-French relations in the west. For this reason five divisions had crossed the Pruth River heading north in anticipation of a French invasion. The Russians were scattered to secure the extensive net of fortresses, and only a small contingent was still available for a regular field campaign.

On the Ottoman side the situation did not seem any better. Troops returning from the previous year's campaign were in a sorry state. Desertions and loss of war materiel made a resumption of operations problematic at short notice. Furthermore, in August 1810 Russian troops managed to join the Serbs taking advantage of the Ottoman involvement in the defence of Rüsçük. The war was going badly in the Caucasus. Here, the Czar had replaced Gudovich with Count Tormasov in 1809, but the only significant success came the following year when the Russians captured the fortress-port of Poti. In the summer an Ottoman offensive was repulsed by General Paolucci at Akhalkalaki, but in November the Russian attempt to seize Akhaltsikhe failed due to a plague epidemic, which, however, affected both sides.[244] In

---

240 Amburger, *Friedrich von Schubert. Unter dem Doppeladler*, p.205.
241 Mikhaïlovskiï-Danilevskiï, and Mikaberidze, *Russo-Turkish War of 1806–1812*, vol. II, p.89.
242 Amburger, *Friedrich von Schubert. Unter dem Doppeladler*, p.217.
243 Nikolai Kamenskoi died in Odessa on 4 May 1811.
244 Martens, *Allgemeine Geschichte der Türken-Kriege*, vol. II, p.279.

1811, Tormasov was recalled at his own request and replaced by Paulucci in Transcaucasia, while General Rtishchev took control of the northern region. Further Russian troops were withdrawn between March and April 1811 as relations with France worsened and the Czar needed more soldiers to counter the threat from Napoleon. In the summer the Ottomans and Persians agreed to a joint attack on Gyumri. However, on 30 August a Kurd in Persian service assassinated the *paşa* of Erzurum and this caused the alliance to break down and the coalition forces to be disbanded. Paulucci sent a body of troops against Akhalkalaki. After a forced march over the snow-covered mountains, avoiding the main roads, the Russians stormed the fortress at night on 9 December, managing to get over the walls before the defenders were aware of them. By the following morning Akhalkalaki had fallen with the loss of only 30 dead and wounded soldiers. The Porte replied on 21 February 1812, when 5,000 Ottomans besieged Akhalkalaki, but failed because of the shortage of siege artillery. Three days later they were defeated at Parghita. Paulucci was recalled to the west, and Rtishchev became commander of the forces on both sides of the Caucasus Mountains, but no further actions occurred.[245]

Given the degree of loss of soldiers and materiel it is legitimate to question the actual nature of the army called upon to defend the Ottoman Empire in 1811. For the Porte, it was necessary to find not only new resources, but also leaders capable of restoring confidence and imposing discipline on an army that had known almost nothing but defeat. Thus, following the successful defence of Silistra in 1809, the Sultan promoted the brave Laz Aziz Ahmed Paşa as grand vizier and commissioned him to direct the campaign on the Danube. He managed to gather a field army of about 60,000 men, comprising regular *kapıkulu* soldiers as well as irregulars from Rumelia and Anatolia. In early June the Grand Vizier summoned a war council to discuss the situation. Since the enemy held the right bank of the Danube, the most pressing urgency was to remove him from his major strongholds. Thus, the first move was to retake Rüsçük, which was seriously damaged after the last siege and appeared to be an easy conquest.[246]

However, before Ahmed Paşa arrived before Rüsçük, Kutuzov recrossed the Danube with his 18,000 men and took a position three miles south of the town. Reconnaissance did not reveal the actual position of the approaching Russians, and when the Ottomans approached to besiege Rüsçük on 22 June, Kutuzov outflanked the enemy columns from the rear and successfully routed them back with a surprise assault. At the end of the day the Russians suffered 800 casualties but maintained control of Rüsçük. The Ottomans claimed 1,500 casualties, but still maintained a large numerical superiority. Kutuzov surprised his adversary by razing the defences of Rüsçük and moving his army across the Danube back into Wallachia, taking with him 635 Bulgarian families.[247]

---

245 Valentini, *Précis des dernières guerres des Russes contre les Turcs*, pp.84–88.
246 Martens, *Allgemeine Geschichte der Türken-Kriege*, vol. II, p.287.
247 Valentini, *Précis des dernières guerres des Russes contre les Turcs*, p.101.

On 28 August 1811, after waiting for supplies and pontoons from Sofia, Ahmed Paşa resolutely crossed the Danube and entered Wallachia. Upon reaching the left bank of the Danube, the Ottoman forces managed to establish a small bridgehead along the river in the vicinity of the village of Slobozia. Over 6,000 janissaries with large provisions fortified their positions. Within a week a further 36,000 men with 56 pieces of artillery arrived on the Danube and joined the field army. Ahmed Paşa left Ismail Bey with 30,000 men on the right bank and headed east.[248] He intended to besiege Vidin outflanking the Russian field army, isolate it from its supply lines and then destroy it. The plan was strategically valid, but had its risks. Among the greatest danger, there was that of dividing forces between the banks of a great river like the Danube. Furthermore, Ahmed Paşa had not taken into account the quality of the troops that had arrived as reinforcements. These were in fact mercenaries recruited by the *ayan* contractors, and they were without pay for weeks.[249]

The Russians under General Kutuzov encamped on the north bank of the Danube in late September 1811, in a Russian coeval print (author's archive). In 1811 the Ottoman attempt to retake Rüsçük turned into a nightmare when in early October Laz Aziz Ahmed's army was encircled by the Russians at Slobozia. As the days and weeks went on, Ottoman casualties increased not only due to enemy pressure, but also to lack of food and supplies. The agony lasted until 14 November. According to an eyewitness, the Ottoman camp was 'a living hell with thousands of soldiers rotting while others were laying helpless with legs or arms amputated'. At the surrender of the Ottomans, and after so many episodes of mutual ferocity that occurred during the war, the feeling of humanity prevailed. Noting the sorry state of the prisoners, General Kutuzov undertook to save as many lives as possible. Ottoman commander Çapanoğlu thanked Kutuzov personally, and the Russian general offered him his own best horse.

Kutuzov immediately reacted to the enemy offensive by moving his headquarters from Giurgiu to Slobozia, not far from the Ottoman bridgehead, while controlling the enemy march with two divisions of mixed Russian-Moldavian troops, which had been returned to his command. Meanwhile, he was fortifying his position, extending embankments and trenches on both sides of the Danube. Ahmed Paşa now found himself threatened on one flank and at risk of being isolated. Thus, he arrested the march and moved to Slobozia. On 30 September Ismail Bey attempted to open a way

---

248 Aksan, *Ottoman War*, p.276.

249 Joucherau de Saint-Denys, in *Histoire de l'Empire Ottoman*, vol. II, p.177, states that 10,000 Albanians deserted the army during the march from Sofia to Rüsçük.

crossing the Danube in order to resume the siege on Vidin, relieving the main army by flanking the Russians. The Ottomans tried twice to cross the river, but after the second failed attempt, Ismail Bey's troops were depleted both due to casualties and desertions, and were now no longer considered a serious threat.[250] On the night of 1 October Kutuzov took the initiative and secretly sent a detachment of 7,500 men commanded by Lieutenant General Markov across the Danube to the right bank. The next morning, Markov's forces surprised and overwhelmed the Ottoman troops at their camp near Rüsçük. Even though the Ottomans outnumbered three times the Russians, they panicked and scattered, suffering 2,000 casualties killed, wounded, or captured.[251] With the loss of the troops protecting his back, the Grand Vizier was now completely surrounded at the bridgehead. Kutuzov then moved quickly to end the battle by initiating an all-out artillery assault upon the enemy bridgehead. The bombardment was directed onto the Ottomans from all directions including from a small mid-river island on which the Russians constructed a battery, and from a flotilla on the Danube. As the days and weeks went on, Ottoman casualties increased not only from artillery fire but also due to lack of food and supplies. The Ottomans started to feed themselves with anything possible, even dead horses. The famine combined with cold, rain and the lack of firewood spread illness and disease. Ahmed Paşa somehow reached the right bank of the Danube and headed to Constantinople to beg the Sultan for a truce with the Russians.[252]

Finally, on 25 October, both sides agreed a ceasefire and food was offered to the starving Ottoman troops. Kutuzov tried to save as many lives as possible by offering the Ottomans the option to surrender with the promise to release them in the spring. Three weeks later, on 14 November 1811, Ahmed Paşa finally agreed to a truce and formally surrendered to Kutuzov. Of the 36,000 soldiers that crossed the Danube to establish the bridgehead at Slobozia it was estimated that 2,000 men successfully deserted; 12,000 men surrendered and were taken captive, and 22,000 lost their lives through warfare, starvation, or disease. According to an eyewitness the Ottoman camp was 'a living hell with thousands of soldiers rotting while others were laying helpless with legs or arms amputated.'[253] Kutuzov, affected at the horrible sight of this, transferred 2,000 sick and wounded to Rüsçük and ordered that they would be treated as guests rather than enemies.

Although the Porte was in no position to propose conditions, the Sultan was aware that Czar Alexander desired to reach an agreement quickly and held out for better terms. The negotiations were continuous, and 12 meetings took place before the end of November. In January 1812 Ahmed Paşa informed the Sultan about the terrible condition of the army. Mahmud assured him that any thoughts of continuing the war should be abandoned; therefore, the Grand Vizier should be authorised to complete the negotiations as he decided. Finally,

---

250 Mikhaïlovskiï-Danilevskiï, and Mikaberidze, *Russo-Turkish War of 1806–1812*, vol. II, p.93.
251 Amburger, *Friedrich von Schubert. Unter dem Doppeladler*, p.221.
252 Martens, *Allgemeine Geschichte der Türken-Kriege*, vol. II, pp.298–299.
253 Amburger, *Friedrich von Schubert. Unter dem Doppeladler*, p.239.

after further months of negotiations, Russia and the Ottoman Empire signed the Treaty of Bucharest on 28 May 1812. It was just at this time, however, that Bonaparte began the invasion of Russia, forcing the Czar to sign the peace on Ottoman terms despite the Sultan's military defeats on the field. Alexander I returned both Moldavia and Wallachia to the Sultan, leaving only Bessarabia to Russia. Here, the Pruth River was established as the new border between Russia and the Ottoman Empire. The Czar also had to return all his gains on the Danube, and in the Caucasus, except for the Georgian province of Meskheti. In exchange, he did get the Ottomans to agree to respect Serbian autonomy and to refrain from punishing the Serbs for their role during the war. The Russians did at least regain their commercial position and the right to protect Christians and to station consuls in the Ottoman Empire, thus enabling them to instigate revolts and undermine the Sultans' rule from within.[254]

The First Serbian Uprising, 1804–1813

With the return of Belgrade and northern Serbia to the Ottoman Empire in 1791, the Porte had restored the garrisons with janissaries and irregular mercenaries. Both these corps were particularly brutal and corrupt. Soon, incidents and reciprocal reprisals made coexistence between the soldiers and the local population difficult. In 1792 the janissaries' power in the province was contested when the sultan, Selim III, ordered them to leave Belgrade. The janissaries though refused to comply, which led the Porte to call on the Serbs for military support. After years of turmoil and disorders caused by the local *ocaks* with the outside support of the *ayan* Pazvandoğlu Osman, the Porte escalated the confrontation with the rebel troops.[255] To eliminate the financial base of their power, *yamaks* were prohibited from holding lands in the province in any way. The *yamaks* and their partisans found welcome refuge in the neighbouring provinces, in particular across the Drina in Bosnia. In order to strengthen Serbian support against the seditious soldiery, in 1793 and 1796 Selim proclaimed a *firman* that gave unprecedented rights to Serbs. Among the most notable, taxes were to be collected by the local *obor-knez*; freedom of trade and religion were also granted. There, the eighteenth century had seen the rise of powerful Muslim feudal *beys* who, strengthened by the arrival of large numbers of janissaries from the lost provinces north of the Danube, were able to make themselves entirely independent of the Ottoman officials, usurping both their revenues and powers. At the same time, they were supported by the thousands of Muslim refugees from the ceded areas of Serbia, Slavonia, Croatia and Dalmatia, who were very bitter

---

254 Shaw and Shaw, *History of the Ottoman Empire and Modern Turkey*, vol. II, p.14.
255 In 1793, the powerful *ayan* of Vidin, Pazvandoğlu Osman launched a series of raids against the Serbs, causing much instability and famine in the region until he was defeated by the Serbs at Kolari. In September 1797, Pazvandoğlu invaded again the *paşalik* of Belgrade in support of the Janissaries. At the end of November, the Serbian chieftains Aleksa Nenadović, Ilija Birčanin and Nikola Grbović led the militiamen to Belgrade and forced the besiegers to retreat to Smederevo..

against Christians, and extremely sensitive to any sort of concessions to them in the fear that they might be expelled from their homes once again.

Notwithstanding the politics of appeasement, the new century saw an even more drastic erosion of the Porte's authority that finally drove Serbia to open revolt. In 1799 the janissaries returned to their quarters after pledging allegiance to the Sultan and shortly afterwards the troubles resumed with higher intensity. The murder of the able *paşa* of Belgrade, Şinikoğlu Hacı Mustafa, on 15 December 1801, opened a new phase in the history of Serbia, since it resulted in the proclamation of the *sancak* of Smederevo – ruled by the local janissaries, now known as *dayıs* (renegades) – independently from the Ottoman government, and in open defiance of the Sultan. These janissaries also controlled the local *yamaks*, in order to extend their rule on the whole province. The janissary chiefs divided the *sancak* into 10 *paşaliks* and immediately suspended Serbian autonomy, drastically increased taxes, land was seized, and forced labour introduced. In 1802 the Porte attempted to curb the *dayı* janissaries and their *yamak* clients to restore direct Ottoman rule with an expedition led by the governor of Bosnia, Bekir Paşa. The expedition aimed to prevent any further flow of supplies to the rebels from their sympathisers in the Empire. The Porte also requested the Austrian border authorities prevent the flow of supplies to Belgrade from the north, and Bekir Paşa appointed Hasan Paşa as the new governor of Belgrade, with the task of securing the cooperation of the Ottoman forces in Serbia. Unfortunately, Pazvandoğlu's control of the area between Vidin and Sofia prevented the Porte from mounting a major offensive against the rebels or sending more than a token amount of arms and ammunition to the loyal forces. However, arms coming into Serbia from Bekir Paşa, together with a supply from Austrian agents sent in the hope of using the expected revolt for their own ends, did provide encouragement for resistance. In response to the threat of revolt, *yamaks* and *dayıs* terrorised the population and executed 72 local leaders in January 1804, hoping to stifle resistance by depriving the Serbs of their natural leaders.[256] Consequently, many Serbs escaped into the mountains and joined the rebel *hayduks* who had resisted the janissaries' established authority. In the spring they began large-scale raids into the lowlands, attacking not only the *dayıs* and their clients, but also the Turkish commoners and *timars*, who responded with further retaliations. The struggle opened a 'reign of terror'[257] that caused suffering and despair to the entire population, while transforming Serbian resistance to *dayıs* and *yamaks* into a revolt against the Porte.

The *hayduk* bands now grew into major resistance movements in all parts of Serbia. They were independent and spontaneous corps, responding to local grievances, and coordinating their efforts more by example than anything else. Of particular importance were the bands in the northwestern Serbian district

---

256 Leopold von Ranke, *History of Servia and the Servian Revolution* (London, 1847), p.119. According to the author, the severed heads of the leaders were put on public display in the central square in Belgrade to serve as an example to those who might plot against the rule of the *dayı*. Some 'skulls towers' were actually built in the surrounding villages.

257 Shaw, *Between Old and New*, p.318.

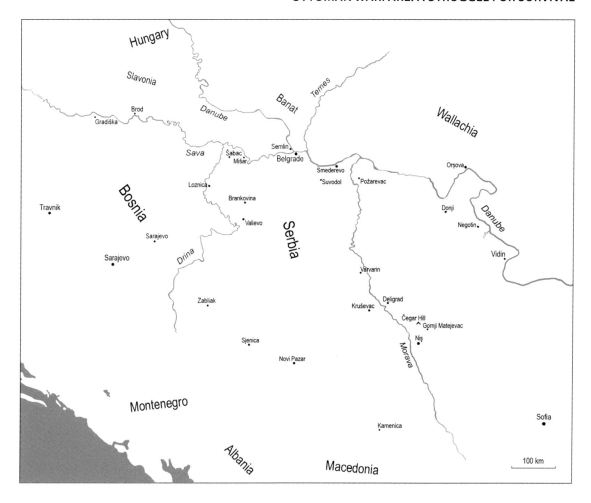

Map 9. The First Serbian Uprising, 1804–1813

of Šumadija, south of Belgrade between the rivers Morava and Kalubara. In 1802, they agreed to coordinate their efforts under the direction of a former soldier of an Austrian *Freikorps* named Đorđe Petrović, but better known as Karađorđe. Returned to civilian life, he became a pig merchant who had previously distinguished himself in the fights against the *yamaks*. Karađorđe soon achieved such success in Šumadija and wide repute throughout Serbia that early in 1804 the *dayı* chiefs tried to conciliate him by offering the monopoly of tax collection in return for his acceptance of their rule. The parties did not achieve an agreement, and the fighting resumed. With the breakdown of negotiations, the rebels redoubled their attacks on Ottoman officials, *timars* and others considered as enemies. Still preserving the guise of loyalty to the Sultan against *dayıs* and *yamaks*, Karađorđe and his followers received large quantities of arms and ammunitions from the Bosnian Bekir Paşa and even from Wallachia, as well as from other Ottoman neighbouring officials and *ayans*. On 12 March 1804 the Porte even issued a *firman* that legitimated the armed Serbian resistance against *dayı* and *yamak* oppression, inviting the officials and people of Serbia to join them, and promising tax

Hadži Mustafa Paşa murdered by the *dahije* on 15 December 1801, in a popular print published in 1802 (author's archive). This episode marked the beginning of the crisis that three years later led to the First Serbian Uprising.

exemptions for nine years following the conclusion of peace, giving impetus to the movement.[258]

Four days later Požarevac and Šabac were captured and their garrisons massacred. At the start of April 1804 Karađorđe had a force of 30,000 men under his command,[259] most of whom marched on Belgrade and Smederevo, while the balance went through Šumadija disarming the local *yamaks* and forcing them to submit. By the end of the month the entire district was under Serbian control with the exception of Belgrade and Smederevo. In the meantime other leaders had raised similar uprisings elsewhere. In the north-west the communities of Brankovina formed their own resistance movement under the leadership of Jacov Nenadović, brother of one of the *knez* killed in January 1804. By the end of April the Serbs held most of the north-west corner of Serbia between the Drina and the Save, including the important forts of Valievo and Šabatz, although to secure their surrender they had been compelled to allow their *yamak* garrisons to retire to Belgrade with all their arms and ammunition. The Porte, which feared that the Serb movement might get out of hand, sent the former Paşa of Belgrade, and now governor of Bosnia, Bekir Paşa, to officially assist the Serbs, but in reality to keep them under control. The Serbs demanded that the *dayıs* be deprived of all power

---

258 Tatjana Katič, 'Serbia under the Ottoman Rule', in *Österreichische OSTHEFTE*, Jahrgang 47, 2005, p.156.

259 Shaw, *Between Old and New*, p.319.

and the *yamaks* forbidden to hold any rural properties, in accordance with the original reform issued in 1793. The Serbs would be officially pardoned by the Sultan, and orders would be issued prohibiting the exaction of any vengeance from them once order was restored. The Ottoman representatives seemed agreeable to the Serbian proposals, but the *dayıs* in Belgrade took advantage of the absence of the rebel chiefs to attack their strongholds around the city, burning and pillaging villages as they went. Karađorđe broke off the negotiations on the grounds that the Porte would be unable to guarantee *dayıs* obedience to the terms.[260] The fighting resumed during the summer of 1804. The Serbs now received considerable amounts of arms and money from the merchants of Zemlin with the compliance of the Austrian authorities, and the Serbian *hayduk*s were transformed into a regular army under the direction and leadership of Serbian officers sent by the Habsburgs.[261] Bekir's approach was delayed during most of June by revolts among the Bosnian *yamaks*, who sought to protect the interests of their counterparts in Belgrade.

In the meantime the siege of the Belgrade citadel continued. In mid June 1804 Nenadović and Karađorđe led a combined force along the Danube to Požarevac, which they captured after a short siege. They then moved on to Smederevo. At first they assured the garrison that if it surrendered noone would be punished since it had not participated in the misrule. But the defenders refused the demand, and Smederevo was also put under siege. Belgrade was therefore now entirely circled by the Serbs, from the Save all the way around to the Danube. Karađorđe and other Serbian leaders met with a group of Ottoman officials and agents sent from Constantinople and demanded that thereafter all the forts of the province be garrisoned by Serbians and that the Porte provide assistance against the *yamaks* continuing to operate in the south of the province. The events preceded plans, and Serbian bands moved to clear the *yamaks* out of southern Serbia on their own. A summer of intense fighting brought them success. The power of the *dayıs* and *yamaks* was finally destroyed outside Belgrade, and the Serbian movement was greatly strengthened as a result.

The janissary commanders of Belgrade, besieged by both Serbs and Ottomans, finally surrendered the city to Bekir Paşa in July 1804, in exchange for their safety. An Ottoman garrison took possession of Belgrade. The *dayıs* had previously fled crossing the Danube. Bekir Paşa ordered the surrender of the *dayıs*; meanwhile Karađorđe sent his lieutenant, Milenko Stojković, to pursuit the renegade janissaries. They entrenched in the island of Ada Kale and refused to surrender, but Stojković encircled and captured them. The survivors were beheaded on 5 and 6 August 1804.[262]

After these events Bekir Paşa ordered the Serbs to disband their forces; however, since the *dayıs* still held important towns such as Užice, the Serbs were unwilling to dispose of their arms without further guarantees.

---

260 Shaw, *Between Old and New*, pp.320–321.

261 Shaw, *Between Old and New*, pp.320–321.

262 According to other sources, it was the *paşa* of Orşova who intercepted the fugitives and executed them. See Ranke, *History of Servia*, p.149.

Nor did the flight of the *dayıs* mean that the *yamaks* were entirely bereft of their power. In western Serbia along the Drina they still held a number of forts and mountain strongholds from which they continued to threaten the surrounding areas as they had in the past. In Belgrade, leadership of the *yamaks* was assumed by a mercenary named Guşanatz Ali, who managed to retain possession of the upper citadel while demanding that Bekir provide the back pay owed his men by the *dayis* before he left.[263] Bekir Paşa was now trying to restore normal conditions to the province. The governorship was turned over to Skopljak Süleyman Paşa, who confirmed the elected Serbian *knez* and decreed that they would have the sole right to collect taxes. Efforts were made to persuade the *timars* to leave their fiefs and settle in the towns, where they would receive the tax revenues collected by the *knez*. Unfortunately Bekir soon had to send a large number of his men back to Bosnia to curb the riots caused by *beys* and *sipahis* and to meet Montenegrin raids from the south. The *yamaks* and their supporters in Belgrade took advantage of the absence of Bekir's troops to imprison him in his own palace and regain control of the citadel and part of the town. They began to attack Serbs in the streets and to arouse Serbian–Ottoman animosity in order to make impossible any agreement injurious to their interests. After forcing Bekir to empty his treasury to provide their overdue wages, they allowed him to leave and return to Bosnia with the remnants of his force.

Though the *yamaks* were now in control of Belgrade, they met resistance not only from the Serbian *hayduks* but also from Süleyman Paşa and his Ottoman garrison. During the winter and early spring of 1805 the *yamaks* devastated the countryside and caused a new famine in Belgrade, but they lacked sufficient strength to overcome their opponents. The military situation remained at a stalemate, while the province rapidly fell into chaos. Further negotiations between the parties were also favoured by the Austrian governor of Slavonia, who offered his mediation, and among the delegates were included agents of the princes of Moldavia and Wallachia who had been instructed by the Sultan to urge the Serbs to accept his terms.[264] However, talks broke down: the Porte could not accept an agreement guaranteed by foreign power, and the Serbs refused to lay down their arms. Fearing a Christian uprising the Porte issued a decree to disarm the *hayduk*s on 7 May

---

263 Shaw, *Between Old and New*, p.324.

264 Michael Boro Petrovich, *A History of Modern Serbia, 1804–1918*; (New York: Harcourt Brace Jovanovich, 1976), vol. I, p.50: The Serbs demanded the following terms: 1 – the Sultan would recognise Karadorde as chief of the Serbs, with the sole right to levy and collect taxes and to direct the administration of the country; 2 – no Muslim would be allowed to settle anywhere in Serbia outside Belgrade without the permission; 3 – all Ottoman customs and justice officials in the provinces would be replaced by Serbs; 4 – all fortresses in the provinces would be garrisoned jointly by equal numbers of Ottoman and Serbian troops, and Karadorde would be allowed to maintain a special personal guard of 500 *hayduk*s of his choice; 5 – the Serbs would pay a regular annual tribute of 500,000 piasters and would provide the Ottoman governor with funds sufficient for his own maintenance and that of his staff; 6 – the Ottoman fulfillment of the agreement would be guaranteed by a foreign power.

1805, asking the Serbs to rely on regular Ottoman troops to protect them from the *dayıs*; the Serbs summarily ignored the decree. For the first time the will of the Sultan had been defied, and the resistance thus became a revolt.[265]

The failure of negotiations and the news of uprisings in southern Serbia finally forced the Porte to consider the Serbs rebels and plan more vigorous action against them. A full-scale expedition against them was prepared, and all the governors and district commanders in Bosnia, Macedonia and Thrace were ordered to prepare their forces to join it. Hafiz Mustafa Paşa, currently governor of Niş, was appointed new governor of Belgrade, ostensibly to conduct negotiations with the rebels but actually to command the expeditionary army that was to be assembled at Skopje.[266] While the Serbians waited impatiently for news of the negotiations from Constantinople, they were joined not only by large numbers of Serbians but also by Christians from Bulgaria, Montenegro, and Albania who came to help him. In late May, having lost any hope of finding an agreement with the Porte, Karađorđe moved to take up positions along the Drina and at Niş, to set up a defence against possible attacks from the west or south. On 15 June 1805 he took Kruševac, north-west of Niş, and finally learned of the Ottoman plans from a captured official. He immediately moved west towards Bosnia, and on 12 July he ambushed and dispersed on the Drina an Ottoman column on its way to join Hafiz Paşa at Niş.

In July Hafiz Mustafa finally left Skopje with 20,000 irregulars of foot and horse and headed for the Morava, where he hoped to join the Bosnian force for a joint attack on the Serbs. Karađorđe sent a contingent of 5,000 footmen under Stoiković to intercept the Ottomans, and at Ivankovac, on the Morava, the two commander came together on 18 August 1805. Stoiković refused Hafiz's proposal to join him in exchange for a remunerative office in Belgrade, and tried to avoid armed confrontation, but when the *paşa* moved to assault his troops, the battle began. From a favourable position on the hills the Serbs repulsed the assault, and with the sudden arrival of reinforce under Karađorđe routed the enemies, who suffered heavy casualties. The Ottomans

---

265 Nevertheless, Karađorđe decided to make a final attempt to negotiate a settlement with the Porte. On 14 May 1805, Alexei Lazarevich, Archbishop of Belgrade, and Stephen Yivkovich, a wealthy merchant, left for Constantinople with a new proposals. Since Serbia had been ravaged by three years of intestine war and could no longer afford to pay the taxes required by a regular province, it would be lowered to the rank of a district, and the governor replaced by a *muhassil*. The district would then be divided into twelve communes, each ruled by an elected prince, with a grand-prince at Belgrade representing the Serbs in all dealings with the *muhassil* and other Ottoman officials. All taxes would be collected by agents of the *knez*, including those on fiefs, whose holders thereafter would have to reside in Belgrade and receive their revenues through the *muhassil*. The *yamaks* would no longer be allowed to live in the province, and order and security would be cared for jointly by the major *knez* and the *muhassil*, both of whom would be allowed to maintain armies for this purpose. See also Shaw, *Between Old and New*, pp.324–325.

266 Shaw, *Between Old and New*, pp.324–325. These orders were actually sent three days before the Serbian delegation arrived from Belgrade, but they were kept secret, and negotiations were begun so as not to warn the Serbs of the new danger.

fled, abandoning all the baggage and artillery. On 19 August Hafiz Paşa, who had been seriously wounded, died while trying to rally the remnants of his army at Niş. Thus, the first Ottoman effort to quell the rebels met an unexpected and staggering defeat. Now the Serbs felt they had nothing to fear from the Porte since they controlled almost all of Serbia with excepting only Belgrade and Smederevo. Preparations were planned to improve the army and a permanent senate was elected with its members chosen in each district by the local priests, monks, notables, and town majors. With this business out of the way, the sieges of Belgrade and Smederevo were renewed. On 21 November 1805 Smederevo surrendered and the garrison was allowed to retire to Vidin, but all the artillery, munitions, arms, and provisions passed to the Serbian troops. The city became the seat of the first Serbian government, and Russia recognised the new state.

Involvement in other provinces and foreign interference delayed the Ottoman reaction until early summer 1806, when the Porte proclaimed the 'Holy War' against the rebels. Irregulars from Anatolia and Bosnia were gathered in Sarajevo, and French military advisors also joined the army for the upcoming campaign. Regular forces were also assembled in Constantinople, but exclusively artillerymen and a few *kapıkulu*

OTTOMAN WARFARE: A STRUGGLE FOR SURVIVAL

The Battle of Mišar, fought on 12 August 1806, painting by Afanasij Scheloumoff (1839).

infantry.[267] The governor of Belgrade, Skopljak Süleyman, held command with Kulenović Mehmed Beg, chief of the Bosnian irregulars. Further delay postponed the beginning of the operation to the end of July. The Ottoman army numbered about 40,000 men, but just a minority could be considered as sufficiently trained for a field campaign. Warned about the Ottomans marching from Travnik, Karađorđe discussed the plans with Nenadović. The two Serbian leaders discussed the strategic situation and decided to build a sconce on top of the Mišar hill, between the River Sava, the wood and the villages Zabar, Jelenča and Mišar. The fortification was placed in a north–south direction with the guns placed at the southern corners, in order to face the approaching Ottomans from the main road, and securing the position by a possible assault from behind.[268] About 7,000 infantry and 2,000 cavalry manned the strong position. On 11 August the scouts of the Ottoman cavalry sighted the enemy and engaged them in a

---

267 Jucherau de Saint-Denys, *Histoire de l'Empire Ottoman*, vol. II, p.226.
268 Ranke, *History of Servia*, p.189. The sconce measured 300 × 280 metres and was made with earth in shape of a square. The improvised fortification had a palisade as protection, and trenches around the four sides. Two cannons were placed on each of the southern corners.

THE OTTOMAN ARMY OF THE NAPOLEONIC WARS 1789–1815

Illustration depicting the Ottomans handing over Smederevo, Belgrade, Šabac and Užice to the Serbs between November 1806 and June 1807. The Serbs were the first Christian population to have successfully risen up against the Porte. Their uprising ultimately became a symbol of the nation-building process in the Balkans, inspiring unrest among neighbouring Balkan peoples.

series of skirmishes that lasted four days. On 12 August Süleyman Paşa realised that he had enough forces for a general assault. The battle resulted in a confuse melee with the two sides involved in a series of assaults and retreats. The Ottomans were close to prevailing but Serbian resistance, led by their own commanders, did not give way, until the rebel cavalry charged the Ottomans causing the panic among Süleyman Paşa's troops. The battle ended with the collapse of the Ottoman centre and the exposure of the right and left columns. The Ottoman lost 3,000 men including the Bosnian commander Kulenović Mehmed; the Serbs claimed 500 casualties.[269]

No major actions occurred until November. Now the geostrategic scenario was worsening for the Ottomans. News concerning Russian mobilisation on the border along the Dniester River meant that St Petersburg aimed to remain in the Principalities of Wallachia and Moldavia. The Russian progress in the area could reverberate in a closer contact between them and the Serbs, allowing the arrival of arms and supply against the Porte without an obstacle. The Ottoman government was worried about

---

269 Ranke, *History of Servia*, p.189, p.202.

the materialisation of such an event, since it could mean the definitive loss of Serbia. It seemed that little remained to prevent a complete break-up of the Empire, in Europe as well as in Asia. At this point it was inevitable that the Ottomans should once again become the focus of European diplomatic action.

In the midst of an incandescent political situation, both domestically and internationally, the Porte prepared for a new war by sacrificing considerable resources. Before the Russians moved, the Ottomans gathered troops for another offensive against Serbia. This time the army comprised soldiers from the newly formed *nizâm-ı cedid* regiments, alongside janissaries and other *kapıkulu* soldiers, but to further increase the strength, irregulars were also enlisted in Albania, Bosnia, Thrace and Anatolia.[270] The *paşa* of Scutari, Bushati Ibrahim, held the command of the army. The Ottomans tried to surprise the Serbs with a winter campaign. In mid November 1806 the Ottoman army, numbering almost 55,000 men with 50 field guns, left Sofia heading to Niş and in early December entered Serbian territory.[271] The march had been slowed down by the difficult weather conditions and cold temperatures: the cavalry had lost many horses, and supplies were slowed down by snowy roads. The Serbs' informers warned Smederevo just in time to mobilise all the available forces and move them south. A war council was met and soon ordered the placing of the troops at Deligrad, north of the River Morava. The Serbian government established Karađorđe as both the military and political leader of the insurrection, but he was not without opposition.[272]

The village of Deligrad was crossed by the old 'royal road', which ran along the Morava to the east and was an obligatory passage for any army heading for Belgrade. On 6 December 1806 the Serbs arrived at Deligrad, laid camp and prepared to face the Ottomans. The Serbian right wing numbered 6,000 men under the command of Mladen Milovanović guarding Bela Palanka. The centre consisted of 18,000 troops deployed on the Kunovaci hill. The left wing comprised 6,000 men under the veteran Milenko Stojković, with an additional 4,500 reserve troops to guard from any possible enemy flank attack.[273] Stanoje Glavaš commanded the cavalry whose task was to delay the enemy progress as much as possible. Tomo Milinović directed the artillery and made significant effort by good positioning and frequent relocation of the guns. Entrenchments and palisades protected the Serbian position along the whole length of the battlefront. For four days the Ottomans tried to force the passage with continuous assaults, but each time they were repulsed. The failure of the winter offensive, the heavy casualties suffered, and the harsh environmental conditions, forced Ibrahim Paşa to negotiate a six-week truce with the Serbs. Meanwhile, on 20 December, the Porte declared war on Russia.

---

270 Jucherau de Saint-Denys, *Histoire de l'Empire Ottoman*, vol. II, p.243.

271 Martens, *Allgemeine Geschichte der Türken-Kriege*, vol. II, p.272.

272 Vladimir Stojančević, 'Karadjordje and Serbia in His Time', in Wayne. S. Vucinich (ed.), *The First Serbian Uprising, 1804–1813. War and Society in East Central Europe*. New York (Columbia University Press, 1982), p.31.

273 Ranke, *History of Servia*, p.202.

The truce allowed the Serbs to complete the conquest of the country. After a successful siege with 25,000 men, Belgrade surrendered on 31 December 1806; on 8 January 1807 Karađorđe proclaimed the city capital of Serbia.[274] The Ottomans opened new negotiations with the Serbs. Belgrade demanded largest autonomy within the Ottoman Empire, which was initially accepted by the Sultan, who wanted to make sure that the Serbs would not join the Russians in the impending conflict. An agreement was reached between the Serbs and the Ottomans that would have ended the insurrection, but the Russo-Ottoman war was still going on. The Serbs were now forced to choose between Russia and the Ottomans; they threw in their lot with the Czar. Once the decision had been made, Karađorđe ordered the elimination of Ottoman delegates at Belgrade However, Karađorđe's efforts to secure a conjunction with the Russians on the Danube failed in April 1807, proving that his troops were unable to penetrate the barrier formed by the Ottoman garrisons in the area.[275]

In June 1807, Russia and Serbia formerly concluded an alliance in which Serbian volunteers would join the Russian army in return for money, arms, and other necessities.[276] However, it was not long before events in international politics upset the strategic scenario in the area. The Treaty of Tilsit, signed on 7 July 1807 by France and Russia, left Serbs and Ottomans alone in the Balkan arena; even more dramatic for the Porte, Selim III had been deposed on 29 May. Unexpected new developments occurred during the year, including the failure of the peace accords between Russia and the Ottoman Empire. Peace talks between the Ottomans and Serbs failed again, but no major actions occurred in 1808, since the Porte was involved in domestic troubles and diplomatic efforts to settle a peace with Russia, and the evacuation of the enemy army from the Principalities.[277]

The war resumed in 1809. New Sultan Mahmud II was well aware that he would never break the Serbs without first depriving them of Russian support.[278] If the Russians were too strong to be repulsed from the Danubian area, the Serbs could be deprived of their base on the river. In order to achieve this result, it was necessary to exploit the Danube fleet so that a strong body of troops could be landed between Orşova and Požarevac. The operation

---

274 Mutual accusations between the Serbs and the Ottomans did not make it possible to establish the number of deaths among the Muslim population in Belgrade. According to some sources, all adult males were executed, and women and children forcibly converted to Christianity. The slaughter was accompanied by widespread destruction of Muslim property and mosques. See Dennis Washburn, Kevin Reinhart (eds), *Converting Cultures: Religion, Ideology, and Transformations of Modernity* (Leiden and Boston, MS: Brill, 2007), p.88.

275 See also the section 'War against Russia and Britain, 1806–1812.'

276 Elodie Lawton Mïjatović, *History of Modern Serbia* (London, 1872), p.34.

277 Stojančević, 'Karadjordje and Serbia in His Time', p.35.

278 News concerning the presence in Belgrade of the Russian agent Rodofinikin referred that he was reorganising the government and army, and special efforts were being made to organise the population en masse and to transform the various semi-independent rebel bands into regular disciplined regiments under a unified command. See in Shaw, *Between Old and New*, p.393.

could be successful, as the Serbs had no river force to repulse the landing. However, large sums of money would have to be invested in refreshing the Danube fleet, arming new units, and above all challenging the Russian artillery, which could be deployed on the left bank. In the immediate future, it was therefore necessary to plan a diversion.

In March 1809 the Ottomans launched several raids against Smederevo, in the hope of triggering a rebellion among the Muslim population in the region. However, the best opportunity for the Porte came in the spring when the Serbs launched an offensive against Novi Pazar and Niş. In May 1809 the Serbs captured Sjenica and repulsed an Ottoman attack on the village of Suvodol in early June. Before the end of the month managed to seize the first objective of the campaign, but the second one offered greater resistance. On 15 April 10,000 Serbs, under Miloje Petrović as commander-in-chief, approached the villages of Kamenica, Donji and Gornji Matejevac, heading for Niş. The Serbs began the siege by digging six entrenchments around the town, each held by a corps under its respective chief. The Ottoman commander was the former governor of Egypt Hürsid Ahmed Paşa, who had 7,000 irregular infantrymen inside the fortress and in the surrounding area, alongside the janissary *ocak* approximately 1,000 men strong.[279] However, the lack of modern siege artillery did not facilitate the Serbs in their task, forcing Petrović to blockade the fortress waiting for the enemy surrender. But time was running out in favour of the defenders, who were waiting for the relief force gathering between Travnik and Skopje. On 30 May the Ottoman vanguard was sighted coming from the south. The Ottomans numbered about 20,000 men, comprised of the *kapıkulu* infantry from the garrisons of Rumelia. The Ottomans tried to outflank the enemy, but Petrović sent a large contingent to halt their progress. However, this action weakened the besiegers and offered to Hürsid Paşa the opportunity to try a sortie on day 31. Early in the morning the Ottomans assaulted the main enemy entrenchment on the Čegar hill, which offered fierce resistance. A Serbian eyewitness described the fight and its epic conclusion:

> The Ottoman troops attacked five times, and the Serbs managed to repulse them five times. Each time their losses were great. Some of the Ottoman troops attacked, and some of them went ahead, and thus when they attacked for the sixth time they filled the trenches with their dead so that the alive went over their dead bodies and they began to fight against the Serbs with their bayonets, cutting and stabbing their enemies. The Serbian soldiers from the other trenches cried out to help Stevan [Stevan Sinđelić, the Serbian chief commanding in the entrenchment of Čegar hill]. But there was no help, either because they could not help without their cavalry, or because Miloje Petrović did not allow it. When Stevan saw that the Ottoman troops had taken over the trench, he ran to the powder cave, took out his gun, and fired into the powder magazine. The explosion was so powerful that all of the surroundings were shaken, and the whole trench was caught in a cloud of dense smoke. Everyone that was in the trench was killed, as was everyone in the vicinity of it.[280]

---

279 Jucherau de Saint-Denys, *Histoire de l'Empire Ottoman*, vol. II, p.245.
280 Stojančević, Vladimir, *Prvi srpski ustanak: Ogledi i studije* (Belgrade: Vojna knj., 1994). pp.90–98.

The explosion forced the Serbs to leave the siege and to retreat into the town of Deligrad, where they built a new defensive line. After the battle Hürsid Paşa ordered that the heads of the Serb dead be collected and skinned, and the skulls be built into a tower, which was erected along the road to Constantinople as a warning to anyone revolting against the Ottoman Empire.[281] The Ottoman victory did not drive the Serbs out of the Danube, but it did take away their initiative. Minor clashes also took place in the north of Kosovo. Lacking numbers and adequate military training, the Serbs failed to establish a corridor to Montenegro and gain access to the Adriatic Sea, which Karađorđe had described as one of his key aims.[282]

On 10 August the Ottomans assembled a further 20,000 horse and foot from Albania, Bosnia and Rumelia under Bushati Ibrahim Paşa and joined with the winning relief force at Čegar hill, they headed to Belgrade. After a series of clashes at Deligrad the Serbs abandoned their position and withdrew to Belgrade. To crush the rebellion, the Ottomans had to prevent the conjunction between the Serbs and the Russians at all costs. In 1810 the Porte planned two offensives against the rebels. The first aimed to expel the Serbs from the Morava, in order to separate them from the Russian army in the Principalities, and the second had to threaten Belgrade with a diversion along the Drina River. From a strategic point of view the plan was well drawn, but the Serbs could manoeuvre by internal lines and deal with the threat according to the moment. In May 1810 the Porte ordered Hürsid Paşa to gather as many troops as possible and move north along the Morava. The Russian offensive on the Danube delayed the preparation and Hürsid was able to move only in July with just 12,000 men. As soon as the news reached Karađorđe he sent to the south a small observation corps, and awaited the enemy. Meanwhile a corps of 2,500 Russians under General Joseph O'Rourke joined the Serbian army in August and soon headed to Varvarin. On 5 September Hürsid Paşa spotted the Russo-Serbians and moved against them in open ground near Varvarin, but the Russian square succeeded in repulsing the uncoordinated assault. The Serbs under Karađorđe and Jovan Kursula, who had been held in reserve at the outset of the battle, emerged from the wood and defeated the exhausted Ottomans. Hürsid Paşa withdrew his remaining troops back to the camp behind Varvarin, and eight days after moved through Kruševac to Niş.[283]

While the attempt to free the Morava from the Serbian presence was heading for failure, in mid September about 30,000 Bosnian irregulars under the command of Vidajić Ali Paşa moved down the River Drina to the Tičar field near Loznica, west of Belgrade. The fortified village was defended by 1,200 Serbs led by local *knez* Anta Bogićević. Estimating that the defence

---

281 Mijatović, *History of Modern Serbia*, p.156. The 10-foot-high skull tower contained 952 Serbian skulls embedded on four sides in 14 rows.

282 Wayne S. Vucinich, 'The Serbian Insurgents and the Russo-Turkish War of 1809–1812', in W. S. Vucinich (ed.), *The First Serbian Uprising, 1804–1813. War and Society in East Central Europe* (New York: Columbia University Press, 1982). pp.141–145.

283 Vucinich, 'The Serbian Insurgents and the Russo-Turkish War of 1809–1812'.

OTTOMAN WARFARE: A STRUGGLE FOR SURVIVAL

The skull tower of Niş, engraving from Felix Philipp Kaunitz, Serbien. Historisch-etnographische Reisestudien aus den Jahren 1859–1868 (Leipzig, 1868). This macabre building was erected by the Ottomans after the battle of Čegar, fought on 31 may 1809. The tower was 4.5 metres (15 ft) high, and originally contained 952 skulls embedded on four sides in 14 rows.

would be unable to resist, Bogićević requested aid from Luka Lazarević who held the command of the region. Learning of the Ottoman landing, Karađorđe sent a message to his lieutenant Petar Dobrnjac urging him to send further reinforcements as soon as possible. Before the end of September 10,000 rebels with artillery from the Šabac and Valjevo districts under Lazarević and Jakov Nenadović as well as the Cossacks of Joseph O'Rourke's Russian corps marched to join the Serbian defence. Karađorđe also hastened to relieve Loznica from the Morava. On 18 October, after a first engagement in the night between both reconnaissance parties, the fight began. Serbian sources exalt the bravery of the defenders, who resisted for eight hours, repulsing the Ottoman assaults. However, the casualties suffered by the two sides seems to be the result of skirmishes than an actual battle. The Serbs claimed 121 dead and 178 wounded, while the Ottomans, according to the same sources, suffered three times more casualties.[284]

These victories effectively liberated Serbia, but independence proved short-lived. Internal differences and shortage of ammunition weakened the Serbian defence, allowing the Ottomans to advance further north. Diplomacy intervened to open a negotiation but Austria and France, now involved in a war, did not support the talks. Russia, in turn, insisted on signing a peace treaty and acted without informing the Serbs. In 1810–11, attempts to agree a ceasefire alternated with skirmishes and raids. The Serbs sought to avoid isolation from their Russian allies, and the Porte could not allocate resources and troops because of the disastrous military situation on the northeastern border.

---

284 Ranke, *History of Servia*, p.238.

Deserted by Russia in 1812, the Serbs refused overtures for a peace, as agreed in the Treaty of Bucharest signed by the Porte and Russia, and continued the war, but with disastrous consequences. Grand Vizier Hürsid Paşa was stationed in Sofia during the recently completed hostilities with the Russians, and from April he seized all the forts still in Serbian hands, opening the way to Belgrade. The Ottomans could exploit the lack of co-ordination of the Serbs, who were involved in a bitter internal dispute for the leadership and there was increasing opposition to Karađorđe's method of government. The Grand Vizier gathered regular troops from the army of the Danube and joined them with irregulars, primarily Albanians and Bosnian Muslims; the latter performed their task brutally, and were accused of committing gruesome acts against the local population.[285] The news caused a mass exodus of people across the Danube. In early October 1812 Karađorđe also fled to the Austrian Empire, joined by around 100,000 other Serbs fleeing the Ottoman advance, including 50,000 from Belgrade and its environs alone.[286] By October 1813 the Ottomans had retaken control of Belgrade. Miloš Obrenović surrendered to the Ottomans, followed by the other chiefs before the end of the year. Hürsid Paşa declared a general amnesty, though Karađorđe and some senior Orthodox clerics were specifically exempted, and called on Serbs to return home. Some 30,000 reputedly did so.[287]

The new governor of Belgrade, Maraşli Ali Paşa, appointed many Serbian leaders, among them Miloš Obrenović and Stanoje Glavaš, to local administrative offices. This was accompanied by an attempt to pacify the region by eliminating many of the powerful local *ayans*. However, harsh imposition of order had the opposite effect of reigniting the riots a few months later.

The Ottoman–Egyptian Saudi War, 1811–1818

Political hostilities and distrust did not cease between the Saudi-Wahhabis and the Ottomans after the truce of 1807, but both sides agreed to declare mutual exchanges in the Hijaz for securing the pilgrims' route to Mecca. Occasional skirmishes occurred along the frontier, but the truce lasted for

---

285 Petrovich, *A History of Modern Serbia*, vol. II, pp.81 and 84. Foreign eyewitnesses reported on these terrible acts: 'In one day alone, 1,800 women and children were sold into slavery at a Belgrade market.' … 'Serbian women and children were raped and sometimes taken by force to harems. Outside Stambul Gate in Belgrade, there were always on view the corpses of impaled Serbs being gnawed by packs of dogs.'

286 Ivan Ninić, *Migrations in Balkan History* (Belgrade: Serbian Academy of Sciences and Arts, 1989), p.93.

287 Article VIII of the Treaty of Bucharest recognised the right of the Serbs without committing either side to full Serbian independence. There is considerable evidence that Mahmud II ordered the commanders stationed in the Danube fortresses to implement Article VIII of the treaty by declaring a general amnesty and peaceful takeover of the Serbian garrisons. See Shaw, *Between Old and New*, p.392.

some time. Rumours of a new war already sounded in early December 1807, when Muhammad Ali of Egypt was ordered to crush the Saudi state by Sultan Mustafa IV, but internal strife within Egypt prevented him from giving full attention to the campaign and the insecure peace continued again. In 1811, after new hostile acts in Iraq and Syria, the Saudi emir denounced the Porte and called into question the validity of his claim to be caliph and guardian of the sanctuaries of Arabia. In response, Sultan Mahmud II ordered again Muhammad Ali to gather an army and invade the Hijaz to resume Ottoman control in the area. The Porte contributed only part of the funds, but granted Muhammad Ali the incomes of looting and requisitions in enemy territory. As for the troops, the Ottoman–Egyptian army was only that in name, as it comprised exclusively the governor's contingents. Moreover, the wily Albanian governor took advantage of the campaign to drive his most uncouth ranks out of Cairo.[288]

In May 1811 Muhammad Ali advanced, encountering some resistance, but his well-trained and equipped troops easily defeated the enemy, and before the end of the year he seized Mecca. In 1812 the Ottoman–Egyptians improved their conquests and seized further localities, opening the route to Medina. Before summer, however, the Saudi-Wahabbis intensified their actions to oppose the enemy and were able to achieve some success in the Valley of Al-Safra (the Yellow Valley). Here they met Muhammad Ali's son Tusun Paşa, who was marching through the valley with a force comprising artillery and equipment for the planned siege of Medina. Tusun was ambushed by the Saud Al-Kabeer forces with 200 cavalry and about 10,000 footmen, and they successfully repulsed the enemy after three days of fighting, forcing the Ottoman–Egyptians to withdraw back to their base at Yanbo. However, a better-coordinated assault achieved success in November when Tusun, supported by 10,000 troops under his father, headed to Medina and seized the city with a storm that cost 600 Saudi casualties.[289] This campaign marked the end of the first phase of the war, as no major action took place in the two years that followed, with the exception of the usual raids and skirmishes of the desert war. In one of this actions, in early 1815, one of the main Wahhabi chiefs, Bakhroush bin Alass, of Zahran tribe, was captured and beheaded by Muhammad Ali in Al Qunfudhah. In the spring of 1815 Ottoman forces inflicted large-scale defeat on the Saudis, forcing them to agree a truce. Under the terms of the treaty the Saudis had to let go of the whole Hijaz. Wahhabi leading Emir Abdullah ibn Saud was forced to acknowledge his state as a vassal of the Porte and obey the Sultan unquestionably.

However, neither Muhammad Ali nor the Ottoman Sultan confirmed the treaty. Suspicious of Abdullah, the Porte resumed the war in 1816. With the assistance of French military advisors, 12,000 Egyptian troops were led by

---

288 Khaled Fahmy, *Mehmed Ali: From Ottoman Governor to Ruler of Egypt* (London: Oneworld Publications, 2012), p.30.

289 Ira M. Lapidus, *A History of Islamic Societies* (Cambridge: Cambridge University Press, 2002). p.572.

Muhammad Ali's elder son, Ibrahim Paşa. In spring, they penetrated into the heart of Central Arabia, besieging the villages of Qasim and Najd. Waging a war of extermination between 1816 and 1818, the Ottoman–Egyptians pillaged the area, forcing the inhabitants to flee and seek refuge in remote regions and oases. By 1817 Ibrahim had overrun Rass, Buraida and Unayza.[290] Saudi armies put up a fierce resistance at Rass where they resisted a siege for three months. Faced with the advance of Ottoman–Egyptian forces Abdullah bin Saud, the leading Saudi Emir, retreated to Dariye.[291]

Ibrahim advanced towards Dariye during the early months of 1818, easily routing Saudi resistances and arrive at the capital by April 1818. The siege would last until September 1818, with the Egyptian-Ottoman army waiting for Saudi supplies to run out. On 11 September 1818 Abdullah offered surrender in exchange for sparing Dariye. However, Al Dariye would be razed to ground under orders of Ibrahim. It was not until the end of September that the Saudi-Wahhabi state ended with the surrendering of all its leaders, while Abdullah bin Saud was sent to Constantinople to be executed alongside several other Wahhabi *Imams*.[292]

The Second Serbian Uprising, 1815

As a result of the abuses committed by the Ottoman garrison in Serbia, new riots and reprisals occurred in 1814. On 27 September a former Serbian officer named Prodan Gligorijević (known simply as Hadži-Prodan) triggered an armed rebellion in the district of Čačak, but after two months of siege the rebels were finally defeated and the survivors sentenced on 30 December. However, Gligorijević escaped capture.[293] After the failure of the revolt the Ottomans inflicted more persecution on the Serbs, including higher taxation and forced labour. In March 1815 Serbian leaders had several secret meetings and decided upon a new rebellion, The revolutionary council proclaimed an uprising in Takovo on 23 April 1815, with the *knez* Miloš Obrenović chosen as the leader, while Karađorđe was still in exile. Obrenović and his

---

290 David Commins, *The Wahhabi Mission and Saudi Arabia* (London: I. B. Tauris, 2006), p.37

291 Commins, *The Wahhabi Mission and Saudi Arabia*, According to the Saudis, en route to Dariyya the Egyptian–Ottoman troops executed every male over 10 years of age.

292 Geoff Simons, *Saudi Arabia: The Shape of a Client Feudalism* (Houndmills, Basingstoke and London: MacmMillan, 1998), pp.156–157. Over 250 members related to the Saud family and 32 members related to the Al ash-Sheikh were exiled. In December 1819, Ibrahim Paşa returned to Egypt after formally incorporating Hijaz into the Ottoman Empire. However, they were unable to totally subdue the opposition forces and Central Arabia became a region of permanent Wahhabi uprisings. In the 1820s, Prince Turki ibn 'Abd Allah ibn Muhammed ibn Saud , gathering growing support from tribes and groups that opposed the Turkish occupation, would lay Siege to Riyadh in 1823. By August 1824, Saudi forces would capture Riyadh in a Second Siege, thus establishing the Second Saudi State with Riyadh as its capital.

293 Sima Milutinović-Sarajlija, *Istorija Srbije od početka 1813e do konca 1815e godine* (Belgrade, 1888), p.488.

OTTOMAN WARFARE: A STRUGGLE FOR SURVIVAL

The execution of the Serbian rebels involved in the Hadži-Prodan uprising of 1814, oil painting by Nikola Milojevič dated to 1863.

supporters were anxious to forestall Karađorđe and keep him out of power. The Serbs managed to receive help from the Czar, who prohibited Karađorđe from returning to the Balkans to take part in the Second Serbian Uprising.

The first major clash occurred a few weeks later. On 4 May, Miloš Obrenović headed with a corps of 4,700 Serbian rebels to Ljubić, where they dug four entrenchments next to each other reinforced with palisades and artillery posts to guard the Morava river crossing. The Ottoman regional commander, the skilled and valiant Imsir Ćaja Paşa, managed to gather enough troops in Bosnia and prepared the offensive. On the morning of 8 May, 8,000–10,000 Ottoman cavalrymen under Kara Mustafa with some artillery crossed the Morava and began to target the enemy with two field guns. Soon the Ottomans approached the first entrenchment but they were repulsed by Serbian fire, which was very effective at short range. Without losing heart the Ottoman commander bypassed the first entrenchments, leading his cavalrymen against the enemy in the second entrenchment, and assaulting them to the flanks and rear. This time the action succeeded and the Serbians fled to the third entrenchment. The retreat caused chaos and disordered the defenders. Serbian accounts of the battle stated that in this critical phase Tanasko Rajić, the commander of the second entrenchment, rallied his men and exhorted them for the last stand. Obrenović saw the chaos growing in the third entrenchment and soon realised the danger. He sent 200 cavalrymen under Milić Drinčić to restore order, but called them back when Mustafa approached with his reserve. Then the Serbian commander sent 3,000 footmen to support the resistance. To worsen the situation, the Ottomans learned about the death of the valiant Imsir Ćaja Paşa, who had been killed two days earlier in an ambush. The news threw the Ottomans into despair, and they fled in disorder pursued by the enemies. Obrenović lost 1,500 men, but the Ottomans lost Kara Mustafa, killed during the escape, and 6,700 casualties including prisoners. The Serbs captured all the enemy's baggage, weapons and ammunition. The news of the victory filled the Serbs with confidence, encouraging them to rise up against the Sultan.

Between May and July the Serbs prevailed on the weak Ottoman forces at Čačak, Palez, Požarevac and Dublje and managed to reconquer the whole *paşalik* of Belgrade before the end of the summer. Miloš advocated a policy of appeasement: captured Ottoman soldiers were not killed and Muslim civilians were released. His announced goal was not independence but an end to misrule. After the French defeat in Belgium, which was a prelude to a more direct involvement of Russia, the Porte agreed for a truce in September 1815. With this agreement Serbia gained some autonomy but remained under Ottoman sovereignty, even Obrenović was left in power as its absolute ruler. After the killing of Karađorđe Petrović in 1817, Obrenović became the leader of the Serbs with the title of Prince.[294] The country existed under an uneasy arrangement between the Ottoman Empire and Russia, in which the Sultan held suzerainty over Serbia, which, however, enjoyed the protection of Russia. The agreement might not have been entirely negative for the Porte, but in fact it opened the way for other nationalist movements in the Empire with devastating consequences for its survival.

---

294 Petrovich, *A History of Modern Serbia*, vol. II, p.166.

4

Dress, Equipment and Ensigns

The concept of uniform was unknown in the Ottoman army, at least that introduced in the West, but the permanent *kapıkulu* corps wore a codified dress as early as the sixteenth century. These rules still existed in the turn of the century, but they dealt with the 'court' dress. Usually the Ottoman clothing style is divided into three periods: the one before the conquest of Constantinople, the one established by Süleyman the Magnificent in the mid sixteenth century, classified as 'the Imperial Style', and the last introduced after 1720 which lasted until the 1830s. In this period, traditional Ottoman Turkish dress had undergone some transformations. The elegance and simplicity of the traditional models had given way to a pronounced tendency towards eccentricity and gigantism. The iconography of those years shows eloquent examples of this trend. During the eighteenth century the Ottomans began to take an interest in Western invention and consumer goods. This interest would have a marked effect on the Ottoman dress, on textiles and occasionally accessories, as well as weapons, especially firearms. Western clothing was rarely included, since the dress aesthetics of the Ottomans and the Europeans were still too different. Exposure to Western Europeans was probably most likely via non-Muslim citizens of the Ottoman Empire because it was these communities in which business interactions most frequently occurred. An increase in the number of Ottoman sumptuary decrees registered official uneasiness with deviations from mandates in this period.

In fact, originally, the place of each individual in Ottoman society was determined by a combination of his class, institution, *millet*, and position, and indicated by his dress and headgear. These provided instant indications of his rights, privileges and duties and thus enabled everyone else to treat him properly and avoid violating or infringing on them in any way.[1] The clothing regulations thus played an important part in maintaining the social fabric of the community. Since the social order, and the clothing regulations which went with it, had broken down almost completely in the 1790s, Sultan Selim III assumed that evils occurred mainly because of failures to observe the old

---

1 Shaw, *Between Old and New*, p.77.

clothing regulations, which made the status of individuals unclear.[2] Members of the military corps wore the clothing set aside for artisans and merchants, because they were more artisans and merchants than they were soldiers. Since individuals no longer limited themselves to the clothing and headgear prescribed for them, it was impossible to tell their rank and position merely by looking at them and numerous disputes and conflicts resulted. With this simple analysis, the solution was obvious. Decrees were issued requiring all subjects to wear only those garments, hats, and decorations to which they were entitled by law. Heavy punishment was provided for violators, and inspectors were sent out into the streets and markets to check on compliance. The Sultan himself began to roam his capital in disguise to uncover violators and turn them over to his officials for punishment.[3] These reforms met with temporary success in the capital, and were initially firmly imposed mainly in the army, but the final result was probably less effective than expected.

The Sources for Ottoman Military Clothing

There are many sources relating the appearance of Ottoman soldiers from the later eighteenth century onwards, but identifying Ottoman soldiers before 1826 is a not easy task since some irregular corps and janissaries dressed in a similar way when they went on campaign. In turn, certain irregular corps were distinguished by clothing of the traditional costume of their country of origin, or by specific features that qualified them as soldiers, but with few differences compared to the civilian dress. This is the case of the Albanian *arnavuts*, who usually wore in their 'national' costume. Bosnians also had their particularities, who identified them as *panduk*.

Some Turkish collections published in the early 1900s also contribute to making difficult the identification of the different costumes.[4] Most of the surviving items are late nineteenth and early-twentieth century re-enactment costumes created for parades in Turkey, as well as theatrical costumes and modern reconstructions that have ended up in private collections and even museums. By examining the existing iconography and comparing it with written sources, it is difficult to identify such subjects are generally classified as 'Ottoman soldier', *sipahi* or even janissary. In many cases, the same figure receives different denominations depending on the source, or it is wrongly identified in the original source, making in turn all subsequent

---

2   Shaw, *Between Old and New*, p.78: 'Jewish and Christian merchants who had amassed huge fortunes had begun to flaunt their wealth by wearing the more prestigious satins and silks set aside by law and custom for members of the ruling class.'

3   Shaw, *Between Old and New*, p.78.

4   Among the most unreliable sources is Mahmud Sevket Paşa's *L'Organisation et les Uniformes de l'Armee Ottomanne* (Constantinople, 1907). This book deals with Ottoman military clothing from the fourteenth century until the early 1900s, but regarding the period before 1830, the author haphazardly collects images from various works, containing subjects belonging to very different periods. These costumes are without any critical apparatus, as was common for this type of text.

reconstructions inaccurate. Recent studies on the clothing of the Ottoman military corps also repeat such inaccuracies. The variety and substantial absence of well-defined rules undoubtedly contributes to making it difficult to reach a firm conclusion, but some of these inaccuracies could be avoided by a careful examination of the contemporary sources. In this regard, many relatively well-known sources have been ignored in modern studies on the Ottoman army. These documents present a very wide range of examples and although some works do not have a detailed description of the subjects depicted, they are very useful for determining any regional characteristics, or the homogeneity of the equipment, and other details. In particular, the paintings commissioned by Robert Aisle and Stratford Canning offer a very interesting view on the dress of the Ottoman soldiers between the 1780s and early 1800s. Especially in the second case, there is first-hand information on the characteristic feature of the Ottoman military dress with all its oddities and extravagances.

Alongside these sources, classic works dealing with military clothing were published in England, France and Germany, but most of these rely upon a restricted group of texts: the aforementioned Mouradgea d'Ohsson, *Tableau Général de l'Émpire Othoman* (1824); Dalvimart's *The Costume of Turkey* (1804);[5] McLean, *The Military Costume of Turkey* (1818).[6] All these works supplied material to many other authors for their illustrations dealing with orientalism's vogue in the early nineteenth century. There are also some valuable Ottoman sources illustrating soldiers and common people, published in souvenir albums. These publications were very popular among collectors in previous centuries, printed in the Ottoman Empire as *muraqqa*, ('book of costumes'), composed usually by putting together images from different sources. Among the most important, first place goes to the *Fenerci Mehmed Albümü*, illustrated in early 1800;[7] *Costumes Turcs* of the 1790s

---

5   Octavien Dalvimart (1767?–1816) worked in Britain as painter and engraver, and then in Paris. According to the prologue of the first edition of his work, he travelled in the Ottoman Empire from 1796 to 1800, always drew from nature. His elegant work was first published in 1802, and again in 1818 and 1820. It includes sixty drawings of human types from the Ottoman Empire, including military subjects. The explanatory texts, in English and French, are based on extracts from works by B. De Tott, J. Dallaway, G.A. Olivier, M. Montague, J. Pitton de Tournefort, d'Ohsson and others.

6   Thomas McLean, *The Military Costume of Turkey, Illustrated by A Series of Engravings. From Drawings made on the Spot* (London, 1818). The work includes 30 watercolours made from life by the French contemporary artist de Molleville. This work is reputed among the primary source on the Ottoman Army in the early 1800s.

7   Little is known about Fenerci Mehmed. The limited information about this artist comes from an article published in 1912 by Sherif Abdulkadir Huseyin Hasim. Since Sherif did not publish his sources, his work remains the only relating the Fenerci Mehme's life. The name Fenerci derives from his previous occupation: Mehmed was in fact a lantern (*fener*) maker and became a painter only after his shop burned down in Fethiye. The various portraits depicted in the album can be divided into three main categories: characters who belonged to the political life of the court; characters who worked in the Topkapı Palace, and members of the army in both daily and parade attire. The third is the largest group, and it is certainly the most interesting, because

of the Diez Collection,[8] and the anonymous album entitled *Les portraits des differens habillemens qui sont en usage à Constantinople et dans tout la Turquie* (before 1809).[9] These three major collections especially focus on the military and provide very detailed information about some lesser known corps and ranks.

Generalities

Thomas Walsh summarised in a few lines the attire of the Ottoman soldiers he encountered during the Egyptian campaigns:

> All the Turks wear turbans, loose jackets, short pantaloons, morocco loafers, and a sash round the waist, in which they constantly carry a long dagger and a brace of pistols. Their heads are close shaved, and covered by a small scull-cap, which is hidden under the turban.[10]

Turban, *kaftan* coat, and *salvar* loose trousers are probably the best-known items of the Ottoman dress. As many as 90 different styles of trousers have been identified in traditional Ottoman dress, differing somewhat in cut but all having the deep crotch and loose fit. Other important features are the layered *cepken* sleeveless coat, *entari* long waistcoat, and the short jackets designated as *hirka*, *mintan*, or *salta*, and *yelek*. The aulic *kaftan* also shows different versions with *üst-kurku*, *divoan-kurku*, *erkan-ı kurku*, and the traditional janissary *dolama* and *ciubbeh* being the most widespread. The layering of *kaftan* and waistcoats was an important feature of the dress aesthetic as well. It served to mark status as much as it served practical purpose. Usually, the more coats that were worn, the more formal the attire. Sleeves were tailored to allow all the layers of luxurious fabric to be visible. Some *kaftans* had extremely long sleeves that would be worn pushed up on the arm, displaying rich folds of fabric. These snug-fitting

---

supplies many details about the new military corps introduced by Sultan Selim III. Soldiers from different units, ranks and in everyday and parade attire are depicted, providing a comprehensive panorama of the Ottoman military at the time, and a very useful guide in identifying each subject the artist could have been encountered in Constantinople.

8   Heinrich Friedrich von Diez (1715–1817) was a Prussian Ambassador to the Porte. His collection approximately contains 450 paintings, drawings, and calligraphies, as well as unfinished sketches and study sheets which he acquired in Constantinople during the period 1786 to 1790. Although the majority of these artworks date back to the fourteenth and fifteenth centuries, the collection includes an album dating the 1790s depicting the dress of some irregulars from Anatolia.

9   Anonymous, *Les portraits des differens habillemens qui sont en usage à Constantinople et dans tout la Turquie* (Early 1800) in R. Naumann and K. Tuchelt (ed.), *Türkische Gewänder und Osmanische Gesellschaft im achtzehnten Jahrhundert* (Graz: Akademische Druck – u. Verlagsanstalt, 1966).

10 Thomas Walsh, *Journal of the Late Campaign in Egypt, Including Descriptions of that Country, and of Gibraltar, Minorca, Malta, Marmorice, and Macri: With an Appendix Containing Official Papers and Documents* (London, 1803), p.53.

DRESS, EQUIPMENT AND ENSIGNS

Ottoman horsemen and foot soldiers, illustration from Thomas Walsh's *Journal of the Late Campaign in Egypt* (London, 1803).

sleeves could have buttons to the elbow. The long sleeves could also be pulled down over the hands in cold weather, which is the most probable reason that this pattern appears in the dress of Anatolians from an early date. Outer coats might have wider short sleeves that could be easily worn over narrower long sleeves. Aulic and court *kaftans* might have long false sleeves that were fastened or only attached by buttons to the top and back of the shoulders, so that the sleeves would hang down the back when not pulled over the arm. This was the common pattern of the *üst-kurku* and other court *kaftan*. These oversleeves might also be wide, and either long or short, but always designed to reveal the snugly fitted undersleeves of the *entari* or other outer garment as well as their own lining and fur. However, the full sleeves gathered to a cuff, known as a bag sleeve, is a distinctively Ottoman variant of this fondness for extravagant pattern, and remained in vogue until the nineteenth century.

The edges of outer coats and *kaftans* were often tucked up into a sash. These were caught up not only for convenience for physical activity but also to display the sumptuous variety of colours and materials in the under-layers of clothing. One or more sashes, usually a bulky length of colourful fabric tied

THE OTTOMAN ARMY OF THE NAPOLEONIC WARS 1789–1815

Janissary *sakka* (water carrier), by Olivier Dalvimart (1802). Note the shape of shoulder straps of the *salta* jacket, which are always associated with this rank. The rules of Ottoman society prescribed precise norms on hair, moustache and beard. Every *kapıkulu* soldier had to shave his head and sometimes let a tuft of hair grow on the top of his skull. The moustache, of all shapes and sizes, was flaunted by every soldier as well as adult male; the beard was instead reserved for the ruling classes, but exceptions were frequent. The officers of the janissaries, the *kapıkulu* horsemen, as well as *timars*, *zeamets*, princes, governors and naturally all the members of the court and government, wore a beard – the symbol of virility par excellence – outlining their leading status.

An *aşçıbaşı* (chief cook) outfit displayed in the Askeri Museum of Constantinople. This was a non-commissioned officer rank in the Janissary corps. Each *orta* had its own *aşçıbaşı* who was responsible for both supervising the food preparation and the raising of the novices. He also had the authority to punish or imprison them for low-level crimes.

DRESS, EQUIPMENT AND ENSIGNS

The *mufti* blesses the cannons in an Austrian print of the late eighteenth century. Although there are no indications as to the colour of the Ottoman artillery carriages, the available iconography seems to leave no doubt that they were of natural wood and that even the metal parts were not painted.

around the waist whose fold could carry weapons, knives, daggers, bags and other items, were a common feature in the Balkans and Western Anatolia too.

Some outermost coats were intended to be simply cast over the shoulders, the sleeves left to hang down. The presentation of outer coats manufactured of rich cloth, in brocade or embroidered, and possibly trimmed or lined with furs was a typical feature of the formal reception of honoured guests by the Sultans. The more elaborate the coat, the more highly regarded the guest.

Ottoman headdress shows in this period an equally huge variety. The Turkish term *tülpend* is the source of the word turban and refers both to the turban and the cotton cloth used for wrapping formal headdress. Because of the requirement that the head should be covered during daily prayers, covering the head at all times became the norm. In addition, the necessity of touching the forehead to the ground for prayer precluded hats with wide brims.

Among the common people a simple turban might be only a scarf wrapped and knotted around the base of a hat, in this case the right term is *sarik*, which means 'wrapper'. The turban was the most common headdress and usually consisted of fine wraps of white cotton over the base of a substantial hat, or *kavuk*. A typical Ottoman *kavuk* in the late eighteenth century consisted of a low red, green or black flat-topped round hat. Some *kavuk*s, typical of the

Egyptian Mamluks as well as of the Ottoman court, were a taller version, with the top distinctly flaring out.

Ottoman turbans in this period were frequently quite tall; the specific size and colours denoted particular court and military ranks, as carefully established by decrees. Military and government senior personnel might also wear various forms of tall and unusually shaped hats, usually decorated with plumes and feathered crests as particular marks of status and bravery. As an exclusive prerogative of the heads of the greatest dignitaries, the *mücevveze* was an actual sculpture of fabric. Shaped like a quadrangular sugar loaf, this turban was made with layers of white muslin and decorated with a band of golden silk. The *mücevveze* was the classic turban worn by the grand viziers, but in some late-eighteenth century iconography this turban is worn by the *kapudan paşa* and other viziers.

Court turbans followed the traditional sumptuary codes, but with some modifications. The other two classic turbans were the *selimi* and the *kallavi*. The *tulpend selimi*, so called because it was introduced by Sultan Selim I (1512–20), was cylindrical in shape and could measure up to 70 cm in height. This turban was usually manufactured with the finest fabrics, usually white muslin, or entirely in silk in the most expansive models, and ended at the top with a characteristic convex shape. Usually the *selimi* was decorated with feathers or *surguç*-aigrette. The *kallavi* turban, equally cylindrical in shape, but smaller than the previous one and slightly flared at the top, still existed for court ceremonial. The *kallavi* resembled a vase and occasionally *selimi* and *kallavi* both had a piping of silver fabric on the front. A third model, similar to the latter turbans, but with the wraps applied vertically, appeared in the eighteenth century with the name *yusufi*. To make a turban like these, about 20 metres of fabric were used, wrapped around the *kavuk*, or applied in several layers and shaped as to give it the desired shape. The classical turban with the cloth twisted in more than one spiral, and with one end falling on the back, was common among the janissaries and in the rest of the *kapıkulu* infantry, who normally wore them in active service on campaign. Substantially similar to the previous one, the turban was also worn by the *ulufely sipahis* both out of service and on campaign. The turban intended for high-ranking officers was the *paşali kavuk*. This headdress was subject to a series of rules to distinguish the rank of the owner. The classic *paşali* ranged between 35 and 50 cm in height. This turban had a characteristic cylindrical shape and a slight flaring at the top; almost always the drape hung over the inner *kavuk*. On the top, the classic grey heron plumes were inserted, and their number established the rank of the officer. This *plumet* took the name *balikcil* and was fixed to the turban with a precious metal setting, aigrette-*sorguc*, which gave its name to the whole *plumet*. The *sancakbegs* adorned their headdress with a single *sorguc*, while *paşas* could have two, and the sultan up to three. The classic pumpkin-shaped turban was the *tulpend örf*, which compared to the other models was considered the most outdated, however it continued to be worn throughout the seventeenth century, particularly in religious circles. Some essential turbans were only composed by the *kavuk* with one or more spirals of cloth around the edge, or, alternatively, by the knotted wrap.

Egyptian Mamluks favoured coloured turbans with particularly complex local patterns, as per the headdresses depicted in the paintings of Carle Vernet and Jean Luis David, illustrating the episodes of the French campaign in Egypt. Colourful turbans also met the taste of the Kurdish tribes of eastern Anatolia and northern Iraq, where the influence of the peoples of the Caucasus and Iran was more marked. In Anatolia, since the beginning of the eighteenth century, scarves were used to form the casual peasant turbans made by wrapping a rolled scarf around the head over a brimless cap and often simply knotting it, with the ends hanging down or striking out of the roll. These scarves might have macramé fringe, or attached needle lace edgings known as *igne oya* or simply *oya*, in the form of petal or leaves. Some iconographic sources suggest that the *oya* became common also among the nomadic eastern Anatolian communities and Turkmen tribes. There were some extensions into eastern Greece, Thrace, northern Syria and the southern Balkans, all areas belonging to the Porte and exposed to multiple influences from the east.

The *mücevveze* turban depicted by Jean-Étienne Liotard, in the alleged portrait of grand vizier Hekimoğlu Ali Paşa (mid eighteenth century). Preserved in the National Gallery, London.

The typical janissary headdress, 'the blessing sleeve of Allah' or *ak börk*, belonged to court ceremonial and was therefore used only on parade, or in quarters on active service. The shape of this characteristic headdress had changed little over the centuries, but by the mid 1700s the *ak börk* appears to have been reduced in height and tended to flare out at the side corners. The front side always displayed the traditional copper case, which originally contained a wooden spoon. This item was detachable and was often a prized work of art individually crafted for the janissaries as well as other *kapıkulu* members.[11] Even the non-commissioned janissary officers and junior officers wore headdress similar to those of the common soldiers; the greater or lesser richness and elaboration of the spoon case and other items marked rank and authority in the corps. Generally the *odabaşi* decorated his headdress with large plumage; the *corbaci*, on the other hand, wore on parade a white cloth cap, ending with a heron-shaped headpiece, adorned with a large white feather; around the base a circular band of felt was decorated with a golden cord like the one used for the janissary's *ak börk*. This headdress was known as *kalafat*. The headdress was the peculiar item of all the other members of the *kapıkulu* infantry. The *acemi-oglanis* wore indifferently in parade or in active service the *kulah*, a felt hat painted in pale yellow with a characteristic conical shape.

---

11 McLean, *The Military Costume of Turkey* p.28: 'In strict conformity with such ideas of military parade, they (the Janissaries) have each of them a wooden spoon, where with they eat their *pilau* ration of rice and which they wear instead of a feather, stuck into a copper tube, which is affixed in front of their bonnets.'

THE OTTOMAN ARMY OF THE NAPOLEONIC WARS 1789–1815

The *silâhdar ağa*, from the *Fenerci Albümü* (early 1800). The Ottoman elegance and self-indulgence of this period was in many ways comparable to the fantasy world created by Louis XVI and Marie Antoinette in the years before the French Revolution. In both societies, court life was an idyllic refuge from national troubles that the rulers were poorly prepared to face.

In the *kapıkulu*, particularly among the janissaries, it was usual to decorate turbans and other headdress with thin metallic strips fixed to a medallion: the *celeng*, a special distinctive brooch issued to soldiers as a sign of bravery. By the late eighteenth century the *celeng* had become a diamond-jewelled central flower with leaves and buds and seven outward rays, arranged upwards from the flower. Contemporary descriptions relate that the *celeng*s were of five different classes.[12] The *celeng*s for rank and file were usually iron, while the ones issued to the commanders were of gilded metal. Ottoman soldiers are known to have received a rectangular gold plate called a *ferahi* that was instituted by Sultan Mahmud I who ruled from 1730 to 1754. The *ferahi* had two sides, with the reverse displaying text invoking Allah's virtues and the obverse featuring the *tugra* of the Sultan. Surviving examples of the *ferahi* dating to the mid eighteenth century have three sewing holes along the top of the plate indicating that these were attached to the headdress or to a cloth halter to be worn around the neck.

In the Asian regions of the Empire local typical headdresses represented an alternative to turbans, such as the cap with a felt or fur brim, typical of Eastern Anatolia, Armenia and Kurdistan, and very widespread throughout the Caucasus and Central Asia; the most expansive models were made with the precious *kedife* velvet. A popular headdress coming from the Western regions but widely spread also in Anatolia was the cylindrical-shaped felt hat, usually black, in some cases with the wrap rolled up at the base and with the two ends falling over the shoulders.

Coeval iconography of Bedouins and Arabs depicts the features of traditional dress with few changes. Though Count Constantin de Volnay gives a negative judgement,[13] in Egypt, Syria and Iraq military dress retained some typical characteristics. Mamluks continued to wear loose trousers, usually of red cloth, and layered coats, while Moors and Arabs mostly wore loose gowns or tunics combined with loose, unfitted coats in natural colours or sometimes in pale grey-blue. Although most of these long gowns did not open down the front, many resemble the Ottoman *kaftan* in silhouette as well as in the sleeves, which were normally wider.

---

12 Mouradgea d'Ohsson, Ignatius, *Tableau Général de l'Émpire Othoman, tome septième, contenant l'état actuel de l'Émpire Othoman* (Paris, 1824), p.412.

13 Volnay, Constantin-François de Chasseboeuf, comte de, *Voyage en Syrie et en Égypte, pendant les années 1783, 1784 et 1785,* (Paris, 1787), vol. I, p.115: 'The armies of the Mamluks and Turks, are but a confused mass of horsemen without uniforms, of horses of all sizes and colours, marching without observing either ranks or distributions.'

DRESS, EQUIPMENT AND ENSIGNS

Grand vizier riding in incognito in Constantinople, after the *Fenerci Albümü* (1809). The presence of such a large number of depictions of military attire as well as diplomatic and political members of the Sultan's entourage sustain the hypothesis that Fenerci Mehmed made this album for a foreign diplomatic or tradesman, who would have needed a handy guide to identify who was who at the court of the Sultan. The authoritative historian Suraiya Faroqui notes that often these costume albums were commissioned to 'identify the dignitaries of the palace with whom the envoys had to interact during their missions'. It is plausible that this impressive album was purchased by a member of the diplomatic entourage in Ottoman Turkey at the end of the nineteenth century, which was later acquired by an Ambassador to Iran at the beginning of the twentieth century.

The *Kapıkulu* Dress Code

The Ottomans were among the first to establish sumptuary rules and laws concerning the army. The dress code mainly concerned the court and the members of the *kapıkulu* and the general lines were resumed in the 1790s by Sultan Selim III. In the first volume of his *Etat Militaire Ottoman*, Kabaağaçlızade Ahmed Cévad Beg provides a description of the clothing worn by the members of the standing army officers and in the last years of existence of the *kapıkulu* corps.[14] According to the author, the clothing of janissaries and senior commanders changed its pattern little throughout the eighteenth century, and maintained its traditional colours and accessories. The *yeniçeri ağa* wore the traditional *kalafat* headgear in the shape of a heron's head manufactured of red cloth, or alternatively a turban with the white wrap twisted at each side of the *kavuk* cap, also in red. A sleeveless *kaftan* lined with fur, called a *üst*, was tailored of white silk. At the back two long false sleeves, also lined with fur, completed the garment. Under the *üst* he wore the silk *entari* waistcoat always in white. A large belt in gilded metal with a

---

14 Kabaağaçlızade Ahmed Cévad Beg, *Etat Militaire Ottoman, depuis la fondation de l'Empire Ottoman jusqu'à nos jours* vol. I (Constantinople, 1882), pp.182–191.

DRESS, EQUIPMENT AND ENSIGNS

Murad Bey enters Cairo with his retinue, 1790s (author's archive). Note the fellayn and the footsoldiers preceding the bey uniformly dressed. Luigi Mayer (1755–1803). Italian-German artist, Mayer was one of the earliest and most important late eighteenth-century European painters of the Ottoman Empire. He was a close friend of Sir Robert Ainslie, the British ambassador to the Porte between 1776 and 1792. In fact, the bulk of his paintings and drawings during this period were commissioned by Ainslie. Mayer travelled extensively through the Ottoman Empire between 1776 and 1794, and became well known for his sketches and paintings of panoramic landscapes of ancient sites from the Balkans to the Greek Islands, Turkey and Egypt.

kancar dagger, both decorated with precious stones and corals, was worn over the waistcoat. Red *şalvar* trousers and yellow *mest* shoes completed the *ağa*'s dress. The *ağa*'s 'ordinances' wore their own dress comprising a white *yusufi* turban over a red *kavuk* with a tassel, and red *kaftan, mintan* and *şalvar* for the *yamaği*; the same but with *mintan* and *salvar* in black for the *moumci*. As for the *noumci*, he wore a red *ciubbeh* with sleeves, long *entari* and yellow leather *mest*; the headdress was the *kalafat*.

The *falakaci ağa*, who accompanied the commander or the grand vizier during the inspection in the city, wore the same *kalafat* headgear but in white fabric. His coat was the *dolama* in pink with flared sleeves, worn over *çakşir* loose trousers and yellow *mest* shoes or *basmak* boots. The *kul kâhya* wore the white *ak börk* of the janissaries with two *sorguçs*-aigrettes fastened on the front and back of the large edge of golden wire. The *kaftan* and waistcoat were like those of the *yeniçeri ağa* but in turquoise cloth; shoes or boots in yellow leather. The *bas-çavuş* wore the *ak börk* of red cloth with a single aigrette; *dolama kaftan*, waistcoat and trousers all in red, and yellow leather *mest* shoes. As for the *orta çavuş*, he wore the janissary *ak börk* with double *sorguç* and brown leather *mest*.

The lining fur of the senior officers' kaftan was the same used for the *yeniçeri ağa*'s clothing.

Senior officers of some janissary *ortas* had particular garments and colours. Sometimes the description is limited to a few brief indications, such as the *sekban başi* wearing a large *kaftan*, while more details are given for the *zagarci başi*, who wears the same dress of the *kul kiaya* with *kalafat* and two *sorguçs*. Some *çorbacis* retained traditional items, for example the commander of *Orta* 54, the *talimhaneciler*, always wore the turban with the insignia of a *paşa* and on parade he carried a bow and quiver with arrows.

The officer responsible for the *fodalhoran* pensioners wore the same dress as the *çorbaci*, but with the janissary *ak börk* with a single *sorguç*. The same dress identified the *muhzir ağa*, except for the golden brocade sash. The *kaftans* of the *çorbaci* were similar to the janissary *ağa* but in turquoise.

The *çorbaci* – *orta* commander – wore a white *kalafat* headdress with plumes, and a red or turquoise *ciubbeh kaftan*, with false sleeves and *salvar*.

The *bayrakdar*-ensign had a blue headdress in the shape of a truncated cone with a white wrap at the base. His *ciubbeh*, *entari* and *salvar* were of unspecified colour. When in service without the ensign, he carried a wooden stick.

The *orta çavuş'* headdress was the *kalafat* with plume as for the *çorbaci*, and regarding this rank, Cévad quotes an original piece of clothing preserved in Constantinople, comprising *dolama kaftan*, *entari* and *şalvar*, without information about colours, and red leather *mest*. Only for the *kaftan* is it possible to establish with some certainty that it was of the traditional turquoise colour, as specified by Cévad Beg. He provides also some information about the dress of the *yamak* officers, who wore the same clothing as the *yamaği ağa* but with red leather *yemini* shoes.

Cévad provided some interesting detail on the dress of the *asçi-uşta* of the janissary, which was different depending on the *orta* to which they belonged. The *asçi* of *Orta* 32 wore a leather coat with brass and leather buttons. Under this heavy garment he wore an apron of leather with buttons as for the coat. Chains and other metal accessories hung on the front. *Mintan, şalvar* and black leather shoes completed the elaborate costume.

The *asçi* dress also appears in a coeval description by William Wittman:

> He is clothed in a large habit of dark coloured leather, covered over with devices of plated metal, which render it extremely weighty, in so much that on days of ceremony, when he is decorated with all the insignia of his office, what with the pressure of this habit, or tunic, and that of the other parts of his dress, which, being also covered with plate of metal, are equally cumbrous and oppressive, he requires the aid of two persons to assist him in walking.[15]

---

15 William, *Travels in Turkey, Asia-Minor, Syria, and Across the Desert Into Egypt During the Years 1799, 1800, and 1801, in Company with the Turkish Army, and the British Military Mission: To which are Annexed, Observations on the Plague and on the Diseases Prevalent in Turkey, and a Meteorological Journal.* (London, 1803), p.181.

DRESS, EQUIPMENT AND ENSIGNS

This description has many similarities with the only known complete example of early nineteenth century Ottoman military clothing. This is the *asçi*'s leather and embossed brass 'uniform' preserved in the Askery Museum in Constantinople. This is one of the few examples that have survived intact to this day, considering that after 1826 much of the evidence and documents relating to the janissaries was destroyed by order of the government, in order to erase the nefarious memory of the corps.

Other *asçis* wore particular dress identifying their *orta*. In *Orta* 1, the *asçi*'s headdress was a *kalafat* decorated with *igne oya* fringes lace edgings fastened on the back. The coat, presumably a *hirka* jacket, had very long sleeves, which reached the knee. He wore a *dolama kaftan*, *mintan*, and *şalvar* of blue cloth; metal belt with daggers, and red footwear with violet gaiters and leather straps completed the clothing. As for the *asçi* of other *ortas*, they wore *kalafat* headdress, *ciubbeh* with sleeves close by a couple of buttons, *mintan*, *şalvar* and metal belt.

During ceremonies the *asçi* was usually accompanied by a couple of adjutants, the *karakoulluk*s, who wore a red *salta* over *mintan* and *şalvar*, a belt with metal fittings, and red leather footwear. According to Cévad Beg their turbans had a pointed shape and were wrapped with 'light-coffee' calico, fastened by several metal pins: this kind of headdress is confirmed in some coeval iconographies. Concerning the *civelek*-cadets of the janissaries, they still wore the distinctive headdress of the *acemi-oğlani* consisting of the tall pale yellow pointed hat. These young men were nearing the end of their apprenticeship and served in the *orta* alongside the veteran janissaries, wearing the traditional *dolama kaftan*, *şalvar* and *yemine* loafers.

Finally, the ordinary janissaries wore the *dolama kaftan* in turquoise or other colours, with green and red the most widespread. This garment seems the item has changed a lot of its original form. The late eighteenth century *dolama* has lost collar patches and cuffs, and also the typical long front flaps have been removed. In the late eighteenth century, the general pattern consisted of a wide coat with short tight sleeves, deprived, however, of its original elegance. In the seventh volume of his *Tableaux*, Mouradgea d'Ohsson provides a possible explanation for this decay. Despite the fact that the number of janissaries had increased considerably by the mid eighteenth century, the Porte never modified the original regulation, which provided the distribution of 'Salonika cloth of various colours' once a year for the manufacture of 12,000 *dolamas*. This arrangement, therefore, left most of the janissaries without the cloth for their new *kaftan*s. The same author specifies that also

A *çorbacı* in ceremonial dress, from Diez's album of Ottoman Costumes (1790s). He is wearing a red kaftan with short sleeves, with additional long false sleeves and white sable fur lining (white with black spots) and edging, over an azure blue *entari* waistcoat. White *halafat* with a broad golden brim with huge ostrich feathers and a smaller black feather aigrette.

the fabric for the headdress and for the seven shirts for each soldier was insufficient, and the latter was in such narrow pieces that it was used to make straps. The result was that those who were left out had to provide for themselves and consequently they introduced changes and simplifications, which, however, affected the quality of the clothing.[16]

The distribution of fabric and other stuff for the clothing included the footwear. This item, *mest* shoe or *yemine* loafers, were manufactured of leather or fabric with a reinforced sole. The general rule prescribing the wearing of yellow leather footwear only to janissaries of the *ortas ceemat*, and of red leather for *böluk* and *segmen* seems to have been no longer observed in the late eighteenth century. According to Ahmed Cévad, the yellow leather shoes were common footwear of the *çorbacis* without reference to the category to which they belonged. Mouradgea d'Ohsson, instead, claims that red leather shoes were only exclusive to the *bölüks*, and that all NCOs had black shoes.[17] The matter remains particularly entangled, since coeval eyewitnesses relate clear information.[18] The original sumptuary code prescribed yellow shoes for *cebeci* and *topçu*, and even the *ulufely sipahis* were easily recognisable by their yellow leather boots and shoes.

Despite the details provided in his work, Cévad Beg does not give information on *odabasi* and other non-commissioned janissary officers, or on other specialities of the *kapıkulu*.

Timar-sipahi after Octavien Dalvimart's *The Costume of Turkey, Illustrated by a Series of Engravings; with Description in English and French* (London, 1804). This fine book of hand coloured engravings depicting the dress and customs of soldier and common people living in the Ottoman Empire. The descriptions accompanying the coloured illustrations incorporate notes by the French artist who drew the images. According to the introduction, he travelled during four years starting in 1796, and always drew from real life. Such costume books were popular with audiences in Western Europe for whom the Ottomans were somewhat mysterious.

Campaign Dress

The sumptuary code, however arbitrarily respected both in the capital and (probably even less) in the border garrisons, concerned only official occasions prescribed by Imperial protocol.[19] In this regard, an 1802 description suggests

---

16 Mouradgea d'Ohsson, *Tableau Général*, p.342.

17 Mouradgea d'Ohsson, *Tableau Général*, p.344.

18 McLean, Thomas, *The Military Costume of Turkey, Illustrated by A Series of Engravings. From Drawings made on the Spot* (London, 1818): 'The Janissaries, on occasions of ceremony, are obliged to wear red shoes'

19 In the 1780s, the Polish writer Ian Potocki wrote about the decision to prohibit the Janissaries in garrison on the Black Sea to wear Tatar bearskins: 'because the Turks have great contempt for them [the Tatars]'. Potocki, Ian, *Viaggio in Turchia, in Egitto e in Marocco* (Rome: Edizioni E/O, 1980), p.9.

that the 'janissary uniform' on campaign was restricted to the headdress and trousers only, 'and they have no limitations concerning the colour of their clothes. They must, however, generally wear large blue trousers.'[20] On the same matter the English diplomat John Philip Morier, who accompanied the Ottoman army in Egypt, stated that janissary dress 'is more uniform than that worn by other troops.'[21] He added further information specifying that:

> their dress is better calculated for walking than the generality of Eastern dresses are; the trousers are smaller, and fit close to the leg in the form of gaiters.

About this topic, McLean adds:

> The janissaries are obliged to wear great blue breeches, and a particular sort of bonnet, the other part of their dress may be of what colour they please; their uniform, with the above exceptions, only consisting in the cut.[22]

Another Englishman, William Wittman, writes that also on campaign the janissaries were the best equipped and dressed soldiers of the Ottoman army:

> They may still be considered as the most select and regular of the Turkish troops. They are at the same time the better and more uniformly dressed and equipped than the other soldiers.[23]

Concerning the janissary officers, Morier provides some interesting details:

> A regular gradation is observed in the rank of their officers; all of whom, from the bayrakdar or ensign, to the binbaşi or colonel, are distinguished by the shape of their turban.[24]

The same author specifies their equipment:

---

20 Dalvimart, Octavien, *The Costume of Turkey, Illustrated by a Series of Engravings; with Description in English and French* (London, 1802), plate 34.
21 Morier John Philip, *Memoir of a Campaign with the Ottoman Army in Egypt, from February to July 1800: Containing a Description of the Turkish Army, the Journal of Its March from Syria to Egypt, General Observations on the Arabs, and on the Treaty of El-Arish, with an Account of the Event which Followed it.* (London, 1801), p.10.
22 McLean, Thomas, *The Military Costume of Turkey, Illustrated by A Series of Engravings. From Drawings made on the Spot* (London, 1818), p.78.
23 Wittman, William, *Travels in Turkey, Asia-Minor, Syria, and Across the Desert Into Egypt During the Years 1799, 1800, and 1801, in Company with the Turkish Army, and the British Military Mission: To which are Annexed, Observations on the Plague and on the Diseases Prevalent in Turkey, and a Meteorological Journal.* (London, 1803), p.236.
24 Morier, *Memoir of a Campaign with the Ottoman Army*, p.11.

> Besides a musket, they carry a pair of pistols and a large knife, which are fastened to their waist by a sash.[25]

The use of such a large individual armament puzzles the Prussian General Georg Wilhelm von Valentini, who specifically remarks on the encumbering clothing of the Ottoman soldiers:

> It may be easily conceived that his number of weapons, his long and loose garments, and more particularly his enormously wide breeches which the janissary is obliged to hold when running, render him incapable of making any rapid movement.[26]

Encumbering clothing and equipment was also a feature of the cavalry. On parade *sipahi ulufeli*s still wore a rich and elaborate dress, including shield, armour and chainmail; their horses had saddle blankets and accessories always of exquisite workmanship. Similarly the Mamluk chiefs, who went into parade and battle with items dating back at least two centuries. This was also a common trend among the Eastern Anatolian cavalry, and also some Georgian or Circassian chiefs wore chainmail and defensive pieces such as breastplate and gauntlets.

Wittman describes Grand Vizier Yusuf Ziya Paşa's retinue at the battle of Heliopolis:

> Some of them were enveloped in curious network coats of mail of steel ... Others again were clad in party coloured dresses. While a part of them were armed with spears, or lances, from twelve to fourteen feet in length, others carried short, twisted, rifle-barrel guns, the rest muskets, carbines ... The whole of them wore swords and pistols in sashes fastened round their waist.[27]

Ordinary cavalrymen followed the usual trend of the infantry, and therefore wore more practical clothing, but retained the typical large weaponry. Coeval descriptions of *deli* light horsemen include weapons like sabre, lance, carbine, and pistols. As for the dress, Morier states that the *deli* wore the same clothing as the Ottoman cavalry, and were distinguished only by a hollow cap of sheepskin, made in the form of a cylinder and tied about the head with a handkerchief.[28]

On campaign, *kapıkulu* cavalry and infantry were provided with woollen coats to defend themselves from the cold. These overcoats were of various colours, almost always provided with pointed caps. The cloaks of the cavalry reached a considerable width, and usually also covered the horse; the cloaks of the foot troops reached below the knee; the soldiers also used them as blankets for the night. Cloaks and overcoats were also common among the

---

25 Morier, *Memoir of a Campaign with the Ottoman Army*, p.10.
26 Valentini, *Précis des dernières guerres des Russes contre les Turcs*.
27 Wittman, *Travels to Turkey*, p.266.
28 Morier, *Memoir of a Campaign with the Ottoman Army*, p.16.

DRESS, EQUIPMENT AND ENSIGNS

Balkan and Anatolian irregulars, who used local patterns. Balkan cloaks were long below the knees and tailored in several layers to make them waterproof. They were given various names: *kaban*, *kaput* or *kabanica*, but always provided with a hood and complete with long sleeves to protect the arms in the cold season. To allow greater freedom of movement, under the armpits were openings from which the arms came out, with an aesthetic result similar to the courtly Ottoman *kaftans*. At other times the soldier covered himself with a simple cloak, or with a fleece of mutton or lamb's wool.

Alongside the *kaftan*, used also as overcoat, Bosnian irregulars wore the *koret*, the typical short Balkan jacket. It had a single breast and was closed by an 'olive' button inside a loop of cord; but the most important element of male dress was the *jacerma*, the richly decorated doublet, piped with silver cord, or with applications in metal, the so-called *kov* and *tucle*, which resembled a breastplate. Similar items were also common in Serbia and Macedonia. In turn, the Bosnian *koret* was not very different from the Albanian *xhamadan*. This was a traditional short jacket still worn as traditional Albanian costume

Henry Alken (1785–1851) had probably never seen a Mamluk, yet this did not matter to his customers. What they wanted was an attractive illustration of renowned horsemen and their noble animals. However, Alken offers an accurate pictures of the low-rank Egyptian horsemen on campaign, particularly the horse's equipment.

THE OTTOMAN ARMY OF THE NAPOLEONIC WARS 1789–1815

A Mamluk chief in full armour, by Georg Moritz Ebers (1837–1898). A Romantic image of the full armour of the Mamluk elite, which was mainly for parade purposes. This attire was common for the Eastern Anatolian cavalry too, and also some Georgian or Circassian commanders wore chainmail and defensive weapon like shield, breastplate and gauntlets.

DRESS, EQUIPMENT AND ENSIGNS

Plate illustrating the drill of the *nizâm-ı cedîd* infantry, after Rayf Mahmoud Efendi, Tableau des Nouveaux Reglemens de l'Empire Ottoman (Constantinople, 1798). Note the first line depicting officers: from right: 1. *bimbaşi*, colonel; 2. *Lieutenant Colonel*; 3. *Adjudant Major*; 4. *Capitaine*; 5. *Lieutenant*; 6. *Sous Lieutenant*; 7. *Porte Drapeau*; 8. *Sergent Major*. The number of buttons qualifying the ranks from Sergeant Major to Lieutenant Colonel.

in modern-day Albania, as well as in Kosovo, North Macedonia, Serbia and Montenegro. Scholars state that here are more than 200 different kinds of clothing in all Albania and the Albanian inhabited regions. The *xhamadan* was shorter compared to the Bosnian jacket, but could carry the same elaborated decoration on the breast. Another difference between *koret* and *xhamadan* was the occasional presence in the latter of long open sleeves.

The attire of the Albanian irregulars must have appeared to Europeans as a mixture of the barbaric and the exotic, but definitively it aroused a unanimous impression of magnificence. All this is evident when Morier describes the war dress of the Albanian irregulars he saw in Egypt:

> They wear a breastplate of silver, and a species of armour covers their legs; many of them walk in sandals; the fore part of the head, as far as the middle of the crown, is shaved, and only a tuft of hair hangs loose on the back part of the head; a red scull cup of cloth comes far over their eyebrows, and gives them a very fierce look. Their fire-arms are in general beautifully ornamented in silver and gold; their muskets are light and are made like a tomahawk at the but-end. I imagine to be used in self-defence in cases of necessity.[29]

The area of origin of the Balkan warriors could be identified also by their footwear. Usually, the populations of the plains or the coast had

---

29 Morier, *Memoir of a Campaign with the Ottoman Army*, p.13.

opanke or *bivce*, consisting of a linen sock collected in a sole of bound skin with strings over the foot, and then passed around the ankle. Volunteers from the mountains also wore woollen gaiters, usually in dark brown or black, high to mid calf, or below the knee. The gaiters were decorated with coloured cord, small pieces of glass or metal buckles; the season determined their thickness. The sole was attached to the foot as in the *opanke*, but the name of the footwear *tozluci* or *terluci*, reveals its Illyrian–Albanian origin. Albanian irregulars also wore gaiters of bright colours with elaborated embroidery, laces and accessories, and these were widespread also among the population coming from the coast.

The Uniforms of the *Nizâm-ı Cedîd*

By the late 1790s evidence of Western influence in military dress exponentially increased with the policy of reforms introduced by Sultan Selim III. Although the essential traditional pattern would still be maintained, this trend would have a marked effect on Ottoman military dress, The introduction of Western features and style influenced the dress established for the *nizâm-ı cedîd*'s troops. These were the first actual Ottoman uniforms, since they established a common dress and equipment for all the soldiers, and specific distinctions in order to identify specialties and ranks within the corps.

The uniform established for the first regiment was a mixture of Ottoman and European, more precisely French, military clothing. A description dating back to the early 1800s states that it consisted of a tight-fitting single-breasted red jacket; trousers of blue or grey cloth wide at the thigh and close to the ankle; a blue cloak; and a red headdress like that of the *bostanci* seraglio's corps.[30]

Weapons and equipment, which had to conform to those of the other Ottoman military corps, were instead of French manufacture, such as the musket with bayonet, the ammunition pouches and sabre-briquet.

It is said that the bonnet of the *bostancis* was the characteristic headdress of the *nizâm-ı cedîd*'s uniform, as it served to confuse the new troops with the gardeners of the seraglio so as not to provoke the reaction of the janissaries. In this regard, Mouradgea d'Ohsson provides some information about the uniform of the *süratçi* light artillery, which also included the red bonnet of the *bostanci*.[31]

There are many coeval prints relating the uniform of the *nizâm-ı cedîd* soldiers but just a few are actually Ottoman sources, which have been both neglected in modern reconstructions. One of the most accurate images is without doubt the table depicting the drill in the *Tableau des Nouveaux Reglemens de l'Empire Ottoman*, by Mahmoud Rayf Efendi, printed in 1798. The description is perfectly coherent with the image, but the plate also shows some officers, including an ensign. They are wearing a large *dolama kaftan* over a short jacket similar to the one issued to the common soldiers, but with laces

---

30 Jucherau de Saint-Denis, Antoine, Baron de, *Histoire de l'Empire Ottoman depuis 1792 jusqu'en 1844* (Paris, 1844), vol. II, p.113.

31 Mouradgea d'Ohsson, *Tableau Général de l'Émpire Othoman*, p.371.

DRESS, EQUIPMENT AND ENSIGNS

Right: Officer, *sous lieutenant* of the *nizâm-ı cedîd* infantry, first regiment, after Mouradgea d'Ohsson, *Tableau Général de l'Émpire Othoman* (Paris, 1824)

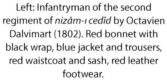

Below: Infantrymen of the first regiment of the *nizâm-ı cedîd* army, from the *Fenerci Albümü* (early 1800).

Left: Infantryman of the second regiment of *nizâm-ı cedîd* by Octavien Dalvimart (1802). Red bonnet with black wrap, blue jacket and trousers, red waistcoat and sash, red leather footwear.

341

THE OTTOMAN ARMY OF THE NAPOLEONIC WARS 1789–1815

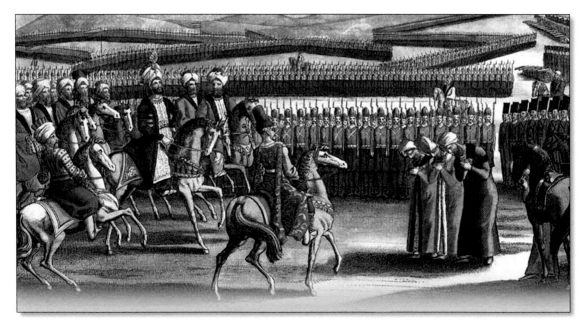

Above: Sultan Selim III inspecting the *nizâm-ı cedîd* infantry and artillery, in an early 1800 French print. Note the artillerymen on the right wearing blue coats and tall black headdress, while the infantry is wearing red and blue.

Right: Officer of the *nizâm-ı cedîd* (New Order Army). The original illustration appears to display on the hat some kind of decoration. A modern reconstruction of this illustration shows an elaborate floral gold badge on the front of the hat. More likely this was written text on the *ferahi* as usually worn on the headdress.

DRESS, EQUIPMENT AND ENSIGNS

on breast like the lanyards in Hungarian style. Large round buttons are visible on both sides of the long coat, from one to five, according to the rank. Another figure on the extreme right wears the same *dolama kaftan* but with laces like the ones on the short jacket; loose *şalvar* trousers, and a waist sash, identifying him as a *colonel*. Unfortunately, the source does not supply information about the colours.

Another very interesting image concerning the New Model Army uniform is the one from the *Fenerci Mehmed Albümü*. Here, a common *nefer* infantryman wears a red short jacket carrying six black cords and 'olives' buttons on both sides. The jacket is trimmed in black along the sleeves and the edges until the collar. A large black *kusak* sash with yellow piping hold the bandolier, which here is of black leather, while the coeval European iconography shows the same of white painted leather. French and later also British equipment was delivered to the *nizâm-ı cedîd* corps, including weapons.[32] Although footwear had to follow the Ottoman sumptuary code, this soldier has tight black leather boots in Hungarian style.

The first regiment, also known as *Levend Çiftlik*, where it had its quarters, is the unit of the *nizâm-ı cedîd* which has the most detail, while uncertainty persists about the uniforms of the other units. Dalvimart depicts a soldier wearing a blue single-breasted short jacket, blue *şalvar* trousers, red slouch hat with black wraps and tassel, and red leather *yamine*. Equipment and weaponry are in perfectly European style. This is very probably the uniform issued to the second, or Üsküdar, regiment, but it is not confirmed by the Ottoman iconography. Some clues are provided by a French print approximately dated 1803. The scene depicts the sultan, who is inspecting his new model infantry and artillery. One infantry regiment is deployed in the background with the artillery on the right. The infantry seems to be the *Levend* regiment, despite the headdress that is a tall white turban. Behind them, another regiment could be the *Üsküdar* regiment, if the blue uniform is assumed to be real, since the first regiment is dressed with red jacket and dark grey trousers.

Further information about the *nizâm-ı cedîd* is provided by the Ottoman sources, which add several interesting details.[33] These are two figures from a pre-1809 collection depicting two soldiers with special characteristics. The first is probably a NCO wearing 'quarter dress' consisting of a short white single-breasted jacket and trousers, with a 'button' embroidered in red on both sides of the breast, while the second figure is a musketeer dressed with single-breasted green jacket and cap, dark grey *şalvar*, and black shoes. It is difficult to attribute this uniform, but it could be that worn by one of the regiments recruited in Anatolia, which arrived in Constantinople in the dramatic turmoil of 1807. A third figure from the same collection possibly depicts the uniform of the *nizâm-ı sekban* infantry raised in 1808 by Grand Vizier Alemdâr Mustafa Paşa.[34]

---

32 Dalvimart, *The Costume of Turkey*, plate 39.
33 Anonymous, *Les portraits des differens habillemens qui sont en usage à Constantinople et dans tout la Turquie*, figures 38 and 39.
34 Anonymous, *Les portraits des differens habillemens*, figure 90.

Weapons

For the Ottoman Turks the weapons embodied a cultural meaning inherited from the nomad warriors of the Central Asia. The high spiritual significance of the weapons was reflected in the great quantity of mottoes and proverbs in which sabres and daggers took on ethical and religious meanings. The same blades or the plates of the armour, and even the rings of the iron ribs, were engraved with words or lines from the Koran. The major arms production centres in Ottoman Europe were in Edirne and Constantinople, where the famous arsenal of St Irene was operating from the end of the fifteenth century. In Asi, there were important centres in Smyrna, Baghdad, Damascus and Yerevan. All these arsenals produced firearms, as well as armour and blades.

The very symbol of the Ottoman world, the sabre, or more precisely the curved blade sword, was the noble weapon par excellence. Among the Mamluks, despite the fact that they were armed with six firearms: a rifle, a blunderbuss and two pairs of pistols, the sabre remained the most prestigious weapon. Even the firearm seems to be an extension of the sword because, as remarked by William Wittman, the Mamluks do not reload their weapons after firing, and a servant who follows them into battle provides for this task.[35]

In the Turkish language it is called *kiliç* and indicates not only the curved sabres, but also all the weapons with the characteristic curvature because *kiliç* simply means 'sword'. With the exception of the *sakkas* and *acemi-oglanis*, sabres were part of the equipment of all *kapıkulu* soldiers and Ottoman troops, both on foot and on horseback. The maximum size of the blades could reach up to a metre, but generally the smaller ones were preferred, lighter and more manageable.

The superb blades of the most admirable Damascus steel or those with showy decorations on precious metal were naturally the prerogative of the senior commanders, but also sabres of natural metal were conspicuously decorated with calligrams and ornamental figurations gathered in medallions, the *higab*, endowed with talismanic meanings. Among the recurring motifs, a prominent place belonged to the name of God, 'Allah', as well as the typical crescent, or the six-pointed star, the so-called *khateh Süleyman*, the seal of Solomon. The hilt was made of horn, wood, or bone; sometimes there were ivory or velvet covered hilts with encrustations of turquoise and coral in the richer models. The shape of the hilt establishes the age and place of production of the sabres. The hilt had a cross shape with straight uprights and an oval or pointed end, and extended symmetrically along the direction of the blade and ended with a more or less pronounced rounding. Appearing as early as the late sixteenth century, the *karabela* hilt would have given its name to a new type of sabre with a less curved blade compared to the *kiliç*, and in the eighteenth century became the typical *kapıkulu* infantry side weapon.

Another type of sabre, with a straighter and broader blade, made its appearance in Anatolia, spreading throughout the Empire and becoming

---

35 Wittman, *Travels to Turkey*, p.236.

DRESS, EQUIPMENT AND ENSIGNS

Left: Late eighteenth century Ottoman *qiliç* manufactured of steel, silver, wood, rubies, almandine, spinel, nephrite and turquoise. It belonged to a senior officer. Blade length 80 cm, overall length 92 cm. (Hermitage Museum, St Petersburg)

Below: Ottoman *pala*, with sword-knot, early 1800s. Blade length 72.5 cm, overall length 85.5 cm. (Hermitage Museum, St Petersburg)

Ottoman *pala* and scabbard, early 1800s. Blade length 72.5 cm, overall length 85.5 cm. (Hermitage Museum, St Petersburg)

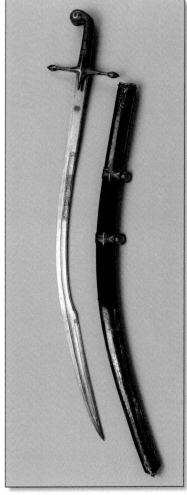

THE OTTOMAN ARMY OF THE NAPOLEONIC WARS 1789–1815

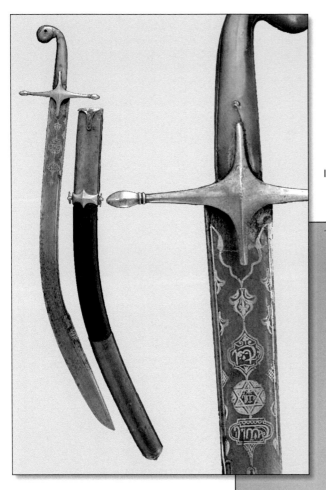

Left: Mamluk *pala*, wood, brass, iron, steel, leather, late eighteenth century. Blade length 73.2 cm, overall length 86.2 cm. (Private collection)

Right: Ottoman *qiliç* manufactured from steel, silver, copper, wood, leather, velvet, horn, metal thread blade. Late eighteenth century. Blade length 79.5 cm, overall length 93.7 cm. (Hermitage Museum, St Petersburg)

DRESS, EQUIPMENT AND ENSIGNS

Tatar or Ottoman sabre, manufactured in steel, wood and brass; scabbard of brown leather and iron fittings. Late eighteenth century. Blade length 81 cm, overall length 95.5 cm. (Private collection)

THE OTTOMAN ARMY OF THE NAPOLEONIC WARS 1789–1815

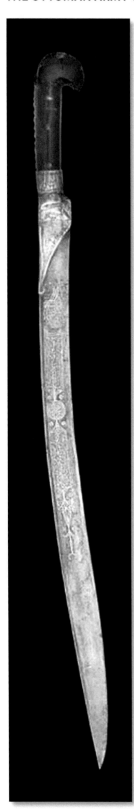

Far left: Balkan *yataghan* with scabbard, dating 1805–06; steel, silver, copper alloy, horn, wood. Blade length 68.5 cm, overall length 83.2 cm, scabbard length 73.5 cm. (Hermitage Museum, St Petersburg)

Left: Gold damascene *yataghan*, Ottoman signed manufactory (Husayn), dating 1813. Overall length 75.6 cm. (Private collection)

popular also in Europe, especially after the French campaign in Egypt. Its name was *pala*, recognisable for the very short blade and for the thickness of the counter-cutting edge. The section of the blade had the shape of a 'T' and in general the overall weight was higher than the other sabre. At the beginning of the eighteenth century the *pala* was used especially by the cavalry, much appreciated for its power and manageability. By the late seventeenth century *palas* with hilts ending with a more rounded end made their appearance. These models were the first types of pistol grip, a pattern destined to last for over two centuries and typical of the classic Ottoman and Mamluk sabres. These creations imitated the hilts of the Arab–Syrian sabre, particularly suitable for delivering the slash without running the risk of losing the weapon. In Egypt, sabres were already produced with very curved blades at the end of the seventeenth century, while in Syria the blades maintained a more upright shape.

The scabbards for all the sabres were made with two strips of wood covered with leather or velvet; metal reinforcements, and rings for the straps completed the whole. At other times the sheaths were entirely metal decorated with stones and other precious materials. Even on scabbards, the Ottoman artisans vented their passion for ornamentation. The most common motif was floral decorations, similar to the *Iznik* ceramics of the classical age. Often the upper end was flared outward to facilitate extraction of the weapon; another flare was used for housing the hilt.

Alongside the sabre, daggers and knives mainly equipped the janissaries and other infantrymen, who carried them alone or in pairs under their sashes. Among the most common knife, the *kancjar* was recognisable by the slightly curved cutting blade and a straight T-shaped hilt. Some models reached 60 cm in length, but usually the *kancjar* ranged between 35 and 45 cm, including the hilt. This knife was the most widespread throughout Anatolia and the Caucasus, where there was also another type of knife, with a straight and double-edged blade, called a *kincal*. It was not unusual to see both these weapons among the panoply of the Ottoman or Egyptian Mamluk infantrymen and horsemen. However, the most popular and widespread dagger was the *yataghan*. This weapon became the favourite dagger among the *kapıkulu*, especially within the janissaries. By the eighteenth century the *yataghan* was a large knife with a long, single-cutting S-shaped blade. The origin of the *yataghan* is probably to be found in the Balkans and more precisely in Albania, but in any case similar weapons already existed throughout the Mediterranean in ancient times. The blades always had a decoration that thickened the edge at the base of the blade, in order to strengthen the insertion point into the hilt. This latter constituted the sign of identification for the *yataghan* and was formed by a hilt without a guard terminating with two 'ears', or 'wings', with a typical rounded shape similar to a femoral head. The end of the scabbard carried a metal sphere or the stylised head of a monstrous animal. The length of a *yataghan* exceeded 55 cm, and some specimens even 70 cm. Several eyewitnesses recalled how the Albanian irregulars used a long *yataghan* instead of the sabre. Other war knives came from Arabia and among the most common was the *djambiya*, easily recognisable by the curved blade and the 'J'-shaped metal scabbard.

Ottoman *tüfenk*, mid eighteenth century. Manufactured of steel, copper, gilt copper, ivory, assorted gems, wood, mother-of-pearl. Length 154.3 cm, calibre 15.4 mm. Mark on the lock *Muhammad Ayyubi*. (Metropolitan Museum of Art, New York)

DRESS, EQUIPMENT AND ENSIGNS

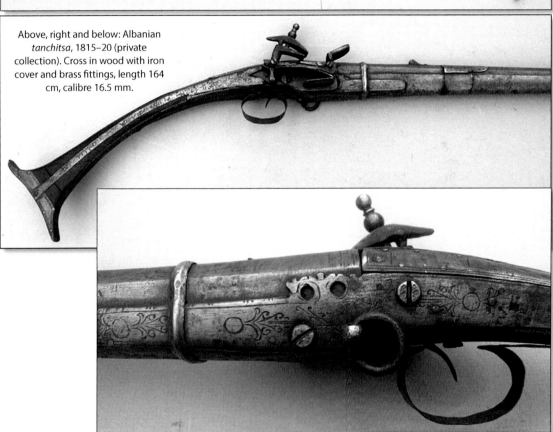

Above, right and below: Albanian *tanchitsa*, 1815–20 (private collection). Cross in wood with iron cover and brass fittings, length 164 cm, calibre 16.5 mm.

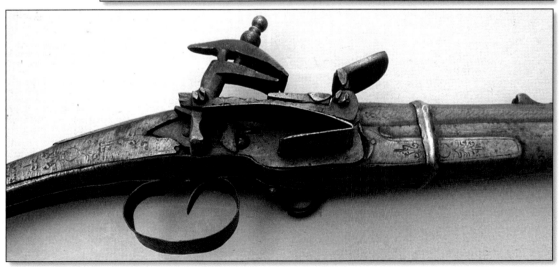

THE OTTOMAN ARMY OF THE NAPOLEONIC WARS 1789–1815

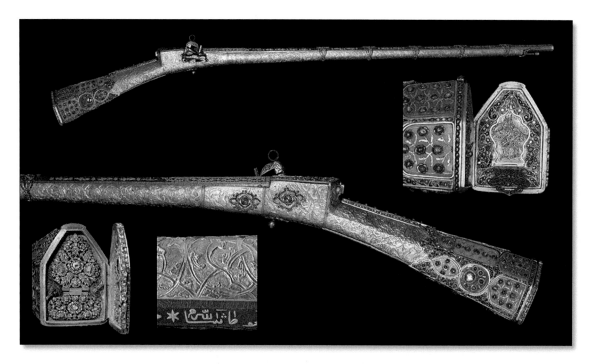

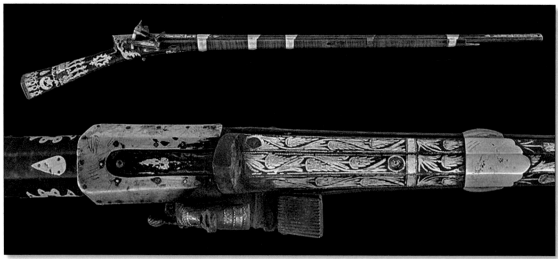

Ottoman *tüfenks*, (Askery Museum, Constantinople). Note the fully decorated metal cover of the first weapons. Length 138 and 140 cm, calibre 14.8 mm. These weapons were intended for the janissaries, and because of their aesthetic and artistic value they have been preserved, while ordinary *tüfenks* are very rare.

DRESS, EQUIPMENT AND ENSIGNS

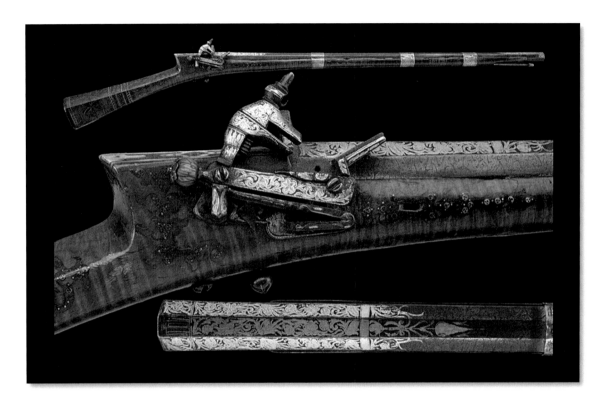

Above: Ottoman short *tüfenk*, early 1800s. A superb weapon manufactured in Constantinople or Smyrna, with octagonal, ribbed, damask barrel finely engraved and gilded at the ends with floral motifs, the base with a three-hole elevation, sights, engraved and gilded tang; beautiful michelet-style battery, decorated and adorned with a fluted coral sphere; wooden case with bone and brass inlays, partially decorated with green floral motifs; length 112 cm, calibre 12.5 mm. (Private collection)

Below: Balkan musket (Macedonia), late nineteenth century, manufactured of steel, silver, mother-of-pearl. Length 134.4 cm, calibre 17 mm. (Hermitage Museum, St Petersburg)

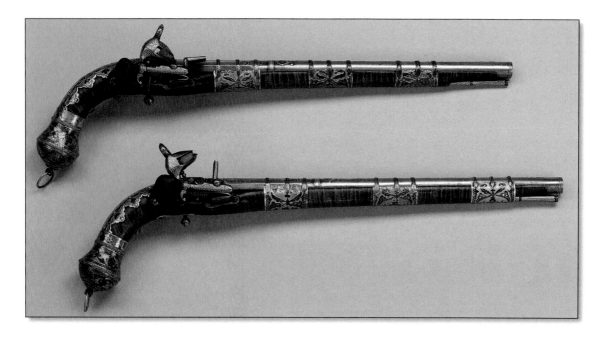

Above: Ottoman pistols, early nineteenth century. Manufactured of steel, brass and wood. Length 49 cm, calibre 14.2 mm. (Private collection)

Below: Ottoman or Balkan pistol, late eighteenth century, European lock and barrel (probably French). Manufactured of steel, silver, gold. Length 57.1 cm, calibre 16.5 mm. (Metropolitan Museum of Art, New York)

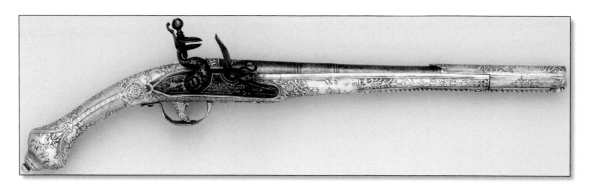

DRESS, EQUIPMENT AND ENSIGNS

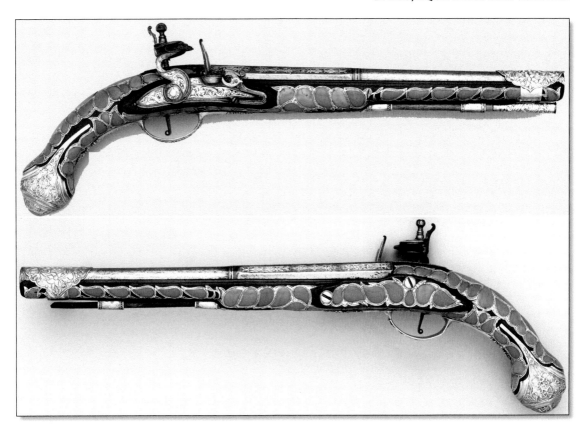

Above: Pair of Ottoman pistols, early 1800s. French lock and barrel. Manufactured of wood, steel, silver, corals, gold. Length 51 cm, calibre 16.5 mm. (Metropolitan Museum of Art, New York)

Below: Ottoman double-barrelled pistols with dagger, early 1800s. Length 51 cm, calibre 14 mm. (Hermitage Museum, St Petersburg

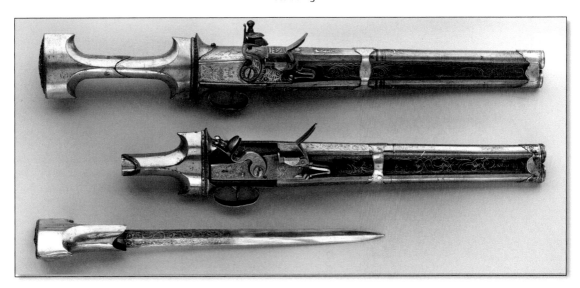

THE OTTOMAN ARMY OF THE NAPOLEONIC WARS 1789–1815

Saddle pistol holsters. Above: late eighteenth century. Length 42.7 cm. Green fabric with gold and silver embroideries, red leather and brass fittings. Right: Early 1800, leather embroidered with silver. Dimensions 41.3 × 12.5 cm. (Hermitage Museum, St Petersburg)

Below: Ammunition bag, late eighteenth century. Velvet, leather, silver, tin, braid and corals. Dimensions: 21.0 × 14.0 × 3.7 cm. (Hermitage Museum, St Petersburg)

DRESS, EQUIPMENT AND ENSIGNS

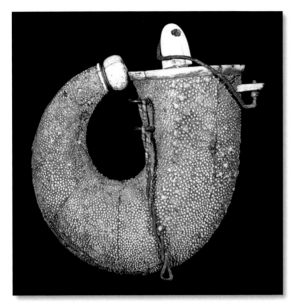

Left: Ottoman ivory powder flask with brass fitting, early 1800s. (Private collection)

Below: Eastern Anatolia or Iranian iron powder flask, 1790s. (Private collection)

Left: Mamluk steel powder flask, early 1800s. (Stibbert Museum, Florence)

THE OTTOMAN ARMY OF THE NAPOLEONIC WARS 1789–1815

Above: Brass powder flask, Syria or Iraq, early 1800s. (Private collection)

Right: Brass powder flask, Egypt or Syria, early 1800s. (Private collection)

DRESS, EQUIPMENT AND ENSIGNS

Above and right: The front and back of an Ottoman iron shield, early nineteenth century. (Private collection)

Below: Ottoman or Mamluk iron shield, early nineteenth century. (Private collection)

Along with daggers, the *kapıkulu* infantry and cavalry went into battle with one or two pistols under their waist sash or in a holster. Sometimes the cavalry also carried one or two pairs of pistols. Scholars outline that one of the symptoms of the Ottoman Empire's military crisis can be seen precisely in the immobility of their technology. The flintlock musket was introduced in the second half of the seventeenth century, but this kind of mechanism did not change and remained practically unmodified until the early nineteenth century. The Ottoman flintlock mechanism was very similar to the Catalan system; in the Western world it was identified as the Spanish *patilla* system. Ottoman firearms were altogether shorter than the Western European manufactures, but not much heavier; on average a *tüfek* reached 120–140 cm in length and weighed 4.5 to 6.5 kg. The calibre was heavier than Western ones, between 12 to 16 mm, and some weapons reached calibres of 18 mm. In siege warfare long muskets called *dahlian* were also used. Several muskets dating back to the late eighteenth centuries are preserved in the Askeri Museum in Constantinople and in the major collections of Ottoman trophies around the world, allowing scholars to examine the great variety of designs and decorative techniques. Most of the wood is painted in red, azure or black, but there are examples entirely covered with velvet, or with tortoiseshell tassels. Some muskets show all the wood painted in white, or more rarely in black; while turquoise, coral and mother-of-pearl are mixed in refined ornamental combinations. Even the metal parts show elaborate decorations, sometimes the firing mechanism, and almost always the fixing bands of the barrel, are in brass. Some muskets have the barrel in black polished metal and provided with decorations on gold or silver. A *tüfek* captured by Russians in 1797, now preserved in the Hermitage Museum of St Petersburg, is completely covered with gilded metal with blue and red stones, while the barrel is of Damascus steel. Not only the muskets issued to the *kapıkulu* infantry were the most lavish and most artistically ornamented, since the weapons of the Mamluks were also to be noticed for their beauty. One musket captured by French in Egypt and now preserved in the Musée de l'Armée in Paris has been manufactured of briarwood with decoration in metal and precious stones.

Since the previous century, a musket shaped with a characteristic stock had begun to spread. It was the *tancitsa*, the typical firearm of the Albanian *arnavuts*. A marked difference between the *tancitsa* and the Ottoman *tüfek* lay in the length. In fact the Balkan weapons could reach a total of 165 cm, the calibre rarely exceeded 14 mm and also the weight was much lower. These muskets were equipped with a mechanism identical to the Ottoman ones and were easily recognisable by the curved and very thin stock, ending in the shape of a fish tail. The parts in wood were often covered with iron, stones or silver, and abundantly decorated in the same style as the *yataghan* daggers. Similar in length, but with a different cross, the Bosnian weapons were equally decorated with metal.

The Balkan cavalry, and especially the Mamluk horsemen widely used the blunderbuss *tüfek*. This firearm was considered more effective than pistols, because the blunderbuss could shoot multiple projectiles, the horseman loaded it more easily, and not least the blunderbuss had a notable psychological effect on the enemy. Two basic blunderbuss models are known, both characterised by the shape of the barrel: one with a pentagonal section as for the *tufek*, and another type with a stock similar to the Balkan model; in both cases it was common to weight the wood with the insertion of metal elements according to the decorative style characteristic of the place of production. Small blunderbusses were used both in Asia and in Europe with the name 'blunderbuss-pistol', and measured no more than 60/70 cm; instead the classic Ottoman blunderbuss reached a metre in length and could be held up like a gun. The calibre was usually more than 15 mm.

The firing mechanisms mounted on these weapons were always the traditional Spanish *patilla* type, but starting from the eighteenth century French flintlock mechanism were imported, especially in Egypt and the Maghreb. However, as early as the mid seventeenth century, several Western European firing mechanisms began to be imported for completing the production of muskets in the Ottoman arsenals and this continued until the nineteenth century.

The large variety of calibres made it difficult to produce balls fit for all the *tufeks* issued to the *kapıkulu* soldiers, therefore the *cebeci* distributed to the soldiers a barrel of lead, with which the men themselves prepared the ammunition balls, cutting the barrel with an axe or a knife.

Ensigns

The ordinary ensigns of the Ottoman army can be divided into three categories based on the elements depicted on the field. The subdivision allows scholars to establish some rules to identify the hierarchy and the usage. The first category includes the *sancaks* bearing only inscriptions, usually of a religious nature and in Arabic. These were usually the large banners that signalled the commanders at the head of their contingents.

The text and words on the flag came mostly from the Koran; otherwise the artisans used the traditional hadiths, the mottoes of the Prophet, to formulate short slogans. The most important of the inscriptions was the *shahada*, the profession of faith of the Muslims. The inscriptional ensign could also carry short invocations or only the name of Allah, composed in elegant calligrams forming a medallion. The inscriptional style, clear and logical, came from the ancient insignia used by Islam, and for a certain period it remained simple and austere even in the Ottoman area; then, in the eighteenth century, it became more sophisticated. The writings were ever larger and more elaborate, forcing the artisans to set up a special compositional discipline. The inscriptions were applied on the *sancak* in different ways on the field and on the edges, collected in medallions or cartridges; on the verso they were repeated inverted to respect the symmetry of the decoration. Regarding their size, the variety is even bigger. There are generally flags of considerable size, such as *sancaks* of 470 cm in length and 270 cm in height; in most cases their shape is trapezoidal. Because of their large size they were hoisted to a pole planted in the ground in the centre of the encampment, or on the tower of a fortress.

THE OTTOMAN ARMY OF THE NAPOLEONIC WARS 1789–1815

Right: Mamluk standard bearer – *tugh* – by Carle Vernet (author's archive). The *tugh* was the most important Ottoman ensign, which identified the rank of the owner. According to William Wittman, the grand vizier had an ensign as commander-in-chief, the *serasker* with the rank of a *paşa* had three horsetails; the *çarcaci başi*, and the janissary *ağasi*, two horsetails; the *cebeci başi*, one horsetail.

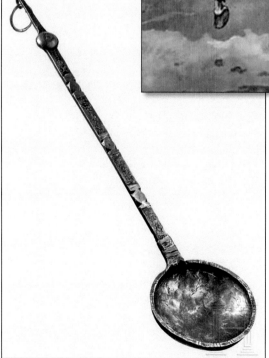

Left: The preservation of *kazan* and spoon (left) was a point of honour and the loss a real misfortune. If this happened as a result of a battle, the soldiers to whom it had been entrusted were not allowed back into the *orta*, and the whole unit suffered permanent humiliation.'

The ensigns depicting figurative elements constitute the second category of *sancak*; those formed simultaneously by inscriptions and symbols belong to the third and last category. The most famous of the astral symbols, destined to become the Ottoman heraldic symbol par excellence in the nineteenth century, was undoubtedly the crescent, or half-moon. The crescents depicted on the Ottoman flags are of two types. The first is very similar to a new moon in the first quarter, and is then called 'open crescent'; the other appears as the eccentric conjunction of two circles, in which the smaller one touches the circumference of the larger, and in this case it takes the denomination 'closed crescent'. The latter type is the most common, in the form associated with one or more stars, and abounds on the Ottoman flags until the twentieth century. Even the star, together with the crescent or alone, appears in a great variety of forms. When it was formed by the crossing of two equilateral triangles, it was known as 'the seal of Solomon' and identified the concept of royalty. In another case the star presented eight tips, the result of the conjunction of two squares, but these were rarer. The last astral symbol used on the Ottoman *sancaks* was the *czintamani*, consisting of three diskettes similar to three closed crescents, arranged in a triangle with the tip pointing upwards. No explanation of its meaning has yet been identified; according to some theories, it would imitate the leopard's fur, while other scholars identify the Central Asian shamanic signs symbolising the domination on the three elements of the world: earth, air and water. The use of astral symbols on flags would seem to follow hierarchical rules. In general these images appear on the *sancaks* issued to the single units, such as the janissary *ortas*, but in some cases, above all the crescent, they are formed by inscriptions, or enclose the calligrams on the large banners of the *paşas*. A figurative symbol largely adopted in the army's flag was the double-bladed sword, the *dhu al-fiqar* (Zulfiqar/Zulfikar), commonly known as 'the sword of the Prophet' or also 'the sword of the janissaries'. The representative style followed two main trends: a traditional one, with a straight bifid blade; the other depicted the Zulfikar with curved blades like a sabre. Often the final knob had the appearance of a dragon's head or the shape of a crescent; at other times the hilt ended in a snake's head. Each janissary *orta* carried its *sancak* in battle, while the tents were decorated with different symbols and colours to identify the unit. Some drawings are extremely realistic and natural, contravening the strict rules on Islamic figurative art, and allow the easy recognition of the *orta* to which they belong. Some symbols allude explicitly to the unit when it represents the original task or qualification assumed. Therefore, the dog is the symbol of *orta* 71, *samsoncu*, and the dromedary identifies *Orta* 1, the *deveci*, originally tasked with escorting the army baggage. The same symbols were tattooed on the hand or on the forearm of the soldiers; instead, on the flags, appeared more easily the crescent, the Zulfikar, or combinations of two or three colours arranged in various patterns. The janissary corps had a further and singular symbol that distinguished them, the *kazan*, the cauldron that was carried on parade in all ceremonies and preceded by the *aşçi* of the *orta*.

Each army detachment and each unit received its own *sancak*, while the smaller units received small-sized banners, the *bayrak*, closely related to the tactical division of the military corps. The *paşa* and *sancakbeg* each had their own banners, with which they led their contingents; other flags belonged to the janissaries' *orta*, the artillerymen and the *sipahis* of the *kapıkulu*. These latter carried yellow, red, white, green, white and green, white and red standards depending the unit that formed the corps.

Mouradgea d'Ohsson gives a summary description of the great janissary flag in the 1780s. This *bairak* was designated *Imam-Azam* in honour of the illustrious doctor of Islamism, and consisted in a white silk banner with text after of sura 61, *surat as-saff* (the Battle), verse 13: *nasrun min Allahi wafathun qarihun wabashshiri lmu'mini* (the help of God and an easy victory proclaims glad news for the faith), embroidered with golden wires. In turn, Wittman states that the white field was also the ensign of the grand vizier,[36] According to Cévad Beg, the janissary banner bore as its main symbol the prophet's sword, the Zulfikar.[37]

Valentini remarks on the extensive use of flag, standards and coloured flames, the latter on the cavalry lances, bearing various symbols, like crescent, a hand coloured with blood or a sabre.[38] With him, Wittman describes the use of ensigns in the Ottoman army in Egypt:

> Each of the Pachas has his respective standard, which is very large; and the devices, or religious professors, by whom the Turkish army is accompanied, have also their sacred banners, the colour of which is usually green. In addition to this, each of the small companies, consisting of from twenty-five to thirty privates, belonging to the corps of infantry, carries a small flag or banderole. Among the Arnauts these little flags are still numerous. The necessary influence to be drawn from the employment of such a multiplicity of standards, banners and flags is, that those who have the charge of them must not only diminish in a considerable degree, in the field of battle, the effective force which would otherwise have been brought into action, but even shackle and impede the military operation.[39]

The variety of colours and shape of the Ottoman flags had as a counterpoint the substantial uniformity of the most typical ensign, the *tugh*, also known in the West as a 'horsetail'. The classic *tugh* consists of two parts. The larger upper part is a long wooden pole with a gilded metal ball on the top, three or four circular brush-like layers of horsetail beneath, and four or six falling braids; the baluster-shaped stem is covered with intricate and colourful horsehair plaitwork, while in the middle there is a loosely falling black, white, red or green horsetail. The stem is in the lower part. It is covered with the

---

36 Wittman, *Travels to Turkey*, p.250: 'The vizier's tent was known exteriorly by two gilt balls placed on the extremities of the tent poles; and near to its was displayed a large white flag, having on it an inscription in Arabic characters '.
37 Cévad Beg, *Etat Militaire Ottoman*, p.183.
38 Valentini, *Précis des dernières guerres des Russes contre les Turcs*, p.33.
39 Wittman, *Travels to Turkey*, pp.231–232: 'How mistaken therefore is the calculation that, independently of the ideas of grandeur and magnificence which the Turks attach to these trivial objects, they have the effect of inspiring the enemy with terror and dismay?'

same plaitwork, is hollow and reinforced at the bottom with a metal band. Altogether the tugh could measure between 200 and 350 cm. In the *tughs* still existing, the metallic globe is never perfectly spherical, its shape being oval, slightly flattened at the top, or onion-like. Like flags and standards, the *tughs* were also assigned to the various military units. Each janissary *orta*, as well as *cebeci* and the two divisions of the *ulufely sipahis* received one *tugh* and during the march they carried it at the head of the column. More than the *sancak*, the *tugh* served to establish the rank of the owner. The *ulufely sipahis* marched with seven *tughs* when the sultan was present and five if the command of the army belonged to the grand vizier. Their *tughs* were the highest flags, and in the encampment they were planted in the ground in front of the commander's tent. Four *tughs* signalled the presence of a vizier, three for or *paşa* and only one for the *sancakbeg*. The *tugh* was the actual war ensign of the Ottoman army and therefore used across the Empire. The Egyptian Mamluk *begs* carried *tughs* like the Ottoman ones, as did the Tatars. The princes of the vassal states, such as Wallachia and Moldavia, also had their own *tughs* when they joined the Ottoman army on campaign.

Appendix

Grand Viziers (1789–1815)

1786–1789	Koca Yusuf Paşa
1789	Cenaze Hasan Paşa
1789–1790	Cezayrli Gazi Hasan Paşa
1790–1791	Rüsçüklu Şerif Hasan Paşa
1791–1792	Koca Yusuf Paşa (second term)
1792–1794	Damad Melek Mehmed Paşa
1794–1798	Zağferanbolulu İzzet Mehmed Paşa
1798–1805	Kör Yusuf Ziya Paşa
1805–1806	Hafız İsmail Paşa
1806–1807	Keçibynuzu Ibrahim Hilmi Paşa
1807–1808	Çelebi Mustafa Paşa
1808	Alemdâr Mustafa Paşa
1808–1809	Çavuşbaşi Arnavut Memiş Paşa
1809–1811	Kör Yusuf Ziya Paşa (second term)
1811–1812	Laz Ahmed Paşa
1812–1815	Hurşid Ahmed Paşa
1815–1818	Mehmed Emin Rauf Paşa

Tableau Général – Janissary Garrisons (1750)

Garrison	Janissaries
Widdin:	5,440
Belgrade:	5,039
Shabaiz:	307
Baghdad:	4,914
Bassorah:	319
Kouran:	203
Choezni:	2,134
Benedr:	4,134
Ibraila:	1,512
Salonique:	1,289

Garrison	Janissaries
Nisch:	1,180
Nikopol:	980
Fekké:	174
Kilhouroun:	175
Oczakow:	1,551
Ada Kalessi	99
Bosna:	961
Antivari:	133
Zwornik:	244
Giurgiu:	739
Methoni:	655
Coron:	275
Chorinte:	482
Castel de Chorinthe:	103
Lamin:	311
St. Maure:	882
Castel de St. Maure:	173
Bénefsché:	244
Ténedos:	333
La Canea:	945
Metelin:	937
Chio:	994
Methymne:	201
Negroponte:	994
Candie:	1,553
Damascus:	722
Tarabulus:	167
Jerusalem:	259
Jaffa:	810
Temrek:	108
Taman:	803
Ori in Mingrelia:	446
Acho:	127
Rubate:	496
Sougoudjik:	158
Trebisonda:	131
Erzindjan:	182
Amasra:	122

Garrison	Janissaries
Bagdadtjik:	110
Akhatzik:	510
Chehriban:	113
Orpha:	91
Kutais:	178
Hassan-Kale:	170
Unieh:	178
Kerassunde:	146
Batoum:	375
(undefined)	102
Soskhat:	123
Erzeroum:	668
Kars:	2,143
Van:	1,379
Fach:	588
Dessoum:	895
Gelibolu	150 (*acemi oglanlar*)
Lemnos:	253
Akinti-Bournou:	685
Bagdad:	….
Constantinople:	….

Source: Kabaağaçlızade Ahmed Cévad Beg, *Etat Militaire Ottoman, depuis la fondation de l'Empire Ottoman jusqu'à nos jours* (Constantinople, 1882), vol. I, pp. 167–168.

Glossary

acemioğlan	novice soldier
akçe	silver coin; *asper*
alay	large tactical corps
alemdâr, bayraktar	standard bearer
arabacı	waggoneer
askeri	tax-exempt military class; military
avariz-i divaniye	extraordinary taxes
ayan	provincial magnate, notable, warlord; Ottoman provincial officials
azab	infantryman; local infantry
binbaşıi	colonel
bölük	company
bostancı	gardener-palace guard
boyar	landowner; notable, ruler in Wallachia, Moldavia
cebeci	armourer
dayı	renegade janissaries of the Serbian garrisons
defterdar	chief accountant
deli	irregular light horsemen
derebey	provincial notable; warlord; also *ayan*
devşirme	levy of Balkan Christians
divan	council of state
enderun	sultan's private apartments in palace
esame	muster roll; but also Janissary pay and ration ticket
fellahin	Egyptian peasants
firman	Sultan's edict
gazi	warrior for the faith
gönüllü	volunteer, irregular light cavalry
hayduk	mercenary, marauder, brigand, thief, highwayman, (Serbian) freedom fighter
humbarac	bombardier; mortar corpsman
iltizam	tax-farming, awarded by auction

kadi	judge
kadiasker	chief military judge
kantar	unit of measure = 56.449 kilograms
kapıcıbaşı	chief gatekeeper of the palace
kapudan paşa	chief admiral
kaymakam	substitute official, commander-in-chief
kethüda kahya	deputy, substitute, grand vizier's second-in-command, steward
kleft, klepht	Greek bandit
kuruş	unit of money, silver coin equal to 120 *akçes*; piaster
lağımcı	sapper
levend	irregular mercenary
miri levend	state-funded mercenaries
muhassil	senior public official in charge with tax collection in a province's district
müstahfız	local fortress guard
nazır	supervisor
obor-knez	(Serbian) title of an elected local native Serbian chiefs, especially in the *paşalik* of Belgrade
ocak regiment	the janissary corps
ocaklık	group of tax farms supporting janissaries
okka	unit of weight = 1.282945 kg
orta	janissary battalion
palanka	wooden fort; small outposts on frontier
panduk	Bosnian irregular of foot
reaya	peasants
sancak	district, standard
sekban	category of janissary corps; mercenary
serasker	commander; regional commanders
serdengeçdi	janissary volunteer for shock troops
silihdar	Sultan's esquire; sword-bearer
süratçi	rapid-fire artillery
timar	land grant, fief
vali	governor of province
vilayet	province
topraklı	provincial cavalry forces, timariot
yamak	A janissary who did not perform an active role, so was without pay when not engaged. He benefited from full tax exemption like the janissaries, and could exercise a trade while waiting for an employment in the corps when a place became available.

Colour Plate Commentaries

Plate A

1 – Janissary *çorbaci* (1790–98)
This figure is portrayed in an Ottoman costume album dated in the 1790s, and wears the dress of the janissary's senior officers for ceremonial duties and parade in the last quarter of the eighteenth century. The large *divoan-kürkü kaftan* with long false sleeves on the back, and sable fur lining, worn over an azure *entari* waistcoat, was originally an exclusive of the higher dignitaries, but later was gradually adopted by the officers of the *kapıkulu*: an allusion to their growing influence in affairs of state. This aulic *kaftan* characterised the clothing of Ottoman court staff, marking the age of the Imperial style begun under Süleyman the Magnificent. The headdress in the shape of a heron, the *kalafat*, was the main distinctive of the *orta*'s commanders and comprised a huge ostrich plume – the *süpürge sorguçlu* – with a smaller black feather aigrette inside a golden holder. Gigantism and exaggerated use of accessories for the clothing of the *kapıkulu*'s members appeared as early as the beginning of the eighteenth century. Curiously, this trend seems to indicate how janissary clothing became more elaborate as the fighting capability of the corps declined.

Source: *Costumes Turcs* (1790s) vol. I, Folio 85: *Çorbacı*; Diez Collection, Library of the British Museum.

2 – *Sipahi ulufely* in full armour, late eighteenth century
During the eighteenth century the *sipahi ulufely* had become more a palace corps than a fighting force, but despite the loss of military prestige it retained an important position in the *kapıkulu*, and its members benefited from privileges and rewards deriving from the proximity to the sultan. This *sipahi* appears in a painting attributed to Konstantin Kapidağli, dating to the last years of the eighteenth century. The gilded mail shirt and round shield belong to the parade dress, but the musket and other items are coherent with the war equipment of the Ottoman cavalry in this period. Originally the units composing the *kapıkulu* cavalry were identified by their standards rather than their dress. These *sancaks* were in yellow, red, white and green. The first two belonged to the two wings into which the corps was subdivided, while the others identified the two subdivisions of the left wing. Other authors report different information about the *sancaks* carried by the *sipahi*, and describe

six 'banners', of which the first four were identical to the aforementioned *sancaks*, plus one with white and green bands and another in white and red.

3 – *Hasseki agasy*, 1790–1810

The 300 selected *bostancis* served inside the Seraglio to attend the Sultan personally, and whenever he went out 60 of them, known as *hassekilar*, accompanied him as bodyguards. Amidst the great variety of dress in use in the Ottoman court, the one issued to the *hasseki* is the most homogeneous. All contemporary iconographic sources show the *hassekis* wearing large kaftan of brocaded or other decorated fabric, usually of red, which also was the distinctive colour of the *bostanci* corps. The large red floppy hat was another distinctive item of both *bostanci* and *hasseki*, and later became the headdress of the 'New Order' Army's soldiers since the raising of the first infantry regiment.

Source: *Hasseky-agassy, ou lieutenant du bostanji bachi*, in Grigoriy Sharopenko's *Album of Turkish Costumes* (1867), Collection of the New York Public Library.

Plate B

1 – Janissary *kara koullaçi*, 1807

It is unclear to what extent the janissaries retained any sort of uniform in the early nineteenth century, since the contemporary iconography shows them wearing a great variety of clothing. This NCO (the assistant of the *asçi* senior cook), wears a classic *dolama kaftan* under a short *hirka* jacket trimmed with fur. Apparently this janissary is wearing a kind of city dress, as can be deduced from his largely informal appearance. The broad turban also appears to have been typical of the Janissaries of Constantinople in this period, but the colour pink is uncommon and probably served to mark the soldier's rank.

Source: *Fenerci Mehmed Albümü* (1800–1825)

2 – Janissary on campaign, 1790–1800

Although the Janissaries' dress was influenced by the province where they served, many commentators report that *kapıkulu*'s soldiers were generally recognisable by the better quality of their clothing and equipment. The source from which this janissary comes qualifies him as a *serdengeçdi*, namely a member of the parties who performed the assaults. However, nothing differentiates him from the common janissaries on campaign, perhaps apart from the black turban. He wears a *yelek* doublet over a short *mintan* jacket, and loose *salvar* trousers. These latter, usually in turquoise, blue or azure, are typical of the janissaries' campaign dress.

Source : 'Serdenguesti, soldat Janissaire en tenue de combat', in Joseph Gabriel Monnier, *Recueil de costumes et vêtements de l'Empire ottoman au 18ᵉ siècle* (1786), Manuscript 65, figure N. 104; City Library of Bourg en Bresse (France).

3 – Janissary junior officer, *cavuş*, **1800–1802**

Janissary parade dress was largely abandoned on campaign in favour of more practical items. This was perhaps only to be expected; but surprisingly, officers maintained a more formal clothing, including the large *dolama kaftan* with long tails instead of the short coats or jackets. This typical coat had fixed its pattern in the sixteenth century, and apart for minor changes it was manufactured for almost three centuries following the sumptuary rules prescribed for Ottoman society. However, the cut was entirely conventional since all the janissaries tailored their clothing privately and only the cloth was issued by the government. Some details are characteristic of the style in vogue at the end of the eighteenth century, in particular the very large size of the lower part, which required a complicated method of securing the flaps under the waist sash. According to the original source, only the wrapped spiral turban replaced the uncomfortable janissary headdress, as was usual on campaign.

Source: Plate XVIII – *Subaltern Officer of the Janissaries* – in Octavien Dalvimart, *The Costume of Turkey, illustrated by a series of engravings; with descriptions in English and French* (1802).

Plate C – Ottoman Kaftan and *Ciubbeh*, 1790–1826

1 – *Erkan-i kürkü* kaftan
2 – *Ust kürkü* kaftan
Together with the *divoan-kürkü*, these were the kaftans worn by dignitaries and senior army officers, including the members of the Imperial family and sultan. Like the *divoan-kürkü* kaftan, represented on Figure 1 of Plate A, these could also be lined with sable fur.

3 and 4 – Janissary *dolama* kaftans. The simple kaftan with more or less long and wide sleeves is widely represented in contemporary iconography as the ordinary coat of janissaries on or off duty. Figure 4 shows the regular pattern of the kaftans worn by the janissaries; however, like the previous, this is a much simplified version of the traditional kaftan, and the lining appears to be the only special feature of the prestigious coat. In this period janissary kaftans are usually without collar patches and flap cuffs, and buttons are also often absent. The most common colours were turquoise, azure, red and green, but yellow and violet kaftans appear in some iconographic sources.

5 – Turkish *ciubbeh*. It was the ordinary coat of common people in the Ottoman Empire, and was also occasionally worn by janissary rank and file and irregular soldiers. The major differences from the kaftan were the sleeves, which generally did not go beyond the elbow, and the absence of an inner lining. The numerous variants had sleeves that were more or less wide, or in the width of the breast.

Plate D

1 – Irregular infantryman, 1786–1800

Thomas Walsh summarised the dress and equipment of the Ottoman soldiers in the first years of the nineteenth century. He wrote: 'All the Turks wear turbans, loose jackets, short pantaloons, morocco slippers, and a sash round the waist, in which they constantly carry a long dagger and a brace of pistols … Their heads are close shaved, and covered by a small scull-cap, which is hidden under the turban.' This figure includes all the items described by Walsh, except for the turbans. However, it is not only the uncommon headgear that marks this irregular, described in the sources as 'Infantryman from Bursa' in Western Anatolia. This figure was first depicted in the Monnier collection dated 1786, where the same 'harlequin' pattern of the sleeveless *yelek* jacket appears in the clothing of an assistant to the janissary *aga*, and in the one of a 'buffoon'. A third version is also included in the *Costumes Turcs* of the Diez Collection. It is difficult to establish what kind of connection existed between the clothing of these three figures, but surely the multicoloured pattern must have been of no small value. In the early years of the following century, the same *bursali* irregular was portrayed for the collection commissioned by Stratford Canning with some minor differences in the colours and shape of the jacket.

Joseph Gabriel Monnier, *Recueil de costumes et vêtements de l'Empire ottoman au 18ᵉ siècle* (1786), Manuscript 65; City Library of Bourg en Bresse (France).

2 – Anatolian *levend*, 1800–1809

It is generally also known that *levend* was the term which the Ottomans applied to the marine soldiers employed on the fleet. One feature of the *levend*'s dress was the shirt sleeves rolled up to show bare arms, however this was a typical feature of all the male population living on the Black Sea coast. The Ottoman *levends* were volunteers coming from the coastal *eyelet*, and the Ottoman provincial governors raised them to serve on ships and in coastal forts on the Black Sea. Marine soldiers also served on the Nile, Danube and Euphrates river flotillas. The typical command unit in the Ottoman Danube gunboat flotilla consisted of 10 vessels and 300 soldiers. This could be the standard organisation at the end of the eighteenth century, assuming that each of the 12 vessels on the Danube had 28–30 *levends* on board. The same term was later applied to all the irregular infantrymen coming from Anatolia, while the marine soldiers received another denomination. In fact, in 1800 Wittman mentions 'a well dressed *galangis*, or Turkish marine'. The *galangis* may have been part of the later corps of New Order Army rifle-armed marines, established and organised into two 500 man regiments in 1804. It should be noted that this unit still existed in 1826, it is traditionally called the *galeonjees*.

Source: *Fenerci Mehmed Albümü* (1800–1825)

3 – Anatolian irregular infantrymen

The same source from which the previous figure comes shows other irregular soldiers passing through Constantinople on their way to the war fronts on the Danube in the early nineteenth century. This soldier shows the characters that would become typical of the mid-century *bashi bozouks*. In particular the jacket with false back sleeves, the *çepken*, was typical of the Kurdish population of eastern Anatolia and Northern Iraq. Like the previous infantrymen, this man carries pistols and dagger under the sash. This weaponry was appropriate for close combat, which the Ottomans performed better compared to their European enemies. Even facing an enemy well trained in the use of the bayonet, the Ottomans troops showed great effectiveness, for example in the episode that occurred in the final phase at the siege of Acre in 1799, when the French troops were pushed back by the Ottoman garrison. According to a battle report, 'the bravest amongst [the French] fell by the sabre and the poniard of the Turks, one in each hand proving an overmatch for the bayonet'. In 1810, during the battle of Batin, it was a similar story when a Russian infantry column was destroyed entering the Ottoman trenches. Janissaries and irregulars engaged the enemy with their daggers, 'and the brave soldiers who crossed the embankment left their heads in the hands of the Turks, who fought like desperadoes.'

Source: *Fenerci Mehmed Albümü* (1800–1825)

Plate E

1 – Provincial *sipahi*, 1800–1802

The cavalry raised by the provinces were reckoned the principal strength of the Ottoman Empire in the previous century. However, the strong decline of the traditional Ottoman tactics on the eighteenth century battlefields relegated the *toprakli sipahis* to second line duties. According to several European commenters, the Ottoman provincial horsemen acted like mounted infantry more than actual cavalry. Furthermore, the quality of these troops was often poor. They had no discipline or tactical training, their weaponry was often obsolete, and they were seldom tested by being called upon to perform. The English diplomat David Morier wrote that:

> a considerable number of volunteers follow the Ottoman armies on campaign. These irregulars, as they are then called, are not an actual military force, since these troops, which come under the denomination of volunteers, consist of religious enthusiasts, who sell the little property which they possess at home, and come from the most remote parts of the empire to follow the standard of Mahomet: as soon as their little fortune is expended, they return home. Many there are, of this class, who have all their lives been plunderers or assassins, and who follow an army in the hope of plunder.

There are not many images depicting these mounted soldiers, and the *sipahi* portrayed by Octavien Dalvimart is certainly one of the most interesting.

The French traveller reports that this *sipahi* came from the Asiatic provinces of the Empire. He wears a *salta* jacket over a shorter sleeveless *yelek*. The tall hat is wrapped in a spiral of multicoloured fabric, typical of the late eighteenth century Ottoman dress. The large *sermali* breeches were common in Egypt, and possibly this detail qualifies him as belonging to one of the armies engaged in the campaigns against the French after 1799.

Source: Plate XLIII – A Sipahi – in Octavien Dalvimart, *The Costume of Turkey, illustrated by a series of engravings; with descriptions in English and French* (1802).

2 – *Delibaşi*, 1800–1809

Deli cavalrymen were recruited in most provinces of Asia and Europe among the Muslim population living on the borders. They formed semi-permanent corps of light cavalry who performed duties such as scouting, intruding, and escorting supply, and at the end of the eighteenth century, the *delis* formed a considerable force of light cavalry which was also employed in Egypt against the French. They wore no uniforms, but were generally identified by the tall black hat. According to contemporary accounts the *delis* rode small horses with an 'English saddle': possibly a light version as distinct from the large Ottoman saddles. This officer is based on the *delibaşi* portrayed by Fenerci Mehmed, presumably in Constantinople in the first years of the nineteenth century. He wears a fur-trimmed *kaftan* with oversized sleeves and a brocade *entari* waistcoat, which qualify him as a wealthy man. The waist sash and holster to carry weapons were common across the Empire and very widespread among both cavalrymen and infantrymen. Like the latter, the *delis* received prizes for each successful action. The English diplomat David Morier pointed out the rewards granted for the enemy heads brought to the Grand Vizier during the Egyptian campaign. He wrote that these generous prizes fuelled an 'improper trade' among the Ottoman soldiers: 'a principle of self-interest seems to pervade all ranks; and this is carried so far, that I have seen the heads of their own companions (*sic*) displayed before the vizier at the battle of Heliopolis, merely to receive the reward attached to every man who brings the head of an enemy.'

Source: *Fenerci Mehmed Albümü* (1800–1825).

3 – Georgian Horseman, 1780–1815

The rough appearance of the Georgian mounted warriors is noted by several travellers and military officers who visited or served in the Caucasus. A chainmail shirt and outdated metal protection coming from the weaponry of the past continued to be worn especially by the Georgian highlanders until the early twentieth century. This horseman is typically armed with a Persian curved sword, a firearm slung across his back and a pair of pistols carried in the broad cummerbund beneath the sash. This item gave support when riding, especially over long distances. On campaign the Georgians horsemen served like the *deli* and *lesghis* light cavalry, and usually carried a lance. As was customary in the Caucasus, the Georgians rode without spurs,

COLOUR PLATE COMMENTARIES

controlling the horse instead with a short wooden handle and a thick, stiff thong of plaited leather. This was suspended from the wrist when not in use. Horses were small, and generally strong. Ottoman Georgia was only a small part of the modern-day state, but the vassal rulers provided troops against the Russians until the definitive loss of the region in 1878.

Source: Reconstruction after contemporary reports and late nineteenth century photographs depicting Kevsur highlanders from Georgia.

Plate F – Mamluk and Egyptian Clothing

1 – Mamluk striped *kaftan*, usually worn under a cloak or a larger coat in cold season. The Mamluk *kaftan* was longer and narrower than the Ottoman one.

2 and 3 – Egyptian *gibbeh*, manufactured with undyed cloth, or in pale blue and vermillion red among the most widespread colours. The *gibbeh* was usually manufactured without lining and was the coat of ordinary urban Egyptian people, as well as of low-rank Mamluks. Although the *gibbeh* had short and wide sleeves, in the interior regions of Syria and Iraq it was also manufactured with long sleeves.

4 – The popular *gibbeh* influenced the clothing of the ruling class. This coat, called the *faragieb*, belonged to the clothing of the high-ranking Mamluks and *beys*, and could be lined with silk or brocade. The *faragieb* was usually worn over a *kaftan*.

5 – Egyptian *eri* cotton shirt, usually of natural colour or dyed in pale blue. This was the main garment of the Egyptian *fellahins*, who wore this with a cloak or a *gibbeh* in the cold season. Thomas Walsh describes an Egyptian *fellahin* wearing a long pale blue cotton shirt hanging loose to the heels. The *eri* was also a common feature of Bedouin dress.

6 – Cotton *eri* shirt manufactured with collar and open sleeves, usually worn by the wealthy Egyptians.

Plate G. *Nizâm-ı Cedîd* Soldiers and NCO

1 – *Nefer* private soldier, *Levend* (1st) Infantry Regiment, 1800–1808
There are several versions of the uniform established for the new military corps introduced by Selim III at the end of the eighteenth century. This figure is based on the drawing by Fenerci Memhed and considerably differs from those depicted in other sources. All the clues gleaned from an examination of the figures portrayed by the Ottoman artist show that he saw the subjects in person and took note of details that could hardly be the result of his own invention. The bayonet is suspended from a black leather strap with a

brass oval fitting, and the footwear, a pair of half-leg boots, are also of black leather. Note the jacket with Hungarian lanyards and the black piping on the shoulders and sleeves' edges.

Source: *Fenerci Mehmed Albümü* (1800–1825).

2 – NCO in quarter dress, 1800–1808

This collection of Ottoman subjects portrayed by an anonymous painter includes some figures belonging to the new military corps raised in the 1790s. This figure is identified as a NCO of the *nizâm-ı cedîd* infantry. The undyed jacket and loose trousers seems to be a quarter-dress garment introduced in imitation of the one used in some European armies. The jacket is presumably worn over the red coat of the regular uniform, like the contemporary Austrian *kittel*, which was used for saving the uniform during the exercises. Note the red 'star' and half circle on the breast of the coat, which replace the brass button used as distinctive of rank in the regular uniform.

Source: Figure 38, in *A Collection of 89 original Drawings, in water-colors, of Publick Officers and others in Turkey* (Constantinople, before 1808).

3 – Anatolian *nefer* private soldier, 1802–1808

The same source as that for the previous figure portrayed this 'Soldier of the Ottoman army in the nineteenth century' with dress and equipment close to the style introduced for the *nizâm-ı cedîd* infantry. He carries a European musket with bayonet and French ammunition pouch, both clues for qualifying this soldier as a member of Selim's New Model Army. However, the information about the regiments quartered in Constantinople indicates that they wore red or blue coats, but the green cap suggests that he did not belong to the European regiments, since they had *bostanci*-style headdress. Therefore, he could belong to one of the regiments raised in Anatolia by Abdurrahman Paşa, governor of Karaman and Alaiye, who introduced a system of military conscription throughout Anatolia to provide men for raising nine infantry regiments.

Source: Figure 37 in *A Collection of 89 original Drawings, in water-colors, of Publick Officers and others in Turkey* (Constantinople, before 1808).

Plate H

1 – *Humbaraci başi* bombardier officer, 1808–15

The clothing issued to the technical corps and New Order Army shows influences from the European-style uniforms and ultimately seems to follow a major regularity compared to the *kapıkulu*. The *humbaraci* bombardier corps had existed since the end of the seventeenth century, but the technical reforms introduced between 1770 and 1775 opened the way to the introduction of the new military corps. In the early 1800s the *humbaracis* were generally in green, retaining the classic cylindrical tall black felt headdress as a distinctive feature. Note the combination of clothing of this officer, which includes a kaftan worn under a short *hirka* jacket with gilded brass buttons as a distinctive of rank.

Source: *Fenerci Mehmed Albümü* (1800–1825).

2 – Artillery officer, 1800–07
The officers of the 'New Order Army' are often depicted wearing *kaftan*, while rank and file have short jackets, and this possibly occurred also in the artillery. However, during the reign of reformer Selim III, the artillery uniform changed several times, and the date of any particular version is difficult to establish. Having to necessarily refer to existing iconography, it seems that in the last years of the eighteenth century, artillerymen of the *nizâm-ı cedîd* wore blue coats and trousers, and tall black headdress. The officer illustrated here appears in the *Fenerci Albümü*, and shows similar characteristics to the *suratçi* 'rapid artillery' uniform represented by Antoine-Laurent Castellan in 1812. The colours are more or less the same and the main difference consists in the headdress – here a turban – and the coat, a *dolama kaftan* with oversized sleeves and a pair of large brass buttons as distinctive of rank. In this case, however, he has only a couple of buttons, whereas officers usually have two or more pairs.

Source: *Fenerci Mehmed Albümü* (1800–1825).

3 – Horse artillery trumpeter, 1800–1807
A mixture of Ottoman and European-style clothing and accessories composes the uniform of this bugler portrayed by Fenerci Mehmed in the early 1800s. The result is a decidedly unprecedented hybrid that prefigures the Ottoman uniforms introduced in the 1830s. Other illustrations concerning the horse artillery show interesting details, including a pointed blue saddle cover with red brim edge, dark grey rolled cloak, and black leather harnesses with brass fittings.

Source: *Fenerci Mehmed Albümü* (1800–1825)

Plate I – Ottoman, Balkan and Mamluk Clothing

1 – Ottoman-Turkish *salta* jacket
2 – Ottoman-Turkish *mintan* jacket
3 – Bosnian *jacerma* doublet
4 – Greek-Albanian doublet
5 – Ottoman-Turkish *yelek* doublet
6 – Greek-Albanian *fustanela* skirt
7 – Balkan loose trousers of coloured cotton
8 – Ottoman-Turkish *salvar* loose trousers
9 – Mamluk *sernali* trousers for cavalrymen
10 – Ottoman-Turkish trousers
11 – Albanian trousers

Plate J

Mamluk elite *amir* horseman

Studies of the history and culture of the Islamic world have suffered from Western scholars' deeply engrained abhorrence of the perceived 'slave' condition. In reality, the relationship between a slave, or freedman client as he typically became, and his master-patron was very different in Islamic societies. Moreover, the Islamic world had a distinctive basis of authority, especially in the Mamluk Egypt where legitimacy of rule was a prize to be won, like any other. Though slavery or bounded labour played a minor part in the agriculture, individuals of slave origin played a significant role in domestic life, the service of the elite and, mainly, in the military. Moreover, it became commonplace for people who had once legally been slaves to rise to positions of influence and authority, and states ruled by such men were not rare. This phenomenon seems bizarre to a modern Western world but underpinning it was a form of slavery far removed from that seen in the Classical Age and much of the medieval Western world. The Mamluk society retained the bonds with the medieval tradition and continued to import its 'slaves' from the Caucasus and other neighbouring regions. The hierarchy of the households had its own *bey*-chief who usually appointed warriors coming from his native country, and formed his personal retinue. The elite horseman was known as the *amir*, and in wartime also provided the officers for the larger contingents. This Egyptian-Mamluk *amir* is based largely on drawings by Carle Vernet, and wears characteristic local elite attire, consisting in the multicoloured turban, the rich weaponry including a blunderbuss, and the elaborate horse equipment. Note the typical long saddlecloth which covers most of the horse's back and hangs down on either side. This was also a feature of Caucasus horse equipment, and maintained unaltered by the Mamluks in Egypt. The Mamluk saddlecloths could be manufactured of velvet, and richly decorated with gilded metal and silver thread, and embroidered with silk. The edges were usually adorned by tassels of golden or silver silk. Sometimes, the bridle might be similar decorated with bosses, pendants and other precious accessories.

Plate K

1 – Egyptian Mamluk, 1790s

Though there is few information about specific colours, the colour of *kaftan* or *gibbeh* could identify retinue or household. In a print after a drawing of Luigi Mayer, dating the 1790s, some horsemen belonging to the powerful Murad Bey wore yellow coats, while the escorting footmen appear all dressed in azure coat with trousers and cloaks of red. Rank or status was indicated by the quality of the Mamluk's clothing and by his weapons. Indeed, more specific to the Mamluks themselves was the rich weaponry, which included a pair of pistols, daggers, a *pala* curved sword and a blunderbuss. Note the pistol holster secured to the waist as typical of all the Ottoman cavalry of this age.

Source: 'Murad Bey enters Cairo', *c.* 1792, painting by Luigi Mayer.

2 – Syrian mounted marksman and dromedary, 1797

Camels, and more often dromedary, were largely used by the Mamluks and Bedouins as a mobile force. Tactically, they were used in a similar way to pick-up cars armed with heavy weapons in modern day Libya and Somalia. A French account of the battle of Chobrakit in 1798 reports that Bedouin warriors mounted on 'camels' targeted the enemy with small saddle-mounted cannons. The 'cannons' were perhaps the Ottoman *habus*, or large-bore rampart-muskets. The use of dromedaries is documented in other regions. William Browne took note of the personal armed retinue of the paşa of Damascus during a parade occurred in July 1797. He saw two groups of 15 and 30 men mounted on dromedaries, with 'musquetoons' fitted to the saddles; of this group of soldiers, it was said that 'this destructive instrument of war has passed from the Persians to the Syrians'.

Reconstruction after W. G. Browne, *Travels in Africa, Egypt, and Syria, from the Year 1792 to 1798* (London 1799).

Plate L

1 – Bosnian cavalryman, *c.* 1800

The Bosnian population had adhered to Islam en masse, and during the Ottoman rule they provided large contingents of soldiers who often proved to be trustworthy and valiant warriors. The Bosnian *panduks* were mainly foot soldiers, but during the wars against Austria and Russia the local governors raised corps of light cavalry capable of facing Hussars and Cossacks. This Bosnian mounted soldier is wearing very distinctive clothing. The headgear with black sheep fur is characteristic of Bosnia, but the *ciubbeh* and trousers are typically Ottoman-Turkish. Note the short cape apparently worn in imitation of the Hussar pelisse. He is armed with a pair of pistols and carries a captured Austrian Model 1769 light cavalry sword.

Source: *Fenerci Mehmed Albümü* (1800–1825).

2 – Kurdish Horseman, late eighteenth century

In the eighteenth century, as today, the Kurds formed a large community settled in southeastern Anatolia, northern Iraq and Syria, whose relations with Constantinople were not very different from those between the central power and the *ayans*. Therefore, some chiefs acted as local lords by carrying out lootings at the expense of the neighbouring communities. The warfare of the Kurds is described as 'predatory incursions', and contemporary reports stated that some tribes lived by continual pillage and warfare. Despite these excesses, the Ottomans relied on the Kurds to guard the Iranian border, where an undeclared war loomed for a long time. The Kurds had a reputation as excellent warriors and they considered the capacity to withstand hardship and fatigue a basic requirement for any good soldier. As a consequence of their allowance, the Kurds might be called on to serve in any part of the Empire, mounted, armed and dressed at their own expense, and the Porte made good any deficiencies and supplied food, pay and heavy equipment. There was not much difference in the clothing of the Kurds from that of the Arab populations of Syria and Iraq or the Mamluks; however, due to the colder climate of the regions where they lived, the dress comprised more layers and heavier garments, such as cloak and overcoat. Kurds are described as mounted soldiers, but several period illustrations depict them as footmen too.

Source: reconstruction after Carl Tilke and Wolfgang Bruhn, *Das Kostümwerk. Eine Geschichte des Kostüms aller Zeiten und Völke* (Berlin, 1941).

Plate M

Muhammad Ali's Albanian foot soldier. The Albanians maintained in Africa their traditional dress with cotton *fustanela* skirt and short sleeveless jacket, as well as Balkan weapons, such as the *tançitsa* musket and *yataghan* knife. (Reconstruction by the author after contemporary prints. With the kind permission of the web magazine *History & Uniforms*)

Plate N

Albanian *arnavut* infantrymen. The western European travellers and artists were impressed by the Balkan costumes, and the magnificent attire of the Albanian soldiers became iconic to represent the most exotic scenarios. The figures above are portrayed in Wittman's *Travels in Turkey* and represent two Albanian foot soldiers in Egypt in 1800–1802; note the muskets of European manufacture. Left, below: another *arnavut* of the early 1800s portrayed by Fenerci Mehmed (*Fenerci Mehmed Albümü* (1800–1825)). He wears a large *dalmatica* overcoat possibly of leather over a *xhamadan* short jacket and doublet. Note the loose trousers worn under the *fustanela* skirt secured to the legs by the gaiters of boiled wool. Right, below: Albanian footman depicted in the *Costumes Turcs* of the Diez Collection, dating to the 1790s. Note the jacket with lanyards on the breast, and the cap with cords on the back.

Plate O

1 – Cavalry standard depicted in an Austrian print illustrating a war episode of the Bosnian campaign of 1788. Approximate dimensions 80 × 200 cm

2 – Infantry ensign, Egyptian campaigns 1800–1802, reconstruction after William Wittman's *Travels to Turkey*. Approximate dimensions 120 × 220 cm

3 – Infantry ensign, depicted in the *Fenerci Mehmed Albümü* (1800–1825). Although banners of various colours and shapes were still used at the end of the eighteenth century, the crescent, or half moon, became the official symbol of the Ottoman Empire. During the reign of Selim III (1789–1809),

COLOUR PLATE COMMENTARIES

the Ottoman State flag began to take a form approximating to the modern day Turkish flag, except for the eight-pointed star.

4 – *Humbaraci* artillery standard, *c.* 1800, after Kabaağaçlızade Ahmed Cévad Beg, *Etat Militaire Ottoman, depuis la fondation de l'Empire Ottoman jusqu'à nos jours*.

5 – Ensign of janissary *orta* 25, late eighteenth century; dimensions 95 × 126 cm. Collection of the Hermitage Museum, St Petersburg. A janissary ensign could carry either colours only or figurative imagery, as well as abstract symbols as in this case. However, note on the pole the silhouette of a fish as an additional symbol. The same symbols carried on the ensign were usually tattooed on the right arm or on the back of the hand. Octavien Dalvimart depicts a Janissary showing a tattoo representing a fish, which nearly covers the entire upper arm.

6 – Ensign of an unknown infantry regiment of the *nizâm-ı cedîd*; size 122 × 101 cm, fringes included. In the last years of the eighteenth century, regimental ensign were adopted for the newly raised military units. This flag carries in the centre the *tughra* (monogram) of Sultan Selim III. Askery Museum, Constantinople.

7 and 8: Ensigns of Muhammad Ali, 1810–11. Muhammad Ali introduced a new ensign which eventually became the first Egyptian national flag. The three crescents and stars perhaps symbolised his victories in three continents: Europe, Asia, and Africa, or his own sovereignty over Egypt, Nubia, and the Sudan. The second ensign became the personal flag of Muhammad Ali.

Plate P

1 – *Sancak*, late eighteenth century, dimensions 234 × 228 cm. Collection of the Hermitage Museum, St Petersburg. This is a well-preserved large banner with multiple figures. Usually these large ensigns belonged to the senior commanders.

2 – Ensign of the janissary *orta* number 56; dimensions 100 × 130 cm. Collection of the Hermitage Museum, St Petersburg. *Orta* 56 had been originally assigned to the surveillance of the Golden Horn residences, and quartered close to the naval arsenal of Galata. This particularity created confusion among some authors, who identified them as naval janissaries, a branch which did not exist.

3 – Inscriptional *sancak*, early nineteenth century; dimension 153 × 255 cm. Private collection, Malaysia.

4 – Another well-preserved *sancak* of the late eighteenth century, dimensions 150 × 235 cm. Collection of the Hermitage Museum, St Petersburg. This ensign carries inscriptional motif, medallion and symbols, including open crescent and *zulfiqar* sword, following the traditional pattern of the Ottoman ensign established in the seventeenth century. This *sancak* possibly belonged to a *paşa*, and became a Russian trophy during the war of 1787–1792.

5 – Large *sancak* with *zulfiqar* and inscriptions dating to 1819; approximate dimensions 150 × 260 cm. Askery Museum, Constantinople. Many of these large flags are today preserved in Turkey, and this suggests that they were only used for ceremonies and parades at the sultan's court.

Bibliography

Coeval Sources

Beaujour, Felix, *A view of the Commerce of Greece, Formed after an Annual Average, from 1787 to 1797* (London, 1800)

Browne, William George, *Travels in Africa, Egypt, and Syria, from the Year 1792 to 1798* (London, 1799)

Abd al-Rahman al-Jabarti, History of Egypt (1711–1821), by J.. Hathaway (ed.), (Princeton NJ: Markus Wiener, 2004)

Doguereau, Jean-Pierre (General), *Journal de l'expédition d'Égypte, publié d'après le manuscrit original, avec une introduction et des notes, par C. de La Jonquière, chef d'escadron d'artillerie breveté* (Paris: 1904)

Jucherau de Saint-Denis, Antoine, Baron de, *Histoire de l'Empire Ottoman depuis 1792 jusqu'en 1844, Tome I–II* (Paris, 1844)

Morier, John Philip, *Memoir of a Campaign with the Ottoman Army in Egypt, from February to July 1800: Containing a Description of the Turkish Army, the Journal of Its March from Syria to Egypt, General Observations on the Arabs, and on the Treaty of El-Arish, with an Account of the Event which Followed it.* (London, 1801)

Mouradgea d'Ohsson, Ignatius, *Tableau Général de l'Émpire Othoman, tome septième, contenant l'état actuel de l'Émpire Othoman* (Paris, 1824)

Porter, James, *Turkey: Its History and Progress. Journals and Correspondence of Sir James Porter* (London: 1854)

Rayf Efendi, Mahmoud, *Tableau des Nouveaux Reglemens de l'Empire Ottoman* (Constantinople, 1798)

Sadik, Ahmed, *Vakai-Hamidié, Chronique depuis 1185 (1771) jusqu'à 1205 (1790)* (Constantinople, 1838)

Schmidt, Jan, 'The Adventure of an Ottoman Horseman: the Autobiography of Kabudlı Vasfî Efendi, 1800–1825', in J. Schmidt (ed.), *The Joys of Philology: Studies in Ottoman Literature, History and Orientalism (1500–1923)* (Constantinople: The Isis Press, 2002), vol. I, pp.166–286.

St John, James A., *Egypt and Muhammad Ali; or, Travels in the Valley of the Nile* (London: 1834)

Thornton, Thomas, *The Present State of Turkey; Or, A Description of the Political, Civil, and Religious, Constitution, Government, and Laws of the Ottoman Empire ... Together with the Geographical, Political, and Civil, State of the Principalities of Moldavia and Wallachia,* Part I–II (London, 1809)

Valentini, Georg Wilhelm von, *Précis des dernières guerres des Russes contre les Turcs, avec des considérations militaires et politiques; traduit de l'Allemand par Eugène de la Côste* (Paris, 1825)

Volnay, Constantin-François de Chasseboeuf, comte de, *Voyage en Syrie et en Égypte, pendant les années 1783, 1784 et 1785, tome I–III* (Paris, 1787)

Walsh, Thomas, *Journal of the Late Campaign in Egypt: Containing Descriptions of that Country, and of Gibraltar, Minorca, Malta, Marmorice, and Macri; With An Appendix; Containing Official Papers And Documents* (London, 1803)

Wittman, William, *Travels in Turkey, Asia-Minor, Syria, and Across the Desert Into Egypt During the Years 1799, 1800, and 1801, in Company with the Turkish Army, and the British Military Mission: To which are Annexed, Observations on the Plague and on the Diseases Prevalent in Turkey, and a Meteorological Journal.* (London, 1803)

General Documentary Sources

Ágoston, Gábor and Bruce Masters, *Encyclopedia of the Ottoman Empire* (New York, NY: Facts on File, 2009)

Bombaci, Alessio, Stanford J. Shaw, *L'Impero Ottomano – Storia Universale dei Popoli e delle Civiltà*, vol. VI (Turin: Utet, 1981)

Boyar, Ebru, *Ottomans, Turks and the Balkans. Empire Lost, Relations Altered* (London, New York: Tauros Academic Studies, 2007)

Driault, Edouard, *La politique orientale de Napoleon: Sébastiani et Gardane 1806-1808* (Paris, 1904)

Faroqhi, Suraiya N. (ed.), *The Cambridge History of Turkey, vol. 3 – The Later Ottoman Empire, 1603-1839* (Cambridge: Cambridge University Press, 2006)

Faroqhi, Suraya N., Bruce McGowan, Donald Quataert, Şevket Pamuk, *An Economic and Social History of the Ottoman Empire, volume II. 1600–1914* (Cambridge: Cambridge University Press, 1999)

Hanioğlu, Sükrü M., *A Brief History of the Late Ottoman Empire* (Princeton, NJ: Princeton University Press, 2008)

Lavallée, Théophile, *Histoire de l'Empire Ottoman* (Paris, 1855)

Lewis, Reina, *Rethinking Orientalism: Women, Travel and the Ottoman Harem* (London: I. B. Tauris, 2004)

MacLean, Gerald, *Looking East. English Writing and the Ottoman Empire before 1800* (New York, NY: Pearlgrave, 2007)

Mantran. Robert, *L'Empire ottoman du XVIe au XVIIIe siècle. Administration, économie, société* (London: Variorum Reprint, 1985)

Philliou, Christine M., *Biography of an Empire. Governing Ottomans in an Age of Revolution* (Berkeley, Los Angeles, London: University of California Press, 2011)

Ortayli, Ilber, *The Empire's Longest Century* (Istanbul: Kronik, 2021)

Özoglu, Hakan, *Kurdish Notables and the Ottoman State. Evolving Identities, Competing Loyalties and Shifting Boundaries* (New York, NY: State University of New York Press, 2004)

Shaw, Stanford J., *The Financial and Administrative Organization and Development of Ottoman Egypt, 1517-1798* (Princeton NJ: Princeton Legacy Library, 1958)

Shaw, Stanford J., *History of the Ottoman Empire and Modern Turkey Volume I: Empire of the Gazis: The Rise and Decline of the Ottoman Empire, 1280–1808* (Cambridge: Cambridge University Press, 1977)

Shaw, Stanford J., Ezel Kural Shaw, *History of the Ottoman Empire and Modern Turkey Volume II: Reform, Revolution, and Republic: The Rise of Modern Turkey, 1808*Shaw, *1975* (Cambridge: Cambridge University Press, 1977)

Somel, Selcuk Aksin, *Historical Dictionary of the Ottoman Empire* (Lanham, MD: Scarecrow Press, 2003)

Tezcan, Baki, *The Second Ottoman Empire. Political and Social Transformation in the Early Modern World* (Cambridge: Cambridge University Press, 2010)

Vaughn Findley, Carter, *Enlightening Europe on Islam and the Ottomans* Shaw, *The History of Oriental Studies, Volume 5* (Leiden, Boston MS: Brill, 2019)

Webb, Caroline and Webb, Nigel, *The Earl and His Butler in Constantinople. The Secret Diary of an English Servant among the Ottomans* (London: I. B. Tauris, 2009)

Winter, Michael: *Egyptian Society under Ottoman Rule 1517–1798* (New York, London: Routledge, 1992)

Ottoman Military History

Aksan, Virginia H., *Ottoman Wars, 1700–1870. An Empire Besieged* (London and New York, NY: Routledge, 2007)

Cezar, Mustafa, *Osmanlı Tarihinde Levendler* (Istanbul: Çelikcilt Matbası, 1965)

Chandler, David, *The Campaigns of Napoleon*, vol. I (Italian Edition, Milan: Rizzoli, 1992)

Fahmy, Khaled, *All the Pasha's Men: Mehmed Ali, his Army, and the Making of Modern Egypt* (Cairo: American University in Cairo, 2002)

Glenny, Misha, *The Balkans: Nationalism, War, and the Great Powers, 1804-1999* (New York: Penguin, 2001)

Hickok, Michael Robert, *Ottoman Military Administration in Eighteenth-Century Bosnia* (Leiden-Boston, MS: Brill, 1997)

Hochedlinger, Michael, *Krise Und Wiederherstellung: Österreichische Großmachtpolitik zwischen Türkenkrieg und Zweiter Diplomatischer Revolution, 1787–1791* (Berlin: Duncker & Humblot, 2000).

Kabaağaçlızade Ahmed Cévad Beg, *Etat Militaire Ottoman, depuis la fondation de l'Empire Ottoman jusqu'à nos jours* vol. I (Constantinople, 1882)

Kabaağaçlızade Ahmed Cévad Beg, *Tarih-i Askeri Osmânî* (Constantinople, 1882), vols II–III

Martens, Carl von, *Allgemeine Geschichte der Türken-Kriege in Europa von 1356 bis 1812*, vol. II (Stuttgart, 1829)

Mikhaïlovskiï-Danilevskiï, Aleksandr Ivanovich, Alexander Mikaberidze (eds), *Russo-Turkish War of 1806–1812*, vols I–II (West Chester OH: Nafziger Collection, 2002)

Petrovich, Michael Boro, *A History of Modern Serbia, 1804–1918*, vol. I (New York, NY: Harcourt Brace Jovanovich, 1976)

Raymond, André, *Le Caire des Janissaires: l'apogée de la ville ottomane sous 'Abd al-Rahman Katkhud* (Paris: CNRS, 1995)

Stojančević, Vladimir, *Prvi srpski ustanak: Ogledi i studije* (The First Serbian Uprising: Trials and Studies) (Belgrade: Vojna knj, 1994)

Shaw, Stanford J., *Between Old and New. The Ottoman Empire under Sultan Selim III, 1789–1807* (Harvard, MA: Harvard University Press, 1971)

Uyar, Mesut, Edward Erickson, *A Military History of the Ottomans. From Osman to Atatürk* (Santa Barbara, CA: ABC Clio, 2009)

Ustun, Kadir, *The New Order and Its Enemies: Opposition to Military Reform in the Ottoman Empire, 1789–1807* (submitted in partial fulfilment of the requirements for the degree of Doctor of Philosophy in the Graduate School of Arts and Sciences: Columbia University, 2013)

Uzunçarşılı, İsmail Hakkı, *Osmanlı Devleti Teşkilatından Kapukulu Ocakları* (Ankara: Türk Tarih Kurumu Basımevi, 1988), vol. II

Ottoman Military Clothing and Weapons

Anonymous, *Les portraits des differens habillemens habillemens qui sont en usage à Constantinople et dans tout la Turquie* (early 1800- before 1808) in R. Naumann and K. Tuchelt (ed.), *Türkische Gewänder und Osmanische Gesellschaft im achtzehnten Jahrhundert* (Graz: Akademische Druck - u. Verlagsanstalt, 1966)

Anonymous, *Recueil de costumes et vêtements de l'Empire ottoman au 18ᵉ siècle* (1786, Joseph Gabriel Monnier's Collection, Fonds Patrimoniaux, Bourg-en-Bresse)

Castellan, Antoine-Laurent, *Moeurs, Usages, Costumes des Othomans, et abrégé de leur histoire; par A. L. Castellan, auteur de Lettres sur la Morée et sur Constantinople* (Paris, 1812)

Dalvimart, Octavien, *The Costume of Turkey, Illustrated by a Series of Engravings; with Description in English and French* (London, 1802)

Fraser, Elisabeth, 'Heinrich Friedrich von Diez and Costumes Turcs', in C. Rauch and G. Stiening (eds), *Heinrich Friedrich von Diez (1751-1817): Freethinker, Diplomat, Orientalist* (Berlin: De Gruyter, 2020)

Fulgenzi di Loreto, Eugenio and Raffaele, *Litographie et Taille Douce* (Smyrna, 1838)

Jacob, Alain, *Les Armes Blanches du Monde Islamique* (Paris: Jacques Grancher, 1985)

Lebedinsky, Iaroslav, *Les Armes Orientales* (La Tour du Pin: Editions du Portail, 1992)

McLean, Thomas, *The Military Costume of Turkey, Illustrated by A Series of Engravings. From Drawings made on the Spot* (London, 1818)

Moreno, José, *Viage à Constantinopla, en el Año de 1784, escrito deorden superior* (Madrid, 1790)

Sertoğlu, Midhat, *Osmanli Kiyafetlerı. Fenerci Mehmed Albümü* (Constantinople: Vehbi Kaç Vakfi, 1986)

Tilke, Carl Max, *Orientalische Kostüme in Schnitt und Farbe* (Berlin, 1923)

Tilke, Carl Max, Wolfgang Bruhn, *Das Kostümwerk. Eine Geschichte des Kostüms aller Zeiten und Völke* (Berlin, 1941)

Articles and Essays

Ágoston, Gábor, 'Ottoman Warfare in Europe 1453–1826', in J. Black (ed.), *European Warfare, 1453–1815* (London: Macmillan, 1999): pp.118–144

Ágoston, Gábor, 'Military Transformation in the Ottoman Empire and Russia, 1500-1800', in *Kritika 12, Explorations in Russian and Eurasian History*, n. 2 (Spring 2011), pp.281–319

Ágoston, Gábor, 'Firearms and Military Adaptation: The Ottomans and the European Military Revolution, 1450–1800', in *Journal of World History*, vol. 25, N. 1 (March 2014), pp. 85–124

Aksan, Virginia H., 'Manning a Black Sea Garrison in the Eighteenth Century: Ochakov and Concepts of Mutiny and Rebellion in the Ottoman Context', in *Ottomans and Europeans: Contacts and Conflicts* (Constantinople: The Isis Press, 2004), pp.251–261

Aksan, Virginia, 'Ottoman Military Recruitment Strategies in the late Eighteenth Century', in V. Aksan (ed.), *Ottomans and Europeans. Contacts and Conflicts* (Constantinople: Isis Press, 2004), pp.191–207

Aksan, Virginia H., 'Mobilization of warrior populations in the Ottoman context, 1750–1850' in *Fighting for a Living* (Cambridge: Cambridge University Press, 2013), pp.331–351

Aksan, Virginia H., 'The Ottomans, Military Manpower and Political Bargains 1750–1850', in M. Sariyannis (ed.), *Political Thought and Practice in the Ottoman Empire* (Rethymno: Crete University Press, 2019), pp. 435–448

Anscombe, Frederick, 'Albanians and Mountain Bandits', in F. Anscombe (ed.), *The Ottoman Balkans, 1750-1830* (Princeton, NJ: Markus Wiener Publishers, 2006), pp. 87–114

BIBLIOGRAPHY

Anscombe, Frederick, 'The Balkan Revolutionary Age' in *The Journal of Modern History*, vol. 84, No. 3 (September 2012), pp.572–606

Bayraktar, Uğur, 'From salary to resistance: mobility, employment, and violence in Dibra, 1792–1826', in *Middle Eastern Studies*, vol. 54, N. 6 (2018), pp.878–900

Bowden, James, 'The Army of Egypt in the Years 1801–1832' in *History & Uniforms* N. 6–7 (2016), pp.81–89 and pp.65–73

Dykstra, Darrel, 'The French occupation of Egypt, 1798–1801', in M. W. Daly (ed.), *The Cambridge History of Egypt. Volume Two. Modern Egypt, from 1517 to the end of the twentieth century* (Cambridge: Cambridge University Press, 1998), pp. 113–138

Ghali Ibrahim, Amin, 'L'expédition d'Egypte vue par les auteurs égyptiens', in *Revue du Souvenir Napoléonien*, N. 291 (1977), pp.20–37

Grant, Jonathan, 'Rethinking the Ottoman Decline. Military Technology Diffusion in the Ottoman Empire, Fifteenth to Eighteenth Centuries', in *Journal of World History*, vol. 10, N. 1 (Spring 1999), pp.179–201

Hathaway, Jane, 'The Military Household in Ottoman Egypt', in *International Journal of Middle East Studies* N. 27 (1995), pp.39–52

Ibtesam, Kh. Mohammed, T. Hoger, Khalil Tawfeeq, A. Murad, 'Early Ottoman Reactions Towards French Invasion of Egypt in 1798', in *Humanities Journal of the University of Zakho* (Kurdistan Region, Iraq), vol. 8, No. 1 (March 2020), pp.69–79

Inalcik, Halil, 'Military and Fiscal Transformation in the Ottoman Empire, 1600–1700', in *Archivum Ottomanicum* 6 (1980): pp.283–337

Katič, Tatana, 'Serbia under the Ottoman Rule', in *Österreichische OSTHEFTE*, Jahrgang 47, 2005, pp.145–158

Kaçar, Mustafa, 'Osmanlı imparatorluğu'nda askeri teknik eğitimde modernleşme çalışmaları ve Mühendishanelerin kurulugu (1808'e kadar)', in *Osmanlı Bilimi Araştırmaları* (Istanbul, 1998), pp.69–137

Levy, Avigdor, 'Military Reform and the Problem of Centralization in the Ottoman Empire in the Eighteenth Century', in *Middle Eastern Studies* 18 (1982), pp.227–249

Malik, Jamal, 'Muslim Culture and Reform in 18th Century South Asia', in *Journal of the Royal Asiatic Society* 13, no. 2 (2003): pp.201–249

Mert Sunar, Mehmet, 'When grocers, porters and other riff-raff become soldiers: Janissary Artisans and Laborers in the Nineteenth Century Istanbul and Edirne', in *Kocaeli Üniversitesi Sosyal Bilimler Enstitüsü Dergisi* (17) 2009, 1; pp.175–194

North, Jonathan, 'Attack along the Danube: The Russo-Turkish War of 1810', in *The Napoleon Series* (July 2000), pp.1–10

Sariyannis, Marinos, 'Ruler and State. State and Society in Ottoman Political Thought', in *Turkish Historical Review* n. 4 (2013) pp.92–126

Spillmann, Georges, 'Les auxiliaires de l'Armée d'Orient (1798-1801). La création de corps auxiliaires égyptiens er syriens', in *Revue du Souvenir Napoléonien*, N. 304 (1979), pp.7–15

Stanford J. Shaw, 'The Established Ottoman Army Corps under Sultan Selim III (1789–1807)', in *Der Islam*, N. 40 (1964), pp.142–184

Shaw, Stanford, J., 'Origins of Ottoman Military Reform', in *The Journal of Modern History*, vol. XXXVII (1965), pp.291–306

Tolga, Esmer U., 'The Confessions of an Ottoman Irregular: Self-Representation and Ottoman Interpretive Communities in the Nineteenth Century', in *Osmanlı Araştırmaları – The Journal of Ottoman Studies*, XLIV (2014), pp.313–340

Örenç, Ali Fuat, 'Albanian Soldiers in the Ottoman Army during the Greek Revolt at 1821', in B. Çinar (ed.), *The Balkans as a Crossroad: Evaluating Past, Reading Present, Imagining Future* (Tirana: IBAC, 2012), pp.502–524

Öztürk, Temel, 'Egyptian Soldiers in Ottoman Campaigns from the Sixteenth to the Eighteenth Centuries', in *War in History* (2016), vol. 23, pp.4–19

Yeşil, Fatih, 'Drill and Discipline as a Civilizing Process: The Genesis of the Modern Soldier in the Ottoman Empire, 1789–1826', in S. Faroqhi and B. Ergene (eds), *Ottoman War and Peace. Studies in Honor of Virginia H. Aksan* – The Ottoman Empire and Its Heritage Politics, Society and Economy, vol. 68 (Leiden, Boston MS: Brill, 2020), pp.101–123

Vucinich, Wayne S., 'The Serbian Insurgents and the Russo-Turkish War of 1809–1812', in W. S. Vucinich, (ed.), *The First Serbian Uprising, 1804–1813. War and Society in East Central Europe* (New York: Columbia University Press, 1982). pp.141–194

Zens, Robert, 'Provincial Powers: The Rise of Ottoman Local Notables (*Ayan*)' in *History Studies*, vol. 3, March 2011, pp.433–447